LEARNING & MEMORY

LEARNING & MEMORY

Howard Eichenbaum

BOSTON UNIVERSITY

_____

W. W. NORTON COMPANY
NEW YORK LONDON

W. W. Norton & Company has been independent since its founding in 1923, when William Warder Norton and Mary D. Herter Norton first published lectures delivered at the People's Institute, the adult education division of New York City's Cooper Union. The Nortons soon expanded their program beyond the Institute, publishing books by celebrated academics from America and abroad. By mid-century, the two major pillars of Norton's publishing program—trade books and college texts—were firmly established. In the 1950s, the Norton family transferred control of the company to its employeed, and today—with a staff of four hundred and a comparable number of trade, college, and professional titles published each year—W. W. Norton & Company stands as the largest and oldest publishing house owned wholly by its employees.

Editor: Jon Durbin
Project editor: Sarah Mann
Production manager: Jane Searle
Editorial assistants: Alexis Hilts and Robert Haber

Composition by Matrix.
Manufacturing by The Maple-Vail Book Group—Binghamton.
Book design by Chris Welch Design.

Library of Congress Cataloging-in-Publication Data
Eichenbaum, Howard.
     Learning & memory / Howard Eichenbaum.—1st ed.
         p. cm.
     Includes bibliographical references and index.

ISBN: 978-0-393-92447-3 (hardcover)

1. Learning, Psychology of. 2. Memory. I. Title. II. Title: Learning and memory.
BF318.E33 2008
153.1—dc22
                                    2007040630

W. W. Norton & Company, Inc., 500 Fifth Avenue, New York, NY 10110
www.wwnorton.com

W. W. Norton & Company, Ltd., Castle House, 75/76 Wells Street, London W1T 3QT
1 2 3 4 5 6 7 8 9 0

BRIEF CONTENTS

Contents

PREFACE

Modern science is now unraveling many mysteries of our existence. Recent advances in astronomy have allowed us to explore the expanse of the universe and delimit the extent of our solar system. We have characterized the Earth, from its depths to the upper ranges of its atmosphere, and we are coming to understand the complex interactions that compose our ecosystems. All these developments enrich our understanding of human existence, but the deepest understanding of who we are will come from investigations of human beings, particularly the human brain.

As the seat of cognition, emotion, and action, the brain houses the components of human nature. Moreover, one specific faculty of the brain underlies what it means to be a unique human being: the faculty of memory. Although the background of our makeup is largely determined by our genes, the specifics that distinguish each one of us are a matter of *memory*. Each person's memories reflect a lifetime of experiences, as well as the learned skills, acquired preferences, and aversions that compose a distinct personality. We learn to talk, to use a particular language, and eventually to speak with the unique accent, syntax, and vocabulary that characterize our personal speech. We learn about ancient and modern history, our family tree, and a network of friends and foes, as well as our own unique position in that network. All this knowledge, and much, much more, composes the vast and complex organization of memories that we use every day. So, the study of memory is also a search for self-understanding that promises to reveal how we came to be who we are.

The nature of memory—its basic biological structure, its psychological characteristics and organization, and its longevity—have been investigated by philosophers, writers, and scientists for hundreds of years, and each approach offers a distinct avenue for understanding memory. Philosophers through the ages have examined memory through introspection, offering prescient proposals about its nature that remain relevant in modern experimental research. Beginning with

Hermann Ebbinghaus's pioneering work in the late 1800s, psychologists have explored the parameters of human verbal memory. Since the turn of the century, scientists like Edward Thorndike and Ivan Pavlov have explored the rules of learning in animals. Neurologists since Franz Joseph Gall in the early 1800s and Theodore Ribot in the late 1800s have attempted to localize memory and explain how it is permanently laid down, basing much of their work on case studies of amnesic individuals. Neurobiologists since Santiago Ramón y Cajal in the late 1800s have sought the nature of the cellular and molecular processes that mediate memory within the brain.

For several succeeding decades, scientists in these various fields studied human memory, animal learning, the neurology of amnesia, and the neurobiology of memory independently, and as interest in the problem of memory increased, each perspective's literature flourished. Often the phenomena investigated in each of these fields were very different, or at least seemed so. For example, most early studies on humans focused on verbal memory, whereas most studies on rats involved maze learning or gradually acquired habits, making the different approaches' findings quite difficult to reconcile.

Recently, however, the rise of modern methods of psychology, cognitive science, animal behavior, and neuroscience has fostered a broader, interdisciplinary body of knowledge, and the conclusions from these diverse approaches have substantially converged, deepening our understanding of both the psychology and biology of memory. For example, neurobiologists studying communication between neurons have discovered that specific molecules that enhance or weaken neuronal connections underlie the mechanisms for incorporating new learning into memory. Other studies investigating how reflexes work revealed that stimuli that do not initially affect behavior can come to evoke reflexes (the conditioned reflex). Such studies have led the way to understanding the basic parameters of learning. Also, what began as a neurosurgeon's heroic attempt to alleviate one patient's severe epilepsy has led to our understanding that learning and memory exist in multiple forms supported by different brain systems.

Over the last thirty years, researchers have combined more sophisticated psychological and biological approaches to discover the distinguishing characteristics of different kinds of learning and memory, and to understand the similarities in these processes between humans and animals. Accordingly, basic knowledge about the cells, circuits, and systems of the brain has substantially enhanced progress in the science of learning and memory. Our understanding is not yet complete, but the convergence of disciplines has brought about major successes. This book provides a progress report on our successes in characterizing the different forms of learning and memory from a combination of the psychological and neurobiological perspectives.

My motivation in writing this introductory text comes directly from the convergence of disciplinary research on learning and memory. Like many of my colleagues, when I reviewed potential textbooks for my learning and memory course, I became frustrated when I couldn't find one that synthesized the psychological studies on humans and animals and incorporated neurobiological studies as well. Due to the separate origins of psychological studies on humans and animals and on the neurobiology of memory, current textbooks focus on one disciplinary perspective at the expense of the others. There are, for example, several very good texts on animal learning, and these have been expanded to include associated issues of behavioral modification. But these texts provide, at best, a cursory treatment of the literatures on human learning and memory and on the neurobiological approach. Similarly, several texts focus on the psychology of human learning and memory, either specifically or as part of a broader treatment of cognitive science. But these books provide scant consideration of research on animal learning and on the neurobiology of memory. A few newer texts have attempted to include the psychology of learning and memory in both humans and animals, but these books merely juxtapose the two literatures in adjacent sections and hardly consider the neurobiological evidence. It was thus that I responded with excitement to the invitation from Jon Durbin at Norton to write such a synthesis myself. This is the first full-length, introductory text to integrate our knowledge of the psychology and neurobiology of learning and memory in both humans and animals.

We believe that our text offers many distinctive features. Most importantly, our integrative, interdisciplinary approach incorporates both animal and human research throughout. We have organized the text around multiple memory systems for intellectual and pedagogical reasons, so that students can move from simple to more complex forms of learning and memory. To engage students with the material, we emphasize stories, applications, examples, and human neuropsychological patient studies throughout all the chapters. Each chapter also includes "Learning & Memory in Action" boxes that show how research from the field applies to various aspects of daily life. We have created a robust art program of 175 photos and drawings designed to help students understand how our brains learn and remember and to enhance their understanding of the scientific process. To help students focus on core principles, each chapter opens with a few Fundamental Questions, includes Interim Summaries of major sections, and concludes with a Chapter Summary and Reviewing the Concepts questions. Just as importantly, we have used Kandel-style section headings throughout, as one more way to focus on core concepts and scientific processes.

Writing this book has been a rewarding intellectual enterprise, and I hope the results will prove useful to readers. Importantly, this project would not have been a success without the collaboration of editors at Norton, including Jon Durbin and

Aaron Javsicas early on, and subsequently Sarah Mann, art editor Gabe White, copy editor Margaret McDonald, and editorial assistants Robert Haber and Alexis Hilts. Their efforts have added considerably to the clarity and coherence of the story this volume tells.

I would very much like to hear from both instructors and students who use this text in the years to come. Please feel free to email me with your thoughts or concerns about the book.

Howard Eichenbaum
Boston University
hbe@bu.edu

PART I

FOUNDATIONS

The Nature of Learning and Memory

One day I walked into the elevator in a large office building and pressed the button for the upper floor where I would meet a colleague. On the way up, the elevator stopped and several people crowded in, pushing me to the back of the car. I found myself squeezed behind a young woman. At first there was nothing remarkable about this event. Then I smelled perfume— a scent that was at once pleasant, familiar, and out of place. What was that smell? Why was it so meaningful yet remote? I was transported mentally 35 years back in time . . . to high school! I felt like a student again, standing in the crowded hallway, wondering what class I was headed for. Then I remembered particular people, especially a girlfriend who wore that perfume. Her name came back to me, and the mystery was solved: She wore that perfume. I mulled it over, enjoying this olfactory journey into my past and recalling several nearly forgotten high school friends. Later I remembered that the perfume was Shalimar, a popular scent at that time.

This unexpected rush of memories happened in seconds. How did I learn and retain so much information? How did the faint cue of a perfume I last sensed so long ago evoke such a powerful memory? And why did the recollection unfold as it did, beginning with a sense of familiarity and importance, then a feeling of being in a particular place and time, and then the rush of images of specific places and people, and finally names and circumstantial details?

———————————

WE TAKE LEARNING and memory for granted. We use them all the time and in virtually everything we do. Do you ever think about what memory is and how it works? Memories are processed and stored by the brain, but brain science alone will not provide a complete understanding of memory. Memories can be relived like videos of our personal experiences, and memory has been described as a storehouse of accumulated knowledge about the world. But it is more than a large collection of video clips and a library. Beneath our conscious awareness, memory contributes to a multitude of acts of perception, coordination, and emotion. For example, we learned to distinguish cars from other objects, to drive a car, and to be afraid at the sight of a car careening at us. How does memory help us accomplish these things?

This chapter has two purposes: to convince you that learning and memory play a central role in our mental lives, and to introduce you to the major themes of the science of learning and memory, which are also the main themes of this book.

Fundamental Questions

1. What are the contributions of genes and experience to our individuality?
2. How big are the roles that learning and memory play in our everyday lives?
3. What do early conceptions of learning and memory have to do with the modern science of learning and memory?
4. What are the central principles of organization for understanding how learning and memory work?

Memory Defines Our Individuality

How much of who we are is determined by our genetic makeup? How much is determined by learning from and remembering experiences? This, of course, is the *nature–nurture debate*: the long-standing and continuing controversy over human nature. This issue frequently comes up in cases of unusual individuals. When we hear about mass murderers, terrorists, and the like, we wonder whether a prepotency or genetic determination might incline someone to violence, or whether violent tendencies are learned from abusive parents or a harmful social context. The more positive exceptions are our heroes, star athletes, political leaders, or famous scientists and thinkers. Did they inherit their intelligence, skills, and drive or learn these from others? Two overall points will help explain what makes each of us unique. First, genes operate in a general, statistical way to set the boundaries of our behavioral capacities. Second, the memories we accrue by learning from experiences shape our individual characteristics within the boundaries determined by our genes.

Genes Set the Range of Our Capacities but Do Not Determine Who We Are

Half a century of DNA research has highlighted the importance of genes. Of course genes play a major role in determining our externally apparent characteristics—

from our facial features to our particular tastes in music and food. Decades of research indicate that genes set the general range of our intellectual capabilities and determine the scope of our perceptual abilities and emotional sensitivities. And genes contribute to our predispositions for particular personality types, preferences, aversions, and abilities. Thus there are many well-characterized examples of relationships between genetic constitution (called the *genotype*) and observable mental and physical qualities and abilities (the *phenotype*). Consider the research showing that the male genotype is better at spatial memory than the female genotype. Thus, for example, males generally outperform females in navigating within a large building to find their way back to a starting position (Postma et al., 2004). Conversely, females are better at memory for some nonspatial details of specific experiences; these differences may be due to differences in sex hormones and their effects on brain development. Such studies show that genes in some way contribute strongly to certain cognitive capacities.

However, the relationship between genotype and phenotype is general and statistical. The genotype characterizes the range and distribution of a particular phenotype over a population (see Figure 1.1). In other words, genotype–phenotype correlations tell us more about populations than individuals. Thus, continuing with the example of sex differences in spatial and nonspatial memory, the full range of male spatial and nonspatial memory abilities overlaps considerably with that of females. So although the population of males generally performs better than the population of females in spatial memory tasks, some females surpass some males in this area, and vice versa for nonspatial memory. Individuals' qualities can fall anywhere in the broad range described by these correlations.

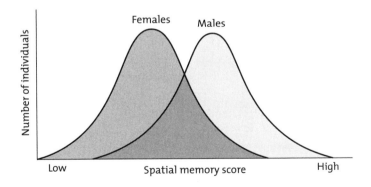

FIGURE 1.1 Overlapping distributions of scores on an ideal test of spatial memory.

Our Individual Personalities and Intellect Result from a Lifetime of Learning and Memory

Genetic predispositions characterize the *range* of our capacities, not the specific ways in which we use those capacities. Consider once more the finding that males tend to excel at some aspects of spatial learning and memory. That superior general capacity does not give any individual man the memory of any particular building. Likewise, some people have a strong predisposition for expertise in music or art. But if they are untrained in these skills, the phenotype may not be observed. Even among those who can learn to play instruments readily, the ability to play a violin (or any particular instrument) is not innate. Thus, in a general and statistical way, genes influence how we think and even the general topics we think about (food, sex, power, and so on). But that is where genetic influence stops. Genes do not influence the particulars of what we think about (fast food or particular dates or bosses, respectively).

We are programmed to babble, but we *learn* to speak a particular language. We *learn* to speak a particular language fluently and accumulate many facts and concepts to speak about. And we *learn* our personal memories from childhood accidents to first dates to first jobs. These memories of a lifetime of first-person events constitute a unique personal history.

We are genetically programmed to crawl, then to walk, then to run. But the refinement of motor coordination, even for these basic skills, relies on substantial experience and learning. Moreover, the development of specific skills depends critically on our ability to learn through extensive practice. Most of us learned to ride a bike. Now you do this easily. But do you remember how difficult and scary it was as you began to learn? Some of us learn to dance, swing a baseball bat or tennis racket, or play the piano. And we learn to do each of these with a personal style. These are examples of a broad variety of unique, specialized learned skills we pursue and use every day, effortlessly.

Some people are nervous and easily provoked, whereas others are mellow and imperturbable. These are examples of genetic predispositions for a comfortable level of stimulation. But we *learn* to appreciate forms of music and art that make us feel at ease or get us excited. A few specific fears may be genetically programmed (such as fear of snakes). But mostly we learn to fear particular people, dark alleys, or perhaps the music that precedes a shark attack in a summer action movie. Our individual personalities are defined as we learn a broad range of attractions, aversions, comforts, and neuroses.

In sum, the study of memory can reveal how we came to be who we are. Our genes set broad limits on the characteristics we develop. Our experiences and the ways in which we integrate them compose the details of our individuality. Understanding how memory works has led us to a greater general appreciation of the complex interactions between the mind and brain, and especially of how memory influences cognition, emotion, and consciousness.

Memory Plays a Pervasive Role in Daily Life

We usually speak of the capacity for learning and memory as an isolated ability, like the ability for athletics or music. But learning and memory can also be viewed as features of all our abilities. In this view, **learning** is the feature by which we can alter our skills, change our dispositions, add to our knowledge, and generally benefit or suffer from experience. And **memory** is the expression of that learning, revealed in alterations of our performance across a broad range of daily activities. Learning and memory influence many aspects of everyday activities simultaneously—from the simplest perceptions and movements to the most complex thought processes.

Memory Is Involved at Multiple Levels during Everyday Behavior

Think about the different levels in which your memory comes into play as you read this textbook. You remembered that Chapter 1 was your assignment and that this book was the text for the course. You instantly recognize the text as English, even if you know other languages; and you know how to find the first page of the assigned chapter and read down the page from left to right. Your knowledge of the structure of English-language books has already served you well.

You begin to read this chapter, and the letters are elements you remember. This may sound trivial; but compare how readily you read the current text with the next sentence printed in an unusual font. *Is this sentence as easy to read as the text of the previous sentence?* It probably requires just a little more time to read that last sentence, at least at first; but if you read it a couple of times, it becomes easy. So your memory is at work—first in recognizing letters and words in a familiar typeface, then in learning a new typeface.

Next consider your memory's role in recognizing words. Read the following text aloud: "Is-thay ext-tay is in ig-pay atin-Lay." Was this difficult? If you remember pig Latin from childhood, you can soon read it quickly and can translate the sentence into "This text is in pig Latin." Now let's put that recovered language to use: "Is-thay entence-say ould-shay e-bay ick-quay oo-tay ead-ray." You probably read and understood that sentence more readily than the first, demonstrating that you have reacquired a general facility with pig Latin. So even the simple act of reading requires memory at several levels: from recognizing letters in a particular font, to recognizing combinations of letters that compose words, to recognizing and using language rules to learn a new language, to translating text into speech. Memory is critical to the simple act of reading at an amazing number of levels.

Now consider any thoughts you had when you encountered the pig Latin examples. Did that experience spark memories of learning to speak pig Latin and perhaps of the friends with whom you shared that language? Did you remember any particular people or events or just a feeling of what childhood was like?

Interim Summary

Memory, accumulated over a lifetime of learning, constitutes the individuality of every human being. Genes set the range and limits of our mental and physical capacities. But the specifics of each person's intellect, personality, and talents result from learning and the expression of memory throughout life. Along with the myriad acquired physical and mental skills we take for granted, we learn to fear dangerous situations, and we learn to appreciate particular styles of music and art. These broad learned aversions and enjoyments are elements of our personalities. We learn to speak and understand our particular languages. We learn world history, our family trees, and our own autobiographies. The vast contents and complex organization of our memories make each of us unique.

Amazing Cases of Amnesia

Another way to appreciate the central and pervasive role of learning and memory is to consider what life would be like without them. A loss of learning and memory capacity is called **amnesia**. Symptoms of amnesia have many possible causes, including major depression, head trauma, strokes, brief anoxia (loss of oxygen), normal aging, Alzheimer's disease, and many other ailments.

In many cases, amnesia causes partial memory loss, noticed as merely an increased forgetfulness of everyday events or an increase in the amount of study required to learn new information. But some cases involve a severe learning and memory impairment that may contrast with otherwise intact perceptual and cognitive capacities. Next we will consider case studies that illustrate the devastating effect of losing learning and memory capacity. A *complete* loss of learning and memory, including both the storehouse of memories you have accumulated to date and the ability to form new ones, would render you frightened and confused. However, even a limited impairment can be devastating. Many individuals lose certain components of memory while retaining other perceptual or intellectual abilities. These cases have helped researchers understand how memory works and recognize its broad importance.

A "Prisoner of Consciousness" Repeatedly Awakens

Consider Clive Wearing, a man described by Dr. Jonathan Miller in a television program titled *Prisoner of Consciousness.* Wearing (Figure 1.2) is a British musician who suffered an infection by the herpes simplex virus. This virus sometimes causes encephalitis, or brain inflammation, that leads to permanent brain damage. In Wearing's case the damage was diffuse and widespread, but the effects on intellectual capacity were specific and dramatic. He lost the capacity to form new lasting memories, a phenomenon called **anterograde amnesia.** In addition, Wearing lost some of his memories formed prior to the damage, a phenomenon called **retrograde amnesia.** Wearing's memories lost from retrograde amnesia date back for only a variable period of years prior to the onset of amnesia. A combination of anterograde and partial retrograde amnesia is a common pattern in memory loss following brain damage.

Wearing's disorder is particularly striking because his amnesia is severe and tragic in its emotional consequences. Wearing lives in a constant state of feeling that he has just awoken from a long sleep; he feels this sense of awakening each time there is a mere shift in focus during an otherwise continuity of wakefulness. He keeps a diary detailing the dates and times when he "regains consciousness." Wearing is obsessively committed to the notion that he has suddenly recovered his conscious state and is now well, and he becomes upset when this view is challenged. Thus he lives without a sense of the past or future, remembering experiences for only a few minutes while they are within his attention. Whenever the topic of activity or conversation turns, the emotional event wherein he "regains consciousness" begins again.

FIGURE 1.2 Clive Wearing with his wife, Deborah.

Notably, substantial components of Wearing's memory are intact. He can remember and use information long enough to carry a conversation. He knows his name and can generally describe his life before the memory loss, including highlights such as singing for the Pope and directing Handel's *Messiah* in London. His musical skills are remarkably spared. Thus he can still sight-read music and can sing a complex piece while accompanying himself on the harpsichord. On the other hand, much of his specific knowledge of facts and personal events in his musical career are lost. In one striking example, he wrote a book before suffering the memory loss, but he knows nothing about this topical material now.

A "Lost Mariner" Has a Vivid Past but Lives Only in the Present

Another remarkable case is Jimmie G., an amnesic man described by Dr. Oliver Sacks (1985) in his book *The Man Who Mistook His Wife for a Hat*. Jimmie G. suffered from Korsakov's syndrome—the destruction of neurons in the prefrontal cortex, temporal lobe, and mammilary bodies resulting from a combination of chronic alcoholism and associated poor diet. Jimmie grew up normally with a special interest in math and science. In 1943 he was drafted into the navy. Jimmie was a natural for radio and electronics and became a submarine radio operator. He pursued a long career in the navy and retired in 1965. Subsequently Jimmie ceased working, led an aimless life, and began to drink heavily. In 1970 he suffered a period of unconsciousness and delirium typical of Korsakov's syndrome. Over the following weeks, the confusional aspects of the disorder dissipated, leaving partial memory impairment.

As in Clive Wearing's case, Jimmie G.'s amnesia is selective to particular aspects of memory. Jimmie's retrograde amnesia can be dated to approximately 1945. Memories of his childhood and wartime experiences are vivid. His knowledge about the ships, radios, and science he used in the military is intact. But Jimmie is "stuck" in 1945. For example, Jimmie was shown a picture of the warship *Nimitz*, which was commissioned in 1975 and named for deceased Fleet Admiral Chester W. Nimitz, who had commanded the Pacific fleet in World War II. Jimmie was amazed at the ship's ultramodern design and could not understand how a new ship could have the name of a living admiral. When shown a picture of the Earth taken from the Moon, he wondered how that photograph could have been created. Jimmie panicked when he saw a current picture of himself, much older and grayer than his 19-year-old self of 1945. He wondered if the event was a nightmare or if he was crazy. Yet moments later, when Jimmie was distracted, he forgot the event and politely introduced himself to the doctor with whom he had just carried out such an upsetting conversation.

Other than his memory, Jimmie G.'s intellectual capacities are normal. However, his memory impairment affects everything he does. For example, Jimmie is good at arithmetic calculations, but only those that can be solved quickly. If a problem has many time-consuming steps that involve remembering earlier parts, he becomes lost. As another example, Jimmie can reproduce the periodic table of chemical elements from memory acquired before his brain damage; but he leaves out elements discovered after 1945.

Sacks characterized Jimmie as "isolated in a single moment of being, with a moat or lacuna of forgetting all around him. . . . He is a man without a past (or future), stuck in a constantly changing, meaningless moment." The nature of a sense of self without the contributions of memory is worth emphasizing. When Sacks asked Jimmie how he felt about his state, he responded, "I cannot say I feel ill. But I cannot say I feel well. I cannot say I feel anything at all." Jimmie could not say that he was miserable, nor could he say he enjoyed life. When he was engaged in a game or puzzle, Jimmie would become keenly involved. But this, he felt, was meaningless play. The hospital staff once employed Jimmie's intact typing skill, giving him a job typing forms from hand-written notes. Jimmie worked proficiently and with some satisfaction in his efforts. Yet this satisfaction was superficial because he could not hold thoughts about what he was typing. It was no more than a mechanical transformation of words to keystrokes, lacking content to contemplate for interest. Jimmie does derive meaning and enjoyment from attending church services, where he becomes absorbed in the feeling of the moment and in the context of memories of his religious upbringing. Jimmie also enjoys gardening and, interestingly, has somehow learned his way around the hospital garden, even though each day he is reintroduced to it. We will study how amnesic individuals exhibit the acquisition of unconscious habits in Chapter 6.

Interim Summary

Amnesia reveals what it is like to lose the ability for learning and memory. Amnesia following trauma or brain damage usually preserves what was learned early in life—basic knowledge such as language and identity as well as memory for common objects (such as houses and faces) and specific examples (your parents' house, your mother), along with childhood experiences. Anterograde amnesia is loss of the ability to form new memories, and retrograde amnesia is loss of memories acquired shortly before the event that caused the amnesia. During a conversation, amnesic individuals can usually hold relevant information in mind. In contrast, their ongoing lives are locked into the present: They cannot learn from new experiences or remember earlier events. Note that these qualities of amnesia are similar in the cases of Clive Wearing and Jimmie G. Keep in mind these features of the impaired and spared cognitive capacities that are hallmarks of amnesia.

The Study of Learning and Memory Has a Long History

For thousands of years, philosophers have pondered the qualities of memory, and writers have analyzed its pleasures and agonies. For over a hundred years, psychologists have examined the nature of learning and its consequences in memory. Neuroscientists have explored the basis of learning and memory in the structure of the nervous system. Given such a broad and deep interest, it should not be surprising that several perspectives on the nature of learning and memory have generated distinct bodies of knowledge. This section outlines some prescient ideas of the early philosophers, then introduces some early psychologists who pioneered research on human memory and animal learning.

Ancient Philosophers Proposed Ideas Central to Today's Views of Learning and Memory

Modern ideas about learning and memory originated with introspection and logical analysis of how learning and memory might work. The ideas derived from this approach foreshadowed current conceptions of learning and memory that have come from technologically driven scientific investigations. For most of the 20th century learning and memory researchers failed to acknowledge these early philosophical contributions. But as the saying goes, "Those who forget history are condemned to repeat it." And repeat it modern scientists did. Modern "discoveries" about learning and memory have been hailed as breakthroughs; and in the modern era, they indeed have broken new ground integrating neuroscience and psychology. However, the fundamental insights of the current era can also be viewed as resurrecting many basic theories of the ancients. The major thinkers considered here had profound insights that remain key to our modern understanding of learning and memory.

Aristotle Distinguished Familiarity from Recollection

Aristotle (c. 350 B.C.) distinguished two forms of remembering: one he called *memory* and the other *reminiscence*. In making this distinction, Aristotle (Figure 1.3) conceived memory as a replication of a sensory perception, whereas reminiscence involved replaying an entire experience. Thus Aristotle proposed that memory is an extension of the senses that incorporates the passage of time since the actual sensory experience. He envisioned a memory as a replicate of a perceived object on some sort of recording device, perhaps comparable to an instant photograph or audiotape. Remembering, then, is a passive "reperception" of the recorded object, independent of its original context.

Aristotle contrasted this form of sense-based memory with reminiscence, which, he asserted, involved the active replay of an entire experience, triggered by an ini-

FIGURE 1.3 Aristotle.

tial memory of one event in that experience. This first memory would lead to a
recovered sense of the situation and flow of events that compose the experience.
Thus Aristotle viewed reminiscence as a process of recovering single items in succession. The difference Aristotle conceived between memory and reminiscence is
recognized today in the distinction we make between familiarity and recollection.
Familiarity is a passive sense of knowing a previously experienced stimulus, like
an object or a discrete event; **recollection,** on the other hand, involves actively
reconstructing the flow of events in a complete experience. In Chapter 9 we will
consider modern psychological and biological distinctions between familiarity and
recollection.

Notably, Aristotle also took a stand on differences between humans and animals with regard to these different kinds of remembering. He asserted that "other
animals (as well as man) have memory, but, of all that we are acquainted, none
. . . except man, shares in the faculty of recollection." You may judge this claim
for yourself when you read the evidence concerning recollection in animals in
Chapter 9.

Maine de Biran Distinguished Conscious Memory from Habits and Emotional Memory

Two thousand years after Aristotle, a less familiar philosopher using the pen name
Maine de Biran (1804/1929) offered a prescient view of different forms of memory. Maine de Biran began with the assumption that there is a simple, automatic
mechanism for associating events, which he called "habit." He proposed that the

habit mechanism underlies three different forms of memory. Maine de Biran called the most complex form *representative memory,* and he argued that this involves the ability to consciously relive and think about a prior experience. He viewed this kind of memory as unique in its access to consciousness and in the flexibility with which we can think about and use memories to solve novel problems in daily life.

The other two forms of memory Maine de Biran identified, *mechanical memory* and *sensitive memory,* differed from representative memory in two important ways. First, neither of these forms of memory could access consciousness. Second, both of these "unconscious" forms of memory had rigid limits on their expression. That is, they could be expressed only under circumstances closely resembling the learning experience, and they could not be used to solve new problems. Specifically, Maine de Biran believed that *mechanical memory* involves learning a movement through repetition. In his view, mechanical memory uses the habit mechanism to improve the speed or coordination of an action through practice. Thus as we practice coordinated movements, such as parking a car or serving a tennis ball, we get better at them, and we exhibit this improvement within the execution of the movement without any effortful recollection of how these movements are performed. Indeed, Maine de Biran distinguished mechanical memory as a form of habit learning that—unlike representative memory—does not generate a recalled idea.

Maine de Biran called the other form of unconscious and inflexible memory *sensitive memory,* which he argued occurs during emotional experiences. Maine de Biran proposed that during such an experience, sensitive memory works when the habit mechanism retrieves a feeling without recalling the circumstances in which the feeling became associated with that type of emotional situation. For example, many people have learned that flashing lights in a hallway are associated with danger in the building. When the lights begin to flash, we may feel our hearts race and a sense of concern and arousal, even without recalling the times this has happened before. We reexperience the acquired emotion without an effortful recall of similar experiences or their emotional consequences.

Both forms of unconscious memory express simple associations. Mechanical memory associates stimuli with movements, and sensitive memory associates stimuli with their emotional significance. Each of these works without conscious recall. Maine de Biran added that although these forms of memory are unconscious, they can cause inflexible and obstinate behavior, as anyone with an irrepressible habit or uncontrollable fear knows.

Maine de Biran was remarkably ahead of his time in realizing the distinction between conscious and unconscious forms of learning and memory and in distinguishing between three types of memory. Later in this book we will examine modern studies that separate acquisition of unconscious habits, similar to Maine de Biran's mechanical memory; learning of emotional reactions, similar to Maine de

Biran's sensitive memory; and the complexities of conscious memory, identical to Maine de Biran's representative memory.

William James Distinguished between Habits and Memories and Envisioned Memory as a Network of Associations

At the threshold of experimental psychology, William James (1890/1918) distinguished between memory as a complex cognitive phenomenon and habits founded in a simple automatic mechanism. James was guided by observations from biology that identified reflex pathways in the nervous system through which a stimulus (such as a pinch) automatically generates a specific motor response (withdrawal). Influenced by the descriptions of these *reflex arcs,* James suggested that nerve impulses in reflex paths more readily traverse paths previously taken. Thus, he wrote, habits form when reflex paths become well worn. Like Maine de Biran, James attributed great importance to habits as the building blocks of more complicated behaviors. James said that practiced behaviors and skills are mediated by sequentially linked discharges that "awaken each other in succession" through connected reflex paths. He held that this kind of chain reaction mediated the production of learned movement sequences.

James distinguished active memory from the acquisition of skills and from a sense of familiarity. James emphasized the warmth and intimacy of recollection from the cold repetition of practiced movements and from the passive feeling of familiarity for a reexperienced stimulus or event. In addition, James characterized memory in terms of its structure as an elaborate network of associations, vastly richer and more complicated than a connected series of habits or a general sense of familiarity. Thus the underlying foundation of recall involves a complex set of systematic associations between particular memories.

James's interest in the biological basis of memory led him to assert that memory depends on two aspects of the physiology of habit mechanisms. First, he suggested that the persistence of a memory depends on our innate capacity for strengthening its reflex pathway. Second, he proposed that access to a memory depends on the number of pathways through which we associate an item. James emphasized that associational links are more malleable than reflex pathways, and he argued that the key to remembering is building many diverse associations with our experiences, weaving memories into a network of systematic relationships. The capacity to search through our network of associations, he wrote, is the basis of conscious recollection and can lead to creative use of memory to address new problems. James admonished his students not to simply rehearse learned material because repetition would not help form diverse associations that support creative use of memories to address new questions. James also distinguished two forms of conscious memory. He differentiated *primary memory,* the ability to hold and manipulate information in mind for a short period, from the permanent memory store he called *secondary memory.*

These fundamental distinctions between unconscious impressions and conscious memories were initially lost in experimental psychologists' efforts to characterize memory as a single system. However, the distinctions were rediscovered and confirmed by modern cognitive and neuroscience research, as we will see later in this chapter. James's distinction between primary and secondary memory was also confirmed much later by cognitive science and neuroscience (see Chapter 12).

Herman Ebbinghaus Developed the Systematic Study of Human Memory

The era of experimental analysis of memory began with the German psychologist Herman Ebbinghaus (1885/1913), who performed the first rigorous studies of human memory capacities. Ebbinghaus rejected the use of introspection and abhorred the complexity of early elaborate explanations of how memory worked. Instead he developed several techniques to control the nature of the material to be learned and generate quantitative and objective assessments of memory. In essence, he tried to reach a scientific understanding of memory.

How did Ebbinghaus do this? First he needed an experiment that would allow rigorous control of the learning process. To accomplish this, he needed learning materials that were uniformly simple so he could test the reliability of memory across new learning experiences and compare memory across changes in the amount of material to be learned, the duration of retention, and other variations of the learning task. Ebbinghaus's solution was to invent the *nonsense syllable:* a meaningless consonant–vowel–consonant letter string (such as *ket, poc,* and *baf*). With this device he avoided the influences of what he called "interest," "beauty," and other features that might affect the memorability of real words. In addition, nonsense syllables simultaneously equalized the length and meaning of the items by minimizing the former and eliminating the latter. To quantify memory, Ebbinghaus invented the measure of *savings*—a method of scoring that measured retention of memories by the reduction in the number of trials or amount of time required to relearn material. In addition, he was the first to employ mathematical and statistical analyses to describe and test the reliability of his findings.

Ebbinghaus's work, performed entirely with himself as the experimental subject, provided a wealth of information about learning and forgetting, the amount of information that can be learned, and the effects of practice on retention and subsequent savings. He also provided the first evidence showing that humans remember the order of items in which they are learned, and he demonstrated that the linkage between items in a learned sequence weakens with the number of intervening items in the list. In these studies Ebbinghaus quantified in the laboratory something we observe in remembering everyday experiences: The more extended and complicated your day, the more difficult it becomes to remember what happened when. The importance of the order of items for our ability to recall experiences will be explored in detail in Chapter 9.

A Separate Line of Research Developed Theories about the Elements of Animal Learning

At the turn of the 20th century, while Ebbinghaus began studying human memory, other pioneers in psychology began to investigate animal learning and develop theories about its basic elements and rules. One early landmark was Ivan Pavlov's discovery of **classical conditioning,** a behavioral protocol in which an initially neutral stimulus is consistently paired with a stimulus that automatically produces a reflexive response. Pavlov (Figure 1.4) was a Russian physiologist who began his career examining how the nervous system controls digestion. He found that when food excites the taste sensors in the mouth and gullet, nerve signals travel through the brain stem to the stomach, where they stimulate the release of gastric fluids.

Pavlov's later studies showed that dogs produced salivary and gastric secretions at the mere sight of food, without having tasted anything—a phenomenon called *psychic secretion.* Pavlov also noticed that this phenomenon was unreliable: Salivation tended to decrease when the dogs were shown beef repeatedly. Conversely,

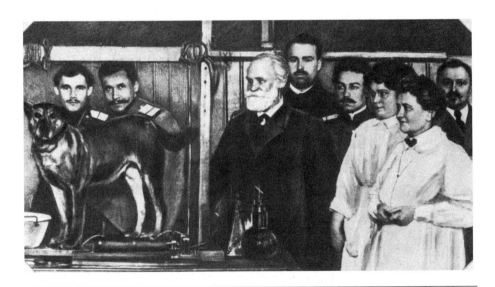

FIGURE 1.4 Pavlov and his staff.
They are shown here with his famous conditioning apparatus and a subject of his classical conditioning studies.

seemingly arbitrary events that preceded the sight of food could trigger salivation, such as when the person who regularly provided food entered the testing room. By studying psychic secretion, Pavlov formalized the perspective that learning is based in the *conditioning* of reflexes by reliable contiguity of an arbitrary stimulus (like the sight of a person) and a stimulus that automatically, and unconditionally, produces a particular behavioral response (such as food producing reflexive salivation). Pavlov's experiments with the conditioning of salivary reflexes became the model for later studies of how basic motor responses are learned—a subject that is the focus of Chapter 5.

Edward L. Thorndike and John B. Watson Studied How Animals Learn Responses for Rewards

Another turn-of-the-century landmark in animal learning theory was the research of psychologist Edward L. Thorndike, who investigated the basic mechanisms of learning using an approach called **instrumental conditioning**—a behavioral protocol in which rewards or punishments that follow particular behaviors tend to alter the probability of that behavior. Thorndike invented an apparatus called the *puzzle box:* a cage with a door that was locked by a latch on the outside that could be manipulated from the inside (Figure 1.5). Thorndike observed how cats placed in the puzzle box learned to flip its latch to open the door and obtain food just outside. The initial learning was by *trial and error:* The cat's behavior appeared random, but eventually the cat would open the latch. Over repeated training trials, the random behavior gradually diminished. Instead the animal appeared to intentionally manipulate the latch and could open the door readily. Thorndike concluded that the cat had formed an association between the latch as the stimulus (S) and the appropriate manual response (R), and that learning was based on the **stimulus–response (S–R) association.**

Following Thorndike, John B. Watson heralded the view that all learning could be reduced to a set of S–R associations. In one of his most famous experiments, Watson trained rats to run a maze and then sought to determine what kind of information the rats were using to guide their behavior by eliminating each of the rats' senses one after another. He found the rats could still run the maze using only the sensory feedback from the contractions of their muscles. The observation that animals could learn a maze based only on muscle sensations led Watson to conclude that learning can be reduced to a chain of acquired reflexes. By 1913 Watson was so convinced that he wrote a manifesto beginning a movement called **behaviorism.** This school of thought asserts that we can understand all learning in terms of simple stimulus and response associations, without considering less measurable concepts such as consciousness, insight, or intent.

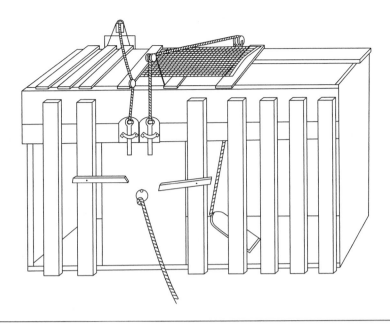

FIGURE 1.5 One of Thorndike's puzzle boxes.
To open the door, the animal had to step on the peddle inside the box, shown to the right
of the door (after Thorndike, 1898).

Interim Summary

The idea that there are different forms of memory dates back to Aristotle, and many
distinct forms of learning and memory proposed long ago prefigured aspects of learning and memory studied today. Two key distinctions include (1) the difference
between familiarity of stimuli and recollection of experiential circumstances and
(2) the differences among learned motor habits, emotional responses, and conscious
memories. Early psychologists, including William James, elaborated on these ideas;
but they receded into the background when researchers like Herman Ebbinghaus
emphasized learning and memory as simple processes of association. Parallel studies of animals described two key forms of learning: classical conditioning, which consistently associates a neutral stimulus and another stimulus that elicits a reflexive
behavioral response; and instrumental conditioning, which alters the probability of
specific behaviors by reward and punishment. Thus, whereas early views espoused
multiple forms of learning and memory, the first experimentalists considered learning and memory as a single faculty of the mind and sought to reduce its basis to simple associations. As we will see next, this approach had only limited success.

Modern Scientific Approaches to the Study of Learning and Memory

The pioneering work just described provided the basis of the modern scientific approaches used in studying learning and memory. These approaches highlight the development of hypotheses that can be tested empirically. For example, Watson's hypothesis that all learning can be reduced to stimulus–response associations contrasted with the hypothesis that animals have conscious memories of their prior experience in a maze. A critical feature of the hypothesis testing approach is that experimenters must provide an **operational definition** for each hypothetical construct—that is, they must have an observable measure of each proposed mental function. Experimental analyses of learning and memory involve constructing operational definitions and testing hypotheses based on those definitions. Thus, in the example of maze learning, experiments were designed to predict the specific choices animals would make if their performance were guided by stimulus–response associations or instead by conscious memory of previous experiences in the maze.

Correlational and Experimental Studies of Memory

Two general approaches are pursued in learning and memory research. One approach seeks correlations between psychological or biological variables. Correlational studies identify likely substrates or consequences of learning and memory; they can characterize changes in behavior and biology in great detail. However, the correlational approach does not tell us definitively whether any particular change is essential to learning or memory. Thus a study that shows a correlation between variable A and variable B does not tell us whether A causes B, B causes A, or both A and B are caused by some other unidentified variable. The other approach involves experimentally manipulating one variable and observing the effects of that manipulation on another variable. Such experiments require preselection of a variable or variables to be manipulated, and this preselection is often based on initial correlational studies that suggest a relationship. Then a subsequent experimental analysis can test whether changes in one variable have a causal role in affecting another variable.

CORRELATIONAL STUDIES In correlational studies, we observe changes in some behavioral, anatomical, or physiological parameter as human or animal subjects learn or express memory. Some changes may be observed at only the behavioral level—such as the tendency to emit a particular verbal response or choice in humans or a particular action or choice in animals. For example, memory of emotionally charged events is generally more detailed than memory of neutral events.

Do we think longer and deeper about emotional events, and is this why we remember them better? Or do hormones released during emotional arousal directly influence how well memories are stored? The correlation between emotional content and detail in memory does not answer these questions, but it has inspired experiments.

In many biologically oriented studies, experimenters track changes in the anatomy, biochemistry, or activity of brain cells or circuits during or following learning. For example, neurophysiological studies that monitor the activity of single brain cells (neurons) have found that patterns of neural activity in the visual cortex are modified during learning about important visual stimuli. Does this mean visual memories are stored in the visual cortex? Or could the changes in activity patterns of visual neurons be driven by memories stored in other brain areas that connect with the visual cortex? Again, the correlational study does not tell us the location of the memories' storage, but this kind of correlation demonstrates the nature of neural activity patterns associated with memory and inspires experimental studies that can trace the sites of memory storage.

EXPERIMENTAL STUDIES The other general approach involves directly or indirectly manipulating some behavioral or biological variable and determining the consequences of these manipulations on learning or memory. In experimental studies, it is important to distinguish the **independent variable** (the variable the experimenter determines independent of the subject's control) and the **dependent variable** (the variable generated by the subject that the experimenter measures). For example, in studying the role of emotional content in memory, the experimenter could manipulate the level of arousal by giving the subject a drug that elevates or depresses emotional arousal as the independent variable, and then measure the detail of memories as the dependent variable.

An appropriate **control group** is a critical part of any experimental analysis. In principle, a control group is a set of subjects who are treated exactly like the group that receives a manipulation of the independent variable (called the **experimental group**); but the independent variable is not manipulated in the control group. In the example of the study of emotional arousal and memory, the experimental group might receive an injection of a drug that creates arousal, whereas the control group might receive an injection of saline fluid that has no biological effects. Thus the control group would be treated exactly like the experimental group, right down to the detail of receiving an injection; but the drug that influences arousal would be left out.

Sometimes it is difficult to produce perfect control that leaves out only one influence. For example, an experimenter wanted to determine whether contiguity of a neutral stimulus and a painful stimulus was essential to learning an association between the stimuli. To examine this, an experimental group of rats was trained to press a lever to receive regular food rewards. Then occasionally a light stimulus was presented for a few seconds, followed by a brief shock. This experimental group rats learned to cease pressing the lever when the light stimulus came on, showing that they had learned the association. The control group received the same light stimulus and shock, but these were always separated in time. The experimenter thought this procedure exquisitely controlled for the contiguity of the two stimuli while giving the control group both kinds of stimuli. However, the control group rats actually pressed the lever more when the light came on, suggesting the light had become a "safety signal" predicting that the shock would not occur. The control group had received a *negative contiguity*—the two stimuli never occurred together. To address this problem, the experimenter created a different control group for which the light and shock stimuli were independently presented, so they occurred occasionally together and at other times far apart. This group's rats did not alter their rate of lever pressing when the light came on—but they did get ulcers, which are a consequence of the unpredictability of painful events. The lesson of this study is that there is no perfect control for learning. Rather, animals and people learn any contingency or lack of it between salient variables.

Investigators alter training or testing protocols or manipulate brain function in various ways. In some cases the variable involves direct manipulation, such as in the drug study previously described. But sometimes there are natural variations of a variable. In learning and memory research, important examples of this can be found in studies of unusual individuals, such as people with exceptional memory ability or particular types of brain damage. In general, researchers can make the strongest conclusions with a sufficiently large number of subjects in each experimental and control condition to allow statistical analyses of the reliability of any observed differences in the dependent variable. But often observations gleaned from individual case studies are compelling.

A final consideration in the design of experimental studies is the possibility of a **confounding variable:** an unintended independent variable occurring along with the intended independent variable that could change the dependent variable. For example, imagine an experiment showing that damage to brain area A affects learning task 1 but has no effect on learning task 2. We might want to conclude that brain area A is critical to task 1 and not task 2. However, perhaps task 1 is easier, and damage to brain area A affects difficult tasks more than easy tasks. Or maybe task 1 is just more sensitive to any kind of brain damage. Here task difficulty and sensitivity are potential confounding variables with the kind of learning that task 1 represents. One way to remove this confounding effect is to identify another brain area B that, if damaged, affects learning task 2 but not learning task 1—the opposite findings of the effects of damage to brain area A. The full pattern of results cannot be explained by differences in difficulty or sensitivity of the two tasks because performance of each task is affected by damage to one brain area and not the other. This pattern of findings is called a **double dissociation** because the effects of each of two types of brain damage are dissociated or distinguished from the effects of the other.

In general, both correlational and experimental approaches are valuable. Correlational approaches can provide considerable detail about associated variables and generate new ideas about variables to manipulate in subsequent experiments. And experiments can be designed with appropriate controls and elimination of confounds to test the causal roles of variables in learning and memory processes.

Themes of This Book

Four closely related themes guide the current science of learning and memory and are also the main theses of this book:

1. Learning and memory are closely intertwined stages of information processing. Learning is the process that generates memories; memories reflect successful learning.
2. Major insights into learning and memory have come from studying the brain. Neurobiological studies provide insights into how memories are represented in the brain, and they provide data that allow us to test psychological theories.
3. Together, psychological and biological studies have revealed multiple forms of learning and memory, each with its own domain of information, rules of organization, and brain pathways.
4. Humans and other mammals share much in the nature of their learning and memory systems and the brain structures that support them. In addition, virtually all animal species share cellular and molecular mechanisms that underlie memory. The neurobiological approach has bridged the distinct lines of study of human memory and animal learning. Merging evidence from humans and animals allows us to understand learning and memory across many levels of analysis, from simple neural circuits to human cognition.

Theme 1: Learning and Memory Are Closely Intertwined Stages of Information Processing

Learning and memory do not reflect separate phenomena but instead are the opposite ends of a continuum of information processing: from acquiring information during learning, to organizing and storing memories, and finally to retrieving and expressing memories. Although studies of human memory and animal learning have run separate courses and dealt with different issues, both lines of study have encountered the same controversies. Researchers in both camps want to understand whether learning and memory can be reduced to simple associations or require more complex ways of representing information. Over this point of controversy, the fields of human memory and animal learning have converged.

In the early part of the 20th century, when the behaviorist approach was at the peak of its influence, most human memory research was guided by the rigorous methods introduced by Ebbinghaus and the notion that human memory could be reduced to a predictable set of events governed by simple laws. But some researchers in the separate fields of human memory and animal learning remained skeptical about the explanatory power of behaviorism. They believed that learning and memory are more complicated than simple stimulus–response associations.

In the field of human memory research, British psychologist Frederic Bartlett's work (1932) contrasted with the reductionist view that human memory can be reduced to simple associations. Bartlett had people read a brief mythical tale about a war between a South American Indian tribe and ghosts. The story contained both ordinary events and surreal events that were described in only fragmentary detail. When, after a delay, Bartlett asked his subjects to repeat the tale, he found that people did not remember all aspects of the story equally well. Rather, they were more likely to forget the surreal events or distort them to fit their understanding of cause and effect. Bartlett's insights about the structure and richness of memory have proven critical for modern views of conscious recollection. Bartlett showed that memory cannot be explained based only on association and repetition. Rather, new memories are woven into an organization of prior knowledge that strongly influences what is remembered.

At the same time, Edward Tolman's research (1932/1951) in animal learning challenged the behaviorist view that learning can be reduced to stimulus–response mechanisms. Tolman used the same species (rats) and maze learning tasks as the prominent S–R theorists so his ideas could be tested against those of the behaviorists using the same experimental variables. Though the behaviorists discounted mental processes that could not be directly demonstrated and measured, Tolman aimed to identify the underlying cognitive mechanisms, purposes, expectations, and insights that guided behavior; his studies revealed certain capacities rats use to solve maze problems that cannot be explained in terms of simple S–R mechanisms. For example, Tolman and his students observed that rats could take novel routes through a maze when trained routes were blocked (Figure 1.6). Tolman theorized that these rats could not have acquired the novel responses through previously rewarded behaviors and must have instead used general knowledge of the maze as a guide. Bartlett and Tolman were among the first memory researchers to endorse **cognitivism**—the belief that learning cannot be explained by simple S–R associations but requires a more elaborate network of knowledge and expectancies.

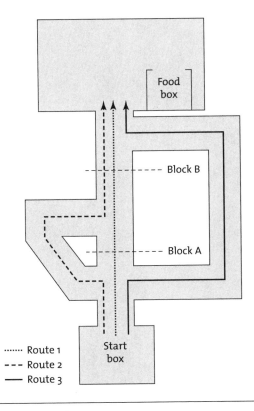

FIGURE 1.6 One of Tolman's mazes.
The rats first learned the three possible routes through the maze. When no blocks were inserted, rats preferred route 1. When block A was added, rats would immediately take route 2. When block B was added, rats seemed to realize that route 2 could not be followed to completion, and they took route 3.

AN EXAMPLE BATTLE BETWEEN BEHAVIORISTS AND COGNITIVISTS The battle between behaviorism and cognitivism was not resolved by Barlett's and Tolman's groundbreaking studies; rather, it continued into the middle of the 20th century. A compelling example of many battles about this issue is a set of experimental studies that pitted the behaviorist view against the cognitivist view in predicting strategies animals use to solve a simple maze problem. The experiments used a T-shaped maze in which the rat began each trial at the base of the T and was rewarded at the end of only one of the upper arms of the T—for example, the one reached by a left turn as the rat reached the top (Figure 1.7A). The maze was open to views of various stimuli in the room, so the animal could see spatial cues outside and within the maze.

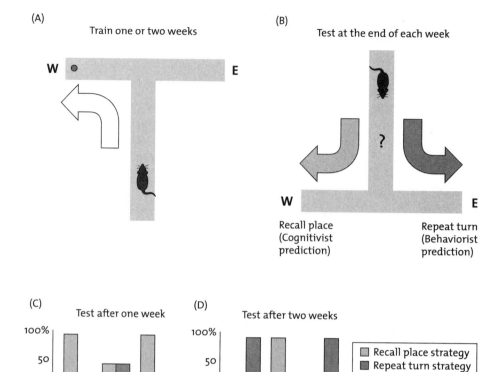

FIGURE 1.7 The T-maze task.
A. Training to take a left turn to reach the west side of the maze. B. Test of strategy. C. Effects of inactivation of the striatum (Str), hippocampus (Hipp), or no treatment (N) on performance measured as the percentage of animals that chose the recall place strategy (light gray bars) or repeat turn strategy (dark gray bars) when tested after one week of training. D. Effects of inactivation of the same brain areas when the animals were tested after two weeks of training.

Behaviorists and cognitivists offered different accounts of what the rats learned in this situation. According to behaviorist theory, learning involves the association between stimuli in and around the maze (S) and the rewarded left turn response (R) as a conditioned S–R. According to this view, animals acquired the association between seeing the choice point in the maze and turning left, and this association was reinforced by food rewards. Behaviorists call this strategy *response learning:* Rewards increase the likelihood of a particular (left turn) behavioral response to a stimulus (the choice point) without reference to the animal "thinking" about what happened last time it took a left turn at the choice point.

In contrast, according to the cognitive account, the rat's learning involved acquiring general knowledge about the layout of the environment using the visible spatial cues around the room and the memory of previously finding food at a particular location in the room defined by the spatial cues outside the maze. According to this view, when rats repeated the task, they used their cognitive capacities to explicitly remember where the food was (on the west side of the room) and then utilized any responses required to reach the place where the reward should be. This strategy, called *place learning,* differs from response learning in two ways. Place learning involves knowledge about the whole environment and memory of each experience in it, whereas response learning involves specific, limited stimulus–response associations. Also, place learning can be expressed in a variety of ways other than previously rewarded behaviors, and it can even support novel responses such as taking different turns through the maze if those are necessary to reach the reward.

The crucial test that would reveal the rats' learning strategy involved rotating the T-maze 180 degrees so the choice arms still ended in the same two places in the room, even though the two arms had switched places, and the start point was at the opposite end of the room (Figure 1.7B). To envision this situation, imagine that during the initial training, the start point was in the south end of the room, so the arm of the maze with the reward would be on the west side of the room, whereas the arm with no reward would end on the east side. When the maze was rotated 180 degrees, the start point would move to the north, and the two arms would still end in the east and west. To determine which kind of learning supported maze behavior, researchers first trained animals with the T-maze in its initial orientation, then presented a single "probe" trial that tested which kind of learning was used by examining the rats' subsequent choices.

Behaviorists predicted that in the probe trial the rats would continue to execute the previously reinforced left turn response at the choice point, leading them to the east end of the room, where the rats had not found food during training. In contrast, the cognitive account predicted that the rats would seek the remembered location of food—the west end of the room—even though this required switching their response to a right turn at the choice point. Thus a single test with the rotated maze would examine the rats' underlying strategy.

Many experiments ensued, with mixed results. In general, place learning was favored, but under some conditions response learning was preferred. Place memory predominated when salient visual cues outside the maze differentiated one goal location from the other; but whenever external cues were minimized, response memory would predominate. Other studies reported that rats employed place memory early as they began to succeed in learning the task, and later they switched to response memory. Such a pattern of results did not, of course, declare a "winner" in the behaviorist versus cognitivist debate. Instead these results suggested that both types of representation are available to rats, which might use either strategy depending on salient cues or response demands.

These studies showed that both behavioral and cognitive strategies exist, and either can be employed to solve maze problems. In addition, these studies demonstrated how strongly learning and memory are intertwined. For this seemingly simple maze problem, subtle differences in the available stimuli or the amount of learning altered the nature of the resulting memory. In perhaps the most striking demonstration of how learning and memory are intimately linked, it was found that early successful learning resulted in cognitive memory, whereas subsequent additional learning resulted in behavioral memory. Later in this book you will read about several additional situations in which learning can result in different forms of memory for the same experiences. These findings necessitate that we view learning and memory as intertwined: Learning is how memories are created. In other words, the important issue is not how learning and memory differ, but how they coordinate in producing different types of representations in the mind and brain.

Theme 2: Major Insights about Learning and Memory Have Come from Studies of the Brain

You have already read about some interesting contributions of brain science to studies of learning and memory. In particular, case studies of amnesia have revealed that learning and memory can function (or fail) separately from perception and other aspects of intellectual function, and that there are different stages of memory formation. Also, these studies have distinguished between different forms of memory based on the nature of the information stored and the ways memory can be expressed. You may recall, for example, that the amnesic man Jimmie G. was able to learn his way around the hospital's garden even while consistently experiencing it as a new and unfamiliar place. This surprising combination of intact brain function and impairment suggests a distinction or dissociation between the cognitive memory of previous visits to the garden and the behavioral memory that allowed Jimmie to navigate its paths with ease. That is, when one type of memory breaks down while another kind is preserved, this suggests that the two types of memory are dissociated, meaning they are supported by separate brain systems.

More recently, new brain imaging technologies monitoring humans performing memory tests have confirmed that distinct brain regions play different roles in memory processing. Also, animal studies have been crucial in identifying the distinct functions of brain areas that mediate memory. In some animal studies, distinct brain areas are selectively removed, and the effects of this surgery on memory can be studied in detail. Researchers have compared these changes to the firing patterns of neurons in the same brain areas of intact animals to determine the kind of information represented in these brain areas. Experimental studies of humans and animals have revealed the circuitry of multiple memory systems in the brain. In addition, neurobiological studies of the cellular and molecular bases of memory have identified changes in connections of brain circuits that underlie memory. And these studies have revealed a cascade of molecular events that cause permanent changes in connections between elements of these circuits.

A key example of how neurobiology has contributed to our understanding of learning and memory relates to the theoretical battle between the cognitive and behavioral perspectives on maze learning in rats—a battle that neurobiological studies have sometimes helped to reconcile.

Recall that the psychological studies did not resolve the controversy; rather, they showed that both behavioral and cognitive strategies could be used to solve the T-maze problem. How can both models be solutions? What determines which strategy is used? These questions have been resolved through neuroscience, and the implications are important and broad, providing an example of different forms of learning and memory. In a landmark experiment, Mark Packard and James McGaugh (1996), taking advantage of previous findings showing that rats switch between place and response memories depending on their level of training, examined the roles of specific brain areas in supporting each kind of memory. They trained the rats for a week in the T-maze task, then assigned them the rotated maze probe trial. Subsequently these rats were trained for another week with the maze in its original orientation before a final additional probe trial. As in the earlier studies, rats initially used place memory, reflected in their strong preference during the first probe trial for the earlier location of food. However, after the additional week of overtraining, the rats' choice behavior changed, reflecting response memory on the final probe test. So under these training circumstances, rats acquired both types of memories successively. Their initial acquisition of place memory fit the cognitivist view, but subsequent overtraining developed response memory consistent with behaviorist theory.

But Packard and McGaugh's experiment went beyond merely showing anew that rats use both response and place learning. They also examined whether different brain systems support these types of learning and memory. Before training, Packard and McGaugh implanted the rats with needles that allowed them to inject specific parts of the brain with local anesthetic during the probe tests to silence certain brain cells for several minutes—either in the hippocampus or in the striatum. The rats were always trained without drugs; but during both probe tests, the rats received infusions of either the anesthetic or a placebo (saline solution) into one of those brain areas.

The striking effects of the anesthetic differed depending on when and where the drug was infused. In the first probe trial after one week of training, rats with anesthetic injected into the striatum behaved just like rats who received the placebo in the same brain area. With or without anesthetic in the striatum, they were predominantly guided by place memory, showing that this kind of memory did not depend on the striatum (Figure 1.7C). In contrast, during the same initial probe trial, the rats with anesthetic injected in the hippocampus showed no preference for one end of the maze over the other: The behaviors they learned during the week of training seemed unavailable. This indicates that they relied on their hippocampus for the place memory, and that only this representation had been created at that stage of learning.

During the second probe test after two weeks of training, a different pattern emerged (Figure 1.7D). Whereas the placebo-infused rats now showed that they had acquired response memory (continuing the left turn response that led to food during training), animals given anesthetic in the striatum lost their response memory for the left turn and instead showed a striking opposite preference for turning right, toward the *place* where rewards had been obtained during training. Meanwhile, the rats with anesthetic injected into the hippocampus in the later probe trial maintained guidance by their response memory.

Combining these data shows clearly that multiple forms of memory develop at different times in training. Rats initially develop and use place memory, which depends on the hippocampus. We know this because when the hippocampus was anesthetized, the rats lost their ability to select the correct place. At this early point in training, the S–R representation had not yet developed: The rats could not resort to response memory when the hippocampus was inactivated. Instead, with no alternative form of memory, they randomly chose to turn either left or right.

After further training, the situation changed—the rats developed response memory. We know that this form of memory depends on the striatum because striatum inactivation affected their performance. Furthermore, it appears that after further training, response memory predominated over place memory, although the latter could be "uncovered" by inactivating the striatum where the response memory was stored. Note that these results, showing that hippocampal inactivation selectively eliminates place memory whereas striatum inactivation selectively eliminates response memory, constitute a double dissociation—the strongest form of evidence for distinct functions of these brain areas.

The two kinds of learning demonstrated here closely match the properties of the two different forms of memory described by William James. Response learning correlates with James's description of a habit as a practiced, ultimately rigid overt movement associated with a particular stimulus. Place learning is much like James's concept of memory as network of associations that can be flexibly applied to solve new problems; this kind of memory also resembles explicit or declarative memory (discussed in the following pages) because it involves remembering events that occurred at a particular place.

Theme 3: The Concept of Multiple Memory Systems Unifies the Study of Learning and Memory

A chief observation in the experiment that probed rats' methods of learning and remembering mazes was that learning and memory exist in multiple forms, each of which operates with unique principles and depends on a distinct brain system. These findings offer compelling evidence that elements of both the behaviorist and the cognitive views are right. There are distinct forms of memory—one involving memory of a place and the other involving acquisition of a turning response—and they are distinguished by both performance characteristics and the brain pathways that support them.

Perhaps the most convincing proof of the existence of multiple forms of learning and memory comes from observations of people with amnesia. The cases described earlier revealed selective loss of some aspects of memory while other learning abilities were still supported by those individuals' intact brain systems. Further amnesia studies have identified which brain areas support particular forms of learning and memory.

One particular study of amnesia has shown a remarkable double dissociation between the systems that support cognitive memory and emotional associations (Bechera et al., 1995). This work examined three people with selective damage to either the hippocampus or the amygdala (two temporal lobe structures). One subject suffered from Urbach–Wiethe disease, a rare disorder that destroys amygdala tissue while sparing the adjacent hippocampus. Another subject experienced multiple cardiac arrests; the associated oxygen loss shrank the hippocampus but spared the amygdala. The third subject suffered herpes simplex encephalitis, which damaged both the amygdala and the hippocampus.

This study focused on a classically conditioned association between a neutral visual stimulus and a loud sound (Figure 1.8A). Subjects were initially shown different colors on a computer screen to habituate them to the visual stimuli. The first trials conditioned the participants to associate a particular visual stimulus with the startling loud sound. Each of three different colors appeared on the screen in random order for two seconds. After a particular color (red) was presented, the participants would hear a brief, loud boat horn sound. When the loud horn was unexpected, it produced involuntary emotional responses, including sweating, which could easily be measured with electrical recordings of skin conductance.

Normal control subjects showed skin conductance changes at the sound of the boat horn, along with robust conditioning to associate the sound with the color red. The subject with selective amygdala damage showed normal skin conductance responses to the boat horn but failed to learn the association between the color red and the sound of the horn (Figure 1.8B). In contrast, the subject with selective hippocampus damage showed normal skin conductance changes at the

(A) **Conditioning task**

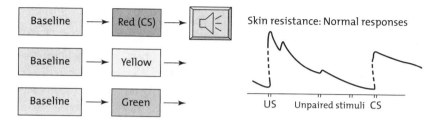

(B) **Results of conditioning**

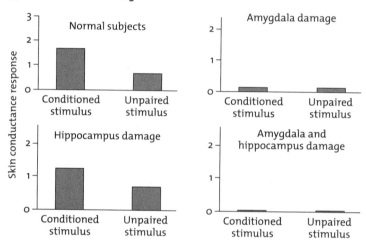

(C) **Declarative memory for the task**

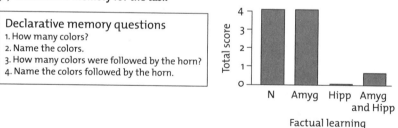

FIGURE 1.8 Emotional learning.
A. A loud boat horn followed the red stimulus but not the yellow or the green stimuli. Skin resistance changed after presentations of the boat horn (the US) and, after training, the red stimulus (the CS)—but not the yellow or the green stimuli, which were not paired with the boat horn. B. Normal subjects showed strong conditioning, whereas those with amygdala damage did not. After training, subjects were asked questions about their memories of the training experience. C. Normal subjects recalled the training events, whereas those with hippocampus damage did not.

sound of the boat horn and normal conditioning to the color stimulus. The sub-ject with combined amygdala and hippocampus damage failed to condition, even though he showed the skin conductance response to the boat horn.

After the testing sessions, the subjects were asked several questions about the relationships between the stimuli (Figure 1.8C). Normal subjects and the subject with selective amygdala damage answered most of these questions correctly. But both subjects with hippocampus damage had trouble recollecting the task events. These findings simultaneously show that (1) a conditioned emotional response to a particular color depends on the amygdala and (2) explicit memory of the details of a conditioning experience depends on the hippocampus. This evidence that diverse forms of memory for a single learning event are affected differently when particular brain areas are damaged strongly supports the notion of multiple mem-ory systems mediated by various brain structures.

Theme 4: The Underlying Bases of Learning and Memory Are the Same in Humans and Animals

Combining the views and experiments from the early philosophers and modern psychological and neuroscience experiments has allowed a tentative classification of memory systems (Table 1.1). The primary distinction is between **cognitive memory** (also called declarative or explicit memory), in which memories can be consciously recalled, and **behavioral memory** (also called nondeclarative or implicit memory), in which memories are expressed though changes in behavior, typically the speed with which we execute a behavior or change our preferences and aversions without conscious recollection.

Behavioral memory includes simple forms of memory that involve the habitu-ation and sensitization of behavioral responses to repetitive stimuli. This form of memory also encompasses simple forms of associative learning, including classi-cal conditioning and instrumental learning—basic paradigms that emerged early in thinking about learning mechanisms. Another simple form of memory involves

TABLE 1.1 A Taxonomy of Memory Systems.

Behavioral Memory	**Cognitive Memory**
Simple forms	Working memory
Habituation	
Sensitization	
Perceptual learning	Episodic memory
Procedural learning	Semantic memory
Emotional memory	

perceptual learning and memory: the improvement in perception of categories of stimuli that we are required to discriminate. Also, consistent with Maine de Biran's ideas, there are distinct systems for procedural learning (the acquisition of reflexive behaviors and habits) and emotional memory (the acquisition of attractions and aversions to otherwise neutral stimuli).

Cognitive memory also features distinct subtypes. Some are relatively short-lived—including short-term memory, which involves information that passively lasts a few seconds, and working memory, which involves information we keep in mind by active rehearsal or manipulation. The two principal subtypes of long-term cognitive memory are episodic memory, which provides a permanent record of personal experiences, and semantic memory, which we use to permanently organize factual information. This text will explain these types of memory in detail, in terms of both their psychological characteristics and the brain systems that support them.

The advances from the study of human memory, animal learning, and neuroscience are converging to comprehensively explain memory with considerable consistency between humans and animals and across species of animals. Both the psychological and neurobiological approaches have distinguished successive stages of memory processing, including separate properties of information processing associated with the acquisition, manipulation, storage, and retrieval of memories; these distinctions are found in both humans and animals. Also, each of these approaches has distinguished multiple forms of learning and memory in humans and animals. Some kinds of memory involve complex conscious thought, whereas others involve simple mechanisms that can be expressed unconsciously during task performance. The realization that there are distinct stages and different forms of learning has generated convergence among the different approaches. This book will explore this synthesis of knowledge about learning and memory.

Interim Summary

Early studies of human memory and animal learning ran separate but parallel courses. Both research areas were beset by controversy between behaviorists, who thought learning and memory could be reduced to associations between stimuli, behavioral responses, and reinforcers; and cognitivists, who believed that complex mental processing and memory organization play a major role in the determination and expression of learned behavior. Recently the behaviorist and cognitivist perspectives have merged in studies showing that both humans and animals have multiple forms of memory that are mediated by distinct systems in the brain. Modern research has generated a taxonomy of memory systems that distinguishes a cognitive memory system from several behavioral memory systems. Behavioral memory includes simple forms of memory, like habituation and sensitization, as well as perceptual, procedural, and emotional memory. Cognitive memory includes working memory, episodic memory, and semantic memory. Outlining the psychological and neurobiological distinctions between these systems is a goal of this book.

Chapter Summary

1. Learning and memory contribute to our individuality. Whereas genes confer the range of capabilities to which we can aspire, our individuality is accumulated as a lifetime of memories. Learning and memory pervade every aspect of our daily lives, contributing to all our perceptual, emotional, behavioral, and cognitive activities. And they encompass many levels of behavioral expression—from how we perceive the world around us, to coordinated movements, to our attitudes and dispositions, to conscious recollection of facts and events.

2. The absence of memory is devastating. People who suffer amnesia usually recall some knowledge acquired early in life, including who they are, basic knowledge about language and things in the world, and personal childhood memories. However, amnesias are often stuck in the present; they may lose their sense of the continuous flow of time and of the future.

3. Early philosophers recognized distinctions between conscious recollection and simpler forms of memory, and between the acquisition and unconscious expression of habits and emotional dispositions. The first experimental psychologists sought to reduce memory to elemental rules of association but could not explain complex forms of memory expression with these rules. Observations from neurobiological studies have also boosted our understanding of learning and memory.

4. Although the different perspectives reflected by philosophy, psychology, and neurobiology began with dissimilar approaches and questions, a major theme of this book is that the observations from many approaches have converged on a comprehensive account of how learning and memory form a continuum from initial processing of incoming information to the organization, retrieval, and eventual expression of a stored memory.

5. A second theme of this book is that the observations from neurobiological studies have contributed strongly to our understanding of learning and memory, allowing us to test psychological theories and validating the distinctions in various kinds of memory—such as differences among conscious memory, stimulus–

response habits, and emotional conditioning. And the convergence of findings from neurobiological studies is evident in the parallels between the characteristics of different types of memory originally described by the ancient philosophers and pioneering psychologists and the distinctions in capacities associated with particular brain areas (demonstrated in studies of human amnesia and studies of selective brain area inactivation in animals).

6. A third theme is that multiple forms of memory are mediated by distinct brain memory systems. The two major categories are cognitive memory and behavioral memory, and these both have subtypes. Within cognitive memory, working memory maintains and manipulates information in consciousness; episodic memory allows us to remember specific experiences; and semantic memory lets us create and update a warehouse of knowledge about the world. Within behavioral memory, perceptual learning involves alterations in behavior associated with sensory stimuli; procedural memory gives us conditioned reflexes and habits; and emotional memory is the acquisition and expression of attractions and aversions.

7. The fourth theme of this book is that this memory taxonomy applies to both animals and humans. Of course there are differences in the intellectual capacities of humans and animals. But as you will read in the chapters that follow, the basic wiring diagram of the brain—including the systems that support different types of learning and memory—is essentially the same across mammalian species. And there are corresponding similarities between humans and animals in the kinds of information processed by these systems. These similarities give us insight into the evolution of the brain's cognitive functions and an appreciation of the primitive thought functions shared by animals and humans.

KEY TERMS

learning (p. 7)

memory (p. 7)

amnesia (p. 8)

anterograde amnesia (p. 9)

retrograde amnesia (p. 9)

familiarity (p. 13)

recollection (p. 13)

classical conditioning (p. 17)

instrumental conditioning (p. 18)

stimulus–response (S–R) association
    (p. 18)

behaviorism (p. 18)

operational definition (p. 20)

independent variable (p. 21)

dependent variable (p. 21)

control group (p. 21)

experimental group (p.21)

confounding variable (p. 22)

double dissociation (p. 23)

cognitivism (p. 24)

cognitive memory (p. 33)

behavioral memory (p. 33)

REVIEWING THE CONCEPTS

- How do learning and memory define us as individuals?

- Is memory an isolated function or a pervasive instrument in our daily lives?

- How can the study of amnesia (the loss of learning and memory capacity) tell us about normal learning and memory?

- How do scientists study learning and memory?

- What were the contributions of philosophy and psychology to our early understanding of learning and memory?

- How has modern research led to a convergence of views about learning and memory?

- What are the major forms of learning and memory in humans and animals?

The Neural Bases of Learning and Memory

Jenny had been feeling ill. Her stomach was growling continuously, and she was nauseated for several hours each evening after dinner. Jenny's doctor recommended an endoscopy to examine her stomach, and the next week she went to the hospital day surgery clinic for the brief procedure. The examination involved placing a thin, flexible tube containing a video camera (called an *endoscope*) into her nose, down her throat, and into her stomach to examine its lining. The procedure did not require anesthesia because there would be no cutting. However, inserting the tube into the nose and snaking it down the throat can be uncomfortable. Jenny was nervous. Even the efforts of the kind nurse who prepared Jenny for the procedure could not calm her.

Realizing this was a major issue, the doctor gave Jenny a powerful tranquilizer called midazolam (its commercial name is Versed). This drug produces conscious sedation, a state in which the patient is awake and aware but somewhat tipsy, and alleviates anxiety and discomfort. Fifteen minutes after administering the drug, the doctor tested Jenny's ability to stand steadily and to walk a line down the corridor. She was woozy and a bit embarrassed at her awkward performance in these simple tasks. Jenny then lay on the surgical table, and the procedure began. She saw the scary tube coming and felt it enter her nose and pass down her throat. She gagged a little; but strangely, she felt unconcerned; the tranquilizer was working.

The whole event took only two hours. When she arrived home, she took a nap. After she woke, her husband asked how she felt about the experience. Jenny was aware that the procedure occurred but remembered few details. She recalled driving to the hospital and meeting the doctor, and she remembered the name of the nurse who prepared her for the procedure. But she recalled little of what transpired after she took the drug. She couldn't remember the tests for her ability to stand steady and walk a straight line; she had forgotten the questions the doctor asked before the procedure; and she could scarcely recall the feared endoscopic procedure itself.

Midazolam is a tranquilizer drug classified as a benzodiazepine. Also in this class of drugs is diazepam, known by its commercial name Valium. When these drugs are absorbed into the bloodstream, they rapidly enter the brain. There they specifically affect nerve cells, particularly at the connections between cells, called *synapses*. Benzodiazepines block the chemical signals that let cells change how strongly they are connected to one another. As you will read in this chapter, changing the strength of nerve connections is a fundamental mechanism for forming lasting memories. This mechanism, called *long-term potentiation (LTP)*, is essential for forming memories. Thus Jenny remembered the events before she took the midazolam but hardly any details that happened while she was under the influence of the drug.

––––––––––––––

BECAUSE OUR CAPACITY for learning and memory is based on brain function, studying nervous system anatomy and physiology reveals the most fundamental mechanisms of learning and memory. These studies tell us which brain structures play a role in learning and memory, and how the brain circuitry that supports memory is organized. In addition, studying the brain shows us how the brain's elements change during learning—the brain's "code" for information processing and storage. And by observing or manipulating brain function during behavior, we can test hypotheses about components and functions of learning and memory and how those functions work together.

Learning changes behavior as a result of experience, and behavior is generated by the brain—so memories must be embodied in brain structure and function. Therefore, understanding learning and memory requires learning how brain structure and physiology support the representation of information.

Fundamental Questions

1. How are memories stored in the brain?
2. Are memories stored in a special location in the brain, or are they distributed in many areas?

Cells, Circuits, and Systems

Memories are represented in the brain at three levels of structure: cells, circuits, and systems. **Cells** are encapsulated structures that are the basic functional units of all body organs, and they are typically specialized for a particular physiological function within each organ. In the brain, **neurons** are cells that are the basic elements of information processing. Understanding the anatomy and physiology of neurons tells us how information is encoded and transmitted in the activity of individual cells. **Circuits** are groups of interconnected neurons that cooperate to represent stimuli, thoughts, and actions. Knowing how neural circuits are formed shows us how memories are represented in the brain. **Systems** are circuits interconnected to form pathways for information to flow through the brain. Distinct systems represent different types of physical stimuli (like vision and hearing) and allow emotional responses, thinking, and coordinated action. The information encoded within these systems is organized into distinct streams of processing, which are coordinated to support learning and the expression of memories. The following sections summarize fundamental knowledge about the brain's structure and information processing at these levels.

Neurons: The Cellular Units of Information Processing

In the 19th century, anatomists examined thin brain slices to observe their fine structure, hoping to uncover the basic anatomical units of brain function. But brain cells are all gray and packed closely together, so the slices showed no clear delineation of the tissue components. The early anatomists tried several stains to color the cellular elements within brain tissue, revealing a microscopic network of cells connected by thin fibers. However, the network appeared to be a jumble of interconnected threads because brain cells are closely intertwined and because the stains colored all cells similarly. This observation inspired the **reticular theory of brain circuitry,** suggesting that the brain's wiring involved a fixed network of fine wires, like a spider's web.

To examine this idea, Spanish anatomist Santiago Ramón y Cajal refined a staining method (originally developed by an Italian anatomist named Camillo Golgi), called a *black reaction* because of its color, that impregnated the membrane surrounding nerve cells with silver particles, darkening their appearance (Figure 2.1; Cajal, 1894; for a review of the history of these discoveries, see Finger, 2000). For reasons still unknown, unlike previous staining methods, the black reaction randomly colored only a small fraction of the neurons in any area of brain tissue. The result was that only a few cells were stained; so when Cajal examined particularly thick brain sections, he saw a few individual cells standing out clearly against a pale background. Using this method, Cajal discovered that the brain was not a reticular network but instead was composed of separate nerve cells connected to one another by specialized elements.

Cajal also identified specific neuron components (Figure 2.2). He could distinguish the cell body (the large part of the neuron, composed of a cell membrane

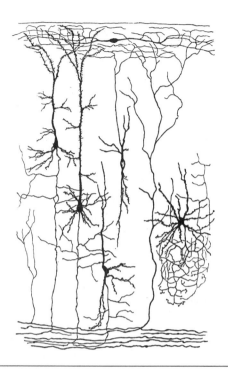

FIGURE 2.1 Section of the cerebral cortex stained using Cajal and Golgi's method.

and chemical machinery inside) from two types of fine extensions of the cell's membrane: many branching fibers called **dendrites** (extensions of the membrane that receive information from other neurons) and a single larger **axon** that sends information to other neurons. Viewing thick brain slices, he could follow all extensions of a cell membrane that connected with other cells. He found elaborate cell endings branching with many connections to multiple parts of another cell or to multiple cells. However, he observed no evidence of the stain continuing into the next cell, as the earlier reticular network theory would suggest. Cajal concluded that cells must communicate without joining their membranes.

Combining these observations, Cajal proposed the **neuron doctrine:** the hypothesis that the brain is composed of discrete nerve cells that are the essential units of information processing. He asserted that the cells are connected, that these connections somehow allow communication between cells, and that collections of interconnected cells form large-scale networks for information processing and memory. Cajal's preparations and their evidence were elegant, and he convinced other anatomists and physiologists that each cell was contained within a membrane and was separate from, although in contact with, other cells. These observations won him, along with Golgi, the Nobel Prize in 1906.

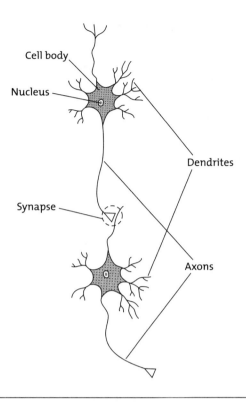

Cell body

Nucleus

Dendrites

Synapse

Axons

FIGURE 2.2 Components of neurons.

Cajal also made fundamental discoveries about the operation of neurons by studying their anatomy. In particular, Cajal observed that in sensory areas the dendrites of cells are oriented from the outside world toward the body of the neuron, and the axon points from the cell's body toward the brain. From these observations Cajal deduced that information flows one way—from the dendrites to the cell body and then to the axon—and that the information is subsequently conveyed by a specialized connection, providing communication with the dendrites of another nerve cell. Cajal realized that information flowing into a neuron from many other cells must be integrated somehow. Then the axon had to carry the integrated signal from the neuron to other cells.

Within this model of neural functioning, Cajal described many different types of neurons that we now realize are suited to specific functions in different parts of the nervous system (Figure 2.3). These types of neurons differ in the kind of inputs they receive and in where their outputs reach, but they all operate on the same basic biological principles explained later in this chapter. So, each neuron's specific role in integrating information is mainly a consequence of its connections within brain circuits.

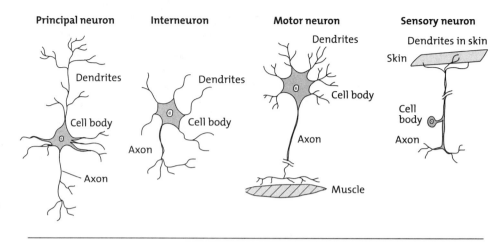

FIGURE 2.3 Types of neurons.

- **Principal neurons** have a highly organized set of dendrites and an axon that may connect with local cells or extend many millimeters to send signals to another brain region.

- **Interneurons** receive and send signals within a local region in the nervous system.

- **Motor neurons** have many branching dendrites, and each neuron has a single axon that extends over a long distance to send signals to muscles.

- **Sensory neurons** have specialized dendrite endings to receive signals from sensory organs in the eyes, ears, nose, skin, and more.

Cajal and others have since identified many variations on these patterns.

Finally, Cajal considered memory. In comparing the brains of several species, he noticed that the brains of more evolutionarily advanced animals (such as carnivores and primates) had more connections between nerve cells than those of less advanced animals (like the platypus). He concluded that this greater network connectivity could be the basis of greater intellectual power. Furthermore, Cajal speculated that learning could increase the number and intensity of the connections, which might underlie skills such as playing a musical instrument. Cajal's suggestions that the number and strength of neural connections underlie memory and that these connections can change in response to mental activity still guide current research into the cellular bases of memory. Cajal's ideas about memory were correct.

Learning & Memory in Action

What Happens to the Brain When We Age?

As people age, their ability to learn and remember deteriorates. People forget everyday events, such as where they put their keys or the name of a person they just met. And there is some truth to the saying that "you can't teach an old dog new tricks" (or at least it's more difficult). But this deterioration, called *cognitive aging,* is not inevitable and does not occur at the same pace in all people. Some folks are sharp in their eighties or nineties. Other people begin losing memory in their early sixties. What is different in the brains of these people? Are they losing brain cells at different rates?

Scientists, examining the brains of people who died at different ages, have compared various brain measures with cognitive status at the time of death. This examination involves staining neurons, using modern improvements of Cajal's methods that stain all the neurons and still show them separately. Sampling methods are used to count the number of neurons and the number of connections between neurons in many brain areas. Such studies show that people who suffer mild cognitive aging, associated with a selective deterioration of memory and not other cognitive abilities, do not lose brain cells. The overall brain cell counts, including brain areas critical for learning and memory, are the same as in the brains of people of the same age with intact memory.

This finding has led to laboratory studies of animals, where we can examine the anatomy and physiology of the animals' brains at different ages. Like humans, animals show different courses of cognitive aging. For example, at about two years of age, some rats have impaired learning and memory, whereas others perform as well as younger rats. Many detailed examinations have shown what differs in the brains of these equally aged animals. Old rats that display cognitive aging, like old people whose memory is beginning to deteriorate, do not lose brain cells. However, connections between neurons are degraded in the old rats whose memory is poor. The number of connections in some brain areas is low, and the strength of the remaining connections is compromised (we will soon discuss how this is measured); this can have major consequences for memory (Wilson et al., 2006). These findings demonstrate Cajal's insight: It's not the number of cells—it's how well connected they are! This knowledge is directing much current research on developing drugs that can improve the formation of neural connections.

Neural Information Processing Depends on Signal Conduction and Transmission

Understanding how brain circuits work requires that we consider the physical bases of communication in the nervous system. This communication involves electrical conduction of signals over substantial distances *within* neurons—that is, through the dendrites, the cell body, and the axon of each neuron (Figure 2.4). In addition, signals also travel *between* neurons via chemical transmission from an axon of one neuron to the dendrites or cell body of the next neuron across the **synapse.** A synapse is the connection between two neurons, including three main components: the presynaptic elements, the postsynaptic element, and the synaptic cleft.

What kinds of signals carry information within and between neurons? In synapses and dendrites the signals, called **synaptic potentials,** which are relatively small and variable in size, *decrease* as they travel along the dendrites toward the cell body. The neuron cell bodies *add together* the small and varying synaptic potentials. If they reach a particular threshold at the origin of the axon, the cell fires and generates a much larger signal called the **action potential,** which has a constant size and travels along the axon over long distances. When this action potential arrives at the synapse, chemicals called **neurotransmitters** transmit the signal to activate the synaptic potential in the dendrite of the next neuron. The most important property of a synaptic potential is its size—and therefore its influence on the cell in generating an action potential. The important properties of action potentials are their rates and firing patterns. These electrical and chemical signals are

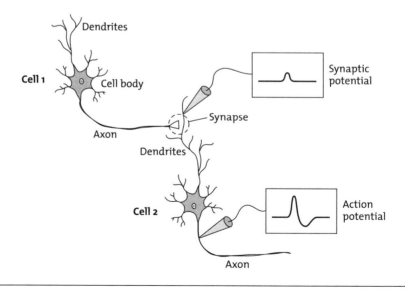

FIGURE 2.4 Types of signals in neurons.

crucial for our consideration of learning and memory because learning influences both the size of synaptic potentials and the firing patterns of neurons—and thus the encoding of memories.

Neurons' Electrical Properties Underlie Signal Communication

How are these signals generated and carried within and between neurons? Let's examine neurons' basic electrical properties. Neurons have a natural electrical potential, or difference in charge, between the inside and outside of their cell membranes. This is known as their **resting potential** (Figure 2.5A). In neurons, both the resting potential and action potential arise from differences in the concentrations of electrically charged molecules, particularly sodium (Na+) and potassium (K+), inside and outside the cell membranes. These concentration differences exist because the cell membranes contain channels that let some of those molecules move into or out of the cell. When the neuron is at rest (that is, when it's not firing), the channels allow primarily K+ to flow. Typically more K+ is inside the cell than outside, so some K+ flows out of the neuron, leaving a negative charge inside the cell. This charge difference generates a resting potential that is typically about −70 millivolts (thousandths of a volt, abbreviated as mV). That's pretty small compared to the potential of a battery (typically 1.5 volts or more)—but it is sufficient to power our most complex thoughts and memories!

So far we have considered the cell at rest. What happens when the cell is called into action? The resting potential is disturbed when synaptic transmission changes the cell membrane's permeability to a molecule, typically Na+ (Figure 2.5B). Unlike K+, Na+ is more concentrated outside the cell because an active cell membrane mechanism pumps Na+ molecules out of the cell. Synaptic transmission briefly increases the membrane's permeability to Na+, so this positively charged molecule flows from its higher concentrations outside the cell into the cell where it is less concentrated, raising the membrane synaptic potential from −70 mV to a less negative or even a positive value. This synaptic potential spreads passively and almost instantaneously, but it dissipates as it travels toward the cell body. Indeed, the size of the potential in a dendrite depends critically on the distance it must travel, so synaptic potentials created in very distant dendrite branches can become tiny by the time they reach their cell body. If the total synaptic potential that reaches the beginning of the axon is above a particular threshold, an action potential is generated. A change of about 15–20 mV in potential is enough to fire a neuron and generate an action potential.

Action potentials have quite different properties than synaptic or dendritic potentials. An action potential is much larger than a synaptic potential. Moreover, unlike the variable size of synaptic potentials, an action potential is "all-or-none." Either the threshold for activation is not reached, and the dendritic potential dis-

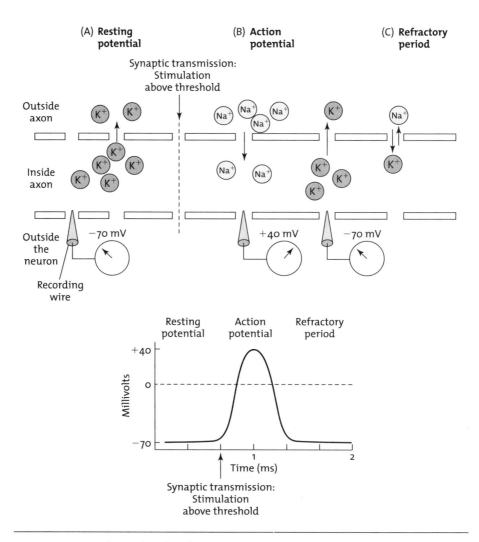

FIGURE 2.5 Charged molecules in the resting potential, action potential, and the refractory period.
A. The resting state involves predominantly the movement of K+ molecules from the inside to the outside of the cell, resulting in a −70 mV resting potential. B. When the cell is stimulated by synaptic transmission above a threshold, Na+ molecules flow inside, resulting in an action potential of +40 mV potential. Shortly after, additional K+ subsequently flows outside the cell, restoring the potential to −70 mV. C. Following the action potential, a cellular pump exchanges Na+ for K+ to restore the balance of molecular concentrations.

sipates rapidly—or the threshold is reached, and the full action potential appears. Furthermore, once created, an action potential maintains its size as it travels through the axon, regardless of the distance involved. This amazing mechanism propagates signals faithfully over long distances.

The Electroencephalogram (EEG)

Recording actual human brain synaptic and action potentials would require inserting electrodes through the skull. However, we can learn about these signals and their electrical fields by placing electrodes outside a person's head in a procedure called an *electroencephalogram* or *EEG*. To record an EEG, a technician attaches many conductive surfaces around the head, each making electrical contact with the scalp at a particular position relative to brain areas underneath. Even though individual synaptic and action potentials involve tiny voltages, the coordinated activation of these potentials creates sufficiently large signals to measure with such external electrodes. These signals do not resemble the small individual synaptic or action potentials. Rather, many synaptic and action potentials occurring in a brain area simultaneously are recorded as summed activity by the electrodes, which appears as a wave in the EEG. So an EEG reflects the degree of simultaneous or coordinated activity of many neurons. When the degree of coordinated neural activity is high, the EEG contains large waves. Conversely, when different synapses and neurons are active at different times, the EEG waves are small and irregular.

Chemical Signals Control Neuron Activity

Once an action potential reaches the end of an axon, how is its signal transmitted to the next neuron? In 1921 physiologist Otto Loewi investigated the idea that chemical agents could stimulate and modulate the actions of the nervous system (see Finger, 2000). Most physiologists at the time believed that communication across neurons was accomplished primarily by an electrical signal. However, some people thought there might also be chemical transmission or modulation of the electrical signal. Loewi devised an experiment to test whether a chemical mechanism was involved in transmitting information between nerve cells.

Loewi removed a frog's heart and bathed it in a neutral solution, where it continued to beat for a substantial period. He electrically stimulated the nerve attached to the heart that slows heart rate. Loewi then removed some of the bathing solution and placed it in a different chamber holding another beating frog heart. After a few seconds, with no direct stimulation of the second heart's nerve, the second heart also slowed. This demonstrated that a chemical agent produced in the stimulated heart—and absorbed in its bathing solution—could slow heart rate. Loewi also performed a complementary experiment: He showed that bathing solution taken after stimulation of a different nerve accelerated heart rate could accelerate a nonstimulated heart. So at least two chemical agents communicate between nerves and the heart—one that slows the heart and another that speeds it up.

These chemicals, called neurotransmitters, are molecules secreted by one neuron to affect the activity of another. The neurotransmitter that slows heart rate is acetylcholine, and the neurotransmitter that accelerates heart rate is noradrenaline. Subsequent research has shown that similar chemical transmission regulates the activity of all neurons. Considerable work has refined our understanding of how these two neurotransmitters work. In addition, we have identified many other neurotransmitters, some of which play critical roles in memory.

Chemical Transmission Supports Communication between Neurons at Synapses

How exactly does chemical communication between neurons work? As we discussed earlier, neurons are connected by synapses. A synapse is composed of two main parts: the **presynaptic element** (the enlarged end of an axon) and the **postsynaptic element** (a specialized area of the dendrite or cell body with receptors for the neurotransmitters), and these two elements are separated by a small gap called the **synaptic cleft** (Figure 2.6). The presynaptic element packages neurotransmitters into **synaptic vesicles**—tiny packets that allow neurotransmitters to travel between neurons. When an action potential arrives at the presynaptic element, the synaptic vesicles bind with the membrane of the presynaptic element and release their neurotransmitters, which diffuse across the synaptic cleft. After the neurotransmitters reach the postsynaptic element, they bind briefly to **receptors,** which are specialized molecular structures in the postsynaptic element that receive neurotransmitters and generate synaptic potentials.

How exactly do neurotransmitters generate synaptic potentials? When an action potential reaches a presynaptic element, channels there allow calcium ($Ca++$) molecules to flow inside (Figure 2.6). The resulting rise in $Ca++$ within the presynaptic element fuses vesicles with the cell membrane, thus releasing a neurotransmitter into the synaptic cleft. The neurotransmitter then diffuses across the synaptic cleft and binds with receptors in the postsynaptic membrane. In many synapses, this process opens $Na+$ channels in the postsynaptic membrane; $Na+$ flows into the postsynaptic cells, causing an **excitatory postsynaptic potential (EPSP).** An EPSP is called *excitatory* because it brings a neuron closer to its threshold for generating an action potential.

However, there are many types of neurotransmitters and many types of receptors, even for the same neurotransmitter. This variation allows considerable regulation of the duration and type of postsynaptic potentials. One major variant of synaptic transmission occurs at synapses that are *inhibitory* rather than excitatory. Here receptor activation opens channels for chloride ($Cl-$), which is a negatively charged molecule concentrated outside the cell membrane. In this situation, the

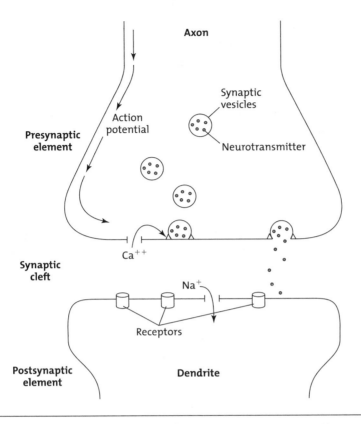

FIGURE 2.6 The synapse and synaptic transmission.

postsynaptic element becomes even more negatively charged (below −70 mV), resulting in an **inhibitory postsynaptic potential (IPSP).** Conduction of an IPSP to a neuron's dendrites inhibits the generation of an action potential. The EPSPs and IPSPs that reach a neuron at the same time add together to determine whether the threshold for an action potential will be reached. And the rate and pattern of EPSPs and IPSPs determine the rate and pattern of the neuron's action potentials.

After a short period determined by the chemical properties of the neurotransmitters and receptors, the binding process is interrupted by an unbinding and diffusion of the neurotransmitter or by other molecules in the synapse that destroy the neurotransmitter. The neurotransmitter or the products of its breakdown are reabsorbed by the presynaptic membrane and repackaged into new vesicles. Thus neurotransmitters are recycled for reuse in synaptic transmission.

Most Drugs That Affect the Mind Modify Synaptic Transmission

Most street drugs that influence our thinking and emotions work by affecting the functions of neurotransmitters. For example, cocaine is a stimulant that causes intense euphoria. Cocaine produces a "peak experience" that makes people feel good about themselves and think they can do anything. Cocaine was discovered by the Incas and was at times used by Shakespeare, Robert Louis Stevenson, Freud, and Sir Arthur Conan Doyle's genius detective Sherlock Holmes. It was an active ingredient in many salves sold to cure everyday problems, including the popular drink Coca-Cola in its original formulation. Unfortunately cocaine can also cause sudden heart failure in people who abuse it or take an overdose. Cocaine is also highly addictive. People who use it a lot and then try to stop "crash": They feel anxious, depressed, despondent, irritable, and immensely tired, and they have an intense craving for more cocaine.

Cocaine works by blocking a mechanism through which the neurotransmitters norepinephrine and dopamine are reabsorbed into presynaptic sites. These neurotransmitters stay in synaptic clefts longer, where they can again bind to receptors and continue to activate the postsynaptic cells. Thus cocaine enhances synaptic potentials at synapses that use the neurotransmitters norepinephrine and dopamine. Such receptors are prevalent in particular locations in the nervous system, and the enhancement of synaptic function there explains the effects of cocaine. For example, in the emotional system of the brain, norepinephrine and dopamine are major excitatory neurotransmitters; so one immediate effect of cocaine is to induce the feeling of an emotional high. At the same time (as discussed earlier), norepinephrine is the neurotransmitter that accelerates heart rate. Cocaine can speed the heart so severely that the heart spasmodically contracts and cannot pump blood. Finally, when someone becomes addicted to cocaine, the brain and body reduce the number of receptors for norepinephrine and dopamine—almost as if trying to become less sensitive to the drug's effects. Consequently, when cocaine is withdrawn, there are fewer receptors and less activation of the emotional system, resulting in the "crashing" syndrome.

This example illustrates how many street drugs operate by influencing multiple functions of neurotransmitters, resulting in syndromes of both short-term and lasting effects. But remember that many prescription drugs used to treat mental disorders—from depression to memory loss—also work by enhancing neurotransmitter function in various ways.

Interim Summary

Cajal discovered that the brain is composed of many individual neurons, each of which is composed of a cell body, several dendrites, and an axon. Cajal correctly envisioned that memory relies on the number and strength of connections between neurons. Neurons communicate across synapses with two kinds of signals: synaptic potentials and action potentials. When synaptic transmission occurs, sodium (Na+) flows into a dendrite, resulting in a synaptic potential that varies in size depending on the strength of the connection. The synaptic potential dissipates as it travels; but if the remaining potential is above a threshold, an action potential is generated at the beginning of the axon. The action potential is much larger than a synaptic potential and remains at a constant size as it travels along the axon. When an action potential reaches the end of an axon, tiny vesicles containing a neurotransmitter fuse with the presynaptic membrane and release the neurotransmitter, which then diffuses across the synaptic cleft and binds with receptors in the postsynaptic site, resulting in a synaptic potential.

There are different types of neurotransmitters. Those that bind with postsynaptic receptors to open channels for Na+ to flow into the postsynaptic site and cause an EPSP are excitatory. Those that bind with postsynaptic receptors to open channels for chloride (Cl−) to flow into the postsynaptic site and cause an IPSP are inhibitory. The many neurotransmitters and types of receptors cause variation in the size and duration of EPSPs and IPSPs.

Interconnected Neurons in Brain Circuits Serve Specific Functions

Around the same time that Cajal was revealing the fine structure of the brain, British physiologist Charles Sherrington (1906) discovered the simplest brain circuit—the **reflex arc**, in which a sensory stimulus leads to a specific, involuntary muscular or behavioral response. Consider, for example, the pain withdrawal reflex that can pull your hand away from a hot pan you have mistakenly grabbed (Figure 2.7). The circuit for this reflex involves pain sensory receptors in the skin of the hand, whose axons

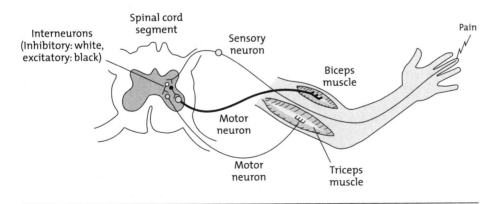

FIGURE 2.7 Circuit of the pain withdrawal reflex.
Shown are both the circuit that uses an excitatory interneuron (the black cell body) to activate the biceps muscle, flexing the arm, and the related circuit that uses an inhibitory interneuron (the white cell body) to inhibit activation of the triceps muscle.

travel into the spinal cord to synapses with interneurons—cells that communicate between neurons within a local region. The spinal interneurons connect with motor neurons, whose axons travel from the spinal cord back down the arm to the biceps muscle, which flexes the arm. Sherrington called this kind of circuit a *reflex arc* because the skin pain initiates nerve signals that are sent to the spinal cord and then "reflected" back to the arm to execute its withdrawal movement. Such reflexes can be generated without conscious or voluntary effort.

When Sherrington began his work, the involuntary nature of reflexes was already recognized. In addition, others had demonstrated the existence of complex coordinated movements supported in the spinal cord without brain guidance. For example, even following decapitation, skin stimulation could produce jumping movements in frogs or coordinated flying wing movements in birds. However, the circuitry that accomplished simple reflexes and complex coordination was still mysterious.

Some of Sherrington's work paralleled Cajal's investigations of anatomical connections between distinct neurons. Sherrington measured the speed at which nerve impulses are conducted and noted that this communication rate slowed where neurons connect. He also found that conduction between neurons was mainly one-way. Sherrington concluded that there must be a specialized connection from the axon of one cell to the dendrite of the next cell.

In addition, Sherrington identified and studied the physiology of excitatory and inhibitory synapses. He discovered *reciprocal innervation*, a circuit mechanism by which every action by one muscle is coordinated with an opposing action of complementary muscles. For example, the arm has both a biceps muscle that can flex it and a triceps muscle that can extend it. The pain withdrawal reflex is usually evoked when someone contracts the triceps, extending the arm to touch a painful stimulus. When the reflex is engaged, the biceps is contracted to withdraw the arm, while the triceps is inhibited.

Sherrington showed that these relatively complex circuits for coordinated actions can operate even when the brain is disconnected from the spinal cord. He speculated that the basis for behavioral sequences made up of smaller component motions might be a "chaining" of reflexes, wherein each successive coordinated movement would be elicited by its predecessor.

Are Memories Represented in Reflex Circuits?

Sherrington envisioned that excitatory and inhibitory reflex elements could account for all complex actions of the nervous system. He proposed that the most complex aspects of perception, action, and memory were embodied in reflex arcs within the cerebral cortex, whereas lower centers mediated more specific and simpler reflexes.

How might reflexes be involved in learning and memory? As we discussed in Chapter 1, behaviorists believed that learning and memory can be explained by associations between stimuli and behavioral responses: After previously neutral stimuli have been followed by appropriate rewards, those stimuli can elicit specific behaviors. Sherrington's suggestion that reflex arcs might be the framework for stimulus–response (S–R) representations later served as a foundation for behaviorism. Indeed, for the first half of the 20th century, the popular view was that learning was mediated by a strengthening of circuits between sensory neurons that perceive important stimuli and motor neurons that control behavioral responses to those stimuli. This learning was thought to take place at various levels of the spinal cord and brain for different types of learned behavior.

Enthusiasm about the parallels between Sherrington's reflex discoveries and the principles of behaviorism led early neuroscientists to look for reflex pathways in the brain, particularly in the cerebral cortex. Their findings, however, were disconcerting. For example, pioneering neuroscientist Karl Lashley suggested that S–R learning might be supported by the development of new connections between the sensory processing area at the back of the cerebral cortex and the motor controlling areas at its front end.

To examine this hypothesis, Lashley trained rats to solve mazes, then carefully placed cuts between the sensory and motor areas of the rats' cortexes, expecting that an appropriate cut would disconnect the stimulus from the learned response and eliminate the corresponding memory. He then tested the animals to see whether they had retained their maze memory. However, Lashley failed to find a specific circuit for memories; no particular cut "disconnected" the rats' retention of maze learning. So Lashley tried larger cuts, removing whole areas of cortical tissue. Again, no specific brain damage eliminated a particular memory. Rather, memories generally degraded depending on the extent of tissue damaged in the cortex. In a pessimistic end to his career, Lashley concluded that "learning is just not possible" (Lashley, 1950). His findings were considered a repudiation of the behaviorist view that learning could be understood in terms of connections between sensory stimuli (S) and behavioral responses (R). Could the cognitivists be right about the need for a more complex mechanism than S–R?

Are Memories Stored in Brain Cell Assemblies?

In 1949 Donald Hebb proposed a possible reconciliation of the behaviorist and cognitivist views in a theory that could account for Lashley's observations. Instead of simple S–R, sensory-to-motor circuits as a basis for memory, Hebb proposed that diffuse brain circuits of neurons could strengthen their connections to operate as a **cell assembly**—a group of interconnected neurons representing a perception or concept. Hebb suggested that a cell assembly formed when the cells were active together, and this collective activity would somehow enhance the structural connections between the cells. He asserted that different cell assemblies could use some of the same cells and that memories were encoded within the activities of whole cell groups rather than in individual cells. Hebb envisioned cell assemblies as networks of cells distributed across a wide expanse of the cortex, not dependent on any particular cells or connections. This concept was consistent with Lashley's findings that rats' maze memories were not stored at discrete sites and could not be disrupted or erased with any particular surgical cut. Rather, the overall performance of the cell assembly was expected to degrade in proportion to the amount of cell loss, as Lashley had observed.

How might such cell assemblies form? Hebb proposed that the synapse was the likely site for structural changes in the neuron that could support memory. His most famous postulate describes how repetitive activity might cause permanent structural change and stabilization:

> When an axon of cell A is near enough to excite a cell B and repeatedly or persistently takes part in firing it, some growth process or metabolic change takes place in one or both cells such that A's efficiency, as one of the cells firing B, is increased. (p. 62)

Hebb suggested that repeatedly activating a particular circuit could stabilize intercellular cooperation within a cell assembly. Initial presentations of a stimulus might set off neural firing that would feed back through circuits to the initially activated cells, such that the overall pattern of activation would reverberate through the circuit. According to Hebb's synaptic postulate, each cycle of activity would strengthen the synapses at circuit connections, and the neurons involved would thus form a cell assembly representing a thought or an action. Additionally, when parts of the circuit were reexcited by only part of the initial input, the entire assembly would tend to reestablish itself. (Today we call this *pattern completion*. For example, when you hear words of a familiar phrase such as "Give me liberty, or . . ." you readily complete this pattern with " . . . give me death.") Hebb's postulate about the growth of cell assemblies has become a guiding theme of research into the cellular basis of memory representations.

Since Hebb's era, neuroscientists have made tremendous advances in understanding the mechanisms underlying the creation of cell assemblies that support memory. One leap came with the discovery of **long-term potentiation (LTP),** which is a cellular mechanism for strengthening connections between neurons. LTP is most commonly studied in the hippocampus—a brain structure that is important for memory, easy to find, and relatively simple. Characterization of LTP mechanisms has been greatly facilitated by the development of the *hippocampal slice* preparation, in which thick sections of the hippocampus are taken from the brain of a rat or mouse and kept alive in a petri dish (Figure 2.8). This preparation lacks the normal inputs and outputs of the hippocampus but provides clear access to cells and internal circuits.

The phenomenon of LTP was discovered by Tim Bliss and his student Terje Lomo, who were exploring the physiology of the hippocampus. They observed that after repetitive high-frequency electrical stimulation of one pathway, a synapse showed two signs of increased efficiency (Bliss & Lomo, 1973):

1. A single stimulation caused a more rapid increase in the excitatory synaptic potential.
2. A single stimulation recruited more cells that reached the action potential threshold.

These changes in the synaptic and cellular responses lasted for several hours, which is why Lomo called the phenomenon *long-term potentiation* (LTP). Many researchers now consider LTP the basic mechanism by which cells enhance their synaptic connections to form cell assemblies.

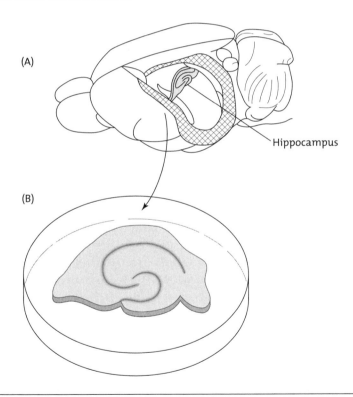

FIGURE 2.8 The hippocampal slice preparation.
A. Cutaway view of the rat brain exposing the hippocampus inside, and a view of the slice that is taken through the hippocampus. B. Slice of hippocampus tissue in a petri dish.

How does LTP work? Consistent with Hebb's hypothesis, inducing LTP in neurons requires two synaptic events: a presynaptic signal and an increase in the potential of the postsynaptic cell. Both are ordinarily accomplished when a synapse is activated repetitively in rapid succession. The initial activation produces action potentials in the postsynaptic cell and an associated increase in that cell's potential, whereas the following stimulations provide simultaneous presynaptic signals. LTP can also support an association between separate synaptic connections that are simultaneously active. When stimulation at one synapse is sufficient to produce an action potential in the target cell, simultaneous stimulation of another synapse, even if weak, will provide concurrent presynaptic activation. As a result, both synapses have LTP and are "associated" so that stimulating either one activates the cells as if both inputs were stimulated. This phenomenon, called *associative LTP*, supports new associations between stimuli or between stimuli and responses.

The molecular mechanism of the most common type of hippocampal LTP involves special properties of a combination of synaptic receptors. The most frequent excitatory neurotransmitter in the hippocampus is the amino acid glutamate. Glutamate receptors include two types: NMDA receptors and AMPA receptors (both these names are acronyms for very long words). These receptors work together to induce LTP. When the postsynaptic site is at rest, AMPA receptors are ready for glutamate to bind, but NMDA receptors are blocked by magnesium ($Mg++$) molecules (Figure 2.9A). When the presynaptic neuron is first activated, glutamate is released and binds to AMPA receptors, which allows sodium ($Na+$) to enter the postsynaptic site, causing an excitatory postsynaptic potential (EPSP). This is the typical excitatory synaptic function described earlier in the chapter.

However, when the initial activation causes an action potential in the postsynaptic neuron, something unusual happens at synapses that undergo LTP. The increased potential in the postsynaptic cells removes the $Mg++$ and unblocks the NMDA receptors (Figure 2.9B). If the same presynaptic neuron (or a neighboring neuron that also connects to the postsynaptic cell) fires soon after the initial activation, the released glutamate binds to both the AMPA and the unblocked NMDA receptors. This binding of glutamate to NMDA receptors is important because, unlike AMPA receptors, NMDA receptors allow calcium ($Ca++$) to enter the postsynaptic cell.

The $Ca++$ that enters the postsynaptic neuron engages a host of molecular events that activate previously inactive AMPA receptors (Figure 2.9C). These receptors immediately make the postsynaptic cell more sensitive to input from the presynaptic cell. Also, $Ca++$ helps the cell synthesize new proteins called neurotrophins, which enlarge the synapses and permanently sensitize them. High-resolution optical methods have detected new postsynaptic receptors growing on dendrites shortly after LTP is induced.

(A) **Normal synaptic transmission**

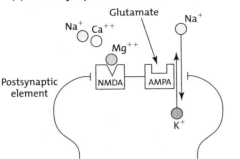

(B) **Depolarization at synapse during LTP**

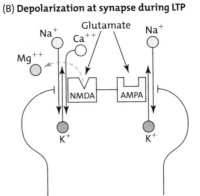

(C) **Calcium enters the postsynaptic site**

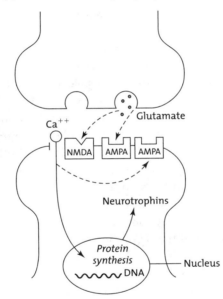

FIGURE 2.9 The molecular basis of LTP.
A. Normal synaptic transmission. B. During depolarization. C. Ca++ enters the postsynaptic site.

If synaptic change could only *increase* synaptic efficacy, all synapses would eventually become saturated—that is, raised to a maximum level of efficacy at which no further learning could occur. But there is also a mechanism of depotentiation or **long-term depression (LTD)** of synaptic efficacy. In general, LTD occurs when either presynaptic activity or postsynaptic activity occurs alone.

Although LTP was discovered in the hippocampus, LTP and LTD have now been demonstrated in several brain areas, including the amygdala, the striatum, and areas of the cerebral cortex known to play vital roles in learning and memory. LTP and LTD are increasingly being considered universal mechanisms for altering the efficiency of connections between neurons.

LTP and Memory May Share the Same Cellular Mechanisms

LTP is definitely not memory: It is a laboratory phenomenon involving massive activations never observed in nature. However, the cellular mechanisms of LTP are apparently also the cellular mechanisms that support memory. Evidence for this comes from two main sources: studies showing that learning produces synaptic physiology changes similar to those caused by LTP and studies showing that blocking LTP can prevent learning.

Some evidence that learning changes synaptic efficacy has come from studies of brain areas other than the hippocampus. For example, John Donoghue and his colleagues demonstrated the generalizability of LTP mechanisms to other brain areas and another form of learning (Rioult-Pedotti et al., 1998). In these experiments, rats were trained to retrieve food pellets through a small hole in a box. Initially the rats' movements were labored, and they often dropped the pellets. However, over one or two practice sessions, the rats refined their motor coordination to obtain pellets rapidly.

Following this training, Donoghue and colleagues removed the rats' brains and measured the connection strength among cells within the area of the motor cortex that controls paw movements. They accomplished this by measuring excitatory synaptic potentials (EPSPs) in the motor cortex after stimulating axons that connected neighboring cells. For the same input stimulation intensity, the EPSPs on the side of the brain that controlled the trained paw were consistently larger than those on the opposite side of the brain. Furthermore, they found it difficult to induce LTP by electrical stimulation in the trained side of the brain, but not in the untrained side. Thus training was followed by a localized increase in synaptic efficacy that saturated the involved neurons' capacity for LTP. These observations suggest that synaptic potentiation resulting from motor learning uses the same synapses and same mechanisms as the synaptic enhancement produced by LTP— providing strong evidence for common cellular mechanisms of learning and LTP.

The chief limitation of the approach just described is that the studies merely show correlations between aspects of LTP and memory. The converse approach would be to bolster the case for cause-and-effect links between the mechanisms of LTP and memory by blocking LTP and determining whether memory is prevented. Compelling data for a potential connection between the molecular bases of LTP and memory have come from experiments in which a drug or genetic manipulation blocking LTP also prevents learning.

Some early, strong evidence supporting this connection between LTP and memory came from studies of spatial learning by Richard G. M. Morris and his colleagues (Steele & Morris, 1999). Morris developed a maze learning task requiring hippocampal function in rats. The maze involved a swimming pool in which the water was made opaque by a milky powder; an escape platform was slightly submerged (Figure 2.10). Rats are good swimmers, but they prefer to find a platform and stand. Typically they are trained to find the platform from four starting positions around the periphery of the maze, and they show learning by finding the platform more quickly. At the end of training, their memory is assessed using a probe test in which the platform is removed. A rat exhibits good memory and effective learning by swimming directly toward the platform location and circling that area of the maze as if expecting to find the platform.

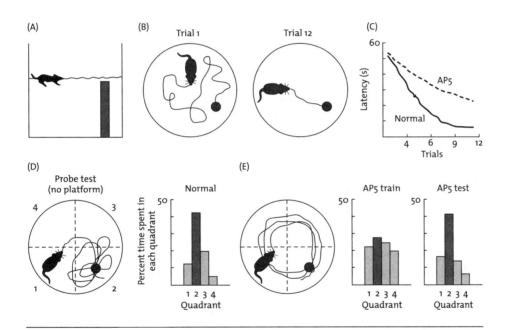

FIGURE 2.10 The water maze and LTP.
A. A side view of the water maze with a rat swimming and a submerged platform.
B. Overhead views of the rat's swim path on trials 1 and 12. C. Time (latency) to find the platform over the course of training. D. Swim path of a trained rat on the probe test and percentage of time spent in the quadrant of the maze that previously had the platform (dark gray) and in other quadrants of the maze. E. Swim path for the probe trial of a rat treated with AP5 during training and distribution of time in maze quadrants if AP5 was given during training (left) or only during the probe test (right).

Morris and his colleagues examined the effects of AP5—a drug that selectively blocks NMDA receptors, which are essential for the induction of LTP, and not AMPA receptors, which support normal synaptic transmission. AP5 prevented new spatial learning in the water maze in a specific way. Drug-treated rats swam normally but did not reach the platform as quickly as normal rats. Indeed, the drug-treated rats often swam in circles around the maze, which is an efficient way to eventually run into a platform without knowing its exact location. In the probe tests, normal rats tended to swim in the former vicinity of the platform; but drug-treated rats showed little or no such bias, indicating that they did not remember the platform location (see Chapter 8 for further discussion of this task). In additional experiments, the researchers tested the effect of AP5 on information retention by administering the drug after training was accomplished; but the drug showed no effect in these tests. This is consistent with the theory that NMDA receptors are required only for the induction of LTP, not for its maintenance.

Learning & Memory in Action

Can Genetic Alterations Improve Memory?

Knowing about NMDA receptors has helped us understand and develop new drugs that can affect memory. One example was discussed at the beginning of this chapter. The drug midazolam that was used during Jenny's endoscopic surgery is a potent blocker of NMDA receptors. Based on what you have read about the role of NMDA receptors in synaptic change and memory, you can now appreciate how this drug can eliminate memory of a stressful experience. Are there also ways to improve memory using our knowledge about NMDA receptors?

Early evidence suggests that such improvements are possible—at least in mice. Genetic modification pioneer Joseph Tsien and several colleagues have created mice with extra NMDA receptors, and LTP can be induced more readily in the brains of these genetically modified mice than in normal mice (Tang et al., 1999). Furthermore, the genetically modified mice are superior learners. Might genetic modifications be applied one day to improve memory in humans as well?

You may imagine that parents would be interested in a technique, not yet possible, for inserting a gene to increase NMDA receptors in their developing fetus. This seems tantalizing, but we don't know what side effects could occur; one might be a tendency to have seizures. And it's not clear whether we should always want to learn as quickly as possible rather than accumulating new information gradually enough to integrate it with experiences. Also, researchers might seek drugs that can increase NMDA receptors; such discoveries could lead to the development of a pill that students might take before studying for tests. Developing such "cognitive enhancers" is indeed a major interest of many pharmaceutical companies that are searching for treatments of memory disorders, such as Alzheimer's disease, as well as drugs that might enhance normal memory.

Interim Summary

Reflex arcs are relatively simple circuits in which a sensory neuron sends signals to interneurons, which in turn send signals to motor neurons, resulting in muscle movements. A variety of such reflexes are located in the spinal cord, and they usually have complementary reflexes that perform the opposite action. The coordinated excitation and inhibition of complementary opposing reflexes can produce complex functions such as walking. Sherrington proposed that a hierarchy of coordinated reflexes, extending all the way to the cerebral cortex, could be the basis for complex functions, including learning and memory. Lashley pursued experiments that sought to disconnect sensory from cortical areas of the brain, expecting to disrupt pathways from areas that process sensory stimuli to those that process motor responses. These experiments failed to find such pathways and instead showed that the amount of brain damaged determined the degree of learning impairment. This observation led Hebb to propose that memories might be represented by large neuron networks, called cell assemblies, that form when active neurons reliably engage the firing of neighboring cells, strengthening connections between all neurons in the network. This increased connection efficacy between neurons increases the likelihood of reactivating the entire cell assembly that represents a memory.

Lasting increases in synaptic efficacy, called long-term potentiation (LTP), occur when an initial neural activation unblocks NMDA receptors, causing a second activation that allows $Ca++$ to enter the cell. This influx of $Ca++$ has several consequences that increase the ease with which that neuron is subsequently activated. Additional studies have shown close associations between LTP mechanisms and those of real memory. The same changes in synaptic efficiency that characterize LTP also occur as a result of real learning; and interventions that block LTP impair memory too.

Brain Systems Serve Psychological Functions

In the early 1800s the young German physician Franz Joseph Gall wondered how the human brain is organized and where memories are stored (see Finger, 2000). He was struck by individuals' varied personalities and mental capacities. He thought these disparate mental faculties were due to brain differences. Gall speculated that the many independent psychological traits were served by specialized brain organs. Gall called his theory **organology** (later called *phrenology*) and suggested that individual differences in psychological faculties were associated with variations in the development of particular brain organs.

Gall realized that proving this theory would require comparing the sizes of specific brain areas in people with different mental capacities. It was not possible in Gall's time to examine the brain directly in living people, so he boldly assumed that the size of the skull area overlying a faculty-specific organ would be larger in people whose psyche emphasized that faculty.

Exploiting this assumption, Gall investigated his theory by carefully observing individuals' variations in particular psychological faculties and correlating those traits with unusual features of their skull anatomy. Gall sought people with special talents (such as writers, diplomats, and musical and mathematical prodigies) as well as people with behavioral abnormalities (the mentally ill, the unintelligent, and criminals). He interviewed people extensively to characterize their behavioral qualities and carefully examined their heads. Based on his categorizations of their abilities and the skull features he found, Gall inferred relationships between skull surface peculiarities and unusual aspects of behavior. For example, he observed that people who had an outstanding memory for stories had bulging eyes. Gall suggested that enhanced development of an organ in the frontal lobes specialized for verbal memory.

In addition, Gall collected hundreds of animal skulls and compared their anatomical features with those of human skulls. He sought relationships between animal behavioral propensities and psychological faculties of humans that shared certain features of skull anatomy. For example, Gall noted a skull area that was larger in carnivores than in grass-eating animals. A similar skull area was quite large in a successful businessman who gave up his profession to become a butcher, in a student who was fond of torturing animals and became a surgeon, and in a pharmacist who became an executioner. Based on this evidence, Gall localized the faculty of "destructiveness, carnivorous instinct, or tendency to murder" to an area above the ears. Thus Gall devised a system of faculties localized to specific brain areas, some shared by humans and animals and some exclusively human.

Gall's specific assignments of cortical areas to particular functions were completely wrong due to two major flaws in his methods. First, as you can appreciate in the examples discussed, Gall's interpretations of personalities or mental faculties were subjective and based on relatively few case studies. Second, Gall assumed a close correlation between skull and brain anatomy and did not examine the brain directly. It turns out that skull anatomy has many influences, of which the size of brain areas underneath is modest.

Subsequent clinical and experimental work failed to support Gall's map of functional assignments. However, these later studies demonstrated that different mental functions are indeed accomplished by specific areas within the cerebral cortex—the part of the brain that lies just beneath the skull. For example, years later French physician Paul Broca identified an area in the left frontal lobe that is critical to speech production; similarly, Carl Wernicke discovered an area in the left parietal lobe that is crucial in language comprehension (see Finger, 2000). Other experiments by physiologists demonstrated that stimulating particular cerebral cortex areas produces specific muscular movements and that a "map" of the body's motor functions exists in the parietal lobe. Gall was wrong about the specifics; but he correctly guessed that the cerebral cortex is composed of multiple functionally distinct areas, each of which serves a particular role.

Modern Phrenology: Functional Brain Imaging

Since Broca's and Wernicke's initial descriptions of specific cortical areas that support language, there have been many discoveries about the functions served by different areas of the cortex, revealed by loss of those functions when specific brain areas are damaged. For example, areas in the back of the cerebral cortex are required for vision, and complex thinking relies on the front of the cortex. In addition, modern technologies have let scientists identify functions of specific cortical areas in humans with intact brains. One of the foremost of these technologies is called *functional magnetic resonance imaging* (fMRI).

To produce an fMRI, technicians place a person's head in a scanning device with large electromagnets and an array of sensors. Brief magnetic pulses are presented while the subject performs a task. The powerful magnetic pulses cause molecules in the brain that respond to magnetic energy to twist slightly and then return to their original orientation when the pulse ends. One molecule that twists in response to magnetic pulses is hemoglobin, a primary component of blood with two features that are crucial for fMRI scanning. Hemoglobin contains an iron molecule, which makes it twist in response to the magnetic pulse; it is also the blood molecule that carries oxygen to the body's cells.

During an fMRI scan, the degree to which hemoglobin twists depends on whether an oxygen molecule is attached to or has been released from the hemoglobin to be consumed by cells. This is handy because when brain areas are active, they consume more oxygen. So highly active brain areas respond differently to the magnetic pulses than less active areas, and this difference registers in the magnetic signals recorded by the fMRI sensors around the head. Sophisticated computers use the sensors' signals to construct an image of the brain's structure, highlighting the more active areas.

The earliest fMRI studies confirmed that the brain areas then thought to be necessary for language functions are precisely the areas activated in normal human subjects performing relevant language tasks (Figure 2.11). Now fMRI has identified many functions of other cortical areas, generating a modern "phrenology" of

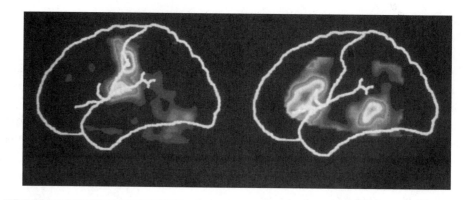

FIGURE 2.11 Examples of fMRI images taken during different language-related tasks.

the cerebral cortex. The powerful tool of fMRI has become a key method used to explore brain function in learning and memory.

The Brain Operates Hierarchically

The nervous system is composed of two main components—the central nervous system and the peripheral nervous system (Figure 2.12). The *central nervous system* itself also has two main parts—the brain and spinal cord. The central nervous system is built to receive sensory information and send action commands to the body through a system of major *nerves* (bundles of axons). The *cranial nerves* connect to the brain, and the *spinal nerves* connect to the spinal cord. The several types of cranial nerves differ considerably in whether they deliver sensory information to the brain, conduct commands out of the brain, or both; in the kinds of information they conduct; and in the locations where they connect to the brain. Spinal nerves are more uniform: They all conduct sensory information into the spinal cord and send commands that originate in motor neurons out from the spinal cord to the body's organs and muscles. These spinal nerves carry signals in and out of the *peripheral nervous system,* which has two major components: the *somatic nervous system* that controls skeletal muscles and the *autonomic nervous system* that controls the body's organ functions.

Now let's work our way through the human brain from the bottom up (Figure 2.13). The brain is divided into three levels that develop at different times during the gestation of an embryo—the hindbrain, midbrain, and forebrain.

THE HINDBRAIN The *hindbrain,* which is continuous with the spinal cord, contains many cranial nerves and groups of neurons, called *nuclei,* that coordinate

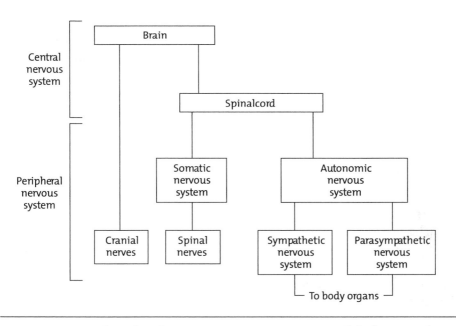

FIGURE 2.12 Hierarchy of nervous system components and their connections.

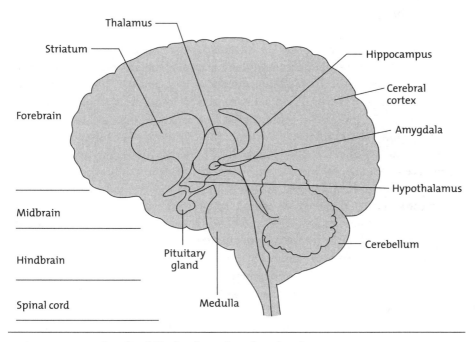

FIGURE 2.13 Levels of the brain and major structures.

impulses to and from the spinal cord and cranial nerves. The hindbrain serves a variety of crucial purposes, including control over respiration and level of arousal (that is, sleep and wakefulness). It connects with several important cranial nerves, including those to the heart, circulatory system, and diaphragm (controlling respiration); and it plays a significant role in maintaining wakeful arousal and orchestrating sleep. On the surface of the hindbrain is the **cerebellum**, a large structure that supports fine coordination of movement. It also is essential for learned coordination between specific sensory stimuli and adjustments to movement, such as blinking in anticipation of an air puff. Recent evidence suggests the cerebellum may play a role in various aspects of language and other cognitive functions.

THE MIDBRAIN Just above the hindbrain is the *midbrain*. Part of the midbrain contains centers for coordinating vision and hearing with movements; these areas are vital to our ability to orient to potentially important stimuli. Another part of the midbrain controls basic orienting movements, such as gazing toward moving objects, and reflexive behaviors, including escape or freezing behaviors that can be conditioned.

THE FOREBRAIN Above the midbrain is the *forebrain,* which has two principal subdivisions whose appearance and functions are quite different. The lower subdivision contains the *thalamus*—a set of nuclei with various purposes in communicating information from the lower brain areas to the cerebral cortex. Some of these functions involve relaying sensory information. Other thalamus functions involve coordinating various cerebral cortex areas to select which stimuli receive conscious attention. At the bottom of the thalamus is the *hypothalamus,* which regulates basic survival behaviors like eating, sleeping, and sex. It is vital for emotional activities and responses. In addition, the hypothalamus is connected to the *pituitary gland*—the most important gland of the hormonal system because it directs the functions of other glands throughout the body. The hypothalamus controls the pituitary gland through axons that connect it to pituitary glandular cells, giving the hypothalamus direct control over the secretion of hormones related to stress, reproduction, and digestion.

On the surface of the forebrain are two roughly symmetrical *cerebral hemispheres,* which contain many structures vital to complex aspects of cognitive and emotional life. We will focus on a few here that are particularly important to learning and memory. The **striatum** consists of nuclei that control posture and movement. These nuclei let us coordinate movements to execute a specific objective, such as walking or grasping; this system helps us learn habitual movement patterns and physical skills. The **hippocampus** is part of the cerebral cortex that, in evolutionary terms, was one of the first cortical areas to develop; it is essential to conscious memory. The amygdala coordinates emotional responses to stimuli.

In humans, the largest component of the cerebral hemispheres is the **cerebral cortex**. The cerebral cortex is characterized by an organization of neurons unlike other parts of the brain. Its neurons are arranged in layers; so if the cerebral cortex were removed and smoothed out, it would look like a large multilayered sheet. This sheet is crumpled and folded many times, giving the outside of the brain its bumpy surface.

The cerebral cortex is divided into roughly symmetrical halves—the *cerebral hemispheres*, which are connected by a bundle of axons called the *corpus callosum*. Each hemisphere is divided into four lobes: the *occipital lobe*, the *parietal lobe*, the *temporal lobe*, and the *frontal lobe* (Figure 2.14). These lobes, along with the areas within them, have distinct functions in processing sensory information, controlling movement, thinking, and storing learned information.

The Cerebral Cortex Has Three Levels of Organization

The cerebral cortex can be thought of as the chief organ of the brain, like the CEO of a company. Like a CEO, the cortex receives information that has already been substantially processed by a series of different brain systems (like employees within departments). These systems are the main functional areas of the brain, and the

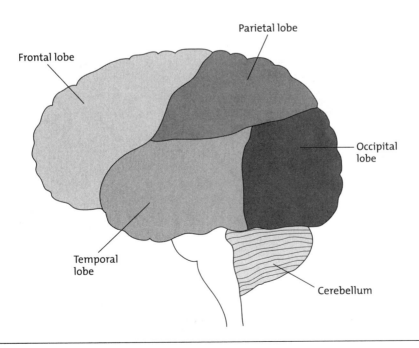

FIGURE 2.14 Lobes of the cerebral cortex.

modifiability of neural connections within each of these systems supports a particular aspect of learning and memory. So understanding the brain's functional systems, and how these systems support learning and memory, depends on a clear conception of how information is organized by the cerebral cortex. This section describes three organizational levels of the cerebral cortex.

The first level of cortical organization involves a distinction between the left and right cerebral hemispheres. The two hemispheres are symmetrical in appearance and to some extent in their functions (with a few differences). Each hemisphere mainly controls functions of the *contralateral* (that is, opposite) side of the body. Thus your right cerebral hemisphere perceives sensory information primarily from the left side of your body and controls movements of the left side of your body, whereas your left cerebral hemisphere perceives stimuli from and controls mainly the right side of your body.

The second level of cortical organization involves distinctions among functions of the cortex areas within each hemisphere. The posterior, or rear, part of the cortex has distinct areas for processing different types of sensory information. The *occipital lobe* processes visual input; the *temporal lobe* handles auditory stimuli; and the *parietal lobe* handles the touch-based senses (Figure 2.15). Other parts of the

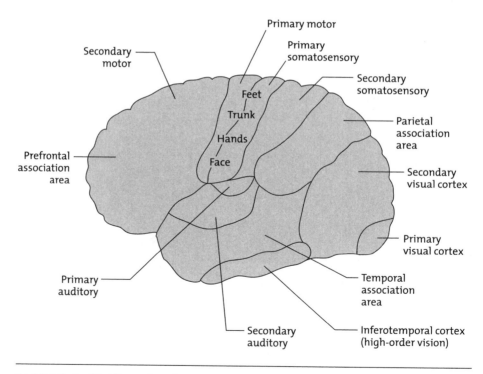

FIGURE 2.15 Hierarchy of sensory areas of the cerebral cortex.

cortex analyze smell and taste. The anterior, or front, part of the cortex is composed of areas specialized for movement control. Some of these areas coordinate movements of specific muscle groups, such as those that focus our eyes. Other areas are involved in consciously holding and manipulating information and organizing and retrieving memories. Cortical areas are categorized into *primary somatosensory areas* that process the details of sensory information (such as detecting edges of contrast or color); *secondary somatosensory areas* that process more complex sensory features (such as movement, depth, or distance of stimuli); and *association areas* that identify complex stimuli and control our perception, coordinated action, thinking, and attention.

The third level of organization involves how information is represented within each area of the cortex. A characteristic of primary cortical areas is that each one is systematically arranged; a *topographic map* is an organized representation of a specific kind of sensory input onto the surface of the cortex (Figure 2.16).

For an example of sensory processing that demonstrates the three levels of cortical organization, consider what happens when you look at a picture (Figure 2.16A). A chief component of vision involves organizing the visual fields, which compose the full view of the environment centered on the point in space where your eyes fixate. At the hemispheric level of organization, the left and right halves of the visual field are each represented in the opposite-side hemisphere, following the rule of contralateral representation. So if your eyes focus on the center of the picture, the left half of the image is represented in the right hemisphere and the right half of the image is represented in the left hemisphere. At the next organizational level within each hemisphere, the primary visual cortex is organized as a systematic representation of places in the visual field. Locations in the visual field close to the fixation point are represented near the midline of the occipital lobe; locations far from the fixation point are represented along the outside surfaces of the occipital lobe.

In the parietal cortex lies the primary *somatosensory* (touch) cortex (Figure 2.16B). Following the rule of contralateral representation, the left side of the body is represented in the right hemisphere, and vice versa. Within each hemisphere, the somatosensory area represents skin areas, with the toes and genitals represented in the depths of the hemisphere at midline; spreading laterally are representations of the trunk, the arms and hands, and then the head. Adjacent to the somatosensory cortex, the frontal lobe contains a similar contralateral topographic mapping of muscle movements. Within each hemisphere, movements of the feet are represented at the midline. Extending sequentially along the surface of the cortex are representations of muscle movements in the body, the arms, and finally the face.

These cortical maps adapt and change remarkably in response to the environment. When the cortex is deprived of a particular sensory input, the cortical zone representing the affected area is unresponsive—at first. But over time, the unstimulated cortical zone begins to respond to sensory input from adjacent zones. For

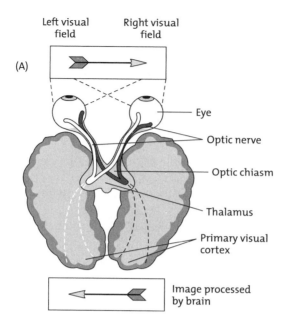

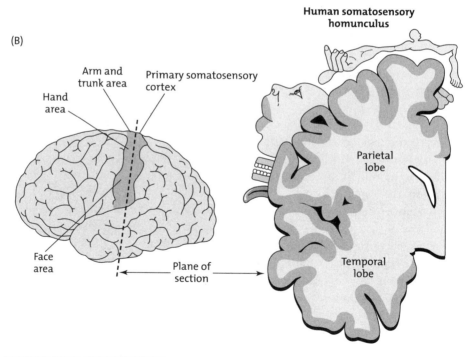

FIGURE 2.16 Topographic maps in the cortex.
A. Visual system. B. Somatosensory (touch) system.

example, if a finger is lost, initially the primary somatosensory area that represents the finger is unresponsive because its corresponding body part is no longer encountering stimuli. But over time, that cortical zone acquires a representation of the adjacent fingers. This suggests that sensory inputs compete for cortical representation and that the extent of their representation depends on their level of activity. This notion has been confirmed experimentally: Increasing the activity of one finger can cause its cortical representation zone to expand, pushing into the neighboring zones representing other fingers.

Association areas serve the most complex cognitive and emotional functions. For example, an area in the temporal lobe called the **inferotemporal cortex** (see Figure 2.15) is specialized to analyze complex visual information and identify familiar objects, including faces. Damage to this area can make a person unable to identify family or friends even though vision is otherwise normal. In the parietal cortex are association areas that help us conceptualize the layout of important stimuli in space. Damage to this area can cause spatial disorientation. Association areas in the frontal cortex direct attention to important issues and stimuli and are involved in memory, thinking, and planning.

Neurologists Use Nervous System Anatomy to Locate Damage

The highly specific organization of the nervous system allows neurologists to identify locations of damage in that system by examining its function. Thus, for example, neurologists can localize damage to the spinal cord or spinal or cranial nerves by identifying loss of sensory or motor functions in the body. Damage to a spinal nerve low in the back causes loss of feeling and movement in the legs and feet. Hiccups that do not go away can be caused by damage to the vagus nerve, which is the 10th cranial nerve. Rhythmic involuntary eye movements suggest damage to the midbrain area that controls eye movements. Specific abnormalities of function offer clues about where in the nervous system there may be a disorder, and they tell us how those areas control particular functions.

Neurologists can also localize the site of brain damage or tumors by examining the behavior of their patients, using their knowledge about the organization of the cortex. Thus, for example, damage to the back of the brain can cause loss of vision, whereas damage to the front of the brain harms motor functions. Similarly, loss of function on one side of the body indicates brain damage in the opposite hemisphere.

The Brain Is Organized by Functional Systems

Gall was also wrong about the idea that any particular function is entirely performed by a specific brain area. Instead the brain's functional systems are composed of sets of connected brain structures that work together. There are four major types of functional systems: sensory systems, motor systems, an emotional system, and cognitive systems. Information about the external world is sent through several stages of **sensory systems** to specialized parts of the cortex. Behavior is accomplished via commands from the cortex to our **motor systems**. In addition, cortical output is directed to an **emotional system** to mediate our appreciation of rewards and punishments. Finally, the cortex itself contains two **cognitive systems** that accomplish higher-order information processing: one that organizes multiple sensory information pathways and another that supports the acquisition and application of rules and plans.

SENSORY SYSTEMS: HOW DO WE PERCEIVE? Sensory systems follow a fairly standard organizational plan—routing information from sensory organs to the thalamus, which passes the information to a hierarchy of cortical processing areas. The sensory organ (eye, ear, nose, or the like) sends input to the brain via a specific cranial nerve, and the data arrive first in the spinal cord, hindbrain, midbrain, or thalamus (depending on which sense is involved). The thalamus performs initial processing to identify the stimulus and directs the information to the primary cortical area for that sense. This primary sensory area in the cortex then sends output to one or more secondary cortical areas. These areas perform further sensory analyses, and their output is sent to tertiary areas through a hierarchy of sensory processing, ultimately reaching the association areas of the cortex.

For example, the visual pathway begins with connections from the eyes' retinas through the second cranial nerve (the optic nerve) to the midbrain, which directs orientation to important visual stimuli, and to the thalamus (Figure 2.16A). The thalamus sends the information to the primary visual cortex in the occipital lobe. From there visual analysis proceeds through a hierarchy of secondary visual cortical areas that analyze color, shape, motion, depth, and location of stimuli (Figure 2.15). Eventually the information reaches the highest cortical areas for vision—both in the parietal associations areas that analyze the location of relevant visual stimuli and in the inferotemporal cortex, which analyzes the form of complex visual stimuli. Our auditory and somatosensory (touch) systems have a similar organization.

MOTOR SYSTEMS: HOW DO WE COORDINATE MOVEMENTS? Organizing information to control and coordinate voluntary movements begins with specialized areas in the cerebral cortex and proceeds into two subsystems (Figure 2.17). At the top level of motor processing is the primary motor cortex. An additional important structure is the premotor cortex, which is central in preparing for and coordinating movements. These motor cortical areas work closely with the striatum and the cerebellum. Each of these structures plays a major role in a circuit that

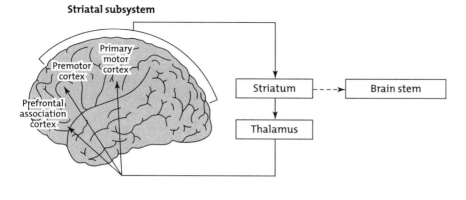

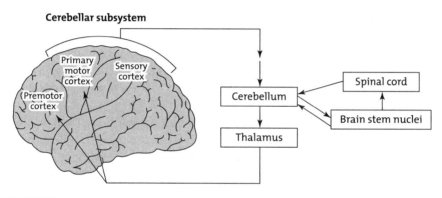

FIGURE 2.17 Motor systems.

begins with downward projections from the cortex and ends in a thalamic route back to the cortex. However, these two pathways differ in the sources of their cortical input and output, their brain stem and spinal cord connections, and their functional roles.

The **striatal subsystem** focuses on the functions of the striatum. The striatum receives input from the entire cerebral cortex and is topographically organized. The striatum projects to parts of the thalamus specialized for motor control; these connections form loops back to the premotor and motor cortex and the prefrontal association cortex. Notably, there are few projections of this circuit to the voluntary motor circuits, so it is apparently not involved directly in controlling motor output. Instead its connections to the premotor and prefrontal cortex suggest that the striatal subsystem contributes to higher motor functions, including planning and executing complex motor sequences.

The **cerebellar subsystem** centers on the cerebellum, a distinctive structure of the hindbrain that has remarkably regular internal circuitry. It has several distinct subdivisions associated with different sensory and motor functions. The cerebellum receives cortical input from the sensory and motor areas. Like the striatal system, the cerebellum has an output loop to the motor and premotor cortex. The cerebellum receives somatic sensory inputs directly from the spinal cord. Based on these spinal connections, the cerebellum is believed to contribute directly to movement execution and to habit acquisition via learned reflexes and body adjustments to changing environmental input.

EMOTIONAL SYSTEMS: HOW DO WE FEEL? The brain system that mediates emotion involves forebrain structures that reconcile emotions and automatic behaviors attributed to emotions. There have been many theories about the brain circuits that support emotional expression. One early theory, proposed by James Papez (1937), suggested that emotion is controlled by a circular set of connections among the medial surface of the cortex, the hippocampus, the hypothalamus, and parts of the thalamus that project to the cingulate cortex. Papez thought that interactions between the medial cortex and the hypothalamus could integrate our thoughts, originating in many cortical areas, with emotional expression, generated by the hypothalamus.

Recent research has focused on pathways to emotional memory through the **amygdala** (Figure 2.18). This structure lies in a central position between cortical information processing and hypothalamic outputs that mediate behavioral responses. The amygdala lies deep in the temporal lobe, just in front of the hippocampus, in an area with many highly interconnected nuclei or groups of neurons. Sensory inputs from the thalamus and cortex project directly to some of these nuclei. Within the amygdala there is considerable interaction among the nuclei, and outputs from amygdala nuclei orchestrate an enormous range of influences on behavior. Some of these include connections to the thalamic and cortical areas that provided sensory input, which may provide emotional "color" to sensory stimuli. Other amygdala outputs travel to functional systems important for different forms of memory—specifically the striatum and hippocampal regions—which may influence memory processing by those systems. Amygdala outputs are also sent directly to the autonomic and voluntary motor systems to generate bodily forms of emotional expression, such as increases in heart rate, blood pressure, sweating, and the release of stress hormones, as well as behaviors like freezing and increased vigilance.

COGNITIVE SYSTEMS: HOW DO WE THINK? Association areas of the cortex provide the highest levels of information processing that underlie our greatest cognitive capacities. One main cognitive system connects virtually all higher cortical areas and the hippocampus; another focuses on the **prefrontal cortex,** the area in front of the motor cortex.

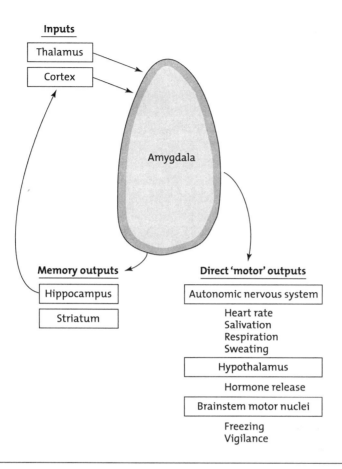

FIGURE 2.18 The emotional system.

The **hippocampal system** consists of the hippocampus and the immediately surrounding cortex called the **parahippocampal region** (Figure 2.19). The hippocampus, an evolutionarily ancient cortical area, is at the pinnacle of the hierarchy of cortical processing streams and plays a vital role in memory. Only highly processed sensory information reaches the hippocampus; but these inputs come from virtually all higher-order cortical processing areas. Sensory information enters the primary cortical areas and passes through multiple secondary and tertiary stages of sensory processing that are segregated by sensory modality. The highest sensory areas project to the *association areas* in the parietal and temporal lobes. A similar hierarchy exists for processing stages in the motor cortical areas, which ultimately project to association areas in the temporal and frontal lobes. Each of these areas combines information from specific senses for a particular higher-order

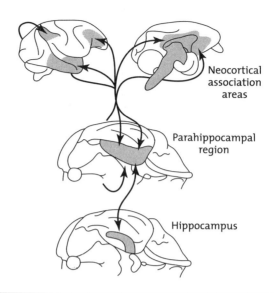

FIGURE 2.19 The hippocampal system.
Arrows indicate two-way communication between brain areas.

function. For example, the parietal lobe association areas process spatial information derived from visual, auditory, and somatosensory inputs; association areas of
the temporal lobe combine these inputs differently to identify the objects we perceive or manipulate. The precise function of the frontal cortex is less well understood, but it also combines different streams of sensory information to determine
the significance of stimuli and the rules and plans for manipulating them.

The outputs of these areas provide inputs to the parahippocampal region. This
area serves some functions in memory itself and in turn connects to the hippocampus, which has complex internal circuitry. Following its processing, the outputs of the hippocampus travel back to the parahippocampal region, and from
there information returns to the cortical association areas that provided the inputs.

The prefrontal system contains the prefrontal cortex and its network of connections with multiple cortical association areas. The prefrontal association cortex lies just in front of the motor area in the frontal lobe. This area is small in most
animals, although in primates and especially in humans it is more elaborate. The
phenomenal expansion of the prefrontal area in primates and humans is correlated
with the evolution of intelligence (Figure 2.20). The human prefrontal cortex is a
diverse area with several distinct subdivisions. These areas are strongly connected
with specific parts of association areas in the parietal and temporal lobes, and they
support working memory—our capacity to hold information for sustained attention and cognitive manipulation.

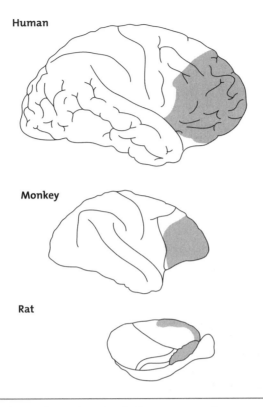

Human

Monkey

Rat

FIGURE 2.20 The prefrontal cortex in humans, monkeys, and rats.

Memory Systems Lie within the Brain's Functional Organization

A central theme of this book is that diverse types of learning and memory emerge from the different functional systems of the brain. How do the various types of memory listed at the end of Chapter 1 map to the functional brain systems described in this chapter? We have seen that our capacity for each domain of memory is distributed throughout multiple cortical zones as well as other brain systems. So memory is distributed throughout the brain, not localized to specific centers. However, memory is not distributed throughout the brain homogeneously. Instead the particular forms of memory introduced in Chapter 1 are supported by specific brain pathways. Some brain areas are involved in multiple forms of memory, whereas others are part of only one memory system.

The simplest forms of learning, including habituation and sensitization to specific stimuli (Chapter 3) and classical conditioning, are not identified with specific pathways (and hence not pictured) but rather are supported within different systems depending on the stimuli and behavioral responses involved. Some forms of learning and memory are accomplished mainly within the cerebral cortex. Perceptual learning (Chapter 4), involving our capacity for categorizing and identifying stimuli, depends on modifications of the cortical areas mediating specific types of stimuli (visual, tactile, and the like). The prefrontal cortex and its interactions with other cortical areas support conscious manipulation of information and working memory (Chapter 12).

Pathways critical to other forms of cognitive and behavioral learning and memory entail interactions between cortical areas and other parts of the brain's functional systems. The pathway supporting permanent organization of cognitive or declarative memory uses connections from many cortical areas to the hippocampus and back to the cortex to support episodic and semantic memory (Chapters 8 through 11). Procedural learning—the acquisition of conditioned reflexes (Chapter 5) and habits (Chapter 6)—is supported by cortical pathways to the subsystems for motor planning and coordination; it is expressed through motor outputs in the brain stem and spinal cord that control voluntary movement. Emotional learning (Chapter 7) depends on cortical pathways to the amygdala; the outputs of this system are expressed through the hypothalamus, autonomic nervous system, and endocrine system, which support autonomic behaviors in response to emotional provocations. This anatomical scheme can be a useful framework for understanding how the brain mediates the different forms of memory discussed in succeeding chapters. A preliminary outline of some brain pathways of the major memory systems is provided in Figure 2.21.

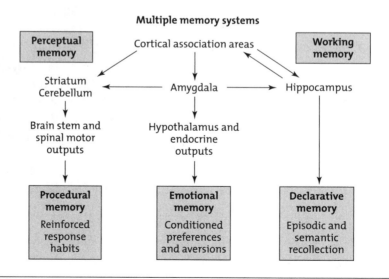

FIGURE 2.21 Outline of memory systems of the brain.

Interim Summary

The brain is hierarchically organized. Lower levels accomplish basic tasks; higher areas, including the cerebral cortex, perform more complex processing and control the lower parts of the system. The spinal cord, via the cranial and spinal nerves, receives information for all the senses and controls the muscles. The hindbrain coordinates inputs and outputs to the spinal cord and controls simple functions such as respiration, heartbeat, and our state of arousal. The midbrain coordinates orientation to important stimuli. The forebrain contains many different areas that control a variety of functions—including most prominently the cerebral cortex, which has numerous areas involved in specific sensory, motor, or cognitive functions and provides a repository for vast amounts of information. The cerebral cortex is a multilayered sheet of nervous tissue that forms maps of our sensory and motor world. The left half of the cortex represents the right half of the world, and the right half of the cortex represents the left half of the world; we call this contralateral representation. The posterior (back) half of the cortex has several areas representing distinct senses, including vision, touch, and hearing; there is a hierarchy of distinct areas that serve more basic or more complex functions in each sense. The anterior (front) end of the brain has a hierarchy of areas that control motor functions. Each cortical area that serves a simpler function has a topographic map in which specific parts of the sensory or motor function are controlled by neighboring areas within the cortical representation.

In addition, the brain is organized into functional systems. Sensory systems allow us to perceive external stimuli. Motor systems let us produce coordinated movements. The emotional system mediates how we feel rewards and punishments. Cognitive systems support our thoughts. The anatomical pathways of these systems span the levels of the brain: Simpler aspects of functions are accomplished at lower levels, and more complex aspects are supported by higher levels. Each of these systems is involved in one or more brain memory systems. Thus learning and memory are distributed throughout the brain—but in highly specific pathways within the known functional systems.

Chapter Summary

1. Biology explains the basis of learning and memory as a central function of the brain. Within the framework of neurobiology, memories can be reduced to changes in connections between neurons; and different kinds of memories can be reduced to the distinct brain pathways that support each kind of memory. Furthermore, neurobiology offers an approach that helps us understand the different types of learning and memory.

2. Each form of learning and memory arises out of the distinct types of information processed by a particular functional system. Accordingly, different information content and rules of operation for each type of memory emerge from the special properties of each system. Research on the neurobiological basis of memory focuses on three levels of brain structures: cells, circuits, and systems.

3. Research at the cellular level is aimed at understanding neurons, the basic units of information processing in the brain. Neurons are composed of four elements: the cell body; dendrites, which collect signals from other cells; the axon, which conducts signals through the length of the cell; and the synapse, which transmits signals to the next cell.

4. Conduction of electrical signals within neurons involves alterations of the neurons' resting potential—a polarization of the cell membrane due to the outflow of potassium (K+) from the cell. When a signal arrives from a dendrite, the cell may change its potential as the result of an influx of sodium (Na+) into the cell membrane. If this potential change reaches a particular threshold at the beginning of the axon, an action potential is initiated and carried along the entire length of the axon. When the action potential reaches the end of the axon, calcium (Ca++) flows into the presynaptic site, resulting in docking of synaptic vesicles and release of a neurotransmitter. The neurotransmitter diffuses across the synaptic cleft to the next neuron and activates receptors within its postsynaptic site, inducing changes in the cell potential at excitatory and inhibitory synapses. The likely mechanism for memory is modifiability of the synapses, which changes the efficiency of a presynaptic neuron's excitation or inhibition of a postsynaptic neuron.

5. Research on brain circuits explores memory representations formed by many neurons operating cooperatively. The simplest neural circuits are reflex arcs, composed of sensory neurons, motor neurons, and related interneurons. Even simple reflex circuits integrate excitatory and inhibitory influences to control behavior. Early experiments showed that complex memories are not stored in reflex circuits but are likely embodied in distributed circuits called cell assemblies.

6. Cell assemblies form by repeated activation of interconnected cells, changing the synaptic efficacies among cells within the assembly and thus representing a particular experience. Substantial evidence has demonstrated that learning changes synaptic efficacy in the relevant brain circuits and that blocking synaptic plasticity prevents new learning.

7. Brain systems involve hierarchies of control by which sensory systems send information through several stages to distinct cortical areas in each cerebral hemisphere; perceptions are elaborated at progressively higher levels of cortical processing into the association areas. Motor control is guided by cortical areas through

two subsystems—one involving the striatum and the other the cerebellum. Emotion is processed in the cortex and at several levels, with the amygdala as a central station controlling emotional expression. Cognitive functions are accomplished by the hippocampal system, which organizes cortical representations, and by the prefrontal system, which analyzes regularities and discovers rules of behavior and planning. Later chapters will describe the functions of these pathways in different forms of learning and memory.

KEY TERMS

cells (p. 40)

neurons (p. 41)

circuits (p. 41)

systems (p. 41)

reticular theory of brain circuitry
   (p. 41)

dendrite (p. 42)

axon (p. 42)

neuron doctrine (p. 42)

principal neurons (p. 44)

interneurons (p. 44)

motor neurons (p. 44)

sensory neurons (p. 44)

synapse (p. 46)

synaptic potentials (p. 46)

action potential (p. 46)

neurotransmitters (p. 46)

resting potential (p. 47)

presynaptic element (p. 50)

postsynaptic element (p. 50)

synaptic cleft (p. 50)

synaptic vesicles (p. 50)

receptors (p. 50)

excitatory postsynaptic potential (EPSP)
   (p. 50)

inhibitory postsynaptic potential (IPSP)
   (p. 51)

reflex arc (p. 53)

cell assembly (p. 55)

long-term potentiation (LTP) (p. 56)

long-term depression (LTD) (p. 60)

organology (p. 63)

cerebellum (p. 68)

striatum (p. 68)

hippocampus (p. 68)

cerebral cortex (p. 69)

inferotemporal cortex (p. 73)

sensory systems (p. 74)

motor systems (p. 74)

emotional system (p. 74)

cognitive systems (p. 74)

striatal subsystem (p. 75)

cerebellar subsystem (p. 75)

amygdala (p. 76)

prefrontal cortex (p. 76)

hippocampal system (p. 77)

parahippocampal region (p. 77)

REVIEWING THE CONCEPTS

- How do the electrical properties of neurons support signal communication within cells?

- How do the chemical properties of synapses support signal transmission between cells?

- What are reflex arcs, and how do they work?

- What are cell assemblies, and how do they represent memories?

- What is long-term potentiation, and how is it related to memory?

- What are the three major levels of the brain, and which structures does each level include?

- How is the cerebral cortex organized?

- What are the major functional systems of the brain?

- How are memory systems related to the brain's functional organization?

PART II

Unconscious Forms of Learning and Memory

Simple Forms of Learning and Memory

A college buddy of mine came from a quiet rural farming area, where evenings were filled with cricket noise and occasional coyote whines. After college, he longed for bright lights and busy urban streets. So after receiving his degree, he moved to New York City. He was a skilled writer and quickly found a job in advertising—but it took him a lot longer to get a good night's sleep than to settle into his profession. His apartment was on a busy street, and traffic was flowing 24/7. Night after night, he lay sleepless for what seemed like hours, listening to cars, trucks, and buses pass his window. Each night he would initially be bothered by the noise. But after a while his mind would drift to other thoughts, and eventually he would fall asleep. Over several weeks, the time it took him to fall asleep decreased until he fell asleep readily, as if the traffic noise did not exist. Six months into his new life in New York, he traveled home for the holidays, where he was surprised to find that he couldn't fall asleep because of all those crickets chirping.

* * *

One Halloween I took my younger son in costume around the neighborhood. He ran from one house to another, charging up to each door, shouting "Trick or treat!" and eagerly collecting candy. Then we came to the house of a neighborhood prankster. At first it seemed like every other house decorated for the holiday, except that there was a large barrel next to the front door. "Trick or treat!" my son shouted as he approached the door. Unlike at other houses, there was no immediate response; we waited quietly. As we tried to hear if anyone was home, a large arm, cloaked in black cloth, reached out slowly from a knot in the wooden barrel, and then it grabbed my son's hand! He was terrified.

After the initial scare, he battled the barrel's arm, won, and was rewarded with a handful of candy. As we left, he claimed that the initial scare was no big deal. But for a while, each time we heard kids shouting somewhere down the street or heard tree branches creaking in the wind, my son froze for a moment. After several minutes of collecting candy without another scare, he had forgotten and no longer responded to the noises and sights of the night. But on the way home, we had to pass the house with the barrel by the door. Even in the midst of discussing his impressive candy collection, my son became wary once again as we approached the barrel.

Habituation and sensitization are pervasive events in our everyday lives. They keep us from constantly attending to unimportant events and raise our vigilance to potentially important future events. In everyday life, we are constantly bombarded by stimuli: clocks ticking, air conditioners humming, exit signs glaring, conversations murmuring nearby. Like my friend who moved to New York, we are initially distracted by these novel stimuli. Yet after a time most of these stimuli do not attract our attention. Our capacity to "tune out" inconsequential repetitive stimuli is called **habituation**. And like my son at Halloween, when we experience something shocking, like a loud bang in the street or a scary TV scene, we become more aware of and responsive to stimuli for a substantial period. This phenomenon, the opposite of habituation, is called **sensitization.** Habituation and sensitization are simple forms of learning and memory that occur in all species. They occur in a broad variety of situations—from invertebrates' self-protection to rodents' social behavior to human babies' learning which stimuli are important. Habituation and sensitization happen to be the easiest kinds of learning and memory to understand in terms of their cellular and molecular mechanisms.

Fundamental Questions

1. How do habituation and sensitization differ from learning about relationships between stimuli?
2. How do habituation and sensitization contribute to daily life?
3. How does the brain accomplish these forms of learning and memory?

Habituation and Sensitization Are Nonassociative Forms of Learning

Habituation and sensitization are the simplest of forms of learning: They change our behavior after simple exposure to a stimulus. They are considered forms of **nonassociative learning** because their effects require no specific association with actions or consequences. For example, the traffic sounds my friend in New York got used to were not associated with any particular positive or negative outcome that he needed to act on; and the ability of the black-cloaked arm to grab my son was not associated with any painful consequence yet was sufficient to sensitize his subsequent reactions to other stimuli. By contrast, **associative learning** links otherwise unrelated stimuli, or a stimulus and a reward or punishment, or a stimulus and a behavioral response. My son's wariness in approaching the barrel was due to learning and association between that stimulus and the scary arm that came out of it.

Habituation Occurs within Brain Circuits

Habituation is a form of learning in which behavioral responses diminish following repetition of an irrelevant stimulus even though the stimulus is perceived by sensory receptors. Habituation differs from nonlearning situations such as adaptation and fatigue, in which stimulus repetition can also diminish responses. A straightforward way to distinguish the different situations that lead to diminished responses is to consider their influences within simple reflex circuits (Figure 3.1).

The simplest reflex circuits consist of three main stages: a sensory receptor that detects a stimulus, an interneuron that relays the sensory signal to motor neurons, and motor neurons that drive muscle contractions. Motor response decreases could be caused by diminished sensory receptor sensitivity. For example, visual receptors decrease their light sensitivity if a bright light shines into the eye; we call this *adaptation*. Similarly, touch receptors in skin become less sensitive when pressure is maintained on the skin for a long period. Decreases in the sensory signal due to this kind of adaptation are not considered a form of learning even though they diminish behavioral responses. Also, when we repeat a movement many times, muscles become *fatigued*. Muscle weakness or incapacitation due to fatigue

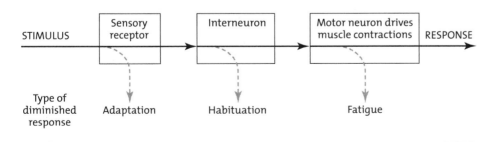

FIGURE 3.1 Comparison of habituation, sensory adaptation, and muscle fatigue.

also lessens behavior responses; but fatigue, like sensory adaptation, is not considered a form of learning. Habituation can occur even in simple reflex circuits. In these cases, scientists have shown that habituation of a reflex is due to changes in interneuron operation, not sensory receptor adaptation or muscle fatigue.

Imagine a mouse that is placed into a chamber and exposed to a loud, startling noise several times. At first the mouse responds to the noise with a large jump; but with each successive noise the size of that movement becomes smaller, and eventually the animal does not move at all. How can we distinguish whether the behavioral change is due to sensory adaptation, muscle fatigue, or habituation?

In this case, sensory adaptation would reduce the responsiveness of the auditory receptors and would be expected to decrease *any* kind of response to the loud sound because the sound would not be heard. By contrast, habituation is response specific; that is, it decreases only the response executed repetitively following a particular stimulus. Therefore, we can distinguish habituation from sensory adaptation by testing whether the mouse still exhibits other types of responses to the sound, such as a brief acceleration of heart rate, even when it no longer jumps. Or we could play the sound from a different location and examine whether the animal orients to the new origin of the sound. If these other responses are intact, we can conclude that the diminished jumping response to the sound is not due to sensory adaptation.

Another possible reason that the mouse stops jumping in response to the sound could be muscle fatigue. As any athlete knows, muscle fatigue results from overuse of particular muscles, and it impairs movement in those muscles regardless of the stimuli that generate the desire to move them. In our mouse experiment, we could distinguish habituation (which is stimulus specific) from muscle fatigue (which is not) by presenting a different type of startling stimulus. Instead of a loud noise, we might present a bright light flash; the mouse would jump again, showing that its muscles still generate the startle response to a new stimulus. Now we have shown that the diminished behavioral response is both stimulus *and* response specific, unlike either sensory adaptation or muscle fatigue. Sensory adaptation and muscle fatigue would exhibit specificity only to the stimulus *or* to the response, respectively. Habituation occurs somewhere in the circuit after particular sensory signals are received and before specific behavioral responses are generated. So it is specific to both the stimulus and the motor response.

Interim Summary

Habituation and sensitization modify our responsiveness to stimuli. They do not require specific reinforcement or association with rewards or punishments, and both of them are considered nonassociative forms of learning and memory. Habituation is specific both to the stimulus that initially generated the response and to the behavioral response that is reduced. By contrast, nonspecific loss of responses to a stimulus is likely due to sensory adaptation; loss of the capacity to produce a particular response to any stimulus is likely due to muscle fatigue. Therefore, habituation is reflected in both stimulus and response selectivity.

Habituation Helps Us Study Recognition Memory

Habituation is used by researchers to investigate certain kinds of learning and memory that were previously considered inaccessible. For example, scientists interested in the minds of infants and animals obviously can't rely on direct reports from their subjects. However, habituation and its opposite, dishabituation, cause subtle but measurable behavioral changes that reveal whether a stimulus is recognized or perceived as novel. Researchers have employed a variety of protocols to examine habituation. The following sections examine how habituation has been used to answer various questions about recongition memory in human babies and animals.

Can Infants Perceive Adult Speech?

Habituation has been used extensively in studies of infants' memory because they cannot speak or use other coordinated motor responses to learned stimuli. In the typical situation, an infant sits on his or her parent's lap facing a screen or table on which objects appear (Figure 3.2). The first time a novel object appears, the infant looks directly at it for a prolonged period, smiling and showing interest, and its heart rate and breathing rate change as well. In the laboratory, infants are sometimes given an artificial nipple, and their intensity and rates of sucking are measured by sensors in the nipple; a novel stimulus typically causes a brief increase in sucking.

FIGURE 3.2 Experimental arrangement for habituation in looking responses by infants.

After repeated exposures to a particular stimulus, the infant pays less attention: The duration of looking and the strength of facial and sucking responses diminish. After several exposures, the infant may show no response at all, indicating that habituation is complete. For a different stimulus, however, the looking, sucking, and other responses return. This **dishabituation,** or recovery of the behavioral response, occurs with a new stimulus because habituation is stimulus specific.

Dishabituation tells us that the infant perceives the new stimulus as different from the habituated one. Experimenters can exploit this phenomenon to explore perception and recognition in infants. For example, suppose we initially habituate an infant's responses to a red picture. Will the infant dishabituate to a pink version of the same picture? If so, we can conclude that the infant can distinguish between red and pink.

This technique has been used to examine whether and when infants can make a variety of perceptual distinctions. For example, one question about the development of language comprehension is when children can distinguish between the sounds "pa" and "ba"—two fundamental elements of speech. To determine when infants perceive this distinction, we can test babies' reactions at different ages to a series of sounds. First a baby hears "ba . . . ba . . . ba" and then "pa . . . pa . . . pa." Even at a few months of age, babies who have habituated their responses to repeated "ba" sounds will dishabituate when "pa" is presented, showing that they detect the difference. This technique has been used to examine a broad range of perceptual and intellectual capacities in infants.

How Long Can Animals Remember a Stimulus?

Animals are usually curious about a novel object and will investigate it for sustained periods. However, when the stimulus is presented again after an extended single exposure, they typically show habituation, especially if the now familiar object is presented with a new object that elicits investigation. The *preferential viewing test* uses this pattern of initial investigation followed by habituation to study recognition memory in monkeys and rats. Monkeys are shown a picture of a scene for a fixed period. Then, following a variable delay, two scenes are presented: One is identical to the original scene and the other is novel. The monkey typically habituates to investigation of the first stimulus within one exposure, so it spends more time investigating the novel stimulus in the test. Most monkeys spend about twice as much time visually exploring the novel scene as the familiar one. With rodents the same test uses three-dimensional objects. The rat is initially given an identical pair of objects to sniff and manipulate. Then, following a variable retention interval, the rat is presented with two objects—one identical to the original pair and the second one novel. Like the monkeys, the rats typically spend about twice as much time investigating the novel object as the familiar one. This test measures how long monkeys and rats can recognize a picture or an object they have experienced just once.

Can Animals Identify Individuals of Their Species?

Do animals distinguish and recognize other individuals in their social community? The answer to this question can tell us when in evolution social behaviors dependent on individual recognition, such as mating and dominance, appeared. Also, if animals can recognize other individuals, we can examine the critical stimuli and brain systems that support individual recognition through studies of animals.

Robert Johnston and his students have used habituation/dishabituation tests to explore the abilities of golden hamsters to perceive and remember odors of other hamsters. Before their work, it was generally thought that hamsters and other mammals generated individual scents, called *pheromones*, to convey information about their identity to other animals. But Johnston wondered how to prove that hamsters actually identify other individual hamsters by their pheromones.

In a series of experiments, Johnston (1993) examined the nature of scent memory in hamsters. Each experiment collected samples of the different scents hamsters generate, including the scents generated by special glands on the animals' flanks and ears as well as females' vaginal secretions and males' urine. One study examined whether an "observer" hamster could distinguish between two other hamsters (we will call them hamster A and hamster B). To test this, Johnston and his students sampled hamster A's flank gland scent by rubbing a glass slide against its flank. They presented this slide to the observer hamster and watched its behavior (Figure 3.3A). The observer sniffed the scent intensely during a 5-minute measurement period. After a delay that varied between 1 second and 30 minutes, they presented the same flank gland scent again and measured the sniffing time—repeating the procedure five times. Each time the stimulus was presented, the observer spent less time sniffing the odor; it had habituated to the scent (Figure 3.3B). Then, on the sixth trial, the experimenters presented flank gland scent again, but this time the odor was collected from hamster B. The observer now spent substantially more time sniffing the odor: It showed dishabituation of the sniffing response, indicating that it could distinguish hamster A from hamster B by their flank gland scents. Furthermore, using this technique, Johnston and his students found that hamsters could remember the scent of other individuals for at least 30 minutes. They also showed that hamsters of one species can use some scents to distinguish individuals of other hamster species.

Johnston and Jernigan (1994) went further. They wondered what signals male hamsters used to distinguish female hamsters in their mating behavior. Do the males find females using only general sex differences in the chemical composition

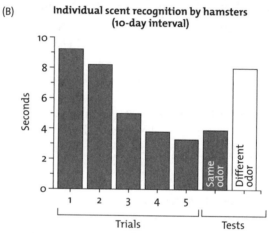

FIGURE 3.3 Individual scent recognition by hamsters.
A. A subject hamster sniffing one of two odors presented on a glass slide. B. Time spent sniffing the familiar odor across successive presentations (1–5) and time spent sniffing the familiar odor from the same hamster or the odor from a different hamster on a final test trial.

of a particular scent? Or might the males recognize particular females by a combination of their scents, providing a unique signature for each female?

To distinguish between these alternatives, Johnston and Jernigan first familiarized a male observer hamster with two different females (X and Y), allowing substantial social interaction between the male and the females without mating (Figure 3.4A). Then they habituated the observer hamster to the vaginal secretion of female X. Subsequently, instead of presenting the females' vaginal secretions as the test stimulus, they presented the flank gland scent of either female X or female Y to different observers. Flank gland scent differs chemically from vaginal secretions. So if dishabituation is based on perceiving a difference in chemical compo-

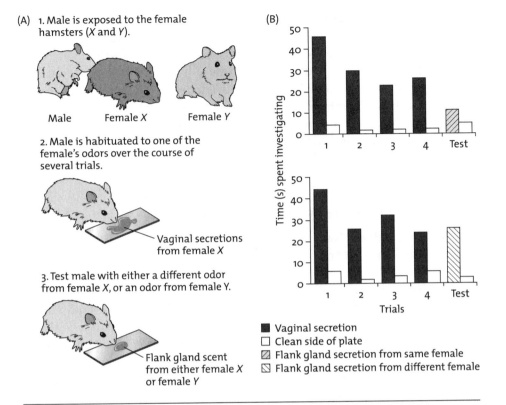

(A) 1. Male is exposed to the female hamsters (*X* and *Y*).

Male   Female *X*   Female *Y*

2. Male is habituated to one of the female's odors over the course of several trials.

Vaginal secretions from female *X*

3. Test male with either a different odor from female *X*, or an odor from female Y.

Flank gland scent from either female *X* or female *Y*

(B)

Time (s) spent investigating

Trials

■ Vaginal secretion
☐ Clean side of plate
▨ Flank gland secretion from same female
▧ Flank gland secretion from different female

FIGURE 3.4
A. A test for recognition of individuals, not chemical differences. B. Time spent sniffing vaginal secretion during repeated exposures (Trials 1–4) and flank gland scents during the test.

sition, the observer should dishabituate with the shift from vaginal secretion to flank gland scent, regardless of the source's identity.

However, when observers habituated to the vaginal secretion of female X were tested with the same female's flank gland scent, they did not dishabituate. Instead they behaved as if they were already habituated to this new scent from the same female. Other observers presented with flank gland scent of female Y did dishabituate, reacting to the odor as a new, unfamiliar stimulus. Thus the observers' behavior was not guided by the chemical differences between the females' different types of scents. Rather, they recognized the distinction between the two females as individual animals, each identified by her unique combination of odors (Figure 3.4B).

An additional part of the study showed that if the male was not preexposed to the females, it dishabituated when flank gland scent of either female X or female Y was presented. This showed that, lacking the opportunity to become familiar with all of a female's scents, the male used only the chemical differences between flank gland and vaginal scents. Clearly, in the original test the male associated the different scents of each female. After the association was formed, the chemical differences between vaginal and flank gland scents were unimportant to the male observer, but the differences between the identities of individual females were significant. These experiments demonstrate that hamsters use combinations of pheromone signatures to identify and remember other individuals and that the habituation/dishabituation test is useful in exploring their perception and memory.

Learning & Memory in Action

How Do Advertisers Use Dishabituation to Direct Attention to Their Products?

Dishabituation can be applied in numerous situations where habituation has diminished responsiveness. For example, teachers vary the loudness or tone of their voices to keep students' attention. Parents present novel objects or funny facial expressions to infants when they appear bored with familiar toys. A sophisticated use of dishabituation is practiced by advertising professionals to entice commuters to pay attention to billboards. Consumer polling has shown that commuters cease paying attention (that is, habituate) to billboards they see in the same place every day. So advertisers periodically change their displays to attract fresh attention.

Interim Summary

Habituation and dishabituation can be used in combination to examine perceptual and cognitive processes in humans and animals. Subjects are initially presented with a stimulus to which they naturally orient and explore. Then they are habituated to that stimulus by repetitive or continuous presentation, resulting in diminished orientation and exploration. Subsequently a novel stimulus is presented. If the new stimulus is perceived as different, the response is dishabituated, as reflected in renewed orientation and exploration. This procedure can determine what kinds of stimulus changes are perceived by the subject. The habituation technique has shown when infants perceive changes in language sounds, whether animals distinguish between other individual animals, and how long animals and humans remember a stimulus they have previously explored.

Primitive Nervous Systems Reveal the Biology of Habituation

Eventually we would like to understand the brain circuits that underlie habituation in everyday human situations, such as my friend's habituation to New York traffic noise. However, detailed examination of the brain circuits that support human habituation is difficult because of the complexity of the systems that support this kind of habituation. Indeed, even simple forms of habituation, such as that of reflexes, is difficult to study in humans or other higher species because of the complex circuitry involved. So researchers have simplified the problem in two ways: by studying habituation in invertebrate species with more primitive nervous systems and by studying these creatures' simplest reflex circuits.

This chapter has already introduced the distinctions among adaptation, fatigue, and habituation that are observed in reflexes. Here we consider in detail the biological mechanisms underlying reflex circuit habituation in a relatively primitive invertebrate species. Invertebrates are superb animals in which to study nervous function cell biology because their nervous systems have many fewer neurons than those of most vertebrates; also, their neurons are large and can be identified by their unique, stereotyped appearance within each animal. These qualities let researchers identify exactly the same cells in each animal and study virtually all the major cells involved in a functional circuit.

In pioneering studies, Eric Kandel and his colleagues have examined the behavioral, anatomical, and physiological properties of habituation and sensitization in *Aplysia,* a large sea snail (reviewed in Squire & Kandel, 1999). Most of their studies focused on the gill withdrawal reflex (Figure 3.5A). When the snail is at rest, it extends its gills from the abdominal region, along with a fleshy continuation of the gill called the siphon. Ordinarily the siphon assists the flow of aerated water over the gills for respiration. However, the gill is a delicate organ that is easily damaged. Therefore, when there are signs of danger, the snail can withdraw the gill and siphon. In the laboratory, a small flap called the mantle shelf ordinarily covers the gill and siphon. The mantle shelf is retracted when the animal is relaxed and the gill and siphon are extended. The defensive reflex can be initiated by a gentle stroke of the siphon with a paintbrush. This causes rapid withdrawal of the gill under the mantle shelf.

Rapid, lasting habituation can be observed in the *Aplysia* gill withdrawal reflex. To accomplish this, the experimenter first elicits the reflex by stimulating the siphon with a paintbrush, resulting in withdrawal of the gill. When the siphon is stimulated again, the reflex is smaller. After several repetitions it becomes quite subdued. Furthermore, following only 10 stimulations, the reflex may remain habituated for only 15 minutes. But after four days of such training, the habituation can last weeks. The longer-lasting habituation is a simple form of learning, to be sure; but its lasting property indicates that it is indeed a form of long-term memory.

(A)

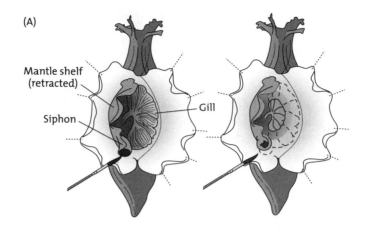

Mantle shelf
(retracted)

Gill

Siphon

(B)

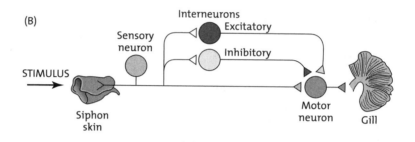

STIMULUS

Siphon
skin

Sensory
neuron

Interneurons

Excitatory

Inhibitory

Motor
neuron

Gill

FIGURE 3.5
A. The gill withdrawal reflex in *Aplysia*. B. The circuit for habituation of the gill withdrawal reflex.

Kandel and his colleagues sought to characterize the nerve cell circuit involved in the reflex and to determine the mechanism of lasting habituation. A sketch of the normal reflex circuit shows just one of each type of cell in Figure 3.5B. All the relevant circuit cells are in a single ganglion, or cluster of cells, in the abdomen. About 40 sensory cells are embedded in the skin of the siphon, and these connect with six motor neurons that operate the gill muscles. The neurotransmitter for the synapses is glutamate. There are also clusters of both excitatory and inhibitory interneurons—cells that receive input from the sensory cells and control the motor neurons. When the stimulus is initially applied to the siphon, the sensory neurons are excited, and these excite the interneurons and gill motor neurons. These inputs converge and cause the motor neurons to discharge action potentials repeatedly, producing a vigorous withdrawal response.

The researchers studied the physiology of this circuit by placing electrodes in the different types of cells and recording synaptic potentials and action potentials during habituation. Following several siphon stimulations, habituation was observed (Figure 3.6). The sensory neurons still produced action potentials, so the habituation was not the result of sensory adaptation or any other change in the responsiveness of the sensory neurons to the stimulus. However, the synaptic potentials in the interneurons and motor neurons were smaller, reducing the likelihood of generating action potentials in the motor neurons. Eventually, even though the sensory neurons were still responding vigorously, no action potentials were observed in the motor neurons. This suggested that the crucial change necessary to store the memory happened in the connections between the sensory neurons, the excitatory interneurons, and the motor neurons. This hypothesis was confirmed by examination of the connections between the sensory and motor neurons. The motor neurons generated successively smaller and shorter synaptic potentials with each stimulation, and these synaptic potential decreases mirrored the fading behavioral responses.

Next Kandel and his colleagues wondered what stage in the process of neural communication was affected by habituation. Focusing on the direct connection between sensory and motor neurons, they asked whether habituation takes place in the sensory neuron, the motor neuron, or the gill itself. They found that the receptors in the postsynaptic sites of the motor neurons were equally sensitive to the neurotransmitter, so the decreased sensitivity had to be located in the presynaptic (sensory) neurons. However, the sensory neurons were producing normal action potentials in response to the stimuli. So why were the motor neurons not responding? Kandel and his colleagues found that the diminished response was not due to a decrease in the sensory neurons' action potentials or the motor neurons' sensitivity. Instead there was a substantial decrease in the number of synaptic vesicles released from the sensory neurons for each action potential they

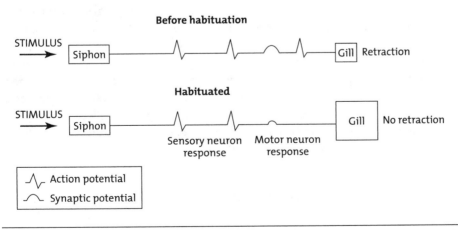

FIGURE 3.6 Habituation of the gill withdrawal reflex.
Electrical responses of the sensory and motor neurons before and after habituation.

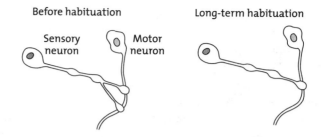

FIGURE 3.7 Anatomy of cell connections involved in habituation in *Aplysia*.

produced. The researchers used an electron microscope to observe the numbers and locations of synaptic vesicles in the presynaptic elements before and after habituation; the number of available vesicles did not decrease, but fewer of them docked onto release sites after action potentials in habituated animals.

Additional studies found that extended training weakened the connections between sensory neurons and their motor neurons, along with substantially reducing the number of synaptic contacts between sensory neurons and interneurons and between sensory neurons and motor neurons (Figure 3.7). So habituation can be explained by changes in synaptic efficacy, both through mechanisms that control transmitter release and through altered anatomical connections.

Interim Summary

A habituation circuit has been described in a model invertebrate species, *Aplysia*. The studied habituation reduces gill withdrawal responses to external stimulation of the siphon of the gill—a natural reflexive response to a potentially dangerous stimulus. The circuit for this reflex involves touch-sensitive neurons in the siphon, which connect via interneurons to motor neurons that control gill withdrawal. During habituation, the sensory neurons remain responsive to stimulation, and the motor neurons and muscles do not tire. A major component of the observed habituation is the result of fewer neurotransmitter vesicles docking at the synapse between sensory and motor neurons. In addition, long-term habituation of this reflex is accompanied by loss of synaptic connections between the sensory and motor neurons.

Sensitization Increases Responsiveness

Now let us consider a quite different phenomenon: sensitization, which increases the magnitude of behavioral responses to stimuli. In the example provided at the beginning of this chapter, on Halloween my son increased his responses to startling stimuli following a frightening event. Is sensitization just the opposite of habituation for particular types of stimuli?

Even though sensitization and habituation both change the magnitude of responsiveness, they diverge in other properties (Table 3.1). The consequences of habituation and sensitization can combine to control the magnitude of a response to a particular stimulus, but the origins and mechanisms of control by these processes differ. Habituation operates within a specific pathway from sensory analysis of a stimulus to the motor circuit that generates a particular response. In contrast, sensitization alters the state of an entire organism and its responsiveness across a broad range of stimuli and responses. Habituation is specific to both a particular sensory stimulus *and* a particular behavioral response. Sensitization, however, influences many reflex circuits. For example, after the Halloween scare, my son became overly responsive in reacting to a variety of stimuli. His heightened reactions were apparent in his nervousness about many sights and sounds.

Habituation and sensitization also differ in other ways. Habituation occurs whenever almost any insignificant stimulus is presented multiple times, whereas sensitization occurs only for emotionally arousing stimuli. Habituation and sensitization also vary in time course. When a stimulus is repeated frequently, the resulting habituation involves a short-term diminished response to that particular stimulus. Such short-term habituation typically is followed by a *spontaneous recovery* of the response after several hours. Repetitions of the stimulus over extended periods can cause longer-term habituation. For example, my college friend fell asleep the first night after a phase of short-term habituation to the nearly contin-

TABLE 3.1 Characteristics of Habituation and Sensitization in Both Simple and Complex Brain Circuits.

Habituation	Sensitization
Specific to particular stimulus and response	General to a variety of stimuli and responses
Results in decreased response magnitude	Results in increased response magnitude
Specific to a particular brain circuit	Heightens responses in many circuits
Occurs after repetition of a variety of types of stimuli	Occurs only after emotional stimuli
Exhibited in both the short term and long term	Normally lasts only for a short period

uous city noise; but his response to the noise spontaneously recovered by the next night. He repeated that short-term habituation for several nights before long-term habituation allowed him to sleep easily despite the city noise.

In contrast, sensitization is usually temporary. A loud noise or scary event typically sensitizes us for several minutes; this duration depends on the intensity of the arousing stimulus. Also, habituation and sensitization can interact: A sensitizing stimulus can temporarily cancel habituation. Thus an upsetting phone call at night caused my college friend to notice the city noise for the rest of that night.

Learning & Memory in Action

Why Do Horror Movies Heighten Our Responses to Benign Events?

Do you ever wonder why you sit at the edge of your seat, heart racing, throughout a horror movie, and then jump every time an unexpected event occurs? Filmmakers excel at taking advantage of the phenomenon of sensitization. Early in many such movies someone suffers a horrible attack. For example, do you recall the beginning of *Jaws,* when a young couple goes swimming at night? That's when we hear that drumbeat foretelling the shark taking its first victim. Subsequently our attention is heightened each time we see people in the water, especially when the drumbeat begins. We are scared even when an unrelated, mundane sudden event occurs, such as a girl screaming in surprise when a companion kicks sand at her. We jump—showing a heightened startle response as a result of sensitization from seeing the initial shark attack.

Sensitization Can Be Studied in Aplysia

In the gill withdrawal reflex of *Aplysia,* sensitization has been studied using a protocol in which initially the animal's tail is stimulated with an electric shock, which increases the robustness of the gill withdrawal response to subsequent siphon stimulation by a paintbrush. A single strong tail shock produces sensitization that lasts for minutes, whereas a series of four to five tail shocks sensitizes for a few days. The circuit that mediates this form of learning involves the same cells as habituation, plus sensory neurons that innervate the tail and additional interneurons (Figure 3.8). Thus, with the addition of cells and connections that provide input from the sensitizing stimulus, the same circuit mediates both habituation and sensitization. In habituation, the diminished synaptic response is *homosynaptic* because

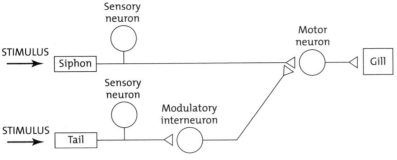

(A) **Sensitization circuit**

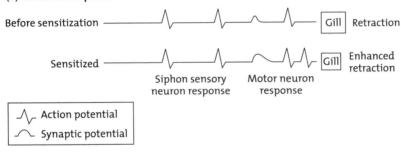

(B) **Electrical response**

FIGURE 3.8
A. schematic diagram of the circuit for sensitization of the gill withdrawal reflex.
B. Electrical responses at successive points within the circuit shown.

the events that cause the habituation occur within the same synapses that support the reflex. However, because sensitization increases many reflex pathways, the increased responsiveness must be caused by some influence outside of, or in addition to, the pathway for each affected reflex. Therefore, sensitization involves a *heterosynaptic* mechanism because it is accomplished by cells and synapses outside the reflex pathway for each affected behavior. When the gill withdrawal reflex is sensitized in the laboratory using electric shocks, the increased responsiveness is accomplished by the tail sensory pathway.

Unlike habituation, sensitization of the gill withdrawal reflex does not directly change the siphon's sensory neuron. Rather, the shocks to *Aplysia's* tail activate the tail's sensory neurons. The sensory neurons, in turn, connect via synapses to a *modulatory interneuron*.

Understanding how sensory neurons influence interneurons requires distinguishing between two types of receptors (Figure 3.9). The typical types of receptors,

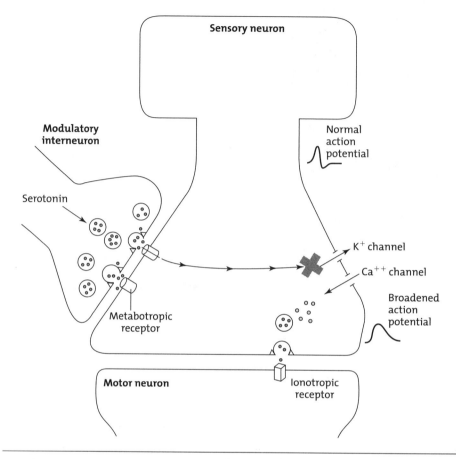

FIGURE 3.9 Interaction between a sensory neuron, a modulatory interneuron, and a motor neuron in *Aplysia* sensitization.

called *ionotropic receptors*, are found in dendrites and are switched on by neuro-transmitters. They allow charged molecules to flow into the dendrite, inducing a postsynaptic potential. The modulatory interneurons in this circuit use different receptors. *Metabotropic receptors* are activated by transmitters or other molecules, but they do not open channels or directly change the membrane potential. Rather, they engage specific chemical reactions that influence transmitter release.

We know quite a bit about how sensory neurons interact with interneurons in the circuit that supports sensitization in *Aplysia*. The modulatory interneurons release the neurotransmitter serotonin, which acts on the metabotropic receptors of the sensory neurons. Consequently, a series of molecular steps inhibits the pre-synaptic K+ channels (indicated with an X in Figure 3.9), prolonging the duration of the action potential. This consequently causes the Ca++ channels of the pre-synaptic elements to stay open longer so that more Ca++ flows into the presynaptic elements. The resulting increased Ca++ concentration in the presynaptic elements increases the number of vesicles docked for each action potential, increasing neurotransmitter release. This, of course, heightens motor neuron response—and hence magnifies the behavioral response to any stimulus.

The studies of sensitization and habituation discussed in this chapter show how the neuron mechanisms discussed in Chapter 2 are pulled into play and modified to accomplish changes in neurons and circuits. These changes, in turn, support behavior modifications that are the basis of learning and memory. In the case of *Aplysia,* habituation can be explained by changes in neurotransmitter release in the short term and changes in the number of synapses in the long term. Sensitization is more complex but still can be reduced to cellular mechanisms that control how well cells connect. In this case, sensitization is accomplished by interneurons whose neurotransmitters hold open channels in the sensory neurons to increase neurotransmitter release. The consequential reflex enhancement is observed at the behavioral level as sensitization. These cases provide compelling examples of understanding a form of learning and memory in terms of cellular and molecular events in neural communication.

Interim Summary

Sensitization differs from habituation. Whereas habituation is specific to both a particular stimulus and a particular response, sensitization modulates a variety of responses to many stimuli. Habituation and sensitization also vary in their longevity. Habituation can be homosynaptic (involving changes within the circuit that supports the affected behavior), whereas sensitization is heterosynaptic (involving a different circuit that can modulate many other behavioral pathways). Sensitization of the gill withdrawal reflex in *Aplysia* is accomplished by interneurons that modulate neurotransmitter release by the siphon sensory neuron in the gill withdrawal circuit.

Chapter Summary

1. Both of the simplest forms of learning, habituation and sensitization, involve changes in behavior following exposure to a stimulus. Habituation decreases responsiveness to repeated presentations of the same stimulus. It is specific to both the particular repeated stimulus and the evoked response. In contrast, sensitization involves a state change in which an arousing stimulus increases an organism's responsiveness to a variety of stimuli.

2. Habituation and sensitization are simple nonassociative mechanisms that change an organism's responsiveness to stimuli, so they are pervasive in their importance to everyday life. In both of these phenomena, the memory of the stimulus is reflected during learning as either a decreased or increased responsiveness to it. Biological studies of habituation and sensitization have shown that we can understand these basic phenomena from the behavioral level to the level of neural circuits and cellular changes.

3. In addition, habituation has been used extensively to study various aspects of perception and memory. These experiments typically involve initial presentation of a stimulus, then presentation of a different stimulus to reactivate the response (dishabituation) compared to the original stimulus. The habituation/ dishabituation paradigm has been used to reveal capacities of infants and animals that cannot be studied by explicit verbal inquiry. Such studies have shown that infants and animals can perceive and remember specific individuals and objects and suggest that many brain systems can be influenced by the repetition of stimuli, leading to diverse consequences for behavior. It is important to acknowledge the distinction between habituation and sensitization as learning paradigms from other kinds of learning that can be accomplished through stimulus repetition.

4. The cellular bases of habituation and sensitization have been studied extensively in the gill withdrawal reflex of the invertebrate *Aplysia*. Habituation decreases the number of synaptic vesicles released from the sensory neuron that connects with motor neurons, and it diminishes synaptic connectivity in the long term. Sensitization affects sensory neurons by the action of modulatory neurons, which activate a cascade of molecular messengers in the sensory neuron to extend the period and amount of transmitter release in the sensory to motor synapse. These findings provide insights at the most basic level into the inner workings of simple forms of memory.

5. Research into the mechanisms of habituation and sensitization has shown that both types of learning are caused by changes in connectivity between cells in reflex circuits. In habituation, memory is accomplished through diminished connectivity; this is based on less transmitter release in the short term and loss of synapses in the long term. Recall from Chapter 2 that Cajal predicted that learning and memory would be based on changes in the extent and strength of connectivity between neurons in the brain. The cellular changes observed in the *Aplysia* models of habituation and sensitization are precisely what Cajal predicted.

KEY TERMS

habituation (p. 88)
sensitization (p. 88)
nonassociative learning (p. 88)
associative learning (p. 89)
dishabituation (p. 92)

REVIEWING THE CONCEPTS

- What are habituation and sensitization? How do they differ from each other and from associative learning?

- How does habituation differ from sensory adaptation and muscle fatigue? When you see a laboratory animal's response levels to a stimulus decreasing, what kinds of experimental procedures can help pinpoint which of these processes is the cause?

- How can we use habituation and dishabituation to study perception and memory in babies and animals? Why would these techniques be particularly helpful for studying such subjects?

- How are habituation and sensitization accomplished by neural circuits in *Aplysia?*

Perceptual Learning and Memory

For a few years during graduate school, I helped my mentor investigate perception and memory in rhesus monkeys. When I was introduced to this research, there was much to learn about how to test monkeys for perceptual and memory capacities. But another form of learning I had not anticipated was surprising. The technicians and senior graduate students could identify individual monkeys, and they often discussed what humans they looked and acted like and even named the monkeys after their human counterparts. Furthermore, the monkeys had come in groups from different sources, and my colleagues could readily identify every monkey's group origin by its facial appearance.

At first all 20 monkeys in our lab looked the same to me. But as I listened to the daily banter about the monkeys and worked with each one in turn, I began to differentiate between them as individuals. After a few weeks I could see that they looked different. Some were younger or older; some had happy or curious or scowling expressions; and there were subtle differences between monkeys that came from different groups. Eventually I too could identify each monkey. And when new animals came into the lab, I could immediately see each animal as distinct and discuss its unique features, and I could classify it based on its group. My success was deemed complete when I could join my colleagues in naming each new monkey based on its likeness to a current political figure, popular entertainer, or faculty member.

———————————

AS THIS STORY shows, we learn to perceive differences in sensory features and remember specific images in a variety of everyday situations. As we grow up, we learn to detect and discriminate many types of sensory stimuli—from different kinds of people we interact with to different kinds of foods we eat on different occasions, to makes of cars, to tools we use. We become familiar with and think about many stimuli we see often. Some of these images we struggle to remember, like someone's face or name. Others are frightful scenes we saw on the street or in a movie that we would rather forget.

Like habituation and sensitization, perceptual learning and memory are good examples of the continuity of learning and memory. We learn by merely perceiving, and we express our memories in the increased fluency with which we identify familiar stimuli. Like other simple forms of learning, perceptual learning is pervasive across species and is biologically based in the brain areas that support different kinds of sensory processing. But unlike other forms of learning and memory, perceptual learning and memory are special in what is learned, how it is learned, where the memories are stored, and in how memory is expressed. In other words, perceptual learning has different rules than other simple types of learning.

Fundamental Questions

1. Do perceptual learning and memory involve a "tuning up" of our perceptual system, or do they constitute a distinct form of learning and memory?
2. What are categorical perception, perceptual skill learning, and repetition priming? In what common situations do we use each of these mental processes?
3. How are each of these phenomena accomplished by the brain?

Characteristics of Perceptual Learning and Memory

We will consider two types of perceptual learning and memory. **Perceptual skill learning** improves the ability to detect, discriminate, and classify sensory stimuli of a particular category. Perceptual skill learning is a general capacity for sensory analysis, not memory for a specific stimulus. This type of perceptual learning changes our ability to detect or identify a sensory stimulus following extensive experience with similar stimuli. For example, when I learned to identify individual monkeys, my experience with a variety of individuals improved my general ability to distinguish individual monkeys. This type of perceptual learning lets us tailor and enhance our ability to gather and recognize sensory information.

The other type of perceptual learning considered in this chapter is **perceptual memory**, which is the unconscious formation and representation of specific previously experienced stimuli and the expression of these representations by unconscious changes in performance of tasks involving those stimuli. Perceptual memory involves learning and remembering specific sensory stimuli—typically independent of any effortful recollection. In many situations mere exposure to specific stimuli can leave a lasting impression. Words, sounds, and pictures we have recently experienced tend to come to our minds more readily than less recently experienced stimuli.

Two key properties distinguish perceptual learning and memory from cognitive memory (our everyday capacity to consciously recall events and facts). Chapter 1 distinguished between cognitive memory—the conscious remembering and explicit expression of memory—and behavioral memory, which is the unconscious acquisition and implicit expression of memory through changes in task performance. These distinctions characterize perceptual learning and memory as a type of behavioral memory. First, perceptual learning can occur with increased exposure to a particular sensory stimulus, even without conscious, intentional retrieval of prior information. And perceptual memories can be expressed implicitly (that is, automatically) through improvements in the ability to distinguish and identify sensory stimuli. Second, perceptual learning and memory are supported by a variety of the brain's sensory processing areas. Unlike other types of memory, there is no single brain "system" for perceptual learning and memory. Instead they happen throughout each sensory system and at every stage of perceptual processing.

In Chapter 2 we toured the distinct systems in the cortex that process information from each sensory modality, including separate areas for vision, touch, hearing, and olfaction. Information processing in each of these systems is hierarchical, involving early processing of elementary features and then more complex features. Correspondingly, perceptual learning and memory are exhibited in all sensory modalities and across a range of processing levels.

Perceptual learning changes how we process specific sensory information. In some cases it increases our ability to detect previously imperceptible stimuli. In other cases, such as learning to distinguish between individual monkeys, perceptual learning improves our ability to perceive differences among similar stimuli. Some perceptual learning, including acquired appreciation of types of art or music, involves analysis and identification of complex features of stimuli. Perceptual learning can be specific to a particular type of sensory information processing or to a particular stimulus; or it can improve our performance for an entire category of stimuli, such as a genre of music.

Perceptual learning and memory also differ from other types of learning and memory in the rules of learning that apply. Perceptual learning is typically non-associative: This type of learning can happen without rewards or punishment or associations between stimuli. (Occasionally, though, we see examples of perceptual learning that involve stimulus-to-stimulus associations.) In this way, perceptual learning and memory are like habituation and sensitization; but perceptual learning and memory do not simply diminish or increase behavioral response. Instead this kind of learning and memory facilitates perceptual processing and identification without changing the response to the stimulus. Perceptual learning can vary in the role of attention and effort and in the longevity of the memory. Some types of perceptual learning and memory occur passively as a result of experience, but others require strong attention and effort. Also, some types of perceptual memory can last months or years, whereas other types last only minutes or hours.

Interim Summary

Like habituation and sensitization, perceptual learning involves a simple, nonassociative form of memory, and this type of memory typically is expressed without conscious awareness or intentional information retrieval. Perceptual learning and memory occur within different sensory processing streams and at different levels of sensory processing. Because of the variety of brain areas in which perceptual learning and memory can occur, the rules of learning, the specificity of memories, and the longevity and other properties of different types of perceptual learning can vary considerably. Next we will discuss several examples of perceptual skill learning and perceptual memory.

Perceptual Skill Learning: Identifying Stimuli

Perceptual skill learning involves accurate detection, discrimination, and categorization of sensory stimuli. Through training, we can perceive what we previously could not even with considerable effort. Some examples of perceptual skill learning are experts trained in areas such as motifs in paintings, orchestral moods in chamber music, subtle perfume scents, and regional differences in Scottish whiskeys. In each of these areas, novices cannot even detect distinctions that spur considerable discussion or argument among experts. In the opening vignette, my initial impression was that all the monkeys looked the same; later I became an expert at monkey identification. How did I learn this?

One influential idea is that perceptual skill learning involves four main mechanisms: attentional weighting, feature imprinting, differentiation, and unitization (Goldstone, 1998). *Attentional weighting* involves increased focus on important perceptual features. For example, in learning to identify individual monkeys, I attended to differences in eyebrows, eye spacing, and other facial features I had previously ignored. *Feature imprinting* involves acquiring representations of stimulus features that serve as templates for comparison with later stimuli. I learned to identify categories of facial features that allowed me to group animals or compare their similarities and differences. *Differentiation* is the process by which we learn to separate stimuli that were previously indistinguishable. Those features of monkeys' faces had completely eluded me at first. *Unitization* is the process by which parts of a stimulus that were previously considered separate are composed to form a single percept. By the end of my training, each monkey's face became a composite image that I could readily identify.

These components of perceptual learning are highly related processes that vary in their prominence among different *types* of perceptual skill learning. We will consider two prominent types of perceptual skill learning. Categorical perception is our ability to identify stimuli that vary along a continuum as belonging to meaningful categories of stored representations, ranging from categories of colors, to speech sounds, to faces and more. **Stimulus detection** is our ability to acquire expertise in perceiving stimulus features in difficult tasks such as aligning or orienting fine line stimuli.

Learning & Memory in Action

Can Someone Really Be a "Born Expert"?

We have all marveled at how experts in paintings or orchestral music can identify and characterize at length qualities of their art forms that we scarcely detect. Do these experts have an innate superior capacity for perceiving a domain we do not appreciate, or could we too be experts if we had the interest and training? To investigate the basis of expertise in wine tasting, Mats Bend and Steven Nordin (1997) had professional wine tasters and untrained people perform a series of olfactory tests. The researchers surveyed the abilities of their subjects to *detect* weak concentrations of specific odors, to *discriminate* weak concentrations of different odors, and to *identify* common household odors. Wine tasters were no better than the control subjects in odor detection, but they were superior to the controls in discriminating and identifying some odors. These findings show that expertise in discrimination and identification of one flavor domain extends to a larger range of olfactory stimuli. But expertise in wine tasting does not alter our innate sensitivity for odors. Thus training in perception may generally improve the ability to discriminate and classify beyond the domain of trained stimuli.

Categorical Perception: Classifying Stimuli

Both human and animal studies have shown that subjects can learn to categorize according to either simple or complex properties. During category learning, subjects deemphasize stimuli features that may have been salient for previous purposes and learn to emphasize features that reliably predict new categories. In general, even complex or abstract features can be categorized with amazing ease. For example, pigeons can be trained to selectively attend to the feature "contains human" across a variety of photographs that contain or do not contain images of humans—or even to identify a particular human across different photos (Herrnstein, 1990).

How we learn to categorize has been studied in detail though explorations of the natural phenomenon of **categorical perception:** our ability to classify into discrete categories stimuli that vary along a continuum of the given stimulus dimension. For example, the visible spectrum of hues is a continuum of light wavelengths. Yet we perceive a rainbow as bands of distinct colors (each containing graded shades within each color) rather than as a fully continuous gradation of hue across the entire spectrum. Correspondingly, it is easier for people to distinguish light frequencies that cross a perceived boundary between colors (such as that between blue and green) than those involving shades of a single color, even when the magnitudes of the wavelength differences are the same. Other examples of categorical perception can be found in each sensory system and for both simple and complex features.

In hearing, for instance, the phonemes /be/ (pronounced "bee") and /de/ ("dee") are perceived by humans as distinct categories even though they differ only in the pitch of a specific transition, and the pitch of this transition can vary in normal conversation. When experimenters systematically manipulated that transition frequency to create intermediate sounds, people identified the intermediates as one of the two categories (either /be/ or /de/) and did not classify them as a sound in between. Also, similar to wavelengths in the visual spectrum, people find it difficult to discriminate between variations of different sounds that fall within one of the two categories. Conversely, people find it easy to make even fine distinctions between sounds that are on opposite sides of the category boundary.

Because even young infants and animals show this form of categorical perception, many researchers believe that perceptual categories are innately built into our perceptual systems. However, there is also evidence that category boundaries are subject to learning. For example, a categorical boundary within a language, such as /be/ versus /de/, is more discriminable to speakers of that language than to those who speak a language that does not include that boundary (see Goldstone, 1998); and the location of categorical boundaries depends on the language we have learned to speak (Williams, 1977). Categorical perception of phonemes is considered fundamental to our ability to identify words across a broad range of speakers and accents.

Categorical perception of more complex stimuli has been examined in studies of facial recognition. Faces are complex objects that are distinguished by many features. At the same time, we typically recognize a particular face with great accuracy in a variety of conditions where critical features are altered—such as in different lighting conditions, in gray scale or color, or with different facial expressions and hair arrangements. Yet all humans are experts at recognizing human faces, particularly those of relatives and other people with whom they are familiar. Because representations of individual faces cannot be innately programmed and therefore must be learned, are faces perceived categorically, as are colors and phonemes?

In a series of experiments, Beale and Keil (1995) examined whether individual faces are perceived categorically. They showed college students photos of pairs of famous people such as Bill Clinton and John F. Kennedy, or Arnold Schwarzenegger and Clint Eastwood, and created "morphed" photos that were composed as intermediates between the pairs to represent a range of gradations between the images of the two famous people. They asked the students two kinds of questions. First they presented each morphed photo individually and asked the students to categorize the photo as one of the two famous people. Then they presented pairs of the morphed photos that were 20 percent apart in gradations, with the pairs taken from the full range of gradations. With each pair, they also presented a target item that was identical to one of the photos and asked the students to judge which of the two stimuli matched the target. Students consistently judged the morphed photos at either end of the range as the appropriate famous person; only over a narrow part of the range where the gradation was near 50 percent were the students inconsistent (Figure 4.1). Such an abrupt shift in categorization is a hallmark of categorical perception. In the matching task, the students performed better in choosing between alternatives that bridged across the category judgment boundary than when they had to distinguish a pair of stimuli that were both on one side of the boundary. These are the standard characteristics of categorical perception.

Perhaps the students were using a particular feature that differed between the faces to make their category judgments (see the next "Learning & Memory in Action" box about sexing baby chicks p. 118). To address this issue, Beale and Keil again presented pairs of morphed photos of famous people and asked new subjects which of the two pictures was a better likeness of one of the famous people; later the subjects categorized each photo. To make this judgment, the subjects had to rely on their own mental representations of the famous people. Again the subjects judged the photos as belonging to distinct categories, reflecting a sharp shift in their assignments between the pair of famous people from which the photos were derived. Also, at the same boundary, the subjects peaked in accuracy in the better-likeness judgments. So when there were no specific features to distinguish between photos, subjects still showed strong categorical perception.

Finally, Beale and Keil asked whether categorical perception of faces occurs only for familiar faces or is a general property of face perception. They repeated the better-likeness experiment with pairs of highly familiar faces (such as Dustin Hoffman and Michael Douglas), with faces of moderate familiarity (like Cary Grant and Jack Lemmon), and with unfamiliar faces of nonfamous people. The

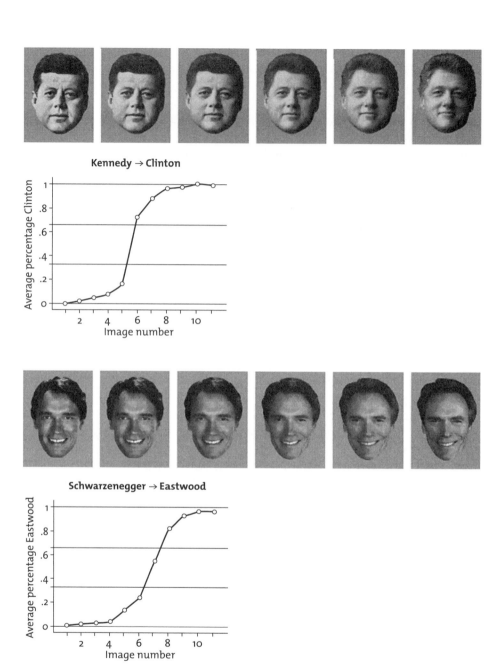

FIGURE 4.1 Categorical perception of faces.
Continua of highly familiar faces and subjects' judgments of these faces as belonging to one of the categories.

sharpness of the categorization judgments was strongly associated with the degree of familiarity of the faces: Subjects strongly categorized highly familiar faces, weakly categorized moderately familiar faces, and did not categorize unfamiliar faces. So categorical perception is not a requisite processing function of face perception. Instead we categorically represent and classify faces only with extensive experience.

People Can Learn to Detect Stimulus Features

Perceptual learning also includes acquisition of the ability to identify and distinguish stimulus features that were initially undetectable or undistinguishable. The development of increased sensory acuity with training, known as perceptual skill learning, has been known for over 100 years and extends across a broad range of sensory tasks, such as color discrimination, the ability to judge the orientation of lines, and the ability to identify pitch. Perceptual skill learning can support *hyperacuity*, the ability to discriminate at a finer grain than is supported by the acuity of individual sensory receptors (Gilbert, 1994). For example, people can be trained as experts in judging whether two vertically aligned lines are exactly in line with one another or are slightly offset (Figure 4.2). This skill, called *vernier acuity*, can become so good that experts can make the in-line versus out-of-line judgment at a resolution finer than that required to detect dots with diameters smaller than the thickness of the lines.

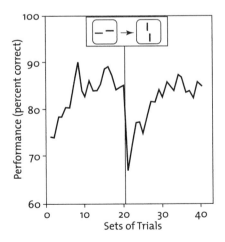

FIGURE 4.2 Vernier acuity test.
Subjects improved over trials with training for one orientation (horizontal or vertical); but performance dropped and had to be trained again when the orientation was switched.

This kind of learning does not require overt discovery of a particular relevant feature or feedback on correctness of judgments; rather, extensive experience and exercise are needed with the detected feature. Characteristically this type of perceptual learning works only within the particular task and the particular range of perceptual features in which training occurred. For example, vernier hyperacuity is restricted to the eye that was trained, the part of visual space where the stimuli were judged, and the orientation of lines that was experienced. Notably, only the early stages of visual processing have segregated areas for processing stimuli presented in one eye, in one part of visual space, and in particular orientations: Higher visual processing areas do not make such distinctions. These limits on the generalization of vernier acuity learning have led to the view that brain areas involved in early stages of perceptual processing are the sites for this form of perceptual learning. Considerable neurobiological research has been guided by this notion.

Learning & Memory in Action

How Can Farmers Distinguish between Male and Female Baby Chicks?

In the poultry industry, it's important to separate cocks from hens shortly after the chicks hatch. Yet male and female newly hatched chicks look identical to all but the most expert eyes for sexing day-old chicks. Novices find it extremely difficult to classify baby chicks as male or female, but experts can categorize them correctly 98 percent of the time at a rate of 1,000 chicks per hour. In the past, it typically required years of practice for people to become proficient at sexing chicks. But once it was discovered that the critical feature is the shape of the cloacal (anogenital) area, novice judges could be readily trained (Biederman & Shiffar, 1987). In this example, whereas training of professional sexers at one time required prolonged practice, it turns out that a specific anatomical feature is sufficient to categorize nearly all animals. However, categorization of even complex stimulus properties can be accomplished in both humans and animals.

The Neurological Basis of Perceptual Skill Learning

Direct evidence from studies of brain activation during perceptual learning shows that some types of perceptual skill learning occur in the first areas of the cerebral cortex that support visual sensation. In one experiment, subjects judged the tilt of a set of parallel lines compared to a 45 degree orientation (Schiltz et al., 1999).

Some subjects compared the test stimuli to a 45 degree clockwise orientation reference line. Other subjects used a 45 degree counterclockwise orientation for the comparison. Over several thousand-trial training sessions, subjects improved by 10 to 30 percent in their abilities to judge whether particular target stimuli were different than the reference orientation. However, the improved judgments were observed only when comparisons involved lines compared to the trained reference line, not for the opposite orientation. Thus subjects trained to compare lines in a clockwise orientation did not improve on comparisons in a counterclockwise orientation, and vice versa. Brain scans taken as subjects performed this task showed several active areas of the visual cortex during perceptual learning (Figure 4.3). Brain activation related to the selective improvement in discrimination for the reference orientation was limited to early stages of visual processing, consistent with the view that the most detailed aspects of perceptual skill learning occur in the first stages of processing within the sensory system.

Perceptual skill learning has four main properties that involve the specificity of what is learned, the role of attention, the speed with which learning occurs, and the role of sleep (Karni, 1996). First, the specific visual experience determines the type of changes induced in performance and in the nervous system. That is, perceptual learning is quite feature-specific, so its results are limited to the sensory

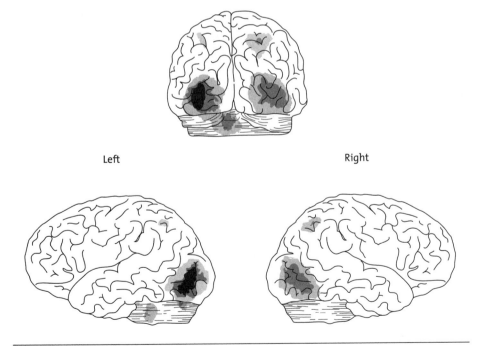

Left   Right

FIGURE 4.3 Brain areas active during line orientation judgments.

parameters targeted for training. For example, a person trained to differentiate minute changes in line orientation will improve at perceiving only line orientation and not line length, thickness, or other features. Also, if stimuli are presented in a particular part of visual space during training, learning is restricted to that region of visual space.

Second, attention and motivation influence the extent of learning. For example, in some of the line orientation experiments just described, the subjects were exposed to lines of both orientations but were told only one of these orientations was the relevant stimulus for making judgments. In such a situation, learning occurs only for the relevant stimulus and not the irrelevant stimulus that receives equal exposure.

Third, perceptual skill learning is based on a slow incremental process by which the cerebral cortex is modified to "tune in" the relevant stimulus dimension. Single brief training sessions can change performance and the brain, but these temporary changes quickly reach a plateau. By contrast, lasting memory requires repeated training over several days, suggesting that the underlying cortical changes require considerable time to mature or consolidate.

Fourth, sleep may be essential for performance improvements in perceptual skill learning. For example, in an experiment by Stickgold, LaTanya, and Hobson (2000), people trained in a perceptual skill task showed maximal improvement between 48 and 86 hours after the initial training. To examine the role of sleep in subjects' improvement, some subjects were deprived of sleep for 30 hours after initial training, then allowed two full nights of sleep before final testing (Figure 4.4). Subjects who were allowed to sleep normally showed substantial improvement after three days of training, but subjects who had not slept the night after learning showed no improvement during that same period. It appears that critical processing during sleep somehow solidifies memories, facilitating performance change.

The generality of this finding has been extended to the consolidation of perceptual learning associated with speech comprehension. People who listen to computer-synthesized speech initially find it difficult to understand. Subjects were given a single 8-hour session of training, followed by 12 hours of wakefulness or sleep (Fenn et al., 2003). Those who slept during the retention interval showed a 45 percent increase in comprehension of computerized speech, and this improvement lasted eight months. However, subjects who did not sleep showed much less improvement. These findings suggest that sleep following perceptual learning can confer much better retention of what is learned.

Brain Circuits Change during Perceptual Skill Learning

How does the cerebral cortex change during perceptual skill learning? Recall from Chapter 2 that the early stages of sensory processing in the cortex are organized

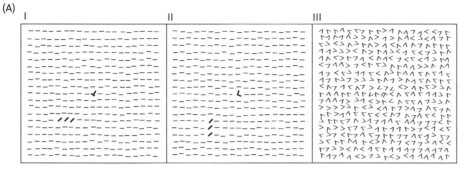

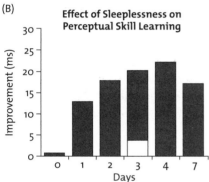

FIGURE 4.4 Sleep and the consolidation of perceptual learning.
A. On each trial subjects got a brief glimpse of an array of horizontal lines plus some tilted lines and a tilted T or L at one of many possible locations in the arrays (I and II). Then, after a brief and variable delay, the subjects viewed a masking stimulus (III) and then had to identify whether the letter presented earlier was a T or L. B. Performance, measured as the minimal delay (in milliseconds) for accurate choices, improved across days in subjects who were allowed to sleep (black bars) but not in those prevented from sleeping (white bar).

as maps of the sensory world. Thus visual space is mapped by circuits of visual neurons that represent adjacent locations in the visual field. Similarly, the body surface is mapped by neurons that represent locations on the skin, and auditory perception is mapped by neurons that represent different frequencies of sound.

Several studies have suggested that these early sensory representations change to support perceptual skill learning. One of the most elegant demonstrations of this kind of perceptual change has come from experiments by Weinberger and his colleagues (1993), who investigated whether neurons in guinea pigs' auditory cortex change their response as a result of learning that specific sounds are important. Initially the researchers recorded the responses of single auditory cortex neurons in an anesthetized animal. They presented a series of sounds at different frequencies, measuring each cell's response to each sound to determine the frequency that generated its highest firing rate. This is said to be the frequency to which the neuron is "tuned" (Figure 4.5). Then the researchers selected a different frequency as the conditioning stimulus and repeatedly presented it paired with foot shocks so that the guinea pig would associate the two stimuli in a way that increased the tone's significance. After training, when the auditory responses of the cells were measured again, most auditory cortex neurons showed an increased rate of firing in response to the initially nonoptimal frequency that had been paired with the shocks. At the same time, the neurons showed reduced responses to other frequencies, including the ones that caused the highest firing rates in the cells before conditioning. That is, the cells retuned themselves to respond more intensely to the relevant stimulus frequency.

In a related experiment, the guinea pigs were trained to discriminate between tones associated or not associated with a shock. The animals' neural responses to the frequency associated with the shock increased; neural responses to the frequency presented alone decreased, as did the responses to all other frequencies,

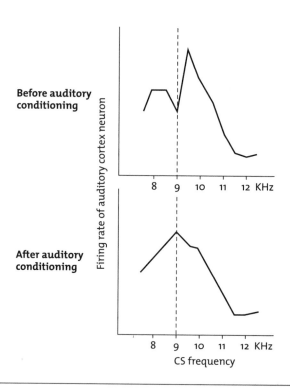

FIGURE 4.5 Retuning of auditory cortex cells by classical conditioning.

including those to which the cells were initially tuned. These effects developed in just a few conditioning trials and were long-lasting. Indeed, the intensity of the conditioned response grew during the hour after training and was maintained for at least 24 hours. Thus retuning of neurons to newly important stimuli can be powerful. Overall, consistent retuning of neurons across the population of auditory cells can shift the topographic map for sound frequencies in the auditory cortex. The map shifts strongly toward greater representation of task-relevant frequencies at the expense of other frequencies in the audible spectrum.

Similar auditory cortical cell retuning toward relevant frequencies has also been observed in monkeys trained to make a difficult pitch discrimination (Recanzone et al., 1993). Monkeys that were trained to discriminate between small differences in tone frequency improved progressively at the task over several weeks. When researchers subsequently recorded the firing patterns of the monkeys' cortical neurons, they found that these cells' firing patterns had changed: They fired faster and more sharply to the trained frequency. Also, the auditory cortex representation grew for the trained frequency (Figure 4.6). Furthermore, these size changes of the cortical representation for the trained frequency were correlated with the improvement in task performance.

Can Perceptual Skill Learning Offset Perceptual Disorders?

These observations of perceptual skill learning in normal humans and animals suggest that some disabilities associated with sensory cortex development disorders might respond well to specific perceptual skill training. One study examined the perceptual skill learning abilities of people with amblyopia, a lack of visual acuity in one eye that occurs when that eye is not used during early childhood. Studies that record visual neurons in animals with experimentally induced amblyopia show that visual neurons that are normally activated by the unused eye have reduced visual responses.

The loss of visual acuity caused by amblyopia has generally been assumed to be permanent. But a recent study showed that perceptual skill training may allow improvement (Levi & Polat, 1996). In that study, adults with amblyopia were trained in the vernier acuity test described earlier. After as few as five 125-trial training sessions, subjects improved by an average of 70 percent. Learning was best for the trained orientation of bar segments and did not transfer to a different visual task. These data suggest that the visual cortical areas affected in amblyopia can still be affected by experience and that perceptual skill training may be useful even in adult treatment.

Other evidence that training can improve developmental defects in perception comes from a study of children with language learning impairments (Tallal et al., 1996). Some forms of language impairment may be due to difficulties in basic sen-

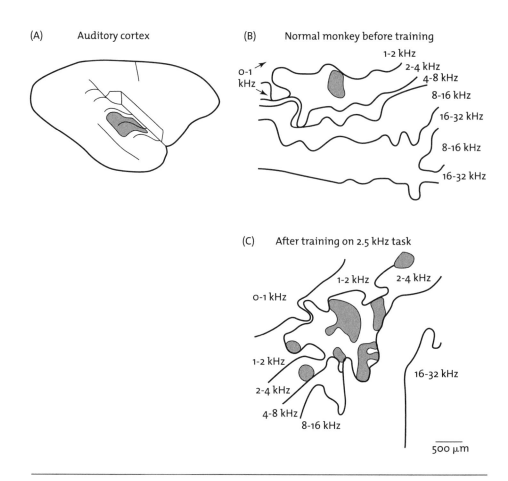

(A)   Auditory cortex

(B)   Normal monkey before training

(C)   After training on 2.5 kHz task

FIGURE 4.6 Auditory cortex representations change with learning.
A. View of monkey brain with auditory cortex shaded. B. Map of frequencies to which neurons in the untrained monkey were responsive. The gray area shows where, before training, neurons responded to the trained frequency. C. Map for the trained monkey. Note the increased size and number of areas responsive to the trained frequency.

sory processing of phonemes, particularly in the identification of fast elements embedded in ongoing speech that allows us to distinguish speech syllables. Tallal and colleagues developed a computer-based set of games with an embedded training program. In each game the child had to distinguish between sounds to advance toward a goal. At first the critical phoneme elements were louder and lasted much longer than normal, so even an impaired child could perceive the distinction. As the child succeeded at each stage of the game, the critical sound was shortened and reduced in volume. Over four weeks, the children showed marked improvements in their temporal processing thresholds. However, a key issue is whether success in a computer game translates into corresponding improvements in speech comprehension. As mentioned earlier, some types of perceptual skill learning do not generalize broadly to situations different than the training stimuli. In this case, the hope is that the acquired perceptual skill will apply to the same phonemes experienced in a variety of contexts.

Some Perceptual Skill Learning Is Independent of Conscious Attention and Memory

Perceptual skill learning may not require that we consciously remember the trained stimulus or even the relevant perceptual dimension during learning. A compelling example comes from studies in which people improved their ability to detect the direction of motion of simple visual stimuli, even when they did not consciously perceive the stimuli. In one study people were asked to identify letters that appeared in the middle of a computer screen while, in the background, an array of small dots appeared to move independently in random directions (Figure 4.7; Watanabe et al., 2001). Although participants perceived the dots' motion as random, 5 percent of the dots were actually moving coherently (that is, in the same direction). Subjects performed well in the letter identification task, identifying letters more quickly after training; but they could not perceive the direction of coherent motion in the dot display. After many letter identification training sessions, subjects were tested for their ability to detect the direction of motion in 5 percent coherent displays. The detection threshold did not increase for these displays, again showing that this degree of coherence fell below the level of perception. However, subjects' ability to detect 10 percent coherent displays had increased considerably as a result of the training. Furthermore, the improved motion detection occurred only for directions of coherent dot movement at or near the exposed direction; the ability to detect other directions of coherent motion did not improve.

How could the subjects in this study learn to detect coherent motion even though they were not aware of the stimuli they learned from? Could perceptual learning occur at an early stage in visual processing below our level of awareness?

In a follow-up study the researchers modified the experiment to address these questions (Watanabe et al., 2002). New subjects were trained in the letter identification task with the "random" dot movement display. This time the display showed a range of coherent motion directions that varied around an average. For example, the average direction might be vertically upward: Many dots would move in different directions, but all the coherent dots would move within 30 degrees of straight up. The investigators applied a clever trick to distinguish early and late visual processing stages. For some subjects, even though the average direction was upward, no dots moved within 5 degrees of that exact direction. This change cre-

(A)

Exposure stage (exposures 1–3)

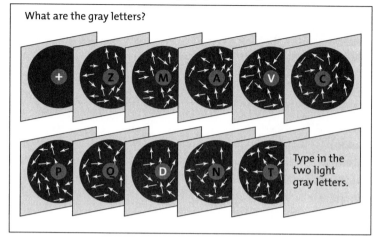

(B)

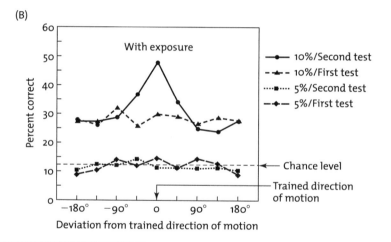

FIGURE 4.7 Perceptual skill learning without conscious attention.
A. The task. B. Improved performance for 10 percent coherent movement in the trained direction of motion.

ated a display in which the direction of *individual* dots' motion differed from their *average* direction of motion. Neurons in the earliest stage of the visual cortex respond only to individual dots and their movement directions, not to the perceived average direction of motion. By contrast, higher visual areas synthesize these individual details to perceive the average motion direction. Therefore, by omitting the directions closest to directly vertical, the investigators could simultaneously expose lower visual areas to more deviant movement directions while exposing more advanced visual processing areas to the average direction.

After training in these conditions, the subjects were tested for their capacity to detect movement direction in these displays. The subjects showed improvement only for the more deviant directions; the improvement was selective for the actually exposed directions and not the average direction subjects perceived. In other words, they showed perceptual skill learning only for the lower-level single dot movement patterns, which were unconsciously processed in lower visual areas, and not for the average movement direction consciously perceived by higher visual areas.

Other evidence for unconscious perceptual skill learning comes from studies of people suffering from cognitive memory disorders: amnesic subjects who cannot consciously recall training. In one experiment, researchers used the vernier acuity test to train normal subjects and subjects with amnesia to judge line alignment. Their scores were based on the threshold at which they could detect the direction of the lines' offset. Training occurred in five blocks of 80 trials, with a week of rest followed by an identical training session. Upon returning to the laboratory for the second training session, none of the amnesic subjects recalled the previous training, the stimuli or procedures, or the investigators. However, most subjects improved in this perceptual skill during the second session, showing substantially lower thresholds for detecting the direction of the lines' offset. In other words, people who lacked conscious recollection of the training performed as well as those who remembered being trained in this form of perceptual skill learning.

Can more complex perceptual skills also be learned without conscious memory? Another domain of perceptual skill learning involves the capacity to classify categories of complex visual information. This ability is often tested using displays of dots arranged in spatial patterns that can be judged as similar to one of several prototype patterns (Figure 4.8). Over many practice sessions, subjects are shown a variety of dot patterns. With practice, subjects improve their ability to appropriately classify each new pattern with the prototype it most resembles.

Hock and his colleagues (1989) investigated whether this task required participants to process entire complex patterns or whether they instead learned the simple components of the patterns and combined their knowledge of these features.

FIGURE 4.8 Prototype patterns for dot pattern classification learning.

This experiment examined the abilities of college students to classify large dot patterns containing subsets of smaller patterns. The students' success in classifying large, complex patterns could not be explained by their success in learning the smaller patterns separately, even when they were instructed to distinguish the smaller sets. Furthermore, the students were equally able to classify the patterns regardless of the patterns' visual field locations, suggesting that pattern categorization occurs at a later stage of visual processing than the perceptual skill learning tasks previously described.

A study of amnesic subjects provides a compelling distinction between their intact capacity for learning a general perceptual skill contrasted with impairment in remembering particular stimuli. Cohen and Squire (1980) were curious about why amnesic subjects seemed to learn and retain *how* to perform experiments while they could not remember *what* they were asked to do. To explore this distinction, Cohen and Squire asked normal individuals and people with severe amnesia to learn to read words presented in mirror image format (Figure 4.9A). Each day the subjects read several sets of three different words as rapidly as possible; the times required for each reading were measured. Half of the words were repeated each day, and half were novel.

There were two main findings. First, all subjects improved their speed in reading mirror image words (Figure 4.9B). For both repeated and novel words, reading times decreased both during sessions and from one session to the next. Furthermore, with the novel word sets, the amnesic subjects performed as well as the normal subjects. That is, despite their memory impairment, the amnesic subjects could acquire the perceptual skill of mirror reading as rapidly and as well as controls.

Second, normal subjects performed faster with repeated word triads than with novel triads. Because familiar and unfamiliar words were mixed within sets, the increased ease of reading repeated words had to reflect memory of those specific words. Here both groups showed learning, but the normal subjects outperformed the amnesic subjects. The difference in improvement with repeated and novel words could be seen most clearly in measuring forgetting across days by the reading time difference between the last block of each day and the first block of the next day. Both groups showed almost minimal forgetting for the novel words, reflecting nearly perfect memory for the general skill of reading mirror image words. By contrast, whereas the normal subjects also showed minimal forgetting for repeated words, the amnesic subjects were quite strikingly impaired, reflecting their specific impairment in remembering the particular words they had been shown. Their mirror reading skill was intact, whereas their memory of particular words was impaired. This demonstrates distinct mental representations of the acquired skill and the words themselves.

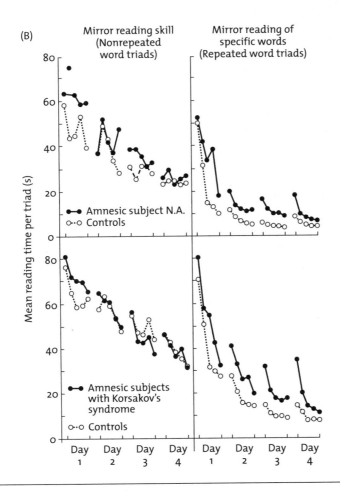

FIGURE 4.9 **The mirror reading test.**
A. Mirror image words. B. Cohen and Squire compared the mirror reading performance of amnesic subject N.A., who had suffered a brain injury, amnesic subjects with Korsakov's syndrome, and normal control subjects. All showed decreased reading times for the general skill of mirror reading (nonrepeated word triads) and for specific words (repeated word triads).

Interim Summary

Perceptual skill learning improves judgments about general stimulus features. This type of learning and memory involves increased attention or focus on particular stimulus features (attentional weighting), learning what features are important (feature imprinting), distinguishing stimuli according to relevant features (differentiation), and combining parts of a stimulus into an important percept (unitization). Two examples of perceptual skill learning are categorical perception and learning to detect stimulus features.

Categorical perception involves qualitative distinctions between stimuli that lie along a continuum but should be interpreted as representing different categories. Examples include our categorization of distinct colors in wavelengths that vary continuously, categorization of phonemes from sounds that vary along an auditory dimension, and categorization of individual faces that vary along many dimensions. Learning to detect stimulus features is most apparent in the phenomenon of hyperacuity, whereby people can learn to discriminate between stimuli at a finer grain than the acuity of individual sensory receptors.

Perceptual learning that requires fine discrimination among stimuli is supported by modifications of neurons in lower-level areas of the cerebral cortex, where neural networks are retuned to represent the relevant dimensions of stimuli presented; a consolidation of the new network representations occurs during sleep. Perceptual skill learning can also occur for more complex perceptual judgments, including classifying visual patterns and reading mirror image words. Perceptual skill learning can occur outside conscious attention and memory, as demonstrated in studies comparing normal and amnesic subjects. (*Note from the author:* Perhaps you have wondered whether it is ethical to perform experiments with subjects who have amnesia. *All* research with human subjects requires the informed consent of the subjects or, in the case of subjects with cognitive disorders, their legal guardians. In addition, all research with human subjects must be performed by accredited researchers and meet rigorous ethical standards.)

Perceptual Memories

So far we have discussed the acquisition of perceptual skills that are specific to a particular feature of stimuli (such as line orientation or direction of movement). But such highly focused skills are also general in that they apply to any stimuli that share the relevant perceptual feature. That is, perceptual skill always applies to a category of stimuli (like the orientation of some *type* of line in the vernier acuity test) and is not limited to skilled perception of an individual stimulus (one *particular* line).

In contrast, perceptual memories are specific to particular stimuli. Perceptual memories are sometimes experienced as a sense of familiarity for a person or an object without the ability to recollect who or what the item is or where and when we experienced it before. In these cases the perceptual memory is conscious—we are aware that the item is familiar—but the memory lacks content other than the perceptual match between the current item and something previously experienced. The phenomenon of déjà vu (the sense that you have been in a new place before) may also be based on a perceptual match between current circumstances and a similar previous experience. Familiarity will be discussed in some detail and compared with recollection of the context in which items are experienced in Chapter 9. Here we will discuss specific perceptual memories in a behavioral paradigm called *repetition priming*.

Repetition Priming Demonstrates Unconscious Perceptual Memories

Many researchers have studied the acquisition of specific perceptual memories as revealed in **repetition priming** (or just *priming*), which is the facilitation of processing of specific materials to which we have been recently exposed. The procedure for demonstrating repetition priming typically involves initially presenting subjects with a list of words or pictures of objects, faces, or other nonverbal materials. Subsequently subjects are reexposed to fragments or brief presentations of whole items. During reexposure, the subject's memory is measured in terms of improvement in their ability to reproduce the whole item from a fragment or by their increased speed in making a decision about the item (Roediger, 1990; Schacter, 1987). For example, a common procedure for examining repetition priming is the **word stem completion** task—a test of verbal repetition priming in which subjects initially study a list of words, then see the first three letters of each word and try to complete it. These tests use words that can be completed in multiple ways. For example, MOTEL has the stem MOT___; this can be completed to form the stimulus word or several other words (such as MOTHER, MOTIVE, MOTOR, MOTION, or MOTTO). Priming is measured by the increased likelihood that the subject will complete the stimulus word presented during the study phase. In another test of priming, subjects are briefly shown a whole word and are asked to identify the word. In yet another version of priming called *lexical decision,* subjects are shown letter strings and are asked to rapidly judge whether each letter string is a legitimate word.

Though the kind of memory priming creates may seem like a vague or hazy version of cognitive memory, research has shown that these are actually distinct, independent forms of memory. Three main lines of evidence have revealed important distinctions between priming and cognitive memory: differences in the content of what is remembered, independence of memory for information revealed in priming and conscious memory, and differences in the brain structures involved in priming and cognitive memory.

PRIMING INVOLVES MEMORY FOR SUPERFICIAL FEATURES WHEREAS COGNITIVE MEMORY INVOLVES MEANING Variations in the type of study of the items have different and even opposite effects on priming and conscious remembering (Jacoby, 1983). For example, in one series of experiments, subjects studied words by reading them aloud (for example, COLD), reading them in a meaningful context (hot—COLD), or coming up with the words themselves in response to antonyms that strongly suggested the target words (hot—?). When subjects were tested for word recognition, self-generated words were consciously remembered best; words read in the context of a meaningful association were remembered next best; and words studied in isolation were least often remembered (Figure 4.10). By contrast, the opposite order of performance was observed when memory was assessed with a task that required subjects to simply read each word. Studied words were identified most quickly if they were presented alone, next quickly if presented in context, and most slowly if the words were generated by the subjects. Thus cognitive memory was best when subjects consciously generated words, whereas priming was strongest when subjects simply read the word with no other conscious processing.

Additional experiments have shown that studying the meanings of words (for example, judging their semantic categories) but not their physical features (such as judging whether they have more consonants or vowels) improves later recognition, whereas both kinds of study improve priming. For example, Peter Graf and colleagues (1982) asked subjects to judge how much they "liked" study words, thereby encouraging them to focus on word meaning, or asked them whether each study word shared vowels with the previous study word, which discouraged attention to word meaning and instead forced subjects to focus on word form.

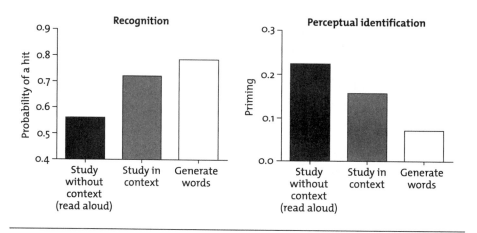

FIGURE 4.10 Different modes of study and repetition priming.
Top: Recognition is better when subjects generate words or study them in context.
Bottom: The opposite pattern is observed for perceptual identification in different modes of study.

They found that subjects consciously recognized the words only in the liking condition and not in the vowel identification condition, but they showed strong priming in both training conditions.

Consistent with the evidence that priming represents superficial features rather than meaning, priming is highly dependent on the exact appearance or sound of a stimulus, whereas our ability to consciously remember a word is relatively independent of those features. For example, changes in the font or case of words or their presentation modality (auditory or visual) between initial exposure and testing substantially diminish priming but have little effect on recognition. Many experiments have shown that repetition priming is typically sensitive to superficial features of the studied items, whereas conscious item recognition is relatively insensitive to superficial qualities.

PERFORMANCE IN PRIMING AND EXPLICIT REMEMBERING ARE STATISTICALLY INDEPENDENT In a seminal experiment showing that priming and cognitive memory for identical information are independent of one another, Tulving and his colleagues (1982) presented subjects with a list of 96 words, then tested them one or seven days later for recognition as well as for ability to complete the words from fragments. To examine whether recognition and priming occurred independently, the investigators compared the probabilities of correct and incorrect identifications in the recognition test and of successful or unsuccessful word completions in the priming test. They found that the recognition and priming probabilities were unrelated and occurred completely independently. In addition, recognition and priming performance had different time courses. Recognition was relatively high on the one-day test but fell substantially on the seven-day test. In contrast, priming was as successful as recognition on the one-day test and was maintained through the seven-day test.

REPETITION PRIMING AND COGNITIVE MEMORY ARE ACCOMPLISHED BY DISTINCT BRAIN STRUCTURES Evidence that repetition priming is accomplished outside the system that supports cognitive memory comes from several studies of priming in amnesic subjects showing that priming capacities can be spared in individuals with drastically impaired cognitive memory. Early evidence came from the successful performance of the amnesic man H. M. on a task called the *Gollins partial pictures task*. In this test subjects were shown a series of cards depicting fragments of a line drawing of a common object like an airplane or a bicycle; the first card of each series contained a few fragments of the drawing, and the last card showed the complete object (Figure 4.11). Subjects were initially shown the most fragmented, least complete images of the items and then were asked to identify the drawn objects; each failure was scored as an error. Next they were shown the second, slightly more complete image in each series, and so on until they could identify

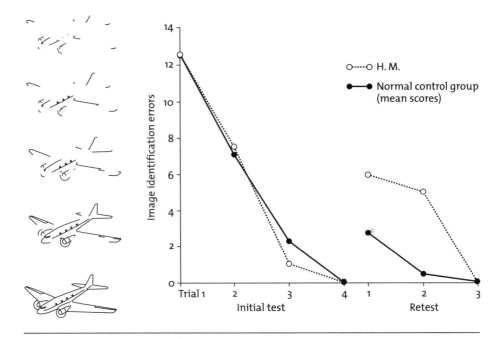

FIGURE 4.11 Gollins figures.
A. In successive pictures the image of the airplane becomes easier to identify.
B. Performance by normal subjects and subject H. M. on multiple tests with the same images.

all the items. After an hour of intervening activity, the entire test was repeated. Because of the earlier experience with the test images, participants could often identify the images using the more fragmented versions of the pictures when they repeated the test, showing that they remembered the first trials. Normal subjects improved substantially during repetitions. H. M. also improved strikingly during test repetitions and showed considerable retention across days of testing. But H. M.'s improved ability to identify fragments of pictures occurred in the absence of any conscious memory of the pictures he had seen.

A more recent study also illustrates the striking dissociation between intact priming and impaired conscious memory in amnesic subjects (Graf et al., 1984). This experiment employed the word stem completion task described earlier. Subjects initially studied a list of words. In the test phase, they were shown the three-letter word stems and were tested for their cognitive memory and for priming of the specific words using different test conditions. In the *free recall* condition, subjects were asked to recollect the studied words—a test that should rely heavily on cognitive memory. In the *cued recall* condition, subjects were presented with the word stems and instructed to use them as cues to recall the words; this condition should also rely strongly on cognitive memory. In the *stem completion* condition, subjects were presented with word stems and asked to simply "write the first word that comes to mind"; this condition specifically assessed priming. The amnesic subjects were impaired in both free recall and cued recall (Figure 4.12), consistent with a cognitive memory deficit. However, they were not impaired in stem completion, indicating intact priming.

Further analysis compared amnesic subjects' performances between the different test conditions. The amnesic subjects did much better in cued recall than they did in free recall (even though they were impaired compared to normal subjects on both tests). So cuing somehow helped the amnesic subjects. Interestingly, the amnesic subjects performed equally well in cued recall and stem completion. This comparison suggests that the cuing facilitated recall by priming the previously experienced words. In contrast, normal subjects did much better in cued recall than in priming, suggesting they used the stems to aid an active search in recalling the words.

Fully intact priming in amnesia is not restricted to namable objects and verbal material. Gabrieli and colleagues (1990; see also Musen & Squire, 1992) showed robust priming by the amnesic subject H. M. in a task designed to make verbal-

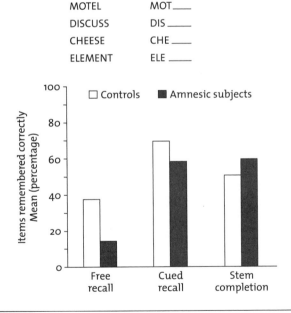

FIGURE 4.12 Repetition priming versus recognition and recall in amnesic and normal subjects.
Top: Study words and word stems presented in the priming test. Bottom: Performance on different types of memory tests of the same items.

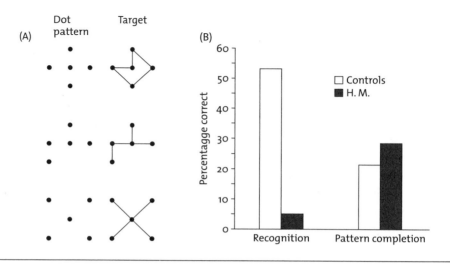

FIGURE 4.13 Repetition priming with dot figures.
A. Dot patterns presented and target line pattern that the subjects formed in the initial presentation. B. Performance in recognition of previously presented patterns and in completion of patterns.

ization difficult. In this test H. M. and normal subjects were shown a set of stimuli, each of which consisted of five dots arranged in a unique pattern (Figure 4.13). For each target pattern, the subject was also shown a corresponding partial dot pattern and was asked to fill in the missing elements of the partial pattern. Then, following other intervening activities, the subjects were given each partial dot pattern again and asked to complete it any way they wished. H. M. displayed a strong tendency to complete dot patterns as he had done before, showing as much priming as the normal control subjects. This intact memory for specific dot patterns was particularly impressive when contrasted with H. M.'s poor performance on a separate test in which he was shown dot patterns and asked if he could recognize which ones he had previously seen. Thus, as observed with verbal materials, H. M.'s unconscious perceptual memory for nonverbal visual patterns was intact, whereas his cognitive memory for the same patterns was impaired.

PRIMING OF ASSOCIATIONS IS ALSO INTACT IN AMNESIA A key issue about perceptual memories is whether priming is restricted to single items or whether new *associations* between stimuli or stimulus features can be learned and expressed through priming without conscious recollection. One form of **associative priming**, which is the facilitation of item processing following a single exposure to a combination of information, involves a variant of the Stroop test (Musen & Squire, 1993). In this task subjects are presented with color names printed in incongruent colors (such as the word *red* printed in green ink) and are asked to name the color of the print while ignoring the contradictory content of the word. Normal subjects are initially slow to name the ink color when it doesn't match the printed word, compared with their speed at identifying the ink color when it matches the printed word. However, normal people improve their speed at naming incongruent ink colors when they repeat the task, reflecting the acquisition of new color–word associations. The new associations are specific to the trained color–word pairs; naming time for colors increases again if the words are printed in new incongruent colors. Amnesic subjects are as capable as normal subjects are in learning and remembering this form of specific perceptual association.

The most striking example of priming complex associations among verbal items is improvement in the time required to read passages of text that have previously been read. To characterize this form of associative priming, Musen and her colleagues (1990) compared rereading times for textual material and the ability to remember the context of the text. The researchers carefully selected two stories of equal length and presented each story first equally often both to normal subjects and to subjects with memory disorders. The subjects were asked to read the stories as quickly as possible but not so fast that they did not understand what they were reading. Each subject read one story three times, then read the other story three times, and then answered questions about both stories. Normal people showed memory for the stories in terms of both faster reading times for each story repetition and their ability to answer questions about the stories. Importantly, the time required for the first reading of the second story was no shorter than that required for the first reading of the initial story—so there was no general acquisition of reading skill during this brief training. The reading skill improvement was specific to each particular story.

In a follow-up study, delays were inserted between the repeated readings. The facilitation in reading speed lasted at least 10 minutes and disappeared within two hours even though the subjects could remember the contents of the story for at least a day. These observations suggest that the text-specific reading skill was distinct from the ability to remember story details—a conclusion reinforced by the findings for subjects with amnesia. Memory-disordered subjects also showed improved reading time, and their performance on text-specific reading was as good as that of the normal subjects, despite a severe deficit in memory of the story contents. It appears that specific perceptual memory links together the words of a paragraph for reading, and this complex perceptual memory is independent of our conscious memory for the reading content.

So far the examples of priming we have discussed all involve **perceptual priming:** the repetition-produced facilitation of processing for the sensory qualities of a stimulus. Other studies have distinguished perceptual priming from **conceptual priming**, which is the priming of entire categories of words. As previously described, perceptual priming is highly dependent on word form and not on semantic analysis. However, priming can also be observed for semantically related categories of words, and in this case priming is not word specific. For example, if subjects are initially given category cues, like *bird,* they show priming for specific exemplars of the category, such as *eagle.* Like perceptual priming, conceptual priming can occur without conscious recollection of the verbal categories and can occur in amnesic subjects. However, unlike perceptual priming, conceptual priming is affected by thinking about the meanings of the study words and occurs even when the category cues and priming cues are presented in different modalities (such as oral and written).

REPETITION PRIMING FOR DIFFERENT MATERIALS IS SUPPORTED BY DIFFERENT AREAS WITHIN THE CEREBRAL CORTEX Tulving and Schacter (1990) proposed that priming may be mediated by a number of cerebral cortex areas, with each functionally distinct area supporting priming for the type of materials it processes. Based on the "hyperspecificity" of priming for the superficial visual features of words (as distinct from their meaning), they suggested that perceptual priming of words occurs at an early stage of word recognition. Also, they suggested that other cortical areas might mediate priming for nonverbal material. For example, in a test of priming for line drawings of objects, people were initially shown a series of drawings that depicted structurally possible real objects and other drawings that could not represent three-dimensional objects (Figure 4.14). Priming was observed only for the structurally possible objects, suggesting that the brain area that supports object priming also processes the perception of images as whole three-dimensional objects.

Studies of individuals with limited brain damage show that brain damage effects on priming vary depending on which area is damaged. This observation supports the notion that different cortical areas mediate different forms of priming. For example, people with Alzheimer's disease are characterized as having damage to the frontal and temporal cortical association areas that mediate higher-order perception and cognition; but the occipital cortex, which performs early stages of visual processing, is spared. Several studies have shown that people with Alzheimer's disease have relatively intact perceptual priming but impaired conceptual priming. But the opposite pattern has been observed in an individual with selective damage to the occipital lobe (Gabrieli et al., 1995). This person showed no visual perceptual priming, despite showing normal recognition memory for the same words and normal conceptual priming. These findings suggest that the prefrontal and temporal cortical areas affected in Alzheimer's disease support conceptual priming, whereas lower-level visual areas support perceptual priming.

Additional evidence for the cortical mechanisms of repetition priming comes from studies using functional brain imaging (Schacter & Buckner, 1998). During

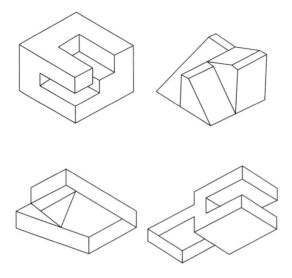

FIGURE 4.14 Possible (upper) and impossible (lower) objects.

repetition priming for words and objects, the posterior areas of the cortex are less active during successive presentations of a stimulus than they were when the same items were first presented. This reduced activity during repetition suggests that less processing is required for neural networks in these areas to identify items that have been recently processed. This conclusion is consistent with the notion that priming facilitates perceptual processing in the relevant cortical areas. Similarly, tasks involving repeated semantic processing, such as classifying words as concrete or abstract, reduce activation in the prefrontal association areas—consistent with the view that conceptual priming facilitates semantic processing in cortical association areas.

Interim Summary

Perceptual memories involve acquiring representations for particular sensory images. Perceptual memories can occur with awareness (as in a sense of familiarity without recollection of where and when an item was experienced) or without conscious awareness (as in repetition priming, where previous exposure to items influences their identification). Priming is highly dependent on superficial (perceptual) features of a stimulus, whereas conscious recall depends more on stimulus meaning. Priming occurs independent of recall and can be fully intact in amnesic subjects who fail to recall the same items. Both verbal and nonverbal complex stimuli can be primed, including associations between stimuli experienced together. Furthermore, conceptual priming—increased fluency for items in a category—can occur independently of perceptual priming. Each of these types of priming is accomplished in the particular sensory cortical area that processes the relevant stimulus dimension.

Chapter Summary

1. Our sensory systems are capable of an impressive amount of learning that can occur independently of cognitive memory. One form of perceptual learning is the capacity to acquire perceptual skills. We can become expert in a broad range of perceptual tasks—from sexing chicks, to identifying faces, to judging fine distinctions in linear alignment. Some of these tasks require focused attention on relevant stimulus features; but in many cases, expertise can be acquired by passive experience. One way to express perceptual skills is our ability for categorical perception: our natural tendency to identify stimuli as belonging to a category of like objects. People learn new categories, and these can be based on simple sensory features or on complex, seemingly abstract qualities. Another way in which perceptual skills are expressed is learning to detect and identify stimulus features that were undetectable before training.

2. The capacities to make categorical distinctions and detect subtle stimulus features are based on modifications of the processing by neurons in particular areas of the brain. Some distinctions are based on tuning neurons in early processing areas; this acquired expertise is specific in scope. Neural modifications for more abstract perceptual processing occur in higher-order cortical areas. Cortical processing modifications require some time for consolidation, and the rewiring appears to occur during sleep. Perceptual skill learning appears as an increase in the cortical surface devoted to the particular information being processed and as improved responsiveness to the relevant perceptual dimensions.

3. Many examples of perceptual skill learning can occur without conscious attention and can occur in people with amnesia who do not acquire ordinary cognitive memories of the stimulus dimensions or categories. This kind of implicit perceptual learning occurs for both specific sensory dimensions and more abstract features. Perceptual memories of specific items also occur independent of everyday conscious memory. This kind of memory is often studied in the context of repetition priming, in which the memory of specific items is revealed in improved or biased identification of previously presented stimuli. Priming can be distinguished from conscious memory in the importance of superficial sensory features (such as type-

face) for priming versus the importance of semantic features (like word meaning) for explicit memory. Also, priming occurs whether or not subjects can explicitly recognize the items. In addition, amnesic subjects typically exhibit normal priming even when they fail entirely at explicit recognition or recollection.

4. Priming occurs for both words and nonverbal patterns. Priming occurs for complex associations such as word pairs, words and the colors they are printed in, and entire passages of text. Like perceptual skill learning, priming is mediated by the perceptual systems that process the relevant materials. In particular, distinct cortical areas may support processing superficial word forms; separate cortical areas may process conceptual word categories.

5. The study of perceptual learning and memory is still young. But we know that the cerebral cortex is remarkably capable of modifying itself both for general analysis of perceptual information and for storing specific perceptual representations independent of other learning and memory capacities.

KEY TERMS

perceptual skill learning (p. 110)
perceptual memory (p. 110)
stimulus detection (p. 113)
categorical perception (p. 114)
repetition priming (p. 131)

word stem completion (p. 131)
associative priming (p. 136)
perceptual priming (p. 137)
conceptual priming (p. 137)

REVIEWING THE CONCEPTS

- How do perceptual learning and memory differ from cognitive memory?

- What is categorical perception? Is it innate or learned?

- What is perceptual skill learning?

- What is the role of attention in perceptual learning and memory?

- How do cortical circuits change to support perceptual learning?

- What is repetition priming? Why are the effects of priming considered perceptual memory?

- Which brain areas support perceptual learning and memory?

Procedural Learning I: Classical Conditioning

On my annual drive home for Thanksgiving last fall, I was in the midst of writing this chapter, and I was thinking about how classical conditioning fits into our everyday lives. We usually think of classical conditioning as a contrived model of learning that happens in the laboratories of scientists who, following in the footsteps of Ivan Pavlov, do things like ring bells and watch dogs salivate. Does classical conditioning also happen in the real world? While pondering this question, I saw the traffic light ahead turn to yellow and moved my foot from the gas pedal to the brake. "Yes!" I thought, "An otherwise neutral stimulus, a yellow light, has come to control my foot!" How did this happen? Of course yellow traffic signal lights are extremely good predictors of red lights that direct us to stop. I had experienced the predictable sequence of yellow light–red light–stop many times. The yellow light had achieved the same power red lights have in evoking my reflexive foot movement to the brakes.

I drove onward to the highway. A sharp curve was ahead; before I reached it, I began to lean in the opposite direction—another conditioned response! The sight of an impending curve predicted that centrifugal forces would press on my body, and I automatically leaned to compensate.

Now I was getting close to the home in which I grew up. I'd exited the highway and was cruising through my hometown. The sight of my old high school made my heart race—an emotional reflex! I'd had many powerful emotional experiences, like exciting sports events and exhilarating (and demoralizing) romances, within that school. And seeing it elicited the feelings I associated with that place and the same emotional responses the actual events once evoked.

Finally I arrived home. My mother came out of the kitchen with the turkey on a platter. I saw that large bird, and my mouth began to water—another example of classical conditioning! I'd eaten that turkey dinner many times, and each time the sight of turkey on a platter predicted turkey in my mouth within minutes. The sight of turkey had achieved the power of the taste of turkey, reflexively evoking salivation. This kind of classical conditioning is an example of what early psychologists called *psychic secretion*: the release of body fluids in response to seemingly neutral stimuli that predict situations in which reflexive secretions will occur. A doctor named Ivan Pavlov, whom you may remember from Chapter 1, studied gastric reflexes and psychic secretions. His work began the formal study of classical conditioning.

MY THANKSGIVING DRIVE home included many examples of classical conditioning, which happens to us often. The familiar events I described expressed acquired associations between previously neutral stimuli (seeing a curve in the road) and consistent subsequent events (driving along the curve) that evoked reflexive responses (leaning). This form of learning, called **classical conditioning,** gives us much of our motor coordination; such conditioning depends on predictable timing of stimuli and responses. Classical conditioning is pervasive in many human and animal learning and memory systems, and it is the predominant type of learning in motor systems. Researchers use classical conditioning to examine the process of learning and, at the same time, measure the memory for acquired associations between different stimuli and responses. This chapter will highlight some examples of classical conditioning that reveal its particular rules, including how association, predictability, and timing of stimuli influence the process.

Fundamental Questions

1. In what ways does classical conditioning occur in daily life?
2. What is the nature of memory representation in classical conditioning?
3. Does classical conditioning apply only to simple motor responses?
4. How does the brain represent conditioned responses?

Pavlov Began the Study of Classical Conditioning

Ivan Pavlov was a theology student, but he became interested in chemistry and physiology. His early research focused on connections between the nervous system and other internal organs, including the digestive system. The prevailing view at that time was that digestive fluids were released into the stomach when food particles stimulated the stomach lining. However, Pavlov suspected that the nervous system acted as a critical intermediary between the food stimulus and the stomach's release of fluids. To investigate this possibility, he developed a novel surgical procedure that allowed him to introduce food either directly into the stomach without letting it travel through the mouth or gullet, or instead into the mouth, allowing the food to travel through the upper gullet and then out the opening without going to the stomach.

Pavlov found that food in the mouth caused the release of gastric fluids even when the food never reached the stomach. He concluded that the two organs communicate via the nervous system: Food excites the taste sensors in the mouth and gullet, transmitting signals to the brain stem. Nerves that innervate the stomach then initiate the release of gastric fluids. This kind of pathway is similar to the muscular reflex pathways that begin with sensory stimulation and end in skeletal muscle contractions (see Chapters 2 and 3). For discovering this reflex arc for digestion, Pavlov received the Nobel Prize in 1904.

By then Pavlov had turned his attention to intriguing reports of "psychic secretion." French physiologist Claude Bernard had described how gastric juices of a horse could begin to flow even when the animal only caught sight of hay—before the food entered its mouth. (Another common example of psychic secretion occurs in new mothers as the letdown, or ejection, of breast milk, which is evoked by the sight, smell, or even mention of their infants.) Pavlov replicated this phenomenon in the dogs he studied, noting that the mere sight or smell of food was sufficient to elicit salivary and gastric secretions. But he also found the phenomenon unreliable. Although the dogs would salivate at the sight of beef, they tended to salivate less after repeated visual presentations of beef. But sometimes salivation was triggered by events that preceded the sight of beef—such as when the person who regularly provided the food entered the testing room. How did this occur? And why was this kind of reflex unreliable, contrasting with the standard observation that reflexes are automatic?

In the experimental protocol he developed, Pavlov focused on the automatic salivation that happened when food was placed in a dog's mouth. He implanted a fine tube into the dog's mouth to collect saliva, allowing him to measure the intensity of this digestive reflex by the amount of saliva produced. Pavlov distinguished the automatic, innate, and reliable reflex from the *conditioned* (learned) reflex. The stimulus that triggered an innate reflex (food in this case) was called the **unconditioned stimulus (US),** and the automatic reaction it triggered (salivation) was called the **unconditioned response (UR).** In this framework, the **conditioned reflex** (the one learned through experience) is composed of an arbitrary, initially neutral stimulus called the **conditioned stimulus (CS),** such as a bell or a light, presented with a US to elicit a **conditioned response (CR),** which typically resembles the automatically generated UR. The general procedure involves presenting the CS for some duration, at the end of which the US overlaps

(Figure 5.1). Early in training, the neutral CS evokes no response; but each presentation of the US automatically evokes the UR. During learning, the CR (which resembles the UR) initially appears shortly before the US; then the CR appears earlier following the beginning of the CS. There are many examples of these stimuli and responses used in classical conditioning (Table 5.1). You can see that the USs in the table would naturally elicit the responses, whereas the CSs, which can be made to evoke the same responses, are neutral stimuli easily manipulated in a laboratory.

Through many systematic studies, Pavlov (1927) identified the importance of two parameters in establishing and maintaining the conditioned reflex: The CS must precede the US by a short interval, and the CS must consistently predict the US. In addition, Pavlov examined the acquisition of the conditioned response as well as its **extinction**—the gradual disappearance of the learned response when

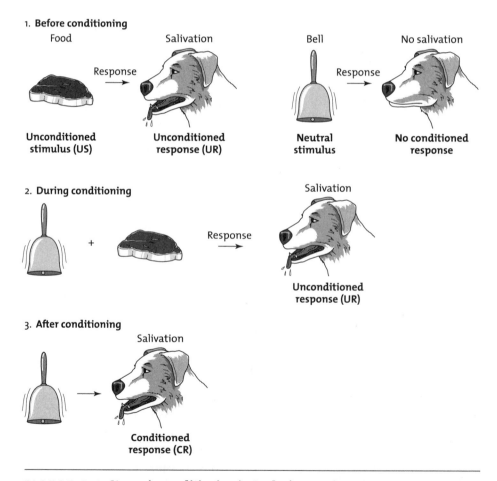

FIGURE 5.1 Stages in conditioning in Pavlov's experiments.

TABLE 5.1 Stimuli and responses in classical conditioning.

Stimulus or Response	Examples
Unconditioned stimulus (US)	Food, loud noises, air puff to the eye
Unconditioned response (UR)	Salivation, startle, eyeblink
Conditioned stimulus (CS)	Tone, light
Conditioned response (CR)	Salivation, startle, eyeblink

the US ceases to follow the CS. Pavlov noted that the CR sometimes reappeared after extinction: When animals were returned to the training situation after extinction the day before, the CR showed a spontaneous recovery (that is, it reappeared without additional training). These and other observations laid the foundations of research in classical conditioning.

Classical Conditioning Provides Protocols for Studying Simple Motor Responses

Classical conditioning has been used extensively to study the association between an initially neutral stimulus, such as a bell in Pavlov's studies, with stimuli that evoke reflexive responses, such as the taste-evoked salivation reflex. The classical conditioning procedure has received widespread attention because it provides straightforward, measurable behavioral responses to stimuli. Researchers can systematically manipulate the features of these stimuli and their timing. Through many studies, we have learned a lot about what kinds of stimuli effectively result in conditioning and about the critical role of timing the stimulus presentations. But although the laboratory procedures used to explore this kind of learning are artificial, conditioning occurs naturally in many situations.

Using classical conditioning, researchers have gotten neutral stimuli to evoke a broad range of simple reflexes involving muscular movements, like the knee jerk reflex, and responses of internal organs, such as cardiac acceleration. The classical conditioning protocol can be used to study many different forms of learning, so it is important to distinguish classical conditioning as an experimental protocol from the specific kinds of memory that are formed during the conditioning procedure. For example, pairing tones with particular tastes can condition reflexive salivation. In addition, this conditioning experience also creates conscious cognitive memories of the stimuli, the responses, and the entire learning experience.

Eyeblink Conditioning: Classical Conditioning of an Elementary Motor Response

If you have visited an eye doctor, you may have been tested for glaucoma with a procedure in which the doctor directs a small, quick burst of air at your eyeball, causing you to blink. The same reflexive eye blinking in response to a mild air puff has been examined extensively in both humans and animals (Gormezano et al., 1987). In a typical experiment, the subject is fitted with a headband containing a nozzle pointed at an eye and a device that records the blink. The US is a brief, gentle puff of air directed at the eye or, in some cases, a mild electrical shock to the area surrounding the eyelids. The CS is typically a light or tone. The UR is typically a rapid, vigorous eye closure, and the learned CR is usually a gradual, less intense blink. Some studies measure the strength and timing (or *latency*) of the onset of the CR, but the most common measure of learning is the percentage of trials in which a CR occurs.

The findings for classical conditioning of the eyeblink reflex are remarkably similar across species. The capacity for classical conditioning of this reflex develops over the first few months of life in human infants and over the first several days after birth in rats (Ivkovich et al., 1999). Although most studies of eyeblink conditioning have used animals, interest is growing in the study of human eyeblink conditioning because of its simplicity and the ability to control aspects of the learning situation (Woodruff-Pak, 1999; Steinmetz, 1999).

Common Conditioning Procedures

As Pavlov recognized, a key feature of classical conditioning is the timing between the CS and US. Several variations of the basic classical conditioning protocol have let researchers examine the underlying basis for this relationship (Figure 5.2). Four such variations are particularly important:

1. **Delay conditioning:** The prototypical procedure involves presentation of the CS for a short period, usually less than one second, with the US presented during the last part of the CS period. Thus, for example, the CS might be a tone presented for 500 milliseconds and the US a 100-millisecond air puff presented during the last part of the CS period. The time between the onset of the CS and the onset of the US is called the **interstimulus interval (ISI)**. Another important temporal measure in classical conditioning protocols is the time between successive presentations of the CS and US, called the **intertrial interval (ITI).**
2. **Trace conditioning:** This protocol is similar to delay conditioning in that the CS is presented first, followed reliably by the US at a particular ISI. However, in trace conditioning the CS terminates before the US is presented, leaving a gap (or *trace interval*) between the CS and US when no stimulus is present.

Classical
Conditioning
Provides Protocols
for Studying Simple
Motor Responses

149

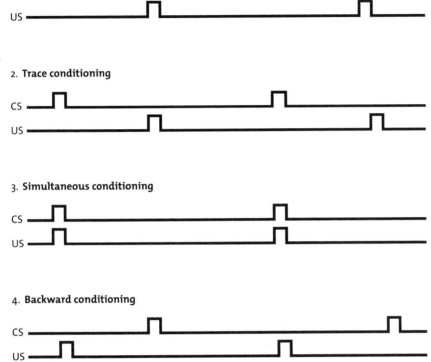

FIGURE 5.2 Pavlovian protocols.

3. **Simultaneous conditioning:** In this procedure, the CS and US are presented at the same time. This might seem to be the most effective way to induce a strong association between the CS and US; but as we will see, it is not the most effective protocol for classical conditioning.
4. **Backward conditioning:** In this protocol, the order of the CS and US is reversed, so the US is presented at a specific interval before the onset of the CS. This technique is used to examine whether the order of conditioned and unconditioned stimuli is critical for learning the association between them.

Control Protocols: Critical Conditions for Learning

Control conditions are also commonly used to test whether the responses learned during conditioning can be attributed to the pairing of the CS and US, as opposed to the effects of repetition of either stimulus alone. Considering this issue helps us understand exactly what subjects learn when they develop an association between stimuli that is strong enough to change their behavior. The assumption in classical conditioning is that the CS and US have become associated or connected in the subject's mind because they happen close together in time—that is, the subject has learned about their *contiguity*. However, as discussed in Chapter 3, behavioral responses can change without stimulus contiguity—even after a single experience with some types of stimuli. Particularly for intense experiences, a single stimulus can cause sensitization, which increases responsiveness to a variety of stimuli. On the other hand, we also saw in Chapter 3 that repetitive presentation of a stimulus results in habituation (a decrease in behavioral responses). The classical conditioning paradigm presents both the CS and US repeatedly and so could diminish reflexive responses to either stimulus. Also, in typical eyeblink conditioning, the US is moderately aversive and could evoke sensitization of responses to any other stimulus. How can researchers be sure whether the effects they observe are caused by habituation, sensitization, or actual classical conditioning?

To control for the possibility that the CS or US alone could change behavioral responses, and to examine any effects caused specifically by the contiguity of the CS and US, experimenters use different types of control procedures. *CS alone* or *US alone* presentations determine whether either stimulus without the other can affect behavior. The *explicitly unpaired CS and US* condition presents the CS and US separated in time and in alternating or random order. This protocol is often used as a control condition for the standard relationship between the CS and US. However, a possible problem with this kind of control condition is that the subject may learn that the CS reliably predicts the *absence* of the US; in cases where the US is aversive, the subject may learn that the CS is a safety signal indicating that no aversive stimulus will occur. Indeed this protocol sometimes produces a change in response to the CS that is *opposite* that of the UR (such as less than the normal spontaneous rate of blinking). To address this issue, another possibility is to time the CS and US presentations independently, which is called *random control*. In this protocol, the CS and US usually occur separately but sometimes can coincide or occur in close temporal proximity. This might seem to be the most valid control for a reliably predictive temporal relationship between the CS and US. However, several studies have observed that even random control procedures result in learning, possibly because a few rare coincidences of the CS followed by the US may be sufficient to support learning.

With these basic conditioning procedures and control conditions in mind, we can examine the properties of classical conditioning, as well as its neurobiological basis.

Interim Summary

Classical conditioning is defined as a consistent predictive relationship between a CS and a US that reflexively evokes a UR. Conditioning is observed when, after repeated pairings of the CS and US, the CS reliably evokes the CR. This procedure has been applied in a wide variety of situations for different types of stimuli and responses, such as eyeblink conditioning in both animals and humans. The standard version of this kind of learning is delay conditioning, in which the CS begins before and continues through the US; the interval between CS onset and US onset is the ISI. Also used are trace conditioning, in which the CS is transient and most of the ISI is an empty trace interval; simultaneous conditioning, in which the ISI is zero; and backward conditioning, in which the US precedes the CS. Conditioning depends on pairing of the CS and US and is usually most effective with delay conditioning.

Variations in Conditioning Reveal Its Basic Properties

There are many variations of the four classical conditioning protocols (delay, trace, simultaneous, and backward conditioning) described in the previous section. Here we consider examples of these types of classical conditioning that have informed us about a number of issues crucial to understanding how the process works: critical timing of the CS and US, how conditioned responses disappear, how different relationships between the CS and US can affect conditioned responses, and how conditioned responses can generalize or discriminate between stimuli.

Gradual Acquisition of a Conditioned Response Depends on Timing

Classical conditioning of motor responses is typically gradual: The conditioning subject must experience many CS and US pairings before the conditioned response grows to its full magnitude and form (Figure 5.3). On the first few trials, there may be no CRs. Indeed, in a study of four- and five-month-old infants, no conditioning was observed during an initial 30-trial session; but this training was required for learning to occur during a second conditioning session (Ivkovich et al., 1999). With additional training, the likelihood and expected magnitude of a CR increase. Note how the gradual, quantitative classical conditioning of motor reflexes contrasts with the rapid, qualitative learning of conscious memories.

The effectiveness of classical conditioning is also influenced by several factors that provide insights into its properties and mechanisms. One of the most significant aspects of this kind of learning is the intensity of the CS and the US. As you

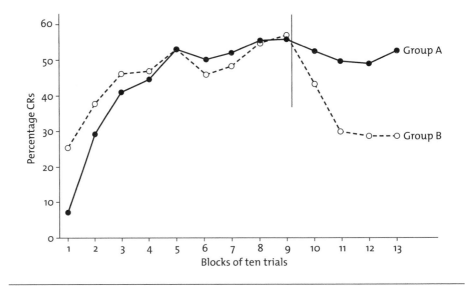

FIGURE 5.3 The acquisition of Pavlovian conditioning.
Group A received a consistently strong US. Group B received the strong US for 90 trials, after which the US intensity was reduced.

might expect, conditioning happens more quickly and attains higher response levels when the CS and US are more intense. Thus in the example shown in Figure 5.3, when the intensity of the US was reduced in Group B, the percentage of trials in which a CR was observed decreased.

In classical conditioning, timing is also critical. As Pavlov discovered, the time between the US onset and the CS onset (the interstimulus interval, or ISI) is crucial to conditioning effectiveness. In general, little learning is observed in simultaneous conditioning, even though a perfectly overlapping CS and US might seem to provide the ideal temporal contiguity of stimuli. Even brief ISIs are not optimal for conditioning. Rather, learning is most rapid at an ideal ISI. In both humans and animals the optimal ISI for classical eyeblink conditioning is about 250–500 milliseconds (Figure 5.4A). Little conditioning is observed at ISIs of less than 100 milliseconds or greater than 2 seconds. The similarity between animals and humans in sensitivity to CS–US timing is remarkable.

Importantly, ISI duration affects CR timing. In his studies of salivary reflexes, Pavlov varied the ISI from a few seconds to a few minutes and observed that the CR onset varied to occur shortly before the US, as if the CR "anticipated" the timing of the US (Figure 5.4B). Studies of human and animal eyeblink conditioning have similarly shown that with relatively long ISIs (like one second), the blink (CR) initially appears just before the puff of air (US), and the timing of the CR progressively shortens so that the conditioned blink (CR) is at its maximum when the

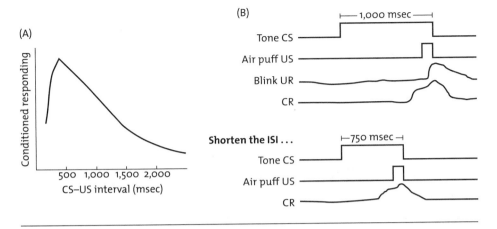

FIGURE 5.4 Classical conditioning at different ISIs.
A. The strength of conditioning is maximal at an intermediate CS–US interval.
B. Conditioned responses in conditioning with different CS–US intervals. The CR is timed
to anticipate the onset of the US.

US occurs. These findings also suggest that the CR is timed to anticipate the US. Given these learning patterns, what do you think happened in backward conditioning when Pavlov presented the US before the CS—that is, when Pavlov gave the dogs their food and *then* rang the bell? Because the CS was not in position to predict the US in this procedure, no learning resulted. These observations show that learning is not limited to an acquired *association* between the CS and US. Rather, during conditioning, subjects also learn the *temporal relationship* between them. Specifically, they learn that the CS predicts that the US will occur at a particular time. Recall that when I was driving home for Thanksgiving, the timing of the yellow signal light in predicting the impending red signal light was vital. The normal interval between these events told me when and how forcefully I should step on the brakes.

Conditioned Response Extinction Is Not Forgetting

There is typically little "forgetting" (actual loss of memory) for a classically conditioned reflex. Even after considerable time, conditioned responses are strong as soon as conditioning trials are again presented. However, this does not mean conditioned responses are permanent and immutable. Rather, if a CS is presented repeatedly in the absence of a US, this reduces the CR, which eventually disappears. In other words, a CS, such as Pavlov's bell, occurring in the absence of a US, such as food, on multiple occasions causes extinction of the conditioned response. For example, as shown in Figure 5.5, following successful conditioning of the human eyeblink response, repeated presentations of the CS tone or light in the absence of the US air puff gradually decrease the probability of the CR blink in response to the light or tone.

Following extinction, the subject behaves just as observed prior to conditioning, showing no response to the initially neutral CS. Therefore, we might conclude that the conditioned response has been unlearned—that is, that the CS–US association formed during conditioning has somehow been eliminated. However, multiple lines of evidence indicate that conditioning's effects are not simply erased from the mind. One such clue is the phenomenon of spontaneous recovery. Following conditioning and extinction in an initial session, typically the subject is removed from the training situation and then brought back the next day for additional testing. Upon presentation of the CS trials on the second day, strong CRs are typically observed even though the response was fully extinguished at the end of the previous day's training. This reappearance of the CR without retraining is known as **spontaneous recovery.** Indeed, after spontaneous recovery, only repeated presentations of the CS alone will reduce and ultimately again extinguish the CR. Typically the CR will spontaneously recover again the next day, though with reduced initial strength. If extinction trials are again presented, the response will diminish further, then spontaneously recover again the next day at a lower level, and so on until the response may completely disappear.

What is the mechanism for spontaneous recovery? Pavlov proposed that just as the initial conditioning can be viewed as the acquisition of an *excitatory association* between the CS and US, CS presentations without the US may lead to a separate *inhibitory association* in which the CS is associated with the absence of the US. According to this view, when extinction is complete, the strength of the inhibitory association has become as strong as the original excitatory association, and the two contradictory associations cancel each other. If this is true, though, why isn't a single extinction session sufficient to cancel the initial training session? A key assumption here is that inhibitory associations are more fragile and tran-

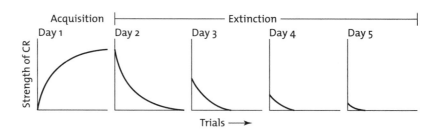

FIGURE 5.5 Human eyeblink conditioning and the reduction of responses during extinction.

sient than excitatory associations; so unlike excitatory associations, they fade with time. After the extinction session, the inhibitory association diminishes between testing sessions; when it becomes weaker relative to the excitatory association, the excitatory association "wins" and the CR reappears. Additional extinction trials strengthen the inhibitory association so that it eventually becomes strong and persistent enough to produce lasting cancellation of the excitatory association.

Here's an alternative perspective: During extinction the repeated presentation of the CS without the consequence of the US causes loss of attention to the CS, regardless of its previously formed association with the US. Conditioned responses cease when the attention level for the CS is so low that it is no longer processed and therefore cannot evoke the CR. According to this view, following an interval between testing sessions, attention is again focused on the CS, which can again elicit the CR, resulting in its spontaneous recovery. These two accounts of spontaneous recovery are not mutually exclusive; perhaps both are correct.

Another line of evidence indicating that conditioned responses are not lost during extinction is the phenomenon of **disinhibition**, in which an extinguished CR reappears not spontaneously but in response to another, typically arousing stimulus. Imagine a situation in which conditioning with a tone CS is completed and followed by extinction so that eyeblink CRs are no longer observed. Now imagine a loud bell sounding shortly before the CS is presented. Typically the CR reappears: It is disinhibited following the noise (similar to the phenomenon of sensitization). According to Pavlov's theory, the fragile inhibitory associations are not only more susceptible than the excitatory associations to the passage of time (as observed in extinction); they are also affected more by the bell. So the loud noise of the bell disrupts the balance between excitatory and inhibitory associations, and the stronger excitatory association trumps the weaker inhibitory one, again generating conditioned responses. According to the alternative attentional account of extinction, the noise, like the passage of time, increases attention to all stimuli, including the CS (an example of sensitization). This results in a recovery of CS processing and renewed generation of the CR.

Finally, a conditioned response can be retrained more readily following extinction than during its initial conditioning. Such **rapid reacquisition** of the CR following its extinction indicates that even when no CRs are observed, at least some subtle association between the CS and US must have been retained. Some rapid reacquisition might be due to spontaneous recovery of the CR. However, even when extinction sessions are repeated until spontaneous recovery ceases, reacquisition of the learned association between stimuli happens more rapidly than original conditioning. Whether spontaneous recovery, disinhibition, and rapid reacquisition involve the same mechanism remains unclear. However, the combined observations for all three phenomena strongly show that once a response is conditioned, it does not disappear following extinction. Some mental representation of the association remains and can be recovered under the right circumstances. These findings clearly distinguish forgetting (true memory loss) from extinction of previously elicited behaviors, which involves new learning to inhibit an unnecessary or inappropriate response.

Conditioning Can Also Involve Learning Not to Respond

As we've just discussed, extinction may involve the development of conditioned inhibitory associations between a CS and the absence of a US. In addition, other protocols have focused explicitly on demonstrating **conditioned inhibition:** the conditioning of a decrease in CRs to a CS. Conditioned inhibition can be observed only when the conditioned response is apparent, so that there is a baseline of CRs that can be reduced by the inhibitory association. Pavlov designed a procedure for demonstrating conditioned inhibition in a single situation that combines excitatory and inhibitory conditioning. One conditioned stimulus (such as a tone) signals the US (food) and is called the CS+. Another stimulus (a light) signals the absence of a US and is called the CS−. On some trials the tone CS+ is followed by the food US in the usual excitatory conditioning protocol; this provides a baseline level of the salivation CR from which we can test inhibition effects. On other trials, randomly intermixed, the tone CS+ and light CS− are presented together without the food US. Salivation responses to the compound tone/light CS+/CS− occur initially but gradually diminish, suggesting that the light CS− inhibits conditioned responses to the tone CS+.

Generalization and Discrimination: Conditioned Responses Transfer to Other Stimuli

Two other common phenomena in classical conditioning are **generalization** (the tendency of CRs to result from a stimulus similar to the CS) and its opposite, **discrimination** (the ability to acquire a conditioned response to one stimulus but no response to a similar but distinguishable stimulus). Typically when animals are conditioned to respond to a specific stimulus, such as a tone of a particular frequency, they are likely to show a CR in response to neighboring frequencies. That is, the CR production transfers, or generalizes, to similar stimuli. For example, when rabbits are extensively conditioned to blink when they hear a tone CS of 1,200 Hz, they will also blink in response to similar tones, producing considerable CRs to tones at 800 Hz and 1,600 Hz and fewer CRs to tones at lower or higher frequencies (Figure 5.6). This pattern of graded transfer, called a *generalization gradient,* occurs for a broad range of stimuli used in classical conditioning.

Generalization typically occurs when animals are trained initially with a particular CS and then tested with a variety of similar stimuli. Discrimination occurs

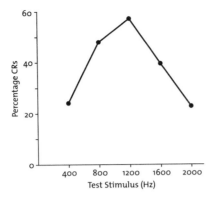

FIGURE 5.6 A typical generalization gradient observed in classical eyeblink conditioning in rabbits.
Note that the response is optimal at the conditioning frequency of 1,200 Hz, and the response is stronger for neighboring frequencies and weaker for more distant frequencies.

when animals are trained from the outset with a combination of the same CS paired with the US and other stimuli presented in the absence of the US. Thus, for example, if an animal is conditioned with a 1,200 Hz tone, it usually shows considerable generalization of the conditioned response to an 800 Hz tone. However, this doesn't mean the animal can't tell the difference between the two tones. If instead it experiences a mixture of trials composed of the 1,200 Hz tone (the CS+) paired with the US and the 800 Hz tone (the CS−) not followed by the US, the difference between the two becomes more meaningful, and conditioning will occur only for the CS+ and not for the CS−. This discrimination can be explained by a combination of excitatory conditioning to the CS+ and conditioned inhibition to the CS−.

Interim Summary

The success of classical conditioning is gradual and depends on optimal timing of the CS and US; learning occurs as the CS consistently predicts US onset. Extinction of the CR is not forgetting. The CR can reappear spontaneously or be inhibited by conditioning with an opposite prediction of the US; can be disinhibited by arousing stimuli; and can be retrained readily. Just as pairing a CS and a US leads to excitatory conditioning, pairing a CS with the absence of a US leads to inhibitory conditioning or conditioned inhibition. Excitatory conditioning and conditioned inhibition combine to determine the extent of generalization or discrimination of responses to a CS.

Learning & Memory in Action

How Do Clinicians Treat Phobias?

Sometimes when people have been exposed to particular stimuli repeatedly in dangerous situations, they develop irrational fears of those and other similar stimuli. A common example occurs when people take elevators to high floors of a building, where they then fear falling. A treatment for such phobias is to gradually expose the person to the fear-producing stimulus. For elevator phobia, a person would be exposed briefly to a view of an elevator, then successively exposed for longer periods. On the first occasion, anxiety might occur immediately and intensively. But after repeated exposures without riding in the elevator, the conditioned anxiety extinguishes. In addition, therapy for this phobia also involves a cognitive component in which the person is encouraged to think about the valuable and important events that will occur when he or she arrives at the end of the elevator ride. This helps people associate positive feelings with arrival at the end of the ride. The combination of extinguishing the conditioned anxiety (the negative UR) and conditioned inhibition of that response by counterconditioning a positive response to the CS often successfully treats specific phobias.

Complex Associations in Classical Conditioning

Several variants of classical conditioning show that this type of learning extends to a broad range of situations (Wasserman & Miller, 1997; Rescorla, 1988). These higher-order forms of classical conditioning may involve increased complexity both in the nature of the associations and in the brain circuits that mediate classical conditioning of motor reflexes (Figure 5.7).

1. *Second-order conditioning:* The standard form of classical conditioning discussed thus far is called **first-order conditioning** because it involves a direct association between a CS and a US. **Second-order conditioning** occurs when animals initially develop a first-order conditioned response, and presentation of the first-order CS is preceded by another CS. Thus, for example, an animal might be trained initially in eyeblink conditioning with a tone CS. When the conditioned response to the tone is established, the animal might see a light before each tone,

1. Second-order conditioning

First stage	Second stage
CS$_1$ ⟶ US	CS$_2$ ⟶ CS$_1$
--→ CR	--→ CR

2. Sensory preconditioning

First stage	Second stage	Test
CS$_2$ ⟶ CS$_1$	CS$_1$ ⟶ US	CS$_2$ -?→ CR
	--→ CR	

3. Blocking

First stage	Second stage	Test
CS$_1$ ⟶ US	CS$_1$ + CS$_2$ ⟶ US	CS$_2$ -?→ CR
--→ CR	--→ CR	

Latent inhibition

First stage	Second stage
CS	CS ⟶ US
	-?→ CR

4. Contextual conditioning

First stage	Test
CS$_1$ ⟶ US	CS$_1$ -?→ CR
CS$_2$ ⟶ US	CS$_2$ -?→ CR

FIGURE 5.7 Higher-order forms of classical conditioning.
In each type, the solid arrow represents the sequence of stimuli presented during training, and the dashed arrow represents the development of a CR as a result of training. A question mark indicates that the CR may or may not be observed, depending on whether conditioning has occurred in the preceding stage. In the bottom panel on contextual conditioning, the rectangle and oval represent different contexts.

with the US discontinued. After several presentations of the light, CRs would begin to appear even though the light was never paired directly with the US. A good example of second-order conditioning was my conditioned braking response to the yellow traffic signal light during my Thanksgiving trip. The original CS was the red light that initially conditioned the braking response. The yellow light predicted the red light and became a second-order CS that produced the same response as the primary CS (the red light).

2. *Sensory preconditioning:* The phenomenon of **sensory preconditioning** is similar to second-order conditioning except that the two CSs are paired before any excitatory conditioning involving the US. In a sensory preconditioning protocol, the light and tone would be paired for several trials before any presentations of the US. Then the animal would be trained with pairings of the tone and the US until CRs were consistently observed. Sensory preconditioning would have occurred if the light alone could elicit CRs. In advertising, a common approach is to expose potential buyers to a combination of the product name and its purpose many times before the buyer uses the product. If use of the product produces positive feelings, the product name itself should produce positive responses.

3. *Blocking and latent inhibition:* Experience with potential conditioned stimuli before training can impair the efficacy of conditioning. In the phenomenon of **blocking** (Kamin, 1968), conditioning is initially accomplished with pairings involving CS1 and the US. Then CS1 is presented in combination with another stimulus (CS2), and conditioning continues as the CS1–CS2 combination is paired with the US. In a subsequent test with CS2 alone, CRs are not evoked. Thus prior conditioning with a stimulus prevents conditioning of a newly added stimulus even though the new stimulus has been paired with a US repeatedly. Similarly, in the phenomenon of **latent inhibition,** a neutral stimulus such as a tone is presented repeatedly without a US before conditioning. Subsequently the efficacy of that stimulus in supporting conditioning is reduced. Both blocking and latent inhibition show that experience with stimuli before conditioning can affect how well they act as conditioned stimuli. A related problem product makers face is that once buyers have been conditioned to associate one product name with the positive values of a product, it is difficult to establish new associations with that product. Many of us are so conditioned to associate "Kleenex" with the tissue we use to blow our noses that it is difficult to learn the names of competitors' tissues; this is an example of blocking.

4. *Contextual conditioning:* During conditioning, information about the environmental context is also acquired, and the CS–US association can become closely bound to environmental cues in what we call **contextual conditioning.** In an example, Penick and Solomon (1991) varied the context in which rabbits were trained in eyeblink conditioning. One group of animals were transported to a distinct testing laboratory in individual boxes; each animal was placed in a large restraining box inside a wooden, well-lit, sound-insulating chamber scented with sandalwood oil. Another group of animals was transported together in an open cart to a different laboratory; each animal was placed in a small restraining box inside a metallic, dimly lit, sound-insulating chamber scented with lemon. Both groups were trained with a 1,000 Hz tone as the

CS and an air puff as the US, and they showed equivalent conditioning over six sessions. Subsequently these animals were retested in the same context or switched to the new context. Continued testing in the same context improved performance, presumably due to the previous training under the same circumstances. But the animals showed considerably fewer CRs when tested in the novel context. So animals learn about the context in which they are trained, and whether or not the conditioned response is expressed depends on this contextual learning.

Contextual conditioning occurs every day in situations where we develop emotional responses to stimuli associated with happy or unhappy events that occurred in a particular context. When I was a child, I used to become anxious at the sight of my dentist walking out of his office to greet me for an appointment. But seeing him on the street did not produce this conditioned anxiety. This place-specific emotional reaction is an everyday example of a contextually conditioned response.

In some situations a context itself can evoke conditioned responses even in the absence of the specific CS. An example is fear conditioning in which repeated presentations of a neutral cue, such as a tone, consistently precede a painful stimulus, such as a shock, that evokes a fearful unconditioned response such as freezing in place. Animals and humans learn to produce conditioned freezing responses to the tone. However, subjects also commonly freeze as soon as they enter the environment or context where they experienced the shocks. This is an example of the context itself becoming a CS.

Interim Summary

Several complex forms of classical conditioning involve combinations of stimuli that interact in their roles as CS. Second-order conditioning occurs when neutral stimuli predict an already conditioned CS. Here the neutral stimulus becomes a CS itself, with the former CS acting like a US; in this way chains of associations can be made. In sensory preconditioning neutral stimuli can be associated by pairing before the conditioning procedure; subsequently when one stimulus become a CS, both can elicit the CR. Blocking and latent inhibition have the opposite effect. In blocking, initial conditioning with one CS prevents subsequent conditioning to the combination of the CS and another stimulus. In latent inhibition, initial presentation of a stimulus without a US makes it less able to become an effective CS in later conditioning. Finally, during classical conditioning animals and people sometimes learn not only about the CS but also about the context or environment in which the CS was presented; so conditioning to the CS is less effective in other contexts, or the context itself can evoke the conditioned response.

The Nature of the Association in Classical Conditioning

Two fundamental issues that Pavlov raised remain the subject of examination in studies of classical conditioning. One issue is the nature of the association with the CS formed during learning. Is the critical association between the CS and the learned response it evokes? Or is the critical association an acquired link between the CS and the US, which then indirectly brings about the conditioned response? The other issue has to do with how the association between stimuli is formed. Is mere contiguity of the CS and the US sufficient to support the learned association between them, or is this contiguity only one of several factors required for learning? We will consider these questions in the next sections.

Is Conditioning Based on S–S Associations or S–R Associations?

Exactly what association is learned in classical conditioning? Pavlov proposed that through repeated presentations of a CS and US, the CS comes to substitute for the US in evoking the CR. Pavlov's *stimulus substitution theory* seems to account for learning in the case of eyeblink conditioning because the CS indeed takes on the property of the air puff in eliciting eyelid closures. However, the stimulus substitution theory falls short of providing a complete explanation for conditioning because the CR and UR are not identical. Typically, even in eyeblink conditioning, UR eyelid closures are stronger and faster than the gentler, more gradual eyelid closures that constitute the CR. More problematic is that not all UR components are duplicated in every CR. When food is presented to condition a salivary response, the unconditioned responses to the food stimulus include chewing and swallowing as well as salivation; yet only the salivation component appears in the CR. In addition, some CRs include components that do not appear in their corresponding URs. For example, in salivary classical conditioning, animals orient toward a salient CS (such as the speaker from which a tone CS originates), which does not occur during presentation of the food US. In yet another circumstance that calls Pavlov's theory into question, a CR may take a form opposite that of its UR. If electric shock is used as a US to produce cardiac acceleration, conditioning causes the CR of cardiac deceleration.

These results do not rule out Pavlov's stimulus substitution theory, but they suggest an alternative to the notion that the CS forms a direct association with the response-generating mechanism. Pavlov speculated that the brain contains distinct areas or "centers" (Figure 5.8) for representing the US (the US center) and the CS (the CS center), as well as another area that generates the UR (the response center). He assumed that an innate connection between a US center and the response center created the unconditioned reflex. Pavlov proposed that during classical conditioning, the CS center somehow becomes directly connected with

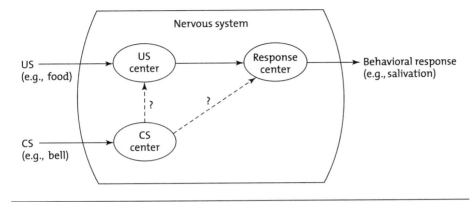

FIGURE 5.8 Possible loci for learning in stimulus substitution theory.
The solid arrow indicates an innate connection between the US and a response center
that elicits the behavioral response. The dashed arrows represent possible learned
connections.

the response center, thus acquiring the ability to make the UR center generate
conditioned responses. Pavlov was basically right about the existence of these centers; we will consider their anatomical locations later when we examine the neural circuitry that supports classical conditioning.

This association between an arbitrary stimulus and a response-generating mechanism is called an *S–R association*. However, if the CR is not identical to the UR,
perhaps the CS center becomes connected with the US center rather than the
response center. According to this view, through pairing of the CS and US, the CS
may develop the capacity to make the subject "think of" the US and then generate an appropriate response that is similar to the UR. Such an association between
an arbitrary stimulus (CS) and the mental representation of the unconditioned
stimulus constitutes what some call an *S–S association*.

If the S–S association idea is correct, Rescorla (1973) reasoned, then manipulating the connection between the innate US and its related response center should
affect the nature of the CR. On the other hand, if the critical connection is between
the CS and response centers directly, then modifying the US–response center connection should not affect the CR. To test the nature of these associations, Rescorla
invented a *US devaluation* procedure in which he first trained a conditioned
response, then separately "devalued" the US, then measured the effect of US devaluation on responses to the CS. Specifically, using a conditioned emotional response
paradigm, he trained rats to press a lever to receive rewards. Next he conditioned
an association between a light CS and a loud noise US that startled the rats, causing them not to press the lever for several seconds. Then, for the rats in the experimental group, he habituated the emotional response to the loud noise by

presenting the noise repeatedly. Rats in the control group received no other noise exposures. Subsequently, Rescorla measured lever press responses to the light CS. In the control group, which had not been habituated to the noise, he observed far fewer lever press responses after the light was presented. However, the rats that were habituated to the noise continued pressing the lever even when the light was presented. The observation that devaluing the US diminishes the effectiveness of the CS suggests a direct link between the US and the CS, thus supporting the notion of S–S associations.

Is Conditioning Based on Stimulus Contiguity or Information?

Pavlov viewed the contiguity of the CS and the US as the critical basis of conditioning. The fact that the strength of the CR depends on the timing of the CS–US contiguity supports this view. However, early observations of blocking (Kamin, 1968) suggested that appropriate temporal contiguity of stimuli is *not* sufficient to produce conditioning. In the blocking effect, recall that initially the CS is conditioned; then it is presented in combination with another stimulus and paired reliably with US presentations. Subsequent CRs are evoked by the original CS but not by the new stimulus. Note that during presentations of the compound stimulus, the new stimulus is paired with the US enough times for the two to form an excitatory association; yet the new stimulus clearly has been blocked from doing so.

Why does the initial CS block conditioning of the new stimulus? Kamin suggested that a US has to be "surprising" to enter a new association. In his protocol, the US is not a surprising consequence when the compound of the CS and the new stimulus is presented because the CS itself already fully predicts the US. This realization was described in an influential account of classical conditioning known as the **Rescorla–Wagner model.** According to Rescorla and Wagner (1972), the effectiveness of the US depends on the extent to which its occurrence or magnitude differs from what is expected based on experience. Quite different from Pavlov, Rescorla and Wagner proposed that the critical issue determining the efficacy of conditioning is the match between the subject's expectancy of the strength of the US and the actual strength of the US. According to their model, learning occurs only when there is a mismatch between the expectancy of a US following the CS and the actual outcome. In real life, this view is another way of saying that we learn mainly from our mistakes—situations in which actual outcomes do not meet our expectations.

In this analysis, whenever the strength of a US is greater than expected, excitatory conditioning will occur for all CSs present. The larger the mismatch between the expectation about the US and the actual US, the greater the amount of conditioning; when the US simply meets expectations, no conditioning will occur.

Conversely, if the US is less intense than expected, inhibitory conditioning will occur for all CSs present. If two or more CSs are presented together, the US expected by the subject is the sum of the expectancies for each CS. (This resembles Pavlov's account of how excitatory and inhibitory associations of equal strength cancel one another.)

Based on these premises, the Rescorla–Wagner model handily accounts for many phenomena in classical conditioning. It predicts that incremental excitatory conditioning will occur when a CS is first paired with a US, and conditioning will strengthen until the subject can fully predict the US based on presentation of the CS. It also explains blocking: After initial conditioning with a CS, the CS fully predicts the US; so when a compound stimulus is presented that includes a new event, the new event does not add to the subject's expectancy and does not cause new conditioning. In extinction and conditioned inhibition, inhibitory conditioning occurs for the CS− to the extent that the expected US does not occur. The response in any subsequent situation is additive, so further presentations of the CS− reduce the likelihood of the CR.

An additional confirmation of the Rescorla–Wagner model came with the novel prediction of what will occur when the magnitude of a US is "overexpected." In this situation, two distinct CSs (such as a light and a tone) are separately paired with the same US until conditioning is complete for both CSs. Subsequently the light and tone are presented as a compound CS followed by the same conditioned US. Later the light and tone are again presented separately, and the magnitude of the CR is measured. The CRs of animals trained with the compound stimulus are weakened in comparison with those of animals trained only with the independent stimuli. Consistent with the Rescorla–Wagner model, presenting the compound CS created an expectancy that the magnitude of the US would be *double* that following either CS alone—derived from the sum of the magnitudes of the US expected from each light and tone. Yet during conditioning with the compound, the magnitude of the US was exactly the same as that presented following either CS alone—less than expected—leading to inhibitory conditioning for the light and the tone. According to this theory, subsequent responses to the light and tone alone should be, and indeed were, reduced.

Interim Summary

Classical conditioning does not link a CS directly to a UR-generating mechanism, forming an S–R association, because the CR is not always identical to the UR. Rather it appears that a representation of the CS forms a direct association with the US in an S–S association. This idea was validated by Rescorla's experiments showing that devaluation of a US affects its CR. Also, mere contiguity (pairing of a CS and a US) is not the critical basis of conditioning: The effectiveness of contiguity can be prevented by prior pairing of the US with another CS (the blocking effect). Instead, according to the Rescorla–Wagner model, a CS is effective only when there is a mismatch between the expectancy of a US and the actual outcome. Excitatory conditioning for the CS will occur only when the strength of the US is greater than expected; conversely, inhibitory conditioning will occur when the strength of the US is less than expected.

Neural Circuits Build Reflex Arcs to Support Classical Conditioning

Two systems have been used as models to study the neural circuits that support classical conditioning of simple motor reflexes. One involves the invertebrate *Aplysia*, which you may remember from the neurobiological studies of habituation and sensitization described in Chapter 3. The other is the rabbit eyeblink paradigm discussed earlier in this chapter. Each system provides insights into different types of neural representations that underlie the classical conditioning of basic motor responses.

Classical Conditioning in Aplysia *Modifies Reflex Circuitry*

One of the simplest animals that displays classical conditioning is the sea slug *Aplysia*. Kandel and his colleagues (Carew et al., 1981) developed a procedure for classically conditioning these animals based on an elaboration of their habituation and sensitization processes and neural circuits, which were discussed in Chapter 3 (Figure 5.9). This protocol combined the same neuroanatomical circuits involved in those simpler learned behaviors, involving two sensory (CS) pathways and a common pathway by which the unconditioned stimulus (US) influences them. One CS pathway directly connects the sensory neurons of the mantle shelf skin to motor neurons that withdraw the gill. The second CS pathway connects siphon sensory neurons to motor neurons. These two potential CS pathways offer the ability to condition one of those paths but not the other. The US pathway indirectly connects the tail via an interneuron to the presynaptic elements of both the mantle skin and siphon sensory neurons.

The classical conditioning protocol that Kandel's team used with *Aplysia* involved the animal learning a discriminative response: conditioning for the mantle CS+ and not the siphon CS−. In some trials the mantle shelf skin was lightly stimulated with a brush; shortly afterward the tail was shocked at a low level insufficient to produce sensitization. In this configuration, the mantle shelf stimulation acted as the CS+ and the tail stimulation was the US. In other trials the siphon was stimulated, and no tail shock was given. Thus siphon stimulation served as

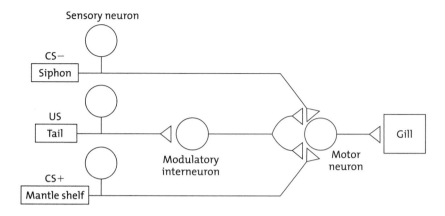

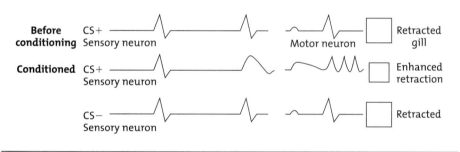

FIGURE 5.9 Classical conditioning in *Aplysia*.
Top: Components of the circuit that supports classical conditioning. Bottom: Neural
activity in components of the circuit before (naive) and after conditioning.

the CS−. Over repeated trials, the animals developed vigorously enhanced withdrawal responses (the CR) to mantle stimulation but not to siphon stimulation.
In other words, the animals learned to discriminate between the relevant CS+
and an irrelevant CS−. As is true of classical conditioning in mammals, timing
was critical: The conditioned response occurred only if the CS+ and US were
contiguous.

What cellular mechanisms could be involved in the association between the
CS+ and US in this neural circuit? The critical cellular mechanisms occur in both
the presynaptic and postsynaptic elements of the reflex circuit and involve electrical activity at the synapses and molecular events in both types of cells (Figure
5.10). The CS+ (mantle shelf stimulation) causes an action potential in the sensory neurons that reaches the presynaptic site, resulting in the influx of calcium
(Ca++), which causes neurotransmitters to dock to the presynaptic membrane

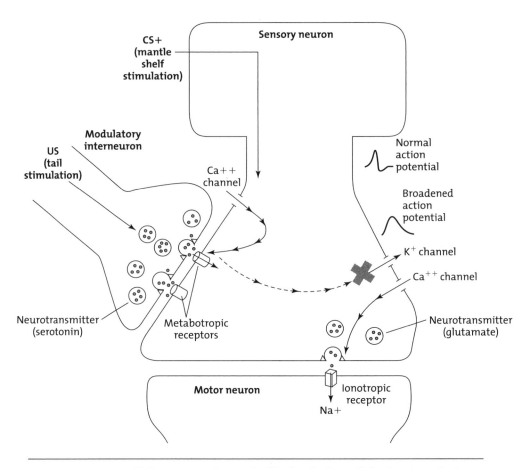

FIGURE 5.10 Cellular events that underlie classical conditioning in *Aplysia*.

and release. Closely following US (tail stimulation) activates a different type of receptors, called metabotropic receptors. When primed by the increased level of Ca++, the US-produced activation of the metabotropic receptors sets off a chain of molecular events that prevent the K+ channel from opening. As you read in Chapter 2, the opening of K+ channels ends the depolarization phase of the action potential. So, the result of prolonging the action potential is that an especially large amount of Ca++ enters the presynaptic element, consequently prolonging neurotransmitter release. This happens only in the mantle sensory neurons (that is, the CS+ pathway). Because the US never occurs with siphon stimulation (the CS−), there is no facilitation of Ca++ entry and therefore no prolonged transmitter release in that sensory neuron (the CS− pathway).

In addition to these presynaptic element changes, a postsynaptic element change also supports the conditioned response. This change involves the same mechanisms as those of long-term potentiation (LTP), which you read about in Chapter 2. You may recall that the neurotransmitter for the reflex pathway is glutamate. This neurotransmitter activates two types of receptors in the postsynaptic elements. One is a conventional receptor that regulates Na+ influx. The other is a special receptor, called the NMDA receptor, that regulates Ca++ flow. During normal reflex operation and habituation and sensitization, the NMDA receptors are blocked by another charged molecule, magnesium (Mg++). However, NMDA receptors have an unusual property: When the membrane potential is reduced (depolarized), the magnesium block is eliminated and Ca++ can flow into the cells.

During classical conditioning the membrane becomes depolarized (more positive) when the CS+ activates the conventional receptors, allowing Na+ influx. This depolarization briefly unblocks the NMDA channels. If a US occurs soon afterward, a long train of action potentials occurs, and the open NMDA receptors allow Ca++ to flow into the postsynaptic elements. The influx of Ca++ results in a cascade of molecular events that creates long-lasting changes to the postsynaptic elements. The fact that classical conditioning in *Aplysia* uses the same LTP phenomenon studied in mammals supports the widely held view that LTP is a cross-species mechanism for memory in many different brain systems.

Classical Eyeblink Conditioning Involves Cerebellum Circuitry

Recent studies have also examined the brain circuit supporting classical conditioning of a simple mammalian motor reflex. Richard Thompson and colleagues pioneered neurobiological examinations of eyeblink conditioning in rabbits (Thompson & Kim, 1996; Christian & Thompson, 2003), and the model they developed has received considerable experimental support (Steinmetz, 1996; Mauk, 1997). Such studies have produced compelling evidence that the cerebellum stores the critical associations for this particular excitatory conditioning.

The cerebellum is a brain structure long associated with motor learning; its circuitry is organized to play a key role in reflex adaptations. The cerebellum has two main components: the cerebellar cortex and the underlying deep cerebellar nuclei. One of the cerebellar nuclei is the interpositus nucleus (Figure 5.11). During classical conditioning, cells in both the cerebellar cortex and the cerebellar nuclei receive two excitatory inputs (one representing the CS and another the US), making these ideal places for forming CS–US associations.

In the circuit shown in Figure 5.11, the unconditioned reflex (UR) pathway carries air puff sensory inputs into a part of the brain stem called the trigeminal nucleus. Outputs of the trigeminal nucleus travel to the cranial motor nuclei either directly or by passing through another brain stem structure called the reticular formation. The cranial motor nuclei send direct motor outputs to the facial mus-

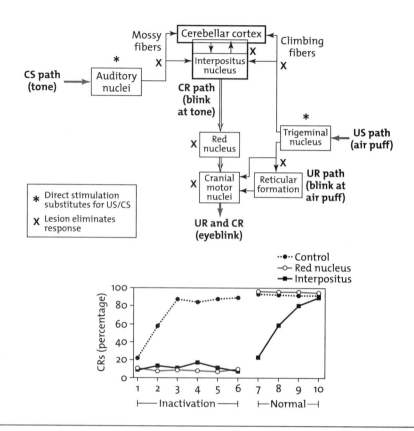

FIGURE 5.11 The cerebellum and the circuit for classical eyelid conditioning.
Top: Schematic diagram of the sensory and motor pathways in the circuit. ✱ denotes
locations in the circuit where electrical stimulation can substitute for a natural stimulus.
X indicates locations in the circuit where a lesion prevents conditioning. Bottom: Course
of conditioning in normal control animals and in animals where neurons were
inactivated in the red nucleus or interpositus nucleus.

cles that evoke the blink. This pathway was difficult to identify; but its vital role
has been demonstrated by an elegant combination of studies showing that (1) cells
in these brain areas fire reliably along with the UR and (2) inactivation of these
brain areas prevents the UR. This pathway puts the US signal near the CS signals
described earlier.

Additional studies have also identified the circuit for the US and CS in the
conditioned reflex (CR). The US input travels from the trigeminal nucleus
through another brain stem area to the cerebellar cortex as well as to one of
the cerebellar nuclei called the interpositus nucleus. The pathway for a tone
CS sends auditory nuclei inputs through the brain stem and then to the cere-

bellar cortex, where the CS and US signals meet and critical synaptic changes occur (Mauk, 1997). The output of this interaction is sent from the cerebellar cortex to the interpositus nucleus, where additional synaptic changes support the development of a CR. The CR output travels from the interpositus to a brain stem area called the red nucleus, which projects to the cranial motor nuclei that control the facial muscles.

The evidence for cerebellar circuit involvement in eyeblink conditioning is substantial. Studies by Steinmetz and colleagues (1996) have shown that electrical stimulation of the auditory pathway can substitute for a tone CS in establishing the conditioned response. Similarly, stimulation of the brain stem area where the air puff US signal enters the circuit can substitute for the air puff. Thus these areas are critical in generating the CS and US signals.

Thompson and his colleagues have provided compelling evidence that the interpositus nucleus of the cerebellum is the critical site of this CS–US association. They have shown that injury or inactivation of the interpositus nucleus impairs the acquisition and retention of classically conditioned eyeblink reflexes, indicating that this area is a vital part of the conditioning pathway. In addition, blocking the molecular events that underlie interpositus nucleus plasticity prevents establishment of the conditioned reflex, demonstrating that crucial changes in cellular structure occur within the interpositus itself.

Additional compelling data come from rabbit eyeblink conditioning studies using reversible inactivations of particular areas (Krupa et al., 1993). Temporary inactivation of the red nucleus or motor nuclei that are essential to producing the CR and UR also prevented the rabbits from outwardly responding to the stimuli during training. However, as soon as the inactivated areas were allowed to function again, CRs appeared in full form. So the circuit that supports the unconditioned eyeblink is not critical for conditioned learning about *when* to blink, but only for producing the actual blinking. In contrast, inactivation of the interpositus nucleus and overlying cortex does not affect UR production, showing that it does not generate motor responses. Yet inactivation of the interpositus resulted in failure of CR development; when the inactivation later wore off, conditioning occurred at the same rate as if there was no previous training (Figure 5.11). These results indicate that inactivating the interpositus specifically prevented learning but not unconditioned blinking—and point to the interpositus nucleus and overlying cerebellar cortex as the essential locus of some sort of memory trace.

Notably, the same cerebellar circuitry is critical to human eyeblink conditioning. In an elegant study exploiting the fact that the left and right cerebellar circuits are specific for the left and right eyes, respectively, Woodruff-Pak and colleagues (1996) conditioned subjects who had experienced damage to either the right or the left side of the cerebellum. The subjects were impaired in acquiring classically conditioned eyeblink responses on the same side of the head as their cerebellar damage; but they normally acquired the conditioned response when trained on the intact side.

Other studies have confirmed the importance of the cerebellum in classical eyeblink conditioning, shedding light on the neural coding that mediates learning in the cerebellar cortex and interpositus nucleus. During training, neurons in both areas increased their firing in response to the CS. During subsequent extinction trials, during which the US was withheld while the CS was presented repeatedly, the CR gradually disappeared as interpositus cells ceased firing. But the neural representation for conditioning remained in the activity of the cerebellar cortex long after extinction. Perhaps this lasting representation supports spontaneous recovery, dishabituation, and accelerated relearning of conditioned responses (Steinmetz, 1996; Figure 5.12).

Finally, a pathway from the interpositus to the inferior olive (a structure deep in the brain stem that activates eyeblink muscle contractions) may influence the efficacy of the US, suggesting a mechanism for conditioned inhibition. Kim and colleagues (1998) used drugs to prevent inhibition in the inferior olive and observed decreased neural output from the olive to the cerebellum. The same drug treatment also eliminated blocking of the conditioned eyeblink reflex. (Recall that in blocking, prior training with one CS prevents learning about another CS presented in combination with the first one.) These findings suggest that during normal blocking, the cerebellar signal inhibits the US representation in the olive and, via that mechanism, prevents conditioning.

Interim Summary

The neural circuitry of two different model systems for classical conditioning of motor responses has been identified and outlined in detail. In the *Aplysia* withdrawal reflex, conditioning requires appropriately timed activation of the CS and US pathway to produce both selective enhancement of neurotransmitter release from the CS sensory neuron and LTP in the motor neuron. In the eyeblink reflex in mammals, conditioning involves complex circuitry where CS and US inputs meet in the interpositus nucleus of the cerebellum. There a trace is stored that engages the reflexive blinking response.

Classical Conditioning Can Illuminate Other Memory Systems

So far we have focused on classical conditioning of elemental salivary and muscular reflexes. This focus let us examine the behavioral properties, neural cir-

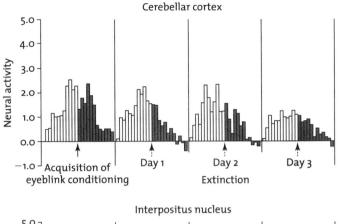

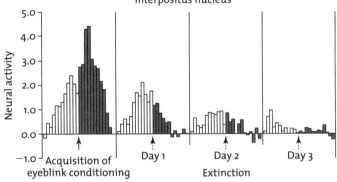

FIGURE 5.12 Firing patterns in the cerebellar cortex and interpositus nucleus during acquisition of the conditioned eyeblink and during three successive days of extinction.
In each panel, neural activity in successive 20-millisecond periods is shown during the CS period and following the US presentation (arrow); in extinction sessions, the dotted arrow indicates when the US would normally have been presented.

cuitry, and mechanisms that support learning in these motor reflex circuits. But classical conditioning as a training protocol is not limited to the study of elemental reflexes. It is also used to study emotional responses and various complex forms of learning.

Among the most widely used types of classical conditioning are methods for conditioning emotional responses. An example is the conditioned suppression paradigm, in which rats initially trained to press a bar at a constant rate are presented with either a light or a tone (CS) paired with a foot shock (US), briefly suppressing the bar pressing. Another example is fear conditioning, in which rats are presented with paired tone CSs and foot shocks. In subsequent memory tests, the tone CS makes the rats freeze and exhibit fearful cardiac and respiratory responses. These emotional conditioning protocols will be discussed in detail in Chapter 7.

Here, to demonstrate the broad utility of classical conditioning, we will discuss two interesting extensions of classical conditioning to other learning supported by higher brain systems.

Taste Aversion Learning Breaks the Rules of Contiguity

One behavioral paradigm that has received widespread attention in studies of classical conditioning is **taste aversion learning.** When animals or humans ingest a food and later experience gastrointestinal distress, they subsequently avoid that food. Most people can recall instances in which they ate something, became ill shortly later, and subsequently avoided that food. Such avoidance persists even when people are certain the food did not cause the illness (perhaps they came down with the flu coincidentally just after a meal). Therefore, the conditioning occurs even when we know that there was contiguity but no causal relationship between the food and the illness. A common example is that people undergoing chemotherapy for cancer often develop an aversion to a food they ate before the therapy made them ill, even though they know it was the therapy and not the food that caused the illness. In animals this kind of learning is sometimes called *bait shyness,* a term borrowed from the observation that mice that survive eating poisoned bait subsequently avoid the trap.

In the laboratory, taste aversion is typically conditioned by having animals consume a novel and appealing flavor (such as sweetened water), then inducing illness by drug treatment or irradiation. Subsequently we can measure learning in terms of a decrease in the normal preference for sweetened water versus tap water. In the taste aversion paradigm, the food is the CS, the illness is the US, and aversion to the food is the CR. This kind of learning is often obvious after a single conditioning trial, unlike the slow process of eyeblink conditioning; and the memory for taste aversion can last a long time. So taste aversion learning is considered an unusual and especially robust example of classical conditioning.

Taste aversion learning is also unique in that it occurs even when the interval between the CS and the US is extended for hours. In one experiment, rats were allowed to drink a sweetened water solution, then irradiated immediately or at intervals ranging from a half hour to 24 hours after drinking. Irradiation at intervals of up to 6 hours produced strong conditioning, and even at 12 hours some conditioning was observed (Figure 5.13A). In eyeblink conditioning, the critical ISI is about a few seconds; so the long effective interval in taste aversion conditioning seems to be an exception to the contiguity principle. But consider the conditions that typically surround taste aversion learning: The effectiveness of long delay conditioning seems appropriate. Usually a poisonous food does not make us ill immediately; rather substantial time is required for the toxin to affect the gastrointestinal organs or enter the bloodstream. So at the usual brief ISI, taste aversion learning would not be adaptive.

Another feature of taste aversion learning is its specificity to flavor as the critical CS. Thus, whereas rats immediately learn an aversive association between a flavor and illness, associations between, say, flavor and shock are not easily acquired. Rats readily learn to avoid a fluid food marked by distinctive visual cues (like water with blue food coloring) when they are shocked for licking its drinking tube. But they do not easily associate other cues with illness (Garcia & Ervin, 1968; Figure 5.13B). This experiment showed that taste–illness and visual–shock combinations have adaptive significance—that is, they belong together—whereas taste–shock and visual–illness combinations do not. These findings shake the Pavlovian assumption that learning can occur between any arbitrary neutral stimulus and any unconditioned stimulus. Instead a new principle for classical conditioning, called *belongingness,* says that the CS and US must "belong" together for conditioning to occur. According to this idea, some types of CS and US stimuli have a natural or adaptive connection and others do not; it remains to be determined how stimuli acquire these natural connections.

Long-delay conditioning and the belongingness of CS–US associations challenge a general principle of CS and US contiguity as the fundamental basis of classical

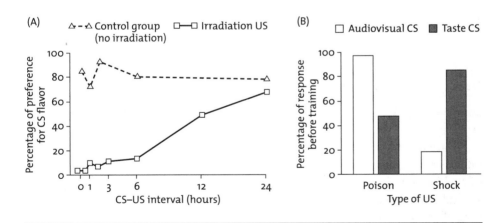

FIGURE 5.13 Taste aversion learning.
A. Success in learning at different ISIs. Animals in the control group are not given the US.
B. Success in conditioning with different CS–US combinations.

conditioning. How does the brain know which ISI and which stimulus pairing are appropriate for different kinds of classical conditioning? The answer is that different brain systems support classical conditioning, but each system has its own operating principles and rules about contiguity. Taste aversion, for example, is mediated by the gustatory cortex, a part of the frontal lobe that processes flavor perception. Damage to this area prevents taste aversion learning.

Learning & Memory in Action

Can Coyotes Be Trained Not to Prey on Sheep?

In the western United States a big problem for sheep farmers is predation of their livestock by coyotes. The farmers hunt coyotes and lay traps with poisons that sometimes also kill other harmless and even endangered species. To solve the predation problem while preserving the coyote population and protecting other wild animals, the principles derived from studies of taste aversion learning have been applied to manage coyotes' predatory behavior in a nonlethal way—specifically by using conditioned taste aversion to teach coyotes not to prey on lambs. Gustavson and his colleagues (1974) exposed coyotes to lamb meat that was tainted with lithium chloride to induce nausea and vomiting. One to three conditioning trials were sufficient to prevent captive coyotes from attacking live lambs that were introduced into their pens. Follow-up studies in the western U.S. and Canadian rangelands have demonstrated the efficacy of this classical conditioning procedure in reducing coyote predation of sheep. The success of this approach has reduced the use of traps and poisons and has preserved the coyote's role in the ecosystem.

Trace Conditioning Requires the Hippocampus

Simple eyeblink reflex conditioning can be accomplished within the cerebellar circuitry described earlier in this chapter, without necessary support by higher brain areas. However, some higher brain areas, including the hippocampus, influence simple reflex conditioning and are necessary for more complex forms of eyeblink conditioning (Solomon, 1980; Disterhoft et al., 1996). For example, several studies have shown that the hippocampus is not required for acquisition of the conditioned eyeblink response in the standard delay conditioning paradigm (the version of classical conditioning in which the CS and US overlap). However, damage to or removal of the hippocampus sometimes accelerates delay eyeblink conditioning (Port et al., 1985). Also, hippocampal neurons develop increased activity associated with the appearance and timing of the CR.

These findings indicate that the hippocampus plays some role in simple eye-blink conditioning.

Other studies involving more complex forms of classical eyeblink conditioning show how the hippocampus may be involved. For example, damage to the hippocampus disrupts learning when subjects are initially trained to blink to a CS+ and not blink to a CS−. Then the CS and US pairings are *reversed:* The former CS+ becomes the CS−, and the former CS− becomes the CS+. Normal animals typically switch their CRs to match the reversed CS–US contingencies. However, animals with hippocampal damage produce CRs to *both* the CS+ and the CS−. In addition, damage to the hippocampus abolishes blocking and latent inhibition (Solomon, 1980), as well as the dependence of conditioning on environmental context (Penick & Solomon, 1991). These studies demonstrate that the hippocampus plays a decisive role in various situations where subjects normally inhibit a conditioned response, which is prominent in all of these paradigms.

In addition, the hippocampus *is* required for the classical conditioning variant called trace conditioning discussed earlier in this chapter (see p. 148). Recall that in the typical version of this task, the CS involves a brief (100-millisecond) tone followed by a silent 500-millisecond "trace" interval punctuated by the US. Trace conditioning therefore challenges the nervous system's ability to associate a CS and a US that are not actually contiguous, although the CS still predicts the subsequent occurrence of the US. Rabbits and humans develop CRs in this form of eyeblink conditioning, and hippocampal neurons also are active during presentation of the CS and US. This variant of eyeblink conditioning is prevented by hippocampal damage (Moyer et al., 1990).

Why does adding a brief trace interval between the stimuli cause their connection to be processed mainly by the hippocampus rather than by the cerebellum? Clark and Squire (1998) suggest that the hippocampus is required in trace conditioning because when the CS and US are not contiguous, learning an association between them requires conscious awareness of the CS–US contingency. As you will read in Chapter 9, the hippocampus plays a key role in such conscious memory. In Clark and Squire's studies, normal and amnesic humans were tested in both delay and trace eyeblink conditioning, then interviewed about their awareness of the temporal relationship between the CS and US. Amnesic subjects with hippocampal damage acquired conditioned responses in the delay conditioning task involving contiguous stimuli but failed to develop trace conditioning. Normal subjects were successful in delay conditioning regardless of their awareness of the contingency, but they succeeded in trace conditioning only when they were also aware of the CS–US relationship.

In a subsequent study, the same investigators either promoted or prevented awareness of the CS–US contingency during delay and trace conditioning in normal subjects (Clark & Squire, 1999). For some subjects, they promoted awareness by explaining the temporal contingency before training. These subjects then watched a movie during training. For other subjects, the investigators prevented awareness. They did not explain the contingency in advance and during conditioning engaged subjects in a demanding task that required them to detect strings of odd digits. The groups prevented from awareness performed well during the delay task but not during the trace conditioning. In contrast, advance awareness of the contingency facilitated trace conditioning. These findings show that human awareness is closely related to success in trace conditioning, and hippocampal damage prevents such awareness and trace conditioning. It appears that hippocampal processing of the CS and memory for the CS–US relationship mediate the temporal gap in trace conditioning—a capacity not supported by the cerebellar system.

Interim Summary

Two examples of classical conditioning show how this formal learning protocol can be applied to other brain systems and other forms of learning and memory. *Taste aversion learning* involves pairing a taste CS with gastrointestinal distress as the US. This form of classical conditioning is unique in that it occurs over long ISIs (hours) and in that only particular stimuli are meaningful in learning to avoid poisonous foods. *Trace eyeblink classical conditioning* involves a variant of standard delay conditioning: A brief blank interval separates the CS and US, challenging brain systems to appreciate the CS–US contingency in the absence of contiguity between those stimuli. Trace conditioning, unlike delay conditioning, requires the hippocampus and involves conscious awareness of the contingency in humans. These examples show that classical conditioning is a training procedure, rather than a form of learning and memory, that can apply to many brain systems with different types of information and different operating rules.

Chapter Summary

1. Classical conditioning is a training procedure that applies to a broad range of situations, learning and memory systems, and species. Classical conditioning is best understood as the predominant form of learning in motor systems. Conditioning in such systems involves several rules of operation and stimuli timing that determine the success of contiguity and make classical conditioning unique among different types of learning and memory.

2. Classical conditioning is a learning protocol in which there is usually a strict temporal relationship between the presentation of an arbitrary stimulus (the CS) and a nonarbitrary stimulus (the US) that reflexively incites an unconditioned response (the UR). The outcome is a conditioned response (CR) that mimics the UR. The CS must predict the occurrence of the US, and the temporal relationship between the CS and US is learned. Learning can be either excitatory (increasing the CR) or inhibitory (decreasing the CR), depending on the extent to which the CS bears new information and the nature of that information. Conditioning occurs when the actual US is not already fully predicted by the CS, and the strength and direction of learning are determined by the mismatch in prediction.

3. Variations of the classical conditioning protocol have shown that extinction is not an unlearning but an inhibition of the conditioned response, which can spontaneously recover in relearning. Excitatory and inhibitory influences from multiple sources can modulate the expression of conditioned responses. Conditioned responses can generalize to stimuli similar to the CS, but we can learn to discriminate between stimuli that predict and do not predict the US. Also, potential CSs can become associated with one another by direct pairing (as in second-order conditioning, sensory preconditioning, and contextual conditioning); a CS can block the effectiveness of another potential CS that confers no new information; and a potential CS can be rendered ineffective by prior presentation without the US (latent inhibition). Each of these effects shows that neutral stimuli can enter a variety of associations with one another and with the US.

4. The neural system for classical conditioning has been characterized in several brain systems. In *Aplysia* conditioning is mediated by modulation of the intensity of sensory motor reflexes. In eyeblink conditioning, a circuit involving the cerebellum and other brain stem areas mediates learning, and a small component of that circuit stores a representation of the CS–US contingency. Conscious awareness of the CS–US contingency is not required for many forms of classical conditioning; but it is required at least sometimes when there is a temporal gap (trace interval) between the CS and the US. In trace conditioning, the hippocampus is crucial in bridging the gap between the CS and the US.

5. Examples of classical conditioning include fear conditioning, which imparts a set of emotional responses to a previously neutral stimulus and is supported by distinct circuitry. Taste aversion learning occurs only for stimuli that are related to feeding and occurs even at very long interstimulus intervals; the critical site of taste memories is in the gustatory cortex. The broad range of circumstances in which these phenomena are observed tells us that classical conditioning is a protocol for generating learning in multiple brain systems.

KEY TERMS

classical conditioning (p. 144)

unconditioned stimulus (US) (p. 145)

unconditioned response (UR) (p. 145)

conditioned reflex (p. 145)

conditioned stimulus (CS) (p. 145)

conditioned response (CR) (p. 145)

extinction (p. 146)

delay conditioning (p. 148)

interstimulus interval (ISI) (p. 148)

intertrial interval (ITI) (p. 148)

trace conditioning (p. 148)

simultaneous conditioning (p. 149)

backward conditioning (p. 149)

spontaneous recovery (p. 154)

disinhibition (p. 155)

rapid reacquisition (p. 155)

conditioned inhibition (p. 156)

generalization (p. 156)

discrimination (p. 156)

first-order conditioning (p. 158)

second-order conditioning (p. 158)

sensory preconditioning (p. 160)

blocking (p. 160)

latent inhibition (p. 160)

contextual conditioning (p. 160)

Rescorla–Wagner model (p. 164)

taste aversion learning (p. 174)

REVIEWING THE CONCEPTS

- What are the basic protocols for different types of classical conditioning and their controls?

- What role does timing of the CS and the US play in the success of classical conditioning?

- Is extinction of a conditioned reflex accomplished by unlearning of the conditioned response or new learning to inhibit the previously learned response? How do extinction and learned inhibition of behavioral responses differ from forgetting?

- How do conditioned excitation and conditioned inhibition of responses interact in classical conditioning?

- What are second-order conditioning, sensory preconditioning, blocking, and contextual conditioning? What do they tell us about classical conditioning?

- Is the association in classical conditioning based on S–S or S–R learning? On stimuli contiguity or on the information contained in events?

- Describe the circuits for classical conditioning of the gill withdrawal reflex in *Aplysia* and the eyeblink reflex in mammals.

- What are fear conditioning, trace eyeblink conditioning, and taste aversion conditioning? How do they differ from the classical conditioning of elementary motor reflexes?

Procedural Learning II:
Habits and Instrumental Learning

There is an old story about students in a psychology class who used what they had learned about conditioning to modify the behavior of their professor. In one version of this story, the professor typically stood behind a lectern at the right side of the room and gave his presentation. The students agreed in advance that whenever the professor moved even slightly to the left, they would show strong attention, nod in approval of the material, and jot down each item said. Conversely, whenever he stood behind the lectern, they would look around, yawn, and frown. Before long, the professor left his usual stance and began moving frequently to the left for short periods before returning to the lectern. As the presentation continued, he moved farther and farther to the left and no longer returned to the lectern. By the end of the class, he was standing in the left corner of the room, delivering his presentation without the notes he had left behind on the lectern.

THIS SORT OF behavior change could have occurred without the professor being aware that his behavior was being manipulated by the students. In this example, the professor's behavior was *instrumental* in producing its consequences (the "reward" of student attention). Therefore, this kind of learning is called **instrumental conditioning.**

Instrumental conditioning is pervasive. For example, child rearing practices carefully apportion rewards and punishments for good and bad behaviors. Do you remember being given a "gold star" for a good act or a "time out" for bad behavior? These reinforcements—that is, rewards and punishments—that occur immediately following particular actions are intended to alter the likelihood of those behaviors. The same ideas predominate methods of training puppies with a carefully designed mix of rewards and punishments that shape their behaviors to our liking. We use reinforcers in all kinds of real-life situations, shaping the behaviors of our significant others, our employees, and more.

Ch. 6 Procedural
Learning II:
Habits and
Instrumental
Learning

184

Instrumental learning creates a particular form of memory called a **habit**, which involves voluntary behaviors that are brought about and influenced by reinforcers (rewards and punishments) presented predictably after the behaviors. In this chapter we will look closely at the brain system that supports the acquisition and expression of habits. We'll also discuss how habits and cognitive memory differ in both their properties and the brain systems that support them.

Fundamental Questions

1. What are the rules of instrumental conditioning?
2. Can we condition any behavior using rewards and punishments?
3. Where in the brain are habits stored?

Instrumental Learning Changes Reinforced Behavior to Reflect Memory

How does instrumental learning differ from classical conditioning? In classical conditioning, the unconditioned stimulus automatically or reflexively evokes a behavior. In contrast, instrumental behaviors are voluntary behaviors whose likelihood is influenced by **reinforcers**—that is, rewards or punishments such as the attention or inattention meted out by the professor's clever students. But distinguishing between reflexive and voluntary behavior can be tricky. For example, when animals are trained to run to the location of a reward, we have no way of knowing whether their behavior is voluntary or automatic.

The most concrete, dependable distinction between classical conditioning and instrumental learning is that in classical conditioning, the unconditioned stimulus always follows the conditioned stimulus *regardless* of whether the subject emits the conditioned response (the CR). By contrast, in instrumental conditioning, the reinforcer is presented *only* if the subject emits the desired response. So in Pavlov's protocol, the food is delivered to the animal at a particular time after the CS regardless of the animal's behavior. In instrumental conditioning, the animal is given the food only when it displays the behavior that is being conditioned to occur. Either way the animal seems to behave as if it figured out the connection. In classical conditioning, the CR *anticipates* the reinforcer: A tone that has been repeatedly followed by an air puff to the eye can elicit a blink before an air puff happens. In instrumental conditioning, the response *is emitted to obtain or avoid* the reinforcer. Thus in both situations, the subject associates an initial stimulus and the consequence it predicts. The main difference is whether the subject's behavior directly affects the occurrence of the reinforcer.

Given these basic differences in how classical and instrumental conditioning are accomplished, are their learning processes fundamentally the same or different? In the past there was considerable controversy over this question. Today distinctions between classical conditioning and instrumental learning have been overshadowed by similarities and differences in what is learned and what brain systems are involved in diverse learning situations. Instrumental conditioning is subject to many of the same classical conditioning phenomena described in the previous chapter—including conditioned excitation and inhibition, extinction and spontaneous recovery, stimulus generalization and discrimination, second-order conditioning, blocking, latent inhibition, and contextual conditioning.

Reinforcers Modify the Predictive Relationship between Stimulus and Response

The formal study of instrumental learning began with Edward Thorndike (1898), whose investigations of animal intelligence you may remember from Chapter 1. Thorndike placed cats in puzzle boxes. The box doors latched outside, and each box had a mechanism an animal could reach from inside, such as a chain to pull or a pole to push that would open the latch. Thorndike would offer food outside the box and observe animals' attempts to escape the box and obtain the food. Although Thorndike intended to examine the intelligence of animals in solving the puzzles, his detailed observations led him to conclude that the puzzle solutions were supported by reinforced habits rather than insight or intelligence. Initially animals displayed a variety of investigatory behaviors; eventually they would open the latch as if by accident rather than by insight or analysis. However, when an animal was retested in the same box, the behavior that opened the latch would occur earlier, so that the escape time diminished across trials.

Thorndike attributed the decrease in problem-solving time to incremental strengthening of a learned connection between the experimental situation and the behavioral response, with the reward reinforcing the successful behavior. He formalized this notion in his proposed **Law of Effect**, which says that if a particular response to a stimulus is followed by a "satisfying event," the satisfying event will strengthen the stimulus–response association, increasing the likelihood that the behavior will be repeated. On the other hand, if a particular response is followed by an "annoying event" (Thorndike's term), the annoying event will weaken the association, making the initial behavior less likely. Note that in Thorndike's conception, the reinforcing event itself is not part of the association. Instead the reinforcer only modifies the association between the stimulus and the response.

Ch. 6 Procedural
Learning II:
Habits and
Instrumental
Learning

186

Reinforcement Alters Behavior in Appropriate Situations

Thorndike's experiments raised several issues that have been clarified in succeeding research. One of these issues is the nature of the relationship between behaviors and reinforcements. Thorndike proposed that contiguity between ongoing behavior and reinforcement is necessary and sufficient to produce learning. His Law of Effect predicted straightforwardly that any specific behavior occurring at the time of reinforcement will increase in likelihood. This central prediction of the Law of Effect has been validated many times in demonstrations of **superstitious learning**. Everyone has seen examples of superstitious behaviors—often little acts that people perform even when they are aware of no causal relationship between the action and its consequences. These behaviors typically are coincidentally associated with successful outcomes, are acquired rapidly, and can be persistent.

Some familiar examples of superstitious learning involve the behaviors of baseball players just before they bat. A particularly powerful example is the routine performed by Nomar Garciaparra, a well-known baseball player. Each time he comes to bat, he tightens his wrist bands repetitively several times, grinds his feet into place in a particular sequence, and then crosses his chest before taking position. Although some components of this behavior may actually influence his batting success, the ritualized nature of his routine is likely more superstition than crucial physical preparation.

Other strong evidence that simple contiguity of behavior and reward is sufficient for learning comes from B. F. Skinner's most famous experiment (Skinner, 1938). Skinner put a pigeon into a small enclosure fitted with a retractable food dispenser and arranged for food to be available at fixed time intervals. There was no predetermined relationship between any particular pigeon behavior and food availability. But despite the lack of an explicit contingency, whatever the pigeon happened to be doing when it received the food reinforcement subsequently increased in frequency. For example, one pigeon that had turned counterclockwise just before receiving food began frequently turning counterclockwise, presumably in hopes of receiving more food. One bird poked its beak into a corner of the test chamber, and another hopped around from one foot to the other. Skinner's explanation was that any behavior that was incidentally or accidentally occurring at the time of reward delivery would be reinforced.

Although Skinner's studies demonstrate the power of contiguity between behaviors and rewards, subsequent studies imply that not all behaviors are equally subject to the Law of Effect. In a key experiment, Staddon and Simmelhag (1971) repeated Skinner's study, more systematically and thoroughly examining the frequencies of a list of behaviors: turning, wing flapping, preening, movement along the chamber wall, orienting to the food dispenser, and pecking. All the pigeons performed certain behaviors, such as orienting to the food dispenser and pecking along the neighboring chamber wall, more frequently near the end of the time interval, just before food was delivered. Thus not all behaviors were subject to the Law of Effect; only particular behaviors called **terminal responses** increased in likelihood when followed by a reinforcer.

Certain other behaviors, called **interim responses,** increased in occurrence in the middle of the interval between food deliveries. Staddon and Simmelhag suggested that these behaviors, including moving and turning along the food hopper wall, were related to searching when food delivery was unlikely. Timberlake and his colleagues have suggested that instrumental conditioning for food reinforcement should be interpreted in light of the feeding system that is activated in hungry animals (Timberlake & Lucas, 1989). Behavioral repertoires in this situation reflect preorganized, species-specific patterns of foraging and feeding. According to this model, when food is not available, animals use specific search patterns. After food delivery, they exhibit behavior focused on getting the food. From this perspective, the behavior patterns observed in these experiments can be viewed as learned alterations of the feeding system repertoire that correspond to reward delivery expectancies, rather than an increase in behavior that occurred contiguous with reward, as characterized by the Law of Effect.

A related set of findings concerns the extent to which particular types of responses can be instrumentally learned. In Chapter 5 we saw that some types of CS–US associations are readily conditioned and others are not. For example, a visual CS is easily conditioned to a shock US and food tastes are readily conditioned to illness; but it is difficult to condition visual cues to illness and tastes to shock (Garcia & Koelling, 1966). Similarly, some types of instrumental conditioning responses are more easily learned than others. Thorndike found that cats were not easily conditioned to execute some types of responses, such as grooming or yawning, to escape from a puzzle box. Based on these observations, he proposed the concept of **belongingness** (discussed in Chapter 5) to explain that certain responses "belong" with a particular reinforcer based on the animal's evolutionary history. Thus behavioral actions on objects a cat can manipulate, such as string pulling and latch pushing, belong with the movement of obstacles such as the puzzle box door, whereas yawning and grooming do not.

This principle was strikingly demonstrated in Breland and Breland's 1961 observations of the "misbehavior" of zoo animals they attempted to instrumentally condition. For example, a pig trained to drop a coin into a box tried to use modified versions of its natural rooting behavior to flip the coin into the air toward the box rather than adopting the seemingly more straightforward behavior of carrying the coin in its mouth and dropping it into the box. When they endeavored to train raccoons to perform a similar task, they were stymied by the raccoons' preoccupation with rubbing coins against one another and dipping them repeatedly into the box without dropping them. The investigators saw that the range of possible

CH. 6 PROCEDURAL
LEARNING II:
HABITS AND
INSTRUMENTAL
LEARNING

188

instrumentally learned responses was limited by the subjects' natural repertoire of innate behaviors. In another systematic investigation of belongingness, Shettleworth (1975) identified six different natural hamster behaviors and attempted to increase the frequency of each behavior in different hamsters through instrumental conditioning. Food reinforcement was effective for behaviors hungry hamsters are likely to perform (such as digging in bedding and rearing and scrabbling at the walls) but not for nonfeeding behaviors (such as face washing, grooming, and scent marking).

Animals Develop Expectations about Behavior and Rewards

Thorndike proposed that instrumental learning involved an association between the stimuli present when the behavior was executed and the reinforced behavioral response, thus leading to the abbreviation *S–R learning*. In this conception, the reinforcer was not part of the association but simply strengthened the S–R bond. However, this original notion has been qualified by subsequent research. A series of influential studies showed that animals develop associations among all three relevant events—the stimulus, the response, *and* the reinforcer (Rescorla, 1988). One line of evidence is the observation that rats can learn different instrumental responses for different types of reinforcements. For example, a rat can be trained to press a lever for food and to pull a chain for water. So animals appear to associate different responses with specific rewards, and they seem to form expectations that particular responses will produce certain rewards.

Another line of evidence comes from studies in which the attractive value of a reinforcer changes after instrumental learning occurs. In this experimental process, called **reinforcer devaluation,** rats are initially trained to make two different responses for distinctive rewards, such as pressing one lever for food and another for sugar water. Subsequently, outside the learning situation, the animal is allowed to consume one of the reinforcers (perhaps the sugar water) and then is made sick by injection of lithium chloride. As described in Chapter 5, this results in classical conditioning of a taste aversion to sugar water. The key test comes next: examining the rate of lever pressing for food and sugar water following the specific devaluation of sugar water. If the rewards only *reinforce* the association between the appropriate lever (stimulus) and the lever press (response), then devaluing a particular reinforcer (sugar water) should have no effect. If, on the other hand, sugar water is part of the association formed between a particular lever and lever pressing, and the animal presses that lever in expectation of sugar water, we might expect a subsequent change in pressing on that lever. In fact, when sugar water is devalued, rats selectively avoid the water-associated lever and prefer the food-associated lever. This preference shows that the reward is indeed a critical part of the learned association.

Another type of experiment highlights the importance of animals' expectations by shifting reward magnitudes. Rats placed at one end of a simple linear alley receive food rewards when they reach the other end. Animals that receive greater amounts of food run slightly faster in the alley than those getting less food. However, if the amounts of food are shifted, the rats that ran quickly for large rewards will run more slowly than the rats that consistently received a small reward. Conversely, rats switched from small to large rewards will run more quickly than rats that always received large rewards. Thus the shift in expectations is more powerful than the actual amount of reward in controlling the animals' instrumental response.

A powerful and tragic demonstration of animal and human awareness of the contingency between behavior and reinforcement is **learned helplessness:** an acquired feeling of futility in which people believe they have no control over their situation. In a series of experiments by Martin Seligman and his colleagues (Seligman & Maier, 1967), animals were initially given painful shocks at unpredictable times. Other animals learned to perform a response that would allow them to avoid the shocks. Subsequently both groups of animals were put in a completely different situation where they could learn to avoid shocks by performing a cued response. The animals that had initially learned to avoid shocks readily acquired the new response. In contrast, the animals that had suffered inescapable shocks made no attempt to learn the new task; they had apparently learned there was nothing they could do to escape shocks.

Seligman extended the concept of learned helplessness to human studies. In one experiment he subjected college students to a series of unpredictable loud noises they could not control. Subsequently the students were asked to solve a series of anagrams, which students not exposed to the unpredictable noises could do well. The subjects exposed to unpredictable noise, however, had considerable difficulty in performing this task, even though solving anagram problems had little to do with the previous noise exposures. Seligman theorized that the earlier experience with uncontrollable unpleasant events produced a sense of helplessness and lack of control that carried over to performance on a subsequent unrelated cognitive task.

Learning & Memory in Action

What Is the Basis of Losing Streaks?

Based on his experimental analyses of animal and human learned helplessness, Martin Seligman (1975) suggested that depression (a lack of affect and feeling) may be attributed to a person's learning that he or she has no control over events. Thus a sudden life-changing illness, such as

CH. 6 PROCEDURAL
LEARNING II:
HABITS AND
INSTRUMENTAL
LEARNING

190

cancer, or a disaster like a flood may be considered a negative reinforcer that is unpredictable and inconsistent with behaviors preceding these events. Under these circumstances, some people can develop a deep sense of loss of control that extends broadly to how they approach not only their specific challenge but also many other life problems. Seligman described the case of a woman whose children had gone to college and whose husband traveled extensively. She felt that these important events were outside her control and developed profound depression.

The idea of learned helplessness has been extended in several directions to elucidate various phenomena. For example, some people have suggested that losing streaks by sports teams may be the result of learning that aversive events cannot be controlled. One study found that indeed teams that lost badly one week were more likely than predicted by their overall performance to lose the next week. Conversely, is it possible that winning provides a false but effective sense of control? How else can anyone explain how the 2004 Red Sox managed to beat the Yankees following a mounting series of successful events during the divisional playoffs?

A practical application of learned helplessness may explain poor classroom performance by some children. Early unexplained failures may create a sense that study and homework behavior does not control outcome. If students view their grades as unpredictable, they may assume they will do poorly regardless of their efforts. Some programs attempt remedial tutoring based on clear assignments, strategies to achieve success, and rewards based on following the specific assignments to reverse such feelings of helplessness and turn around otherwise unsuccessful classroom performance.

Interim Summary

Thorndike's Law of Effect states that reinforcers alter the likelihood of behaviors that precede them. This simple rule explains the development of superstitious behaviors that we acquire because of their history of association with reinforcing outcomes. However, the Law of Effect depends on the types of behaviors, called terminal responses, that tend to occur just before a reward is consumed, as opposed to interim responses that occur preceding reward consumption. And not all behaviors are equally easily conditioned by reinforcers. Rather, behaviors that "belong" with particular reinforcers (like foraging behaviors that precede food) are more easily conditioned by an instrumental contingency. Consistent with this observation, animals develop expectations about rewards that follow their behaviors and act accordingly. For example, they modify their instrumentally conditioned responses appropriately when reward values are altered. Also, behavior can be affected by a learned absence of reinforcer predictability. In particular, animals and humans become "helpless" when conditioned to believe that negative reinforcements are unpredictable and unrelated to their behavior.

Animals Learn about the Environment and Expect Reinforcers

A variety of protocols are used to study instrumental conditioning. Among the most common are mazes and Skinner's operant box. Each of these learning situations has provided deep insights into the processes and neural bases underlying instrumental learning.

Rats in Mazes Learn Rules, Expectancies, and Spatial Layout

In 1901 Willard Small, inspired by the famous garden maze at Hampton Court in London (Figure 6.1), introduced the maze to studies of animal learning. He began what would become an industry of systematic and quantitative studies aimed at identifying the minute details of how rats acquire specific turning patterns in mazes. Some mazes used to study rats' navigational strategies are simple. Perhaps the most common example is the T-maze (Figure 6.2, left), which simplifies maze

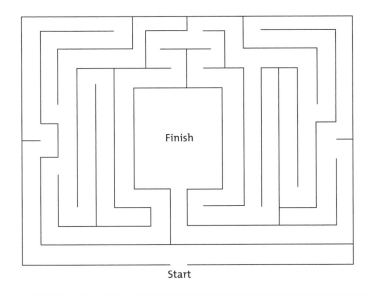

FIGURE 6.1 The maze in Hampton Court.

CH. 6 PROCEDURAL
LEARNING II:
HABITS AND
INSTRUMENTAL
LEARNING

192

navigation to a single turn. Rats begin at one end of an alley and at the other end reach a choice point between right and left goal alleys. In one common test condition, the rat is required to make a particular left or right turn consistently. This condition is called "win–stay" because the rat "wins" a reward by turning in one direction and reaching a particular goal arm, and it must "stay" with that response in subsequent trials to obtain additional rewards. A variation is the "win–shift" version of the task: After "winning" a reward in one goal arm, the rat must then "shift" to the opposite goal arm to receive the next reward. In *alternation learning* the rat continues to "win–shift" over many successive trials, thus alternating between turns to the left and right goal alleys.

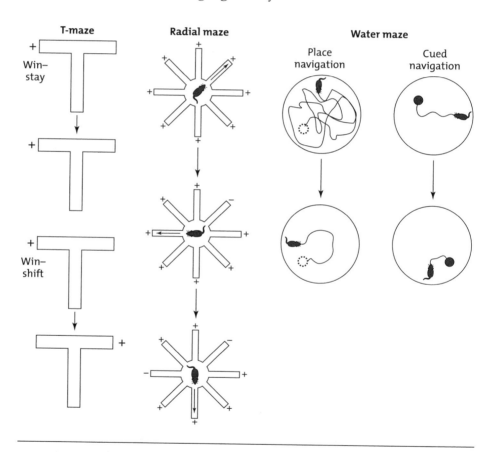

FIGURE 6.2 The radial maze, T-maze, and water maze.
In the T-maze win–stay task, the reward site (+) is consistent across trials; but in the win–shift task, its location is switched between trials. In the radial maze, rewards are found only once at the end of each maze arm. In the water maze place navigation task, the escape platform cannot be seen and is always placed in the same location. In the cued navigation version of this task, the platform can be seen and is moved from trial to trial.

An animal's ability to learn expectancies about rewards in maze learning is seen in comparisons between win–stay and win–shift performance: Rats more readily learn the win–shift task than the win–stay task. This result may seem counterintuitive because the animal most readily learns to *not* repeat the most recently rewarded response. Certainly this result is not predicted by the Law of Effect. It appears that after the rat has eaten the food in one goal arm, it does not expect to find food there on the next trial and instead searches the other goal alley.

The most amazing performance of win–shift behavior is observed in the radial maze, composed of a central platform with multiple goal arms radiating like spokes of a wheel in all directions (Figure 6.2, center). In the win–shift version of this task, each goal arm end is baited with a food pellet, and the rat is allowed to forage. Rats readily learn to visit each arm just once in a trial, collecting all the rewards efficiently by avoiding arms already visited. The rats could have learned to visit the arms in a succession of clockwise or counterclockwise choices. However, the procedure delays each choice by a few seconds, which is sufficient to prevent that strategy. Instead the animals seek food in new maze arms in a seemingly random order without returning to previously searched areas. Rats performed surprisingly well on this task even when there were 17 goal arms, requiring the rat to remember as many as 16 arms visited in each trial (Olton et al., 1977).

Another popular maze task is the water maze (Morris, 1984)—an open swimming pool filled with warm water that is made opaque with the addition of milk powder or water-based paint (Figure 6.2, right). There is no way out of the pool, but a rat can climb on a platform in the water to rest. Across a series of training trials, the rat begins from any of several starting locations and must find the platform to climb on it. In one version of the task, called *cued learning,* the platform is elevated just above the water surface and painted with a dark color so that it is easily visible. The painted, raised platform is usually moved between trials so the rat must learn to approach the visible cue rather than swim to the former location of the platform. Here a simple S–R association between a specific visual cue and the approach response toward that cue supports learning.

In another version of the task, called *place learning,* the platform is set just below the surface of the water with no cue indicating its location. Rather, rats must learn to use environmental cues to remember the platform location. Here learning requires more than a simple S–R association. Because no specific cue indicates the platform's location, the rats cannot simply learn to approach a specific stimulus. And because the animals must swim from different starting points, they cannot learn a specific set of turning responses to reach the platform.

The other common paradigm for studying instrumental learning is the **free operant** technique developed by Skinner. The term *operant* refers to the requirement that the animal must operate on the environment to receive a reward. Thus operant learning is generally viewed as synonymous with instrumental learning.

CH. 6 PROCEDURAL
LEARNING II:
HABITS AND
INSTRUMENTAL
LEARNING

194

Skinner developed the free operant protocol to let the subject control when it executed the response without experimenter intervention. In a typical free operant task, a rat presses a lever or a pigeon pecks a key, and at any time that behavior increases the likelihood of reward. The measure of learning is a change in response rate associated with reward contingency. Mazes also use operant conditioning in the sense that animals' operating responses to the maze environment get specific reinforcements. However, maze experiments involve discrete trials in which the experimenter imposes conditions for when the instrumental behavior is to be executed. Also, the typical measure of learning in a maze is accuracy of choice and the latency to make the choice once the trial has begun, rather than the response rate. The following sections will describe how these paradigms are used to study instrumental learning.

Operant Conditioning Shapes Behavior to Match Rewards

Special techniques have been developed to study operant conditioning. The apparatus used for operant conditioning is typically a small chamber (often called a **Skinner box** after its creator) outfitted differently depending on experimental subject species (Figure 6.3). Rats press a lever to get food pellets delivered into a cup from a gadget that looks and works like a gumball machine. Pigeons have a round panel in the wall, called a key, that they can peck to obtain grain.

In operant conditioning animals typically learn uncommon behaviors, such as a rat pressing a lever or a pigeon pecking a key. The timing of reward consumption is often a bit delayed from the desired operant behavior; even if food is delivered immediately after a lever press or key peck, it is presented a few inches away from the lever or key, and the animal may not even notice the food itself while making the operant response. Because of these features of operant conditioning, a **shaping** procedure gradually modifies the animal's behaviors toward the desired responses. In shaping, the experimenter begins by delivering a reward the first time the animal moves close to the feeder. When the animal first hears the feeding machine deliver the food, it may freeze at the noise. However, eventually the animal finds the food and becomes interested in the feeder. After a few food deliveries, the animal habituates to the noise and (by classical conditioning) associates the noise with the appearance of food in the feeder. At this point the feeder noise has become a conditioned stimulus and is referred to as a **secondary reinforcer.** It takes on a key property of food (the primary reinforcer): It entices the animal to approach the feeder.

Now the experimenter shapes the animal's behavior so that it will perform the desired response. This is accomplished by rewarding successive approximations of the desired behavior. At first the experimenter delivers the food when the animal merely moves toward the lever or key. When the animal increases its approach

FIGURE 6.3 The Skinner box.
Left: Rat in lever-pressing test. The lever is just to the left of the rat. Lights in the box
signal the availability of food when the lever is pressed. Right: Pigeon in key-pecking test.
The pigeon will peck at one of the three keys to generate a food reward that will be
available in the hopper located lower on the wall.

behavior, the experimenter requires the animal to perform the next component
of the conditioned behavior: The rat must contact the lever or the pigeon must
peck near the key before being rewarded. The experimenter continuously requires
a response closer and closer to the full lever press or key peck that automatically
activates the feeder. This procedure resembles the strategy used by the students
mentioned at the beginning of the chapter, who shaped their professor's lecture
behavior so he would stand in one corner of the room.

An interesting variation on this procedure is **autoshaping**. In this protocol,
untrained pigeons are placed into the conditioning chamber. At a regular interval,
the response key is illuminated for several seconds, then food is delivered. As in
the conditioning of superstitious behavior, there is no required relationship
between the desired key peck response and the food delivery. Nevertheless,
pigeons reliably begin to peck the key when it is illuminated before the automatic
food delivery; at that point the feeder activation is made to require a key peck.
The usual interpretation of this phenomenon is that early in conditioning, the
pigeon looks toward the suddenly illuminated key before reinforcement. This association may reinforce the looking behavior. Later, when food is not delivered
immediately upon looking, the pigeon begins to approach the key, and it does this
ever closer to the time of food delivery. According to this view, in later trials, as
the latency between looking at and approaching the illuminated key decreases,

CH. 6 PROCEDURAL
LEARNING II:
HABITS AND
INSTRUMENTAL
LEARNING

196

the animals come even closer to the key and begin to peck at it; that behavior becomes associated with the reward.

However, careful observations of the pigeons show that this interpretation is not correct. Pigeons do not successively look, approach, and contact the key. A study that closely examined the pigeons' behavior at the time of pecking hinted at the actual mechanism of autoshaping (Jenkins & Moore, 1973). Here some pigeons were trained to peck for food and others for water. Detailed observation showed that the pecks differed under these conditions. When the reinforcer was food, the pigeons executed brief, forceful pecks with their beaks open, just like those performed when feeding. When the reinforcer was water, the pigeons instead pecked slowly with their beaks closed and even sometimes made swallowing movements, just like drinking behavior. These observations have led to the interpretation of autoshaping as an example of classical conditioning. According to this view, movement toward the key replicates the unconditioned behavior that was executed when the reward was delivered; the illuminated key becomes a CS as it comes to substitute for the food (US), taking on a similar ability to elicit feeding behaviors. Autoshaping is therefore an example of how instrumental and classical conditioning share many features.

The field of **behavioral modification** applies principles of shaping and instrumental or operant conditioning to a broad variety of situations in education, business, and psychotherapy. These methods can diminish problematic behaviors and increase appropriate behaviors of children in the classroom; teach children with learning disabilities to speak and write more fluently; reduce workplace accidents; and help people lose weight, reduce alcohol consumption, and improve their lives in many other ways.

One example is the use of **token economies** in a variety of situations including classrooms, mental institutions, and prisons. In a token economy, individuals earn tokens for performing or not performing specific behaviors. The tokens can be exchanged for primary reinforcers (such as candy or other desirable goods). In a mental institution, tokens may be given for personal hygiene, appropriate social interactions, participation in group discussions, and productive work activities. These therapies succeed to the extent that specific behaviors can be defined and consistently reinforced with tokens. In some situations a token economy has succeeded as well as other traditional therapies and has reduced the need for medication. Token economies are also often used in classrooms to encourage good behavior and stronger academic performance.

Reinforcement Schedules Determine Behavioral Responses

Real-world reinforcements do not immediately or reliably follow behavior. For example, we often work hard in studying for a test but receive the grade substantially after taking it; and sometimes we do not receive the good grade we expect. Gamblers pay to pull a slot machine lever many times to obtain infrequent rewards. Baseball batters work hard to get a hit about a third of the time. Why do we continue to produce learned behaviors when the reinforcement contiguity is delayed or infrequent? What controls when we continue to generate the behavior and when we quit (extinguish)?

A simple, striking illustration of the impact of irregular response–reinforcement contiguity is the phenomenon called the **partial reinforcement effect.** Animals' behavior is first shaped with rewards reliably following each response. But once the behavior is engaged, we can easily switch to reinforcing only every other response; and we can gradually decrease the reinforcement to only once every 10 responses (or even fewer) and still maintain robust responses. Indeed, under these conditions, when the reinforcement is discontinued, the number of trials required before the animal ceases responding (extinguishes) is considerably *greater* than the number of trials to extinction if every response was rewarded before extinction.

In daily life, partial reinforcement sometimes works against our best intentions. For example, a parent who punishes or tries to extinguish a child's whining for a treat should, in principle, be effective. However, if the parent occasionally gives in and rewards the child, this produces a variable ratio schedule (explained in the following paragraphs) that extends rather than reduces the behavior.

The partial reinforcement effect may seem paradoxical because the learned behavior seems to be stronger for the less rewarded condition—an apparent violation of the Law of Effect. This view comes from the observation that the contingency of partial reinforcement is similar to that of extinction: In both conditions, the subject emits many nonreinforced responses. However, in partial reinforcement the subject may associate many nonreinforced responses with eventual reinforcement. Thus, following partial reinforcement, the subject may continue to respond in extinction because it has learned to expect that one of its responses will eventually pay off.

Much research has focused on the relationship between operant behaviors and patterns of partial reinforcement in an effort to understand how behavior is modulated by unreliable rewards. Four reinforcement schedules have received the most study. In a **fixed ratio schedule (FR),** reinforcement is given after a particular number of responses. For example, in an FR-4 schedule, reinforcement is delivered after each fourth response. In a **variable ratio schedule (VR),** the number of responses required before the reward varies randomly but has a constant average value. In a **fixed interval schedule (FI),** reinforcement is delivered following the first response after a particular amount of time since the last reinforcement. For example, in an FI-15 schedule, a timer begins after each reinforcement delivery; when it has measured 15 seconds, another reinforcement is given after the next response. Finally, in a **variable interval schedule (VI),** the duration of the minimum interval varies randomly but has a constant average period. For example, in a VI-15 schedule, the time before the next response generates a reward might vary between 5 and 25 seconds, with an average of 15 seconds.

Each of these schedules results in a distinct behavior pattern that is typically recorded in terms of the running sum or **cumulative response** over time (Figure 6.4). Gener-

CH. 6 PROCEDURAL
LEARNING II:
HABITS AND
INSTRUMENTAL
LEARNING

198

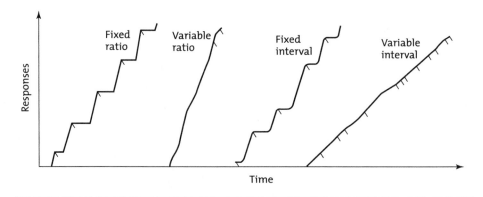

Responses

Fixed
ratio

Variable
ratio

Fixed
interval

Variable
interval

Time

FIGURE 6.4 Operant response patterns for different reinforcement schedules. The x axis represents time, and the y axis represents the cumulative number of responses. The small marks show when reinforcements are provided.

ally response rates are higher in the ratio schedules than in the interval schedules, resulting in a more rapidly rising cumulative response. In fixed ratio schedules the subject usually pauses briefly after each reinforced response; but the cumulative response is more or less linear for both fixed and variable ratio schedules. In a fixed interval schedule, the cumulative response has a scalloped appearance, with an initially slow response rate and then increasing response as the interval times out. This response pattern suggests that the subject anticipates the reward with an increasing rate of behavior. In a variable interval schedule, the time of reward cannot be judged; here the cumulative response is linear, indicating a constant response rate.

Considerable research has examined the response pattern when an animal can choose between two behaviors (usually two levers to press or two keys to peck) that are associated with different reward schedules. For example, a rat might be allowed to respond to a left lever on a VI-15 schedule and a right lever on a VI-30 schedule; that is, rewards can be obtained at a minimum of every 15 seconds on the left lever and 30 seconds on the right lever. After substantial experience, the rat emits a consistent pattern of responses at the two levers to maximize the rewards. This pattern of behavior is described by the **matching law.** The response rates are described by this formula:

$$B1/(B1 + B2) = R1(R1 + R2)$$

B1 = the rate of behavior 1 (left lever presses)
B2 = the rate of behavior 2 (right lever presses)
R1 = the maximal rate of rewards associated with behavior 1
R2 = the maximal rate of rewards associated with behavior 2

In the example, R1 = 4 per minute and R2 = 2 per minute, so B1/(B1 + B2) = 2/3. In other words, the rat will distribute its lever presses between the two levers at a 2:3 ratio, with a greater rate at the left lever. The same formula accurately characterizes choice behavior for variations in the magnitude of reward associated with two behaviors.

Note that this matching law will maximize the reward rate only in a combination of variable interval schedules where an exact interval length cannot be anticipated. In a combination of fixed interval schedules, responding to one lever will always provide a greater amount of reward than responding to the other; so animals will eventually respond only to the lever with the higher rate of reward.

Interestingly, in similar situations humans are sometimes characterized as irrational when they do not consistently select the higher-probability choice but instead pursue what is called **probability matching**. In probability matching subjects select each of several choices in proportion to their rate of success. Thus, in typical experiments, subjects choose between two buttons and are rewarded for predicting which button will illuminate next. Most humans will match their choices to the probabilities of the two buttons becoming illuminated. For example, if the buttons pay off in a ratio of 2:1, human subjects tend to select the buttons in the same ratio even though they would be correct more often if they would consistently select the higher-probability button. In contrast, animals do not probability match; rather, they consistently select the higher-paying button. Sometimes animals really are smarter than people!

Chained Responses Compose Organized Behavioral Routines

We have seen so far that animals can exhibit seemingly intelligent behavior in responding to different reinforcement schedules and in making choices. Here we will extend the scope of instrumental behavior to sequences of responses and stimuli. A straightforward extension of simple instrumental responding is the phenomenon of **response chaining**—which is how animals execute a sequence of operant behaviors, only the last of which results in reward presentation. Some prominent examples of response chaining are the acts animals perform in circuses or similar public shows. Trainers can teach an animal to climb a ladder, then pull a chain, run through a tunnel, push a ball to a cup, slide down a chute, and finally run to the trainer for a reward. How are such complex behavior sequences maintained? The general explanation is that each behavior in the sequence serves as a secondary reinforcer to the next behavior, until the animal finally receives the primary reinforcer (food) from the trainer at the end of the sequence. In other words, completion of the first behavior is reinforced by the stimulus on which the animal acts in the next step of the sequence; the second act is reinforced by the stimulus for the third act; and so on.

But how does the trainer establish the indirect relationship between the initial act in a long sequence and the receipt of primary reinforcement at the end of the sequence? What we never see is that animals most effectively acquire response

CH. 6 PROCEDURAL
LEARNING II:
HABITS AND
INSTRUMENTAL
LEARNING

200

chains using **backward chaining.** In this strategy, animals are first trained to per-form the *final act* in the sequence to obtain the primary reinforcer. Then they are trained to perform the next to last act to get the stimulus for the final act, which results in reinforcement. Next they are trained to perform the third to last act to gain presentation of the next to last stimulus, and so on. Eventually the animal will perform the entire chain even if all the stimuli (the ladder, chute, and so on) are present at once. Response chains are fragile: If one of the stimuli is missing, the chain may be broken so the animal cannot skip a missing part of the sequence.

A related problem is the learning of **serial patterns**. Can animals discover sequential patterns in rewards and respond appropriately? Hulse and Campbell (1975) trained rats to run down a simple alley to receive varying numbers of food pellets in a reliable order: 14 on the first trial, 7 on the second, 3 on the third, and none on the fourth. The animals adjusted their running speed as if they could pre-dict the anticipated reward, running most quickly on the first trial and slowing progressively to the last. A subsequent study showed that the rats were not sim-ply running more slowly as the day went on. They could also learn to match run-ning speed to reward expectation even if the sequence involved both increasing and decreasing reward magnitude changes (such as 14, 1, 3, 7, 0). One explana-tion is that rats might use each item in the sequence as the cue for the next, sim-ilar to the associations that underlie response chaining (Capaldi et al., 1980). However, Roitblat and colleagues (1983) found that inserting new nonrewarded responses in the middle of a sequence did not disrupt sequential pattern respond-ing for the rest of the sequence. Thus the animals were not relying on each indi-vidual association between adjacent items, but must instead have developed knowledge about the overall positions of items in the sequence.

Interim Summary

The performance of rats in mazes has been used extensively to examine how rats learn and remember particular behavioral responses and locations in space. Variants of the popular T-maze protocol include the win–stay rule (rats are consistently rewarded for one type of turn), the win–shift rule (they are consistently rewarded for turning in the direction opposite that of the last response), or alternation (they systematically switch between left and right turn responses). The radial maze has several arms radiating from a central platform; training for this maze most commonly uses the win–shift rule. The water maze is a large pool filled with opaque water with an escape platform submerged at a particular location defined by cues outside the maze.

Other popular protocols for studying instrumental learning involve operant conditioning tasks in which animals are gradually trained to perform an other-wise low-frequency behavior, such as pressing a lever. Behaviors most related to the one occurring just before reward consumption can be autoshaped by drawing attention to the location of the desired response before the reward is delivered.

Partial reward schedules make behaviors resistant to extinction. Typical partial reinforcement schedules can be fixed or variable and involve either the ratio of responses to rewards or the interval between reinforced behaviors. Also, when put into conflict situations where rewards are distributed between two behaviors, animals tend to select the more rewarding behavior alone, whereas humans tend to match their responses to the probability of rewards for each behavior. Instrumental learning can also support the chaining of responses into a long series of behaviors that forms a routine.

Humans' Habits and Skills Combine Cognitive Memory and Instrumental Learning of Motor Programs

The previous discussion suggests that animals can acquire sequential knowledge and behavior that mimic humans' complex skill learning. But how do people learn complex skills and sequences? Much effort has gone into the study of how humans learn to complete sequences and solve other complex skill-learning problems. Some forms of sequence learning that have received attention are straightforward examples of motor coordination such as walking, swimming, writing, typing, playing the piano, and driving a car. Walking and swimming are repetitive and the others not; but all these skills require precise timing and orderly actions. Without that precision, we would fall down when trying to walk and never play a pleasing tune on the piano. How do we become skilled at these procedures, and how do we seem to execute them so effortlessly?

An early view was that skilled motor behaviors are mediated by response chaining mechanisms. For walking, it seems reasonable that the sight of the left leg moving forward and stepping down might act as the stimulus for beginning to raise the right leg and move it forward. We could break these alternate leg movements into simpler elements of muscle contractions that follow in sequence. Those microscopic movements would eventually have to be accomplished unconsciously using sensory feedback from angles of the leg parts and the pressure of stepping down. Also, you can imagine how simple feedback reinforcement might shape and optimize a broad variety of coordinated behaviors. Improvements in timing and positioning of each act in the sequence would result from feedback of our smoothness and speed in executing the sequence.

However, as Karl Lashley (1951) realized, there are several reasons why response chaining does not adequately explain skill learning. First, reaction times are much too slow to have feedback from one movement initiate the next. The

CH. 6 PROCEDURAL
LEARNING II:
HABITS AND
INSTRUMENTAL
LEARNING

202

time it takes a person to react to the sensation of his or her own movements is longer than 100 milliseconds. Yet a pianist can execute 16 finger movements in a second! Second, some people who have lost sensory feedback from their hand movements due to nerve damage can still execute skilled hand movements, even while blindfolded to prevent visual feedback. Third, many of the most common errors made in skilled performance involve sequencing errors, such as when we transpose sequential letters when typing (*raed* instead of *read*). This would seem impossible if each typed letter was the essential stimulus for the next. Fourth, it has been observed that the time required to begin a sequence depends on the length of the sequence to be executed.

These findings led to the notion of a **motor program**—a preprogrammed sequence that is initiated complete with sequencing and timing of its elements. For typing, a motor program would send all the commands for finger movements, initiating them in the appropriate order to produce the correct sequence of typed letters. An advantage of motor programs is that they can complete sequences at any speed. Modern views of motor skill learning contend that the motor program contains a sketch of the general coordination of movements that can be modified as needed to alter the tempo, magnitude, or intensity of the movements or even the specific body parts that are executing the movements (Schmidt, 1988). Examples of this occur when we make fine adjustments to improve the accuracy of our tennis serve, when we change the size of our handwriting, or when we alter the loudness or tempo in playing music on the piano.

Skills Are Learned in Three Stages

More complex forms of human skill learning are accomplished in a series of stages. Anderson (1982) proposed three characteristic stages of the development of a complex skill. The kinds of skills that require these stages are complex, such as learning to type or to drive a standard transmission car. The first **cognitive stage** involves the learner remembering a list of instructions for the sequence to be followed. For example, in learning to type you might think about the word *read*, slowly look at each key on the keyboard, and type the letters one at a time. In driving you might memorize the steps of engaging the clutch, then shifting, then pressing the gas petal, then releasing the clutch. This stage involves cognitive memory, and it is slowly and often awkwardly executed.

The second **associative stage** is also slow. This stage involves substituting for the verbal memory a more direct representation of the sequence of movements that executes the skill. At this stage in learning to type or drive, you become free of having to remember the next step in the sequence. Each step begins to smoothly follow the last. You no longer have to rehearse; you begin to perform the skill without conscious memory. The skill parts have become linked in a procedure that still requires close attention and monitoring—but not anticipatory, conscious, step-by-step commands. You must think about the word to be typed or when shifting must occur, but directions for each sequential step are executed without recalling each step.

Finally, in the **autonomous stage**, the procedure is free of conscious control and direction. You can type by just seeing words, and your hands effortlessly press the correct keys. Similarly, all aspects of driving a car are executed smoothly and virtually outside conscious control. An expert typist can keyboard a page of text in seconds but have almost no idea of its content. Experienced drivers can carry a conversation or think about what they will do at their destination with almost no monitoring of their driving actions. When a skill is fully autonomous, explicit remembering can become difficult. Some expert typists find it hard to describe where some keys are on a keyboard. Seasoned drivers can have trouble telling someone how to change gears in a car—it's easier just to show them. An autonomous skill requires less attention but is less interruptible. It is difficult to type part of a common word or to stop at a particular move in shifting gears.

Interim Summary

We learn a variety of skills and routines in everyday life, including walking, writing, typing, and playing the piano. Some repetitive movements, like walking and swimming, may be learned by response chains in which each sequential action is reinforced by feedback of its success. Other sequential behaviors, such as writing, typing, and piano playing, involve motor programs that occur too quickly for feedback to have substantial influence; these programs can be fine-tuned in amplitude and tempo. Complex skills are learned in a series of stages. In the cognitive stage a learner remembers a list of steps; the associative stage eliminates explicit remembering but still requires conscious attention and monitoring; and the autonomous stage allows the skill to be expressed without conscious control.

Striatal Cortical Pathways Support Instrumental Learning and Skill Acquisition

What brain circuits support our capacity for learning habits and skills? Considerable evidence indicates that skill learning is accomplished by a brain system centered in the striatum, a brain area that was introduced in Chapter 1 (Figure 6.5). The striatum receives input from the entire cerebral cortex, and these connections are capable of neural plasticity. The striatal connections are organized to sort and associate somatosensory representations with the appropriate motor representa-

CH. 6 PROCEDURAL
LEARNING II:
HABITS AND
INSTRUMENTAL
LEARNING

204

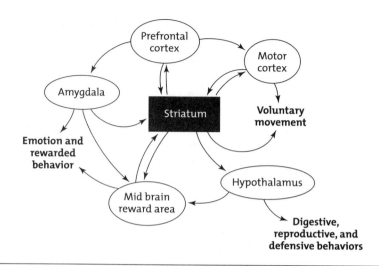

FIGURE 6.5 The striatum as a central structure in instrumental behavior.

tions—such as associating sensory representations of the hand with motor representations that control it (Graybiel et al., 1994).

The striatum is a part of a cortical loop that communicates with nuclei in the thalamus, targeting both the premotor and motor cortex and the prefrontal association cortex. Notably, this circuit projects only minimally to the brain stem motor nuclei and not at all to the spinal cord. In addition, the striatum interacts with many different brain areas involved in a variety of processes such as motivated (food seeking, defensive, and reproductive) behaviors; emotion; and processing rewards. This circuitry shows that the striatum does not directly control motor output but instead contributes to higher motor functions—including, many believe, the planning and execution of goal-oriented behavior (Graybiel, 1995; Schultz et al., 1995; Mink, 1996).

The Striatum Is Critical in Animal Instrumental Learning

Much research has suggested that the striatum plays a pivotal role in S–R learning (Packard & Knowlton, 2002). Evidence for this hypothesis comes from studies of the effects of striatum damage or inactivation in animals. Early studies found that striatum damage impaired learning of a variety of instrumentally conditioned tasks, including conditioned avoidance and discrimination learning tasks based on training with reinforcements.

How do we know that striatum damage specifically affects instrumental learning and not other types of learning or perception, motivation, or motor coordination? This problem has been addressed using **double dissociation,** in which the experimenter typically compares the effects of damage in two brain areas on tasks that demand the same general perception, motivation, and motor coordination but distinct forms of learning and memory. Damage to brain area A affects performance on task 1, but performance on task 2 is normal; damage to brain area B affects performance on task 2, but performance on task 1 is normal. This pattern of results shows that both variants of the task are sensitive to brain damage; that neither locus of damage affects the common perceptual, motivational, or coordination requirements of the tasks; and that each locus of brain damage affects how these capacities create a distinct type of learning.

One striking double dissociation experiment involved training rats with a radial maze (eight arms radiating from a central platform), comparing the win–stay and win–shift rules you read about earlier in this chapter (Packard et al., 1989; Figure 6.6). Both versions of the task used the same maze, the same food-motivated performance, and the same kind of approach responses. The tasks differed only in the behavioral choice necessary to earn a reward, allowing researchers to examine the role of specific brain areas in different kinds of learning. In the win–stay task, four of the eight maze arms were illuminated each day; the rat could consistently approach any lit arm to receive a reward. Rats with striatum damage were impaired in learning this version of the task, but rats with hippocampus damage actually performed better than normal animals. In the win–shift task, all maze arms contained a reward each day, and the rat had to visit each arm just once and then shift to a new arm to maximize its rewards. (When the rat removed food from a particular maze arm, the reward was not replaced.) Rats with hippocampus damage were impaired in this task, but rats with striatum damage performed normally. The win–stay version of the task using illuminated maze arms can be viewed as a prototypical S–R task in that animals must respond consistently to a particular cue (arm illumination). This type of memory depends on the striatum (and not the hippocampus), as the rats' behavior showed. In contrast, the win–shift version of the task requires remembering which maze arms still have rewards and does not support performance based on a consistent S–R association. Instead it requires animals to remember which arms they have already visited; this form of memory apparently depends on the hippocampus and not on the striatum.

Perhaps you recall from Chapter 1 an elegant double dissociation of striatum and hippocampus memory functions. In that study, either the striatum or the hippocampus was temporarily inactivated to determine the roles of these brain areas in different learning strategies for a simple T-maze task. Rats were trained to make a consistent turn to enter a particular goal arm, then tested after one and two weeks of training with the maze rotated 180 degrees. After one week of training, rats tended to go where they had previously received rewards even though they had to turn in the direction opposite that used during training. This *place learning* depended on the hippocampus, not the striatum. In contrast, after two weeks of training, the rats tended to make the same turn they had used during training even

CH. 6 PROCEDURAL
LEARNING II:
HABITS AND
INSTRUMENTAL
LEARNING

206

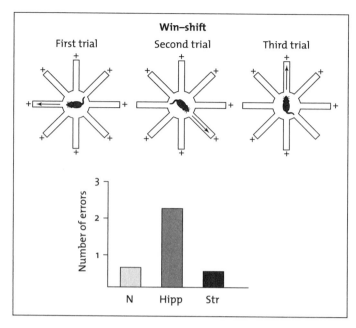

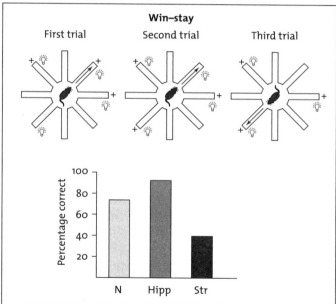

FIGURE 6.6 Hippocampus and striatum lesions and radial maze performance.
In the radial maze diagrams, + indicates an arm that was baited with food, and a light
bulb indicates an arm that was illuminated. N = normal control subjects; Hipp = subjects
with damage to the hippocampus; Str = subjects with damage to the striatum.

Striatal Cortical
Pathways Support
Instrumental
Learning and Skill
Acquisition

207

though this brought them to a different place. This *response memory* depended on the striatum, not on the hippocampus. These findings offer compelling evidence of distinct learning strategies mediated by the striatum and hippocampus and show that neither brain area is required for the perceptual, motivational, or motor coordination demands common to both response and place learning.

Learning & Memory in Action

Why Does Stress Often Cause Forgetting?

When some people are stressed, they say, their thinking shuts off and they struggle through the situation on a sort of autopilot, remembering few details while learning how to react when the same situation recurs. This anecdotal observation suggests that emotional stress might somehow shift the balance of memory systems from the predominant use of a hippocampus-dependent cognitive strategy to the predominant use of a striatum-dependent habit strategy.

To investigate this possibility and identify its neural basis, Packard and Wingard (2004) examined the effects of stress on place and response learning in a maze. They treated rats with a drug that produces anxiety before giving them a maze task. After the drug wore off, the rats were tested to see which strategy they used. Rats treated with a placebo predominantly used a place strategy; those treated with the anxiety-creating drug predominantly used a response strategy. In a second experiment Packard and Wingard infused small quantities of an anxiety-creating drug directly into each rat's amygdala, which sends emotional signals to the striatum and hippocampus (see Figure 6.5). These findings matched those of the general treatment with the same drug. Thus anxiety and stress appear to make the amygdala switch off the hippocampus so that the striatum becomes the predominant learning system.

The Striatum Also Supports Human Instrumental Learning

Our understanding of the striatum's role in human learning and memory comes mainly from studies of individuals with Parkinson's disease or Huntington's disease. Both disorders lead to profound motor deficits. Parkinson's disease causes tremors, rigidity, and akinesia (inability to move) following cell death in the substantial nigra. This cell death depletes the neurotransmitter dopamine in the striatum. Huntington's disease, which is also characterized by lost striatal function, causes irregular movement patterns. As you might imagine, studying people with these diseases to characterize the role of the striatum in human memory is far

Ch. 6 Procedural
Learning II:
Habits and
Instrumental
Learning

208

more complicated than examining animals' brains. In addition to their motor deficits, some people with Parkinson's disease also suffer from depression or dementia; people with Huntington's disease always develop progressive dementia. Furthermore, the drugs used to treat these symptoms can affect cognition. These factors can unintentionally confound or influence experimental results, making them more difficult to interpret.

Despite these limitations, clinical observations of striatum function have demonstrated that people with Parkinson's disease or Huntington's disease show deficits in several skill learning tasks (Salmon & Butters, 1995). In one study, people with Huntington's disease were trained in rotary pursuit (Gabrieli, 1995)—a simple motor skill learning task that requires subjects to maintain contact between a handheld stylus and a metal disk revolving on a turntable. Normal subjects improved with practice, increasing the amount of time they maintained contact with the target; but subjects with Huntington's disease showed virtually no learning. Because Huntington's disease causes specific motor deficits that might make the rotary pursuit task harder, the turntable was slowed so that when the Huntington's subjects were introduced to the task, their initial performance was as good as that of control subjects working with a faster rotating disk. Equating initial performance levels in this way did not reduce the learning deficit; even when the task was adjusted so that the Huntington's subjects' initial performance exceeded that of normal subjects, the Huntington's subjects still failed to show learning. Thus the researchers showed that the striatum contributes to motor skill learning.

A more complex skill learning task in which individuals with Huntington's disease and Parkinson's disease are impaired is the serial reaction time motor sequencing task. In this task, a computer screen shows four lighted panels, each corresponding to a button on the keyboard below. One screen location flashes during each trial, and the subject presses the button corresponding to that location. Unknown to the subject, the locations flash in a repeating order (such as a 12-item sequence in which each of the four locations is flashed three times). Implicit learning of the sequence is measured in two ways. First, as subjects learn the sequence, their average reaction time to respond to a given item gradually decreases. Second, reaction time slows substantially in a test period when the stimuli are presented in random order. The shorter reaction times for the learned series compared to those for a random series reflect learned memory. Subjects with Parkinson's disease or Huntington's disease are typically impaired in motor sequence learning (Willingham & Koroshetz, 1993; Pascual-Leone et al., 1993). Thus the striatum is vital for learning and remembering the order of movements in a skilled routine.

The striatum is also involved in learning S–R associations in humans, just as it is in animals. A striking example of a double dissociation between the roles of the human striatum and hippocampus involves the analysis of an unusual form of habit learning. Knowlton and colleagues (1996) compared individuals in the early stages of Parkinson's disease, who had suffered striatum damage, to amnesic individuals with damage to the hippocampus or the hippocampal memory system. These subjects were trained in probabilistic classification learning, presented in the form of a weather prediction game. The task involved using cues from a set of cards to predict one of two outcomes (rain or sunshine). On each trial, one or more cards from a deck of four were presented. Each card was associated with the sunshine outcome only in a probabilistic way (Figure 6.7). For example, a particular card predicted sunshine in 60 percent of the trials, and a different card predicted sunshine in 40 percent of the trials. The stimuli differed only in the pattern of shapes printed on the cards, and the subjects were not told the probability of sunshine associated with each card. When multiple cards were presented, the correct weather prediction was determined by the average of their probabilities. For example, if one card of a presented pair predicted sunshine in 60 percent of the trials and the other card predicted sunshine in 40 percent of the trials, the average probability was 50 percent. Based on the cards presented in each trial, the subject had to predict rain or sunshine and was then given feedback about the prediction's accuracy.

The probabilistic nature of the task made it counterproductive for subjects to attempt to recall earlier trials because any particular cue configuration could lead to more than one outcome. For example, when presented with the pattern shown in a previous trial, a subject might remember the response she made for the earlier occasion; but the current trial's outcome need not be the same as in that earlier trial, leading to confusion. Instead the most useful information to be learned concerned the probability associated with particular cues and cue combinations, so that learning occurred gradually across trials—much as real-life habits or skills are acquired. This format was specifically designed to eliminate any advantage normal subjects would have in remembering specific prior trials.

Over the initial trials, normal subjects gradually improved from pure guessing (50 percent correct) to about 70 percent correct—about as accurate as possible because the outcomes were probabilistic. However, subjects with Parkinson's disease failed to show significant learning, and this impairment was particularly evident in those with more severe Parkinsonian symptoms. By contrast, the amnesic subjects learned the task, achieving accuracy levels like those of controls by the end of the trials.

After this weather prediction training, the subjects were asked multiple-choice questions about the types of stimulus materials and nature of the task. Normal subjects and those with Parkinson's disease performed well in recalling the task events. But the amnesic subjects were impaired, performing near the chance level of 25 percent correct. What do these results suggest about the relationship between the kind of memory required to learn a skill and the memories we have of particular events—such as the time spent learning that skill? As you probably noticed,

Ch. 6 Procedural
Learning II:
Habits and
Instrumental
Learning

210

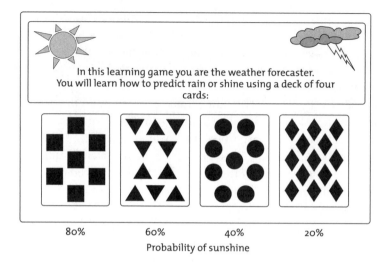

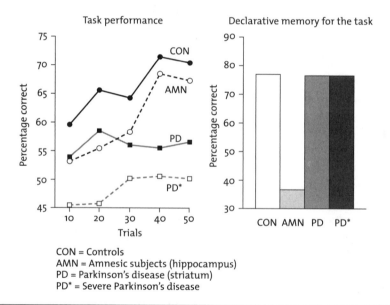

FIGURE 6.7 Weather prediction task.
A. Appearance of the computer screen on a trial using all four cards. B. Performance in
forecasting weather (left) and in memory for the task stimuli and rules (right).

these findings demonstrate a clear double dissociation: Habit learning is disrupted
by striatum damage, and memory for learning events is impaired in amnesia—
providing further evidence that habit learning depends on the striatum whereas
ordinary memory for identical learning materials is accomplished within a sepa-

rate brain system. The amnesic subjects in this study were similar to Jimmie G. (Chapter 1), who learned his way around a hospital garden but professed no memory of having seen it before.

INSTRUMENTAL LEARNING IS INVOLVED IN DRUG ABUSE Chronic abuse of addictive drugs is a complex social phenomenon based partly in learning and brain mechanisms. Two features of addictive behavior make drug abuse particularly problematic. First, addiction is compulsive: Addicts are driven to abuse even when they are aware of its deleterious affects on their lives. Second, addiction is subject to relapse even after seemingly successful withdrawal and periods of abstinence. Substantial recent evidence suggests that S–R learning and its brain system play a central role in these two prominent aspects of drug addiction. Different abused drugs, including amphetamine, heroin, nicotine, and alcohol, have distinct molecular mechanisms; but all increase the release of dopamine in the striatum. This fact has led to the suggestion that the reinforcing effects of drugs may be mediated by the same brain systems involved in learning based on natural rewards (Everitt et al., 2001; Berke & Hyman, 2000; Kelley, 2004). By altering the release of dopamine in the striatum, drugs could change information processing in the striatum and throughout the brain system that mediates S–R learning. Specifically, to the extent that dopamine is a reinforcement signal in the striatum, drugs may achieve some of their dramatic effects by enhancing the operation of the S–R learning system. In addition, the neurotransmitter glutamate and NMDA receptors play a crucial role in plasticity within the circuits identified in Figure 6.5.

Within the frameworks proposed, we typically employ our capacity for foresight and conscious control of long-term consequences to adjust our reward-seeking behavior. However, current theorizing suggests that the effects of drug abuse on striatal dopamine may enhance S–R learning within that system to overwhelm mechanisms of cognitive control, leading to both compulsive behavior and relapse. Consistent with this view, drug-seeking behavior of addicts becomes increasingly stereotyped and ritualized, automatic, inflexible, and stimulus-bound. In particular, self-reports of relapse suggest that addicts lose conscious direction in reacting directly to environmental cues that take control of behavior. Indeed, cravings for addictive drugs depend greatly on contextual cues associated with drug taking. In a hospital setting, cravings usually diminish—but they can become acute as soon as the addict reenters the environment in which drugs were a routine of life. For example, entering a bar is too strong a stimulus for alcoholics, and returning to the social milieu of drug taking often incites rapid relapse in heroin addicts. Similarly, in animal models of drug addiction, following extinction of drug taking, reintroducing environmental cues associated with former addictive behavior provides powerful cues for reinstatement of drug taking. Considerable research on dopamine, NMDA receptors, and striatal system function is providing a possible new avenue of success in treating addiction.

Ch. 6 Procedural
Learning II:
Habits and
Instrumental
Learning

212

The Striatum Is Activated during Habit Learning in Humans

Functional neuroimaging studies provide another way to explore the role of the striatum in human learning and memory, with results closely paralleling studies of people with brain damage. In these studies, subjects perform an instrumental learning task while their brain activity is measured by blood flow changes in the striatum and other brain areas. Increases in striatal activation have been associated with learning finger movement sequences (Seitz et al., 1990; Seitz & Roland, 1992) and with learning to press buttons following a sequence of panel lights on a computer screen (Grafton et al., 1995). Neuroimaging studies have also documented striatal activation during perceptual and cognitively based skill learning tasks like probabilistic classification in the weather prediction task (Poldrack et al., 1999). Taken together, the neuropsychological results and neuroimaging evidence show that the role of the striatum in habit or skill learning encompasses a variety of learning abilities that involve multiple stimuli and response choices and that show gradual, incremental performance improvement across trials.

Striatal Neurons Are Activated during Habit Learning

Recent neurophysiological studies have confirmed the involvement of the striatum in S–R learning and have revealed how the striatum represents memories. Several studies have described neurons in the striatum that fire in anticipation of movements, suggesting that striatal activity might be associated with the relationship between behavioral contexts and responses (Mink, 1996). Also, neurons that project from the brain stem into the striatum and use dopamine as a neurotransmitter fire with the expectation and reception of rewards (Schultz et al., 1993; Schultz, 2006). Moreover, these dopamine neurons carry signals to the striatum about the predictability of rewards contingent on a stimulus. Recall from Chapter 5 that Rescorla and Wagner (1972) showed that conditioning occurs only when a stimulus adds predictive value regarding a reinforcer. An added stimulus that does not alter predictions is not learned, as shown in the phenomenon of blocking. Consistent with these behavioral findings, once a contingency between a stimulus and reward is established, adding a nonpredictive stimulus does not activate the striatal dopamine neurons, whereas these neurons do respond to a stimulus that adds predictive value (Figure 6.8). The combined findings for neurons in the striatum and elsewhere in this circuit have led researchers to suggest that the striatum uses knowledge about the behavioral context and reward predictions to plan behavioral responses (Schultz et al., 2000; Graybiel et al., 1994).

In addition to these observations about simple and conditional motor responses, other data indicate a prominent role for the striatum during sequence learning.

Kermadi and Joseph (1995) trained monkeys to fixate on a central location and memorize a sequence of panels that were illuminated in order on a computer screen, then look at and subsequently reach toward each panel in the correct order (Figure 6.9). Many striatal neurons responded to the visual instruction stimuli while the monkeys fixated on the initial point or during their eye or arm movements. Furthermore, the responses of many neurons depended on the sequential order of the targets: They responded to a visual cue only if it was in a particular position in the three-item sequence. Notably, these cells fired in anticipation of each item in the sequence, demonstrating again that the striatum participates with other structures in anticipating behavior sequences.

These neurophysiological observations converge with anatomical and behavioral data to suggest that the striatum plays a critical role in habit learning by resolving competition among multiple sensory and response options, particularly as we learn response sequences. The striatum houses circuitry for cortical sensory input and direct motor outputs, which are both necessary to associate stimuli with specific behaviors. Furthermore, the striatum receives reward signals capable of reinforcing associations of stimuli and responses. So the striatum is a key component of a pathway for habit learning involving the acquisition of stereotypes and unconscious behavioral patterns, and this pathway can mediate S–R behavior independent of circuits for other forms of memory.

Interim Summary

In both animals and humans, the striatum plays a central role in habit and skill learning. Animal experiments have shown double dissociations between the effects of damage to the striatum versus the hippocampus. Striatal damage causes deficits in S–R learning in which a specific cue (such as a light) should be approached or a particular response (like a left turn) should be executed to receive reinforcement; however, striatal damage does not harm memory of a reward's location or the reward value expected. By contrast, the hippocampus is not essential for S–R learning but instead supports memory for where rewards were obtained.

Humans with Parkinson's and Huntington's diseases have striatal dysfunction, resulting in motor coordination deficits and S–R learning impairments in both simple motor skill learning tasks and complex sequence learning tasks. Complementary studies of striatum physiology show that the striatum is activated when humans learn finger movement sequences, as well as during S–R learning in a probabilistic classification task. In animals performing S–R and sequencing tasks, striatal neurons are activated when the animals anticipate movements or rewards; these neurons also fire in association with learned movement sequences.

CH. 6 PROCEDURAL
LEARNING II:
HABITS AND
INSTRUMENTAL
LEARNING

214

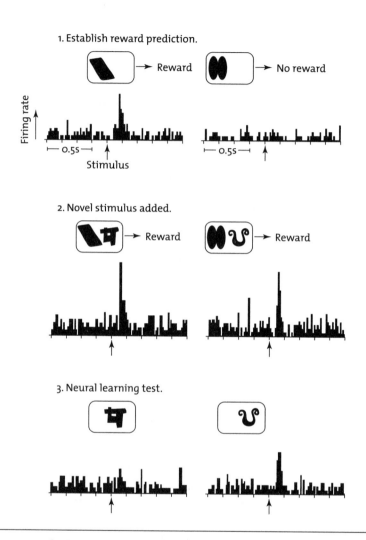

FIGURE 6.8 Blocking of neural predictive responses in a dopamine neuron.
The top panels show that this cell fires after presentation of a stimulus that predicts reward and does not fire after a different stimulus that predicts no reward. The middle and bottom panels show that adding a second stimulus to the reward-predicting stimulus does not further activate the cell; but adding a second stimulus that changes the reward prediction of the formerly negative stimulus activates the cell.

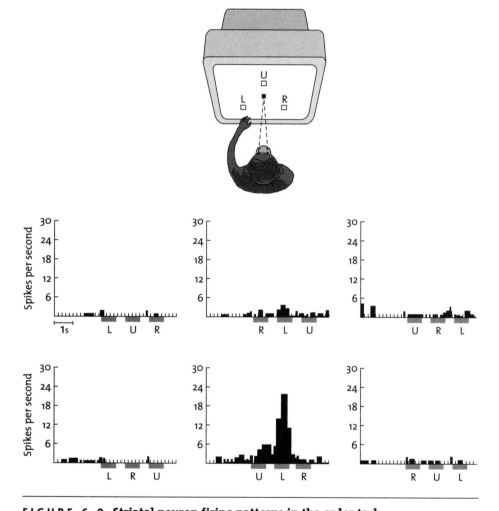

FIGURE 6.9 Striatal neuron firing patterns in the order task.
R, U, and L refer to stimulus positions in the right, upper, and left, respectively. Note the activation of this neuron selectively during the middle part of the ULR sequence.

CH. 6 PROCEDURAL
LEARNING II:
HABITS AND
INSTRUMENTAL
LEARNING

216

Chapter Summary

1. Instrumental learning lets us acquire specific reinforced behavioral responses. Habits are based on predictable consequences of actions. Habit acquisition pervades studies of learning and memory using mazes and a variety of operant conditioning tasks in animals; it is also prominent in human skill learning and implicit learning of specific responses to stimuli and response sequences.

2. Unlike classical conditioning, in which the US is delivered regardless of the response, in instrumental learning the reinforcer is provided only when a particular behavior is emitted. As embodied in Thorndike's Law of Effect, behaviors associated with positive reinforcement increase in likelihood, whereas behaviors associated with negative reinforcement decrease in likelihood. Many superstitious behaviors increase in occurrence when associated with reinforcement; but only some behaviors (called terminal responses) that occur near the time of reinforcement obey the Law of Effect. Behaviors must be consistent with their reinforcers—that is, they must be related or "belong" to the rewards—to be learned. In instrumental conditioning, animals learn associations between a stimulus, a response, and a reinforcer and can act distinctly for each such association; animals behave according to their reward expectancy for a given stimulus and response.

3. Various mazes have been used to study instrumental learning. Rats can learn to return to maze locations consistently associated with rewards (win–stay), and they can remember specific locations and not return to already visited places (win–shift). Another prominent example of instrumental learning is the free operant task, in which rats and pigeons can emit specific responses at any time and are reinforced according to ratio or interval schedules. Animals can learn reward schedules, match their response distributions to the reward probabilities of multiple response choices, learn to chain operant responses, and learn serial patterns. Humans also learn sequences of behaviors called skills. Skilled performance is acquired in stages and is mediated by motor programs that contain the sequence of coordinated movements.

4. Instrumental and skill learning are supported by a brain system that involves cortex and striatum circuitry. Animal and human studies have shown that instrumental learning of reinforced responses depends on the striatum. Many of these studies have distinguished striatum-dependent habit learning from hippocampus-dependent memory of specific places or events. Correspondingly, striatum neurons are activated during instrumental and skill learning, particularly that involving learning behavior sequences.

5. Chronic drug abuse shares many features with the phenomenology and circuitry of the instrumental learning system. Addictive conduct can be character-

ized as an exaggerated instrumental behavior that dominates conscious control of the consequences of actions. Instrumental conditioning is also relevant to the shaping of behaviors in many clinical and workplace situations.

KEY TERMS

instrumental conditioning (p. 183)

habit (p. 184)

reinforcers (p. 184)

Law of Effect (p. 185)

superstitious learning (p. 186)

terminal responses (p. 187)

interim responses (p. 187)

belongingness (p. 187)

reinforcer devaluation (p. 188)

learned helplessness (p. 189)

free operant (p. 193)

Skinner box (p. 194)

shaping (p. 194)

secondary reinforcer (p. 194)

autoshaping (p. 195)

behavioral modification (p. 196)

token economy (p. 196)

partial reinforcement effect (p. 197)

fixed ratio schedule (FR) (p. 197)

variable ratio schedule (VR) (p. 197)

fixed interval schedule (FI) (p. 197)

variable interval schedule (VI) (p. 197)

cumulative response (p. 197)

matching law (p. 198)

probability matching (p. 199)

response chaining (p. 199)

backward chaining (p. 200)

serial patterns (p. 200)

motor program (p. 202)

cognitive stage (p. 202)

associative stage (p. 202)

autonomous stage (p. 203)

double dissociation (p. 204)

REVIEWING THE CONCEPTS

- How does instrumental learning differ from classical conditioning? What associations are learned in instrumental learning?

- What is the Law of Effect, and what role does it play in instrumental learning? Are all behaviors equally subject to the Law of Effect?

- How do superstitious behaviors appear? How can we get rid of them?

- How do rats solve maze problems?

- How is behavior affected by reinforcement schedules?

- How are response chains acquired?

- What are the psychological stages of skill learning in humans?

- Which neural pathways support habit and skill learning?

- How are instrumental conditioning mechanisms involved in drug abuse?

CHAPTER 7

Emotional Learning and Memory

t was a bright fall day in Boston when I turned on my computer and resumed work on a grant application. A few hours into the morning, one of my postdoctoral fellows rushed into my office and told me that a disastrous thing had happened: An airplane had crashed into the World Trade Center in New York! I thought a lot of people might be hurt, or maybe it just crashed into the roof or at the ground; I'll wait a while and then turn on the news. But several minutes later, the colleague rushed back into my office telling me another airplane had hit the World Trade Center. My first reaction was disbelief. Then, in a second, I realized this could not be an accident. Of course I, and everyone else, rushed into a room with a TV and followed the story for the next hour. While watching the news coverage, we all witnessed the collapse of the World Trade Center towers. We were thunderstruck, aghast in thinking about how many people must have died. I worried about friends who worked and lived in New York and wondered if they were OK.

Later our university shut down for the day, and I tried to reach my friends in New York without success. Over the days that followed, more information about the attack became clear. I was vaguely aware of the phrase "Al Qaeda" before, but now it became the unforgettable name of a terrorist group. I would eventually reach my friends, some of whom were by then involved in the search for survivors.

As you probably do also, I have a vivid memory of the events of the morning of September 11, 2001. I can remember exactly where I was sitting, who came into my office to alert me to the news of each crash, and how I thought and responded. These memories run chills down my spine. I vividly recall watching the first news with my lab colleagues. I generally remember the main events that occurred later that day, but not as well as those surrounding the time of the crashes and the buildings falling. Why is the memory for these shocking events so strong and vivid?

_____

THE PRECEDING STORY is an example of a flashbulb memory, the kind of vivid, detailed memory people have for emotionally laden events. These are usually negative: public events including disasters such as 9/11 and presidential assassination attempts, as well as private events such as hearing about the death of a family member. They can also be emotionally charged positive occasions, such as winning a contest or proposing marriage. Flashbulb memories are striking examples of two ways in which emotion and memory are related. First, emotional memory is a distinct form of learning and memory, separate from cognitive learning and memory. Cognitive memories can be brought to mind and are usually expressed by conscious, voluntary speech or action. In contrast, our expression of emotional memories is involuntary and visceral, such as the chills running down my spine when I remember 9/11. Second, strong emotions at the time of learning can make cognitive memories of the factual events that occurred particularly strong, detailed, and long-lasting. This chapter will consider both emotional learning and memory and how emotions can influence cognitive learning and memory.

Fundamental Questions

1. Are emotional learning and memory truly distinct from cognitive memory?
2. Do emotions merely enrich all memories, or are particularly emotional memories encoded in a special form?
3. How can we get rid of strong, negative emotional memories?

Emotion and Memory Mix at Multiple Levels

Emotion is a chief type of behavioral output; as such, it's one way we express our memories, especially those that have strong emotional content or meaning. We predominantly think of memory expression in terms of conscious recollection and explicit, usually verbal, expression. At the same time, however, emotional memories are typically expressed by emotional components of our behavior—from our tone of speech, to flushing of our faces or sweating, to a sense of trepidation in our bodies as in my emotional memory for 9/11. Emotional memories are also expressed as biases and preferences toward particular items or classes of items to which we have been exposed, such as a brand of wine we've heard about in an advertisement. On another level, our factual memories are colored by their emotional associations. The people and events we remember after emotional experiences are often characterized by us as scary, comforting, or any of a broad range of emotional features. On yet another level, memories surrounding emotional experiences are often remembered better or especially vividly. The emotions themselves, or perhaps the heightened arousal that accompanies emotional experiences, can enhance our memory for objective facts and events perceived during an emotional experience. These aspects of emotion and memory occur automatically and usually without conscious intent or even conscious awareness. In this chapter we will consider how emotional memory can be expressed distinctly from cognitive memory of an event, and we will consider how emotions influence our cognitive memory of emotionally charged events.

Emotional Learning Can Occur without Conscious Recollection

I still feel a bit nervous when I see a pre-9/11 picture of the World Trade Center in New York, and only after that initial feeling do I recall my experiences during that day. I would have expected the opposite sequence—that seeing the picture would have reminded me of the events of 9/11, which would elicit my nervous feelings. Can we have emotional memories independent of factual ones?

In a classic case study of amnesia, French neurologist Claparède (1911) was carefully documenting the forgetfulness of a woman with Korsakoff's disease, a severe memory disorder. To test her capacity to learn, at the outset of an office visit, Claparède planned a surprising and mildly traumatic experience for her. He greeted the woman with their customary handshake but had a needle hidden in his hand to prick her finger. As you might imagine, she expressed her shock and dismay—but then appeared to forget the incident. Upon her next arrival at his office, the woman refused to shake Claparède's hand because "sometimes people hide needles in their hands"—although, even with considerable prompting, she could not recall the painful incident.

Later Damasio and colleagues (1985) described a similar case of intact emotional learning in an amnesic man named Boswell. Even during extended stays in a hospital, Boswell had not learned to recognize any of the hospital staff—not surprising because of the severity of his amnesia. However, he consistently seemed to like some of the staff with whom he had positive encounters.

In a more formal study of whether amnesic people can remember affective information, normal and amnesic subjects were shown pictures and biographical descriptions of two individuals, one characterized positively and the other characterized negatively (Johnson et al., 1985). When questioned after a delay, the normal subjects typically recalled the biographical narratives and then characterized the individuals accordingly with positive or negative descriptions. In contrast, the amnesic subjects could not recall the individuals or their biographies but strongly preferred the "good guy" over the "bad guy." These and other case studies (see Tobias et al., 1992) show that memory for emotional aspects of experience can indeed function separately from the ability to recollect objective information from the same experiences.

Daniel Tranel and Antonio Damasio (1985) directly compared memory for faces and for emotions associated with faces by assessing recognition and emotional responses to photos of family members' faces. When people see pictures of family members, they normally recognize their relatives. They also respond emotionally to these pictures, and these emotional responses can be detected in brief skin resistance changes that do not occur when they view unfamiliar faces. In this experiment, the researchers tested both recognition and skin resistance responses of people with a disorder called *proposagnosia*—an inability to recognize familiar faces due to localized cerebral cortex damage. Even though these subjects could not consciously recognize their relatives' faces, they exhibited normal skin resistance differences in response to pictures of family members versus strangers.

The combined results of these studies suggest that people can learn about the perceptual features of faces and their affective associations even without conscious recognition. We apparently acquire perceptual memories, can attach affective values to them, and can express these emotional memories through covert changes in attitude and automatic emotional responses independent of the mechanisms we use to consciously identify the same stimuli. Thus emotional learning and memory involve a distinct form of memory that occurs independent of cognitive memory. They occur automatically and outside of conscious control, and they can be observed even in amnesic subjects who lack conscious memories of their emotional experiences.

Animals Learn Attractions and Aversions Independent of Other Aspects of Memory

The study of emotional memory has been formalized in many animal studies that seek to identify the critical properties and neural basis of emotional memory. Some prominent experiments have focused on learning to fear previously neutral stimuli. Joseph LeDoux and his colleagues (1990) developed a simple and now widely used method for studying how rats learn to fear a previously neutral tone. In this classical conditioning protocol, rats are initially placed in a small chamber with a grid floor. The rats are allowed a few minutes to explore and habituate to the new environment. Then a tone is presented for 30 seconds and terminated with the presentation of a brief electrical shock through the grid floor (Figure 7.1A). Typically the animals freeze and show fear for a few seconds after the shock, then become more relaxed. Training continues with a few more pairings of tone and shock. Then the animals are removed for the day. In later test sessions, the animals are placed back into the training environment and, after several seconds, are again presented with the tone, but not the shock. The animals now show a conditioned fear response to the tone alone (Figure 7.1B). Learned fear can be measured in multiple responses, such as increased arterial blood pressure, heart rate,

(A) Training

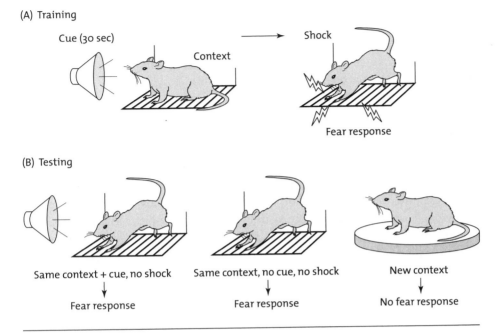

FIGURE 7.1 Cued vs. contextual fear conditioning.

and respiration, as well as motor responses like increased alertness and a freezing response that includes crouching and complete immobility. Also, we can measure fear by observing decreases in normal behaviors that would ordinarily occur. For example, if the animals had been trained to press a bar for water, a cessation of bar pressing and drinking water could indicate fear.

In addition to the conditioned fear responses a rat shows in response to the tone, it typically displays the same fearful behaviors when it is placed back into the training environment, even before hearing the tone (Figure 7.1B). This has led to a major distinction between two categories of stimuli that become associated with the shock. First there is fear conditioning to the specific cue: the transient stimulus that is temporally associated with the onset of shock (in this case, the tone). There is also fear conditioning to the context: a variety of unchanging stimuli in the training environment that are present throughout the trials and constitute the background within which specific cues and shocks are paired.

Although distinguishing between the conditioned effects of cues and context might seem difficult, certain objective distinctions work well. First we can separately test cued and contextual fear. This is typically accomplished by initially placing an animal in a training context for an extended period (a minute or two), without presenting the tone cue, and measuring contextual freezing alone. Then we can remove the animal and place it in a different environment that causes no fear symptoms (Figure 7.1B). After confirming the absence of fear in the novel environment, we present the tone and measure conditioned fear specific to it.

Second, fear of a cue and fear of a particular context can be conditioned separately. How can a cue be conditioned without also conditioning its context? As you might imagine, the context's complex combination of environmental features requires the rat to integrate many stimuli through exploration. If we prevent this integration by allowing only a brief initial exploration period before pairing the tone and shock, later tests will show cued fear conditioning but no contextual conditioning. Likewise, we can independently produce contextual conditioning in the absence of cued conditioning by initially exposing the animal to the environment, then presenting unpaired tones and shocks at separate times. This procedure creates strong contextual fear responses; but without the appropriate timing to form a predictive link between the tone and the shock, the animals show no conditioning to the tone cue.

Phobias: An Example of Fear Conditioning

Phobias (irrational fears of specific stimuli), along with many other anxiety disorders, have historically been considered psychiatric conditions that arise due to conflicts in upbringing. However, a simpler explanation of these disorders may be that they are unfortunate consequences of the rapidity, strength, and generalization characteristics of fear conditioning. For example, Freud wrote about a boy named Hans who, at the age of 5, witnessed a horse falling and subsequently (even into adulthood) became anxious and fearful around horses. Freud believed this horse phobia stemmed from Hans's unconscious anxieties about his relationship with his mother, whereby Hans came to fear horses as a cover for an underlying fear of castration. However, perhaps instead the pairing of the previously neutral stimulus (the horse) and the traumatic event (seeing it fall) induced fear conditioning that generalized to all horses.

Interestingly, phobias ordinarily occur not about meaningless or completely neutral stimuli but more often about particular stimuli that we are prepared to fear; and fear conditioning may explain how we come to think of some stimuli as innately fearful. For example, Susan Mineka and colleagues (1984) showed that laboratory-reared monkeys do not fear snakes when they are alone with a snake at first exposure. However, if the mother is present, she reacts strongly to the snake, causing a fearful reaction in the infant monkey. The pairing of the snake stimulus and the mother's fearful reaction appears to be sufficient to result in fear conditioning to snakes, and it is easy to see how this is passed through generations and can appear innate. Related findings show that human phobias to the same common stimuli are not equivalent. People who fear snakes do not show heightened responses to spiders, and the reverse is true for spider phobics. Thus although both snakes and spiders are stimuli to which many people develop phobias, neither is more innate than the other. More likely, both are stimuli of which we are especially prepared to become fearful with conditioning.

Fear Conditioning Can Influence Other Behaviors

Recall from Chapter 3 the story of Halloween night, when my son was scared by a prankster's hand reaching out of a barrel. After his fright, he became sensitized and reacted strongly to otherwise innocuous events, startling at the sound of leaves rustling in the wind or kids shouting down the street. How does a fearful response spread its effects to seemingly unrelated behaviors?

Michael Davis and his colleagues (1994) developed a technique for measuring the effects of conditioned fear on a natural reaction known as the *startle reflex*. This protocol uses as its test behavior an unconditioned reflexive behavior in which, when a rat hears a loud sound, it moves or jumps suddenly because it is startled. Startle responses are influenced by the rat's emotional status: When the animal is relaxed, the magnitude of its startle reflex is smaller, and when it is nervous, the startle reflex is potentiated (enhanced). In the typical protocol for fear-potentiated startle, animals are initially exposed to pairings of a light or a tone with a foot shock in an environment outside a startle chamber. Subsequently, in the startle chamber they are tested for the effect of the conditioned stimulus on their reflexive startle response to a loud noise. Following initial pairings of a cue and shock, the startle reflex becomes much stronger in the presence of the conditioned light or tone (Figure 7.2). In addition, we can distinguish cued and contextual conditioning in the fear-potentiated startle

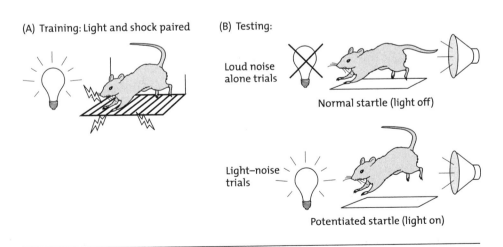

(A) Training: Light and shock paired

(B) Testing:

Loud noise alone trials

Normal startle (light off)

Light–noise trials

Potentiated startle (light on)

FIGURE 7.2 Fear-potentiated startle.

protocol by measuring the intensity of the startle response in the environment used in initial cue–shock pairings (to test contextual conditioning) or in a different environment (to test cued conditioning alone).

Positive Emotional Associations Can Also Be Conditioned

Can we also condition positive emotions in animals? It might indeed be adaptive to learn to be attracted to stimuli that have positive emotional consequences. Two protocols for measuring positive emotional conditioning involve variations of some familiar tests discussed earlier. A common procedure for conditioning positive emotion in animals is the paradigm called **conditioned place preference**. This test uses the same kind of radial maze described in Chapter 6, with multiple arms radiating around a central platform like wheel spokes. In this test animals separately acquire different responses to two maze arms: conditioned attraction to one and habituation to another (Figure 7.3). During the initial conditioning, all

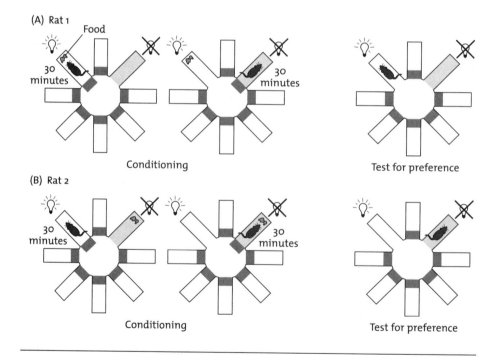

FIGURE 7.3 Conditioned place preference.
In separate experiences, a rat is confined with food in either an illuminated arm (Rat 1) or a dark arm (Rat 2) then confined in the altenate arm without food. In subsequent testing, the rat is allowed to move freely between those arms.

maze arms are blocked except one that is illuminated and one that is dark. A rat is exposed to each of these two arms, one at a time. Each rat is conditioned to associate either the lit or the dark arm with food by being confined in that arm for 30 minutes with plenty of food. In separate trials, the same animal is confined to the other arm for the same period, but no food is available. Thus for half of the rats, the lit arm is associated with food and the dark arm is not, whereas for the other rats the opposite associations are conditioned. In the subsequent test session, no food is placed in the maze, and the animal is allowed access to both the lit and dark arms and the connecting platform between them. The experimenters assess relative preference for the two arms by measuring the amount of time spent in each arm over a 20-minute session during which the animal can explore freely. The expected outcome is that the rat will spend considerably more time in the arm that was previously associated with food than in the one that was not associated with food.

This version of the radial maze task emphasizes strong, distinct emotional associations with a particular location that are based on the presence or absence of food. At the same time, this protocol requires no specific behavioral response to obtain a reward, as is typical of instrumental conditioning, where animals must choose and then approach the appropriate maze arm (you read about this win–stay task in Chapter 6). Also, this procedure does not require memory of specific experiences in the radial maze, unlike the win–shift task in Chapter 6. So emotional memory for maze arm preferences is distinct from a habit of approaching specific maze arms and from cognitive memory for recently visited arms.

Much like fear, positive emotional learning can also spread to other behaviors; a particularly impressive demonstration involves a protocol called **second-order conditioning**. In this procedure, animals are trained to associate an initially neutral stimulus with a reward. That stimulus is then used as a reinforcer to condition another stimulus and response. In one version of this protocol, each time thirsty rats approached a water dispenser to drink, a light was turned on, so they were trained to associate the light with their approach to the water dispenser (Everitt & Robbins, 1992). Subsequently the animals were trained in a different chamber to discriminate between two levers they could press. Pressing one lever was followed by the light, although the water dispenser was not filled; pressing the other lever produced no light or water (Figure 7.4A). Because the rats had already associated the light and dispenser with water, they had acquired the properties of secondary reinforcers. That is, their presentation supported learning to discriminate between the levers. The rats pressed both bars somewhat but much more often pressed the bar associated with the second-order reinforcer: the light (Figure 7.4B).

(A)   Stage 1   (B)   Stage 2

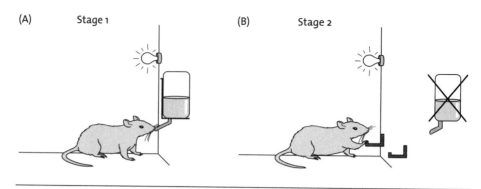

FIGURE 7.4 Second-order conditioning.

Learning & Memory in Action

Why Do Advertisers Bombard Us with Product Names and Images?

In a classic series of experiments on attitude and experience, Robert Zajonc and his colleagues (1968) found that familiarity breeds content or attraction for otherwise neutral stimuli. Inspiration for these studies came when Zajonc discovered a surprisingly strong correlation between the affective connotation of words and how frequently we use them in written language. Zajonc's initial surveys showed that people apply more positive connotations to more frequently used words, even when the words do not have intrinsic affective value. For example, most people prefer *long* to *short* and *above* to *below;* for each of these antonym pairs, the first word is more common in our language than the second. In some cases, even when the desirability of word pair comparisons was explicit and indicated a ranking direction (such as *better* versus *good*), people rated the more common word *good* more positively than the less common word *better!*

Taking this phenomenon into the laboratory, Zajonc and his colleagues asked subjects to participate in an experiment in pronouncing supposedly Turkish words. They read a series of nonsense words—pronounceable but meaningless letter strings such as *jandara* and *ikitaf.* Ratings of "goodness" were closely related to the number of times the nonsense words were read by the subjects. Clear relationships between exposure and favorable ratings were also found for Chinese calligraphy characters that could not be pronounced and for photos of college students; so simple visual exposure was sufficient to produce a preference for familiar items. Furthermore, in an additional study subjects viewed 20 random shapes, each with such a brief exposure period (1 millisecond) that the subjects reported having seen only light flashes (Kunst-Wilson & Zajonc, 1980). In a subsequent test the subjects could not judge which items had been seen any better than predicted by chance; but they were consistently biased in favor of the previously seen stimuli over novel stimuli. These studies provide compelling evidence that mere exposure to perceptual material leaves a memory trace, and its effect is to improve our attitudes toward those items.

Interim Summary

A simple, direct way to study animal emotional learning and memory is the fear conditioning protocol, in which an initially neutral tone is paired with a shock. Subsequently animals express fear (by freezing and other autonomic responses) of the tone as well as of the environment or context in which the tone and shock occurred. Conditioned fear spreads its effects to other behaviors, as is demonstrated in the fear-potentiated startle protocol; here previous fear conditioning causes a light to enhance a reflexive startle response to noise. Positive emotions can also be conditioned. For example, animals can be conditioned to prefer places where they previously received rewards. In humans, mere exposure to an otherwise neutral stimulus can elicit an attraction to that stimulus.

Emotions Influence the Strength of Cognitive Memories

As we've already discussed, the increased arousal and intense feelings associated with emotional events affect the strength of cognitive memories for both the emotional aspects of the experience and its factual details. This phenomenon has been studied in two ways: by interviewing people who have experienced highly emotional events, and via experimental analyses of memory for emotional material.

Flashbulb Memories: Exceptionally Vivid Recollections of Emotional Events

A particularly powerful example of the mixture of emotion and memory is the phenomenon of **flashbulb memories** (Conway, 1995), of which my story about 9/11 is a typical example. Everyone remembers highly emotional life events, which makes sense because they tend to be important, personally meaningful experiences. But in addition to your memories of how you felt in these moments, you probably also recall many mundane details that surrounded the events, such as where you were, what you were doing, what you were wearing, and whom you were with. These flashbulb memories are vivid and full of details, seeming as precise as photographs taken when the flashbulb of a camera fires.

For some people such memories may include a traumatic accident, the breakup of a relationship, or perhaps scoring highest on a test or winning a lottery. These individual flashbulb memories are real, of course; but they are difficult to evaluate experimentally. Typically there is no record of the mundane aspects of the event, so the veracity and completeness of a personal flashbulb memory cannot be measured accurately. Because of this problem, studies of flashbulb memories usually focus on public events witnessed by large populations, for which event details can be validated and surrounding circumstances can be verified for many witnesses. Prominent examples are President Kennedy's assassination, the *Challenger* space shuttle's explosion, Princess Diana's death, and the airplane crashes into the World Trade Center and the Pentagon.

Some studies collect narratives from witnesses to the events; others involve systematic interviews and validation. In 1973 one examination published in the magazine *Esquire* surveyed many famous people, asking where they were when President Kennedy was shot (Berendt, 1973). Julia Child recalled she was eating fish soup in her kitchen. Billy Graham was playing golf and had a feeling something bad would happen. Such memories can be lasting. A collection of narratives by aged individuals recalling where they were when they heard President Lincoln had been shot some 35 years earlier reported vivid memories (Colegrove, 1899). One person recalled she was planting a rosebush when she was told by her husband. Another remembered he was fixing a fence in the morning when he was told by a particular friend.

A formal study of the contents and strength of emotional memories was based on a questionnaire given to many individuals who had experienced a highly emotional public event. In this study, Brown and Kulik (1977) characterized six classes of information that appeared in more than half of the accounts for various public events. People were most likely to report where they were when they heard the news, the events that were interrupted by the news, and what they did immediately following. They were also likely to remember who told them the news and the emotional states of others as well as their own emotional reactions. The amount of detail varied considerably. In addition to the commonly provided categories of information, many records contained idiosyncratic details that did not fit any particular category, such as recalling the current weather or what people were wearing. David Pillemer (1998) reviewed many accounts and studies of vivid memories for major personal and public life events. He found that people tend to strongly believe that their personal memories of momentous events are accurate. These memories typically include details of people's personal circumstances at the time and sensory images that constitute a reliving of particular moments of the experience.

In a systematic study of the accuracy of flashbulb memories, Schmolck and colleagues (2000) interviewed several people from California three days after the verdict in the O. J. Simpson murder trial. This highly publicized event captured widespread attention in the United States. The California trial brought out many differing viewpoints and emotional reactions in the public and in the media. The researchers' interviews contained many objective questions about the trial, along with questions about where and how the interviewees found out about the verdict, their emotional reactions to the case, and the extent to which they discussed the case with others. Then 15 and 32 months later, the same people were interviewed again to assess the accuracy of their memories. At 15 months, most responses were similar to the original ones; but after 32 months, memories showed significant deterioration. Although the memories of about 15 percent of the subjects were perfect or almost perfect 32 months after the verdict, the memories of about 40 percent of the subjects were greatly distorted or lost. The accuracy level was not strongly related to how much people discussed the case, their interest in the trial, or their agreement with the verdict. Instead accuracy was most associated with the intensity of people's emotional reactions to the verdict. Thus so-called flashbulb memories are actually not photographic in detail; it appears that the strength and accuracy of memories, both for the emotion-producing event and for the peripheral details, are influenced by the emotional status of the observer.

Emotion Strengthens Memories of Personal Events

Prospective studies of emotional memories have focused on comparing the accuracy of memories with and without strong affective content. In a pioneering study, Kleinsmith and Kaplan (1963) had subjects study arbitrary pairings of words (called *paired associate learning*). Some of the words had strongly affective meanings, such as *rape, vomit,* and *kiss;* subjects' emotional arousal was monitored by measuring skin resistance changes while they studied the words. When subjects were tested one week later, they recalled the provocative words better than emotionally neutral words.

More recently, Cahill and McGaugh (1995) examined memory for story material presented both visually in slides and verbally in slide narratives. The story was divided into three sections (Figure 7.5). The first and last segments of the story described a set of neutrally affective events: a mother and son arriving at a hospital where the father worked and then leaving. The middle segment of the story differed for two subject groups. The neutral story group heard an account of a mock emergency drill that involved no real disaster or bloodshed. The arousal story group heard about the boy being critically injured in an accident as he arrived at the hospital and being rushed to the emergency room, where his severed feet were reattached by surgeons. The efficacy in producing emotional arousal was measured by subjects' ratings of the events. The sub-

	Narratives accompanying the slide presentation	
Story phase	Neutral version	Arousal version
1	1. A mother and her son are leaving home in the morning.	A mother and her son are leaving home in the morning.
	2. She is taking him to visit his father's workplace.	She is taking him to visit his father's workplace.
	3. The father is a laboratory technician at Victory Memorial hospital.	The father is a laboratory technician at Victory Memorial hospital.
	4. They check before crossing a busy road.	They check before crossing a busy road.
2	5. While walking along, the boy sees some wrecked cars in a junkyard, which he finds interesting.	While crossing the road, the boy is caught in a terrible accident, which critically injures him.
	6. At the hospital, the staff are preparing for a practice disaster drill, which the boy will watch.	At the hospital, the staff prepares the emergency room, to which the boy is rushed.
	7. An image from a brain scan machine used in the drill attracts the boy's interest.	An image from a brain scan machine used in a trauma situation shows severe bleeding in the boy's brain.
	8. All morning long, a surgical team practiced the disaster drill procedures.	All morning long, a surgical team struggled to save the boy's life.
	9. Make-up artists were able to create realistic-looking injuries on actors for the drill.	Specialized surgeons were able to reattach the boy's severed feet.
3	10. After the drill, while the father watched the boy, the mother left to phone her other child's preschool.	After the surgery, while the father stayed with the boy, the mother left to phone her other child's preschool.
	11. Running a little late, she phones the preschool to tell them she will soon pick up her child.	Feeling distraught, she phones the preschool to tell them she will soon pick up her child.
	12. Heading to pick up her child, she hails a taxi at the number 9 bus stop.	Heading to pick up her child, she hails a taxi at the number 9 bus stop.

FIGURE 7.5 Emotionally arousing and neutral stories.
Note that the first and last phases of the stories are neutral, but the middle phase differs in emotionality.

jects were not told they would be tested for their memories of the story. However, two weeks later, they were given a surprise test on the story details. The neutral and arousal groups did not differ in their memories of details in the initial and final parts of the story; but the arousal group was far superior in recalling the middle segment of the story.

Interim Summary

Emotional experiences enhance cognitive memories. A prominent case of this enhancement involves flashbulb memories, in which people have vivid memories of emotionally arousing occurrences, including major life events and public disasters. In most cases, people remember where and from whom they heard about the events and retain images of specific events that are almost a reliving of the experience. Such memories also are exceptionally lasting, and the vividness and persistence of these memories are related to the strength of people's emotional reactions. Prospective studies that compare memories of similar factual materials that vary in emotional content show that emotional arousal can significantly affect subsequent memory.

Neural Circuitry for Expressing Emotions Supports Emotional Learning and Memory

The brain circuits that mediate emotional learning and memory, and the effects of emotion on memory, involve the same neural circuitry that supports our feelings and expression of emotions. This situation is similar to that for perceptual and procedural learning, where learning modifies the circuitry for perception and motor coordination. Emotional learning and memory are accomplished within the same neurons and brain circuits that support the basic processes being learned and remembered. Therefore, before describing the neurobiological basis for emotional learning, we need to look closely at the brain circuits for perceiving and expressing emotions.

A Complex Brain Circuitry Supports Emotional Perception and Expression

The brain areas that mediate our emotional perception and expression are a collection of distinct and interconnected structures—some in the cerebral cortex, others beneath it in the subcortical nuclei, and more deep in the brain stem. Our understanding of the individual contributions of these structures and the full complexity of how they interact has been evolving over the last 75 years and is still rudimentary. Let's begin by tracing a succession of theories about the anatomy and functional role of this system.

In 1937 neuroanatomist James Papez offered the first theoretical proposal of a brain system for the perception and integration of emotions. He differentiated between brain circuits for thought and emotional feeling. He suggested that the stream of thought involved channeling sensory inputs into the thalamus and then to areas of the cerebral cortex on the external surface of the brain. In contrast, he suggested that the stream of emotional feeling followed a path from the thalamus to the cortical areas on the medial surface of the brain. These cortical areas, including part of the orbital prefrontal cortex, cingulate cortex, and parahippocampal gyrus, are known collectively as the *limbic lobe* because these areas lie on the midine margin or *limbus* of each cerebral hemisphere. Papez speculated that these structures constitute a circular circuit for emotion: The cingulate cortex projects to the hippocampal region, which projects to part of the hypothalamus (the mamillary bodies), which then projects to part of the thalamus, which in turn projects back to the cingulate cortex, completing the loop. He hypothesized that the circular nature of this loop might be the reason for the repetitive nature of our rumination about emotional experiences.

In 1949 Paul MacLean added more structures to the circuit and elaborated the notion of a limbic system. He focused on electrophysiological evidence indicating that parts of the Papez circuit receive sensory signals from the internal organs. He proposed that the limbic system composes a *visceral brain*—a system for regulating the internal organs. MacLean proposed further that connections between the limbic system and both lower brain stem areas and higher-order cortical areas support distinct aspects of emotional experience. The pathways through lower brain stem structures, he suggested, mediate instinctive, formulaic behaviors. He called this system the *reptilian brain* because this pathway and such stereotyped behavioral repertoires were fully evolved by the time reptiles appeared. He proposed that the limbic system itself constitutes a *paleomammalian brain* that mediates the involuntary expression of emotion through the autonomic nervous system and hormonal outputs, and he recognized that this system exists even in the lowest mammals. Finally, MacLean suggested that the pathway through the higher cortical areas, the *neomammalian brain,* mediates the conscious experience of feelings. He suggested that conscious experience of emotions may exist only in higher animals and humans, depending on the extent of cortical evolution.

Since the theories of Papez and MacLean, there have been numerous elaborations and modifications to the concept of the limbic system, and the boundaries of this system have become unclear. Recent anatomical evidence has expanded the connections of the limbic system forward toward the frontal lobe and backward toward the midbrain (pons and medulla; Figure 7.6). These interconnections are so strong that anatomist Walle Nauta (1971) proposed that we view this system as a continuum of structures throughout the brain. It has become increasingly difficult to separate the limbic system from other brain systems to which it is connected. Therefore, more recent studies of the neurobiology of emotion and emotional memory have focused on components of this system.

*Neural Circuitry
for Expressing
Emotions Supports
Emotional Learning
and Memory*

235

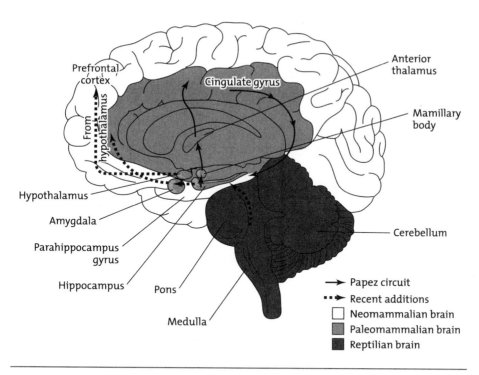

FIGURE 7.6 Pathways in the limbic system.
The shading in the above drawing shows MacLean's proposed reptilian, paleomammalian, and neomammalian systems.

The Amygdala: A Center in the Pathway for Emotional Expression

Recent research has focused the study of emotional memory on the circuits centered in the amygdala, a tiny almond-shaped structure deep in the temporal lobe. The amygdala is central between cortical information processing areas and the limbic circuitry, and it has a variety of output pathways to the cortex, other brain systems, and brain stem areas that mediate hormonal and autonomic responses. Thus the organization of the amygdala, along with its main inputs, internal connections, and outputs, implies that it plays a crucial role in processing emotions.

The overall structure of the amygdala involves several highly interconnected nuclei. Most prominent among these are the lateral nucleus, the central nucleus, and the basolateral nucleus (Figure 7.7). The amygdala's basic circuits of sensory input, internal connections, and multiple output routes work as follows: Sensory inputs from the thalamus and cortex project mainly to the amygdala's lateral nucleus and to some extent to the basolateral nucleus. From the lateral nucleus, signals travel within the amygdala to the central and basolateral nuclei. There are

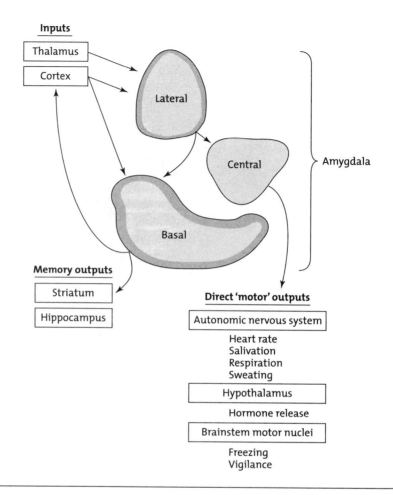

Inputs

Thalamus

Cortex

Lateral

Central

Basal

Amygdala

Memory outputs

Striatum

Hippocampus

Direct 'motor' outputs

Autonomic nervous system

Heart rate
Salivation
Respiration
Sweating

Hypothalamus

Hormone release

Brainstem motor nuclei

Freezing
Vigilance

FIGURE 7.7 Amygdala circuits.

three major types of outputs from the amygdala. One pathway projects from the central nucleus to the hypothalamus and the autonomic nervous system that controls the body's organ functions. Two other pathways originate in the amygdala's basolateral nucleus and project outward to the cerebral cortex and striatum.

Several studies have shown that the amygdala receives sensory inputs from both the thalamus and the cerebral cortex. The thalamus inputs come from the gustatory (taste) area, from areas representing the body's internal organs, and from the auditory area, but not from the main areas of the thalamus that process somatosensory (touch) and visual information. Cortical inputs come through the olfactory areas and association areas.

The amygdala's three main output pathways support distinct aspects of emotional expression (Figure 7.7). Some output travels back to the cerebral cortex to

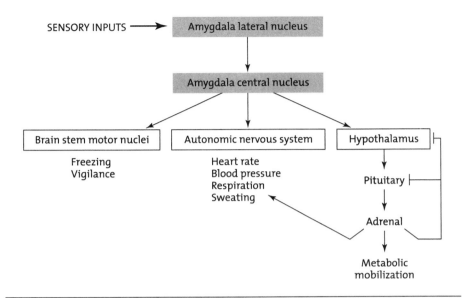

FIGURE 7.8 Output pathways of the amygdala.

support our conscious emotional feelings. A second stream of output is sent to other memory systems, including the striatum, which (you may recall from Chapter 6) is a critical structure in habit learning, and to the hippocampus, which is essential for cognitive memory.

The third set of outputs from the amygdala includes direct control circuits for several types of involuntary emotional responses. These circuits originate in the central amygdala nucleus and involve three streams of outputs (Figure 7.8): (1) projections to the brain stem to generate stereotyped behavioral responses such as freezing and facial expressions; (2) projections to the autonomic nervous system to control the "fight or flight" response that increases heart rate and blood pressure, diverts blood flow from the gut to the brain and muscles, and mobilizes energy stores; and (3) projections to the hypothalamus, which in turn sends neural projections and hormonal outputs to the pituitary gland causing the release of epinephrine and glucocorticoids by the adrenal glands. These hormones stimulate the fight or flight response by activating target organs of the autonomic system.

This complicated scheme supports the correspondingly broad range of responses associated with emotional experiences. Highly emotional states induce several responses, including increases in heart rate and respiration; decreased salivation and digestion; and increased vigilance and freezing.

We still have a great deal to learn about these complicated circuits, but we know that the amygdala is positioned to play a critical role in all the diverse aspects of emotional expression. The amygdala receives both lower-order and complex sensory inputs, and it can influence our thoughts and our memories. It directly supports the expression of emotional memories through a range of involuntary responses.

The Amygdala Is Critical to Emotional Expression

Several lines of evidence have confirmed the existence of limbic system circuits that are involved in emotional expression. In 1937 Kluver and Bucy described an affective disorder syndrome in monkeys that resulted from removal of the temporal lobe. The Kluver–Bucy disorder was characterized by *psychic blindness*: a blunting of emotional reactions to novel, frightening objects. Part of this disorder involved the muting of normal aggressive behaviors, as well as other abnormalities of social behavior. This part of the disorder has been attributed to amygdala damage.

Recent studies have focused on the human amygdala's role in emotional perception (Adolphs et al., 1994, 1995). These studies have measured the capacity of people with amygdala damage to recognize emotional facial expressions, and they included a famous subject (S. M.) with a rare disorder known as Urbach–Wiethe disease. This condition damages the amygdala while sparing the neighboring cortex and hippocampus. S. M. showed a specific impairment in recognizing fearful, surprised, and angry facial expressions. She also had trouble recognizing other aspects of people's emotions but showed no general deficits in language, memory, or perception. S .M. recognized familiar faces, even ones not seen in a considerable time; and she could perceive fearful faces as expressing emotion but did not characterize the expression as fearful. The investigators concluded that S. M. could perceive facial expressions; but due to her amygdala damage, she did not generate responses associated with fear.

These findings are supported by other observations showing that some amygdala neurons in monkeys and humans respond selectively to faces (Heit et al., 1988). Brain imaging studies have shown that the human amygdala is activated specifically in response to viewing fearful faces, although some responses to other facial expressions were also observed (Breiter et al., 1996; Figure 7.9). These data show the importance of the amygdala as a crucial part of a brain system specialized for perceiving and understanding information related to emotion.

The Circuit for Emotional Memory Storage Centers on the Amygdala

The most thoroughly studied examples of emotional memory involve the brain system that mediates fear conditioning, examined by Joseph LeDoux, Michael Davis, and their colleagues. This research focused on specific amygdala circuit elements that support the learning of fearful responses to a simple auditory or visual stimulus. The significant amygdala pathways include auditory sensory inputs via

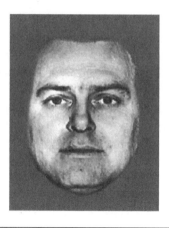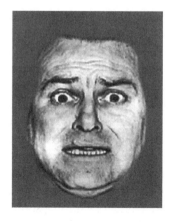

FIGURE 7.9 Examples of neutral (left) and fearful (right) expressions.

the brain stem to circuits through the thalamus or cortex that project to the lateral amygdala nucleus. The lateral amygdala nucleus then projects into the central nucleus, which is the source of outputs to subcortical areas that generate a broad range of fear-related behaviors, including autonomic and motor responses.

LeDoux and his colleagues focused on the input connections to the amygdala (LeDoux, 1992, 1996), examining the role of this circuitry in animals using a tone-cued fear conditioning task. Animals with lateral amygdala damage displayed normal unconditioned autonomic and motor responses following foot shocks. However, in subsequent testing of conditioned tone cue responses, they showed dramatically reduced reactions to the tone—in both autonomic measures (heart rate and blood pressure) and motor responses, in particular freezing. Subsequent efforts investigated whether the auditory lateral amygdala input circuits via the thalamus or the auditory cortex are essential for emotional memory. The researchers found that destroying *either* the part of the thalamus that sends auditory input to the lateral amygdala *or* the entire auditory cortex that projects to the amygdala did not reduce autonomic or freezing responses. However, eliminating *both* these inputs produced the full effect seen after lateral amygdala lesions. Thus for this simple type of conditioning, either direct thalamic input (which offers crude sound identification) or the thalamo-cortical input pathway (which allows sophisticated identification of auditory signals) is sufficient to mediate conditioning.

Additional experiments tried to identify the neural basis of contextual fear conditioning. These studies found that amygdala lesions blocked conditioned freezing responses to both contexts and tone cues. In contrast, hippocampus damage selectively blocked contextual fear conditioning, sparing conditioned responses to tone cues. Combining these data with anatomical knowledge suggests that the full circuit mediating fear conditioning involves multiple pathways to the amygdala

(Figure 7.10). The most direct pathway is from areas within the auditory thalamus to the amygdala; but a secondary path to the amygdala through the auditory cortex can also mediate tone-cued conditioning. Contextual fear conditioning involves a less direct pathway by which multimodal information arrives in the hippocampus and then is sent to the amygdala.

Additional studies by LeDoux and his colleagues have characterized neural representations in auditory pathways to the amygdala. In the parts of the thalamus that project to the amygdala, some cells respond to tones and others respond to foot shock stimulation. Furthermore, some cells that project to the amygdala acquire heightened responses to simultaneous presentation of both tones and somatosensory stimuli during conditioning. Cells in the amygdala's lateral nucleus that receive thalamus input also respond to auditory stimuli; some cells are selective to particular tones, whereas others respond more broadly. Fear conditioning that uses an auditory stimulus, like a tone, as the CS enhances auditory responses of lateral amygdala neurons; cells that did not respond to tones before conditioning begin to respond to tones afterward. These findings, combined with other electrophysiological data described in Chapter 2, suggest that lateral amygdala neuron responsiveness changes may underlie associations between tones and shocks in fear conditioning.

The Amygdala Plays a Key Role in Human Emotional Memory

Research with human subjects has revealed a similar dissociation between emotional and cognitive memory. In a seminal study, Bechara and colleagues (1995) examined three individuals with selective damage to either the hippocampus or the amygdala. One woman was the previously discussed subject S. M., who could not identify fearful facial expressions. She suffered from Urbach–Wiethe disease,

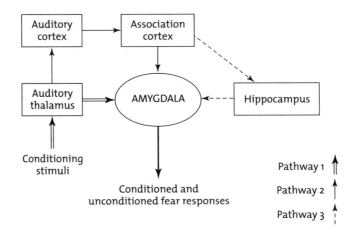

FIGURE 7.10 Circuit for fear conditioning.

a rare disorder resulting in selective loss of the amygdala but sparing the adjacent hippocampus. Another subject in Bechara's study had experienced multiple cardiac arrests that resulted in selective hippocampal damage, sparing the neighboring amygdala. The third subject suffered herpes simplex encephalitis, damaging both the amygdala and the hippocampus.

This study used a form of fear conditioning that involved learning an association between a neutral stimulus and a loud sound (a boat horn) that produced a set of autonomic nervous system responses, previously described in Chapter 1 (see p. 31). As you may recall, all the subjects were conditioned twice: once in the visual modality where the conditioning stimulus (CS+) was a colored slide, and then again in the auditory modality where the CS+ was a pure tone. Subjects were initially habituated to the CS+ as well as to several other stimuli in the same modality (different colors or tones) that would be presented as irrelevant CS− stimuli. Subsequently, during conditioning the CSs in one modality were presented in random order for two seconds each. Each CS+ presentation ended with the unconditioned stimulus (US): a brief, loud boat horn sound. The loud horn startled the participants, producing involuntary emotional responses (UR) including sweating, which was measured through electrical recordings of skin conductance.

Normal control subjects showed skin conductance changes to the US and robust conditioning to the CS+, with smaller responses to the CS-stimuli (Figure 7.11).

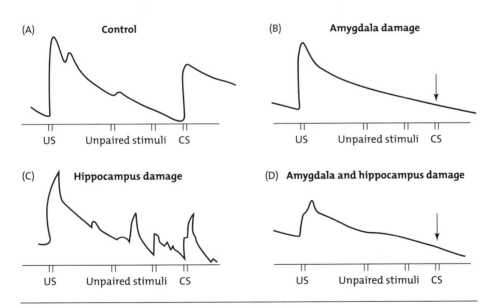

FIGURE 7.11 Fear conditioning in humans.
Each panel shows the emotional responses reflected in increased skin conductance (due to sweating) in response to the unconditioned stimulus (US), the conditioned stimulus (CS), and stimuli that were not paired with the boat horn.

The subject with selective amygdala damage, S. M., showed normal unconditioned skin conductance responses to the loud horn (US) but failed to develop conditioned responses to the CS+ stimuli that predicted when the horn would sound (Figure 7.11B). In contrast, the subject with selective hippocampal damage showed strong skin conductance changes to the US and normal conditioned responses to the predictive CS+ stimuli (Figure 7.11C). This subject also responded to the CS− stimuli but clearly differentiated these from the CS+ stimuli. The third subject with combined amygdala and hippocampus damage failed to condition, even though he responded to the US (Figure 7.11D).

After the conditioning sessions, the subjects were questioned about the stimuli and their relationships (see Figure 1.8C, p. 32). Control subjects answered most of these questions correctly—as did S. M., whose selective amygdala damage seemed to prevent fear conditioning to the CS+ stimuli. However, both subjects with hippocampal damage had trouble recollecting the task events, even though the one with the intact amygdala showed strong conditioned responses during training. These findings demonstrate a clear double dissociation: This form of emotional conditioning is disrupted by amygdala damage, and the ability to remember details of the learning situation is impaired by hippocampal damage.

The Amygdala Is Also Vital in Acquisition of Positive Emotional Memories

The view that the amygdala is essential in mediating stimulus–reward associations is widely held. However, this notion has proven difficult to establish unambiguously in experimental analyses of the effects of amygdala damage. Findings across a broad variety of learning tasks show that amygdala lesions sometimes impair simple stimulus–reward learning tasks—but sometimes they do not. McDonald and White (1993) have suggested that these mixed results may be explained by distinguishing between stimulus–response and stimulus–reward associations. In *stimulus–response learning,* a positive reinforcer increases the likelihood of the behavioral response that has repetitively preceded it. As we saw in Chapter 6, this kind of habit learning is accomplished by procedural learning systems that involve the striatum, not the amygdala. In *stimulus–reward learning,* the reward changes how the subject feels about the stimulus, which can support an increased tendency to approach that stimulus.

To distinguish stimulus–response and stimulus–reward associations in maze learning, McDonald and White performed an experiment with separate groups of animals trained in different versions of the radial maze task. One version was the win–shift task (see Chapter 6), which required animals to remember each maze arm they visited that day and avoid revisiting those arms. Damage to the hippocampus severely impaired performance in that task, but damage to either the striatum or amygdala had no effect. A second version was the win–stay task, which reinforced animals for approaching any illuminated maze arm. In this task, striatal damage caused a severe deficit, whereas hippocampal or amygdala damage had no effect. The third version of the task was a conditioned place preference, in which animals were rewarded while confined in one maze arm and not rewarded while confined in another. In subsequent preference tests, animals with amygdala damage failed to show a normal preference for the maze arm where they had earlier been rewarded, whereas hippocampal and striatum damage had no effect.

This triple dissociation strikingly demonstrates the distinct roles of the hippocampus, striatum, and amygdala in different forms of learning for the same maze and food rewards. In addition (and of particular relevance to the issue of distinguishing stimulus–response and stimulus–reward learning), McDonald and White demonstrated that when animals with amygdala lesions were rewarded for approaching illuminated maze arms, they normally learned to approach those arms. In contrast, the conditioned place preference task avoided conditioning habitual behavioral responses by simply feeding animals in an illuminated maze arm, thus removing the approach requirement. In other words, in this task the positive reinforcer enhanced the attractive value of stimuli independent of any overt behavioral response. The distinction between stimulus–response and stimulus–reward associations was particularly compelling because amygdala and striatum lesions had opposite effects: Amygdala lesions prevented conditioned place preference but not conditioned approach responses, and striatum lesions blocked conditioned approach responses but not conditioned place preference. Thus stimulus–response and stimulus–reward associations are supported by distinct brain systems.

Interim Summary

Emotional learning and memory are supported by the same brain circuits that accomplish emotional feelings and expression. The full brain circuit for emotion is not well understood, but investigators over many years have made substantial progress in outlining several important pathways involving the cortex, thalamus, hypothalamus, and amygdala.

Emotion is accomplished by a circular pathway called the Papez circuit, and a central structure in this circuitry is the amygdala. The amygdala receives sensory inputs from the thalamus and cortex, integrates information within its nuclei, and sends outputs directly to the hypothalamus and brain stem to generate behavioral, autonomic, and hormonal responses. The amygdala, vital to emotional expression, is where inputs from neutral sensory stimuli are associated with emotionally arousing stimuli, thus storing emotional memories. Damage to the amygdala causes deficits in emotional learning in animals and humans even when behavioral or autonomic responses are not affected by the damage. The amygdala plays a decisive role in both positive and negative emotional memories.

Brain Circuits That Support Emotional Arousal and Attention Modulate Cognitive Memory

The amygdala also plays a crucial role in modulating (influencing the efficiency of) the cognitive and procedural learning and memory systems. The amygdala seems to modulate these types of memory in two general ways. First, it influences arousal and attention during learning. Second, it influences the strength of recently acquired memories via hormones that pervade all brain memory systems. These two mechanisms of memory modulation will be discussed in turn.

The Amygdala Plays a Key Role in Emotional Arousal and Vigilance

Emotional arousal and attention during learning are supported by structures in the brain stem and other areas that receive emotional signals from the central amygdala nucleus. These areas project to a structure near the thalamus called the superior colliculus, which controls orienting behavior, and to widespread areas of the cerebral cortex in a pathway associated with vigilance and attention (Figure 7.12). Kapp and his colleagues (1991) showed that neurons in the central amygdala nucleus exhibit rapid changes in firing to conditioned stimuli during fear conditioning, and correspondingly, that lesions in this area block conditioned heart rate responses. In addition to its influence over reflexive responses, Kapp and his colleagues asserted that amygdala activation generally arouses cortical processing mechanisms.

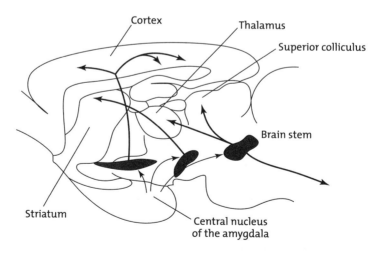

FIGURE 7.12 A rat brain showing the widespread pathways that support emotional arousal and vigilance.
The shaded areas in the base of the forebrain and brain stem receive direct inputs from the amygdala and send outputs to areas that control arousal.

Consistent with these observations, Gallagher and Holland (1994) found that rats with central amygdala nucleus lesions are deficient in acquiring conditioned orienting responses. They initially trained rats to approach a food cup in response to a light stimulus, then paired tone stimuli with the light. Rats with central amygdala nucleus lesions could learn conditioned *approach* responses to visual and auditory stimuli, and they even acquired second-order conditioned approach responses to the tone at the normal rate. However, in striking contrast, conditioned *orienting* responses (rearing on the hind legs and orienting to the light source) were abolished (Figure 7.13). These findings support the notion that the amygdala influences arousal and attention to stimuli, but it does not control behavioral responses to stimuli.

Further studies have yielded additional evidence of the amygdala's essential role in attention during learning. Classical conditioning was used to examine attention shifts caused by changes in what subjects expect following a familiar stimulus (Gallagher & Holland, 1994). Two procedures measured responses to tones and lights, as well as changes in attention to these cues. One procedure involved the blocking paradigm (see Chapter 5), in which pretraining with one stimulus prevents conditioning to a subsequently added stimulus. The reduced conditioning to the added stimulus has been attributed to a lack of attention paid to a stimulus that adds no information. In this study some animals first experienced pairings of a light and food and subsequently developed conditioned expectancy responses to the light. Subsequently all animals were given pairings of a light plus tone and food, then tested for conditioned responses to the tone alone. Animals pretrained with the light alone and food displayed blocking in their diminished responses to the tone alone.

The opposite procedure is unblocking. This process is identical to the blocking paradigm—but during the light plus tone phase, the amount of associated food is changed. This altered amount of food associated with the tone cue adds information and normally results in strong conditioning to the tone. When both normal rats and rats with lesions to the central amygdala nucleus were tested, the lesions had no apparent effect on blocking but prevented unblocking. Combining these results with other studies, Gallagher and Holland argued that a major influence of the amygdala in learning is to increase attention to predictive stimuli.

Distinct Neural and Biochemical Circuits Enhance Emotional Memories

Earlier sections of this chapter discussed how emotional experiences often leave vivid memories. Specific brain circuits and neurochemical bases appear to cause this effect. Recent work shows that affectively charged experiences activate stress hormone production and thus begin a cascade of neurochemical events that influence memory systems (McGaugh, 1996). According to this view, the amygdala is

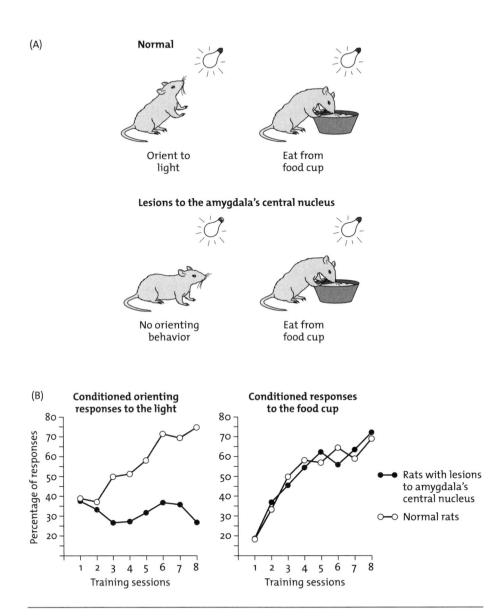

FIGURE 7.13 Effects of amygdala lesions on approach and orientation.
A. Illustrations of orienting (left) response to the light and conditioned (right) responses
to the cup. B. Orienting responses to the light and conditioned responses to the food cup
across training sessions.

a main target of stress hormone activation, particularly that associated with adrenal glucocorticoid hormones and epinephrine. The amygdala, in turn, influences structures including the hippocampus and striatum, whose roles in cognitive memory and habit learning have already been introduced.

Investigations of animal memory facilitation by adrenal hormone activation have focused on a task called *step-through inhibitory avoidance* and posttraining drug injections. In this task a rat is initially placed in a small, bright chamber that is attached to a larger, dimly lit area (Figure 7.14). When a door separating these chambers opens, the rat typically steps through to the larger, dim compartment; the door is closed, and the floor is subsequently electrified. After a brief period of gentle foot shocks, the rat is allowed to escape back to the small chamber. The effect of this training, of course, is to inhibit subsequent entry into the aversive

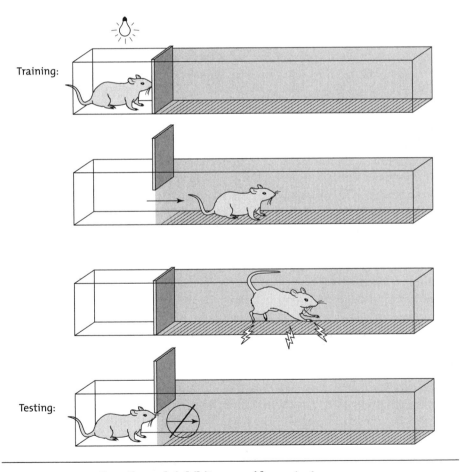

Training:

Testing:

FIGURE 7.14 Step-through inhibitory avoidance test.

compartment. In later tests of memory for this experience, the animal is again placed into the small lit chamber, and the time required for it to step through the door is measured.

Many memory modulation studies involve systemic injection or brain infusion of drugs after this initial learning, which often changes subsequent memory performance. These effects typically require administering the drugs within minutes after training; the drugs have no effect if postponed for an hour or more. Administering the drugs only after the rats' training eliminates the possibility that the drugs are altering perception, arousal, or motor performance during the learning experience. Instead, any effect of a drug given after the learning experience has occurred can be attributed to brain processing that solidifies, or consolidates, the memory.

Extensive evidence shows that certain hormones—specifically epinephrine and adrenal glucocorticoids—can improve memory for inhibitory avoidance, and that these effects are accomplished by the amygdala. In an elegant series of studies, McGaugh and colleagues (1996) revealed some important components of the circuit through which these effects are exerted. Glucocorticoids released during stressful events (or administered by injection directly into the brain in the experimental studies) can directly influence steroid receptors in the brain. Epinephrine does not enter the brain easily, however, so its effects are likely indirect. A strong possibility is that epinephrine stimulates receptors in the vagus nerve, which projects into the brain stem and then to the amygdala. These neurons projecting into the amygdala release norepinephrine (a chemical cousin of epinephrine) in the brain.

The memory-enhancing effects of glucocorticoids are remarkably similar to those of epinephrine, and glucocorticoids' effects appear to be supported by the amygdala's basolateral nucleus. A stimulant drug injected into the amygdala's basolateral nucleus enhances memory, presumably by enhancing the effects of glutocorticoids. On the other hand, lesions of the amygdala's basolateral nucleus block the memory-enhancing effects of glucocorticoids by removing the brain structure they target. Thus converging evidence implies that amygdala storage of emotional memories is influenced by a specific brain circuit activated by stressful events.

But the story does not end there. Stress also affects the intensity of other types of memories besides inhibitory avoidance, as in the flashbulb memory effect discussed earlier; here again hormones and the amygdala play a significant role. Thus although most memory modulation research has investigated the inhibitory avoidance task, studies have also observed that emotional arousal and epinephrine can improve discrimination learning and maze learning. In particular, one experiment showed that these influences extend specifically to memories supported by the hippocampus and striatum. Packard and his colleagues (1994) trained rats in two different versions of the water maze task: one in which learning was cued by a visible marker at the escape site, and another in which the platform was hidden.

Brain Circuits That
Support Emotional
Arousal and
Attention Modulate
Cognitive Memory

249

In previous studies, the same research team had shown that learning the cued platform task depends on the striatum, whereas learning the hidden platform task depends on the hippocampus (Packard & McGaugh, 1992). You may recall from Chapter 6 how rats had drugs infused into the striatum, the hippocampus, or the amygdala, and then after recovery they were trained in a single session on either a spatial or cued maze task. Posttraining hippocampal infusions of amphetamine, which increases norepinephrine in the brain, enhanced later retention in the spatial task, whereas striatal infusions had no effect. Conversely, posttraining striatal infusions of amphetamine enhanced later retention in the cued task, whereas hippocampal infusions had no effect. Posttraining amygdala infusions of amphetamine enhanced retention in both tasks.

A follow-up study examined whether the memory enhancement following amygdala amphetamine infusions happened by means of hippocampal and striatal mechanisms or whether this enhancement required direct amygdala involvement. As in the first study, animals were trained in two versions of the water maze task and then given injections of amphetamine into the amygdala. Before the retention testing, the amygdala was inactivated to keep it from directly affecting retention performance. The experimenters found that inactivating the amygdala did not block the memory-enhancing effects of the injections that they had observed in the earlier study—so the amygdala influenced memory *storage* in the hippocampus and striatum during and after learning rather than memory *expression*.

Additional evidence that emotions can affect different forms of memory, and that this effect is mediated by the amygdala, comes from human studies exploring whether emotional arousal can influence the strength of cognitive memories (Cahill & McGaugh, 1995, 1998). One test discussed earlier used slides to tell subjects two versions of a story (Figure 7.5, p. 232): either a story of a traumatic accident or a control story with neutral emotional content. Recall that normal subjects remembered the emotional component of the story better than the parallel section of the neutral story. The researchers' follow-up study revealed that in contrast, subjects given a drug that blocks norepinephrine (known as a beta blocker) showed no better recall of the emotional story component than of its mundane parts, even though they rated that story component as strongly emotional and their memory for other parts of the story was normal. Memory for the neutral story was not affected by the drug, showing that the drug had no general effect on story memory. A subsequent study has demonstrated that a drug that increases norepinephrine further enhances memory for the emotional component of the story.

Comparing studies of brain-damaged subjects to research with normal subjects has further implicated the amygdala in emotional memory enhancement. S. M., the woman with amygdala damage from Urbach–Wiethe disease, was tested in the emotional story paradigm just described. Compared to control subjects, she failed to show memory enhancement for the emotional part of the story. However, S. M. performed as well as controls on the initial neutral story segment and rated the emotional material as provoking strong feelings—showing that she understood the emotional nature of the material.

Brain imaging studies have shown amygdala activity while normal human subjects view emotional material, and this activation is related to enhanced memory for that material. In one study, during different scanning sessions, subjects viewed film clips that were strong or neutral in emotional content. The amount of activation in the amygdala was greater for emotional films, and memory for the emotional material exceeded that for the neutral stories (Cahill et al., 1996). Furthermore, the amount of amygdala activation was correlated with performance in a delayed test of memory for the emotional films but not for the neutral films.

A subsequent study by Hamann and colleagues (1999) examined amygdala responses in subjects viewing photographs with either positively or negatively charged emotional content, and then surprised the subjects with a memory test a month later. For both pleasant and aversive photographs, the amount of amygdala activation during the original viewing matched subsequent memory for the items. Finally, Kilpatrick and Cahill (2003) further analyzed the data collected earlier by Cahill and his colleagues to examine the relationships between activation of the amygdala and other brain regions. Their analysis revealed substantial influence of the amygdala on the activation levels in areas of the cortex that process emotional material. These data support the notion that the amygdala plays a central role in influencing how the cortex processes cognitive memories.

Learning & Memory in Action

Why Are Posttraumatic Stress Disorder and Anxiety So Difficult to Treat?

Most people have heard about war veterans who, on hearing a loud, startling noise, such as a car backfiring, suddenly begin sweating and shaking, and are driven to take cover as if they were back in combat situations they may have left behind years before. This is a typical example of the symptoms of posttraumatic stress disorder (PTSD). A recent hypothesis about PTSD is that it may be based in an exceptionally strong, maladaptive form of fear conditioning. Anatomical, physiological, and behavioral studies have shown that fear conditioning is rapid and lasting. Furthermore, some of its critical circuits are not cue-specific. So a scenario that could explain PTSD is that in combat, a soldier suffered repeated links between gunfire and the possibility of imminent death. The rapid plasticity within the amygdala formed an association, which served the soldier well in driving him or her to seek cover during subsequent military operations. However, this form of conditioning is both lasting and indiscriminate:

Auditory input to the amygdala crudely codes the stimulus, and that pathway is distinct from the circuit for conditioning to the appropriate *context* in which gunshots were originally associated with a fear of death. The effect of such traumatic experiences on the amygdala has been demonstrated in a brain imaging experiment showing exaggerated amygdala activation in response to threat-provoking stimuli presented to veterans with PTSD (Rauch et al., 2000).

So even long after his or her wartime experiences, when a soldier hears a loud sound that is sufficiently similar to a gunshot, the automatic circuits for cued conditioning from crude auditory input through the amygdala take control. The context, of course, is not right: The soldier is no longer in battle conditions—but context recognition is supported by a separate (hippocampal) pathway. This pathway might tell the soldier that these fears are unfounded, but it does not have sufficient influence to prevent the conditioned fear response mediated by the direct amygdala pathway that supports cued fear conditioning. Indeed, in the brain imaging study just cited, the veterans showed abnormally low activation of the prefrontal cortical area that inhibits the amygdala.

Another way in which the emotional impact of painful memories can go awry is in anxiety and the inability to let go of agonizing memories. Thus people who suffer highly stressful experiences, like assaults or traumatic accidents, often keep returning to the events in their minds, ruminating over what happened and what they might have done to prevent or escape the events. A possible biological explanation may be found in the role of the amygdala and hormonal mechanisms in the enhancement of stressful memories. Thus the stressful aspects of the events enhanced the memories of the painful details—so much so that the memories continue to be recalled at even the faintest cue or absence of other distracting events. One approach to treatment that is currently under investigation is an attempt to ameliorate these lasting effects of traumatic experiences by giving people drugs that block facilitating effects of glucocorticoids and epinephrine on emotional memory consolidation. The idea here is that if the drugs are given before these memories are consolidated, the emotional enhancement of the memories will be reduced.

Interim Summary

In addition to its fundamental role in storing and expressing emotional memories, the amygdala also modulates cognitive and procedural memories. Amygdala activation by arousing events increases vigilance and attention; damage to the amygdala impairs orienting responses and blocks normal increases in attention to stimuli when reward expectancies are altered.

The critical pathway for the modulatory effects of emotion begins with the release of glucocorticoids and epinephrine by the autonomic nervous system in response to emotionally arousing stimuli. These hormones activate the vagus nerve, which projects into the brain stem and the amygdala; there norepinephrine mediates the effects of arousal. The amygdala projects to the hippocampus (where emotional activation enhances cognitive memory) and to the striatum (where emotional activation enhances habit memory). This system modulates memory similarly in animals and humans.

Chapter Summary

1. Emotional learning and memory comprise a distinct memory system that pervades our unconscious lives and supports learning to approach or avoid stimuli independent of cognitive memory and habit learning. At the same time, strong emotional arousal enhances other kinds of learning and memory. We benefit from this system that learns about emotionally important events quickly and strongly; but it can also work to our detriment in the inappropriate expression of strong emotional memories, such as in phobias and anxiety.

2. Emotion and memory interact in multiple ways. Familiarity generally makes us comfortable with known material. We can learn an aversion or attraction to an otherwise neutral stimulus without conscious recollection of previous experiences, as seen most strikingly in amnesia. Emotional events are exceptionally powerful in arousing our memory systems; as a consequence, emotional events are easily recalled, as are their surrounding situations. This phenomenon is especially compelling in flashbulb memories, wherein people have vivid memories of momentous life events.

3. The brain system for emotional perception and expression is complicated; most modern research focuses on pathways through the amygdala. The amygdala is involved in both natural and learned emotional responses. Expression of emotional memories is mediated by several circuits: to the cortex, where memories for emotional events are enhanced; to the base of the brain, which generates arousal; and to other memory systems. Amygdala damage blocks the attachment of affect to neutral stimuli in a variety of tests, including fear conditioning, fear-potentiated startle, conditioned place preference, second-order reward learning, and memory of reward magnitude.

4. Emotional memories can be expressed in a variety of involuntary responses mediated by amygdala outputs. These include outputs to the brain stem nuclei

that control stereotyped behaviors; outputs to the autonomic system, which directs the fight or flight response; and outputs to the pituitary gland, which engages hormonal responses. An additional pathway through the hippocampus is essential for memory of the contexts in which emotional events occurred.

5. The arousal produced by emotional events can facilitate memories of those events. This phenomenon is mediated by hormone release that activates the amygdala to release norepinephrine in other memory systems. Anxiety and posttraumatic stress disorder may reflect overengagement of the memory modulation system.

KEY TERMS

conditioned place preference (p. 226)
second-order conditioning (p. 227)
flashbulb memories (p. 229)

REVIEWING THE CONCEPTS

- What are the unique features of emotional learning and memory?

- Can both positive and negative emotions be conditioned?

- How do emotions influence the strength of cognitive memories?

- Which structures make up the brain circuits that support emotional expression, emotional memory, and the emotional modulation of memory?

- What is the role of stress hormones in the strength of emotional memories?

- What role does the emotional memory system play in anxiety and posttraumatic stress disorder?

PART III

CONSCIOUS FORMS OF
LEARNING AND MEMORY

Cognitive Memory

A 7-year-old boy was walking one day when he was knocked down by someone riding a bicycle; he fell and hit his head on the ground. He was briefly unconscious but otherwise apparently uninjured. Later the boy began to have occasional seizures that were initially minor. However, the intensity and frequency of the seizures grew over several years. Eventually, after he graduated from high school, his seizures became frequent—several minor attacks each day and a major one each week—and he could no longer work as a motor winder. The seizures could not be controlled even with large doses of anticonvulsant drugs, leading physicians to perform an experimental operation in an effort to treat his devastating seizure disorder. The focus of his epileptic activity was suspected to be in the medial part of the temporal lobes, specifically in the region of the hippocampus. To take out the damaged tissue, the surgeon removed the medial part of the temporal lobe cortex surrounding the hippocampus; the amygdala, which lies in front of the hippocampus; and the anterior half of the hippocampus itself. An MRI study later confirmed that the removed tissue included the anterior two-thirds of the hippocampus, as well as the amygdala and the surrounding cortex (Figure 8.1; Corkin et al., 1997).

The operation reduced the seizures' frequency so they could be largely prevented by medication. However, a striking and unexpected consequence of the surgery was a severe loss of his capacity for cognitive memory. When he awoke after the operation, he could no longer recognize the hospital personnel, and he could not learn who they were. His childhood memories and general knowledge accumulated while growing up were intact. But he had lost memories obtained in the several years before the surgery and had virtually no ability to acquire new cognitive memories.

To protect his privacy, this man is known in scientific literature by his initials, H. M.; he is possibly the most studied, famous neurological case study

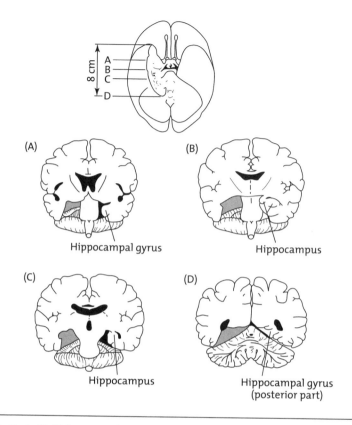

FIGURE 8.1 H. M.'s operation.
The top diagram shows a view of the brain from below and indicates, on the left side of the illustration, the removal of tissue in the medial part of the temporal lobe. The diagrams below are illustrations of sections through the brain corresponding to the levels A through D indicated at the top. In each section, the right side of the drawing shows the normal appearance of the medial temporal lobe structures and the left side shows the areas removed (shaded in gray). Note that the actual surgery involved removal of tissue on both sides of the brain.

ever. H. M.'s case illustrates the nature of amnesia and what life is like without the capacity for cognitive memory. After postoperative recovery, H. M. returned home and lived with his parents. He attended a rehabilitation workshop and became a handyman, successfully performing simple, repetitive jobs. Later he moved to a nursing home, where he participates in daily social activities, watches TV, and solves jigsaw and crossword puzzles. He often solves the same puzzles and reads the same magazines day after day without becoming familiar with the material.

Those who examine H. M. typically remark that within a moment's break in their interactions, H. M. will forget their names, having met them, and all details about any testing that just ended. This author's experiences were no different. My first encounter with H. M. involved transporting him from the nursing home to M.I.T. for some testing in 1980. On the way to the nursing home I had stopped at a nearby McDonald's restaurant and had left a coffee cup on the car's dashboard. I picked up H. M., seated him comfortably in the back of the car, and began the trip to Boston. After a few minutes H. M. noticed the cup and said, "Hey, I knew a fellow named John McDonald when I was a boy!" He proceeded to tell about some of his adventures with the friend, so I asked him to elaborate and was impressed with his detailed memories of that childhood period. When the story ended, H. M. turned to watch the scenery passing by. After a few more minutes, he looked at the dashboard and remarked, "Hey, I knew a fellow named John McDonald when I was a boy!" He related a virtually identical story and answered the same questions similarly. H. M. appeared to have no idea he had just told this elaborate tale. After the conversation ended, he turned to view the scenery again. However, just minutes later, he looked at my dashboard and exclaimed, "Hey, I knew a fellow named John McDonald when I was a boy!" We reproduced the same conversation one more time; then I disposed of the cup under my seat (Eichenbaum & Cohen, 2001).

THE CAPACITY to bring to mind previous personal experiences and factual information, and to use this information to solve novel problems, is called **cognitive memory.** Cognitive memory is what most people think of when they consider memory. Yet cognitive memory is only one kind of memory—quite different from the unconscious learning and memory discussed in the previous chapters. Unlike behavioral memory, which is expressed through changes in our perceptions and actions, cognitive memory involves our everyday conscious remembering of facts and events. In addition, among the most prominent distinctions of cognitive memory is its flexibility—the capacity to generalize across many experiences and employ memories to solve new problems; notably, these properties of cognitive memory are observable in animals as well as humans. Cognitive memory is also characterized by distinct processing stages of encoding memories and subsequently retrieving them.

Fundamental Questions

1. What defines cognitive memory and distinguishes it from the types of behavioral memory discussed so far?
2. What aspects of daily life are compromised in people who lose the capacity for cognitive memory?
3. How can we measure cognitive memory in animals?

Cognitive Memory Is Declarative; Behavioral Memory Is Procedural

This book distinguishes between cognitive and behavioral memory systems. These terms can be applied equally well in characterizing disparate forms of memory in humans and animals. However, various laboratories use somewhat different terminologies for the same phenomena. In human studies, the distinction between *declarative* and *procedural* memory is prominent, mostly because in humans cognitive memory is expressed by explicit (declarative) statements about the contents of memory, whereas behavioral memory is measured by performance of motor or perceptual tasks (procedures).

The terms *declarative memory* and *procedural memory* were originally borrowed from literature about artificial intelligence and applied to human memory capacities (Cohen, 1984). The choice of those terms was intended to emphasize the distinction in computer programs between facts or data that could be directly accessed and routines or processes that could be run to obtain data. For example, solutions to multiplication problems can be found by looking up the answers in a table stored as a database. Each pair of numbers in the database is associated with the specific answer that results when those two numbers are multiplied together. To find the answer, you don't need to do any calculating; you simply check the table or database and "declare" the answer.

Consider the problem $9 \times 5 = ?$, which most of us associate with the number 45 by maintaining a mental multiplication table rather than by working out the problem each time we need the answer. Alternatively, using a procedural strategy to solve the problem, we could derive the solution each time by repeatedly adding 9s five times (or 5s nine times), obtaining the same solution. The distinction between procedural and declarative memory has also been likened to the difference between "knowing how" (procedural), as employed in the acquisition of motor skills, and "knowing that" (declarative), as seen in knowledge of specific facts and events. A key feature of these distinctions is this: "Knowing that" requires conscious direction of attention to the act of remembering, whereas "knowing how" occurs through the performance of skilled actions that does not involve or depend on conscious recollection.

Cognitive Memory Is Flexible and Inferential

A second central feature of cognitive memory is conscious access to memories and the consequent ability to employ the accessed memories in a variety of situations, including novel circumstances. Cohen (1984) characterized the accessibility of cognitive memories as allowing us to compare and contrast information derived from different experiences and to make inferences and generalizations across experiences. This capacity differs considerably from forms of behavioral memory that are typically expressed within repetition of the learning event itself.

How do we measure the capacity to generalize and infer from cognitive memories? A simple, straightforward test of inferential memory expression comes from psychologist Jean Piaget's work with development of cognitive capacities. Among his influential studies of children's stages in developing logical capacities was an experiment in which children first learn a set of premises (exemplars) for comparing items, and then make a logical deduction about the items by combining the premises. For example, the premises might be "Sally is more fair than Sue" and "Sue is more fair than Jane." Based on a combination of these premises, we should be able to deduce that Sally is more fair than Jane. This task is called *transitive inference* because we must make a novel judgment based on learned transitions between premise pairs even though the directly linking item is missing. Piaget viewed this task as a vehicle to study the development of logical thinking. However, the transitive inference task is also a memory test. In particular, it tests the subject's ability to remember the specific premises long enough to compare them, as well as the ability to link them within a network of memories that allows comparisons of all the items.

Systematic studies of transitive inference in children typically involve a larger series of premises that can be linked along a hierarchy. Bryant and Trabasso (1971) had children learn the relative lengths of five colored straws (Figure 8.2A). Each premise was composed of a pair of straws where the children could see only a one-inch segment of each straw until the choice was made. Referring to the straws by alphabetic letters, the children learned in separate trials that straw A was longer than straw B, B was longer than C, C was longer than D, and D was longer than E. The critical transitive inference test was to compare B to D. B and D had each been the longer straw in another comparison, and each had also been the shorter

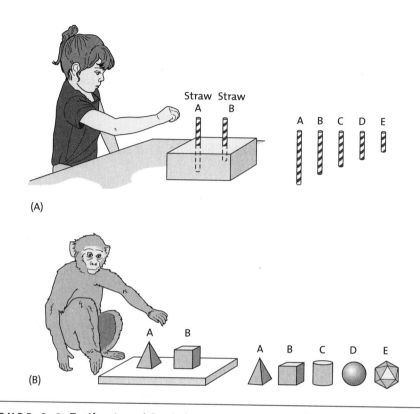

FIGURE 8.2 Testing transitive inference in children and monkeys.

straw in another comparison. So the subjects could not use absolute response values for the straws. Nonetheless, when asked to select the longer straw, children as young as 4 years responded appropriately, choosing the correct straw much of the time. Furthermore, the frequency of trials on which they made the correct inference was equal to the combination of probabilities for the premise pairs B versus C and C versus D. Thus, when memory for premises was accounted for, the children's capacity to compare, appropriately link, and then inferentially generalize to make novel judgments was good.

Do animals have the capacity for inferential generalization in cognitive memory? It seems they do. McGonigle and Chalmers (1977) trained monkeys in a series of pairwise discrimination problems, each involving two differently shaped objects, one of which was heavier than the other (Figure 8.2B). The problems composed the set of premises that involved choosing object A as heavier than object B, B as heavier than C, and so on, much like the straw-length discriminations in the experiment done with children. Following successful training to choose the heavier object in all the premise pairs, the animals were presented with the B versus D pair and rewarded regardless of their choice. The results were remarkably similar to the findings for 4-year-old children. Monkeys were likely to choose B as heavier than D, and the likelihood was predicted by their performance on the premises B versus C and C versus D. These results suggest that relatively simple tests may offer a way to examine animals' cognitive memory.

Learning & Memory in Action

How Do People Make Creative Leaps?

Many "mental leaps" are based on the capacity to use cognitive memory in making transitive inferences. Take, for example, a child who solved the transitive inference problem about Sally, Sue, and Jane. There the logical capacity to make a novel inference about Sally and Jane was attributed to the linking and organization of two premises. Can the same explanation account for creative thought?

One case of creative thinking is the ability to make an analogy—that is, to apply a general rule to new materials that share a common fundamental relationship with the original materials. A good example of thinking by analogy is learning to solve the *matching-to-sample* problem and applying it to new stimuli. In this task, the subject is initially shown a sample stimulus and is then given a choice between two test stimuli: one that is identical to the sample and one that is different. The rule is to choose the test stimulus that matches the initial sample. After initial training in a few problems, children and animals acquire the rule of "sameness" in making the choice and can apply this rule in trials that use completely novel stimuli. Here the explanation might be that children and animals begin by acquiring memories for exemplars of the matching-to-sample experiences. In doing so, they may link these exemplars via their common generic features, including the basic protocol in which a sample stimulus is always followed by a choice test and the sameness rule guides their choice. When presented with a novel sample and test stimuli, they recognize the trial protocol, remember the rule, and apply it to the novel problem. The same explanation can account for a variety of analogical reasoning abilities in humans. For example, the man who invented Velcro attributed his invention to noticing how burrs stick on a dog's fur. Likewise, President Lyndon Johnson thought of how dominoes topple one another in sequence when he described the "domino effect" by which losing a war in Vietnam could cause the spread of communism to Thailand and India (Holyoak & Thagard, 1995). Demonstrations of such analogical thinking in animals in simple problems such as matching to samples suggest that they have the same fundamental ability to conceive abstract relations and apply them to novel exemplars.

Interim Summary

A fundamental characteristic of cognitive memory is our capacity to generalize across memories and use memories in solving new problems. Transitive inference is a prototypical formalization of these characteristics. In transitive inference, we must access multiple memories that share common information, link them via their common features, and then make a generalization in solving a novel problem. Recent studies have shown that animals also have this capacity, suggesting a common fundamental property of cognitive memory across species.

Human Cognitive Memory: Distinct Encoding and Retrieval Strategies

An immense amount of research has delved into the nature of cognitive, declarative memory in humans. Here we will consider some key findings, organizing them by customary divisions between memory encoding, memory retention (or forgetting), and memory retrieval. These events are closely related, and in experimental research we learn about memories only through the success or failure of our subjects at the retrieval phase. But many clever and elegant experimental designs have revealed much about memory encoding and storage as well as retrieval.

Cognitive Memories Are Complex Images Encoded Semantically and Organized within a Schema

Encoding refers to how information is represented in memory. Although many perceptions reach our sensory systems, what we remember depends on how we construct, manipulate, and organize mental representations of that information. Here we consider three key aspects of encoding: imagery, levels of processing, and types of organization.

IMAGERY Imagery is the creation of sensory (usually visual) images of words or other items to elaborate memory content for the items. The ancient Greek poet Simonides is credited with inventing the art of using visual imagery as his primary memory tool to encode large amounts of unrelated information. The sad story of the origin of Simonides's strategy is that he had just left a banquet at which he had spoken when the roof of the building collapsed, crushing the banquet guests beyond recognition. Simonides found that he could recall the faces and clothing of each guest according to where they were sitting in the room; this was the basis of his *method of loci* for remembering lists. He successfully used and taught this memorization strategy of visualizing each list item in a particular place along a route or within rooms of a house.

LEVEL OF PROCESSING How a memory is encoded depends on the level of cognitive processing it receives. The concept of **level of processing** refers to how material is analyzed—from superficial physical qualities of the stimulus to deep levels of its meaning (Craik & Lockhart, 1972). The level at which a stimulus is processed powerfully influences how well the information will be encoded. For example, Craik and Tulving (1975) had subjects study a list of words in one of three ways. The shallowest processing level involved the superficial appearance of the words: Subjects judged whether each word was in capital letters (*FLOOR, mop*). The intermediate level involved phonemic processing—judging whether words rhymed. (Does *FLOOR* rhyme with *MOP?*) The deepest processing level was semantic—judging whether each word fit appropriately in a given sentence. (Does *mop* fit appropriately in "He cleaned the floor with the _____"?) The proportion of words recognized after a delay depended on the level of processing during encoding: Subjects recognized more words after deeper processing (Figure 8.3).

This experiment shows that mere exposure to words does not necessarily lead to memorability. Indeed, Neisser (1982) tells the story of a Professor Sanford who estimated that he had read his family prayers at least 5,000 times at meals. How-

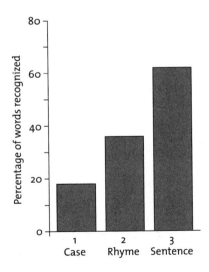

FIGURE 8.3 Depth of processing effect.
This graph shows the proportion of words recognized as a function of the type of processing during the initial study period.

ever, when formally tested, he could scarcely recall the prayers. Another example occurred when BBC radio attempted to inform its listeners about a change in its transmitting frequency. Despite hearing the announcement over 1,000 times, 75 percent of listeners could not recall the new frequency. Interestingly, most listeners were aware of the impending change and could remember its exact date; so even within the same material, some details are processed effectively and others are not.

Further insights about mental activity that supports memory come from studies in which subjects generate material to remember. Slamecka and Graf (1978) had subjects generate for each target word a synonym, rhyme, or associated word beginning with a specific letter. For example, they might ask for a synonym for *rapid* that begins with f (perhaps *fast*) or an associate of *high* that begins with t (*tall*). Subjects were better able to remember words they generated than those they simply read. The depth of processing effect was also apparent in subjects' better memory for synonyms semantically related to the target words than for rhymes, which were more superficially related. A possible explanation for both the depth of processing and generation effects is that greater processing creates additional retrieval routes. Elaborate processing (thinking about words' meanings or associating them with other items) increases the number of associates of target words; when the subject must search for and generate the words, retrieval is vigorously practiced during the encoding phase.

These studies suggest that *intentional encoding*—thinking about word meaning— is superior to *incidental encoding*, which involves thinking about only superficial physical characteristics. But other studies have shown that intent to remember does not really matter. Hyde and Jenkins (1973) asked different groups of subjects to either rate words on a pleasantness scale (deep processing) or to identify whether the words contained particular letters (superficial processing). In addition, half the subjects in each group were told they would be tested for their memory of the words (encouraging intentional encoding); half were told that the judgments were the purpose of the experiment (incidental encoding). Then all subjects were tested for their ability to recall the words. The results showed that intentional encoding alone had no effect on memory. However, subjects better remembered the words they encoded more deeply (Figure 8.4). Thus intention to memorize does not, by itself, improve encoding. What matters is whether such purposeful memorization leads to deeper processing and elaboration, which *do* improve encoding.

So mere repetition does not improve memory. Rather, elaborate processing— creating more retrieval routes and associations—increases the likelihood of later retrieval. An additional issue concerns the timing of rehearsal in memorizing materials. Retention is best when a substantial delay occurs between rehearsals. Thus lots of practice all at once (which many students call *cramming*) is much less effective than the same amount of practice spaced over a longer period. Why? One

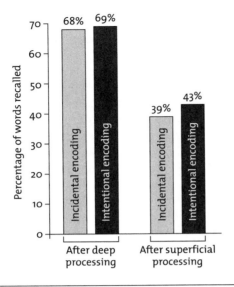

FIGURE 8.4 Intentional/incidental encoding versus depth of processing.

explanation is that greater spacing between study periods allows greater variability in types of associations for item encoding. Thus delays between practice sessions are another way to increase the number of retrieval routes providing access to the target items.

ENCODING ORGANIZATION Encoding organization involves the framework of meaningful connections between items within mental representations. Since the pioneering studies of Bartlett (see Chapter 1), we have known that the encoding of new information is strongly influenced by the **schema**, or prior knowledge structure, of the rememberer. A similar notion is the *script,* which organizes a series of actions into a familiar sequence, such as going to the grocery store. In one famous study, DeGroot (1966) compared the memory of chess masters and novices for board positions selected from real chess games. After brief study, chess masters could accurately reproduce the positions of several chess pieces; novices, however, showed only partial memory and required eight times as much exposure to reach the accuracy of the masters. Later Chase and Simon (1973) replicated this finding, also showing that chess masters recalled no better than novices if the chess pieces were randomly arranged. Apparently the chess masters used their schemata for the appropriate structure of chess to organize their memory for specific pieces. When prevented from using their schemata (when the pieces did not fall into a known framework), the masters recalled no better than novices.

The importance and role of organization were demonstrated in an experiment where subjects read a set of instructions. Some subjects were given an organizational framework for the passage they read, and others read the passage by itself (Bransford & Johnson, 1972). Here's the passage used:

> The procedure is actually quite simple. First you arrange items into different groups. Of course one pile might be sufficient depending on how much there is to do. If you have to go somewhere else due to lack of facilities, that is the next step; otherwise, you are pretty well set. It is important not to overdo things. That is, it is better to do too few things at once than too many. In the short run this may not seem important but complications can easily arise. A mistake can be expensive as well. At first the whole procedure will seem complicated. Soon, however, it will become just another facet of life. It is difficult to foresee any end to the necessity for this task in the immediate future, but then one never can tell. After the procedure is completed one arranges the material into different groups again. They can be put into their appropriate places. Eventually they will be used once more and the whole cycle will then have to be repeated. However, that is part of life.

As you might imagine, subjects who read this passage without an organizing principle, as you've just done, found it difficult to follow and remember its contents. Indeed, subjects who were given no background before reading the passage rated the passage as barely comprehensible. Furthermore, they recalled fewer than 3 of the 18 ideas contained in the passage. A second group of subjects was told after reading the passage that the instructions pertained to washing clothes. However, this did not change either their comprehensibility or memory scores. In contrast, a third group who was told the topic before reading the passage rated its comprehensibility much higher and recalled more than twice as many ideas from the passage. Thus an organizational framework had an impact on memory if it was available at the time of encoding but could not boost memory if provided after encoding.

Implications for Study Strategies

The finding that organization is a key to memory success should help you study for exams. This fact was recognized by William James (1890/1918), a pioneer in the systematic study of psychology who was introduced in Chapter 1. James admonished his students not to simply rehearse the information they heard in lectures. Such repetition, he argued, would only support regurgitation of that information, not lead to diverse associations and creative use of that information in addressing new questions and solving novel problems. James's insights can be joined with the encoding and retrieval features of cognitive memories to offer two suggestions for study strategies.

First, when encoding new information, it is useful to repeat the information; however, such study should not only repeat but also elaborate. Thus, as mnemonists do, try to associate the new information with other related information that enriches the description of the item to be remembered. When you study a name and date, add elaborations about the person and time when the events occurred. Use imagery and think about the implications of this event to encode in depth.

Also, as James emphasized, the elaborated information needs to be not just listed but also organized so that each item is connected with others to which it relates. Do not merely repeat a list of names and dates; instead, look for ways to link them in their historical context so they logically flow from one to the next. Apply an organizational scheme to link them by major themes that are derived from the entire lesson.

These strategies will improve your performance when an instructor asks you to relate information obtained in one lecture to that in another, or to show parallels between information across seemingly distinct domains. These two strategies will help you develop an organized memory to support inferences from your knowledge, much like the examples of transitive inference described earlier.

Retention and Forgetting Depend on Time and Interference

In addition to encoding memories, we also have to be able to retain them for later retrieval. The **retention** of memories (maintenance of information over time) and its opposite, **forgetting** (loss of memories over time), are the subject of much research both as a part of understanding memory and for the practical reason that we would all like our memories to persist longer. Most of this work focuses on the nature of forgetting, for which there are three prominent explanations. The simplest view is that memories' strength may decay as a function of time, making them more difficult to retrieve. A second potential explanation is that new memories may conflict with the information contained in old memories, interfering with retrieval of the earlier stored memories. A third, somewhat similar possibility is that we may lose access to our stored memories if we no longer have access to the cues used for retrieving them. Here we consider evidence for memory decay and interference; the role of retrieval cues in retrieving and forgetting will be discussed in the next section.

The idea that memories decay was investigated exhaustively by Herman Ebbinghaus in his classic studies reported in 1885 (introduced in Chapter 1). Ebbinghaus used himself as his sole subject. In one notable experiment, he learned 169 lists of 13 nonsense syllables (meaningless but pronounceable three-letter strings) and then relearned each list at intervals varying in length from a few minutes to many days. He measured the amount of time required to learn a list for the first time and then measured the time he spent relearning the same list at the test time. By subtracting the relearning time from the time he initially spent memorizing the words, he calculated a *savings* score to reflect the portion of memory retained. Ebbinghaus found that memory decreased rapidly and linearly at first, with a loss of about 60 percent over the initial several minutes. Thereafter the rate of loss slowed considerably: Only another 20 percent loss occurred over many succeeding days (Figure 8.5). Overall the rate of loss is best described as a logarithmic function that Ebbinghaus called the *Power Law*.

This Power Law function that describes the rate of forgetting has stood the test of time and characterizes the retention and loss of memories for a broad range of materials. For example, Bahrick and Phelps (1987) tested university graduates for retention of a foreign language (Spanish) at various intervals after graduation. (Those who used their Spanish frequently after graduation were excluded from the study.) They found exactly the same Power Law function as Ebbinghaus observed, with memory decaying quite rapidly at first, then slowing to approach a nearly constant level of considerable retention for as long as 50 years. Students who had attained greater knowledge while at school retained more memories, but the Power Law function was identical for good and poor learners. Although these studies show that memory indeed decreases with time and that the rate of decay follows a mathematical rule, they do not tell us whether memories are lost. In particular, they do not say whether the performance reduction is a decay of memory strength or whether time allows other processes to intervene.

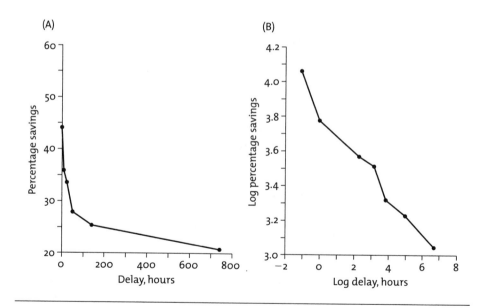

FIGURE 8.5 Ebbinghaus's data on forgetting rates.
The same data are plotted in terms of the amount of information retained (savings) on a linear scale and as a logarithmic function.

Considerable research indicates that **interference**—the processing of irrelevant materials that distract from the intended learning materials, independent of any memory decay—can strongly influence memory retention. There are two kinds of interference. **Proactive interference** involves the negative influence of materials learned before a target item on subsequent memory for the target. For example, focusing on remembering where you parked the car can make you forget to pick up the keys. **Retroactive interference** involves the negative influence of materials learned after the target item on subsequent memory for the target item. For example, looking for the car keys can make you forget why you were going for a drive. In a classic study of retroactive interference, McGeogh and McDonald (1931) had subjects study a list of adjectives. Then, during a delay before testing, the subjects rested quietly, learned unrelated materials, or learned additional adjectives. Subsequent recall was best if the subjects merely rested after the initial study. Somewhat poorer performance was observed if the subjects learned unrelated materials (nonsense syllables or numbers) in the intervening memory period. Retention was considerably poorer when subjects studied other adjectives, and worse when the words had meanings similar to the originally studied items. The standard explanation for retroactive interference, supported by these findings, is that memories of the newer items compete with the older memories and displace or overshadow them.

Proactive interference was documented in studies that observed forgetting of nonsense syllables over relatively brief periods of a day (Underwood, 1957). It seemed unlikely that retroactive interference could explain this rapid forgetting because the subjects were not asked to study other nonsense syllables after learning. Also, it was improbable that they were exposed to such material naturally in the intervening period of their everyday lives. Underwood realized that his subjects had been exposed to many nonsense syllables in previous testing, however, and found that the extent of such prior exposure predicted retention of subsequent lists. Later experiments showed that prior learning can profoundly affect memory for subsequent material. For example, in one study subjects learned three new lists of word pairs every two days, with the test on each list occurring just before they learned the next (Keppel et al., 1968). Memory was good for the initial groups of lists, but performance progressively declined on successive groups (Figure 8.6).

The fact that memories are subject to forgetting and interference provides further suggestions for study habits. First, do not wait to study until the night before an exam. Refresh and update your understanding by rehearsing and integrating new information with earlier knowledge. This is a good way to prevent forgetting and to elaborate and organize your memories. Second, information integration must focus on reducing sources of interference. If, for example, two historical events you're attempting to remember occurred on the same date, this similarity is a potential source of interference. In this case, integrating your knowledge of

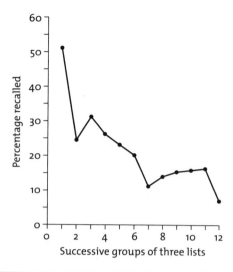

FIGURE 8.6 Proactive interference.
Performance in recall is shown as a function of the number of lists the subjects had previously learned.

the two events should focus on their distinct meanings to help prevent confusion by their common date.

Retrieval: Recall or Recognition of Acquired Memories

Retrieval is the process of searching for and finding a stored memory. It might seem that retrieval depends primarily on how well information is stored. But as we have already learned, memory organization and other information learned before or after encoding can affect retrieval. Studies show that retrieval depends on the use of associations between retrieval cues (including prompts and other cues) that provide access to the target memories.

The distinction between storing a memory and the ability to retrieve it is perhaps best demonstrated in the "tip of the tongue" phenomenon, in which people are sure they know some fact or event but cannot recall it explicitly. Everyone has had this experience; but is it an accurate sense of knowing, or an illusion of knowing? Brown and McNeill (1966) examined this phenomenon by showing subjects dictionary definitions of words. When the subjects could not identify a word but had a "feeling of knowing" the answer, they were asked to guess the number of syllables in the word, its initial letter, and other descriptive information about the word. The subjects were more often correct about these "tip of the tongue" words than about other words for which they reported no sense of vague recollection. In a later study, Hart (1967) asked subjects trivia questions; when they reported the "feeling of knowing" state, they were better at recognizing the answer among several choices presented. These findings show that we can to some extent be aware of a stored memory, even when we cannot access it without further retrieval cues.

Memory retrieval is usually assisted by **retrieval cues:** stimuli available at the time of retrieval that are derived from information that surrounded the target item during encoding. The significant role of retrieval cues can be seen by comparing memory performance under minimal and maximal cuing in two common testing conditions: free recall and recognition. In **free recall**, a subject is given minimal information upon which to retrieve memories—typically merely a request to recall recently studied materials. The opposite extreme condition is **recognition**, in which a subject is shown the item to be remembered, usually along with other items not studied, and is asked to identify whether each item was among those studied. In this condition, the cue is the item itself—obviously the closest possible retrieval cue. An intermediate condition between free recall and recognition is **cued recall**, in which subjects are given a moderate degree of prompting, such as the category of information to be remembered or a part of the item to be recalled. The common finding across many studies is that performance is poorest in free recall, intermediate in cued recall, and best in recognition, which shows that cues are a prominent influence in memory retrieval.

The importance of surrounding information as retrieval cues was illustrated in a series of experiments by Tulving and Thompson (1973). Subjects were asked to study a set of target words along with low-frequency associates—that is, other words only loosely associated with the target words. For example, for the target word *bread, burnt* is a low-frequency associate, whereas *butter* is a high-frequency associate. The experimenters first provided a list of high-frequency associates that the subjects had not studied (like *butter*) and asked the subjects to simply say the first associated words that came to mind. As you might expect, even though these high-frequency associates were not presented for study, they easily brought to mind the target words (*bread*). Then the experimenters asked the subjects to recognize the words they had produced as ones that had appeared on the study list. In this recognition task, performance was poor. Finally the experimenters used the previously studied low-frequency associates as cues to elicit the target words; now the subjects remembered many target words. These results distinguish the memory representations that helped subjects recall the target words when cued by the high-frequency associates from their recall of the target words derived from associations with other words experienced when subjects studied the list. The high-frequency associates prompted target words as part of the subjects' preexisting base of knowledge about those words, whereas the studied low-frequency associates independently prompted target words through associations that were acquired during that specific encoding experience.

Another general influence is the context in which retrieval is attempted. Memories are best retrieved when testing occurs in the same environment or state of the rememberer in which learning originally occurred. A striking demonstration of **context-dependent memory** was reported by Godden and Baddeley (1975) in a study of memory in underwater divers. They were studying divers because a friend who was a diving instructor had noticed that divers typically forgot items they had seen underwater even when quizzed shortly after returning to land. In their formal experiment, Godden and Baddeley had divers learn a list of 40 words either underwater or on land, and then tested them in one of these retrieval conditions. Retrieval performance was substantially better when the divers were tested in the context where their initial learning occurred (Figure 8.7).

Another example of context-dependent memory is **state-dependent learning**, in which retrieval performance of subjects who learn under the influence of a drug or alcohol is typically better when they are tested in the same state of mind. Thus when people study material when they are drunk or under the influence of mood-altering drugs such as marijuana or nitrous oxide (laughing gas), their memory for that material is superior if they are tested in the same drug-induced state than without the drug (Eich, 1980). Similarly, a subject's mood during a test can influence the ability to recall words associated with a particular mood. For example, Teasdale and Russell (1983) had subjects study lists of neutral, negative, or positive words. Then, following induction of a happy or sad state, they asked the subjects to recall the words. Regardless of which mood subjects had been made to feel, they remembered many more words with meanings that matched their mood than words with meanings that did not. The effects of context and retrieval state are much stronger for recall than for recognition. One explanation is that context and state may act as generalized retrieval cues whose necessity is lessened when the target item itself is offered as a strong retrieval cue.

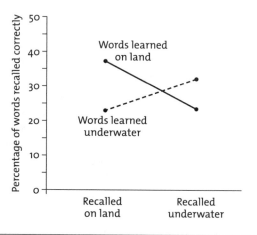

FIGURE 8.7 Underwater divers and context-dependent memory.

This information offers more study strategy tips. Some exam questions may emphasize recognition—such as matching and multiple-choice questions. These are easier as long as they really depend on recognizing the precise materials studied. So a good exam writer alters the test items just enough to make simple recognition based on superficial similarities lead you astray. Other test questions provide just enough information to demand your recall. Do not use such retrieval cues merely to regurgitate the section of a lecture or text that contained the cue. Instead use them to retrieve the network of associations you have studied, and explain how the information retrieved relates to the topic. Also, some students find that they can remember material only in the context in which it was studied—for example, by reading the chapter and anticipating succeeding sections. This will not work for an exam that asks novel questions. So when preparing for an exam, study with someone else who asks innovative questions. This will help you organize your memories and will let you practice answering questions in a format similar to what may occur in a real test.

False Memories Use the Same Mechanisms as Real Memories

Thus far we have seen what studies of encoding, retention, and retrieval reveal about the workings of cognitive memory. **False memories** (claims of remembering events that did not actually occur) can also show us how memories are encoded, stored, and retrieved. Their existence shows that memory failure not only can involve decay or inaccessibility but also can emerge as altered memory. Many powerful demonstrations of memory distortions have occurred both in the laboratory and in more practical environments. One famous study of false memory illustrates the tendency to make deductions about relationships between events not actually witnessed. Bransford and Franks (1971) had subjects study a set of sentences, including the following intermixed among other sentences about unrelated material:

> The ants ate the sweet jelly which was on the table.
> The ants in the kitchen ate the jelly.
> The ants in the kitchen ate the jelly which was on the table.
> The jelly was sweet.

In the subsequent recognition test, the experimenters presented some of the exact sentences that the subjects read and other sentences that included some of the material but also included new ideas from unrelated sentences. In addition, they included some sentences that were logical composites of the sentences presented but were not actually on the initial list, such as "The ants ate the sweet jelly." The subjects performed the same in remembering sentences that they actually read and sentences that were new composites of the same ideas, and their confidence in their judgments was equal for old and recomposed sentences.

Learning & Memory in Action

How Do Mnemonists Perform Their Tricks?

Of particular note in the use of imagery to encode memories are *mnemonists*—people with unusually large memory capacities who use imagery to astounding effect. Among the most remarkable of these cases is a man named Shereshevskii studied by Russian psychologist A. R. Luria (1968). Shereshevskii's capacities were discovered when he was a journalist: His editor noticed that Shereshevskii never took notes but could repeat any instructions or story verbatim without error. In Luria's formal studies, Shereshevskii could accurately commit to memory lists of hundreds of words, long strings of letters, poetry in languages he did not speak, and complex scientific formulas. He retained this material indefinitely and could repeat it forward or backward. Shereshevskii used a superb capacity for imagery and blending of stimuli with a visual or other sensory image. For example, he might describe a particular tone as like "fireworks tinged with pink–red hue" and feeling "rough and pleasant" and "an ugly taste—rather like that of a briny pickle." Shereshevskii was expert at applying the method of loci to encode and retrieve a winding, complicated, and somewhat bizarre route through a complex mathematical formula. There were, however, drawbacks to this otherwise remarkable memory capacity. Shereshevskii's memory was so cluttered with details that he sometimes could not grasp the big picture or sort out important components from superficial ones.

There have been several famous examples and systematic studies of mnemonists (Ericsson & Chase, 1982). Their skill has been attributed to three principles. First, they attach new information to preexisting knowledge to encode information meaningfully, such as associating each item with a room in a house. Second, they organize memories within a structure that links them together, like the relationships between rooms in a house. Third, they practice memorizing information, which allows speedy retrieval searching through their organized memories.

Interim Summary

This overview of encoding, retention, and retrieval processes in cognitive memory converges on a few fundamental features of this kind of memory. Cognitive memory is highly associational. Successful encoding of cognitive memories depends on the number of

Cognitive Memory:
Uses a Circuit of
Cortical Structures
and the
Hippocampus

277

associations created during encoding (depth of encoding). Retention of cognitive memories depends on the number of competing associations created before encoding and during retention (interference), as well as on the passage of time (forgetting). Retrieval depends critically on both specific retrieval cues and the general context associated with encoding. Also, cognitive memories are encoded and stored within a framework of knowledge accumulated prior to the new learning experience (encoding organization). Finally, cognitive memories are those that reach consciousness and can be expressed in tests of recall and recognition, as well as situations that allow inferences from memory.

Cognitive Memory Uses a Circuit of Cortical Structures and the Hippocampus

Studies of amnesic people with specific areas of brain damage have provided a wealth of information about which brain areas are essential for cognitive memory. In addition, functional imaging during cognitive memory performance has provided considerable data about the brain areas involved in cognitive memory. Here we will review some of these findings.

Observations Reveal the Importance of the Hippocampus in Cognitive Memory

One of the most useful ways we have learned about the brain system that supports cognitive memory is through the study of people who have lost that capacity. The most famous of these cases is H. M., the amnesic man introduced at the outset of this chapter (Scoville & Milner, 1957; Corkin, 1984). Formal testing has shown that H. M.'s disorder is highly selective. His impairment is almost entirely specific to memory, as distinguished from other higher-order perceptual, motor, and cognitive functions. His perceptual capacities are ordinary; he performs normally on tests of visual acuity and other perceptual functions. He can recognize and name common objects. H. M.'s intelligence was above average in standard IQ tests before the operation. After the surgery his IQ actually rose somewhat, perhaps because of the alleviation of his seizures. H. M.'s language capacities are intact; he appreciates puns and linguistic ambiguities, and he communicates well and freely.

Also, H. M.'s short-term memory is intact. He can immediately reproduce a list of numbers as long as that of control subjects. His ability to understand and take in pictorial material is unharmed. However, memory deficits in these areas become evident as soon as his immediate memory span is exceeded or after a delay with some distraction. In testing after retention intervals longer than several seconds, H. M. shows almost no memory capacity, as measured by many conventional tests. On the most common clinical memory test, known as the Wechsler Memory Quotient, his score indicates a generally severe memory disorder, and he scores zero on components of the test that assess memory for logical facts from a story, verbal paired associates, and picture recall. Various other tests have shown that H. M.'s memory deficit is global in that he is impaired in every stimulus modality: stories, word pairs, digit strings, new vocabulary words, drawings, nonverbal paired associates, block diagrams, songs, common objects, and object locations. He cannot learn simple mazes, and he fails at delayed recognition of words, nonsense syllables, numbers, geometric drawings, faces, and tonal sequences.

But in contrast to his severely impaired cognitive memory, H. M. has a relatively intact capacity for learning a variety of nondeclarative tasks (Corkin, 1984). For example, H. M. can acquire motor skills at a normal rate. One such test, called mirror drawing, involves the acquisition of sensorimotor skill. In this task the subject sits at a table viewing a line drawing and his or her own hand only through a mirror (Figure 8.8). The line drawing contains two concentric outlines of a star, and the task is to draw a pencil line within the outlines. Errors are scored each time an outline border is contacted. This test may seem simple, but in fact normal subjects require several trials before they can successfully draw the line without errors. H. M. showed striking improvement over several attempts within the initial session, as well as considerable savings across sessions: He consistently made fewer errors on each test. His success in learning this skill contrasted with his inability to recall having taken the test; he had to be shown what to do at the outset of each test day. In addition, H. M. has shown strikingly good performance in a variety of perceptual learning tasks and in verbal and nonverbal repetition priming (discussed in Chapter 4). Additional tests of H. M. and other amnesic subjects with damage to the

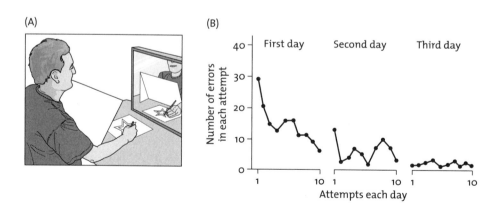

FIGURE 8.8 Mirror drawing by H. M.
A. The subject only sees the reflection of his hand and the star in the mirror. B. The number of errors (crossing of lines on the star) is reduced across successive trials, and this learning is retained across days of testing.

hippocampal region have shown a variety of other intact learning capacities, including intact classical eyeblink conditioning and habits such as the weather prediction task (see Chapter 6) and intact emotional learning (Chapter 7). These studies provide compelling evidence that the hippocampal region plays a crucial and selective role in cognitive memory.

Functional Brain Imaging Shows the Hippocampus Supporting Cognitive Memory

In recent years it has become possible to observe the activity of the human hippocampus as subjects perform cognitive memory tests. These brain images have yielded data that complement the findings from studies of people with amnesia. Whereas studies of amnesic subjects reveal the particular types of memory loss that result when the hippocampus is damaged, the imaging studies show that the intact hippocampus is activated selectively during cognitive memory performance. These studies have provided insights into the fundamental properties of cognitive memory that engage the hippocampus.

In an early brain imaging experiment, subjects studied a list of familiar words and then were tested for implicit or explicit memory of the words while their brains were scanned (Schacter et al., 1996). The implicit memory test presented word stems with the instruction to respond with the first words that came to mind. When subjects correctly provided the previously seen words during performance of this repetition priming test, the hippocampus was not activated. However, higher-order visual areas showed a marked activation change associated with viewing familiar visual–verbal material. The explicit memory test involved recalling the words. Two variations of this task altered the strength of the memory representation. In the deep encoding condition, during initial study subjects judged the words' meanings; in the superficial encoding condition, subjects judged the words' physical characteristics. During the simultaneous memory test and brain scanning, the subjects performed much better in recalling the deeply encoded words than the superficially encoded words (79 percent versus 35 percent respectively), as we might expect from the level of processing effect. Unlike in the priming task, the hippocampus was activated during explicit conscious recollection. This activation was present only during *successful* recollection (the deep encoding condition; Figure 8.9).

Further studies have shown that the hippocampus is especially active when we combine different sources of information for successful recollection. An early study examined whether the hippocampus is activated when we process associations between stimuli; subjects' brains were scanned as they viewed pairs of pictures, each of which included a photo of a person and a photo of a house (Henke et al., 1997). In one condition, subjects were asked if that particular person was likely to

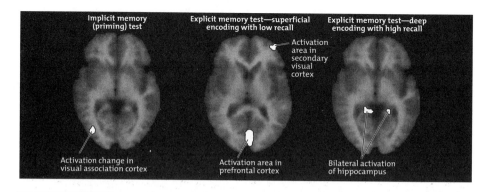

FIGURE 8.9 Hippocampal activation in high- versus low-recall conditions.

be the occupant of that particular house—a question that encouraged subjects to relate the person to the house. In the other (control) learning condition, subjects were merely asked the gender of the person and whether the view of the house showed the inside or outside. This condition did not encourage subjects to associate the person with the house, and recall performance in this condition was poor (28 percent) compared to that of the associative condition (62 percent). The brain scans demonstrated that the hippocampus was much more strongly activated during associative learning than during the control condition.

At the outset of this chapter you read that a hallmark of cognitive memory is the ability to link related memories and make transitive inferences from indirectly related memories. Recent functional imaging studies have shown that the hippocampus is selectively activated when humans use their memories of associations to make transitive inferences for novel questions. In one study subjects initially learned to associate each of two faces with a house and learned to associate pairs of faces. Then, during brain scanning, the subjects were tested for their ability to judge whether two faces that were each associated with the same house were therefore indirectly associated with each other, and for whether they could remember trained face pairs. The hippocampus was selectively activated when subjects made inferential judgments about indirectly related faces, but not during recall of trained face–house or face–face pairs (Figure 8.10; Preston et al., 2004). In another study subjects learned a series of judgments between pairs of visual patterns that contained overlapping elements, as described in the example of transitive inference earlier in this chapter (A over B, B over C, C over D, and D over E). Subjects also learned a series of nonoverlapping comparisons (K over L, M over N, O over P, and Q over R). During brain scanning, the subjects made various transitive judgments between items that required overlapping comparisons (A versus C, A versus D, A versus E, B versus D, and so on) as well as judgments between items from nonoverlapping pairs (K versus N, K versus P, O versus R, and so

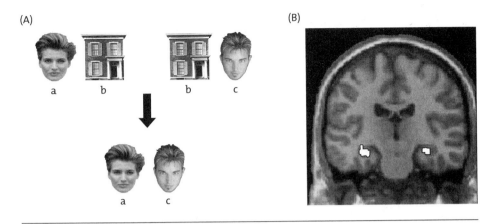

FIGURE 8.10 Transitive inference imaging in humans.
A. Examples of overlapping pairs of face and house stimuli. B. Activation of the hippocampus shown as bright spots in the left and right hippocampus.

forth). Brain images showed that the hippocampus was selectively more active during the subjects' novel, transitive judgments than it was during novel, non-transitive judgments (Heckers et al., 2004). These studies complement the findings for amnesia following hippocampal region damage, showing that the hippocampus is vitally and selectively involved in remembering associations between items and in the flexible expression of those associations.

Interim Summary

The brain system that supports cognitive memory involves the hippocampal region deep in the temporal lobe. Damage to this region causes loss of cognitive memories extending backward and a severe deficit in establishing new cognitive memories. Functional brain imaging confirms the important role of the hippocampal region in cognitive memory. This region is activated during study of novel information, especially during the formation of arbitrary associations and when subjects are linking memories and making inferences from memory—precisely the characteristics of information processing that are fundamental and unique to cognitive memory.

Animal Models Identify the Role of the Hippocampus in Cognitive Memory

Following the case report of H. M. and other amnesic subjects, researchers began to develop animal models of amnesia with hippocampal region damage. The aim of these early efforts at modeling amnesia in animals was twofold. First, our ability to produce selective, circumscribed damage to specific brain regions in animals offers more anatomically specific information about the functions of individual brain structures than the damage that results from human surgeries, accidents, and disease. So we can use animal models to determine more precisely which brain structures are critical to cognitive memory.

Second, to a much greater extent than with humans, investigators can control the nature and extent of animals' experience during learning. Humans arrive in clinics with unique learning backgrounds that differ along many dimensions. In addition, details of an individual's background can be known only to the extent that it has been recorded, and such records are typically vague. By contrast, with animals investigators can dictate all the details of experience they bring to the experimental setting. From the discussion so far, it should be obvious that new learning occurs in the context of previously acquired knowledge, so it is advantageous to know and control the nature and extent of that knowledge. Over the last 40 years, many animal models have been developed and numerous theories proposed to explain the role of the hippocampus and associated areas in cognitive memory. Here a few of the most prominent ones will be described.

Preliminary Studies Suggest the Hippocampus Contains a Cognitive Map

In 1978 John O'Keefe and Lynn Nadel proposed that the hippocampus implements the creation and application of a **cognitive map**—a mental representation of the environment. The notion of cognitive maps had been proposed by psychologist Edward Tolman (1932/1951) as the basis for maze learning in animals. Tolman thought the simple habit learning mechanisms that had been proposed to explain maze learning and other forms of instrumental and classical conditioning (see Chapter 6) were not sufficient to account for all the animals' capacities. Instead he believed that animals were capable of complex mental processes, including the abilities to make plans with expectancies about the outcomes of actions based on those plans. Tolman rigorously tested these ideas, performing several experiments that undermined predictions of conditioning theory. His experiments showed that rats could demonstrate insight by taking a novel roundabout route or shortcut in a maze when such strategies were warranted, even when inconsistent with a previous reward history that favored a different route.

Based on these studies, Tolman proposed that the acquisition of cognitive maps involves a form of cognition distinct from habit formation. Cognitive maps represent places in terms of distances and directions among items in the environment; they are composed as rough representations of the physical environment layout that the animal uses to navigate among salient locations and other important cues. O'Keefe and Nadel (1978) saw cognitive maps as enabling animals to navigate to locations beyond their immediate perception. In addition, they characterized cognitive mapping as a rapid assignment of specific events and landmarks to places within the spatial map. This kind of learning was envisioned as driven by curiosity, expectancy, and purpose rather than reinforcement of specific behavioral responses. O'Keefe and Nadel were first to connect the data about hippocampal function to Tolman's ideas and proposed that the hippocampus mediates cognitive memory, as distinguished from habit learning, in animals as it does in humans.

Compelling evidence in support of the cognitive mapping theory comes from the striking and selective impairment in water maze spatial learning following hippocampal damage in rats. As described in Chapter 6, the water maze task requires rats to find an escape platform hidden beneath the water of a swimming pool. The rats are released into the pool from a variety of starting points and must locate the platform and climb on it to rest from swimming. In initial trials, rats typically require one to two minutes to find the platform. During repeated trials, normal animals rapidly reduce their escape latency; they eventually reach the platform in less than 10 seconds from any starting point.

Morris and his colleagues (1982) showed that rats with hippocampal damage also reduce their escape latencies, showing some extent of learning but never learning to swim directly to the platform as normal rats do. In a subsequent "transfer test" the escape platform was removed, and rats were allowed to swim for one minute with no opportunity to escape the pool. In this transfer condition, normal rats circled near the former platform location. Rats with hippocampal damage showed no preference for the pool area where the platform had been, highlighting the severity of their spatial memory deficit. In a different version of the water maze task, when the escape platform could be seen above the surface of the water (cued navigation), both normal rats and those with hippocampal lesions rapidly learned to swim directly to it. This protocol emphasized the distinction between two types of spatial learning, only one of which depends on the hippocampus. Rats with hippocampal damage could learn to approach the platform when they were guided by a specific local cue. But without an intact hippocampus, they showed no capacity for the kind of cognitive map–based learning that requires understanding relations among distant spatial cues (Figure 8.11).

Powerful complementary evidence comes from O'Keefe and Dostrovsky's (1971) recordings of the electrical activity of rats' hippocampal neurons while the animals explored open environments. Many hippocampal cells increased their firing rates whenever the rats occupied a particular location in the environment. This study and several that followed showed that spatially related hippocampal firing patterns can be observed in many behavioral situations. A clear example occurs when a rat forages for food pellets distributed randomly throughout an open field. The rat continuously searches in all directions for extended periods (Figure 8.12). In this situation many hippocampal cells fire at a high rate only when the rat crosses a particular area, regard-

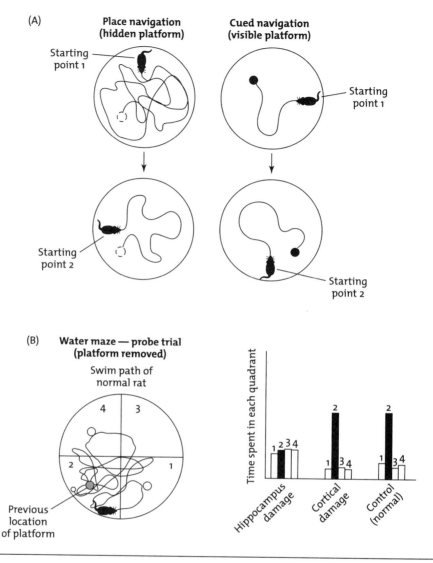

FIGURE 8.11 Morris water maze.
A. Versions of the water maze task. The panels on the left show a sequence of two trials where the rat begins each trial at a different starting location and has to use cues surrounding the maze to find a hidden (submerged) platform whose location remains constant. The panels on the right show a sequence of trials where the platform is visible and changes locations between trials. B. Performance on a probe trial where the platform is removed. Memory is reflected in an increased amount of time spent searching for the missing platform in the quadrant of the maze where it was previously located. The bar graphs compare the amount of time spent in the target quadrant (black) and other quadrants of the maze by animals with damage to the hippocampus or cortex and normal control animals.

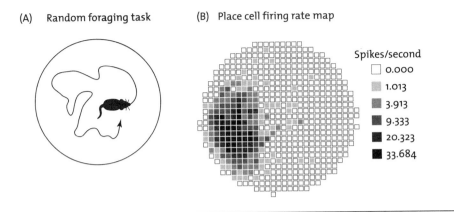

(A) Random foraging task

(B) Place cell firing rate map

Spikes/second

☐ 0.000
▨ 1.013
▨ 3.913
▨ 9.333
▨ 20.323
■ 33.684

FIGURE 8.12 Monitoring a hippocampal place cell in a rat performing the random foraging task.
A. Movement pattern of the rat as it searches for randomly distributed food. B. The firing rates of the recorded hippocampal cell are shown on a map of the area where the rat foraged. Darker shades represent higher firing rates.

less of its orientation within the environment. O'Keefe and Nadel (1978) speculated that these so-called place cells could support cognitive mapping in the hippocampus.

Experiments Suggest a Role for the Hippocampus in Remembering Recent Experiences

In 1979 David Olton and his colleagues proposed an alternative to the hippocampal cognitive mapping hypothesis. He argued that the hippocampus is essential when solving a problem requires remembering a recent experience. He called this *working memory;* but we will not use this term because it now has a different meaning in cognitive and neuroscience literature. In current usage, *working memory* refers to the ability to temporarily hold information *online* while working on that information. As described in detail in Chapter 12, this memory capacity has been tied to the prefrontal cortex rather than the hippocampus. The kind of memory Olton described was more complex: It involved recalling information obtained in a single experience and retaining and using it after a delay of many minutes, even when additional experiences occurred during the delay. Olton and his colleagues distinguished this kind of memory from *reference memory,* which he characterized as memory for information that is useful across all experiences. For a rat in a maze, such reference information includes notions that food rewards are at the ends of maze arms, that the rewards are not replaced as soon as they are eaten but are often replaced between trials, and the like. On a conceptual level Olton described his theory as similar to Tulving's (1983) distinction between *episodic memory* for events tied to a specific time and place, as contrasted with *semantic memory* for knowledge that is time and event independent. Indeed, given that the latter distinction currently predominates over the working/reference memory distinction, it is more appropriate to characterize Olton's notion of hippocampus-dependent memory as memory for unique episodes.

The Olton evidence was generated by experiments with the radial arm maze and the T-maze (see Chapter 6). Olton and his colleagues (1979) compared performance of normal rats and rats with hippocampal damage in a version of the radial maze task that tested memory for different maze arms with distinct reward associations (Figure 8.13). Some maze arms were baited once during each trial, requiring the rats to remember their specific experiences during that test session to avoid repeat visits to those maze arms. Other arms were never baited, requiring rats to learn across sessions not to enter those arms at all. The latter capacity is another example of reference memory emphasizing the fixed stimulus–response associations for these arms. Normal animals perform at high levels on both task components. In contrast, rats with hippocampal damage performed well only in the reference memory component of the task, learning over several trials which arms were never baited. But these rats never performed at better than chance levels, even with extended training, in learning not to revisit baited arms during a single trial. That is, they were unable to learn by remembering their specific experiences. In other experiments, Olton and his colleagues (1979) showed the same selective role of the hippocampus in memory for specific experiences within a T-maze and in tests with nonspatial stimuli.

Recent Evidence Converges on the Relational Memory Account of Hippocampal Function

Intense debate has focused on different predictions and results from experiments testing the cognitive mapping theory and the working/reference memory theory.

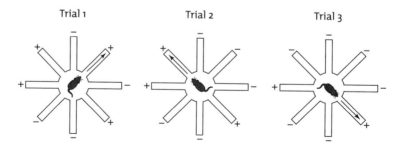

FIGURE 8.13 Radial maze task.
At the outset of testing four of the arms are baited with food (+ signs) and four are not baited (− signs). Across successive trials, the rat can collect a reward only once from each of the baited arms.

One way to interpret these studies' findings together is to consider them as differentially emphasizing fundamental features of episodic and semantic memory.

A cognitive map is a prototypical example of semantic memory. Cognitive maps contain knowledge about the spatial structure of the environment accumulated over many individual episodes. They represent the spatial relationships among cues in the environment, and this structure can be used for navigational inferences. This view of cognitive mapping was highlighted in a study by Eichenbaum and colleagues (1990) demonstrating that rats with hippocampal damage could learn to swim to a particular location in a water maze if they were trained incrementally to take a habitual path from the same constant starting point in each trial. However, the rats with hippocampal damage still differed from normal animals in how they used this learning. Whereas normal animals could use that training to navigate from various new starting points, animals with hippocampal damage could not generalize and apply what they had learned to other routes (Figure 8.14). These findings suggest that the hippocampus links mental representations of different routes to form a memory network of paths through the maze. Like a map, this network allows the animals to navigate via novel routes; that is, it supports flexible memory expression. Without a hippocampus, animals can use only their intact habit learning system to navigate to the platform using the single route (or series of responses) they have been taught.

So what do we make of Olton and colleagues' findings indicating a selective role for the hippocampus in memory for specific experiences? And how do we merge these findings with the essential role of the hippocampus in spatial memory and the phenomenon of place cells? A primary feature of the working/reference memory theory is that the hippocampus is involved in remembering specific prior maze experiences. Recordings from hippocampal place cells have provided evidence that the hippocampus represents individual experiences in a maze (Wood et al., 2000). In this experiment rats performed a T-maze alternation task that depended on memory of the most recent experience. Each trial commenced when the rat traversed the T stem and then selected either the left or right arm (Figure 8.15). To alternate successfully, the rats had to distinguish between their left-turn and right-turn experiences and use their memory of the most recent previous experience to guide the current choice. As animals performed the task, electrodes monitored the activity of hippocampal neurons; as in the previous studies, many neurons were place cells that fired only when the animal traversed a particular location in the maze. An interesting finding of this study was that the firing patterns of many place cells depended on whether the rat was in the midst of a left- or right-turn episode, even when the rat was moving through the central stem of the maze. Other place cells fired when the rat was at a certain point in the maze stem, regardless of which way the animal was about to turn. Thus the hippocampus encoded both the left-turn and right-turn experiences using distinct representations—and even distinct neurons—for each type of episode. The hippocampal memory for this task also included common elements of the maze expe-

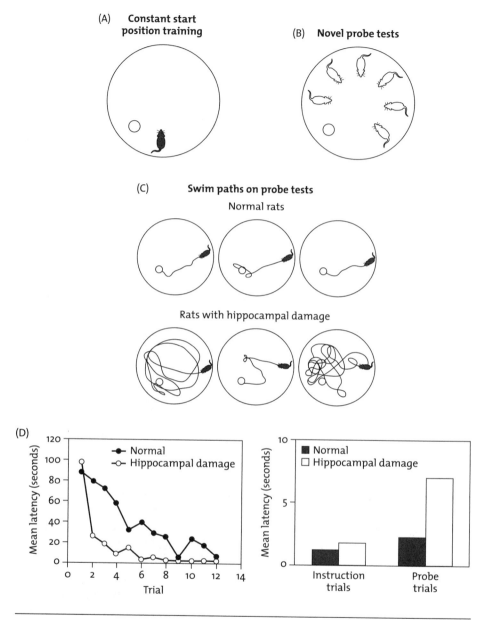

FIGURE 8.14 Water maze learning from a single start point and navigation.
A. The rats are initially trained with several trials always starting from the same
location. B. Subsequently, knowledge of the location of the escape platform is probed
with the rat starting once from each of several new locations (indicated by rat
outlines). C. Swim paths of three normal rats and three rats with hippocampal damage
starting from the location on the right side of the maze. D. Average performance in
learning from the constant starting point (top) and on repetitions of the instruction
trials and the probe trials.

*Animal Models
Identify the Role of
the Hippocampus in
Cognitive Memory*

289

FIGURE 8.15 Firing patterns of a hippocampal neuron and hypothetical representation of memories guiding performance on T-maze alternation.
Circles indicate that each cell fires when the rat is in a particular place and moving in a particular direction. As a group, the neurons represented by light gray circles fire during a left-turn trial, and the neurons represented by medium gray circles fire during a right-turn trial. Some cells, indicated by dark gray circles, represent places common to both types of trials; these could link the representations for left- and right-turn trials.

rience that could link right-turn and left-turn trials, and these commonalities were also represented in a distinct set of neurons.

These observations suggest that place cells are not elements of a static map. Rather, their activity reflects the encoding and retrieval of a specific path through the environment. Furthermore, representations of place sequences appear to be linked by representations of places that are common to multiple types of experiences. The combination of episode-specific representations and linking elements could constitute the basis of the sort of systematic network of memories William James long ago suggested as the basic framework of conscious memory (see Chapter 1).

Relational Memory Accounts for Flexible Memory Expression

The findings discussed so far indicate that the hippocampus supports the creation and flexible use of memory networks to solve maze problems. Can memory networks supported by the hippocampus also be employed to solve other kinds of learning and memory problems? Two related studies show that the hippocampus plays a similar role in both animals and humans: It supports the creation and flexible expression of memory networks for nonspatial as well as spatial information. One study compared the abilities of normal rats and rats with hippocampus dam-

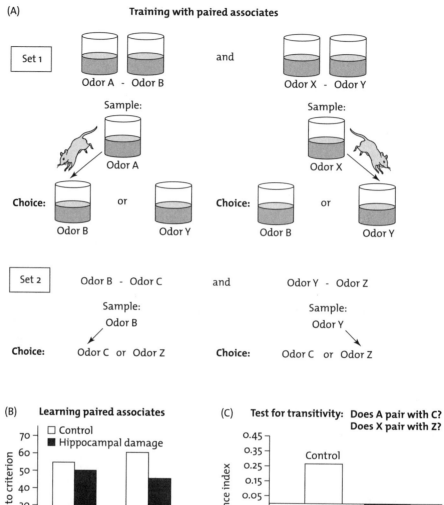

(A) **Training with paired associates**

Set 1

Odor A - Odor B   and   Odor X - Odor Y

Sample: Sample:

Odor A   Odor X

Choice: Odor B   or   Odor Y   **Choice:**   Odor B   or   Odor Y

Set 2   Odor B - Odor C   and   Odor Y - Odor Z

Sample: Sample:
Odor B   Odor Y

Choice: Odor C or Odor Z   **Choice:**   Odor C or Odor Z

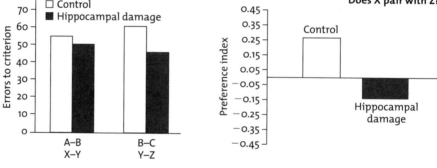

(B) **Learning paired associates**

☐ Control
■ Hippocampal damage

Errors to criterion

(C) **Test for transitivity: Does A pair with C?
Does X pair with Z?**

Preference index

Control

Hippocampal
damage

FIGURE 8.16 Associative transitivity.
A. Design of the experiment. In Set 1, animals are initially trained on two paired
associates (A–B and X–Y). Then in Set 2, they are trained on a second set of two paired
associates with overlapping elements (B–C and Y–Z). B. Animals with hippocampal
damage make no more errors than control subjects do in learning the paired associates.
C. Control rats show strong transitivity as a positive preference for the indirectly
associated odors, whereas rats with hippocampal damage show no transitivity (a
negative preference).

age to learn associations between pairs of odors and to link these representations via common elements to support novel inferential judgments (Bunsey & Eichenbaum, 1996; Figure 8.16). Animals were initially trained to associate pairs of odor stimuli with one another. Initially they learned to associate odor A with odor B and odor X with odor Y. Then they were trained with a second set of paired associates, and this time each association involved an element that was common to the previous pairings: B with C and Y with Z.

Normal rats and those with hippocampal damage all learned the paired associates rapidly. Then the rats were given probe tests to determine whether they organized their representations of the four odor pairs into a network that interleaved overlapping odors or whether they simply learned each problem independently. The probes assessed the capacity for transitive inference, precisely as described earlier in humans. In the scheme here, representations of the pairs A–B and B–C could be organized into a larger network, A–B–C, which should support transitive association of A with C; similarly, X–Y and Y–Z could be organized into X–Y–Z, which should support transitive association of X with Z. In the probe test, normal rats showed strong transitivity; but rats with selective hippocampal lesions were impaired, showing no evidence of transitivity.

An additional experiment (Dusek & Eichenbaum, 1997) has shown that rats can also learn a hierarchical series of odor judgments. That is, they can choose A over B, B over C, C over D, and D over E—and when tested for transitive inference, demonstrate the appropriate choice of B over D. Rats with hippocampal damage can learn the basic premises (A over B and so forth) but do not display transitivity. The combined findings from these studies show that rats with hippocampal damage can learn even complex associations, such as those in the paired odor associates. But unlike normal animals, they do not interleave the overlapping elements of these distinct experiences to form a networked representation that supports inferential, flexible expression of their memories. These animal models clarify the central and general role of the hippocampus in fundamental information processing features of human cognitive memory (Eichenbaum et al., 1999).

Interim Summary

Substantial evidence indicates that animals, like humans, have the fundamental information processing abilities that characterize cognitive memory and that the hippocampus plays a vital role in this capacity. Studies of spatial memory (a good example of cognitive memory) show that animals rapidly learn and easily remember where important events occur, and they can use these memories flexibly to navigate according to expectancies about those events. Also, hippocampus neurons are activated when animals occupy particular locations in the environment. In addition, animals can remember nonspatial information from single episodes and can link nonspatial memories and express this memory organization through transitive inference. Recordings of animals' hippocampal neurons show that the hippocampus creates networks of spatial and nonspatial memories that encode and link memories into a systematic network accessible for flexible memory expression.

Chapter Summary

1. Cognitive memory, which can be distinguished qualitatively from behavioral memory, is our everyday memory for facts and unique personal events. Unlike behavioral memory, it is declarative, accessible to consciousness, and can be expressed explicitly and flexibly in varied situations other than repetition of the learning event. Cognitive memory is supported by a different brain system than perceptual learning, conditioning, habit acquisition, or emotional learning. Cognitive memory exists in animals as well as in humans and depends on the same brain system across species.

2. Encoding of cognitive memories can be accomplished by imagery—especially spatial imagery. Such encoding is facilitated by deep processing of items' meanings, rather than superficial processing of items' physical characteristics. Encoding of cognitive memories also depends on the schematic framework in which new information is represented.

3. Retention of cognitive memories diminishes according to a Power Law. Although memory may decay directly, compelling evidence implies that interference is the primary determinant of whether memories will last or be forgotten. Proactive interference prevents distinctive encoding, whereas retroactive interference diminishes useful retrieval routes.

4. People are often aware of having particular memories even when they cannot retrieve the details. Successful memory retrieval depends on retrieval cues, which are primarily formed as associates of the items during encoding. Retrieval is most successful in recognition, less so in cued retrieval, and most difficult in free recall—corresponding to the number of retrieval cues available in these conditions. Retrieval also depends on reinstatement of the encoding context. Retrieved memories are not exact copies of the encoded information; rather, they are reconstructed, making them prone to false retrieval by appropriate cuing.

5. The brain system that mediates cognitive memory involves the hippocampus and its connected cortical regions. Much of what we understand about the role of the hippocampus in memory comes from studies of human amnesia following hippocampal damage. Such damage causes a selective and severe deficit in the permanent storage of cognitive, declarative memories while preserving perceptual, motor, and

cognitive performance; working memory; memories obtained long before the hippocampal damage; and a variety of nondeclarative memory capacities. Functional brain imaging has shown that the hippocampus is activated selectively during encoding and retrieval of cognitive memories—particularly memory that involves associations between items and the declarative and flexible expression of associations.

6. Animal models prove that animals are capable of cognitive memory and have informed us about the specific role of the hippocampus itself in the basic information processing features of cognitive memory. Investigations of cognitive mapping have demonstrated a significant role of the hippocampus in encoding spatial relationships and flexible expression of spatial memories, capturing the fundamental role of the hippocampus in linking memories. Other work has shown that the hippocampus is also important in memory for specific spatial and nonspatial experiences. Such research has converged on a general model in which the hippocampus encodes the flow of events and the places where they occur and links those experiences into a relational memory network. The next chapters will elaborate the nature of components of the cognitive memory system.

KEY TERMS

cognitive memory (p. 259)

encoding (p. 264)

imagery (p. 264)

level of processing (p. 265)

schema (p. 267)

retention (p. 269)

forgetting (p. 269)

interference (p. 271)

proactive interference (p. 271)

retroactive interference (p. 271)

retrieval (p. 272)

retrieval cues (p. 273)

free recall (p. 273)

recognition (p. 273)

cued recall (p. 273)

context-dependent memory (p. 274)

state-dependent learning (p. 274)

false memories (p. 275)

cognitive map (p. 282)

REVIEWING THE CONCEPTS

- Why is cognitive memory called *declarative* while behavioral memory is called *procedural*?

- How are cognitive memories encoded, retained, and retrieved?

- What is the evidence from human studies indicating that the hippocampus plays a central and selective role in cognitive memory?

- What is the role of the hippocampus in animals' memories?

9

Episodic Memory

Y ou, like almost everyone, have probably had the experience of meeting someone on the street, feeling you know him, and not being able to recall who he is. You see the person and recognize the face as familiar, but the memory doesn't click. Who is he? He waves and says your name. You wave back, but you can't return more than a weak hello. You feel embarrassed. He is substantially older than you. Is he a family friend? But then what is he doing on your college campus? He initiates a conversation: "How's it going?" That question does not tell you much. Because you can't remember how you know him, you are not sure what he knows about you. His face is familiar, and his voice, too, but the memory just won't come. You simply answer, "Fine," deflecting the question, and return with a generic but interested "And how are you today?" He responds, telling about his heavy workload and giving you a clue: "Class seems more difficult every year." OK, he is a professor! He must have been your instructor, but in which class? You now have enough information to ask a more leading question: "Really, I thought our group had to be the most challenging to teach. What do you think has changed?" The professor describes how the upcoming elections complicate his lectures about current events, and you realize that he was your lecturer in political science your freshman year. Now you can recall liking that class and its relevance to your thoughts about society. Some of his lectures were fascinating, and you remember talking with your classmates about what a good speaker he is. You even remember his name—just in time to say, "Nice seeing you again, Professor Jones!" at the last moment.

THIS ANECDOTE CAPTURES the focus of this chapter: **episodic memory,** which is our capacity to consciously recollect specific past events. Episodic memory contrasts with **semantic memory**—accumulated knowledge that is not tied to any particular event but is also subject to conscious recollection. The story emphasizes the difference between **familiarity** (the sense of knowing that a stimulus or situation has been previously experienced) and **recollection** (the ability to bring to consciousness the circumstances of the previous experience). Familiarity is closely bound to the perceptual qualities of a stimulus; recollection, on the other hand, incorporates the meaning of a stimulus, the context in which it was encountered, and many associations of the stimulus that give rise to a vivid reminiscence of the previous event. In this chapter we will consider the nature of episodic memory and the brain system that supports it.

Episodic memory and semantic memory are generally viewed as two components of cognitive memory—our capacity to consciously recollect everyday facts and events. This chapter will further elaborate this distinction, providing a detailed characterization of episodic memory that incorporates (1) the subjective aspects of how we *experience* remembering our personal past and (2) the contents of episodic memories—that is, *what* we remember, distinguishing between the contents of memories involved in recollection and familiarity. We will also consider evidence that the hippocampus plays a special role in episodic memory in both humans and animals.

Fundamental Questions

1. What are the fundamental characteristics of episodic memory? How does it differ from familiarity and semantic memory?
2. Do animals have episodic memory? How can we find out?
3. What specific brain areas support episodic memory?

Defining Episodic Memory

Endel Tulving (1983; see Tulving & Markowitsch, 1998) introduced the distinction between episodic and semantic memory; he began by acknowledging several commonalities of these forms of memory. He emphasized that both are complex, involve diverse kinds of information, and are characterized by rapid encoding of vast amounts of new information. Both abstractly represent information and can be accessed flexibly and used inferentially. All of these qualities distinguish both episodic and semantic memory from behavioral memory. At the same time, episodic memory and semantic memory have major differences. Episodic memory records events and episodes relevant to our personal lives, whereas semantic memory includes general truths, beliefs, ideas, and concepts about the world. Episodic memory is experiential; semantic memory is factual.

Consistent with these characterizations, episodic memory is more sensitive to the context in which specific information is learned. Episodic memories are stored with the knowledge of when and where they are acquired, whereas semantic memory is not bound to the place or other aspects of the context in which knowledge was gained. Episodic memory associates what happened during a specific experience, when it happened, and where it happened. In the example presented at the outset of this chapter, your early awareness that the person was someone you knew could reflect semantic memory because that knowledge was not bound to a particular meeting or its associations. In contrast, your eventual recovery of the what, where, and when information about your previous experiences with your political science professor displays the contents of episodic memories.

Focusing further on the issue of *when,* Tulving directly contrasted episodic and semantic memory in terms of their representations of time. He asserted that episodic memory has a temporal organization: It captures the flow of events in time, and knowledge within episodic memory incorporates the occurrence order of events. Thus in a typical example of a vivid episodic memory for your morning today, you can recall how you awoke, what you dressed in, what you had for breakfast, how you came to campus, and so forth—in other words, the unique events of this day that occurred in a particular order. In contrast, semantic memory is conceptual and not bound to any time of occurrence. Semantic memory contains information like where you live, what kinds of things people generally eat for breakfast, and how college works. It is not specifically concerned with any particular day in your class schedule.

More recently Tulving (2002) has increased his emphasis on the distinction that episodic memory involves *remembering* specific personal past experiences, whereas semantic memory involves simply *knowing* impersonal facts independent of recollecting where these facts were accrued. This characterization focuses on what he calls the *autonoetic* component of episodic memory: the awareness of personal experience that involves yourself as the central feature in the memory. Episodic memories are defined by being experienced—or more properly, reexperienced. Thus Tulving characterizes episodic memory as "mental time travel." He assumes that the capacity for episodic memory is predicated on an ability to perceive subjective time, the feeling of time passing and knowledge of times past, and the notion that there will be events in the future. As such, episodic memory is a fundamental part of our sense of subjective time. This temporal property of episodic memory contrasts with semantic memory's *noetic* property, or simply the conscious knowing of facts. This difference between episodic and semantic memory has created the "remember versus know" distinction central to many current investigations of episodic memory.

Autobiographical Memory

Based on this definition of episodic memory, it would seem that memory of your personal history is an especially good example of episodic memory. However, your autobiography contains both specific events (your first kiss) and factual information for which you do not remember the event (your birth date). This suggests that autobiographical memory may be an independent category of memory. Is there a special store for the memories of your own life? The idea that one's autobiography can be separated from other memories, and selectively lost following trauma, is a central plot in some movies. For example, in the action thriller *The Bourne Identity*, a key premise is that the protagonist Jason Bourne loses all memory of who he is and of his personal life after he is shot and left floating in the sea. Notably, even though he does not know the source of any of his knowledge, he remembers several languages that he speaks fluently, retains information about the geography of Europe, and reveals many skills and much knowledge about how to be a spy.

Autobiographical memory includes factual information that is not bound to any particular experience, such as one's name, place of birth, and other personal data. But most studies of autobiographical memory focus on personal memories of events, such as one's high school graduation, first date, and specific adventures or unique experiences. What kinds of information do we remember about our personal lives? And are personal memories psychologically different from episodic memories of impersonal events, such as your recalling the events in a movie you watched last night?

Some studies have used diaries to examine the nature of information remembered in autobiographical memories. In these studies, people record the events of each day, then are later tested to see what they remember about those events. A particularly well-known example is the study of Marigold Linton (1975), who kept a diary of 5,500 events over six years. Her analyses led to the conclusion that personal memories are most vividly recalled for unique and particularly emotional events. One problem with this approach is that subjects may preferentially record events that are unique or emotional. However, in another experiment students kept diaries of their roommates' experiences; both the students keeping the diaries and the roommates themselves showed better memory for unique and emotional events (Thompson, 1982). A clever study designed to prevent preferential recording of particular kinds of events used pagers that sounded at random times to direct subjects to record the experiences they were engaged in whenever they were paged (Brewer, 1988). The results of this study supported the earlier researchers' conclusions: Unique and emotionally charged events were recalled best. Perhaps unique events are less subject to interference from similar experiences, and the enhanced memory for emotional events may be based on the flashbulb memory effect (an especially vivid memory for highly emotional events; see Chapter 7). These interpretations suggest that autobiographical memories are subject to the same influences as other episodic memories.

On the other hand, some evidence suggests that autobiographical memories may, in fact, have unique features. Studies using specific words like *accident* or *birthday* to cue subjects to recall life events have revealed an interesting difference between the retention of autobiographical memories and impersonal episodic memories. The distribution of dates when remembered experiences occurred is not predicted by the linear Power Law function describing forgetting rates that was outlined by Ebbinghaus (see Chapter 8). Instead these studies show a complex picture of autobiographical memories across the lifespan (Figure 9.1). Few people have any memories from the first two years of life, and most have little memory of their first five years. This phenomenon is called *childhood amnesia*. Over the next several years, from the ages of about 5 to 20, memories increase before a decline ensues. The relatively high number of memories for the period of life surrounding ages 20–30 is called the *reminiscence bump* (Rubin & Schulkind, 1997). Some have suggested that the unusually high rates of memory storage during this period have to do with the many identity-defining "firsts" that occur between the ages of 15 and 25, but the exact reason remains unclear.

Although people are generally not good at remembering actual dates of specific autobiographical memories, they can usually order a series of life events. It is common to use temporal cycles, such as semesters or seasons, to organize a

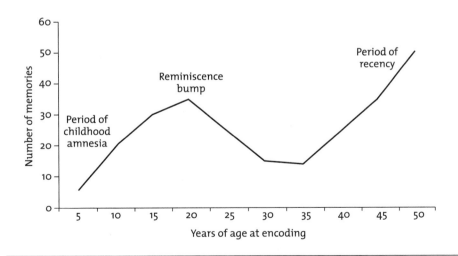

FIGURE 9.1 Distribution of memories across the lifespan for a person approximately 50 years old.
The period of recency covers memories encoded during the most recent 5 to 10 years.

series of episodes. People also use temporal landmarks, such as graduations, births, or beginnings of jobs, to recall the timing of more minor events in terms of what occurred before and after those landmarks. Another factor that distinguishes autobiographical memories is the role they play in our lives. Our identities are defined and bolstered by what we remember about our experiences. So we often relate stories about our past experiences to others, and the vividness of personal memories is influenced by such motivation to recall and by the practice and rehearsal of memories that comes with telling life stories. Thus while autobiographical memory has unique properties, it also seems to be subject to the same rules of interference, association, and emotional enhancement that influence the strength and quality of cognitive memory in general.

Interim Summary

Endel Tulving introduced the distinction between episodic memory (our capacity to replay in mind specific personal experiences) and semantic memory (our general knowledge about people and things and a sense of familiarity for previously experienced stimuli). Episodic memory is characterized in humans by our subjective sense of having experienced an event before and our ability to travel back mentally in time and relive the experience. Such memories contain information about what happened, along with when and where it happened.

Fundamental Properties of Episodic Memory

Some fundamental properties of episodic memory have been identified by distinguishing processes that contribute to our ability to recognize an item that was previously experienced in a test setting. In the example that began this chapter, you immediately experienced a sense of familiarity with the face of the person who greeted you, but no awareness of particular previous experiences or the reason why you knew this person. Subsequently, and after considerable effort, you recollected information about the context in which you knew him and your specific experiences with him. Experimental studies of differences between the qualities of experience in familiarity and recollection have inspired *dual process theories* that view familiarity and recollection as two independent processes that contribute to recognition memory (Yonelinas, 2002).

Several studies support the idea that these two independent processes contribute to recognition; these investigations also suggest key distinctions between familiarity and recollection (Table 9.1). Familiarity is based on finding a perceptual match between the test item and a stored representation of items in mem-

T A B L E 9 . 1 Differences between Recollection and Familiarity.

Recollection	Familiarity
Meaning (deep encoding)	Perceptual match (shallow encoding)
Associative, context, source	Individual items
Slow	Fast

ory, whereas recollection is based on accessing the meaning of the test stimulus in one's prior history. This distinction leads to differences in performance based on familiarity and recollection. During memory encoding, disparities in the level of processing (see Chapter 8) distinguish between later success in memory. Shallow encoding, such as for superficial stimuli characteristics, leads to better performance for familiarity than for recollection. Deeply encoded memories, like those involving stimuli meaning, generate better recollection than familiarity.

Memory retrieval based on familiarity also differs in some important ways from retrieval based on recollection. Perceptually matching a stimulus with a memory to support a sense of familiarity is a relatively fast process compared to recollection, which requires an exhaustive memory search for experiences with the test stimulus. So retrieval based on familiarity is typically faster than retrieval based on recollection. However, if the test stimulus is changed at all from the way it was originally presented, these differences decrease familiarity-based memory but do not affect recollection. Performance based on familiarity tends to diminish relatively rapidly compared to that based on recollection. Conversely, providing clues that lead to false recognition (such as including items in a recognition test that are similar to items presented earlier) reduces the likelihood of correct recollection-based recognition but does not affect familiarity. Finally, because recollection involves forming new associations between otherwise distinct items, the ability to recognize novel *pairings* of familiar items is especially reliant on recollection rather than on familiarity.

Quantifying the Contributions of Recollection and Familiarity to Episodic Memory

Experimental analyses of memory have been developed to characterize and quantify the distinctions between recollection and familiarity and to measure their distinct contributions to recognition memory. A particularly compelling line of studies is based on analyses of **receiver operating characteristics (ROCs)**, a method that measures the ability to identify items from a previously studied list under varying levels of confidence or bias in making the recognition judgment

Learning & Memory in Action

Eyewitness Testimony

Distinctions between basic mechanisms that underlie recollection and familiarity may be important for understanding the phenomenon of eyewitness testimony. Eyewitness testimony is an important example of episodic memory in which people incidentally observe a crime or disaster; sometimes they directly participate in such events unintentionally as victims. Within the context of legal proceedings, eyewitness testimony is typically viewed as crucial to understanding events that occurred and essential to proving cases of misconduct. People are often quite confident about their memories of these emotionally arousing events, and their confidence is taken as a measure of evidentiary accuracy. However, eyewitness testimony is subject to error even when accompanied by a high degree of witness confidence. How could such memories be erroneous? How can eyewitness testimony be influenced, and how can we improve the questioning of witnesses to increase their memories' accuracy?

Eyewitness testimony is subject to two types of errors: misattribution and suggestibility. Both appear to be based on the distinction between the highly associative nature of recollection and the absence of associative information in memories based on familiarity. In his book describing the seven "sins," or sources of error, in memory, Daniel Schacter (2001) tells the story of John Doe 2 in the case of the 1995 bombing of the Oklahoma City federal building. In investigating the case, the FBI interviewed employees of an auto body shop where the main perpetrator, Timothy McVeigh, had rented the van that was used to deliver the bombs. A principal eyewitness testified that he had seen two men rent the van two days before the bombing. He provided descriptions of both men, and these were used to guide a nationwide hunt for two suspects known as John Doe 1 and John Doe 2. McVeigh was captured and identified as John Doe 1. An arrest was also made based on the description of John Doe 2, but this turned out to be a misidentification. Careful examination of the rental records showed that the witness had seen two van rentals on successive days—one involving McVeigh and the other involving two men, one of whom resembled McVeigh. The witness had not distinguished between the two rental incidents and unconsciously retrieved the memories of all the individuals involved. This and many similar cases show that witnesses can unconsciously transfer people or events from one experience into another experience that shares features with it. Such misattributions may be caused by relying on familiarity with particular features and not distinguishing them by the contexts and associations in which they were actually experienced. A laboratory example of this kind of memory conjunction error occurs when subjects study a list of words that includes *spaniel* and *varnish* and later claim to remember the word *Spanish*.

The other type of error prominent in eyewitness testimony is suggestibility (Schacter, 2001). Weak memories can be influenced or even generated by how a questioner extracts information from a witness. This phenomenon was illustrated by an experiment in which memories were generated in Dutch people 10 months after the crash of an El Al cargo plane into an Amsterdam building (Crombag et al., 1996). In response to the question "Did you see the television film of the moment the plane hit the apartment building?" over half of the 193 people interviewed claimed to have seen the film even though no camera recorded the crash and no film was shown on television. Many of these people also provided details regarding whether the plane was burning at the time of the crash and whether the plane fell vertically or hit the building while moving forward. In another example (Loftus & Palmer, 1974), subjects viewed a movie of an automobile crash and then were given leading information while being interviewed about the crash details. Reports of the speed of the cars and other story details were greatly influenced by how the questions were asked.

Other studies have shown that merely suggesting events that were not actually witnessed can generate apparent memories of the events. In one famous experiment, a teenager was asked by his older brother to remember the time the teenager had been lost while shopping in a mall (Loftus & Pickrell, 1995). The teenager could not recall the episode. However, several days later the teenager produced a vivid account of being lost in the mall as a child, even though the event never occurred. And expectations about events that were not suggested can intrude into eyewitness testimony. For example, students were placed in an academic office briefly and told to wait for an experiment to begin. When subsequently asked to recall what they saw in the room, the students correctly reported the presence of an office desk and chair—but many students also recalled seeing books on the shelves although there were actually none. Clearly the expectation of seeing books in an academic office influenced the students to generate those memories. Many studies have now demonstrated that leading questions and expectations about events can strikingly affect eyewitness testimony.

Based on these findings, psychologists have devised methods for retrieving eyewitness information that avoid errors of misattribution and suggestibility (Fisher & Geiselman, 1992). Their interview techniques ask witnesses to recall everything, whether or not they consider it important; to try to reinstate the context of the event they are trying to recall; to recall the order in which events occurred; and to take different perspectives in recalling the events—for example, the perspective of the perpetrator and then of the victim. These techniques avoid leading suggestions and the items that can be identified as familiar, instead emphasizing contextual and temporal associations for episodic recollection.

(Yonelinas 2001, 2002). In a typical experiment using ROCs, subjects begin by studying a list of words. After some delay, they are shown the same items plus an equal number of new items. For each test presentation subjects are first asked whether the item was on the original study list. If they respond yes, they are asked how confident they are about their judgment.

Because the stimuli are usually everyday words, all the test list items are somewhat familiar to the subjects. So performance of this task depends on how strong the sense of familiarity must be for judging a word as "old." If a subject is trying hard not to overlook any items seen previously and therefore liberally judging whether she has seen the items before, she is likely to correctly recognize many items, but she is also likely to misidentify some new items as recognizable; this kind of misidentification is called a *false alarm*. On the other hand, if the subject is trying hard to avoid false alarms and is therefore conservative in identifying old items, she is likely to miss identifying some of the items presented earlier. In ROC analysis experiments, we can measure a subject's personal criterion for judging an item as familiar by asking how confident she is about each judgment. The criterion for considering an item to be familiar is relatively low when she is highly confident about an item; the criterion is relatively high when confidence is low. Variations in performance across different judgment criteria provide the data for the ROC analysis.

Performance in an ROC analysis is typically scored according to the ratio of correct identifications of previously seen items (*hits*) versus false alarms at the different judgment criteria. By this method, the rate of correct identifications based on chance alone lies along the diagonal where the probabilities of a hit and of a false alarm are equal, and good performance is reflected in scoring more hits than false alarms. A typical ROC curve is shown in Figure 9.2. Note that the curve is asymmetrical, with a positive hit rate on the *y* axis. This shape reflects successful recognition even at the most conservative judgment criterion; subsequent performance is characterized by a bowed curve, showing a maximum deviation from the diagonal at a middle criterion, and then reaching the diagonal at the top right corner of the curve where the criterion is most liberal. The combination of these two components of the ROC function (asymmetry and curvilinear shape) is important in distinguishing recollection and familiarity, as you are about to see.

We can clarify the asymmetrical and curvilinear components of the ROC curve by varying the testing protocol in ways that emphasize either recollection or familiarity. One way to emphasize recollection is to present pairs of words to remember as the original study list—for example, *train–cup, phone–clock*. During the test, subjects must judge previously presented pairs (*train–cup*) as old and rearranged pairs (*phone–cup*) as new. Because recollection involves remembering associations between items, performance on this test depends strongly on recollection. Conversely, because all the individual items are equally familiar in the test list, sub-

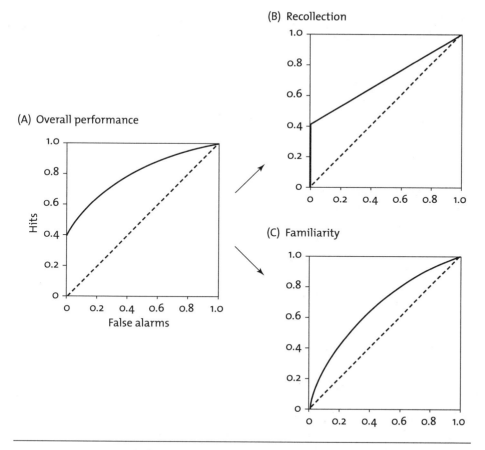

(A) Overall performance

(B) Recollection

(C) Familiarity

FIGURE 9.2 ROCs in humans.
A. Performance based on a combination of recollection and familiarity, typically observed in memory for single words. B. Performance based on recollection only, typically observed in recognition of word pairs. C. Performance based on familiarity only, typically observed in rapid judgments for recognition of single words. The dashed line indicates chance performance.

jects cannot use item familiarity differences to make their judgments. Under these conditions, the ROC function is strongly asymmetrical but linear; that is, the curve has no bow (Figure 9.2B).

The opposite pattern is observed under test conditions that emphasize the use of familiarity. This can be accomplished by forcing subjects to make quick judgments. A sense of familiarity usually occurs immediately when a previously experienced item is presented, whereas recollection involves effortful retrieval and therefore is slower. When subjects are given a list of single items to remember and then tested with a one-second deadline, the ROC function is fully symmetrical and curvilinear (Figure 9.2C). Thus recognition rate graphs using ROC analysis provide a sort of signature for recollection, observed in the function's asymmetry, and a signature of familiarity, observed as the function's curvilinear shape.

Interim Summary

Recollection and familiarity can be distinguished in several ways. One involves the depth of processing of stimuli. Recollection predominates when we think about the meaning of the stimuli, whereas familiarity predominates when we think about the superficial appearance of stimuli. Recollection involves retrieving associates of a memory cue and the context in which the cue was experienced; familiarity involves recognizing features of the cue itself. Familiarity involves a fast perceptual match, whereas recollection involves slower search processes. In addition, recollection and familiarity differ in their contributions to the ROC function: Recollection generates an asymmetric ROC function, and familiarity causes the ROC curvilinear shape.

The Hippocampus Supports Episodic Memory

The idea that episodic and semantic memory function as separate systems was strongly confirmed when studies of an amnesic man known as K. C. provided biological evidence for this distinction. As a result of a closed head injury, K. C. suffered widespread cortical and subcortical damage, including damage to the medial temporal lobe (Tulving & Markowitsch, 1998). K. C. has normal intelligence, language, ability to imagine, and other cognitive capacities, including intact short-term memory. Also, his general knowledge acquired before the injury is mostly unharmed. He can play the organ and chess, as well as several card games—all skills he learned before his accident. He knows when he was born, the names of schools he attended, and the kind of car he once owned. But he has virtually no capacity for recollecting old experiences or forming new episodic memories. He cannot remember everyday events, circumstances, or important information gained through experience. No amount of cuing helps him recall particular experiences. On the other hand, in tests of his capacity to learn new semantic information, K. C. struggles but ultimately can complete simple sentences and word definitions. Because our memory for particular experiences strongly enhances semantic memory formation, the research team working with K. C. concluded that his difficulties in acquiring semantic memories are largely due to his loss of episodic memory, which would ordinarily support the acquisition of semantic knowledge.

Because K. C.'s brain damage is diffuse, his case study offers no clear insight into the neurobiology of episodic memory. However, three other cases in which brain damage resulted from transient anoxia (temporary loss of oxygen) early in life suggest that the hippocampus plays an important role in episodic memory (Vargha-Khadem et al., 1997). In these people, the damage was selective to the hippocampus, sparing the surrounding cortical areas. As these children grew up, it became clear that they had memory difficulties; they were ultimately tested in adulthood and found to be severely deficient in memory for everyday experiences. Despite their impaired episodic memory, these people successfully acquired language skills, literacy, and enough factual knowledge to attend regular schools. Based on standardized IQ testing, all three individuals' semantic memory for vocabulary and general information, as well as their capacities for comprehension, fell within the normal range. They also performed normally in recognition tests involving words and nonwords, as well as those using faces. Several other tests focused on their ability to recognize new associations between stimuli presented in an experiment. They successfully learned associations linking pairs of words or pairs of faces. However, they had trouble learning word–voice and object–place associations, indicating specific areas of deficient associative memory. These findings suggest that stimuli of the same type (like face–face associations) might be associated within the same area of the cerebral cortex so that they do not require hippocampus-dependent episodic memory.

One way in which the capacities of recollection and familiarity have been evaluated in amnesic subjects is through comparisons of performance in recall versus recognition tests. Recall tests demand strong, conscious recollection of the study experience. Therefore, performance in these tests is closely related to the strength and accuracy of recollection. In contrast, recognizing a previously experienced stimulus depends on a combination of recollection and familiarity, as shown by the ROC analyses described earlier.

Consistent with this view, several studies have suggested that recall and recognition are differentially impaired in amnesia. Aggleton and Shaw (1996) surveyed many studies and concluded that people with damage limited to the hippocampus or its connections were nearly normal in recognition memory but were as impaired as people with more widespread damage in tests of recall. Similar evidence was provided by extensive studies of a woman known as Y. R. who, in adulthood, suffered damage limited to the hippocampus and sparing the surrounding cortical areas (Mayes et al., 2002; Holdstock et al., 2002). Y. R.'s performance in 43 recognition tests was relatively normal, but she was deficient in all 34 tests of recall. This contrast between intact recognition and impaired recall spanned verbal and nonverbal stimuli, different kinds of responses, and a broad range of other variables. Within closely controlled variations of object and object–place recognition tasks, Y. R. performed normally when forced to choose the familiar object;

but she had trouble recalling an object from a cue, even when this task was easier for controls than the object recognition task. The sparing of recognition performance was not universal, however. Y. R. was stumped by a yes–no object recognition task that involved close similarities between the target stimuli and alternative choices, and she also had problems recognizing where she had seen a particular object. Holdstock and colleagues (2002) concluded that impaired or normal performance depends not on whether the task involves recognition or recall per se, but rather on whether recognition can be supported, at least in part, by familiarity.

An additional line of evidence supporting the notion that recollection is more impaired than recognition in people with hippocampal damage comes from studies showing that amnesic subjects perform poorly in recognizing associations even when recognition for single items is spared (Giovanello et al., 2003; Turriziani et al., 2004). These experiments found less recognition memory for associations between words, between faces, or between face–occupation pairs, in contrast to normal performance in recognizing single items (Figure 9.3). Thus it appears that recollection depends on hippocampal function but can, at least in part, be supported by familiarity that does not depend on the hippocampus.

The ROC method has provided further evidence for a selective hippocampal role in episodic recollection (Yonelinas et al., 2002). In this study, normal subjects and those with selective hippocampal damage were given a list of words to study;

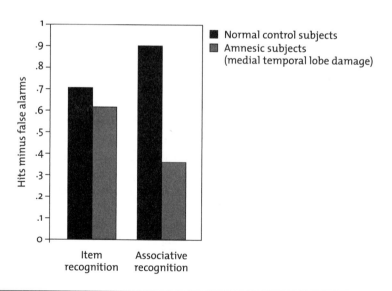

FIGURE 9.3 Single item versus associative memory in amnesia.
Overall performance on hits minus false alarms is compared in normal control subjects and individuals with damage to the medial temporal lobe.

then their memory for the words was assessed using the ROC method described earlier. Normal subjects showed the usual asymmetrical and curvilinear ROC function, indicating that they used both recollection and familiarity to recognize the words from the study list. In contrast, the ROC function of amnesic subjects was symmetrical, demonstrating a deficiency specific to the recollection component of recognition (Figure 9.4).

The conclusion that the hippocampus is selectively involved in recollection is not, however, universal. Some researchers have argued that although recall may more sensitively test memory damage, amnesic subjects are impaired in both recall and recognition (Stark & Squire, 2001). Furthermore, studies of amnesic subjects with damage limited to the hippocampus have characterized their deficits in recall and recognition as equivalent (Manns & Squire, 1999). In one study recognition impairments were apparent across a variety of standard tests, including recognition of faces, words, and other materials; these individuals had equal difficulty in recognizing items based on recollection and those for which their judgments were based on familiarity (Manns et al., 2003). Other studies found impairment of both associative and single item recognition (Stark et al., 2002) and on both the recollection and familiarity components of ROC curves (Wais et al., 2006).

The studies that purport to show a selective role of the hippocampus in recall based on deficits in amnesia have been criticized as inconclusive because selective hippocampal damage is never complete: It spares some hippocampal tissue. Any

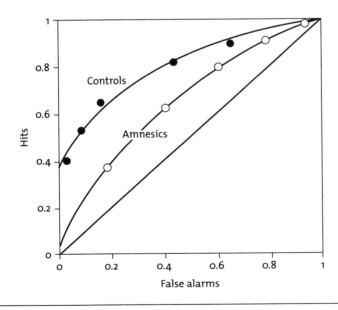

FIGURE 9.4 ROCs in normal control subjects and amnesic subjects.

residual recall or recognition capacity may be mediated by the remaining hippocampal fragment, and the participation of any remaining hippocampal tissue may contribute to semantic memory with sufficient practice—consistent with the common finding that amnesic subjects with limited hippocampal damage are at least modestly impaired in learning new semantic information (Squire & Zola, 1998). The finding of a functional hippocampal segment in one case of early-onset hippocampal damage is consistent with this view (Maguire et al., 2001). Thus comparisons between recall and recognition performance are not conclusive about the selective role of the hippocampus in recollection.

Learning & Memory in Action

Aging and Memory Loss

Older people frequently complain about their memories, and in particular about the loss of their ability to remember everyday events. Many comprehensive examinations of aging adults' learning and memory abilities have provided a wealth of information about aging and memory. Although aging causes some loss of learning capacity and of memory across domains (including classical conditioning, skill learning, and other forms of behavioral memory), the most common and most prominent decline affects episodic memory (Light, 1991; Healy et al., 2005; Yonelinas, 2002). Furthermore, this damaged episodic memory appears to be due to a selective loss of recollection abilities with relative sparing of familiarity. Several studies have shown intact ability to recognize individual items that were previously studied. However, when the words to be remembered (and later recognized) were presented in more than one way, older people tended to have trouble remembering whether they had seen or heard the words and whether they passively read or actively generated the words. When they studied more than one list, they demonstrated impaired episodic memory through their difficulties in remembering what list they saw the words in; sometimes they also had trouble remembering whether they actually saw a word in the experiment or it just seemed familiar because they had encountered it elsewhere.

In recognition tests using ROC analyses, aged adults exhibited poorer recollection functions with spared familiarity functions. Furthermore, aged adults were more prone to memory errors that may result from overdependence on familiarity, such as higher false alarm rates. In a particularly illuminating experiment, Jacoby (1999) presented an initial list of words once, twice, or three times, followed by presentation of a second list. Subjects were then tested for recognition of items that appeared only on the second list. Young adults were better at excluding words they had seen on the first list, presumably because the repeated exposures to the first list helped them associate those words with the specific list in which they appeared. In striking contrast, aged adults showed the opposite pattern: They were more likely to make intrusion errors involving interference from words that appeared more frequently in the first list. They seemed to rely on the familiarity of the words—which was greater for the repeatedly presented first list—regardless of the list in which they had appeared. Jacoby described a practical and sad case in which con artists had relied on this distinctive loss of recollection and spared familiarity that comes with age. The con artists would call their victims and ask for detailed personal information about recent purchases. They called back after several days and, after determining that a victim had forgotten the previous call, would concoct a story in which they spoke of the need for final payment on one of the previously purchased items. The aged victims, relying on the apparent authenticity of the caller who knew about the purchase, would comply with the request by sending a check.

Brain Imaging Suggests a Selective Role for the Hippocampus in Episodic Recollection

The findings for amnesia indicating an important role for the hippocampus in episodic memory are supported by complementary evidence from studies using functional brain imaging in normal human subjects. In one experiment subjects memorized a list of words. During scanning they were first asked to recognize the words and then classify their remembering process as based on memory for the experience of studying or, instead, lacking in episodic detail (Eldridge et al., 2000). The hippocampus was relatively more active in association with correct episodic recollection—but not when subjects made errors or, during their correct recollections, reported lacking experiential details such as where in the list a word was seen (Figure 9.5).

Several additional studies have aimed to characterize the nature of memory processing that activates the hippocampus. For example, several experiments have tested whether the hippocampus is more active during encoding or retrieval of associations among many elements of a memory—a characteristic of context-rich episodic memories (Cohen et al., 1999). Some researchers have reported activation of the hippocampus, as well as many cortical areas, during retrieval of autobiographical experiences (Maguire, 2001). These brain images show that the hippocampus is most active when people are recalling specific experiences at a particular place and time. Perhaps most compelling of these are images showing selective hippocampal activation during retrieval of personal experiences but not during retrieval of less personally important public events about which general

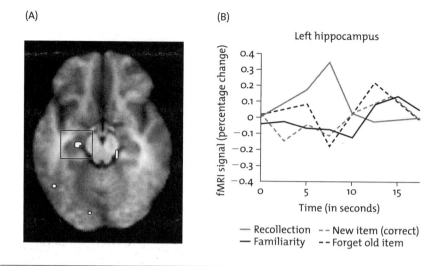

(A)　(B)

Left hippocampus

FIGURE 9.5 fMRI in recollection.
A. Brain scan showing a horizontal section through the brain with the area of activation in the left hippocampus indicated. B. Activation over time in the hippocampus when subjects make correct recollection and familiarity judgments, when they correctly identify new items, and when they forget an old item.

knowledge is sufficient (Maguire et al., 2000). However, hippocampal involvement in processing complex material is not limited to autobiographical details. Its role extends broadly, for example, to recollection of the context of learning in formal memory tests (Davachi et al., 2003; Ranganath et al., 2003). The hippocampus is activated during encoding of multiple items, and it is more active when subjects are required to link the items through systematic comparisons than when subjects learn the items through rote rehearsal (Davachi & Wagner, 2002). Furthermore, the greater the hippocampal activation observed while a subject compared and linked the items, the greater the subject's success in a recognition test.

Some brain imaging studies have demonstrated that different components of the medial temporal lobe may play distinct roles in recognition. This research compared the hippocampus with the surrounding parahippocampal cortical area to determine whether these areas are differentially activated during varying memory demands. For example, Gabrieli and colleagues (1997) showed subjects line drawings of common objects and animals. When subjects were again shown the pictures and recalled the names of the objects and animals, part of the hippocampus was selectively activated. In contrast, when subjects were shown novel or highly familiar pictures, the parahippocampal region was activated. Similarly, Davachi and colleagues (2003) showed subjects words and asked them either to imagine a spatial scene described by each word (such as a garbage dump for *dirty*) or to read the word backward. The hippocampus was activated when subjects successfully encoded the contextual cues, whereas part of the parahippocampal cortical region was activated during successful encoding of the superficial qualities of single words. These observations are consistent with the findings from studies of amnesia that suggest differential roles for the hippocampus in linking multiple distinct items into an integrated whole (Cohen et al., 1999) and for the surrounding cortical areas in familiarity of individual items (Eichenbaum et al., 1994).

However, this theory that the hippocampus might be selectively activated during recollection is not universally accepted. In functional brain imaging, the hippocampus may be more active whenever information needs to be remembered or is recalled, regardless of whether the material is truly episodic. In other words, functional imaging may be incapable of distinguishing between selective activation during recall versus familiarity per se; and it may confound differences in the degree of activation associated with the larger number of elements and contextual information contained in an episodic memory.

Because of these ambiguities, several researchers have turned to animal models. There researchers can study the effects of selective and complete lesions of the hippocampus, directly comparing the effects of hippocampal lesions to those of lesions to surrounding cortical areas. Also, researchers can directly observe animals' neural activity in the hippocampus and surrounding cortical areas, and these findings may reveal important distinctions in the nature of memories represented in these areas. However, controversy surrounds the questions of whether animals are capable of episodic memory and, if they are, how it can be observed experimentally.

Interim Summary

Cases of amnesia demonstrate that episodic memory can be lost while other conscious memory capacities are retained. These studies indicate that selective hippocampal damage can remove the ability to recollect specific experiences or learn simple associations while sparing memory for factual knowledge and the ability to recognize familiar materials. Functional brain imaging in humans has confirmed these findings, showing that the hippocampus is activated during recollection. Furthermore, functional imaging has helped delineate the contents of episodic memory and the distinct roles of different anatomical components of the medial temporal lobe. These studies have shown that the hippocampus is activated during processing of multiple items that are to be associated in memory. In contrast, the parahippocampal region is activated when subjects view stimuli. This distinction suggests that the parahippocampal region supports familiarity of single items, whereas the hippocampus is recruited to associate items in memory and to retrieve those associations during recall.

Episodic Memory May Exist in Animals

Distinguishing the roles of the hippocampus and the immediately adjacent parahippocampal region is difficult in studies of amnesia and with functional imaging because these methods offer only crude anatomical resolution. Therefore valid animal models of episodic memory would help us make more refined anatomical distinctions. However, this raises a key question about animals: Do they have episodic memory?

Since the time of Aristotle, many have distinguished humans' unique capacity to look backward in time to prior events in their lives. For example, Scottish poet Robert Burns concluded his "Ode to a Mouse on Turning Up Her Nest with the Plough" as follows:

> Still thou art blest, compar'd wi' me!
> The present only toucheth thee:
> But, och! I backward cast my e'e
> On prospects drear!
> An' forward, tho' I canna see,
> I guess an' fear!
> —Robert Burns (1785)

Avoiding the issue of autonoetic awareness (awareness of personal involvement in a previous experience), recent studies have sought to identify fundamental features of episodic memory that can be explored in animals (Table 9.2; Griffiths et al., 1999; Morris, 2001; Roberts, 2002; Whishaw & Douglas, 2003). These analyses have focused on three features of episodic memory that can be tested and measured in animals:

1. Episodic memories reflect the information acquired in a unique experience, which could contain associations formed during that specific occasion.
2. Episodic memories are marked by their occurrence at a particular place and time.
3. Vivid episodic memories unfold over time and across space as a sequence of events.

TABLE 9.2 Features of Episodic Memory in Animals.

Acquired in a single experience
Memory for *where* and *when* something happened
Memory for the order of events in an experience

Here we will consider these features of episodic memory and how they can be used to develop animal models and pursue detailed neurobiological investigations.

Episodic Memories Reflect Unique Experiences

Perhaps the most straightforward feature of episodic memories is that they involve information acquired in a single unique experience. Thus it seems reasonable to study memory for unique experiences to investigate episodic memory. However, this definition may include memories that are not truly episodic. In particular, several examples of behavioral memory involve substantial learning and behavioral change following single unique experiences. In humans, these include the phenomena of verbal and nonverbal priming and increased fluency in rereading a text passage. In animals, we see many examples of lasting memory following a single experience in sensory discrimination learning and fear conditioning, none of which depend on hippocampal system function or memory for the "what, where, and when" of an event.

Nevertheless, some studies of animals have revealed an essential hippocampal role in memory based on unique experiences. For example, Olton and his colleagues (1979, 1984) distinguished memory for the occurrence of unique events from memory for associations that do not change over different experiences. He asserted that temporal organization was paramount for event memory and elegantly employed T-maze alternation and radial maze tests to show that rats can remember specific recent visits to maze arms. In these tests, ablation (or disconnection) of the hippocampus consistently caused a profound deficit in memory for specific experiences, but it spared memory for places that had a consistent reward association. This distinction has been explained as a differential demand for remembering specific experiences, dependent on the hippocampus, versus a demand for habits of approaching or avoiding maze arms never associated with rewards supported by other brain systems (see Chapter 6).

Other studies have explored the role of the hippocampus in memory using recognition tasks that involve a single exposure to novel stimuli. These have focused mainly on the widely used *trial-unique delayed nonmatch to sample* task (Mishkin & Delacour, 1975). In this test, initially a novel object is presented as a sample stimulus (Figure 9.6A). Then, following a delay, this same sample is presented along with a novel stimulus, and the subject must choose between them. Specifically, the subject must select against the sample (that is, select the nonmatching stimulus). For example, a toy bear might be the sample object. When it is initially presented to a monkey or rat as the sample stimulus, the animal examines the bear and finds a treat underneath. Then the bear is removed and the animal must remember it for a variable period. Following that delay, the bear and a novel object, such as a red ball, are presented. This time only the ball covers a

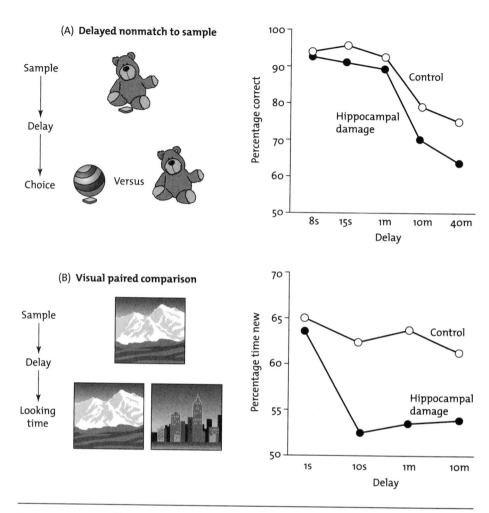

FIGURE 9.6 Effects of damage to the hippocampus in monkeys.
Note the detrimental effects on performance of A. the delayed nonmatch to sample task
and B. the visual paired comparison task.

reward, so the animal must remember that it has already obtained food under the
bear and now must investigate the new stimulus to obtain another treat.

Much literature shows that damage to the entire medial temporal lobe region,
or to the parahippocampal cortical areas surrounding the hippocampus, produces
a severe delay-dependent impairment in this task. Performance is intact when the
delay between exposure to the sample stimulus and the subsequent paired stimuli is a few seconds, but retention deteriorates rapidly thereafter. In contrast, damage that affects only the hippocampus causes either modest (Zola et al., 2000;

Nemanic et al., 2004; Clark et al., 2001; Mumby et al., 1992) or no (Murray & Mishkin, 1998) deficit in delayed performance, even when many items have to be remembered (Dudchencko et al., 2000; Murray & Mishkin, 1998). These observations suggest that parahippocampal cortical areas can support this form of simple recognition, even without hippocampal involvement (Murray, 1996).

On the other hand, different results have emerged from studies using another form of recognition test that exposes monkeys or rats to a novel visual stimulus and then, following a delay, tests their time spent visually investigating that stimulus versus a novel stimulus—a task similar to the habituation–dishabituation test discussed in Chapter 3 (Figure 9.6B). In this test, selective hippocampal damage produces a significant delay-dependent impairment revealed in a lack of preference for the new stimulus over the old one (Zola et al., 2000; Nemanic et al., 2004; Clark et al., 2000). The conflicting observations after hippocampal damage of (1) little or no deficit in the delayed nonmatch to sample task and (2) severe deficits in investigation of novel stimuli suggests there is some unidentified difference between the performance demands of these tasks. Though both tasks seem to test episodic memory for a single, specific encounter with a stimulus, the habituation–dishabituation task seems to differentially demand hippocampal involvement. What is the crucial distinction between the tasks? At this time we do not know. However, consideration of episodic memory in spatial learning sheds light on memory demands that invoke hippocampal function.

Assessing Episodic Memory Using Signal Detection

The mixed findings among recognition tests in animals parallel the inconsistent observations for recognition memory in human amnesia (reviewed earlier in this chapter). This pattern of cross-species observations supports the view that multiple processes sustain simple forms of recognition: One process involves a hippocampus-dependent recollection process, and the other involves familiarity-based processing that does not require the hippocampus (Eichenbaum et al., 1994; Brown & Aggleton, 2001; Griffiths et al., 1999). Because these processes cannot be clearly distinguished in animal studies, testing animals' ability to recognize information gained in unique experiences has been of limited value.

However, recently a novel approach has shown that understanding the contributions of two distinct processes that support recognition—recollection and familiarity—may help researchers make sense of the variable findings about recognition. This approach adapts the ROC analyses that have been used to distinguish the contributions of recollection and familiarity to humans' recognition performance (Fortin et al., 2004). In the ROC analysis protocol developed for rats, the animals are initially offered a sequence of 10 odors. Following a 30-minute delay, they are given those same 10 odors and 10 new odors, mixed in random order. In differ-

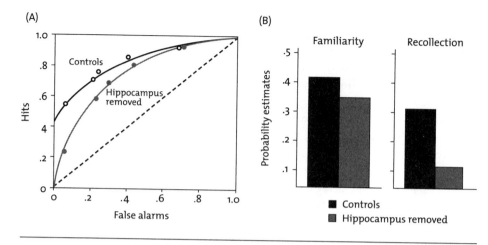

FIGURE 9.7 ROCs in rats.
A. ROC plot. B. Quantitative measures of recollection and familiarity.

ent sessions a rat's tendency to respond to a test item was manipulated by varying how much food was available for responding or not responding to that stimulus. This changed the animal's bias in responding one way or the other, equivalent to the effect of varying confidence levels in human ROC studies. This process allowed the researchers to conduct an ROC analysis based on correct identifications of previously presented items (hits) and incorrect "recognition" of new items (false alarms)—much like the ROC analysis used to study recognition in humans.

The ROC function in normal rats was remarkably similar to that observed in a human verbal recognition task (Figure 9.7). Furthermore, removing a rat's hippocampus reduced performance to a symmetric ROC function that reflected only the contribution of familiarity, and not recollection, to the process of recognizing the odors. These results distinguish recollection and familiarity in an animal model and provide strong evidence of a specific hippocampus role in the contribution of recollection to recognition judgments. Furthermore, these findings suggest that the hippocampus plays a similar role in animal and human recollection.

Episodic Memories Occur at a Particular Place and Time

Other animal studies have been guided by Tulving's characterization of episodic memory as oriented to the time and place of the experience—as distinct from semantic memory, which organizes factual information conceptually and not by where learning occurred. This distinction has been verified in experiments that check animals' ability to remember when and where a specific event occurred as a reflection of "episodic-like" memory (Clayton & Dickenson, 1998; Morris, 2001).

Clayton & Dickenson (1998) investigated animals' memory for when and where events occurred in a clever laboratory experiment that explored the natural hoarding behavior of scrub jays (Figure 9.8). Initially jays stored both worms and peanuts in an array of locations. Because the jays ordinarily prefer eating worms to peanuts, they recover the worms first when they are allowed to seek the stored food within a few hours after hoarding. However, if a multiday interval is imposed between hoarding and recovery, the worms degrade and are not palatable. Under this condition the jays recovered the peanuts first, revealing that they can selectively seek a particular type of stored food and that their choice of which type of food to recover is based on the time elapsed since hoarding. Clayton and Dickenson concluded that the jays remembered what they had stored, as well as where and when they had stored each item. Because these food stimuli were equally familiar to the birds when they were tested, they could not choose on the basis of differential familiarity (and control studies showed they cannot smell the rotten worms).

However, as Roberts (2002) has argued, this protocol more directly tests the jays' sense of how much time has passed since their hoarding rather than revealing a memory of exactly when specific experiences occurred. If this is the case, the jays could rely on signals about the *strength* of their hoarding memories to judge how much time has passed rather than remembering specific information about the timing of the events. Thus jays may learn to prefer worms while their memory for hoarding them is still strong, but not after a few days when their memory is weaker. This kind of memory cue would be quite different from an episodic notion of when an event occurred.

FIGURE 9.8 Testing episodic memory in jays.

Memory for Where a Unique Event Occurred

Other studies of animals' episodic memory have focused on whether animals can remember where a unique event occurred and whether this capacity depends on the hippocampus. For example, in one experiment rats were trained in a variation of the Morris water maze task. The escape platform was placed in the same maze location at the outset of each training session. Then the rat was allowed to swim around until it found the platform in four trials. Learning the new place to escape from swimming was reflected in decreased swim time across the four trials. A large decrease in swim time was observed in the second trial, indicating that the rats remembered the new location after even a single experience. Rats with selective hippocampal damage were severely impaired on this task. Furthermore, when neural plasticity (long-term potentiation or LTP; see Chapter 2) was prevented, rats performed well in remembering the new location for a few seconds, but they had trouble remembering it for a few hours (Figure 9.9; Steele & Morris, 1999). These findings provide strong evidence that the hippocampus is vital to memory for where a unique escape event occurred.

An additional study showed that animals can remember unique positive (rewarding) events and that this kind of memory also depends on the hippocampus. Day and colleagues (2003) initially allowed rats to find different flavored rewards (such as strawberry versus grape) buried in sand-wells at specific locations in a open platform. The experimenters tested the rats' memory for the location associated with a specific flavor by giving the rats tidbits of one of the tasty foods while holding them in a box at the periphery of the platform and then allowing the rats to go to the original location associated with the cued flavor. After a single exposure to a flavor, a normal rat accurately went straight to the location in which that particular flavor had previously been consumed. Inactivation of the hippocampus or blockage of NMDA receptors resulted in poor memory. These findings show that the hippocampus plays an essential role in memory for places associated with unique events.

The hippocampus is also vital in recognizing where objects have previously been investigated. A study using a variation of the habituation–dishabituation task initially exposed rats to two objects in particular places inside one of two chambers (Mumby et al., 2002). In subsequent recognition testing, either the location of the object within the chamber or the chamber itself changed. Normal rats spent more time exploring the reexperienced objects when they were moved to new places in the chamber or presented in different chambers than when they were presented again in the same place and chamber. However, rats with hippocampal damage failed to show this form of recognition. Thus memory for both a particular location in the environment as well as for entire environments depends on the hippocampus.

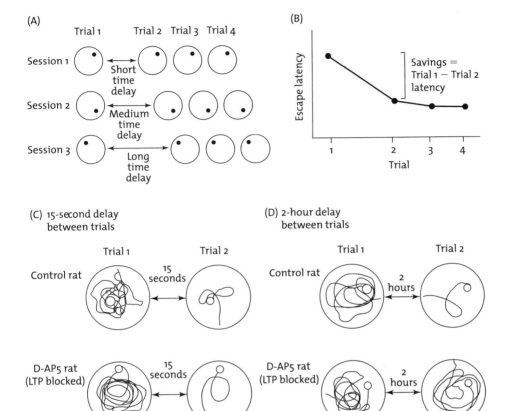

(A)

Trial 1   Trial 2 Trial 3 Trial 4

Session 1

Short
time
delay

Session 2

Medium
time
delay

Session 3

Long
time
delay

(B)

Escape latency

Savings =
Trial 1 − Trial 2
latency

1   2   3   4

Trial

(C) 15-second delay
between trials

Trial 1   Trial 2

Control rat

15
seconds

D-AP5 rat
(LTP blocked)

15
seconds

(D) 2-hour delay
between trials

Trial 1   Trial 2

Control rat

2
hours

D-AP5 rat
(LTP blocked)

2
hours

FIGURE 9.9 Episodic memory in the water maze.
A. Design of the task. Each session was composed of a single trial with the escape
platform in a new location (Trial 1), followed by a variable time delay and then three
further trials with the platform in the same location. B. Memory for the location of the
platform in the first trial each day is reflected in "savings": a decrease in the latency to
find the platform in the same location on the second trial. C & D. Examples of swim paths
of a control subject and a rat given AP-5, a drug that blocks LTP in the hippocampus,
when trial 2 is given 15 seconds or 2 hours, respectively, after trial 1.

Perhaps the strongest evidence that the hippocampus is critical for learning
important events' environmental context comes from studies of fear conditioning
(Phillips & LeDoux, 1992; see Chapter 7 for further discussion of fear conditioning involving contextual cues). These studies use a conditioning protocol to pair
a tone and shock repeatedly so that rats fear the tone. In addition, rats also become
fearful of the context in which the tones and shock were presented, as shown by
freezing behavior and other signs of fear when the animals are returned to the

conditioning environment. Damage to the hippocampus eliminates this contextual fear conditioning without affecting conditioned fear to the tone.

Vivid Episodic Memories Unfold as a Sequence of Events

If I asked you what you did when you woke up this morning, you would recall the sequence of events that led you to this point in the day. You might recall first awaking in bed during a dream, then getting up, showering, brushing your teeth, and so on. Episodic memories like this entail a sequence of events that unfolds over time and space. Therefore, considering how both humans and animals remember the orderliness of events in unique experiences may provide a fruitful avenue for neurobiological explorations of episodic memory.

To investigate the role of the hippocampus in remembering the order of events, researchers have employed a behavioral protocol that assesses rats' memory for experiences with a unique sequence of olfactory stimuli (Fortin et al., 2002; Kesner et al., 2002). One experiment compared the rats' memory for the order in which they experienced odors with their ability to recognize odors without regard for their order (Figure 9.10). In each trial rats were presented with a series of five common household scents. Memory for each series of smells was subsequently probed using a choice test, in which the animals were reinforced for selecting the earlier of two odors in the series. The rats were tested with six types of probes to assess memory over different numbers of intervening items (lags) between presentations of odors in the series. In each trial any pair of nonadjacent odors might be presented as the probe, so the animal had to remember the entire sequence to perform well throughout the testing session.

Normal rats accurately performed sequential order judgments across all lags, and their probe test performance depended on the length of the lag: Order judgments were easier when more time passed between odor presentations. In contrast, rats with hippocampal lesions showed severe impairment. The same rats were also tested for their ability to use recent odor encounters to recognize odors and distinguish them from novel ones. For each trial, a series of five odors was presented in a format identical to that used in the sequential order task. Then the rats' recognition was probed with a choice between one of the series odors and another common odor that was not in the series; the rats received a reward for selecting the novel odor over the one presented earlier. Five types of probes varied the recency of the initially presented odor.

Normal rats and those with selective hippocampal damage learned this task equally rapidly for the different types of probes. Both groups were consistently better able to recognize odors that appeared later in the series, suggesting some forgetting of items that had to be remembered longer and through more intervening items. Thus hippocampal damage did not affect the rate of forgetting in a

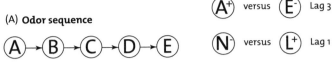

(A) **Odor sequence**

1. **Order probe: "Which came first?**

2. **Item probe: "Which is new?"**

(B)

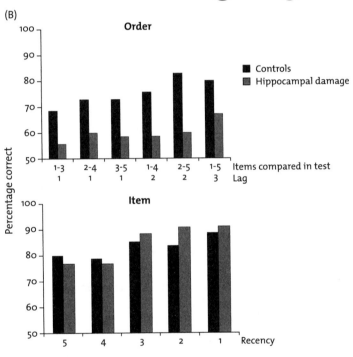

FIGURE 9.10 Odor order task and data.
A. Design of the task. On each trial subjects were initially presented with a randomly ordered sequence of odors selected from a large set. Then they were tested for knowledge about either (1) the order of the odors by judging which of two came earlier or (2) which odors were presented by judging between an odor that was presented and one that was not (+ indicates rewarded stimulus; − indicates nonrewarded stimulus). B. Performance on the order and item judgments as a function of (1) the number of items intervening between the test odors for the order judgment or (2) the recency of the test odor in the item judgment.

test of simple familiarity with individual items, consistent with studies of familiarity and the hippocampus discussed earlier. This finding, combined with the observed deficit in judging the order of items in a series of odors, tells us that rats with hippocampal damage could not use differences in individual items' memory strengths to make the order judgments. So it is also unlikely that normal rats used differences in the strengths of individual memories to solve the problem, but instead remembered the order of odors experienced. Contrary to the argument that animals lack episodic memory because they are "stuck in time" (Roberts, 2002; Tulving, 2002), these observations suggest that animals can recollect the flow of events in unique experiences.

Interim Summary

Evidence from many studies indicates that animals have the capacities for episodic memory's fundamental features. Animals can remember events that were experienced just once and show this ability across a wide variety of tasks. Also, like humans, animals can remember where and when events occurred and the flow of events in a unique experience. The identification of these memory features in animals strengthens the view that animals have all the fundamental traits that are characteristic of episodic memory in humans. In addition, animal studies have revealed a vital role for the hippocampus in each of these features of episodic memory, confirming similar findings from human studies.

Hippocampal Neurons Represent Episodic Memories

How do hippocampal neurons in animals and humans represent episodic memories? A common observation across both behavioral protocols and species is that different hippocampal neurons are activated during virtually every moment of task performance—including during simple behaviors, such as foraging for food, as well as learning-related behaviors and relevant stimuli. The activity patterns of many of these cells show striking specificities, corresponding to particular spatial configurations of stimuli. Activations in the overall network of cells can be characterized as a sequence of firings representing the step-by-step events in each behavioral episode. This general pattern is observed in a broad range of behavioral protocols: classical conditioning, discrimination learning, matching to sample tasks, maze tasks, and so on. When animals are repeatedly given specific stimuli and rewards and trained to execute appropriate cognitive judgments and conditioned behaviors, hippocampal cells are activated with each sequential stimulus and behavioral action.

A potential difficulty in interpreting experimental results is that neural firing associated with various *events,* such as food pellet delivery, occurs consistently in a particular *location,* such as near the food dispenser—so the firing patterns may primarily reflect spatial information. One study addressed this issue by training animals to perform the same behavioral judgments at many locations in the same environment (Wood et al., 1999). Specifically, rats were trained in a recognition memory task: Cups with scented sand were the relevant cues, and during each trial the cup was placed in any one of nine locations so that cup location was incidental (it did not predict rewards; Figure 9.11A). In each trial the rats approached the cup and sniffed the odor, then dug in the sand for a reward if the odor did not match the one presented in the preceding trial or turned away if the odor matched. Because the location of the stimuli that the rats had to judge varied systematically, neural activity related to the stimuli and behavior could be dissociated from that related to location.

Hippocampal cells were active during all aspects of this task performance, supporting the view that the hippocampus encodes a continuous flow of events. Some cells fired only if a rat approached the stimulus cup from a particular location, or fired only when the animal encountered a particular conjunction of the odor, the place where it was experienced, and the match or nonmatch status of the odor compared with the earlier sample (Figure 9.11B). These firing patterns are consistent with the representation of events unique to a particular rarely repeated episode. Other cells' firing corresponded to only one particular feature of the task. Thus some cells fired during a particular phase of the approach toward any stimulus cup. Others fired as a rat sampled a particular odor, regardless of its location or match/nonmatch status. Certain cells fired only when a rat sampled an odor at a particular place, regardless of the odor or its status. Other cells fired based on the match or nonmatch status of any odor, regardless of where it was sampled. The largest proportion of cells that fired when a rat was sampling an odor showed striking specificities: They fired differentially depending on combinations of the odor, where it was sampled, and its meaning (match or nonmatch). These findings show that hippocampal cells encode each successive event in every trial and represent all the features of specific events that compose each unique experience.

A recent study suggests that human hippocampal neurons have properties similar to those just described for rats (Ekstrom et al., 2003). In this experiment, subjects navigated a virtual reality town in which they played a taxi driver searching for passengers picked up and dropped off at various locations. Different hippocampal neurons fired during each moment in the task. Some fired when subjects viewed particular scenes, occupied certain locations, or searched for passengers or drop-off locations. Many cells fired only in association with exact conjunctions of a place and the view of a particular scene.

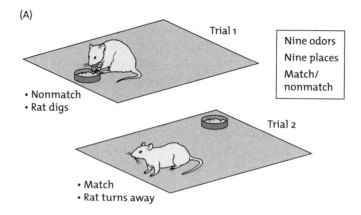

(A)

Trial 1

Nine odors
Nine places
Match/
nonmatch

• Nonmatch
• Rat digs

Trial 2

• Match
• Rat turns away

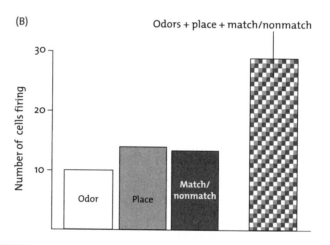

(B)

Odors + place + match/nonmatch

Number of cells firing

Odor
Place
Match/
nonmatch

FIGURE 9.11 The responses of hippocampal neurons in animals performing an odor recognition memory task.
A. The design of the task. On each trial the rat was presented with a single cup of scented sand and could find a reward in it if its odor differed from the odor presented in the preceding trial. B. This graph compares the number of hippocampal neurons whose firing pattern distinguished the particular odors, the place where each odor was presented, each odor's match or nonmatch status, or combinations of these features.

The combined observations from studies of humans and rats show that across species and in numerous behavioral protocols, hippocampal neurons are structured to store information about sequences of events. A subset of hippocampal neurons is selectively activated at every moment throughout task performance, allowing the hippocampus to encode every salient event as it occurs, whether or not that event is critical to the task. The encoded information includes where events occur as well as a broad range of nonspatial stimuli, behavioral events, and contingencies that characterize the task. The hippocampus keeps a running record of everything we attend to, tracking what happened and where and when it occurred (Morris & Frey, 1997). This characterization is consistent with the view that hippocampal networks encode both rare and common experiences as sequences of events, stimuli, and places (Eichenbaum et al., 1999).

The Hippocampus Represents Spatial Routes

As just described, hippocampal neurons' firing patterns encode behavioral events and the places where they occur. Furthermore, sequences of neural activations represent series of events that compose meaningful episodes, and the information contained in these representations both distinguishes related episodes and links them together. Imagine, for example, that you leave your house one day and walk to the grocery store. The next day you also leave your house, but this time you go to the bank. Your episodic memories of these events should each contain a series of events and the places where they occurred along the way to your destination. In addition, suppose the separate journeys to the grocery store and the bank both included a particular intersection. Somehow your episodic memories for the two trips would have to distinguish between the instances of being at that intersection. Can your hippocampus do that?

Compelling data imply that the spatial firing patterns of hippocampal neurons encode sequences of events and the events' places, and these representations are distinguished according to the episode in which they were experienced. In one study, rats were trained in the classic spatial alternation task in a modified T-maze (see Figure 8.15, p. 289; Wood et al., 2000). This task requires that the animal distinguish between left-turn and right-turn episodes and remember the immediately preceding episode to guide the current trial's choice (recall the win–stay and win–shift reward systems discussed in Chapter 6). Thus this task's memory demands resemble those of episodic memory. If hippocampal neurons encode each behavioral event and where it occurred, then most cells should fire during only one type of episode. That is, most cells' firing should be specific to either the left-turn or the right-turn situation. This should be particularly evident when the rat is in the stem of the maze—the corridor of the maze leading to the choice point, which the rat traverses at the beginning of both types of trials.

Indeed, virtually all cells that fired in the maze stem also fired differentially during either the rat's left turn or its right turn. Most cells showed striking selectivity for one trial type, suggesting that they contributed to the mental representations of only one type of episode. Other cells fired substantially during both trial types, potentially linking the left-turn and right-turn representations through the common places traversed. These data demonstrate that the hippocampal network encodes routes through space as sequences of events and encodes specific places that characterize particular episodes as the animal moves through space.

Functional brain imaging studies suggest that the human hippocampus acts similarly. Several imaging studies have been performed on humans engaged in spatial tasks; these studies show a common network of cortical areas activated during different aspects of spatial performance. Furthermore, when humans simply view complex spatial scenes, both the parahippocampal region and parts of the hippocampus can be activated (Epstein & Kanwisher, 1998). Other studies have directly investigated hippocampal activation during recall or encoding of large-scale environments. In one study humans initially explored a virtual reality representation of a town during brain imaging (Maguire et al., 1997). Stronger activation was observed in the right hippocampus during successful recall of routes than while following arrows through a route or during unsuccessful navigational attempts. Similarly, the hippocampus is strongly activated when London taxi drivers recall specific routes through the city (Maguire et al., 1998).

These studies demonstrate hippocampal activation during route retrieval, but they do not distinguish whether such activation reflects recollection of specific routes or generation of routes from maplike representations. Indeed, following initial study of either routes or maps, the hippocampus is activated during subsequent navigation of an environment. One study recently addressed the issue of whether humans encode environments in terms of sequences of places that compose routes or as pieces of a map of the environment (Shelton & Gabrieli, 2002). In this study, subjects' brains were scanned as they explored a large-scale virtual reality environment in one of two ways (Figure 9.12). Under one condition, they explored the environment from a bird's-eye view, encouraging a survey representation resembling a mental map. Alternatively they explored the environment from a ground perspective by entering through a doorway and traversing corridors and rooms, encouraging route representation.

As in previous imaging studies, a common network of cortical areas was activated in both conditions, but there were differences. Survey encoding caused greater activation in the inferior temporal and posterior parietal cortex—areas known to be associated with visual processing, suggesting that survey representations are encoded mainly as complex visual scenes. In contrast, route encoding involved regions not activated by survey encoding, including other cortical areas, the parahippocampal region, and the hippocampus. These findings support the view that the hippocampus initially encodes a large space as episodic representations of specific route-following experiences. These episodic representations can then be recalled and integrated to develop survey representations and to navigate familiar environments. Combining the findings for rats and humans, the data consistently show that the hippocampus represents space in terms of sequences of

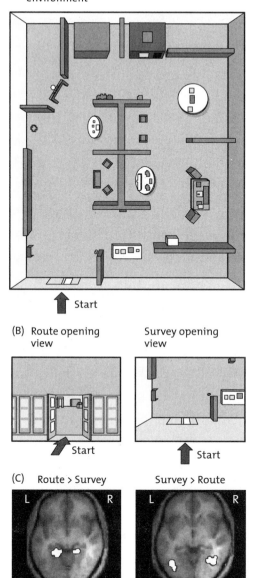

(A) Overhead view of the virtual environment

Start

(B) Route opening view   Survey opening view

Start   Start

(C)   Route > Survey   Survey > Route

L   R   L   R

FIGURE 9.12 Brain activations as subjects encode information in route and survey tasks.
A. A top view of the environment that subjects explored in virtual reality. B. The view at the outset of exploration from either the route or the survey perspective. C. Brain areas more activated in the route and survey versions of the task.

places and the events that occur in these places as we traverse the environment. Furthermore, hippocampal representations of space, like those for nonspatial memory, are fundamentally organized as sequences of events and places where they occur.

Interim Summary

Recordings of single neurons in animals have shown us the contents of hippocampal episodic memories. Hippocampal neurons encode a broad variety of events and where they occur. The hippocampus represents the flow of events in all attended experiences and distinguishes events depending on the episodes in which they occurred, as required to serve our ability to mentally replay experiences during episodic recollection. These properties of episodic representation are also observed in humans, further suggesting that the fundamental nature of episodic memory representation is similar across species.

Chapter Summary

1. Episodic memory is characterized by single-experience learning with enduring memory. Humans and animals share common features of episodic memory, so it is reasonable to expect a continuity of the basic information processing in this kind of memory across species. The hippocampus plays a vital and selective role in this processing.

2. In humans, episodic memory involves the ability to recollect specific personal experiences. This kind of memory is distinguished from semantic memory by its focus on unique personal events and its incorporation of when and where events occurred. The organization of episodic memory is temporal in that such memories are characterized by the flow of events that compose unique experiences.

3. Episodic memory can be selectively lost in amnesia. Several individuals with amnesia, some with selective hippocampal damage, have lost their capacity to recollect specific episodes but can recognize familiar stimuli. The ability to recall unique experiences may depend specifically on the hippocampus. In contrast, stimulus recognition may be supported in part by a sense of familiarity, which may be supported by the parahippocampal region. Functional brain imaging shows that the hippocampus is engaged selectively in episodic recollection, whereas parahippocampal region activation reflects novelty or familiarity of individual stimuli.

4. Animals demonstrate several aspects of episodic memory. They can remember unique events, and they display recollection-like memory retrieval as demonstrated in signal detection analyses. They can also remember the contexts in which they experienced specific stimuli and the order of events in unique episodes. The hippocampus is important to each of these aspects of experience that characterize episodic memory in humans. Consistent with this characterization, hippocampal networks represent events in their context and encode sequences of events and where they occur. These properties of hippocampal networks likely support our subjective experiences of recalling past events.

5. These combined findings suggest that the hippocampus plays a similar role in human and animal episodic memory. The initial characterization of episodic memory as defined by subjective mental replay of past experiences is difficult to study directly in humans or animals. However, recent successes in identifying features of episodic memory that can be observed objectively have allowed considerable progress in characterizing the nature and brain pathways of episodic memory across species.

KEY TERMS

episodic memory (p. 295)
semantic memory (p. 295)
familiarity (p. 296)

recollection (p. 296)
receiver operating characteristics (ROCs) (p. 301)

REVIEWING THE CONCEPTS

- What key features distinguish episodic memory from semantic memory?

- In humans, what is the role of the hippocampus in recall and recognition? What is its role in recollection and familiarity?

- How are signal detection analyses used to distinguish between processes of recollection and familiarity?

- What is the evidence that animals have episodic memory? What role does the hippocampus play in animals' episodic memory?

Early in my graduate studies, I was asked to stop my experimental work briefly so a senior graduate student could use the necessary lab equipment to complete his thesis in time to begin his first job. I had wanted to take some time off from the experimental work to bolster my understanding of neuroanatomy, and at the same time I was yearning to follow a girl to Paris. I took this coincidence seriously and spent the next six weeks in the cafés near the University of Paris, enjoying wonderful café au lait and croissants while working my way through a neuroanatomy workbook.

By late morning my mind was usually boggled with neuroanatomical terminology, so I would wander the streets taking photographs and learning the territory. One of my favorite areas was the Place de Panthéon, an area I came to know well within a couple of weeks.

After my morning work, I usually spent the afternoons taking in the sights. I frequently would take the subway to the Luxembourg Garden, and by exploring the garden and its surrounding neighborhood, I came to know the layout of that area quite well, also. Walking there one day, I started down a small street with apartments and shops I hadn't seen before. I turned a corner and suddenly found myself staring, quite unexpectedly, at the Panthéon.

Until that moment, I had a mental map of the neighborhood of the Luxembourg Garden and another mental map of the area around the University of Paris and Panthéon. Suddenly the two maps merged into a larger framework that covered a substantial section of the left bank area of Paris. I was becoming a Parisian (or at least I thought so) in terms of my knowledge of Paris geography.

YOU HAVE PROBABLY had a similar experience while learning your way around a new place; such experiences are just one example of the formation of semantic memory, our store of general knowledge about the world. Just as my knowledge of two Paris neighborhoods became integrated into a more comprehensive mental map, learning and integrating semantic information across many domains occurs gradually as experiences reveal constancies and regularities about the world. How do our brains organize and store the vast amount of information we learn about geography, history, baseball, or myriad other topics? Where is all this information stored, and how do we access it? How is new information added to an existing framework? This chapter addresses these questions and more.

We first consider the broad scope of semantic knowledge that we acquire during our lives. Next we look more closely at the organization and mechanisms of semantic memory from two perspectives:

1. Models of semantic memory developed from the perspective of cognitive science propose how knowledge might be organized conceptually and then are tested with human performance.
2. Case studies of people with semantic memory disorders, as well as functional brain imaging studies, identify areas of the brain that are involved in processing semantic memories.

Finally we consider how episodic memory and semantic memory interact, allowing us to build our semantic memory storehouse with information acquired in new experiences.

Fundamental Questions

1. What theories have been advanced to explain how semantic knowledge is organized?
2. How do researchers define categories of semantic knowledge?
3. Where is information about different categories of semantic knowledge stored in the brain?

Defining Semantic Memory

What is the capital of France? Who was the second president of the United States? What is a double play? What is hip-hop? Where is the Statue of Liberty? What is the best route from your home to work? Is a dolphin a fish? Each of these questions taps your semantic memory—an incredibly large store of information about countless areas of knowledge.

Your semantic memory store is enormous. Average people have vocabularies of 20,000 to 100,000 words and know the basic geography of the world; the history of their own countries; the lineage of their family trees for at least a few generations; arithmetic; and detailed knowledge of at least one profession, at least one hobby or pastime, hundreds of foods, clothes, TV shows, songs, vehicles, and many more topics. And they can access most of this information in an instant.

This semantic memory storehouse of general knowledge includes our knowledge of words, as its name suggests, and it also includes our knowledge of concepts, scenes, geography, mathematics, and every other class of knowledge, verbal and nonverbal, for all factual information that can be brought to conscious awareness and expressed explicitly. **Semantic memory** is the component of cognitive memory that contains information not bound to any particular event, and it is organized by conceptual properties rather than by the order of experienced events.

Semantic Memory May Be Organized as a Hierarchy of Concepts

One of the earliest, most influential modern models of semantic memory suggested that knowledge is stored in a network of interrelated concepts and that this network is organized as a hierarchy, with specific features at the bottom of the hierarchy and more abstract, general features at the top. Figure 10.1 shows this

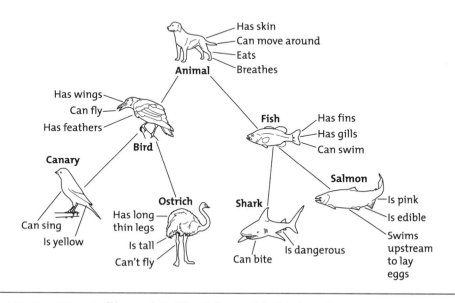

FIGURE 10.1 Collins and Quillian's hierarchical network.

kind of hierarchical network for some components of semantic memory for animals. Note that at the top of the hierarchy are features that define all animals: They have skin, and they can move, eat, and breathe. This general category is divided into major categories of animals, such as birds and fish. These categories in turn are defined by the features that characterize all birds, such as having wings and feathers, and all fish, such as having fins and gills and being able to swim. These categories are divided into subcategories, which are defined by their features, and so on. This is an efficient way to store knowledge. The system does not have to explicitly store information for each **exemplar**—that is, each particular item to be remembered. Instead it can more efficiently store common characteristics of several exemplars at higher levels of the hierarchy. Thus, for example, we do not have to specifically store the information that canaries have wings because that feature is already stored at the higher-level category of birds. At the same time, this kind of network supports inferences about specific exemplars. If I ask you, "Does a canary have feathers?" you can refer to the information at the superordinate level of birds. Even if you cannot picture a canary feather specifically, you can infer that it must have feathers.

This model was tested in famous experiments by Collins and Quillian (1969, 1972). They predicted that if semantic knowledge is organized as a hierarchical network, the amount of time required to answer questions should be related to the number of steps in the hierarchy that must be traversed to find the answer. Verifying a statement about properties within one hierarchy level should be faster than verifying a statement that requires combining information stored at multiple levels. For example, confirming that a canary is yellow should take less time than confirming that a canary is an animal. Also, additional time should be needed in direct proportion to the number of hierarchy levels that must be bridged to verify a statement. For example, it should require more time to verify that a canary breathes than that a canary is a bird. Both of these predictions were confirmed.

This kind of model could be instantiated by a simple mechanism connecting items according to the strength of the associations between them. This notion presumes that features within a level occur together more frequently and therefore are more closely associated than features stored at different levels. For example, the feature *yellow* is closely associated with canaries. *Yellow* appears virtually every time we think of *canary*. By contrast, *breathe* and *canary* hardly ever appear together. Some people wonder whether findings that seem to support a conceptual hierarchy are actually a consequence of frequent co-occurrence of conceptually similar items. But perhaps the associations among related items that we learn through experience become the basis for conceptual hierarchy.

If indeed associations between concepts underlie the construction of hierarchical organizations, exceptions to the orderly hierarchy sequence should occur when strong associations between features bridge large hierarchy distances. Ripps and colleagues (1973) found that some statements about common associations that bridge large distances in a conceptual category are verified more quickly than other statements that involve looser associations among concepts stored closer together in the hierarchy. For example, even though *mammal* is a subcategory of *animal*, the statement "A dog is a mammal" required more time to verify than "A dog is an animal."

Compelling evidence that semantic memories are organized hierarchically from top (more general concepts) to bottom (more specific properties) has come from studying how people retrieve words using the combined cues of the first letter of a word and the higher-order category associated with that word. People tend to come up with an appropriate word faster if given the category cue first, then the first letter of the word, and not the other way around. For example, if given the category *birds,* then the first letter *c,* people are quicker to respond *canary* than if they are initially given the letter, then the category. This finding suggests that giving the category first prepares the subject to search within a coherent and manageable set of words in which the letter *c* can cue a relevant word. Giving the letter *c* first presents too many undirected possibilities.

Also, the notion that semantic organization is based more strongly on associations (the words *canary* and *bird* are associated) than on the logic of conceptual links (a canary really is a kind of bird) explains why some judgments that are equivalent in conceptual distance, but more commonly associated, are made faster. For example, people judge that a canary is a bird more quickly than they judge that a penguin is a bird. This finding suggests that items are stored according to the dominant features that characterize them rather than the logical relations between concepts. Rosch (1973) measured the different amounts of time required to verify a particular sentence when it was completed with different exemplars taken from the same level in a conceptual hierarchy. For example, she tested the time required to verify "I watched a ____ eat a worm" with the blank filled in by *robin, eagle, ostrich,* and *penguin.* Although a hierarchical network places all these birds at the same distance in the hierarchy from what birds eat, some of these exemplars are experienced more frequently than others.

Thus our semantic knowledge of concepts seems to be organized less by conceptual features than by experienced features that are common across exemplars. Some relatively simple concepts, like simple shapes, can be rigidly and unequivocally defined by their features. For example, a square is a closed polygon with four sides that are equal in length. If a shape has these features, it unambiguously is a square. If a shape lacks any of these features, we can unequivocally conclude it is not a square. However, many other categories—especially natural categories—are more complex. For example, in the hierarchy of animals, most people would agree that a defining feature of birds is that they can fly. Some birds, though, such as penguins and ostriches, cannot fly. Most people would be inclined to say that laying eggs is also a defining feature of birds; but other animals (reptiles, fish, and insects) lay eggs too.

These and many other examples challenge the view that we can organize semantic knowledge according to rigid conceptual schemes. An alternative is the idea that through associations, we develop a **prototype:** a simple model of a category of items that share the basic features of the model. Prototypes do not require rigidly defined features; rather they organize items according to the typicality of associating particular features with a conceptual prototype. Exemplars that share more features with the prototype are recognized more quickly and frequently than those that share fewer features with it. Furthermore, organization by prototype allows categories to have fuzzy boundaries, so items can exist within multiple categories or be judged differently by various people. For example, McCloskey and Glucksberg (1978) asked people to assign a number of items to one of the following categories: *fruits, vegetables,* and *precious stones.* They found that some items were consistently placed in the same category and others varied. For example, *tomato* was categorized as a fruit by some people and as a vegetable by others. A tomato sits at the conceptual boundary between prototypes for fruits and vegetables: It looks like a fruit and has seeds, but it is not sweet like most fruits we eat.

Other examples of items that people differently categorize are dolphins, which have many features of fish but are mammals, and penguins, which have some features of fish but are birds. People are unlikely to name dolphins as an exemplar of a mammal or penguins as an exemplar of birds, and they are relatively slow to verify statements that categorize these animals. Rosch and Mervis (1975) explored prototypes by giving two groups of people the names of 20 objects from each of six categories (*furniture, vehicles, weapons, clothing, vegetables,* and *fruits*). One group was asked to list as many attributes as possible for each category. For example, fruits were characterized as round, sweet, yellow or red, and grown on trees; vegetables were characterized as long, not sweet, green, and grown in or near the ground. Few objects were described with all the attributes of their categories, showing that people do not apply rigid conceptual definitions to natural objects. Indeed, certain objects were frequently given from few to nearly all of their category features. The other group of subjects was asked how typical each object was of its category; particular objects were given a typicality rating of good or poor. These ratings varied consistently with the number of features an object shared with its category. Thus apples and broccoli were rated as typical of their categories and have all the features of fruits and vegetables just listed, whereas tomatoes were rated as low in typicality and have features from both categories.

Semantic Memories May Be Stored as Sets of Distributed Networks

A more modern approach to understanding the organization of semantic memory involves *distributed network models* (McClelland & Rumelhart, 1986). In these models, embodied as computer simulations, concepts are represented as patterns of activation across a network of interconnected units. Each unit can be conceived as representing some feature (such as *has wings*) of a concept (*canary*). The units do not have to correspond to a nameable feature or concept; instead they may represent merely some aspect of a feature (perhaps the shape of a wing) that cannot be named. Conversely, a nameable feature, such as *has wings,* might be represented across many units.

The units acquire their specificities through learning. In the typical experiment a network is given a set of inputs (cues) and is required to generate a response. Different network units will be activated according to the initial weights or strengths of connections with other units, leading to an activation pattern of network outputs. Whenever the actual generated output matches the correct response, the connection weights are increased; if the network fails to produce the required output, the activated connection weights are reduced. Through this "learning" process, networks can be trained to process specific auditory input patterns corresponding to the sound of a word in order to produce, for example, a set of outputs corresponding to the word's meaning.

In distributed network models, knowledge is encoded in the different strengths of connections between units. Typically the units are organized into **modules** (groups of units) that correspond to one type of information, such as visual or auditory, or serve a particular function, like input or output. Units within a module are typically more richly interconnected than those between modules. Thus a variety of network models can be created to simulate assorted systems and perform various functions. For example, Farah and McClelland (1991) created a model of semantic memory with three modules corresponding to verbal inputs, visual inputs, and semantic representations, each composed of separate modules for visual and functional units. In this model, visual and verbal inputs are both connected to the semantic representations, but they are not connected to each other. An important characteristic of these models is that they exhibit **graceful degradation**—a gradual rather than catastrophic decay of function when part of the model is compromised. In these experiments, when the network is somewhat damaged, the modules lose only partial function because the network information is distributed across many units. Farah and McClelland's model performed well in associating names and pictures of objects even when 40 percent of its units were destroyed. Other more complex configurations of multiple distributed networks have been created to address how semantic memory incorporates information from episodic memory. Some of these models will be discussed in Chapter 11.

Learning & Memory in Action

How Can Computers Learn to Recognize Speech?

Given the complexities of semantic memory networks, you might correctly surmise that it would be difficult to create machines with semantic memories. However, using theoretical conceptions derived from network models that you have read about here, engineers have succeeded remarkably in creating machines that perform some of the tasks we do so well with our semantic memory. Take, for example, a problem that is central to semantic memory: speech recognition. This might seem to require only a straightforward matching of sounds to word templates, but the problem is not so simple.

Consider first that we must match sounds made by a broad range of human voices with various accents to the meaningful words in our vocabulary. Consider also that speech occurs in many background noises. Yet current systems are remarkably able to understand a large speech vocabulary. Theodore Berger and his colleagues have developed a system that can recognize spoken words from a variety of speakers better than the keenest human ears. Furthermore, the system can identify words even through noise levels a thousand times the volume of the target words. More amazing is that this machine employs a network of only 11 artificial "neurons" with 30 links in an architecture modeled after the hippocampus. The network does not have a preprogrammed set of words. Rather, it learns to match speech patterns to target words through training with a diverse set of input voices, using rules like those in the Farah and McClelland model, much as we learn to recognize speech and match various voices to meaningful vocabulary. Such systems will soon replace the automated answering machines in airport reservation lines and other businesses that are so frustrating to customers. And they will be used by us to tell our radios what stations to tune to, to ask our global positioning systems how to get to our destinations, and to call in our pizza delivery orders.

Interim Summary

An intuitive view of the structure of semantic memory suggests that information is stored as a hierarchy of concepts. The hierarchy is organized with specific exemplar features at the bottom and more general features at the top. Tests of this idea show that answering questions about items that require crossing levels of generality takes longer, consistent with the hierarchical structure. Also, it is easier to answer questions that involve working down, rather than up, the hierarchy. At the same time, associations between specific features and exemplars that have those features are powerful. Thus semantic memory is likely based on a conceptual hierarchy with strengths of associations between features in prototype exemplars modifying how the conceptual organization is used. Distributed network models originally developed by McClelland and Rumelhart have shown that semantic networks can arise through modifications of the initially random connections between units as the network is given partial information and asked to identify particular exemplars. Through reinforcement of accurate connections, the network represents a hierarchy of conceptual features similar to those revealed in human studies. The success of these network models suggests that simple associative principles are sufficient to create conceptual hierarchies.

Spatial Memories May Be Organized as Routes or Surveys

One type of semantic memory that is difficult to represent in words or verbal concepts is spatial knowledge. Nevertheless, spatial knowledge is subject to some of the same variables as verbal knowledge. For example, think about the idea that our mental representations of distances between items in a hierarchy (such as the number of steps in the hierarchy between *canary* and *animal*) depend on the extent of experienced associations in verbal semantic memory networks. A parallel observation is that semantic memories for spatial knowledge are similarly determined by the extent of experience and details of associations about geography. In one study, Moar (1978) gave British citizens a piece of paper with only a vertical line marking the north and south ends of Britain and asked them to draw lines representing the locations of cities and directions between them. From these sketches Moar reconstructed maps of his subjects' conceptions of British geography. As can be seen in the examples shown in Figure 10.2, the nature of the maps depended on where the subjects lived. Thus maps drawn by subjects who lived in the south tended to exaggerate the details of city locations and directions in England, with which they were more familiar; similarly, subjects from the north tended to elaborate the details and directions between cities in Scotland.

How are such large-scale spatial representations constructed? Environments that cannot be viewed in their entirety from a single location must be learned initially by navigation through the environment. So knowledge of the environment initially consists of a set of **routes**—specific paths from one place to another (Thorndyke & Hayes Roth, 1982). However, as experience is accumulated, people can learn locations of objects, along with distances and directions between them, and eventually gain a maplike overview or **survey** knowledge of the environment. Survey learning is richer if the goal is to create a map of the environment than if the goal is merely to get from one place to another in independent trips.

Once acquired, spatial memories are not entirely flexible; like maps on paper, they are easier to use in particular orientations (Shelton & McNamara, 2001).

(A)

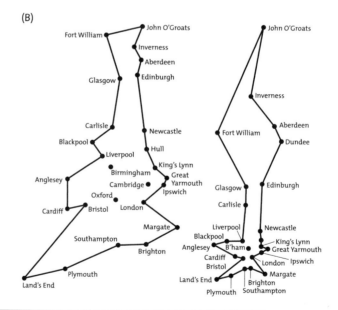

(B)

FIGURE 10.2 Actual and reconstructed maps of Britain.
A. Actual map of Britain. B. Maps of Britain drawn from memory by Moar's subjects. The reconstructed map on the left was made by people from Cambridge, whereas the one on the right was made by people from Glasgow.

When we initially view a room and learn the locations of objects in that room from one perspective, we recall the objects' locations best when viewing the room from the same perspective. However, even when learning occurs from several perspectives, some views are more favorable for accurate memories. The key issue seems to be the use of specific **reference systems,** or perspective views, in creating a survey representation. One reference system is *egocentric,* involving the locations and distances of objects relative to the position and direction of the viewer. In this situation, memory is best from the learned viewpoint. Other reference systems are *environmental:* They are based on the locations and directions of objects in relation to one another, independent of the viewer. The environmental reference frame can vary and depends on the viewer's experience, the structure of the environment, and specific objects in the environment. Thus people designate a conceptual "north" (which might be a sense of "straight ahead" rather than real north), and this creates privileged directions in memory so that retrieval of spatial relations is more efficient in directions aligned with the conceptual north–south–east–west axes. For example, imagine you were asked to memorize the set of objects shown in Figure 10.3 as seen from the view indicated by the arrow. You would find it much easier to point to the clock if you were standing at the book looking at the wood than you would while standing at the lamp looking at the wood. So mental maps seem to be constructed around a particular reference point with items aligned in simple, two-dimensional, 90 degree axes from that point.

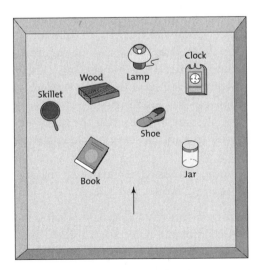

FIGURE 10.3 Example layout of a room with several objects.
The arrow indicates the viewer's perspective.

Like verbal semantic memories, spatial memories are also hierarchically organized (Stevens & Coupe, 1978). People learn object locations in terms of clusters of neighboring elements within a room, such as grouping together the objects on a desk. Then they learn the spatial relations of those clusters relative to each other—perhaps the set of furniture in an office. Progressively higher levels of integration allow us to organize representations of rooms within a building, buildings on a city block, and so on, forming a hierarchy of reference frames (Poucet, 1993).

Learning & Memory in Action

Designing Cities

Knowledge gained from studies of human cognitive maps has aided the work of environmental engineers in understanding how people learn their way around their cities. Conversely, studies by urban planners can show scientists how people organize their cognitive maps in the real world. For example, in his landmark study of cities, Lynch (1960) interviewed people in three sample cities: Boston, Jersey City, and Los Angeles. People were chosen who had lived in each city for a long time and had residences or workplaces in diverse locations throughout the city. The interviews requested descriptions and sketches of the environment, and asked about locations of major landmarks and the routes of imaginary trips. Lynch identified five main elements of peoples' images of their cities:

1. *Paths* are channels along which the observers move; they may occur in the form of streets, sidewalks, canals, or railroads.
2. *Edges* are boundaries that break the continuity of surfaces, including shores, walls, and demarcations between districts.
3. *Districts* are medium-sized sections of a city conceived as two-dimensional areas that people can be "inside of."
4. *Nodes* are strategic spots in a city that the observer can enter and use as a starting or ending point for travel, including road junctions and street corner hangouts.
5. *Landmarks* are other points of reference that the observer does not enter, such as signs, towers, domes, and hills.

These observations suggest that maps are not formed from a blank mental grid into which notable objects are inserted, and the important features of maps are not arbitrarily selected. Rather, our construction of cognitive maps depends on how we travel paths within them, on our ability to use edges to compartmentalize large-scale environments into smaller districts, and on our ability to join those districts by key nodes and landmarks—as described at the beginning of this chapter.

Interim Summary

Associations play a key role in the development of semantic memories for spatial topographies. These associations can occur as we learn sequences of places that compose routes through the environment or as we learn important locations in a global survey of the environment. Once acquired, spatial cognitive maps are easiest to use starting from familiar viewpoints and depend on our reference framework, such as a direction for "north." Like other kinds of semantic memory, spatial maps involve conceptual hierarchies; large topographies have less spatial resolution, whereas small topographies contain spatial detail.

The Organization of Semantic Information Processing

Much of what we know about the brain areas involved in processing specific types of semantic information comes from case studies of individuals with selective damage to particular areas of the cerebral cortex. Many of these people have specific information processing deficits, suggesting which type of semantic information is normally handled in that brain area. Complementary evidence comes from functional imaging studies demonstrating activation of specific brain areas when a particular type of information is processed. The combination of these studies has provided a preliminary mapping of the organization of semantic memory in the cerebral cortex.

Aphasia and Agnosia

Studies of individuals with circumscribed brain damage have revealed considerable insights into the organization of semantic memory in the brain. These studies focus on people with **aphasia,** a disorder of language comprehension or production, and those with **agnosia,** an inability to identify familiar objects.

Within the domain of memory for words, Goodglass and colleagues (1966) reported that people with aphasia following damage to areas of the cerebral cortex sometimes have selective deficits in finding particular categories of words. Some subjects had difficulty naming colors or body parts, others with naming food and kitchen utensils. These observations led to the hypothesis that distinct cortical areas represent different semantic categories of information, an idea first systematically investigated by Warrington and Shallice (1984). Their study described four individuals who developed cortical damage following herpes infections. Each of these subjects had trouble understanding words that referred to living things while having no difficulty in processing names of inanimate objects. In one experiment, the subjects tried to identify pictures of many animals, plants, and inanimate objects. The subjects could name almost none of the living things but accurately identified 80 to 90 percent of the inanimate objects. Similarly, they could offer reasonably elaborate descriptions of inanimate objects but gave, at best, impoverished descriptions of animals and plants. For example, one subject described a wasp incorrectly as a "bird that flies" and a duck as "an animal"—but characterized a submarine as a "ship that goes underneath the sea" and an umbrella as an "object used to protect you from water that comes."

The deficit was apparent for both visual and auditory stimuli and for both rare and frequently appearing items; but sometimes an item could be identified when presented in one modality (perhaps as a written word) and not the other (hearing the word). In a test that assessed these individuals' ability to identify items from 26 verbal categories, one subject scored within the normal range in 14 categories and poorly in the remainder. The categories in which the subject failed were dominated by types of animals and plants, such as insects, fish, and fruits, although he also had difficulty with a few other categories, such as precious stones. By comparison, he performed well on a broad range of categories related to inanimate objects or concepts, including clothing, furniture, vehicles, and sports. However, another subject showed the opposite pattern of selective deficiency. This man had a severe deficit in the comprehension of inanimate object names, whereas his ability to process names of foods, animals, and plants was preserved. The existence of subjects with opposite patterns of deficiency for different categories rules out the possible interpretation that some categories are just more difficult and therefore more sensitive to general brain dysfunction.

Damasio and colleagues (1996) combined studies of individuals with aphasia and brain imaging experiments to extend the notion that different cortical areas mediate distinct categories of verbal knowledge. They tested the abilities of many subjects who had limited damage to different cortical areas to name pictures of people, animals, and tools. They found a broad variability in subjects' deficits: Some people were impaired in naming items from only one category, whereas others' impairments affected combinations of categories. One combination that was strikingly absent was a deficit in naming people and tools, but not animals.

Each subject was then subjected to a brain scan to identify the locus of cortical damage. The scan results explained why the particular combination of people and tools was not observed and offered insight into how representations of these semantic categories are organized. Individuals with deficits in naming people all had damage to the left temporal pole (the tip of the temporal cortex); those with impairment in naming animals had damage to the left anterior inferior temporal cortex; and those with deficits in naming tools had damage in the left posterior temporal and parietal cortex (Figure 10.4). The jobs of these cortical areas were confirmed with a functional imaging study of normal subjects who had brain scans performed as they named famous people, animals, and tools. This study showed

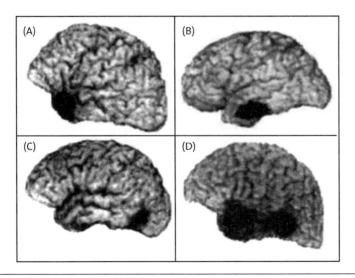

FIGURE 10.4 Scans of subjects with category deficits.
Subject A had a specific deficit in naming people, subject B in naming animals, and subject C in naming tools. Subject D was deficient in all three categories.

that distinct areas of the cortex were activated when subjects named items in each category; these areas corresponded to the damaged areas for which the identical naming functions were lost.

Proposagnosia and Anomia

Some deficits observed in individuals with brain damage can be highly selective, hinting at how knowledge is organized in the brain. A remarkable example of agnosia is the disorder known as **proposagnosia**—the inability to recognize familiar people (Farah, 2004). People with this disorder typically have normal intelligence and memory for a variety of materials, and they readily recognize a large range of objects and line drawings. They also can identify faces in general among other types of stimuli and can point out key facial features, such as the eyes, nose, and mouth. However, they cannot recognize people whom they know. They do not recognize their doctors on sight, and they fail to recognize even their spouses, children, or other family members until they hear their loved ones speak. In testing, they cannot identify pictures of famous people.

One particularly clever experiment with a proposagnosic subject provided insight into the nature of face recognition. This individual and normal subjects were asked to match one of a set of faces presented in the normal orientation to a specific sample face presented either in the normal orientation or upside down.

Normal subjects are much better at matching faces in the typical orientation; but surprisingly, the proposagnosic subject showed the opposite pattern—better performance in matching upside-down faces. This observation suggested that we have a special face recognition mechanism that helps normal people recognize faces in the ordinary orientation and is detrimental for faces that are upside-down. This mechanism was not available to the proposagnosic subject, preventing him from easily recognizing faces in the normal orientation; but it also did not disadvantage him when he had to recognize upside-down faces.

Anomia is a disorder of the ability to name objects. This impairment is a variant of aphasia that has been called *amnesic aphasia* because the main deficit is in remembering the names of objects—an ability central to semantic knowledge. Many cases of anomia have been observed. Some are general to all varieties of objects and any method of presentation. But other cases of anomia are selective to a particular category of objects, such as colors, letters, numbers, or actions; and there have been cases selective to proper names. Other cases are selective to a particular sensory modality such as vision, touch, or smell. Many such disorders can be attributed to disconnections between sensory inputs and verbal comprehension areas. For example, one man could not name objects touched with his right hand but succeeded if the objects were felt with his left hand. Other cases of anomia may be attributable to impaired verbal comprehension. For example, if a subject cannot understand the difference between a fork and a spoon, then it is not surprising that she cannot remember the name of either object. However, in *pure anomia* the individual cannot provide the name of the object but can explain its characteristics or how it is used. For example, a person with pure anomia may not be able to provide the name for a picture of a camel but can describe it as an animal that lives in the desert and can go for days without water. These observations tell us that our memory for the names of things—semantic knowledge at its purest—is a distinct memory capacity.

The Cortex Processes Category-Specific Information

Several functional imaging techniques have identified cortical areas that play distinct roles in category-specific information processing. Kanwisher and her colleagues (1997) identified an area in the ventral temporal cortex that is activated during the processing of face images; she called this area the *fusiform face area* (FFA). The FFA was more strongly activated during passive viewing of intact face images than scrambled ones and more activated during viewing of faces than other images. This finding complements the observations for proposagnosia (discussed a few paragraphs ago), which occurs in people with damage to the ventral temporal cortex. Also, these findings match descriptions of neurons that respond selectively to face images, which researchers have found in the same temporal cortex area in monkeys.

Another study reported the existence of a cortical area specialized for processing spatial information. This area, located in the parahippocampal gyrus, was called the *parahippocampal place area* (PPA; Epstein & Kanwisher, 1998). This time human subjects' brains were scanned as they passively viewed different types of scenes and sets of objects and faces. The PPA was activated when the subjects looked at various views of houses or environmental scenes. But the PPA was not activated when subjects viewed faces or common objects. The PPA's response to scenes with a spatial layout but containing no discrete objects (an empty room) was as robust as the response observed for complex scenes (rooms with furniture) and much stronger than response levels for multiple objects without a spatial background. When parts of scenes were rearranged to eliminate the appearance of a coherent space (they looked like scrambled patterns of puzzle pieces), the PPA response was reduced. So this cortical area appears to be specialized for processing spatial geometry. A subsequent experiment showed that the PPA responds as strongly to changes in the viewpoint of a scene as it does to changes in the scene layout, indicating that the PPA processes viewpoint-specific information about spatial geometry (Epstein et al., 2003).

Another cortical area has been identified as specialized for processing information about human body parts (Downing et al., 2001). This area, localized in the right lateral occipital cortex and called the *extrastriate body area* (EBA), was more active in people viewing photographs or drawings of human bodies and body parts than in people looking at various inanimate objects or their parts. The EBA was activated in response to both faces and other body parts, including hands. The response to whole bodies was greatest, but the response to face parts was greater than that to whole faces. In addition, the EBA seems to be specialized for semantic knowledge of human bodies. The response of the EBA was greater to human bodies or body parts than to various animal bodies or body parts, although the latter response was greater than that to object parts.

These observations raise the question of whether the entire cerebral cortex is organized as a set of modules specialized for processing different categories of semantic information. If so, how many categories are there, and what are they? How can there be enough areas to represent all the kinds of information processed in semantic memory?

Cortical Area Specialization: Category-Specific or Process-Specific Mechanisms

Cortical areas that appear to be category-specific may actually just be well suited to respond to processing demands characterizing certain types of information. Martin and his colleagues (1996) followed the initial reports of specialized cerebral cortex areas for processing living things and inanimate objects (Warrington & Shallice, 1984) by scanning the brains of normal subjects as they silently named items shown in line drawings of various animals and tools. Naming animals and tools activated speech areas, as well as a broad area in the ventral temporal lobe on both sides of the brain. In addition, naming animals selectively activated an area in the left medial occipital lobe, an area involved in early visual processing. In contrast, when subjects named tools, an additional area in the left premotor cortex was activated. Notably, this area was also activated when subjects imagined grasping objects with their right hands. When subjects named tools, another area in the left middle temporal gyrus was selectively activated. This area also became active when subjects generated action words associated with objects.

These observations led Martin and his colleagues to suggest that our capacity to process semantic information about a broad range of information is mediated by a large network of cortical areas. According to this view, specialized processing of different information categories recruits distinct cortical areas suited to processing specific physical attributes or functional properties defining various categories of information. Thus identifying animals may require processing visual details, whereas tool identification may demand information about objects' functions. In this view, the observed cortical processing distinctions for other categories of information would also depend on differences in those categories' processing demands.

Another possible distinction in semantic processing may be related to the difference between distinguishing individual items within a category, as experts do, and holistically processing items as members of their categories. For example, perhaps the so-called face area is really specialized for picking out individual items within a category, such as specific faces. The object processing area, on the other hand, may actually focus on grouping exemplars into appropriate categories—such as understanding that many styles of chairs are all the same type of object. This possibility has been explored in functional imaging studies by Gauthier and her colleagues (1999, 2000). One such study trained human subjects to discriminate between complex objects called "greebles." A greeble is one of a collection of many individual objects, each of which has several feature dimensions; the objects can be grouped into families with similar features (Figure 10.5). With sufficient training, people learned to categorize greebles both as individuals and as members of a family. Following training, subjects' brains were scanned as they viewed a variety of greebles and a variety of faces. The cortical area activated for sorting and grouping greebles was identical with the FFA, the area previously shown to be specialized for face processing.

In a second study, the same researchers examined the cortical areas involved in processing pictures of car models and bird species by expert subjects. The FFA was more active when experts viewed items within their expertise than when they viewed other familiar objects. These studies support the notion that cortical areas

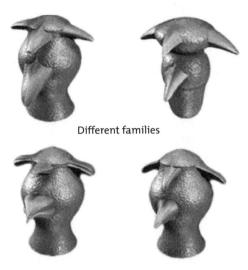

Different families

Different individuals

FIGURE 10.5 Greebles.

are distinguished by the kind of processing they perform rather than the distinct categories of semantic information processed. The FFA is specialized for distinguishing individuals within a category, whereas object processing areas may be specialized for generalizing among exemplars within a category. (See Tarr & Gauthier, 2000, and Kanwisher, 2000, for a discussion of this controversy.)

The debate about whether cortical areas are specialized for categories of information or kinds of processing is leading toward a consensus about knowledge organization in the cerebral cortex. Ishai and colleagues (1999) used functional brain imaging to identify three distinct areas of the ventral temporal cortex that each responded preferentially to faces, houses, or chairs; these areas were in the same cortical locations in different subjects. However, each knowledge category evoked substantial responses in all three cortical zones, and each information category was associated with a distinct pattern of activation across the expanse of the ventral temporal cortex. These data suggest that a large continuous network of cortical areas represents a broad variety of categories and that different network components process distinct categories of information. Similarly, Chao and colleagues (1999) reported distinct but overlapping activation patterns when subjects read the names of or answered questions about either animals or tools, suggesting a distributed network with sites for processing these information categories. And Haxby and colleagues (2001) described an expansive network of cortical areas that were activated while subjects viewed diverse stimulus categories, including faces, cats, and several types of crafted objects (such as chairs and shoes). In a distinct set of overlapping areas, activation patterns reliably corresponded to the knowledge categories being processed. Even in areas that maximally responded to only one category, the response patterns could still discriminate among all the categories (but see Spiridon & Kanwisher, 2002, for a contrary view). Taken together, these findings strongly suggest that semantic memories are represented in a broad cortical network in which different parts of the network have some degree of specialization for a particular information category or kind of information processing.

Interim Summary

Studies of aphasia and agnosia indicate that memories for words and visual stimuli are organized by conceptual categories. Information about specific conceptual categories of items is stored in distinct areas of the cerebral cortex. Functional brain imaging also shows that distinct conceptual categories of stimuli, such as faces, places, and body parts, are represented in specific cerebral cortex areas. A current controversy is whether these anatomically distinct activations arise because of the representation of conceptual categories or because brain areas are specialized to perform different types of processing necessary to identify features that are common to stimuli within one category. These ideas about the brain's basic organization of semantic memory are not mutually exclusive: Conceptual clusters may arise from specializations in brain processing mechanisms.

Episodic Memory Contributes to Semantic Memory

Tulving (2002) has argued that the episodic and semantic memory systems are distinct. But the same information can be processed by both systems, and we can often replay earlier experiences in episodic memory to answer questions about facts acquired in those experiences. On the other hand, as Chapter 8 discussed, many believe that semantic memories synthesize information acquired from episodic memories. Specifically, the hippocampus may encode episodic memories into networks to generalize about the common features among related memories and mediate flexible memory expression. Within this model, the hippocampus contributes to semantic memory by constructing networks of associations called *relational networks* that coordinate memories stored in the cerebral cortex (Eichenbaum et al., 1999). From this perspective, semantic memories are not directly mediated by the hippocampus. Rather, the hippocampus links memories, letting us integrate information and use memories in novel ways. This is often called *flexible* memory expression to contrast it with the stereotyped way in which habits are typically expressed. So semantic memory might be possible without hippocampal involvement.

Supporting this view, some aspects of semantic knowledge can be acquired normally even by densely amnesic individuals with damaged hippocampal systems. Knowlton and colleagues (1992) examined whether people with amnesia can acquire grammar in the absence of episodic memory. They showed subjects nonsense letter strings generated by an artificial grammar that determined general rules for letter string sequencing and length (Figure 10.6). The subjects studied these strings by repeating each string immediately after its presentation. Then subjects were told that the letter strings were formed by complex rules. Subsequently they were shown novel letter strings one at a time and classified them as grammatical or nongrammatical according to whether they conformed with the rules inferred from the earlier examples. Finally the subjects were tested to determine

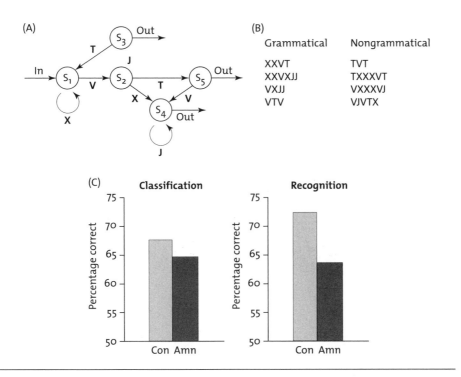

FIGURE 10.6 Artificial grammars.
A. Formal structure of the grammar where each step (S) involves a specific letter.
B. Examples of grammatical and nongrammatical letter strings. C. Performance of normal control subjects (Con) and amnesic subjects (Ams) on classification of grammatical and nongrammatical letter strings and on recognizing previously classified strings.

if they could recognize previously presented grammatical letter strings after a brief study phase. Both amnesic and normal subjects could correctly classify the letter strings in about two-thirds of the trials. However, the amnesic subjects had trouble recognizing the studied grammatical items. These findings show that memory for grammatical structure is separate from memory for the specific examples to which those rules are applied, and acquisition of grammatical semantic structure can proceed normally even in amnesic people.

There is also strong evidence that amnesic individuals can learn to distinguish categories of stimuli even without being able to recall specific stimuli. Reed and colleagues (1999) showed subjects line drawings of cartoon animals (Figure 10.7). Each drawing varied systematically along nine different features—the head, neck, body, and so on. Two variations of each feature were assigned in advance to compose one of two prototypes that therefore differed in all the features. Subjects were told that their job was to assign each cartoon animal as belonging or not belonging in the category called "Peggles," basing their judgments on the overall appearance of the animal. They were shown an animal with all the features that defined Peggles to provide the prototype for that category; the other exemplars they viewed varied in their degrees of distortion from that prototype. During an initial study phase, subjects saw a set of low-distortion exemplars to illustrate the variations of Peggles. Then they were shown many distorted exemplars.

Amnesic subjects performed as well as normal subjects in learning to categorize the cartoon animals. Performance in both groups varied consistently accord-

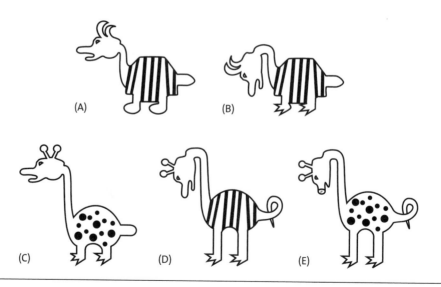

FIGURE 10.7 Examples of cartoon animals.
A is the Peggle prototype, and B through E have successively fewer of the prototype features (E has none).

ing to the number of prototypical features each exemplar included. But in a subsequent test of memory for the categorization task, the amnesic subjects performed poorly in identifying which features composed the Peggles prototype. These findings show that the cortical systems spared in amnesic individuals can acquire knowledge about grammar and object categories.

So amnesic individuals can acquire *general* rules. But can they also learn new *specific* factual information? Some studies have emphasized the relative sparing of semantic memory in amnesic subjects with selective hippocampal damage (Vargha-Khadem et al., 1997; Verfaellie et al., 2000). However, substantial evidence also says that normal acquisition and flexible expression of semantic memories greatly depend on the hippocampal region. Manns and colleagues (2003) examined the severity of retrograde and anterograde amnesia for semantic information in people whose brain damage was limited to the hippocampal region. These individuals had impaired memory of news events for a year or more prior to the onset of amnesia, and they were also impaired for information presented after they became amnesic. They recognized names of famous people but had trouble judging whether these people were living or deceased. Complementary evidence from functional brain imaging shows that a large cortical network, including the hippocampus, is activated during acquisition of everyday factual information (Maguire & Frith, 2004).

Still, Manns and colleagues' subjects acquired substantial semantic knowledge, albeit less than that of normal subjects. Even in cases of severe amnesia following extensive damage to the hippocampal region, there is compelling evidence of some degree of spared semantic learning. Although several studies have shown the partial sparing of semantic memory in amnesia, the most impressive of these may be O'Kane and colleagues' (2004) report that although the amnesic man H. M. was severely impaired relative to normal control subjects, he showed a remarkable amount of knowledge acquired about people who became famous after the onset of his amnesia. When prompted with a first name of a famous personality, H. M. could recall the last names of 12 out of 35 of these people. Further, given choices between a famous name and a fictitious one, H. M. discriminated 87 percent of famous from fictitious names, and he could provide some factual details about a third of the recognized people. These findings clearly demonstrate the successful acquisition of restricted semantic knowledge even in a person with dense amnesia.

Amnesic individuals, including H. M., have also shown striking, though rare, success in acquiring new semantic knowledge in everyday learning situations. For example, five years after his operation and onset of amnesia, H. M. and his parents moved to a new house. In 1966, eight years after they moved, he was asked to draw a floor plan of the house; the drawing captured all the essential elements of the organization of rooms in the house (Corkin, 2002; Figure 10.8). After living in that house for 16 years, H. M. moved into the home of a relative; three years after this move, he was again asked to draw the floor plan of his former home,

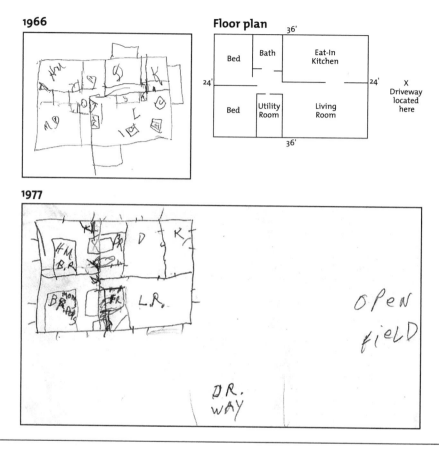

FIGURE 10.8 Drawings by H. M. of the house he lived in from 1958 (five years after his operation) to 1974.

which he did successfully. These observations show that with extensive experience in everyday life, even a person as severely amnesic as H. M. shows some ability to acquire spatial knowledge via slow learning.

A more formal example of successful learning of semantic knowledge by amnesic people has come from a technique called **errorless learning,** in which subjects are gradually trained to provide correct responses without the possibility of explicitly making a mistake. In a striking example of this technique, Glisky and colleagues (1986) used a method of *vanishing cues* to teach amnesic subjects computer language commands. Across many trials, the subjects were shown definitions of commands, such as "a repeated portion of a program" and the matching command LOOP. The subjects would read the command in response to its definition. After several repetitions the last letter was dropped, and the subjects had to complete the command word. The numbers of command word letters provided as prompts were reduced following multiple correct responses until the subjects could provide the entire terms without cues. Even densely amnesic subjects learned 30 computer terms and retained this knowledge for up to six weeks of testing. Further testing, however, revealed that the subjects' memories for these terms were relatively inflexible: They could provide the correct terms only when asked in precisely the same format and failed when the wording of the questions was altered. For example, a subject who successfully learned that the command SAVE is the answer to "What is the command to store a program?" could not recall the correct command when directly asked to store a particular program.

Another remarkable example of spared acquisition of semantic knowledge was provided in a study of learning new semantic information by means of *common ground,* which refers to the information shared by conversation partners to support complex communication. Common ground between speakers and listeners allows them to track and recall new terminology created during conversations. This phenomenon was investigated in a setting that involved amnesic individuals and their nonamnesic communication partners performing a game. At the start of the game, the amnesic subject was given a set of 12 cards, each of which contained a particular shape; the cards were in a predefined order. The nonamnesic partner was given the same cards in random order. The objective of the game was for the partners to collaborate in putting the randomly organized cards in the same order as those given to the amnesic subject using only conversation between the partners to convey the correct order. The game was played several times, each with a different ordering of the shape cards. So the speed with which the partners could complete the task was shortened if they created names for the shapes to facilitate their communication. The amnesic subjects were remarkably good at this task, often succeeding at a normal rate. The partners collaboratively generated labels for the shapes, and they remembered and used these labels in successive trials at the game. The amnesic subjects' success contrasted strikingly with their failure to later learn arbitrary labels for the same kinds of shapes. Thus their success in the game could be attributed to the gradual merging of descriptive characteristics of the shapes with corresponding shape names. Somehow the gradual, collaborative assignment of names to shapes could be acquired without an explicit demand for memory.

Is Semantic Memory Organization Spared in Amnesia?

Does the partial semantic memory deficit following hippocampal damage reflect a *quantitative* difference in overall declarative memory capacity of the medial temporal lobe system (Manns et al., 2003)—or full and selective loss of some specific *quality* of semantic processing? O'Reilly and Rudy (2001) proposed that the hippocampus and cortical areas both have powerful capacities for learning the kinds of stimulus associations that compose declarative knowledge. However, they argued, the hippocampal and cortical information processing mechanisms differ. In their opinion, the hippocampus rapidly learns about individual experiences and prevents interference by separating representations of those experiences. On the other hand, the cortex gradually extracts commonalities of many experiences. This view suggests no ultimate difference in the *content* of these systems' memory representations. Instead it proposes differences in how memory representations are formed in the different systems and in the extent to which they can each form representations based on a single experience.

To address this issue, Bayley and Squire (2002) investigated the capacities of an individual (E. P.) with extensive medial temporal lobe damage. They trained E. P. to remember factual information by presenting novel three-word sentences repeatedly during several sessions over three months. E. P. learned the sentences more slowly than normal control subjects but showed gradual improvement in both cued recall and recognition of the sentences' last words. Unlike control subjects, E. P. never consciously recalled the items, showing no increased confidence in correct choices and no difference in response times for correct and incorrect answers—both of which typically accompany conscious recollection in normal subjects. Also unlike normal subjects, E. P. did not remember sentences if a target word was replaced with a synonym; his memory did not emphasize the sentences' semantic content. These findings are consistent with the previously discussed capacities of amnesic subjects in learning computer language routines (Glisky et al., 1986) and demonstrate that spared semantic memory in amnesia differs qualitatively from that of normal subjects.

Animal models have also provided clues about how hippocampal information processing might explain the findings for semantic memory in amnesic people. In particular, studies of transitive interference, like those described in Chapter 8, have focused directly on the learning of multiple related problems and their integration into memory networks that support flexible, inferential judgments. One study compared the abilities of normal rats and rats with selective hippocampal damage to learn a set of odor problems and to interleave memory representations of these problems to support novel inferential judgments (Bunsey & Eichenbaum, 1996). In another experiment rats learned a hierarchical series of overlapping odor choice judgments (A over B, B over C, C over D, and D over E), then were probed for a relationship between indirectly related items (B over D; Dusek & Eichenbaum, 1997). In both experiments, normal rats learned the series and showed robust transitive inference in the probe tests. Rats with hippocampal damage also learned the initial premises but failed to show transitivity in both experiments. These results show that rats with hippocampal damage can learn even complex associations, such as those in the odor paired associates and overlapping choices. But unlike animals with intact hippocampal functioning, they do not interleave the distinct experiences according to their common elements to form representation networks that can support inferences and flexible memory expression.

Complementary evidence for the role of the hippocampus in networking memories comes from two other studies (introduced in Chapter 8) indicating that the hippocampus is selectively activated when humans make inferential memory judgments. In one such study, subjects initially learned to associate each of two faces with a house and learned to associate pairs of faces. During subsequent brain scanning, the subjects were asked whether two faces that were associated with the same house were therefore indirectly associated with each other and whether trained face pairs belonged together. The hippocampus was selectively more activated during the inferential judgment about indirectly related faces than during recall of trained face–house or face–face pairings (Preston et al., 2004; see Figure 8.10, p. 281). In the other study, subjects learned a series of choice judgments between pairs of visual patterns that contained overlapping elements. The hippocampus was selectively activated during transitive judgments as compared to novel nontransitive judgments (Heckers et al., 2004). Chapter 8 described these studies to show how the hippocampus links related memories. Here we mention these experiments again to show how the linked memories compose a relational network that supports the ability to make inferences from memory.

Combined, these findings suggest that areas of the cerebral cortex can mediate acquisition of grammatical rules, as well as learning information categories and complex stimulus conjunctions that compose semantic knowledge. However, the hippocampus performs an additional type of processing that contributes to cortical memory networking. The results of the transitive inference paradigm point to an essential hippocampal role in linking related memories according to their common features; this linkage builds a network that can support inferences between memory items that are only indirectly related. Such performance suggests how a general networking of memories can underlie the flexibility of declarative memory expression.

Interim Summary

Semantic memory is constructed by the abstraction of regularities across many individual experiences. Episodic memory updates semantic memories. This interaction between episodic and semantic memory is supported by many studies demonstrating a specific role for the hippocampus in organizing semantic memories. Several examples of spared acquisition of semantic knowledge in subjects with severe episodic memory deficits following hippocampal damage show that semantic knowledge can be stored without hippocampal processing. However, such spared semantic memory in amnesia is inflexible, tied rigidly to the exemplars that the subject learned, and impoverished in its use in novel circumstances. This characterization of spared semantic learning holds both for cases of human amnesia and for animal models that require subjects to learn related associations and express them flexibly in novel circumstances.

Chapter Summary

1. Learning semantic information occurs gradually, as knowledge of constancies and regularities about the world accumulates over many experiences. Semantic memories therefore constitute our knowledge about the world. The basic structure of semantic knowledge is embodied in conceptual hierarchies. Human and animal studies indicate that the organization of these conceptual hierarchies is based on associations learned during daily experiences.

2. Brain areas specialized for particular types of information processing store specific categories of knowledge. The hippocampus serves a key role in the process of incorporating new semantic information and in integrating semantic networks so that knowledge gained in past experiences can be used to solve new problems.

3. Early ideas about the organization of semantic knowledge were modeled as networks that stored items according to an efficient and logical hierarchy of features, running from the most abstract and general to the most concrete and specific. Consistent with this notion, experiments showed that more time is required to make judgments across greater distances in the hierarchy.

4. However, an alternative view, also supported by considerable data, is that item features are stored according to the extent of their associations with specific items. This model retains important aspects of the hierarchical order structure, and its association-based organization is consistent with views of the neurobiological basis of associative memory. A further elaboration of this notion is that semantic information is stored in terms of conceptual prototypes, with items organized according to how many features they share with the prototypes.

5. A modern approach to simulating semantic networks involves distributed network models that represent concepts as patterns of activation across interconnected units. In these models, each unit represents a particular feature of a concept, so that knowledge is distributed across the entire network. In computer simulations, these distributed neural networks can "learn" to map input onto output features extremely well, and researchers have simulated many properties of semantic memory using networks of units specialized for different types of information processing.

6. Studies of people with brain damage and functional imaging of normal humans have revealed the nature of semantic memory organization in the cerebral cortex. Semantic knowledge is represented in a broad area of the temporal, parietal, and occipital cortex. Zones within this cortical expanse selectively process

different *categories* of information, such as animals, faces, tools, chairs, houses, and words. At the same time, many of these areas process different *types* of information—for example, distinguishing exemplars within a category, generalizing across exemplars of a category, or imagining the use of an item. These functional specializations combine so that a large network of cortical areas participates in processing every type of information, but a distinct set of components is engaged in any particular category of semantic processing.

7. Semantic knowledge can be acquired by the cortex alone—without involving episodic memory mediated by the hippocampus. Some aspects of semantic processing are accomplished entirely within the cortex, such as acquiring grammatical rules and categorizing objects. However, semantic knowledge obtained without hippocampal processing is rigid and impoverished. Normally the episodic and semantic memory systems interact to interleave information acquired in specific experiences into the semantic network, allowing elaboration and flexible expression of semantic knowledge.

KEY TERMS

semantic memory (p. 335)
exemplar (p. 336)
prototype (p. 338)
modules (p. 339)
graceful degradation (p. 339)
routes (p. 341)
survey (p. 341)

reference systems (p. 343)
aphasia (p. 345)
agnosia (p. 345)
proposagnosia (p. 347)
anomia (p. 348)
errorless learning (p. 356)

REVIEWING THE CONCEPTS

- What is semantic memory? How is it distinguished from other forms of cognitive memory?

- How might semantic knowledge be organized as a conceptual hierarchy? How might it be organized as a set of distributed networks?

- How are spatial memories organized?

- What is the evidence for category-specific processing in particular areas of the cerebral cortex? What kinds of evidence contradict or complicate this view?

- How does episodic memory contribute to semantic memory?

CHAPTER

11

Memory Consolidation

One day when I was about 8 years old, some friends and I were riding our bikes through the neighborhood in search of adventure. As it grew late (without much adventure), a friend and I decided to head home for dinner. At the intersection that divided the paths to our houses, he headed in one direction and I rode in another. Just after we parted, I strained to yell to him the plans for the next morning. Intent on the message, I followed him with my eyes instead of looking where my bike was headed. When I looked back, only a few feet away and directly ahead was a large dump truck. Before I could react, my bike went under the truck, and my head struck its rear gate.

The next thing I recall is sitting in the kitchen of the house where that truck was parked. The woman of the house, a familiar neighbor, was wiping my forehead with a wet cloth and alternately applying an ice pack. When my mother arrived, they considered my condition, as parents do; declared me well; and suggested strongly that I pay more attention next time.

My memory of some parts of this event is perfect; other parts are completely lost. I can see that truck just a few feet ahead—as clearly as I saw it decades ago. But I don't recall the events of the accident or being taken to the neighbor's kitchen. The striking contrast between what I remember so vividly and what I don't remember at all suggests some distinctions between elements of the memory itself. The emotionally charged memory of the sight of that truck was surely enhanced by my moment of panic. At the same time, my memory of *hitting* the truck—an event at least as emotionally powerful as *seeing* the truck—is completely gone.

IN THIS CHAPTER we consider how the strength and persistence of memories can be affected by the events that follow a new experience. Recall H. M., the man who became severely amnesic at the age of 27 after his hippocampus and the surrounding cortical areas were surgically removed to treat his persistent seizures (see

Chapter 8). In addition to his lost ability to form new permanent memories, H. M. also exhibited a striking **retrograde amnesia**—a loss of memories acquired before a traumatic event, which in H. M.'s case included the years before his surgery. One method used to measure H. M.'s retrograde memory loss is called the *Crovitz personal remote memory test* (Corkin, 1984). In this test subjects are given concrete nouns, such as *bike,* and asked to relate them to an experience from any period in their lives, describing what happened and when the event occurred. To assess the consistency of these memories, the test is readministered the next day. Normal subjects typically provide memories from throughout their life spans, often emphasizing recent events that are relatively fresh in mind over more remote experiences. However, for all of the cues, H. M.'s associated memories dated back to when he was 16 or younger, so that his most recent memories were of events that took place in 1942. He had no memories of the end of World War II, his high school graduation in 1947, or any other more recent events. These observations show that H. M.'s retrograde amnesia extended back several years before his surgery.

These two examples of the loss of specific memories acquired prior to trauma demonstrate the phenomenon of **temporally graded retrograde amnesia:** retrograde amnesia that causes greater loss of memories for events that occurred recently before a trauma than for events that occurred more remotely in the past. The cases differ in several ways, most prominently in the type of brain injury and in the severity and extent of retrograde amnesia. My injury was a mild concussion, and my retrograde amnesia extended backward in time for only a few seconds. H. M.'s brain damage was caused by surgical removal of the hippocampal region, and his resulting amnesia extended backward for years. Although the period of lost memories varies quite a bit as these two cases show, temporally graded amnesia is common following brain trauma from many different causes. Major questions researchers pursue are why retrograde amnesia is temporally graded and why the period of lost memories varies so much.

The existence of temporally graded retrograde amnesia suggests that memories that normally would have been formed during experiences are subject to interference for some period after learning, and that this period is finite—other memories obtained longer before the damage are somehow immune to the same disruption. In other words, memories apparently require some time to **consolidate,** that is, to undergo some active process through which they become permanent.

Consolidation can be considered a bridge between initial learning and permanent memory storage. Memory consolidation was first recognized in studies of human retrograde amnesia, and its characteristics have now been elucidated in systematic animal studies. This chapter reviews several case studies of retrograde amnesia to outline the basic characteristics of this kind of memory loss. We then consider early experimental studies that demonstrated the phenomenon of consolidation in humans without brain damage. Further experimental studies in ani-

Studies of
Retrograde Amnesia
Characterized
Memory
Consolidation

365

mals have led to the belief that memory consolidation takes place in two stages. In a brief phase immediately after learning, cellular processes fixate memories. This fixation stage is followed by a second, prolonged process of memory reorganization. The first memory consolidation stage is pervasive across memory systems, and the second consolidation stage is specific to the cognitive memory system. We will examine both phases of memory consolidation in detail to see how these processes allow us to create and organize a permanent memory store.

Fundamental Questions

1. What happens during each stage of memory consolidation?
2. Why are there two stages of memory consolidation?
3. Is retrograde amnesia a failure of memory organization during storage or a failure to retrieve memories?
4. Can the success of memory consolidation be deliberately influenced after learning?

Studies of Retrograde Amnesia Characterized Memory Consolidation

The characteristics of retrograde amnesia just described were also observed in Clive Wearing and Jimmie G., two amnesic men described in Chapter 1. Clive Wearing, the composer and musicologist, lost all the memories he had accumulated for a few years before he became ill with encephalitis. Similarly, Jimmie G. lost 25 years of memories acquired between his early experiences in the navy and the onset of Korsakoff's disease long after his retirement. In both men's cases, it was as if the many events they had experienced during the affected periods had never occurred. How can memories that were established and used be simply erased, and what does this mean about the permanence of memory?

Although references to the idea that memories require time to "ripen" date back at least to the Romans, retrograde amnesia was not studied in detail until 1882. French philosopher and psychologist Theodore Ribot provided the first review of many cases of retrograde amnesia associated with brain damage and head trauma. He examined case reports of 26 people who had been knocked unconscious in accidents such as a fall from a horse or a blow to the head. In each case of memory impairment, Ribot observed that the person lost not only the memory of their accident but also memories acquired over a prolonged period before the accident. Ribot concluded that time was required for memories to become

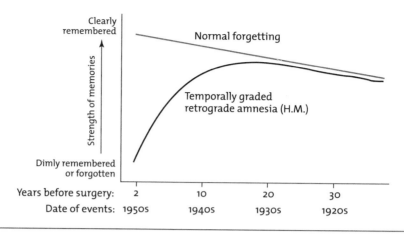

FIGURE 11.1 Retrograde amnesia.
The strength of memories normally declines over time (normal forgetting), so that older memories are weaker than newer ones. Individuals like H. M. who suffer from retrograde amnesia lose more recent memories (that is, events that occurred shortly before injury), whereas memories for events that occurred remotely before the injury are intact.

organized and fixed and that this process can be disrupted by "cerebral excitement" resulting from trauma.

Based on his survey of these cases, Ribot formulated the famous **Law of Regression** (also known as *Ribot's Law*), which says that the likelihood that a particular memory will be lost due to injury is inversely related to the time elapsed between the event to be remembered and the injury (Figure 11.1). In other words, recent memories are more likely to be forgotten after an injury than memories formed much earlier in life. Ribot never used the term *consolidation* to describe normal stabilization of permanent memory, but he is credited with the first thorough characterization of temporally graded retrograde amnesia, which revealed its dependence on brain processes.

Retrograde Amnesia Can Be Induced without Head Injury

Around the same time that Ribot was describing retrograde amnesia in individuals with head injuries, early psychologists Georg Müller and Alfons Pilzecker (1900; see also Lechner et al., 1999) demonstrated that retrograde memory loss can also be observed following events that are not as traumatic as being hit on the head. In a series of experiments Müller and Pilzecker showed that experiences that follow acquisition of new material can affect how well the material is remembered. For stimulus materials Müller and Pilzecker used the nonsense syllables Ebbinghaus (Chapter 1) developed, and they presented these stimuli in pairs. Subjects read the

*Studies of
Retrograde Amnesia
Characterized
Memory
Consolidation*

367

syllables aloud, emphasizing alternate syllables to encourage a sense of pairings of alternately emphasized and deemphasized syllables. Thus, using capital letters for emphasized syllables and lowercase letters for deemphasized syllables, the subjects might read "BAK, pef, KIB, dox, HEG, fuw," and the like, generating the pairings "BAK–pef," "KIB–dox," and so forth. After a delay, the researchers presented the emphasized syllables and asked the subjects to recall each item's paired associate. Müller and Pilzecker allowed a fixed number of training trials on each list and measured memory by the percentage of correctly recalled syllables.

One of Müller and Pilzecker's main observations leading to the concept of memory consolidation was that subjects reported a strong tendency to spontaneously think about the training pairs during the delay before they were tested, even when they tried to suppress deliberate rehearsal. They called this phenomenon **perseveration,** referring to the continued processing of information obtained earlier; and they linked it to the additional observation that sometimes after subjects had correctly recalled a syllable, they reused the same response incorrectly when cued by other items. These perseverative responses were called **intrusion errors**—incorrect responses that involved items experienced earlier but now inappropriate. Also, errors typically involved improper recall of differently paired items from the same list rather than new items the subjects had not studied. The researchers additionally noted that this perseveration and tendency for intrusion errors followed a regular time gradient: They were much more prominent for a few minutes after the original learning than on the next day. The researchers speculated that perseveration might reflect transient brain activity that plays an important role in establishing and strengthening learned associations.

Müller and Pilzecker suggested that perseveration might serve a natural purpose of establishing representations and strengthening the associations between syllables. They postulated that if this were the case, disrupting the perseveration should be detrimental to later recall. They tested this hypothesis by evaluating the effects of material intentionally interpolated between presentation of the initial list and the recall test. For example, in one experiment they initially had subjects study a list of six paired syllables. Then, in an attempt to prevent perseveration, after a few seconds they had the subjects read a second list eight times. Following a six-minute delay, the subjects were tested on cued recall for the initial list. As a control, Müller and Pilzecker had the same subjects study another list of syllable pairs; this time they did not interpolate a distracter list before the testing. Without the distracter, subjects recalled 48 percent of the items; but when the distracter prevented their perseverative tendencies, recall was reduced to 23 percent. They concluded that in the distracter condition, the intense mental activity following the initial list reading inhibited the subjects' ability to form the essential associations. They named this phenomenon **retroactive interference**, describing a process by which events following learning interfere with consolidation of learned material.

In addition, Müller and Pilzecker found that the timing of the interpolated material affected its degree of retroactive interference. In another experiment, they varied the timing of the distracter task from a few seconds to several minutes after initial study. The distracter task interfered most with recall when it was presented at the shortest interval following the material being learned, and its detrimental effects diminished considerably when the interference was delayed by more than six minutes. Finally, they also examined the effect of similarities between the interpolated material and the study material. The subjects read a list eight times and then were immediately asked to describe three pictures of landscapes. Even when the distracter was unrelated to the material being learned, subjects performed much more poorly than if no interpolated task was given. The combination of these studies led Müller and Pilzecker to conclude that perseveration normally follows new learning and that this activity helps consolidate new information in memory. Any disruption of the perseverative process prevents the consolidation necessary for the formation of new associations.

In 1903 William Burnham combined Müller and Pilzecker's findings about perseveration in normal human subjects with Ribot's description of retrograde amnesia following brain trauma. He asserted that retrograde amnesia involves the disruption of a physical process of memory organization in the brain, which underlies a psychological process of repetition and association. Thus he explained the temporal grading of memory loss in amnesia described by Ribot's Law as a consequence of interrupting the brain activity that normally supports the organization of new memories.

Memory Consolidation Can Be Disrupted or Facilitated

Some of the strongest evidence supporting the existence of a period of memory consolidation has come from studies of people who have received electroconvulsive therapy (ECT), which is mysterious in its mechanisms but remarkably effective in cases of severe depression where drug therapies have failed. In this treatment, two electrodes are placed on the subject's head, and current is passed between the electrodes to produce brain seizures. Following clinical observations that individuals receiving ECT could not remember events immediately preceding their treatment, Zubin and Barrera (1941) performed the first experimental studies confirming that ECT causes temporally graded retrograde amnesia. They presented subjects with paired associates prior to shock treatment and subsequently found that the effect of the shock depended critically on the time elapsed between study and the treatment; the significant consolidation period was approximately 30 minutes.

Following this clinical observation, Duncan (1949) explored the effects of electroconvulsive shock on light-cued fear conditioning in animals. He reported a clear,

Studies of
Retrograde Amnesia
Characterized
Memory
Consolidation

369

consistent pattern of retrograde amnesia depending on the interval—from 20 seconds to 14 hours—between training and electroconvulsive shock. Several succeeding studies showed that (1) the poorer performance following ECT was not due to a possible punishing effect of the shock and (2) other kinds of interventions between learning and recall, such as anoxia (lack of oxygen to the brain), temperature changes, and direct electrical stimulation of particular brain areas using implanted electrodes, also hindered recall of recently learned material. Various studies reported widely different durations of the period after learning during which the treatments were effective in disrupting memory, and the duration of this effective period varied across species, tasks, and treatments. These findings led to doubt that any simple fixation process could account for all the findings (reviewed in Polster et al., 1991).

One line of study supporting the idea that consolidation has a physiological basis demonstrated that memory can be enhanced, as well as impaired, by postlearning treatments. McGaugh (1966) trained rats in an inhibitory avoidance task by placing them in a well-lit chamber. Then a door was opened, allowing the rats to step into a larger, darkened, enclosed chamber, which rats normally prefer to the open, bright chamber. Subsequently shock was applied to the rats' feet, and they were allowed to escape back to the illuminated chamber. After a variable delay, the rats were injected with a central nervous system stimulant such as picrotoxin or strychnine. Then, following a substantial further delay, they were tested for memory of the earlier foot shocks by measuring the amount of time they took to reenter the dark chamber from the lit one. Control rats had moderately long step-through latencies but eventually stepped through. Animals injected with the stimulant did not enter the dark chamber, showing stronger learning. So consolidation processes can be enhanced by physiological changes introduced after training, which substantially strengthens the case for consolidation as a physiological process.

A prominent early account of consolidation was Hebb's (1949) dual trace theory. He believed that a transient memory trace is initially established at the level of persistent physiological activity, and that this trace subsequently modifies the active neurons structurally to become more permanent. Hebb proposed that transient memory representations initially activated in the cerebral cortex are embodied and sustained in cell assemblies that **reverberate**—that is, repeatedly recycle information around the cell assembly (Figure 11.2). Repeated coincident activations among the assembly cells cause structural alterations that make reactivation of the entire assembly possible when subsequent memory cues activate only a small portion of the cell assembly. According to this theory, either mental distraction or brain trauma can disrupt this reverberatory activity before the structural changes are complete. Conversely, stimulant drugs might speed or make more persistent the reverberatory activity, enhancing consolidation. Today we

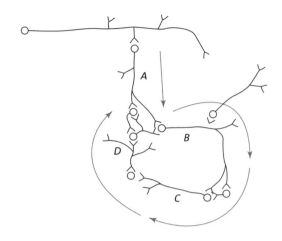

FIGURE 11.2 Hebb's conception of a reverberatory circuit.
Information entering the network from neuron A would cycle among neurons B, C, and D many times.

know that consolidation processes can be enhanced or retarded, indicating that consolidation is an active process. Considerable research is focused on the nature of the reverberatory process believed to mediate consolidation.

Interim Summary

The phenomenon of temporally graded retrograde amnesia demonstrates that for some time newly formed memories are susceptible to disruption. An active process called consolidation appears to transform memories in some way that confers their permanence. Temporally graded retrograde amnesia can occur as a consequence of head injury, brain damage, or retroactive interference by other mental activity. Pioneering investigations using stimulant drugs have shown that consolidation can be enhanced as well as disrupted for some period after learning. The period of consolidation can be brief or prolonged, suggesting different types or stages of memory consolidation.

Memory Consolidation Has Two Distinct Stages

The discoveries about consolidation have revealed two distinct time courses of retrograde amnesia, suggesting the existence of two distinguishable forms of memory consolidation (Table 11.1). This distinction was evident in the examples at the outset of this chapter. In one case the cause of amnesia was a mild blow to the head, and the result was a retrograde amnesia that affected memories for events

TABLE 11.1 Characteristics of Two Forms of Memory Consolidation.

	Fixation	Reorganization
Level of processing	Cellular, molecular	Brain systems
Minimal affective disruption	Electrical, chemical	Brain tissue damage
Duration of vulnerability to disruption	Minutes, hours	Days, months, years

that occurred a few minutes before the trauma. In contrast, the removal of H. M.'s medial temporal lobe structures resulted in retrograde amnesia extending 11 years back. The first case can be explained by disruption of reverberatory activity, but a prolonged retrograde gradient cannot because it is difficult to imagine a reverberatory loop that is activated for years. In his examination of many case studies, Burnham (1903) also recognized a distinction between two classes of retrograde amnesia: one with a brief retrograde time course due to the "shock" of an accident, and another in which memory is obliterated for a long period. Modern researchers see these two classes of retrograde amnesia as different both in the mechanisms underlying the consolidation process and in how long the process lasts. One form of consolidation involves memory **fixation:** stabilization of molecular structure changes within cells and synapses that occurs for minutes or hours. The other form of consolidation involves memory **reorganization:** alterations of our knowledge networks through complex interactions between brain structures lasting for weeks to years after learning experiences. First we will examine the cascading cellular events that immediately follow learning and result in fixation. Then we will consider the prolonged process of memory reorganization and the interactions among brain structures that integrate memories.

Cellular Events Are the First Stage of Memory Consolidation

The cellular processes that fixate memories involve a series of molecular and microstructural events by which short-term synaptic modifications permanently change connectivity between neurons. As you read in Chapter 2, the most commonly studied form of neural plasticity is long-term potentiation (LTP), which is initially induced by the coactivation of AMPA and NMDA receptors in the postsynaptic site of a neuron (see Figure 2.9, p. 59). Subsequently a series of molecular reactions plays a vital role in fixating the changes in synaptic function that occur in LTP (Figure 11.3). Most prominent among these molecular events is the entry of $Ca++$ that occurs during the induction of LTP and the subsequent activation of a molecule called cyclic adenosine monophosphate (cAMP). This molecule has

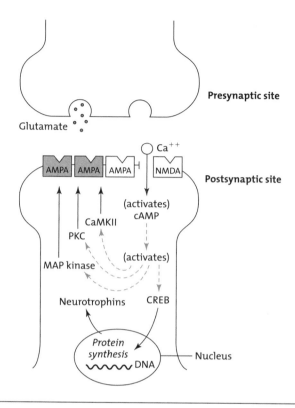

FIGURE 11.3 Molecular events that mediate memory fixation.
The entry of calcium when existing AMPA and NMDA receptors (white symbols) are
activated together causes several molecular events that result in the addition of new
AMPA receptors (gray symbols) as well as growth of the synapse.

many functions. In the fixation process it activates other molecules called kinases, particularly calcium/calmodulin-dependent protein kinase (CaMKII), protein kinase C (PKC), and MAP kinase. These molecules increase the number of AMPA receptors on the postsynaptic membrane making it more sensitive to the neurotransmitter glutamate and thus increasing its response to subsequent stimulation. These cellular events begin immediately with each learning experience and continue to unfold during the minutes and hours after learning. Many studies have shown that pharmacological treatments and genetic manipulations interrupt the functions of cAMP, CaMKII, PKC, and MAP kinase, blocking memory consolidation (Elgersma & Silva, 1999).

In addition, cAMP activates another molecule called cAMP-response element binding protein (CREB). CREB operates within the nucleus of the neuron to activate a class of genes called early immediate genes, which, in turn, activate other genes that direct protein synthesis. Among the proteins produced is neurotrophin, which activates growth of the synapse and increases the neuron's responsiveness to subsequent stimulation (see Figure 11.3). Activated synapses seem to become "tagged" by generated proteins, and this process may activate further gene expression at the nucleus and coordinate associations made with events that produce succeeding activations of the neuron (Frey & Morris, 1997). Many studies using various kinds of memory tests have shown that drugs that inhibit protein synthesis block memory if given before or within minutes after learning; these drugs are not effective if they are delayed (Davis & Squire, 1984). The general finding of these studies is that protein synthesis is not essential to initial learning or to maintaining memories in short-term memory. However, protein synthesis is essential for permanent memory fixation.

These cellular and molecular events on a timescale of seconds and minutes are essential for learning to transition from short-term storage to long-term memory. In principle, these events occur in every brain structure that participates in memory. Molecular events that mediate the permanent structural changes associated with memory have been studied in a broad variety of invertebrate and mammalian brain structures. Various types of interference, from electroconvulsive shock to drugs and behavioral distractions, have been shown to disrupt memory fixation within a brief time window following learning. This window varies considerably across species, tasks, and the type of interference; but it is typically on the order of seconds to minutes and perhaps an hour (Dudai, 2004). The loss of memory is temporally graded relative to when the disruption occurs, and the degree of loss lessens steadily and gradually for progressively older memories. We can use drugs and other treatments to document distinct processes within memory fixation, but it is not clear whether these different phases occur serially or in parallel.

Additional observations suggest that memory fixation processes may be fragile for a period extending beyond several hours (Figure 11.4). To investigate the possibility that memories remain labile for an extended period, Nader and colleagues (2000) trained rats in a fear conditioning protocol and then confirmed that their memory was retained as long as 14 days after. Then they infused a protein synthesis inhibitor into the rats' amygdala either immediately or delayed following the retention test. If the infusion occurred shortly after the first retention test, subsequent memory in a second retention test was impaired. Delayed infusions, however, did not affect subsequent retention. The researchers concluded that the first retention test "reactivated" the fear memory and that this reactivation was followed by a "reconsolidation" phase that required protein synthesis in the amygdala. Currently these researchers are investigating the mechanisms of the reconsolidation effect and the extent to which this phenomenon extends to other types of memory.

Another major area of progress involves studies examining stressful events that cause the adrenal glands to release epinephrine and glucocorticoids. This activation improves the fixation of memories for experiences surrounding stress activation, and the amygdala is essential to this influence on memory (see Chapter 7). Many stud-

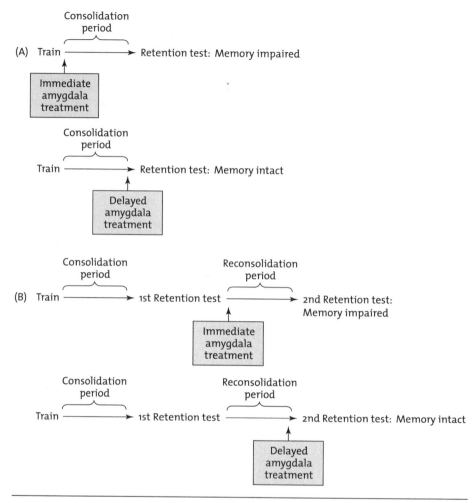

FIGURE 11.4 Memory consolidation and reconsolidation compared.
Treatments produce amnesia if given shortly after training (blocking consolidation) or shortly after a first retention test (blocking reconsolidation), but not if delayed after training or the first retention test.

ies of memory fixation involve systemic injection or brain infusion of drugs after initial learning, with the common result that subsequent memory performance is altered (McGaugh, 2000). These drugs typically are effective only if administered within minutes after training. The posttraining administration procedure eliminates the possibility of the drugs altering perception, arousal, or motor performance during learning. And this methodology provides strong evidence that neurochemical modulation strongly influences memory fixation for several minutes after new learning.

Learning & Memory in Action

Blocking Consolidation of Traumatic Memories

Traumatic experiences, such as violent personal attacks and wartime events, can cause posttraumatic stress disorder (PTSD), a syndrome involving recurring memories of the violent events and severe, often disabling, anxiety. Such emotional arousal can cause the release of norepinephrine, a neurotransmitter that enhances memory consolidation (McGaugh et al., 2002; see also Chapter 7). Researchers are now trying to determine whether interfering with this consolidation process can block the formation of traumatic memories and thus prevent PTSD.

The strategy in these clinical trials is to give the drug propranolol, which blocks the action of norepinephrine, to people as soon as possible after they have suffered traumatic events. In the first of these investigations, 31 trauma victims who were evaluated in the first hours after traumatic exposure were randomly assigned to take either propranolol or a placebo treatment after arriving in the emergency room (Pitman et al., 2002). In subsequent interviews three months later, the investigators did not diagnose fewer cases of PTSD in the propranolol group. However, they did find that propranolol recipients experienced lower measures of stress than the placebo group when they listened to vivid narratives of their traumatic events.

A second study in France reported greater success (Vaiva et al., 2003). In this study doctors in two hospitals identified individuals who came into the emergency room shortly after physical assaults or automobile accidents suffering severe emotional trauma. Some were given an immediate dose of propranolol as well as three daily doses for the next seven days; other similarly traumatized people did not receive the drug. In psychological tests two months following the traumatic events, almost all these people exhibited some PTSD symptoms, but the symptoms' severity was twice as high among those who had not taken propranolol.

These mixed findings do not yet support the use of propranolol as a reliable treatment for reducing the likelihood of PTSD. However, they suggest that under some treatment regimens, it may be possible to use our understanding of memory consolidation to block formation of unwanted memories. Some people believe it is unethical to erase experiences from the memories of trauma victims because such loss of memory for the events precludes learning to deal with the past. Others assert that erasing traumatic memories and thereby preventing the distress of PTSD is no different than eliminating the human experience of any other disease or disorder. What do you think about this issue?

Interim Summary

There are two distinct stages of memory consolidation: a relatively brief stage that depends on cellular and molecular mechanisms of memory fixation and a prolonged reorganization stage that depends on systemic interactions among brain structures. The first stage involves a cascade of molecular events that changes synaptic connections. This stage begins with cellular events similar to those that support LTP, increasing receptors and activating genes that drive protein synthesis, which in turn changes synaptic connections. Under some conditions these molecular processes may be reactivated by reminder cues, and the strength of the fixation process can be modulated by emotional arousal and stress. These cellular and molecular events occur over the first several minutes following learning, so treatments that alter these events over that brief period can enhance or retard memory fixation.

The Hippocampal–Cortical System Supports Prolonged Memory Reorganization

Another form of memory consolidation involves events above the level of cellular physiology. This kind of consolidation occurs at the level of brain systems, specifically the hippocampal–cortical system, and is special to cognitive memory. The timescales of events involved in systems-level consolidation are many times greater than those of cellular fixation mechanisms. It appears that this type of consolidation requires hours, days, months, or years, depending on the species and the nature of the memory tested. Indeed, this consolidation process may continue over a lifetime.

The long timescale of memory consolidation at the brain systems level is closely related to the temporally graded retrograde amnesia previously discussed, in which recent memories remain susceptible to disruption for years. Here we consider the neural processing that underlies long-term memory consolidation. How long does such consolidation last? Which brain structures mediate consolidation? Where are memories stored after consolidation? Are all kinds of memories subject to long-term consolidation? Studies of both human amnesia and animal models of amnesia address different aspects of these issues, painting an increasingly clear picture of hippocampal involvement and the role of hippocampal–neocortical interaction in memory reorganization.

Retrograde Amnesia Following Hippocampal Damage Is Temporally Graded

The main focus of studies of long-term memory consolidation has been characterizing amnesia following hippocampal system damage—in particular the phe-

*The Hippocampal–
Cortical System
Supports Prolonged
Memory
Reorganization*

377

nomenon of temporally graded retrograde amnesia for cognitive memories. The conceptual linkage between the hippocampus and consolidation of cognitive memories began with the earliest observations of H. M. Scoville and Milner's 1957 report about H. M. focused on his amnesia as a particularly good example of Ribot's Law, which states that more recent memories are more likely to be lost after a traumatic event than memories that were acquired more remotely in the past (see Figure 11.1, p. 366). Thus Scoville and Milner characterized H. M.'s amnesia as a severe, striking, selective impairment of recent memory accompanied by spared remote memory capacities. As far as could be ascertained at that point by interviewing H. M. and his family, his retrograde memory loss seemed to date back two years prior to the surgery, with his childhood memories apparently intact.

More recent evaluations confirm that H. M.'s remote memory impairment is temporally limited, although his duration of retrograde amnesia has been extended to at least 11 years (Corkin, 1984). These studies used several strategies to assess H. M.'s memory of material he would have acquired during the decades prior to his surgery. In addition to the Crovitz personal remote memory test already described, other tests evaluated his memory for public events, including naming well-known songs, verbally tested recognition of events, and ability to identify faces of people who became famous in particular decades. For example, a verbal test of recognition for famous events included questions about important public events from the 1940s through the 1970s. H. M., whose surgery was performed in 1953, scored within the normal range for questions about events that occurred in the 1940s, showed borderline-successful recognition for events from the 1950s, and was clearly impaired on events from the 1960s onward.

A test for recognition of public scenes included pictures depicting important scenes from the 1940s through the 1980s, selected so that the famous events could not be deduced from the pictures alone. Subjects, including H. M., were asked if they had seen the pictures before and could identify the events; then further questions were asked about details of the events depicted. H. M.'s scores were deficient in all decades except the 1940s.

Is Retrograde Amnesia Limited to a Particular Kind of Memory?

Temporally graded retrograde amnesia has been observed for both semantic and episodic memories following hippocampal damage. Manns and colleagues (2003) examined the severity of retrograde and anterograde amnesia for semantic information in individuals with damage limited to the hippocampal region. These people had impaired memories of news events for a year or more prior to the onset of amnesia and could not remember events that occurred after they became amnesic. They performed well in recognizing names of famous people but poorly in judging whether these people were living or deceased. In contrast, the same subjects had good access to episodic memories for public events that occurred 11 to 30 years prior to onset of amnesia.

To examine remote episodic memory in amnesia, Bayley and colleagues (2003) gave detailed interviews to subjects with damage limited to the hippocampal region. Whereas these people were severely impaired in recalling both personal experiences and public events that occurred within a brief period before the onset of amnesia, they performed as well as normal subjects in recalling vivid details of autobiographical events and semantic knowledge from memories acquired in the first third of their lives. Thus both episodic and semantic memories that were acquired shortly before the onset of amnesia were lost, whereas both types of memories that were obtained more remotely in the past were retained.

Teng and Squire (1999) examined in detail whether the phenomenon of temporally graded retrograde amnesia also extends to spatial memory. They focused on a subject with extensive damage to the medial temporal lobe including virtually complete hippocampal damage. This man had lived in a California neighborhood during the 1930s and 1940s but had moved away and subsequently returned only occasionally. The spatial memory acquired during these two decades was evaluated by comparing his ability to construct routes between different locations in his former neighborhood, as identified using archival maps of the areas from the relevant period (Figure 11.5). In addition, his ability to plot alternative routes was examined by asking him how to navigate between places when the major route between them was blocked. They also measured the subject's accuracy in pointing toward major landmarks from an imagined position in the neighborhood. On all these tests, the subject scored at least as well as age-matched control subjects who had lived in the same area during the target period and who had also subsequently moved away.

As a follow-up test, the subject and the control subjects were asked to solve the same sort of navigational problems based on knowledge of their current neighborhoods. In sharp contrast to his earlier performance—and unlike the control subjects—the subject failed completely at these tasks, which required more recently learned spatial information. Thus for this subject, the pattern of retrograde amnesia for spatial knowledge matched that of temporally graded nonspatial memory observed in previous studies of many amnesic individuals. So for both episodic and semantic memory, whether the material is spatial or nonspatial, Ribot's Law holds for amnesia resulting from damage to the hippocampal region. Memories acquired recently prior to the onset of amnesia are lost while older memories remain intact.

The Hippocampal–
Cortical System
Supports Prolonged
Memory
Reorganization

379

(A)

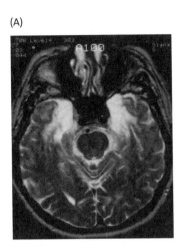

(B)

FIGURE 11.5 Retrograde spatial memory.
A. Brain scan showing the subject's extensive medial temporal lobe damage (white area).
B. Map of the town where the subject grew up, dating from the 1940s. The letters A
through D on the map indicate the locations of some of the landmarks used in Teng and
Squire's (1999) tests of spatial memory.

What Determines the Duration of Retrograde Memory Loss after Brain Damage?

Not all forms of retrograde amnesia are temporally graded. Some retrograde amnesias associated with a variety of etiologies have *flat* gradients: The impairment includes both memories obtained recently prior to the onset of amnesia and memories extending back to early childhood (Warrington, 1996). In addition, some retrograde amnesias show a pattern of memory loss characterized less by the age of the memories than by their nature. For example, one study compared the temporal gradient of retrograde amnesia in four subjects who all had trouble recalling or recognizing faces of people who had become famous during the last several decades. Some of these people showed flat gradients of retrograde amnesia for this kind of facial recognition and for a broad range of other types of information dating to all periods of their life spans. Retrograde amnesia following medial temporal lobe damage often affects memory for personal episodes more severely than semantic memory, and this deficit in autobiographical memory extends back many years, sometimes affecting the entire life span prior to onset.

It has been argued that flat gradients of retrograde amnesia, and particularly loss of autobiographical memories, occur only with damage or suspected damage beyond the hippocampal region. For example, amnesia associated with Korsakoff's syndrome, closed head injuries, seizure disorders, and certain other etiologies often includes damage or cell loss in the prefrontal cortex. Such damage to the prefrontal area is associated with disorders of **source memory**—memory of where and when information was acquired. Such an inability to identify the circumstances surrounding new learning might be expected to cause selective impairment of memory for personal experiences—that is, episodic memory. Also, some individuals with medial temporal lobe damage who have extensive retrograde memory loss also have lesions extending beyond the hippocampal region into the temporal neocortex. This damage could compromise the areas responsible for permanent storage of episodic and semantic memories (Bayley et al., 2003; see Chapter 10). Thus, consistent with the prevalent view that the final repository of memories is in areas of the cerebral cortex, memory loss caused by damage to cortical areas should result in amnesia that does not show a temporal gradient.

Other studies of temporally graded retrograde amnesia have elucidated the duration of retrograde memory loss. In one study of temporally graded retrograde amnesia, Reed and Squire (1998) tied the duration of memories lost in retrograde amnesia to the extent of damage to the medial temporal region. This study involved four individuals who became amnesic without other cognitive impairment following specific brain injury and who, for unrelated reasons, subsequently died and were autopsied, allowing analysis of their brain damage. Two of these people developed amnesia following a brief loss of oxygen. Both had a selective loss of cells within the hippocampus and had limited retrograde amnesia extending only one to two years. The other two individuals had more extensive retrograde amnesia extending back 15 to 25 years. Examining the brains of these more severely amnesic people showed cell loss throughout the hippocampus and also to some extent in the entorhinal cortex (the cortical area surrounding the hippocampus). These studies further confirm that damage limited to the hippocampal region can cause temporally limited retrograde amnesia, and that the extent of the temporal gradient of retrograde amnesia might be associated with the anatomical extent of damage within the hippocampal region.

Animals and Prospective Studies of Retrograde Amnesia

Experimental protocols for studying retrograde amnesia in animals have allowed a major advance in understanding the role of brain structures in memory consol-

The Hippocampal–
Cortical System
Supports Prolonged
Memory
Reorganization

381

idation. The use of animals lets researchers specifically control both the anatomical structures under study and the learning experience before brain damage. These prospective experiments tightly control the learning that takes place before brain damage in order to precisely equalize the nature and extent of information that subjects acquire. Several prospective studies of retrograde amnesia have used different species and various learning and memory protocols. Most of these studies support the notion that damage to medial temporal structures causes temporally graded retrograde amnesia. However, this finding is not universal; and the severity and gradients of retrograde amnesia vary across studies depending on the species, types of tests, and loci of brain damage. Here we consider a few studies that provide examples of retrograde amnesia patterns and the variety of memory tests employed.

To investigate the role of the hippocampus in memory processing following learning new material, Zola-Morgan and Squire (1990) trained monkeys in a series of object discrimination problems where they learned that one visual stimulus was rewarded and another not rewarded at different times prior to removal of the hippocampal region. Animals were trained in 100 object discrimination problems, segregated into five 20-problem sets presented at 16, 12, 8, 4, or 2 weeks before the surgery. Each set of problems consisted of two problems per day, thus requiring a total of 10 days. Performance was typically good in learning, averaging 88 percent correct on the last trial of all the problems. Two weeks after surgical removal of the hippocampal region, memory was assessed for all 100 problems. Normal monkeys performed best with problems that had been learned more recently, with significantly poorer performance on problems learned earlier, thus showing a typical forgetting curve (Figure 11.6). Monkeys with hippocampal damage showed the opposite pattern: They performed poorest on problems presented at the shortest interval before surgery. However, the same monkeys were not impaired on problems presented 8 to 16 weeks before surgery. Thus, following this period of consolidation, the memories no longer relied on the function of the hippocampal region. By documenting the existence of temporally graded retrograde amnesia, these findings also reveal a consolidation deficit in animals with damage limited to medial temporal lobe structures.

Temporally Graded Retrograde Amnesia Follows Selective Hippocampal Damage

The study just described demonstrated temporally graded retrograde amnesia following damage to the hippocampus and surrounding cortical areas. If the hippocampus itself plays a crucial role in memory consolidation, then we should observe temporally graded retrograde amnesia after damage limited to the hippocampus. Some of the best evidence for this comes from studies of contextual fear conditioning in rats. (For details about this protocol, see Chapter 7.)

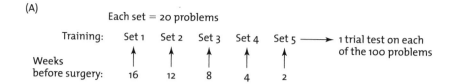

(A)

Each set = 20 problems

Training: Set 1   Set 2   Set 3   Set 4   Set 5 ⟶ 1 trial test on each
of the 100 problems

Weeks
before surgery: 16   12   8   4   2

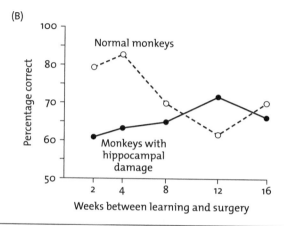

(B)

FIGURE 11.6 Retrograde amnesia in monkeys.
A. Design of the experiment showing when subjects were trained prior to hippocampal damage. B. Performance as a function of time of training for normal monkeys and time of training prior to surgery for monkeys with hippocampal damage.

To examine the role of the hippocampus in memory for contextual fear conditioning, Kim and Fanselow (1992) placed rats in a conditioning chamber and presented a series of 15 tone–shock pairings within a single session. Then they selectively damaged the rats' hippocampi at 1 to 28 days after training. Testing for conditioned fear associated with the shock was conducted separately for the context (the training chamber) and for the tone (Figure 11.7). To test for contextual fear, rats were placed back in the training chamber, and freezing behavior was measured for several minutes. To test for conditioned fear of the tone, animals were placed in a different chamber, and freezing was measured during repetition of the tone. Normal rats exhibited substantial freezing behavior across all retention intervals, indicating virtually no forgetting of the conditioned fear for both the context and the tone.

In contrast, rats with hippocampal lesions showed a temporally graded impairment in contextual fear conditioning. When the interval between training and surgery was one day, they were severely impaired, showing virtually no freezing in the familiar chamber. When the surgery occurred a week after training, the rats retained some conditioned fear; and they demonstrated full retention when the

*The Hippocampal–
Cortical System
Supports Prolonged
Memory
Reorganization*

383

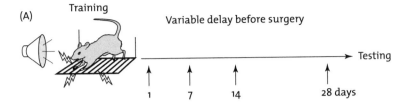

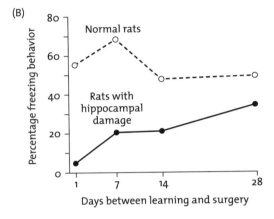

FIGURE 11.7 Retrograde amnesia for fear conditioning.
A. Design of the experiment showing time following training when the hippocampus was damaged. B. Performance as a function of the interval between training and hippocampal damage.

surgery occurred a month after training. In addition, the retrograde amnesia was material specific. That is, at all retention intervals the rats retained their conditioned fear of the tone even when hippocampal damage impaired their memory of the conditioning environment.

Is Retrograde Amnesia Following Hippocampal Damage Limited to Spatial Memory?

We've just discussed the effect of hippocampal damage on memory for the environment where fear conditioning occurred. Because of the importance of the hippocampus to spatial memory, some investigators have asked whether the hippocampus's role in memory consolidation might be limited to memory for places. This question was addressed in a study that examined whether a form of memory with no spatial component also depends on the hippocampus for long-term consolidation. In this study, a temporally graded retrograde amnesia was

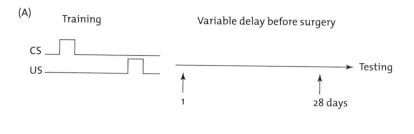

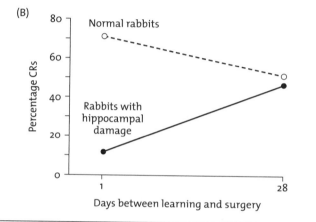

FIGURE 11.8 Retrograde amnesia in trace classical conditioning.
A. Design of the experiment showing time following training when the hippocampus was damaged. B. Performance as a function of the interval between training and hippocampal damage.

observed in rabbits trained in hippocampus-dependent trace (classical) conditioning (Figure 11.8; also see Chapter 5). Kim and colleagues (1995) trained the animals using trace eyeblink conditioning procedures. In each trial, a brief tone CS was followed by a 500-millisecond trace interval and then an air puff US. Daily training continued until the rabbits exhibited eyeblinks during the CS or trace interval consistently. The rabbits then received hippocampal lesions either one day or one month later; after a recovery period, all animals were tested for retention during retraining. Normal rabbits showed complete savings of the conditioned eyeblink at both retention intervals. By contrast, rabbits given hippocampal lesions one day after training were severely impaired, exhibiting no retention of conditioning; indeed they were unable to acquire the task postoperatively. However, when the surgery occurred one month after conditioning, the animals showed as much savings as did control subjects at both retention intervals. Taken together, these animal studies show that the hippocampal region plays a vital role in memory consolidation. It processes information during an extended period of several days to weeks following learning, making memories much less vulnerable to disruption.

The Hippocampal–
Cortical System
Supports Prolonged
Memory
Reorganization

385

What Determines the Duration of the Temporal Gradient of Retrograde Amnesia?

The duration of retrograde memory loss has been examined by studying rodents' temporally graded retrograde amnesia for spatial discrimination problems. In one study, mice were trained in a set of two-choice spatial discrimination problems using a radial maze (Cho et al., 1993). For each problem, the mouse was rewarded for selecting one of two adjacent maze arms, and different pairs of arms on the same apparatus were used for multiple problems. Animals were trained in successive problems separated by 10 days. On the day following training in the final problem, the entorhinal cortex (the cortical area surrounding the hippocampus) was damaged in some of the animals.

Notably, as observed in studies described earlier, normal mice and mice with damage to the entorhinal cortex showed opposite memory patterns in subsequent retention testing. Control mice with intact brains exhibited striking savings on problems presented three days before surgery, with significant forgetting at longer retention intervals (Figure 11.9). Mice with entorhinal damage that was inflicted

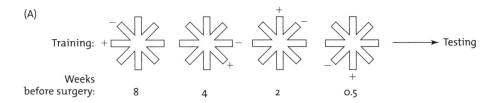

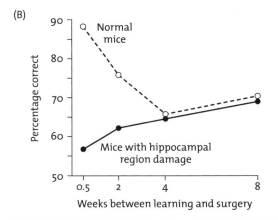

FIGURE 11.9 Retrograde amnesia for maze learning.
A. Design of the experiment showing time of training before the hippocampal region (in this case, the entorhinal cortex) was damaged. + indicates rewarded maze arm; − indicates nonrewarded maze arm. B. Performance as a function of the interval between training and hippocampal region damage.

three days after problem presentation showed almost no retention. When the surgery occurred two weeks after problem presentation, they showed moderate retention; and for problems presented four to eight weeks before surgery, they showed normal levels of retention. Thus this study indicates that the consolidation period for maze learning is between two and four weeks.

A follow-up study using rats replicated these findings about entorhinal lesions, showing a severe retention deficit when the training-to-surgery interval was a few days, with better performance for more remotely acquired spatial discrimination and normal performance for discrimination learned at the longest interval before surgery (Cho & Kesner, 1996). In addition, this study examined the role in spatial memory consolidation played by the parietal cortex—a part of the cerebral cortex essential for spatial cognition and thought to be the site of permanent spatial memories. In contrast to the findings for entorhinal lesions, rats with parietal lesions, though impaired, showed no temporal gradient. Animals with parietal cortex damage were impaired at all retrograde periods tested. These data are consistent with the findings for humans with retrograde amnesia discussed earlier in this chapter, and they support the view that the hippocampal region plays a role in consolidation. The parietal cortex is not involved in consolidation but appears to be a permanent storage site for spatial memories after they are consolidated by the hippocampus.

Although considerable evidence shows that the consolidation of several types of memories depends on the hippocampus, there have also been failures to find retrograde amnesia following hippocampal damage, as well as reports of flat (not temporally graded) deficits. These studies differ in the types of lesion and training, leaving open the critical parameters that determine the extent of the retrograde gradient in animals and humans. Notwithstanding these mixed results, the many successful demonstrations of temporally graded amnesia in animal models, using a compelling range of species and behavioral tests, add to the conclusions from studies of human amnesia. Components of the hippocampal system play an essential role in memory consolidation for a broad range of information, including visual discrimination, contextual fear conditioning, trace eyeblink conditioning, and maze learning problems.

Learning & Memory in Action

Does Sleep Aid Memory Consolidation?

For many years scientists have speculated that memory processing during sleep may contribute to consolidation (Stickgold, 2005). Consistent with this notion, several studies have shown memory improvements for perceptual

The Hippocampal–
Cortical System
Supports Prolonged
Memory
Reorganization

387

and motor learning following sleep. For example, in one study subjects were trained to identify vertical lines against a background of horizontal lines on a computer screen (Stickgold et al., 2000). In a test the following day, subjects allowed to sleep normally showed overnight improvements, but subjects deprived of deep sleep did not improve. Such sleep-dependent improvement extends to several other perceptual learning tasks, including an auditory task involving interpretation of artificial speech (Fenn et al., 2003). In a motor learning task where subjects learn to tap a set of keys in a particular sequence, no performance improvement is typically observed after subjects take a four-hour break, but subjects who nap during that interval show an average of 16 percent improvement in tapping speed (Walker & Stickgold, 2005). Similar improvements follow overnight sleep.

However, the evidence for consolidation of cognitive memories during sleep is less compelling (Siegel, 2001). Studies of many cognitive memory tasks have failed to find any retention deficit for episodic memory tasks following sleep deprivation (Smith, 2001). Although some studies have found improvements correlated with the amount of sleep, these effects could reflect hormonal modulation of consolidation processes rather than a particular kind of information processing that occurs during sleep. In one study, human subjects' overnight improvement for a virtual reality navigation task was correlated with how long they slept (Peigneux et al., 2004). This finding parallels observations that patterns of hippocampal neural activity recorded in alert rats "replay" during subsequent sleep (Louie & Wilson, 2001).

So sleep appears essential to the consolidation of perceptual and motor skills, but its role in consolidating cognitive memories is unclear. For now, if you have an exam tomorrow, get a good night's sleep, but study first!

Interim Summary

A prolonged stage of memory consolidation can be observed in humans and animals, as has been revealed by damage to the hippocampal region. Temporally graded memory loss in humans extends to both episodic and semantic memory and to memory for spatial environments. Human retrograde memory loss can affect a few years or extend several years back, depending on the extent of damage to the medial temporal area. Damage beyond the medial temporal lobe can result in nongraded (flat) retrograde impairment. Prospective studies in animals can precisely specify what was learned and when and how well learning occurred before onset of amnesia. These studies have confirmed the phenomenon of temporally graded memory loss and shown that the loss includes both nonspatial and spatial memory. Temporally graded memory loss can occur following damage limited to the hippocampus, and non-graded (flat) gradients occur following cortical damage, as observed in humans.

Models of Cortical–Hippocampal Interactions Illuminate Memory Reorganization

The mechanisms of long-term memory consolidation have been the subject of many theoretical proposals. It is generally believed that the final repository of long-term memories is the neocortex, and hippocampal processing somehow organizes or facilitates the representation of permanent memories in specific neocortical sites. How does the hippocampal system interact with neocortical processors to store and consolidate memory? Several models of hippocampal–cortical interactions have been proposed, including a number of computational models. Here we consider two recent models that focus on how the hippocampus could mediate a slow reorganization process.

In the first of these models, Alvarez and Squire (1994) proposed a simple network model highlighting basic distinctions in the operating characteristics of the cerebral cortex and the hippocampus. They argued that the cerebral cortex can store an immense amount of information, but cortical representations change slowly and incrementally. By contrast, the hippocampus has limited storage capacity, but it records information rapidly by using rapid LTP mechanisms to change connection strengths. Their goal was to show how these properties instantiated within a simple neural network simulation could demonstrate key properties of consolidation. Figure 11.10A illustrates their model, which simulated two distinct generic cortical areas and a medial temporal lobe (MTL) region. Each neural unit in these areas was connected to every other unit in the model, and the connection strengths could be modified by an LTP-like mechanism. The rate of change in connections between the MTL and the cortex was designed to be rapid but short-lasting, whereas connection changes between the two cortical areas were slow but long-lasting. When new information was presented to the network to set up activations in the cortical areas, the MTL connections changed substantially and rapidly to represent the conjointly active units in the cortical areas, although little permanent change occurred in the cortical representations or their connections. Subsequently, when the MTL area was randomly activated to simulate a subsequent consolidation event, the originally activated cortical input areas were reactivated, incrementally enhancing their connections.

Memory performance of the model was assessed in terms of how well activation of one cortical representation could reactivate the associated representation

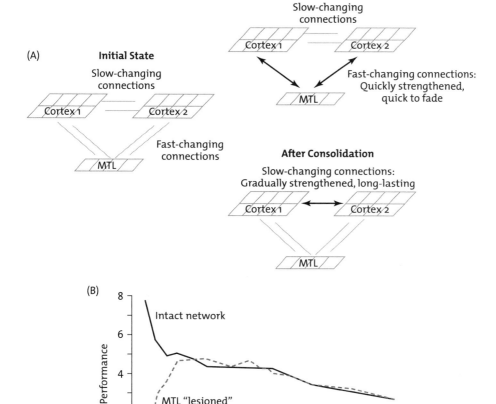

FIGURE 11.10 Alvarez and Squire's model of consolidation.
A. Design of the model. Each array reflects a set of neurons in a cortical area or in the medial temporal lobe (MTL). Initially weak connections are shown as fine lines, whereas strong connections are shown as a heavy two-directional arrow. B. Performance of the model as a function of the number of cycles of simulated neural activity between training and the simulated lesion.

in the other cortical area (Figure 11.10B). To evaluate the model, the investigators activated the neural elements corresponding to the memory representation that had been established in one cortical area of the model, and then checked whether the elements corresponding to the associated representation became activated in the other cortical area of the model. The intact network showed strong performance in activating the associated representations shortly after learning and showed some forgetting over time. By contrast, if the MTL section of the model was removed shortly after learning, memory performance was poor; and the longer the MTL was left intact after learning, the stronger were the consequent memory performances. Accordingly, the model seemed to simulate the essential characteristics of memory reorganization.

McClelland and his colleagues (1995) developed a more elaborate and larger-scale model, extending these ideas and applying them within the context of the distributed network models described in Chapter 10. In their model, cortical representations involved systematic organizations of related items in parallel, multidimensional hierarchies. They envisioned the function of the cortex as identifying stimulus characteristics and sorting items into categories and subcategories within the large-scale organization. As an example, they considered the network illustrated in Figure 11.11A, in which birds and fish are characterized by a set of properties (for example, a robin is an animal that has feathers and wings, is red, and can fly). They noted that computer models of these elaborate parallel distributed networks can readily be trained to sort many animals according to these kinds of characteristics.

However, once a set of hierarchical organizations is established and stabilized within the model, it is difficult to add new items smoothly. This is not because a network cannot be altered to include a new item by repetitive training—it will do so quite well. The problem is that such novel training changes the established network, resulting in **catastrophic interference:** sudden and severe disruption of the representations of relationships between existing network items. New training alters a network so it can identify the item, but the modifications interfere with the network's ability to identify the old information. For example, training the network to identify a penguin, a bird that has characteristics of both birds (wings) and fish (can swim), caused catastrophic interference with the established categories. As a result of this focused training, network performance on overall categorization of birds and fish fell precipitously.

McClelland's solution to the problem of catastrophic interference was to add a new component to the model: a small network that could mimic the function of the hippocampus. This new, small network could rapidly acquire a representation of a new item and then slowly and gradually train the large network to use the new category. When this model was tested, the connection strengths in the hippocampal network changed rapidly and were sent repetitively to the larger cortical network. The cortical network modifications were slow and incremental. In addition to receiving occasional input from the hippocampus, the cortical model was repetitively exposed to the materials it was initially built to represent, thereby creating an interleaved learning regimen. This intermixing of new information with reinforcements of old representations allowed the cortical network to incorporate new information without breaking down due to catastrophic interference. In the

*Models of Cortical–
Hippocampal
Interactions
Illuminate Memory
Reorganization*

391

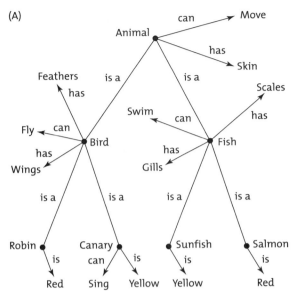

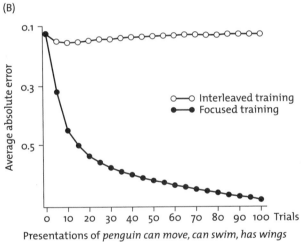

FIGURE 11.11 McClelland's model of consolidation.
A. Propositional network that the model is trained on. B. Performance of the model as a function of interleaved versus focused training.

example sorting task, such interleaved training in categorizing penguins, fish, and birds preserved successful performance on all three categories (Figure 11.11B).

Eventually this interleaved learning produced a cortical representation that no longer benefited from hippocampal activations. Thus the model exhibited a critical feature of memory consolidation: temporally limited dependence on the hippocampus. In addition, though, this model suggests that the required duration of consolidation would not necessarily be constant. Rather, the time required for memories to consolidate might depend on the nature of the information involved, as well as on any other new learning that must be stored during consolidation of information stored earlier. Thus memory consolidation involves lifelong evolution of cortical networks as they gradually approach a state where more interleaving does not alter the network substantially. This conception of memory consolidation also helps explain the various durations of temporal gradients in retrograde amnesia. The consolidation period is typically brief when there is little new information to be stored in an existing framework, and it is typically long when the required changes in the existing framework are large.

Hippocampal Network Processing Contributes to Memory Reorganization

The preceding discussion shows that the hippocampus plays an essential role in memory consolidation for some period following learning, but it does not specify the nature of information processing that occurs during consolidation. One prominent view is that the hippocampus binds together disparate elements of memory representations stored in widespread neocortical areas (Paller, 1997). A corollary view is that during the consolidation period, remembering involves the spreading activation of signals from the hippocampal region outward to cortical areas (Damasio, 1989). Further consideration of the nature of hippocampal representations, combined with our knowledge about cortical–hippocampal circuitry, offers potential insights about how cortical–hippocampal interactions might underlie memory consolidation. As described in Chapters 9 and 10, the hippocampus represents learned episodes as a series of discrete events, each encoded within the activity of a single cell. In this scheme, some cells encode highly specific conjunctions of stimuli and actions, or sequences thereof, that compose rare events occurring in only one or a few learning episodes (such as the sequence of specific events that comprised your walk to class today). Other cells encode common features of similar, related experiences (such as the route you always take to class and the buildings you pass on the way). These representations shared between episodes could support our ability to link an event in recent memory to memories of similar previous experiences.

Eichenbaum and colleagues (1999) have suggested that the representations of events that are common across episodes could play a role in the linking and interleaving processes of memory consolidation that are key features of the models just described. According to this view, each time a related episode occurs, or even when we just think about that episode, the hippocampal cells representing the parts of the episode that are common to similar episodes become active. These

*Models of Cortical–
Hippocampal
Interactions
Illuminate Memory
Reorganization*

393

cells send outputs to the entorhinal cortex, which in turn sends outputs to other cortical areas. Such outputs could activate existing representations of those common events in the entorhinal cortex and other cortical areas. Thus when we have an experience that shares information with other previous experiences, the hippocampus helps us elicit memories of the related experiences.

In addition, simultaneous activation of several related memory representations in the cortex could strengthen connections between the relevant cortical cells. If cortical representations of related episodes activate simultaneously several times, the connections between elements that compose the related memories should also become stronger. Eventually the connections within the cortex can become strong enough that activation within the cortex itself is sufficient to elicit related memories without necessarily involving the hippocampus.

Evidence for the idea that the hippocampus connects cortical representations comes from a study in which monkeys were trained in a visual paired associate task. During the task, researchers recorded neural activity in the parahippocampal region surrounding the hippocampus and in the higher-order visual area in the temporal cortex responsible for object identification (Naya et al., 2001). In each trial, the monkey initially saw the first of an arbitrarily paired set of visual cues; following a delay, the monkey had to choose the pair of the initial cue from two visual cues to obtain a reward. Temporal cortex neurons responded before parahippocampal neurons to visual stimuli that were presented as initial cues. This should be expected because temporal cortex neurons receive visual information first and send the visual inputs to the hippocampal region. The opposite activity sequence was observed in the recall phase of the task. When the monkey had to anticipate the paired associate of the cue, neurons that were directly responsive to the pair when it was shown began to fire in anticipation of that cue, and this memory response was observed in the parahippocampal area before it was seen in the temporal cortex. Thus the memory signal began closer to the hippocampus and spread outward to the visual cortex. This finding is consistent with the view that the hippocampal region links cortical representations to one another—in this case linking representations of visual stimuli in the temporal cortex.

Other experiments have studied the evolution of memory representations in the hippocampus and cortex during consolidation. One study examined metabolic activity in the hippocampal and cortical areas at different times after mice learned a radial maze task (Bontempi et al., 1999). Animals were initially trained to find rewards in particular arms of a maze. Then the activation levels of different brain areas were examined when the animals performed the task at different times following learning. Hippocampal activity was high when the animals demonstrated their information retention 5 days after learning, and at this time the prefrontal and temporal cortex were less activated. Conversely, 25 days after learning, hippocampal activation had diminished considerably whereas the prefrontal and temporal cortex showed greater activation. In addition, the correlation between the level of hippocampal activation and memory performance declined from 5 to 25 days, whereas accuracy became more strongly predicted by cortical activation in the same period. Consistent with these observations, Frankland and colleagues (2004) reported similar results for the time course of consolidation of contextual fear memories. These findings confirm the involvement of the hippocampus early in consolidation and the relative increase in cortical involvement during retrieval as consolidation proceeds.

Interim Summary

Computer simulations of temporally graded retrograde amnesia support the idea that memory reorganization involves interactions between the hippocampus and cortex. In these models, the hippocampus learns rapidly and gradually teaches the cortex new information, which is interleaved with practice of older information. This interaction eventually modifies cortical representations to incorporate the new information, ultimately making the hippocampus unnecessary as observed in temporally graded retrograde amnesia. Firing patterns of hippocampal and cortical neurons support the view that the hippocampus rapidly acquires episodic memories and links recent episodes to other memories that share common information. Other studies show that the hippocampus is essential for expression of memories soon after learning, but eventually cortical activations predominate. These combined computer models and experimental studies clarify how episodic information is woven into a network of memories abstracted from many related episodes.

Chapter Summary

1. Memory consolidation helps establish the permanence and organization of memories in the postlearning period. There are two forms of memory consolidation: One involves the molecular and cellular processes that support the fixation of memory within synapses over minutes or hours, and the other involves interactions within the cognitive memory system that support memory reorganization over a period of many weeks and even years.

2. Through a cascade of molecular and microstructural events, short-term synaptic modifications permanently change connectivity between neurons; this process occurs across brain structures that participate in memory and across species. Memory fixation can be either halted or facilitated by administering postlearning treatments that interfere with this molecular and cellular cascade.

3. Natural modulatory mechanisms can also facilitate fixation in the various memory systems of the mammalian brain. One important modulatory system involves the adrenal glands' release of glucocorticoids and epinephrine, which is triggered by the amygdala during stressful events. This activation improves memory fixation in the declarative and habit systems in both animals and humans.

4. In addition, the cognitive memory system mediates the prolonged reorganization of memories. This process has been identified in temporally graded retrograde amnesia for cognitive memories in both humans and animals. The nature of these mechanisms within the cognitive system is not yet well understood. However, current models propose that the hippocampus rapidly stores indexes of cortical representations, and then slowly facilitates interconnections between cortical representations through a process of repeated two-way interactions between the cortex and the hippocampus. Over an extended period, these interactions ultimately cause the reorganization of and connections among cortical representations in order to incorporate new material into semantic knowledge.

KEY TERMS

retrograde amnesia (p. 364)

temporally graded retrograde amnesia (p. 364)

consolidate (p. 364)

Law of Regression (p. 366)

perseveration (p. 367)

intrusion errors (p. 367)

retroactive interference (p. 367)

reverberate (p. 369)

fixation (p. 371)

reorganization (p. 371)

source memory (p. 380)

catastrophic interference (p. 390)

REVIEWING THE CONCEPTS

- What are the two distinct stages of memory consolidation?

- Describe the molecular and cellular process of memory fixation.

- What is temporally graded retrograde amnesia, and what does it tell us about memory consolidation?

- How might interaction between the cortex and hippocampus support both the prolonged reorganization of memories and the temporally graded memory loss often observed in retrograde amnesia?

Short-Term Memory and Working Memory

Are you good at remembering telephone numbers? Read the following number; then cover the page and try to hold the number in memory for 10 seconds:

90739

You may have succeeded with that one: It's similar to the five-digit phone numbers that were popular in many U.S. towns in the 1950s. Now try the following number:

7654074

How did you do on that one? Probably rather well. Phone numbers in most U.S. towns had just seven digits until the 1990s, when requests for cell phone, fax, and computer telephone numbers required telephone companies to assign more new numbers than combinations of just seven digits would allow. Now try holding this number in memory for 10 seconds:

5368749201

Many people would have difficulty with this one. One way to make it easier would be to break the number into chunks, such as 536-874-9201, which would be more like the system of area codes, exchanges, and four-digit unique numbers that telephone companies use these days. But I suspect you would agree that this size of number is near our memory limits. Imagine how things may be in 10 or 20 years if every member of an even larger population requires multiple phone numbers for cell phones and inventions still to come. Try the following number:

2357819523665

I think you will agree that this is just too much. We've just demonstrated that we have a limited capacity for holding information in our minds for even relatively brief periods. Our ability to store information in our current consciousness without active rehearsal is called **short-term memory;** this kind of memory is defined by how much we can remember, usually for several seconds, before the information is either stored more permanently or lost.

Now try the following. Start with the number 100 and count backward by 7s. How did you do? Here are the answers:

93, 86, 79, 72, 65, 58, 51, 44, 37, 30, 23, 16, 9, and 2

This task is easier in one way but more difficult in another. Although you have to remember only one number at a time, you also have to manipulate that number to perform the arithmetic and hold in mind the rule of subtracting 7. So first you remember 100, then recall the equation $100 - 7 = ?$, and then solve the equation. Next you must remember the solution to the equation (93) and restart the operation on that number.

Here's another task that combines memory and manipulation. Suppose I presented to you the following string of letters, one at a time at a rate of one per second. Don't try to memorize the list, but tell me if each letter is the same as the letter that came two items earlier. So just read each item one at a time, without looking at the other items, and respond yes or no to indicate whether that letter is identical to the item that appeared two back in the series:

x–g–h–g–k–e–p–e–b–s–h–s–n–l–n–z–b–c–s–w–s–w–j–g–j–a

How did you do? Here is the series again; the items that should have received "yes" responses are capitalized:

x–g–h–**G**–k–e–p–**E**–b–s–h–**S**–n–l–**N**–z–b–c–s–w–**S**–**W**–j–g–**J**–a

This task resembles the subtraction task in that it required you to keep a small amount of information in mind while performing an operation on that information. You had to create a running buffer to hold the most recent two items, then match the first item in the buffer to the next item and make your response. Then you had to drop the first item in the buffer, shift the second item to the first position, add the new item as the second one in the buffer, and so on. Again you had to combine holding a few items in memory and performing a mental operation—in this case matching to the first item in the sliding buffer. The ability to hold information in mind while manipulating or actively rehearsing it is called **working memory.** Thus working memory occurs naturally when we are just thinking about something or when we actively try to memorize by repetition or other thoughtful mental activity. Working memory can, in its simplest use, extend the duration of short-term memory indefinitely through active rehearsal. But working memory can perform more complex mental processing as well, as illustrated by the task in which you made judgments about items two back in the list of letters.

Here's one more seemingly simple task: Who were your teachers in your most recently completed year of school? This task requires a substantial memory search. You probably began by recalling the courses you took, perhaps by thinking through your daily schedule. This may have led you to recall particular lectures, which would have brought to mind the images—then the names—of the lecturers. This common sort of memory search is also an example of working memory in action. You had to keep in mind the goal of the search—identifying teachers—and the rule, which was to find the ones from last year. You recalled a day's classes, then their teachers, and repeated this mental activity until you identified them all.

THE TASKS YOU just attempted illustrate how we work with memory. Working memory involves short-term storage of stimuli and the rules for manipulating that information; it can also include a guided search for information from long-term memory. This chapter surveys three related, relatively brief types of memory: a very short-term sensory store, short-term memory, and working memory.

First we will discuss the key features of these short-lived forms of memory, considering the relationships among them. Then we will review psychological studies of working memory that elaborate its component processes. We will also consider the neuroscience of working memory, which shows that the frontal lobes play a central role in both humans and animals. The frontal lobe is a very large part of the cerebral cortex composed of several distinct areas that perform separate functions. Human and animal studies show that these functions are fundamentally the same across species in supporting different abilities to briefly store and manipulate information.

Fundamental Questions

1. How much information can our short-term memory store?
2. What happens in working memory?
3. What brain areas and processes support working memory?

Defining Short-Term Memory

We Have a Very Short-Term, Large-Capacity Sensory Memory Store

Incoming sensory information is first held in a **short-term sensory store** with a fleeting duration and a surprisingly large capacity. This store can house different types of visual or auditory stimuli and can hold up to about 20 to 30 items. Look briefly at the following array of letters:

Z	T	I	K	P
F	G	U	L	N
X	H	A	V	Q

Now, when you look away, how many of them can you recall? Probably you could recite only four or five before losing track. Even so, you probably felt you could have remembered additional letters had your memory not faded so quickly while you were saying the initial four or five. Sperling (1960) investigated this sensory memory capacity using a special procedure that circumvented the usual difficulty of time required for recall. He told his subjects that they would look at arrays of letters such as the one here and then hear a tone indicating which part of the array they should recall. A high tone indicated they should recall the top row; a middle tone meant they should recall the middle row; and a low tone told them to recall the bottom row. Using this test procedure, Sperling found that even after very brief exposures to stimulus arrays of 15 items, people could often recall a large percentage of the items. However, if an interval of just one second was inserted between presentation of the array and the tone, subjects recalled significantly fewer items. Thus we have a very short-term sensory store that has a large capacity but is held quite briefly.

Darwin and colleagues (1972) revealed a similar short-term store for auditory information. They had subjects wear headphones and presented three different nine-item lists of letters and numbers through one or both of the headphone earpieces so that they sounded like they came from the left, the right, or above (when heard from both sides at once). They presented three such lists simultaneously (one to the left ear, one to the right ear, and one to both ears) and then gave a visual signal indicating which list the subject should recall. People could not recall all nine items but performed well in remembering part of the selected list. As with the visual information, this information was held only briefly. If a delay of more than a few seconds was imposed, rapid forgetting occurred. These findings suggest that our sensory memory lets us hold a lot of exact sensory information for a very short period before we select the information to be encoded into long-term memory or forget it.

We Also Have a Short-Term Memory of Limited Size

The telephone number test described earlier is an example of a task that draws on short-term memory. The fact that there are seven digits in a conventional phone number is no accident. That number is based on considerable research showing that most people can accurately reproduce number or letter strings of about seven, plus or minus two, items, with performance falling off considerably thereafter. Indeed 7 is often referred to as the *magic number* because that is the average number of items people can hold in short-term memory. The magic number 7 is most frequently demonstrated in a test called **digit span** where, as in the earlier example, subjects are asked to recall increasingly long lists of numbers until they fail to immediately recall the entire list. The magic number 7 applies to both visual and auditory stimuli.

Thus, following the very large but short-term store of memory for sensory information, a considerably smaller amount of information enters the next phase of short-term memory. A common demonstration of the capacity of this next stage of short-term memory comes from studies of the free recall of longer lists. In this kind of test, subjects read or hear a long list of words and are then immediately asked to recall as many of the words as possible in any order. The number of items usually exceeds the magic number 7—that is, it exceeds the capacity of short-term memory—so recall from a long list contains contributions from both the contents of short-term memory and any items that might have entered long-term memory. In this test researchers focus on **serial recall**, which is the accuracy of recall for each item depending on its position in the list. Serial recall performance is analyzed using a **serial position curve** to show the likelihood that each successive list item will be remembered. The serial position curve typically has a U shape: The highest curve points correspond to the items at the beginning and the end of the list, which are most likely to be remembered. The dip in the middle of the serial position curve shows the typically poorer recall of words in the middle of the list (Figure 12.1). Superior recall of items at the beginning of the list, called the **primacy effect,** is usually attributed to lack of interference from preceding items, which makes the early list items more likely to enter long-term memory. The better recall of items at the end of the list, called the **recency effect,** occurs because

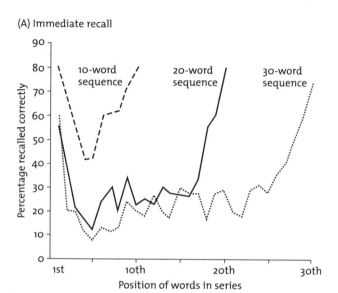

(A) Immediate recall

(B) Recall delayed by 30 seconds

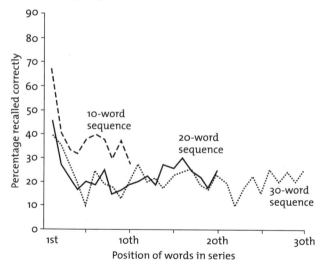

FIGURE 12.1 The serial position curve.
A. Recall immediately after lists of varying length are presented. B. Recall is delayed for 30 seconds during which the subject is distracted.

those later items are still available in short-term memory. As this explanation suggests, the recency effect disappears if even a brief delay is interposed between presentation of the list and recall of the items. Note that the size of the recency effect is about five to seven items, which corresponds to the magic number of items most people can hold in short-term memory.

Despite this size limit of short-term memory, we can increase the amount of information it can handle by efficiently compacting more information into each item stored. This process is called **chunking.** For example, any time you combine sets of digits in a telephone number to remember it, you are chunking the information to improve your recall. By relying on our tendency to chunk information, telephone companies were able to increase the total number of possible phone numbers without making them significantly harder to remember. The new information in a single chunk was presented in the form of the *exchange*—the set of three digits in a phone number that comes before the final four-digit block. The exchange was conceived as a set of numbers that would be common to all phone numbers in a city or district, making this new chunk relatively easy to recall. Pressed to come up with yet more phone numbers, telephone companies then invented the area code—an additional three-digit chunk common to phone numbers that included many different exchanges. Once again, adding this additional chunk made the memory task only a bit larger. Fortunately items that are chunked in short-term memory are also typically stored as the same chunks in long-term memory.

The duration and capacity of short-term memory has been studied by examining the rate of forgetting items when rehearsal is prevented using the **Brown–Peterson test.** Brown (1958) and Peterson and Peterson (1959) asked subjects to read a sequence of unrelated words or consonants such as B–H–D, then immediately start counting backward by threes. After varying intervals for up to several seconds, they asked the subjects to stop counting and recall the items. The subjects' ability to recall all three words or consonants was quite good if the interval spent counting was only three seconds (Figure 12.2). Performance fell rapidly thereafter; when the subjects spent six to nine seconds counting before recall, they could remember only a single item. These data provide a measure of the **forgetting curve** of short-term memory—that is, the rate at which information is lost over time.

The duration and capacity of short-term memory depend on what kind of information must be held in mind. For example, it is easy to remember a list of letters that compose a single word for a long time despite distraction, showing that a chunk of one word enters long-term memory as a single item. Even though the Brown–Peterson test is intended to measure short-term memory alone, it is clear that some items can enter long-term memory and become immune to interference.

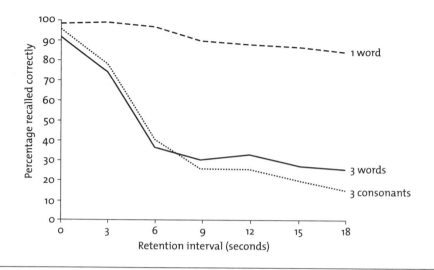

FIGURE 12.2 Brown–Peterson forgetting curves.
Performance as a function of different types of materials to remember and the length of the retention interval, during which subjects are prevented from rehearsing.

Also, studies repeatedly testing subjects with words as cues have found that performance typically deteriorates for short lists of words from the same category (such as *zebra, snake, lion*). Such deterioration is blamed on *proactive inhibition* from earlier items preventing proper encoding of later items. However, when a list of words from a new category (perhaps *table, chair, lamp*) is presented, performance suddenly rises. Similar performance increases occur when subjects switch from lists of numbers to lists of letters or when the background colors of visually presented items change, although the largest improvements come with new item meanings rather than superficial features. This phenomenon, called **release from proactive inhibition,** demonstrates a lasting effect of items that are otherwise forgotten rapidly, suggesting an interaction between long-term and short-term memories.

Short-Term Memory Transitions into Long-Term Memory

William James (1890) was the first to recognize a distinction between short-term and long-term memory. The distinction, best captured later in a model developed by Atkinson and Shiffrin (1968), is that these two forms of memory operate in succession so that information from the very short-term store is sent into a short-term memory buffer just large enough to hold about seven chunks of information. The contents of short-term memory can be rehearsed and eventually are stored in long-term memory (Figure 12.3).

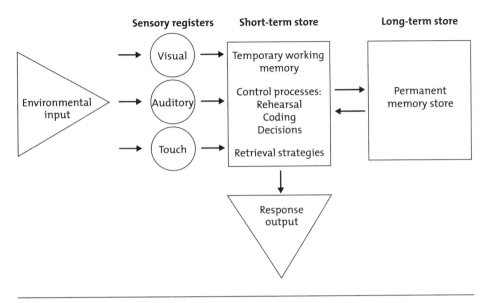

FIGURE 12.3 The Atkinson–Shiffrin model.

According to this model, the purpose of short-term memory is to rehearse items so they have a better chance of being stored in long-term memory. The pattern of remembering items best near the beginning and end of a series, as shown in serial position curves, matches this model. The primacy effect is caused by superior rehearsal of the first few items, which are held and rehearsed longer before the interference of successive items eventually bumps them out of short-term memory. However, other studies have shown that rehearsal by itself does not always improve long-term retention. Glenberg and colleagues (1977) separated the effects of rehearsal and attention by presenting a four-digit number, asking subjects to rehearse an unrelated word for 2, 6, or 18 seconds, and then finally asking for recall of the number. Subjects were told that the experiment aimed to assess their ability to recall the number, and the word rehearsal was a just a distracter (similar to counting backward in the Brown–Peterson test). When the researchers asked the subjects to recall the words they had been rehearsing, they found the subjects' performance quite poor and relatively unaffected by the length of time spent rehearsing. Thus it seems that instead of relying on rehearsal alone, the extent to which items reach long-term memory depends on the processing depth of the material. As discussed in Chapter 8, when words are studied at a semantic level, they are better recalled from long-term memory.

Short-term and long-term memory surely interact. For example, as mentioned earlier regarding release from proactive inhibition, semantic features of information stored in long-term memory can still affect short-term retention of new information. However, analyses of the recency effect also have suggested that the contents of short-term memory differ qualitatively from material stored in long-term memory: Short-term memory tends to rely on perceptual qualities of stimuli, whereas long-term memory depends more on stimuli meaning. This distinction was demonstrated by Kintsch and Buschke (1969), who had subjects study lists of words that included several pairs of either homophones (*bear* and *bare*) or synonyms (*car* and *auto*), and then immediately freely recall the words. The response patterns formed a typical serial position curve, which the researchers analyzed to differentiate errors due to the homophones' acoustic similarities from errors caused by the synonyms' semantic similarities. In the recency part of the serial position curve, which describes recall rates for the last list items, they found more mistakes based on acoustic similarities between homophones. On the other hand, the primacy part of the curve showed that for the early list items, the subjects made more errors based on the synonyms' related meanings. Thus memory for the early list items relied on semantic information (typical of long-term memory), whereas memory for the last items relied on phonetic information (typical of short-term memory).

Are short-term and long-term memory sequential stages of processing, or are they parallel processes working to incorporate the same new information? Compelling evidence that some aspects of short-term and long-term memory are distinct and parallel comes from characterizations of people with brain damage. As you read in Chapter 8, subjects such as H. M., who have anterograde amnesia following damage to the hippocampal system, have severely impaired memory both for recent experiences and for the kind of facts most of us accumulate from day to day. In formal testing situations, amnesic individuals can be severely impaired in acquiring new long-term memories—for example, not recalling a brief story read just seconds before a distraction. But they typically show a normal capacity for short-term memory as measured by the digit span test and the Brown–Peterson test. Also, when tested for serial recall of lists, amnesic people show a loss of the primacy effect and poor performance in the middle of the serial position curve—both considered reflections of items that make it to long-term memory—but intact recency, which reflects the contents of short-term memory (Baddeley & Warrington, 1970; Figure 12.4).

Precisely the opposite pattern of spared and impaired memory performance has been observed in a different type of subject (Shallice & Warrington, 1970). People who have cortical damage in the temporoparietal area have memory spans limited to two or three items. They show a recency effect in the serial position curve limited to the last item listed and exhibit very rapid memory loss in the Brown–Peterson forgetting test. In contrast, they perform quite well in recalling a story after several minutes and in various other long-term memory tests, such as learning word pairs over several trials. Such brain damage is near the area of

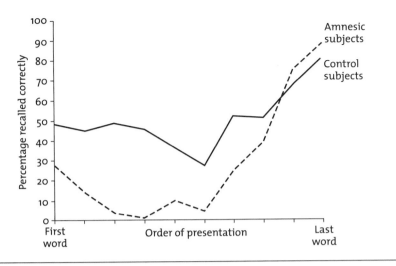

FIGURE 12.4 **Primacy and recency in amnesic individuals.**

the cerebral cortex that processes speech, which is consistent with the idea that short-term memory in these tasks is mediated by phonetic-level processing. These findings support the view that short-term memory involves online processing of perceptual—in this case acoustic—aspects of stimuli, whereas long-term memory involves the meanings that stimuli contribute to received information.

Interim Summary

We have a very short-term sensory store that can briefly hold a lot of visual or auditory information. This mechanism lets us search for specific items we have just experienced and bring that information into other types of memory. We also have a short-term memory that permits us to retain approximately seven items for an extended period; we can effectively augment this store by chunking elements into larger items, such as multiple-digit numbers. Some items held in short-term memory make the transition to long-term memory. However, the simple idea that items move from short- to long-term memory is not supported by experimental analyses. Short-term memory tends to emphasize the perceptual qualities of stimuli, whereas long-term memory emphasizes item meanings. Some people with brain damage have intact long-term memory but impaired short-term memory, whereas others have impaired long-term memory and spared short-term memory. These findings all suggest some degree of independence of the short-term and long-term stores.

Working Memory Is Short-Term Memory with Several Components

Studies of short-term memory do a good job of explaining how we hold information in mind for a few seconds, and they tell us what happens to this information as it enters long-term memory. But these basic observations about how short-term memory works do not address the more complex process of actively manipulating new information to reason and solve problems. To examine how we manipulate information held in short-term memory, Baddeley and Hitch (1974) began to explore the concept of *working memory*—a system more complex and richer than short-term memory but reserved in function for items that are within ongoing conscious control.

Baddeley's (1986) model contains three main interacting components: a phonological loop, a visuospatial sketchpad, and a central executive. Within this model the phonological loop and visuospatial sketchpad are specialized subsystems with dedicated functions, and the central executive serves a control function that uses the information processed by the two specialized subsystems (Figure 12.5).

The Phonological Loop Supports Auditory Rehearsal

The **phonological loop** is a short-term storage space for speech-based information that includes a mechanism for **subvocal speech** (the ability to consciously verbalize words without speaking aloud). Thus this system contains a kind of "inner ear" for hearing unspoken speech and an "inner voice" for talking to ourselves. Both of these are employed for storing the sounds (that is, the phonetics) of words and rehearsal. The system can hold about two seconds' worth of auditory information, which is sufficient to support the kind of short-term memory required in, say, the digit span test.

Baddeley and his colleagues examined the phonological loop's storage capacity by having subjects read aloud lists of words with different numbers of syllables (Baddeley, 1986). The more syllables the words had, the less likely subjects were to recall them; and there was a constant relationship between each subject's reading rate and the number of words recalled. Because the phonological loop can store only as much information as it can process in two seconds, subjects' read-

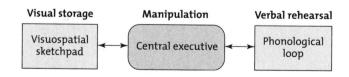

FIGURE 12.5 Baddeley's model of working memory.

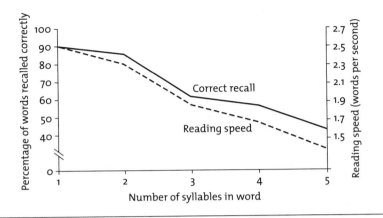

FIGURE 12.6 Recall and reading speed as a function of the number of syllables in each word.

ing rates determine the number of words stored (Figure 12.6). For example, subjects' reading rate for three-syllable words was about 1.8 words per second, and subjects could recall an average of 3.5 such words from the list of 5. Dividing this average memory capacity of 3.5 words by the rate of 1.8 words read per second yields a capacity for the phonological loop of about two seconds' worth of words.

The phonological loop has also been shown to support articulation of words. Evidence comes from studies examining short-term memory for span tests using sequences of letters rather than digits. When subjects repeated sequences of letters back to the experimenter from memory, they tended to make errors involving phonologically similar information. For example, span errors for the list H–F–R–Q–G–R that substitute S for F or V for G are more common than would occur by chance. Also, subjects make more errors when trying to recall strings of letters that have rhyming names (T–B–G–V–Z) than strings of letters with dissimilar-sounding names (Q–C–F–Y–R–K). However, when the items to be remembered are presented in writing and processed visually rather than auditorily, the tendency to erroneously recall phonologically similar items disappears, as does the influence of word length on memory capacity. And other kinds of repetitive tasks, such as tapping a finger while test items are presented, do not suppress verbal memory performance. Thus the phonological loop supports word articulation and stores phonetic information.

Additional evidence showing that articulatory processing occurs during rehearsal comes from studies showing that articulation of irrelevant material can interfere with concurrent memory performance. If subjects are required to speak irrelevant material, such as repeating the word *the* as they listen to a list of words and recall the list in written form, their performance drops dramatically. Simply playing speech in the background during visual study of digits for a digit span test impairs later performance, even if the speech is in a language the subject does not understand.

The phonological loop is thought to serve any task that requires a short articulatory memory, such as counting. This mechanism is probably important in formulating and comprehending long sentences because we need to remember the beginning of a sentence long enough to understand its complete meaning at the end. The phonological loop is also required for second language learning—specifically, for holding in mind a combination of words in a native language while pairing them with words of the same meaning in a new language. The same mechanism can be used to rehearse equivalent words in the two languages.

The Visuospatial Sketchpad Supports Rehearsal of Visual Images

Complementing the phonological loop, the **visuospatial sketchpad** is a separate and parallel system for rehearsing visual or spatial information in short-term memory. This system lets us create and hold in mind a mental image of something we have just seen or imagine what something might look like. Baddeley and his colleagues investigated this component of working memory by asking two groups of subjects to use different strategies to remember a list of 10 words (Baddeley, 1986). One group was instructed to imagine a walk through the college campus and associate each word with a specific campus location. The other group of subjects simply rehearsed the word list without using a spatial visualization strategy. Consistent with the notion of a mental sketchpad for holding images in mind, subjects remembered the words more accurately when they had become associated with mental images. In another experiment, subjects were asked to remember pairs of concrete words (like *bullet–gray*) or abstract words (*gratitude–infinite*). The concrete word pairs, which are more easily visualized, were also more likely to be recalled than pairs of abstract words.

Conversely, interference with visualization compromises memory test performance. For example, in one experiment subjects memorized sentences that included spatially imaginable words (such as *room* or *valley*) or sentences that contained nonspatial words (*apple, book*). At the same time, some subjects performed a visual tracking task in which they held a pointer and used it to track a moving light spot while they heard the sentences. Memory for sentences without a spatial component was unaffected by the concurrent visual tracking task. But the tracking task disrupted memory for the spatially descriptive sentences to the same levels observed for the nonspatial sentences.

The phonological loop and visuospatial sketchpad seem to work independently as distinct components of working memory. Quinn and McConnell (1996) showed this by introducing interfering activities that were intended to affect one or the

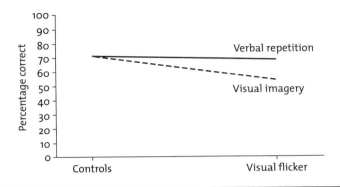

FIGURE 12.7 Word list performance as affected by visual flicker interference.
The visual flicker caused only slight interference for subjects who used verbal repetition
to aid memorization, but for subjects who memorized the list using visual imagery, the
visual flicker had a more detrimental effect on memory performance.

other of the two systems. They had subjects learn lists of words using either visual
imagery or rote verbal repetition. In the background the subjects simultaneously
experienced either irrelevant visual flicker (intended to interfere with processing
by the visuospatial sketchpad) or irrelevant speech (intended to interfere with the
phonological loop). Performance by subjects using imagery to memorize the
words was indeed impaired by concurrent visual flicker, whereas performance by
subjects using rote repetition was unaffected by the visual flicker (Figure 12.7).
Conversely, the rote repetition subjects' performance was impaired by irrelevant
background speech, whereas the performance of subjects using imagery was not.
The observation that each type of interference affected just one type of processing shows that the two systems work independently.

The Central Executive Manipulates Information and Recruits Other Systems

In Baddeley's model the **central executive** performs many tasks to control and
manipulate information in working memory, to access information from long-
term storage sites, and to distribute processed information to various sites for long-
term memory. It can translate information between the phonological loop and
visuospatial sketchpad in a variety of ways (such as by transforming words into
images or vice versa). And the central executive can simultaneously store and
manipulate information. The central executive is composed of many subsystems
for directing attention, keeping goals in mind, and creating and applying rules.
Many of these tasks are thought to take place within the prefrontal cortex; so we
will examine these aspects of the central executive's role later in this chapter when
we consider the neurological basis of working memory.

Baddeley has recently added to the model an additional subsystem called the **episodic buffer,** which stores the sequence of events composing a recent experience (Baddeley, 2000). He proposed this additional subsystem based on the observation that subjects can recall a lot more words when the words make up sentences or coherent ideas. Thus, whereas the number of unrelated words that can be immediately recalled is approximately 7, memory for a sentence can successfully contain 16 or more words. This phenomenon is likely related to the chunking effect, but this raises the question of how chunking is accomplished. Also, prose recall is not subject to interference by concurrent articulation of irrelevant material. These and other findings led Baddeley to suggest that the episodic buffer stores sequences of events that compose specific experiences and can hold this information for several seconds.

In addition, recent functional brain imaging studies also demonstrate separation between elements of the working memory system (Baddeley, 1998). The "inner ear" of the phonological store involves the verbal comprehension area (Wernicke's area) in the left parietal lobe, and the articulatory rehearsal process involves the speech area in the left frontal lobe (Broca's area). The visuospatial sketchpad is served by distinct areas in the right hemisphere, and processing either object-oriented or spatial aspects of visual images elicits a distinctive pattern of brain activation.

Learning & Memory in Action

How Do Waitresses and Waiters Remember So Much?

Expert waiters and waitresses can listen to orders from several people at a table without taking notes and deliver all the orders correctly. How do they do it? One study examined this question by observing expert waitresses in action (Stevens, 1988). Each of five customers placed an order for a hot or cold sandwich, a hot or cold drink, and a dessert. The waitress wrote each order onto a check but left the checks with each customer and then went to submit the orders at various kitchen locations where the different types of food were prepared. When the meals were ready, she collected the items and distributed them accurately to the customers.

How did she do this? As each customer placed an order, the waitress used working memory to manipulate the information, making it easier to remember by clustering the items into three groups: sandwiches, drinks, or dessert. Then she went to different preparation areas to place all the orders of a particular type: all the hot sandwiches in the hot kitchen, the cold drinks where they were prepared, and so on. Next she collected all the orders at each location. This scheme made sense in terms of the layout of the restaurant preparation areas, minimized the load on the waitress's working memory capacity, and maintained a correspondence between the food type organization and the geography of where the customers were located so she could deliver the orders correctly. Finally, by combining food type clustering and spatial organization, she distributed the orders to the correct customers according to where they were sitting. This scheme may seem chaotic; but the waitress's duties provide a superb demonstration of how manipulating information in working memory interacts with long-term memory to accomplish a complex job.

Animals Too Have Working Memory

Substantial research with various species has demonstrated impressive memory for lists of items that closely resembles the working memory observed in humans. For example, rats performing the standard radial maze task, in which they must visit each of several maze arms only once per testing session, show remarkable memory capacity for up to 17 arms (Olton et al., 1977; see Chapter 6). Also, rats and monkeys perform well in delayed matching and nonmatching to sample tasks even for many objects or pictures (Dudchenko et al., 2000; Murray & Mishkin, 1998; see Chapter 9). These high-capacity memory performances suggest that animals may use other forms of memory in addition to (or in place of) working memory to surpass our human working memory magic number of seven items. In particular, animals may use episodic memory, known to have a larger capacity, to perform these tasks.

Other types of behavioral tests aimed specifically at list memory may provide a more appropriate format in which to compare the working memory performance of animals and humans. Wright and his colleagues (1985) directly compared working memory in pigeons, monkeys, and humans using a **serial probe recognition task** for lists of complex pictures. In this task a subject is presented with a list of study items. Then, following a variable delay, the subject is presented with a test item that may have appeared among the study items. Each species performs a specific response to indicate recognition of the test item or a different response to indicate that it was not among the studied items. This test circumvents the need for animal subjects to recall items on the list yet still measures how well subjects remember items at particular serial positions in a list, as is typical of experiments with list memory in humans. This method also lets the experimenter measure retention time precisely for items at each serial position in the study list, allowing quantitative comparison of retention times for the same types of stimulus materials across species.

In this experiment, the animals viewed travel slides and the human subjects viewed slides of patterns made with a kaleidoscope, making it difficult for the humans to use verbal labels or familiarity with the images as memory cues. The task was otherwise similar for all species. For each trial, initially a series of four slides was presented briefly along the top of a screen, with a one-second interval between stimuli. Then, following a variable retention delay, the test stimulus was presented on the lower part of the screen. The humans and monkeys pushed a lever to the right or left, respectively, to indicate whether or not the test stimulus was part of the initial series of four images. Pigeons pecked a right or left key to register their responses.

For all species, when there was no delay between presentation of the list and the test, subjects had trouble recalling the first image displayed in every series of four and progressively improved with each serial position (Figure 12.8). Thus no species showed a primacy effect, and all showed a robust recency effect. As the retention delay was increased, performance improved for the initial items so that the primacy effect appeared in all species. Thus at medium retention delays, the serial position curves were U-shaped for all species, showing both primacy and recency effects. As the retention delay increased further, the recency effect disappeared, as is typical in serial position curves for list memory; this effect was also observed in all species.

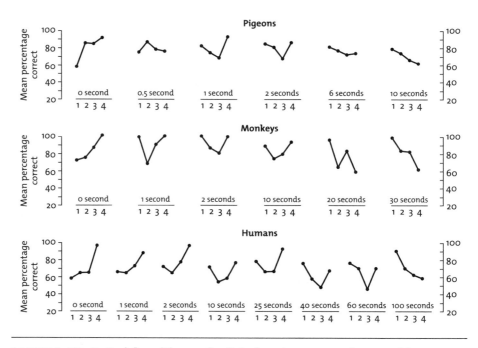

FIGURE 12.8 Serial position probe data for pigeons, monkeys, and humans.

Although the same basic shape of the serial position curve, along with its changes after retention delays, were observed in all the species, the temporal range for these effects differed among species. The described progression of recency-only, U-shaped, and primacy-only curves occurred over retention delays of 10 seconds in pigeons, 30 seconds in monkeys, and 100 seconds in humans. Thus the temporal dynamics of working memory are quite compressed in animals as compared to humans. These findings suggest that the mechanisms governing the fundamental properties of primacy and recency effects are similar across species, but the dynamics are elongated in human working memory.

Interim Summary

Working memory is accomplished by three complementary, interacting functions: (1) The phonological loop supports our capacity for subvocal speech by rehearsing about two seconds' duration of auditory verbal information. (2) The visuospatial sketchpad supports our capacity to hold in mind the appearance of visual images or images described verbally. (3) The central executive manipulates information that is held in short-term memory, calling on the other components of the working memory system and using task rules to alter or make judgments about the information. There may also be a distinct episodic buffer that helps us hold in mind details and the order of events in recent experiences. Studies comparing animals and humans have shown that all species exhibit primacy and recency effects in serial list memory. The strength of these serial position effects varies with memory delay in all species, suggesting similar working memory functional capacities across species.

Working Memory Is Controlled by the Prefrontal Cortex

Working memory involves multiple types of cognitive processing of a broad range of stored material. Correspondingly, working memory relies on a widespread network of brain structures. Considerable evidence points to the prefrontal cortex as the locus of working memory's central executive component, and to a variety of other cortical areas as the mediators of subsystem processes. This section begins with an overview of the anatomy of the prefrontal cortex and early evidence of its functional role. We will consider whether the prefrontal area is directly involved in memory or supports other cognitive processes related to memory; we will also examine whether anatomically distinct subdivisions of the prefrontal area have different roles in working memory. Then we will see how the prefrontal cortex interacts with other higher-order cortical areas to integrate information from short-term and long-term memory.

The Prefrontal Cortex Is the Central Executive of Human Working Memory

Deficits in working memory can arise from a variety of disorders, including some associated with damage to multiple brain areas. Nevertheless, the greatest attention in behavioral studies has been accorded to the prefrontal cortex, befitting its role as the central executive of working memory systems. But the role of the prefrontal cortex is not limited to memory processing. Rather, the prefrontal cortex serves multiple higher cognitive functions involved in personality, affect, motor control, language, and problem solving, each of which contributes substantially to memory.

The emergence of brain imaging techniques has allowed investigators to examine the areas of the human cortex activated during working memory. Among the first of these studies, Jonides, Smith, and their colleagues (1997) characterized areas of the human brain activated during a variant of the spatial *delayed response* task. In this task subjects fixated on a central point on a computer monitor and were shown three dots as target sample stimuli. Following a brief delay with no dots visible, a circle appeared on the screen, sometimes marking a location where a dot had previously appeared. In each trial, the subject had to remember all three target locations to say whether the subsequently presented circle marked a location in that set. The brain areas prominently activated included the dorsolateral prefrontal cortex, the posterior parietal area, and parts of the occipital and premotor areas, revealing a large network of cortical areas involved in working memory. In humans, the spatial delayed response task activated these structures predominantly on the right side of the brain.

Researchers have also examined the same verbal and visuospatial working memory processes that were the focus of Baddeley's model, and indeed imaging shows that distinct brain areas mediate the visuospatial sketchpad and the phonological loop. Tasks requiring subjects to rehearse verbal material activate different parts of the parietal cortex that support these functions. All tasks that call for working memory activate prefrontal areas. In addition, parts of the prefrontal cortex are especially strongly activated when subjects are required to update verbal information—consistent with the idea that this area serves as the central executive of working memory processes.

Also supporting the view that memory processing is secondary to the fundamental role of the prefrontal cortex in complex cognitive functions, neuropsychological studies generally suggest that memory deficits are a consequence of impairments in attention and problem solving (Roberts et al., 1996). For example, one of the best-studied and most profound impairments following prefrontal damage in humans is a deficit in thought function commonly measured using a test called the **Wisconsin Card Sorting Test** (Figure 12.9). A subject is initially given four cards, each of which shows a unique design with colored shapes. The design of each card varies in terms of the

Target card

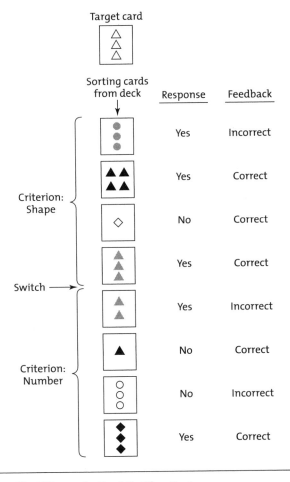

FIGURE 12.9 The Wisconsin Card Sorting Test.

shapes displayed, the number of shapes on the card, and / or their color. Subsequently the subject is given a deck of similar cards and must sort the deck by placing one card at a time onto one of the target cards according to a matching criterion (color, shape, or number) that the experimenter has selected but not revealed. After each card is sorted, the subject is given minimal feedback about whether the card was placed in the correct pile according to the experimenter's sorting criterion. When the subject eventually discerns the criterion and is consistently sorting the cards correctly, the experimenter shifts to a new criterion without warning, which the subject must discover using the same process.

This task contains an obvious working memory component: Subjects must keep in mind the feedback about each sorting decision to discover the correct criterion, then dispense with that pattern and correctly identify, maintain, and apply a new one. Subjects with frontal lobe injuries are severely impaired in this task. However, these individuals do not forget the current sorting criterion, as demonstrated by the observation that they learn and maintain the initial sorting criterion. Instead they **perseverate**: that is, they continue to use a rule or strategy when it is no longer appropriate. These findings show that the prefrontal cortex is essential to the ability to modify learned rules as a task requires, not merely to memory for those rules.

On the other hand, the intact memory for sorting criteria observed in subjects with prefrontal damage (who are also called *frontal patients*) does not mean that these individuals perform perfectly well in all standard memory tasks. They do well at some but show impairment in others (Shimamura, 1995). They perform normally in recalling stories or nonverbal diagrams and in learning verbal paired associates; these findings contrast with the typically poor performance of amnesic subjects in the same tasks. However, frontal patients are inordinately susceptible to proactive interference when they attempt to memorize groups of word pairs in which some words appear in more than one pair. Thus frontal patients have difficulty distinguishing between associations that share the same information. These individuals also show impairments when tested for **meta-memory,** which is a self-assessment of how much we are aware of remembering. Specifically, when frontal patients are asked whether they will recognize previously studied words, they tend to underestimate how much they know. Yet they perform just as well as normal subjects in accurately recalling the words. Similarly, frontal patients perform poorly in remembering the situations in which they learned materials that they can subsequently recall correctly. This deficit in **source memory** (memory for where or when we learned something) has been viewed as a distinctive characteristic of prefrontal damage. Each of these aspects of cognitive processing involves information that is processed during working memory and subsequently contributes to long-term memory.

Another potentially related area of memory impairment in individuals with prefrontal damage is difficulty in remembering the temporal order of recent events. In one study, subjects were shown a long series of cards in rapid succession, each card bearing two line drawings. Some cards also portrayed question marks, indicating that subjects should specify which of the two items shown on the card had appeared more recently in the sequence of preceding images. In some cases both items had appeared earlier, but at different points in the sequence. In other cases one item had appeared before, and the other item was new. Frontal patients could recognize the previously seen items but could not identify their order. In another study subjects were given a list of 15 words and subsequently were asked to reconstruct the order in which they appeared (Shimamura et al., 1990). Frontal patients performed relatively well in freely recalling the words and in recognizing the words when presented on a test list, but they had trouble ordering the items to match the initial list. These observations suggest that the prefrontal cortex plays a critical role in selecting and organizing relevant information and strategies. A deficit in this executive capacity could account straightforwardly for the difficulties of frontal patients on the Wisconsin Card Sorting Test and other tasks that require switching attention. This kind of deficit could also underlie these subjects' impairments in source memory and meta-memory, as well as problem solving and temporal ordering, to the extent that such tasks require inhibiting irrelevant materials and cognitive strategies and selecting appropriate ones instead (Miller, 2000).

Learning & Memory in Action

What Is It Like to Have Prefrontal Cortex Damage?

As the central executive of our conscious lives, the prefrontal cortex is vital to our sense of self and awareness of events in the world. But people with prefrontal damage are not unconscious and they are not completely lost in life, even though aspects of their conscious thought and memory are severely affected. What is it like to have damage to the prefrontal cortex? Baddeley (1986) discussed a particularly interesting case of a man known as R. J., who had bilateral damage to his frontal lobes following a head injury. He was unconscious for several weeks but gradually recovered his physical abilities. Before the accident, he had an IQ of 120 and worked as an engineer. Afterward his IQ dropped significantly, and he showed modest deficits in standard memory tests.

Most bizarre, and perhaps most tragic, were his abnormalities in autobiographical recall. When tested by cuing with common words, he produced a number of colorful memories delivered with complete conviction and contextual detail. For example, when cued with the word *river,* he recalled an incident when he had taken his niece rowing in a river. The episode was filled with details, including information about an injury his niece suffered and their trip to the hospital. However, when subsequently cued with the same word, he produced a completely different story and denied knowledge of the previous incident—which his wife confirmed had not actually occurred. Similarly, when asked about the circumstances of his own accident, he always produced a vivid story, albeit a different one on each occasion. This kind of failure in episodic memory is known as **confabulation** (the production of elaborate false memories), and it is a common consequence of prefrontal damage.

R. J.'s confabulation may have been related to the inflexible thought and tendency to perseverate often observed in individuals with prefrontal damage. In R. J.'s case, this was quite strikingly demonstrated when he one day denied that he was married to his wife. Even when his wife pointed out that they had been married for several years and showed him pictures of their children, R. J. perseverated in his position, acknowledging only that his son did indeed look like him. Baddeley suggested that this pattern of abnormalities could reflect a **dysexecutive syndrome** characterized by an inability to contemplate current and recalled events or to interpret the validity and implications of those experiences to draw reasonable conclusions. R. J.'s experience demonstrates that, unlike amnesic individuals, people with prefrontal damage are not characterized by an absence of memories. Instead they seem unable to identify the relevant aspects of incoming and retrieved information held in working memory, or subsequently to interpret the meaning of that information.

The Prefrontal Cortex Is Composed of Several Distinct Areas

The assignment of the central executive function to the prefrontal cortex is supported by substantial anatomical data. The large size of the prefrontal area in primates and especially humans is impressive and is clearly associated with the evolution of cognitive capacities (Figure 12.10). In addition, the human prefrontal cortex is a diverse area composed of several distinct subdivisions, and there is considerable evidence that these distinct areas play different functional roles. There is also extensive correspondence between the anatomy and functional roles of areas in human and monkey prefrontal cortexes. Although several anatomical areas have been characterized based on structural appearance, most of the functional evidence has been related to four general regions. These include the medial, dorsolateral, lateral, and orbital areas. Most of the attention with regard to working memory functions in monkeys and humans has focused on the dorsolateral and ventrolateral areas, and these areas are distinctively connected with posterior parts of the cerebral cortex. Clear anatomical evidence also shows that some prefrontal regions in rats correspond to those in primates, particularly in the medial and orbital areas (Uylings et al., 2003). Evidence is mixed about whether the dorsal and lateral subdivisions of the prefrontal cortex, which figure prominently in views of primate and human working memory, also exist in rodents. Nevertheless, neuropsychological evidence suggests that the medial and orbital areas in the rodent prefrontal cortex may serve some of the general functions of working memory observed in primates (Kolb & Robbins, 2003).

There are distinctions among prefrontal areas with regard to their inputs from posterior cortical areas. The dorsolateral prefrontal area receives inputs mainly from cortical areas that represent somatosensory and visuospatial information. The lateral prefrontal areas receive inputs mainly from cortical areas that represent auditory and

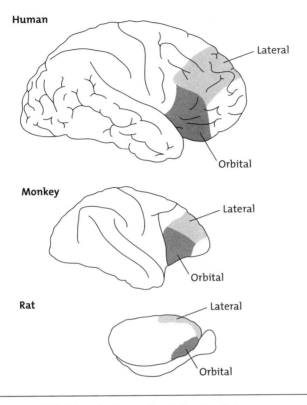

FIGURE 12.10 Subdivisions in the prefrontal cortex in humans, monkeys, and rats.

visual pattern information. In particular, research aimed at distinguishing the various subsystems of working memory has devoted considerable attention to differentiating the visuospatial input to the dorsolateral prefrontal area from the visual pattern input to the lateral prefrontal area. These two types of information—about *where* events occurred (captured in visuospatial information) and *what* occurred (captured in visual pattern information)—are combined when working memory for these aspects of events comes together in episodic memories for what happened where.

Functional Imaging Studies Reveal Distinct Roles of Prefrontal Areas in Humans

To examine potential differences in the functions of prefrontal areas, Smith and colleagues (1996) used different versions of a *three-back* task designed to test working memory for either spatial or verbal material. This task is structured similarly to the two-back test using a series of letters that was presented at the beginning of this chapter. In both the spatial and verbal versions of the task, in a series of trials subjects fixated on a cross at the center of a computer screen and were shown a series

(A) Spatial memory condition

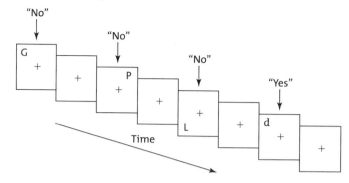

(B) Verbal memory condition

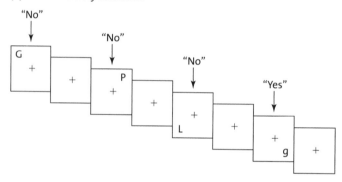

FIGURE 12.11 Three-back tasks.

of letters. In each trial, a different letter was presented in a new place near the edge of the screen, and between letters the subject saw a blank screen (Figure 12.11).

The subject had to keep in mind either spatial or verbal information about the series of letters in order to say whether each new item matched the one seen "three back" in the series. In the spatial memory condition, the subject had to identify whether the screen location of each new item matched that of the item presented three trials back, ignoring the identity of the letters. In the verbal memory condition, the subject had to identify whether each new item displayed the same letter presented three trials back, ignoring the items' locations. Thus both tasks' stimuli were identical, but their memory demands differed according to either a spatial or verbal rule. Brain imaging of subjects during the spatial task showed the most prominent activation in the posterior parietal and prefrontal areas of the right hemisphere. The verbal task also activated primarily parietal and prefrontal areas, but this activation was focused in the left hemisphere. Thus this study identified differences between the cerebral hemispheres in prefrontal function in verbal and spatial memory, revealing the larger network of cortical areas involved in working memory.

Animal Studies Also Reveal Distinct Functions of Specific Prefrontal Areas

As with our considerations of other forms of memory, animal experiments have provided greater understanding of the contributions of specific prefrontal cortical areas to working memory than we can gain from observing humans with brain damage. Not all aspects of prefrontal function in humans discussed here have been studied in animals. However, some characteristics of human prefrontal function have been examined extensively in animals. These studies show that, as in humans, the prefrontal cortex of animals is critical for short-term memory—specifically for components of working memory including shifting of task rules and memory for temporal order.

SHORT-TERM MEMORY Deficits in short-term memory following damage to the prefrontal cortex have been known since the pioneering studies by Jacobsen and his colleagues (1935). These studies focused on the *delayed response task,* which is a variant of the shell game designed for monkeys. In this task, a monkey watched a reward being hidden under one of two plaques. After a delay, the monkey had to remember and choose the location of the reward. Monkeys with prefrontal damage were severely impaired in remembering where the reward was hidden, even for a few seconds. But the same animals rapidly learned which of two places or which of two visual stimuli were consistently associated with a reward. This pattern of results indicates that the prefrontal cortex is essential for short-term memory for a particular event, but it is not crucial for perceptual or motor aspects of these tasks or for making long-term associations between stimuli and rewards.

We now also have data showing that deficits in different kinds of short-term memory result from damage to specific areas within the prefrontal cortex, which is consistent with the heterogeneity of prefrontal connections. These data signify that areas of the prefrontal cortex may be suited for modality-specific processing of information in memory. Most prominent among these findings, selective deficits have been observed in association with damage to each of three key areas of the prefrontal cortex. First, damage to the dorsolateral area produces a severe deficit in the ability to hold spatial information in mind, such as where a reward was hidden, as just described. Damage to a second key prefrontal area, the lateral prefrontal cortex, does not impair spatial short-term memory but does cause severe deficits in short-term memory for objects. And damage to a third key area, the orbital prefrontal cortex, makes olfactory, taste, visual, and auditory discrimination difficult. These impairments are especially notable when animals are required to reassign reward values to different stimuli. Such orbital lesions also result in emotional disorders.

Additional neuropsychological studies have provided parallel evidence of functionally heterogeneous areas in the prefrontal cortex of rats, suggesting that prefrontal functions are common in mammalian evolution (Kolb & Robbins, 2003). For example, damage to the medial prefrontal area in rats causes deficits in spatial alternation, in spatial working memory in the radial maze task, and in the Morris water maze. This finding makes sense given the structural similarities between rats' and monkeys' brains in the connections between the prefrontal region and other areas of the cortex. Specifically, a number of connections in both species' brains are similar: between the medial prefrontal and spatial cortical areas, and between the orbital prefrontal area and the subcortical limbic and olfactory structures. These data indicate that the rodent medial prefrontal area's involvement in spatial memory performance is similar to the dorsolateral prefrontal area's contribution to monkeys' spatial processing abilities. Likewise, several studies have demonstrated behavioral abnormalities in emotion, response inhibition, and olfactory memory after orbital prefrontal lesions in rats similar to those observed in monkeys following lesions to the same prefrontal area.

SHIFTING OF TASK RULES More recent studies of the neuropsychology of prefrontal function in monkeys and rats have suggested a broader role for the prefrontal cortex in cognition as observed in humans. For example, Dias and colleagues (1996) trained monkeys with lateral or orbital prefrontal lesions in a variant of the Wisconsin Card Sorting Test. In this experiment, the animals learned to discriminate compound visual stimuli each composed of a polygon and a line presented on a computer screen (Figure 12.12). First they had to attend to one dimension (the polygon) and ignore the other (the line). Then they learned other discrimination problems that required rule shifting, beginning with one involving an **intradimensional shift**, which required discrimination between new polygons while ignoring new lines. Their next discrimination problem involved an **extradimensional shift**, requiring discrimination between new lines while ignoring the new polygons. Thus intradimensional shifts required learning a new example problem using the same logical rule, whereas extradimensional shifts required changing the rule as well as learning a new example. Finally the monkeys learned a reversal of the last problem; that is, the formerly rewarded stimulus was now nonrewarded, and the formerly nonrewarded stimulus was now rewarded.

The results of this experiment showed that different prefrontal cortex components serve different cognitive demands. Neither the lateral nor the orbital prefrontal lesions affected the monkeys' performance in the intradimensional shift problem, showing that these areas are not required to apply a rule already stored in memory to solve new problems. Monkeys with lateral lesions were impaired in the extradimensional shift problem but not in its reversal. This finding showed that the lateral prefrontal area is needed for switching a logical rule regarding a relevant stimulus dimension but not for associating a new stimulus with a reward when the task structure is unchanged. Monkeys with orbital prefrontal lesions showed the opposite pattern: They were unimpaired in the extradimensional shift but impaired in its reversal, showing that the orbital prefrontal cortex plays a critical role in switching reward

(A) Compound discrimination—attend to polygon.

Trial 1   Trial 2

Intradimensional shift (I)—attend to new polygon.

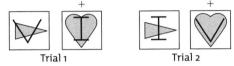

Trial 1   Trial 2

Extradimensional shift (E)—attend to new line.

Trial 1   Trial 2

Reversal (R)—attend to other line.

Trial 1   Trial 2

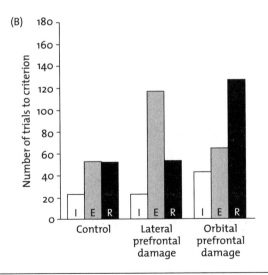

FIGURE 12.12 Attention switching in monkeys.
A. Example stimuli and rule for each stage of testing. B. Performance by experimental
groups on the intradimensional shift (I), extradimensional shift (E), and reversal (R)
stages.

values but not in switching logical rules. Thus both prefrontal areas function in changing behavior based on new contingencies; but the lateral and orbital areas play distinct roles in switching logical rules and reward assignments, respectively.

To examine whether prefrontal cortical areas in rats serve similar functions in rule shifting, Brown and colleagues developed an attentional switching task for rats similar to the version used for monkeys (Birrell & Brown, 2000; McAlonan & Brown, 2003). In these experiments, rats were trained to discriminate between compound stimuli composed of scents and different background media (such as sawdust or stone chips) that were scented, analogous to the foreground and background visual patterns used in the monkey studies. Damage to the medial prefrontal area disrupted performance of the extradimensional shifts but not of intradimensional shifts or reversal learning. In contrast, damage to the orbital prefrontal area produced the opposite pattern: impairment of reversal learning but not of extradimensional or intradimensional shifting. These results duplicate the pattern of findings for lateral and orbital lesions in monkeys.

MEMORY FOR TEMPORAL ORDER Besides supporting the ability to shift attention and behavior between different sets of guidelines, the prefrontal areas also contribute to working memory for the order of events in time. Petrides (1995) investigated the nature of temporal information processed by the prefrontal cortex by examining working memory for temporal order in monkeys with dorsolateral prefrontal lesions. On each test day, monkeys were presented three distinct objects in three successive trials. In the first trial, all the objects had a food reward hidden underneath, so any one could be selected for a reward. After a 10-second delay, the same objects were again presented (with their positions randomized), and the initially selected item was not rebaited; so the subject was required to choose one of the remaining objects to obtain a second reward. In the third trial, the objects were again randomly rearranged, and the monkey had to select the last remaining baited object. Monkeys with dorsolateral prefrontal lesions were impaired in this **self-ordering task,** in which the animal determined the initial order in which the items were selected. However, the same monkeys readily learned to select objects in a particular order when the experimenter presented them repeatedly in that order—that is, in a task not requiring the animal to monitor in working memory its own selections. These findings demonstrate a strong parallel with the studies showing deficits in humans with prefrontal damage. Both species show impairment in monitoring the order of experienced events, and they subsequently fail to remember that order.

In addition, Kesner and his colleagues (1992) have demonstrated that medial prefrontal lesions result in deficits in temporal ordering in rats. In experiments similar to those used with monkeys, rats were trained to enter radial maze arms to obtain rewards. For each trial they were first allowed to visit each of four arms in a predetermined sequence. Then they were given one of two types of memory tests. In the test of temporal ordering ability, they were given a choice of the first and second, or second and third, or third and fourth presented maze arms, with the contingency that another reward could be obtained by choosing the maze arm that was presented earlier in the sequence of arms visited that day. In a control task, the rats were presented with one of the arms that had been visited that day and another arm that was not presented in that trial, and subsequently they were rewarded for reentering the arm visited earlier. Animals were trained in the task preoperatively, then retested after medial prefrontal lesions. They performed well on both tests preoperatively but very poorly on the order test after surgery. The rats performed well when tested for recognition of the first arm presented on each day but were impaired for subsequently presented arms. Thus, like monkeys with dorsolateral lesions, rats with medial prefrontal lesions are more severely impaired in order memory than in recognition.

Combining the findings of these studies suggests strong homologies among the areas and functional roles of the prefrontal cortex across species. In humans, monkeys, and rats, areas of the prefrontal cortex support the ability to select and inhibit information and strategies, as well as the ability to organize information and maintain that information over brief periods. These observations suggest that the essential information processing circuits in the cerebral cortex that support cognition and memory are largely conserved among mammalian species. Differences in mammals' behavioral patterns and capacities are likely due to the overall size and degree of specialization of cortical areas.

Monkey Studies Show How Prefrontal Cortex Neurons Represent Working Memory

The studies just described show that some key functions of the human prefrontal cortex are also provided by prefrontal areas in animals. For these functions, animal studies can provide further insights about how information is processed in the prefrontal cortex at the level of single neuron activity. In the early 1970s neurophysiologists began to study the activity of neurons in monkeys performing the delayed response task (Fuster, 1995). In these studies, one of two keys (left or right) was illuminated as the memory cue. Following a variable delay, both keys were illuminated in the choice period, and the monkey was rewarded for selecting the same key that had been illuminated as the cue. Some cells fired associated with presentation of the left or right cue in both the sample and choice periods. Subsequent work has shown that prefrontal neurons fire selectively associated with visual and spatial properties of memory cues across a variety of working memory tasks. Moreover, many prefrontal neurons begin to fire either upon presentation of the sample item or at the moment it disappears, and many of the same cells continue to fire throughout the ensuing delay period. These **delay cells** number half the recorded neurons in the prefrontal cortex and have received a great deal of research attention because they provided the first evidence of neural activity specifically involved in storing a short-term memory.

Many studies have examined the activity of delay cells, using a version of the delayed response task that trains monkeys to fixate on a central spot on a display and to maintain fixation while a target at any one of eight locations in the display is briefly illuminated (Goldman-Rakic, 1995). Following a delay period when the target must be remembered, the monkey moves its eyes to the location of the former target to obtain a reward. The prefrontal cortex is important to this variation of the delayed response task, and this paradigm also improved researchers' ability to monitor the precise locations of stimuli and eye movement responses.

In a key experiment designed to examine whether different parts of the dorsolateral prefrontal cortex are involved in distinct aspects of the task, monkeys were trained to perform the task and then given small unilateral lesions in that brain area. Subsequently their performance was measured for each of the eight target locations, both in the memory task and in a simple control task where the target light remained lit while the monkeys were rewarded for looking toward it, eliminating the need for spatial memory.

The lesions had no effect on eye movements in the control task, but they did impair the memory task. The lesions caused poor delay-dependent performance for stimuli presented in a particular area of the stimulus display screen. This deficit was observed only when the target was presented in a particular area of the visual field; at longer delays—when the memory demand increased—the magnitude of error in the monkeys' eye movements was greater. These data provided the first evidence of a *mnemonic scotoma*—a deficit in memory for a specific region of visual space. This specific memory deficit differs from a perceptual scotoma, which is the loss of visual perception for stimuli presented in a particular region of visual space.

Correspondingly, recordings of prefrontal neurons in intact monkeys performing this task revealed that the majority of delay cells fired selectively while the animals were remembering a stimulus presented in a particular part of visual space. The delay cells were most active in the part of the dorsolateral prefrontal cortex associated with remembering stimuli presented in that spatial region (Figure 12.13). The delay cells also fired only during trials when a correct eye movement was produced, indicating that the neurons' activity reflected the maintenance of the target location in spatial memory. Subsequent analyses confirmed that most of these cells in fact maintained the memory of the target location, rather than firing in anticipation of the monkeys' responses. To test this question directly, monkeys were trained in both the standard version of the task and an alternative version in which the monkeys were required to move their eyes to the location opposite the illuminated target. Most of the delay cells that fired associated with a particular cue location fired during memory regardless of the subsequent response's direction. The remaining delay cells fired associated with the incipient direction of the eye movement, indicating that the prefrontal cortex also contains information about the intended response.

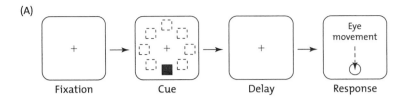

(A)

Fixation   Cue   Delay   Response

(B)   Prefrontal neuron firing pattern

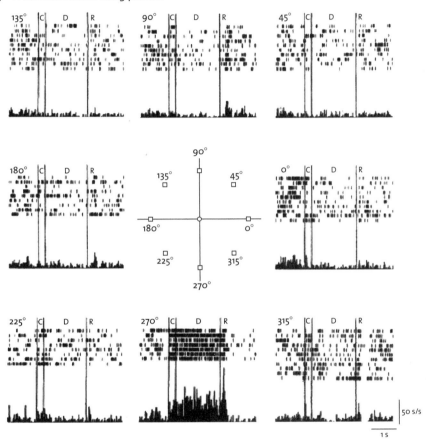

FIGURE 12.13 The eye movement delayed response task and prefrontal cells.
A. Example of events during a single trial. B. Displays showing activity of a single cell
during the cue (C), delay (D), and response (R) intervals of trials in which the cue was
presented in different locations. This cell fires selectively when the memory cue is
presented in the 270 degree position. When tissue in this brain area is destroyed, the
animal cannot remember cues presented in that position. Other cells in the dorsolateral
prefrontal cortex would respond selectively to cues at different positions, and damage to
one of those areas would produce a mnemonic scotoma for cues presented in the
corresponding location in space.

Research at the neural level has also reinforced the view that the prefrontal cortex contains a temporary memory store. Miller and colleagues (1996) compared the capacity of temporal and prefrontal neurons to temporarily retain visual information in working memory. They trained monkeys in a matching to sample task that required the animals to maintain visual memories during a delay of a few seconds. Results showed that a larger proportion of temporal cortex cells responded selectively to visual features, but activity of these cells ceased abruptly if an intervening stimulus was presented during the delay. On the other hand, a smaller proportion of prefrontal cells responded to specific visual features; but these cells maintained elevated stimulus-specific activity during the delay, even when intervening stimuli were presented.

Some evidence from variations of working memory tasks indicates that there can be regional parcellation of short-term storage functions. Particularly striking evidence comes from a study in which Wilson and colleagues (1993) trained monkeys in two variants of the delayed response task. One version was the standard occulomotor spatial delayed response task, although only two target locations were employed (right and left). The other version was a visual pattern delayed response task in which one of two elaborate visual stimuli was presented at the central fixation point; after a delay, the monkey was required to make a left or right eye movement to indicate which pattern matched the sample cue. In the pattern delayed response task, neurons in the lateral prefrontal area were particularly responsive: Over three-quarters of the delay cells differentially fired in association with viewing a visual cue. Some of these cells showed highly selective delay responses. For example, some cells fired specifically in association with one of two patterns when the cues were faces; but they did not differentiate between two other visual patterns (that is, they did not fire to either pattern, or they fired similarly to both). The opposite result was obtained for cells in the dorsolateral prefrontal cortex: Most delay cells fired selectively in the spatial task and not in the pattern task.

Subsequent studies have suggested that the lateral prefrontal area may, however, combine information from different input streams to encode the combinations of stimuli and strategies relevant to virtually any task. In one study, researchers trained monkeys in a variant of the delayed matching to sample task in which subjects were shown a sample target object (Rao et al., 1997). After a delay, they were shown that object again with another object; the objects were each presented in a different location and then removed from view. Finally, after a second memory delay, the monkeys had to move their eyes to the former location of the item that matched the initial target object. Thus the monkeys had to remember two aspects of the sample object. During the initial delay they had to retain the visual properties (the "what" quality) of the first object. During the second delay they had to retain the object's location (its "where" quality). Neurons in the monkeys' lateral prefrontal areas responded to both the "what" and "where" qualities of objects. These data demonstrate that cells in the same area of the prefrontal cortex can represent both visual and spatial information.

Two other studies show that neurons in monkeys' prefrontal cortex encode abstract rules for making decisions. In one study, monkeys performed either a delayed matching or nonmatching to sample task using visual cues. The monkeys were given a signal during the delay to indicate whether they should apply the matching or nonmatching rule when choosing between stimuli (Wallis et al., 2001). The activity rate of prefrontal neurons during the delay depended on both the object to be remembered and the rule in play. In another study, monkeys were trained to distinguish several species of dogs from cats based on exemplars of both kinds of animals (Freedman et al., 2001). Then researchers monitored their prefrontal neural activity while they were tested on "morphs"—computer-generated images of animals that were differing degrees of catlike and doglike. They found that prefrontal cells encoded the abstract concepts of *cat* and *dog* and demonstrated categorical perception, responding similarly to all items in each of the categories (Figure 12.14).

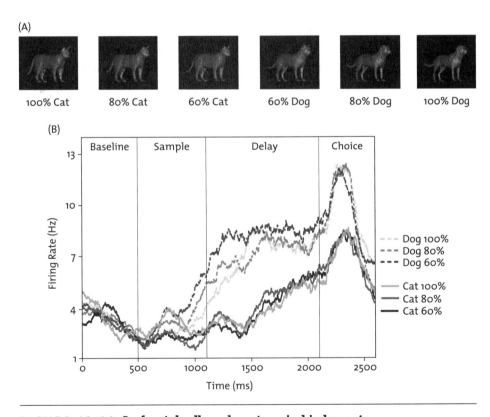

FIGURE 12.14 Prefrontal cells make categorical judgments.
A. Items at each end are examples of a particular cat and dog; items in between show intermediate stimuli. B. Response pattern of a single neuron to different stimuli.

These responses were selective to the prefrontal cortex; cells in the higher visual processing area of the inferotemporal cortex did not show categorical perception and instead fired in response to specific visual features of the animals (Freedman et al., 2003).

Interim Summary

The prefrontal cortex is the central executive in working memory. Humans and animals with prefrontal cortex damage perform poorly in tasks that require holding information in mind, switching performance in response to task rule changes, and memory for temporal order. In addition, specific areas within the prefrontal cortex serve these functions for different domains of information. Correspondingly, in humans the prefrontal cortex is activated during performance of working memory tasks. In monkeys single prefrontal cortex neurons are active during the memory delay when the animal must keep in mind the critical stimulus, and response cells in different parts of the prefrontal cortex can be selectively activated depending on the nature of the stimulus material. In addition, however, when task demands require integration of visual and spatial information or other complex manipulation of information, prefrontal cells process combined visual and spatial information as well as abstract information incorporating how stimuli are categorized according to task rules.

A Network of Cortical Areas Orchestrates Working Memory

The studies just described demonstrate some of the ways in which the prefrontal cortex plays a crucial and central role in working memory. However, recent studies using functional imaging of the entire cortex show that the role of the prefrontal cortex is akin to that of an orchestra conductor; players in this orchestra are distributed throughout other areas of the cerebral cortex (Pasternak & Greenlee, 2005; Postle, 2006). Two studies highlighted here show how different cognitive demands contribute to distributing functional activations among cortical areas during working memory performance.

One of these studies showed that working memory circuits are widespread in the cortex. This study also supported some earlier-described neuropsychological findings from cross-species studies showing that the prefrontal cortex is involved more in strategic processing of items in memory than in mere storage of those items. In this study, Cohen and colleagues (1997) combined variants of the *n*-back task with rapid fMRI scans to compare regional activation levels in the brain during differing demands for executive control in managing more items versus holding items for a longer time. They trained subjects to match verbal stimuli to items presented previously under four different conditions. These included comparisons to items one, two, or three positions back, as well as a zero-back condition in which subjects had to identify a particular stimulus whenever it was presented. Scans were made during stimulus presentation, immediately afterward, and repeatedly during the 10-second delay between trials. The scans showed that areas in both the left prefrontal cortex and the posterior visual areas were activated, but the extent of activation differed depending on the experimental conditions. The prefrontal cortex was most active under high memory load conditions (that is, in the two- and three-back tasks) and less so in the zero- and one-back tasks; the level of prefrontal activation was constant throughout the memory delay. Conversely, the visual areas were more active late in the delay when the memory demand was highest, regardless of the memory load. In addition, the amount of activation in Broca's area, the cortical area involved in speech production, was affected by both factors, with the greatest activation for the highest load at the longest memory delay; this observation is consistent with the view that Broca's area is the site of the phonological loop described earlier in this chapter. These findings identified a large network of cortical areas involved in working memory, and they highlight the importance of the prefrontal cortex in its executive function rather than mere storage.

Another study revealing the extent of cortical activations during working memory focused on the extent to which cortical areas throughout the network contribute to memory specificity and to holding information in mind during a working memory task. In this study, Courtney and colleagues (1997) compared posterior and prefrontal cortical activations in humans performing a working memory task requiring subjects to remember a face over a delay. They compared activations in these areas during presentations of either faces or ambiguous, unpatterned visual stimuli, and also during the memory delay between stimulus presentations. The posterior and prefrontal cortical areas' responses to three components of the task were analyzed: brief and nonselective visual responses, brief and selective responses to faces, and responses sustained over the memory delay. The researchers found that posterior visual cortical areas showed primarily brief visual responses, whereas prefrontal areas exhibited strong delay responses and selective responses to faces. Furthermore, the researchers analyzed the extent to which these task components activated areas throughout the cortex. The most posterior area responded nonselectively across different visual stimuli and was not active during the delay, whereas the most anterior prefrontal areas responded most during the delay and showed selectivity for faces. These findings suggest that in addition to its role of holding information in mind, the prefrontal cortex may also be especially suited to retrieving and using memory representations stored throughout the cortex.

A study that recorded the activity of prefrontal cortex neurons clarified how this retrieval process occurs. In this experiment, monkeys were initially trained in a task requiring them to view a sample visual stimulus and then, after a delay, guess which item from a set had been assigned as the sample's associate (Rainer et al., 1999). After the monkeys learned the paired associates, prefrontal neurons responded selectively to the sample stimulus while it was being presented, and some of these neurons remained active during the memory delay. However, before presentation of the set of possible associates and toward the end of the delay, prefrontal neurons altered their activity to respond selectively to the appropriate paired associate. These findings suggest that prefrontal neurons may have access to stored long-term representations of visual as well as spatial associations, which they can employ according to task demands.

Combining these findings with many other recent studies of cerebral activation during long-term memory retrieval tasks strongly implicates areas of the prefrontal cortex in the process of accessing memories stored in posterior cortical areas (Buckner & Wheeler, 2001; Simons & Spiers, 2003). Distinct areas of the prefrontal cortex may mediate different aspects of working memory's component processes, including specifying cues and performing semantic analysis to guide memory retrieval, monitoring the relevance of remembered information, and rehearsing phonological information to maintain it in memory (Dobbins et al., 2002; Ranganath et al., 2000). Meanwhile areas of the parietal and temporal cortex are involved in recognizing familiar items and perceiving reconstructed memories. The processes that coordinate this orchestration of memory retrieval are still under intense investigation.

The Role of Prefrontal–Hippocampal Interactions in Episodic Memory

Early in this chapter we considered how information is processed from a perceptually based short-term memory, through working memory, to a meaning-based long-term memory. From studies discussed in Chapters 8 through 10, we know that long-term memory depends on the hippocampal memory system. So how does the prefrontal system interact with the hippocampal system in the transition from short-term to long-term memory?

Functional imaging studies have shown that during episodic memory tasks that typically involve the hippocampal region (like memorizing lists of words or pictures), the prefrontal cortex is also active. Furthermore, the level of prefrontal cortex activation during these tasks predicts success in subsequent recall (Buckner et al., 1999). This evidence suggests that the executive functions of the prefrontal cortex contribute to episodic memory. In fact, the prefrontal cortex interacts with the hippocampal region in three ways to support episodic memory processing.

First, when we intentionally memorize materials, our memory will be much better if the information receives in-depth semantic processing based on the items' meanings (see Chapter 8). This kind of deep encoding strongly activates areas of the prefrontal cortex. In contrast, when features of the same words are processed superficially (such as for upper- or lowercase characters), there is little prefrontal activation and consequently poor later memory. Similarly, when subjects are given distracter tasks that direct working memory away from a study list, prefrontal activation is reduced and memory is impaired. Thus one important contribution of the prefrontal cortex to episodic memory is directing the meaning-driven processing that allows us to remember deep encoding of material.

A second contribution of the prefrontal cortex comes into play when we think about our experiences. We contemplate their meaning, manipulate that information, and usually act on it. Then we evaluate the results of those actions. The prefrontal cortex is a major source of information that is sent to the hippocampal region, which (as discussed in Chapter 9) binds together diverse streams of information to compose episodic memories. Not only does the hippocampal region bind episodic knowledge of what happened with where and when it happened; it also incorporates information received from the prefrontal cortex about our subjective experiences of those events. During episodic memory retrieval, we recall not only the events but also our thoughts about those experiences. This introspective aspect of episodic recollection is the most personal quality of our autobiographical memories (Moscovitch, 1992).

Third, when we experience new material, our perceptions are automatically matched with memories organized by the hippocampus—typically allowing us to evaluate whether the new information is familiar and evokes memories of related experiences, or is unfamiliar and requires more thought. This means that while our prefrontal cortex is taking in and processing new information, the hippocampal region is providing information about previous related experiences (or the lack thereof). Correspondingly, the hippocampal region is activated during working memory, especially when the information being held in mind is novel (Schon et al., 2004).

These three types of interactions between the prefrontal cortex and the hippocampal region, supporting a two-way conversation between executive and memory processes, are fundamental to the richness of our recollective experience.

Interim Summary

The prefrontal cortex performs its working memory functions in concert with other areas of the cerebral cortex. Prefrontal areas are activated whenever information must be kept in mind and manipulated, whereas more posterior cortical areas are activated during perceptual and passive storage of specific materials. In addition, the prefrontal cortex plays a key role in active retrieval of memories stored in cortical areas. Thus the executive functions of the prefrontal cortex in memory include both temporary storage and manipulation of information going into memory in the cortical areas and active search processes in retrieving memories from those areas. In addition, the prefrontal cortex and hippocampus interact extensively during working memory, contributing to the richness of both ongoing executive processing and subsequent episodic memory.

Chapter Summary

1. There are multiple forms of memory that hold information for only a brief period. A very short-term sensory store holds both visual and auditory information. Its capacity is large, but its longevity is transient and is interrupted by the act of retrieval. Short-term memory has a capacity limited to approximately seven items, although this capacity can be extended considerably by chunking the information into larger units. Without active rehearsal, the duration of short-term memory is only a few seconds.

2. Short-term and long-term memory can be distinguished by characteristics of the serial position curve that describes properties of memory for items in a list. The primacy effect (enhanced memory for items at the beginning of a list) reflects better long-term memory encoding without interference of earlier items, whereas the recency effect (enhanced memory for items at the end of a list) reflects the contents of short-term memory. Animals also have a capacity for working memory, reflected in primacy and recency effects during serial list learning that resemble these effects in humans.

3. Although the traditional model views short-term and long-term memory as serial stages of processing, substantial evidence indicates that these two kinds of memory are at least partially independent. For example, short-term memory is influenced by superficial perceptual features of items, whereas long-term memory depends on deep semantic processing. Also, neuropsychological studies have identified individuals who have selective disorders of each one of these types of memory but not the other.

4. According to Baddeley's model, working memory contains three main interacting elements: a phonological loop, a visuospatial sketchpad, and a central executive. The phonological loop includes both a perceptual store and an articulatory rehearsal mechanism. The visuospatial sketchpad has similar mechanisms for storage and rehearsal of visual and spatial information. The third component of Baddeley's model, the central executive, controls the other subsystems and performs several processes for focusing attention, adopting task rules, and organizing and

retrieving information. A later addition to Baddeley's model is an episodic buffer, which may store the sequential flow of events in experiences.

5. The brain area most associated with the particular properties of working memory is the prefrontal cortex, which is composed of several functionally distinct sub-areas. The prefrontal cortex is highly elaborated in primates, especially humans, although there is substantial evidence for homologous areas in all mammals.

6. Humans with prefrontal damage have severe deficits in switching task rules, which are reflected in perseveration of rules that are no longer appropriate. They are also particularly susceptible to proactive interference in memory tasks and have trouble with meta-memory (the feeling of knowing), recalling the sources of memories, and remembering the order of events in past experiences. These observations suggest that the prefrontal cortex plays a critical role in selecting and organizing relevant information and strategies.

7. Monkeys and rats with prefrontal damage exhibit many of these same executive control abnormalities, which are reflected in working memory impairments where interference is high, in perseveration, in impairments in switching task rules, and in memory for the order of events. Specific aspects of this impairment pattern differ according to the damaged prefrontal cortex region, and particular areas within the prefrontal cortex are more important for certain modalities of information processing.

8. Neurons in the prefrontal cortex fire associated with maintaining information in working memory during a delay between encoding and retrieval. In addition, prefrontal neural activity can be specific to the particular type of information processing that a task demands; but these neurons can also combine different kinds of sensory information when required. Also, prefrontal neural activity reflects the ongoing application of task rules and processing of abstract concepts used to make decisions.

9. The prefrontal cortex is part of a large network of cortical areas that serve specific functions within working memory, with posterior areas mediating encoding and retrieval of specific information. (The same cortical network, along with the hippocampal region, is involved in encoding and retrieval of long-term episodic memories.) In humans, the prefrontal cortex is highly active during working memory tasks—especially the *n*-back task, which demands both maintenance and manipulation of recently acquired information. Distinct areas within the prefrontal cortex may mediate specific components of executive function, including selection, rehearsal, and monitoring of information retrieval.

KEY TERMS

short-term memory (p. 398)

working memory (p. 399)

short-term sensory store (p. 400)

digit span (p. 401)

serial recall (p. 401)

serial position curve (p. 401)

primacy effect (p. 401)

recency effect (p. 401)

chunking (p. 403)

Brown–Peterson test (p. 403)

forgetting curve (p. 403)

release from proactive inhibition
(p. 404)

phonological loop (p. 408)

subvocal speech (p. 408)

visuospatial sketchpad (p. 410)

central executive (p. 411)

episodic buffer (p. 412)

serial probe recognition task (p. 413)

Wisconsin Card Sorting Test (p. 416)

perseverate (p. 418)

meta-memory (p. 418)

source memory (p. 418)

confabulation (p. 419)

dysexecutive syndrome (p. 420)

intradimensional shift (p. 424)

extradimensional shift (p. 424)

self-ordering task (p. 426)

delay cells (p. 427)

REVIEWING THE CONCEPTS

- What are the different types of short-term memory, and what are the key differences between them?

- Describe the relationship between short-term and long-term memory.

- In what sense is working memory a distinct form of short-term memory, and what are working memory's component processes?

- How does working memory in animals compare to human working memory?

- Which brain areas make up the system that supports working memory? What is the role of the prefrontal cortex in this system?

GLOSSARY

action potential A neuron-generated electrical signal that has a constant size and travels along the axon over long distances.

agnosia A neurological syndrome that causes an inability to recognize familiar stimuli even though basic sensory modalities are intact.

amnesia The loss of capacity for learning and memory. Amnesia can be retrograde, meaning that memories occurring before the onset of amnesia are lost, or anterograde, which is a loss of the ability to acquire or maintain new memories.

amygdala A set of subcortical nuclei in the temporal lobe that coordinates emotional responses to stimuli. The amygdala is critical to emotional memory.

anomia A disorder of the ability to name objects.

anterograde amnesia Loss of the capacity to form new lasting memories.

aphasia A disorder of language comprehension or production caused by damage to brain areas that support language skills.

associative learning Learning that involves linkage of otherwise unrelated stimuli, or a stimulus and a reward or punishment, or a stimulus and a behavioral response.

associative priming The facilitation of item identification or other processing following a single exposure to a combination of information.

associative stage The second stage of skill learning that involves conscious, direct, but nonverbal motor representation of a sequence of movements that executes the skill.

autonomous stage The third stage of skill learning that involves execution of a sequence in the absence of conscious control and direction.

autoshaping An instrumental conditioning protocol in which untrained pigeons are placed into a conditioning chamber and, at a regular interval, a response key is illuminated for several seconds, then food is delivered with no required relationship between the desired key peck response and the food delivery. Nevertheless, pigeons reliably begin to peck the key when it is illuminated before the automatic food delivery; at that point the feeder activation is made to require key pecks.

axon Extension of the neuron membrane that sends information to other neurons.

backward chaining Procedure for training animals in response chaining, by which animals are first trained to perform the final act in a sequence to obtain the primary reinforcer, then trained to precede this behavior with the next to last act in order to get the stimulus for the final act. Then the third to last act is added to the sequence in the same manner, and so forth until the animal is performing the entire response chain.

backward conditioning Classical conditioning protocol in which the order of the CS and US is reversed, so the US is presented at a specific interval before the onset of the CS. This protocol is used to examine whether the order of conditioned and unconditioned stimuli is critical for learning the association between them.

behavioral memory Memories that do not reach consciousness and are expressed by changes in performance when particular actions that were performed during learning are repeated.

behavioral modification The application of principles of shaping and instrumental or operant conditioning to a broad variety of situations in education, business, and psychotherapy.

behaviorism The view that we can understand all learning in terms of simple stimulus–response associations, without considering less measurable concepts such as consciousness, insight, or intent.

belongingness The hypothesis that certain responses "belong" with a particular reinforcer based on an animal's evolutionary history.

blocking A classical conditioning phenomenon in which conditioning to a neutral stimulus is prevented if that stimulus is presented along with another CS already conditioned to produce the CR.

Brown–Peterson test A procedure in which subjects are initially given a list of items to remember, then distracted for a variable period, then asked to recall the list.

catastrophic interference Sudden and severe disruption of the representations of relationships between items in an existing memory network.

categorical perception The ability to identify various stimuli as belonging to meaningful categories of stored representations, such as categories of colors, speech sounds, or faces.

cell The encapsulated biological structure that is the basic functional unit of all body organs; typically specialized for a particular physiological function within each organ.

cell assembly A group of interconnected neurons that represents a perception or concept.

central executive In Baddeley's model of working memory, a system that controls and manipulates information in the visuospatial sketchpad and the phonological loop, accesses information from long-term storage sites, and distributes processed information to long-term memory sites.

cerebellar subsystem A motor system in which the cerebellum receives cortical input from the sensory and motor areas and projects to several motor areas. This system supports conditioning of reflexive responses.

cerebellum A large structure in the hindbrain that supports fine timing and coordination of movement. The cerebellum is essential for learned coordination between specific sensory stimuli and adjustments to movement.

cerebral cortex The largest component of the cerebral hemispheres that is organized as a sheet of several layers of neurons. The cerebral cortex is essential to many sensory and motor functions and is the repository of detailed representations of memories.

chunking Increasing the amount of information stored by efficiently compacting multiple elements of information into each item stored—such as storing a set of three digits as a single three-digit number.

circuits Groups of interconnected neurons that cooperate to represent stimuli, thoughts, and actions.

classical conditioning A behavioral protocol in which an initially neutral stimulus is consistently paired with a stimulus that automatically produces a reflexive response, eventually resulting in the capacity of the initially neutral stimulus to produce the response.

cognitive map A mental representation of the spatial organization of the environment.

cognitive memory Memories that reach consciousness and can be expressed explicitly, typically through language or a broad range of intentional actions.

cognitive stage The initial stage of skill learning that involves the learner remembering a list of instructions for the sequence to be followed.

cognitive systems Systems of the brain that support thinking.

cognitivism The view that learning cannot be explained by simple S–R associations but requires an elaborate network of knowledge and expectancies.

conceptual priming Repetition-produced facilitation of identification or other processing of entire categories of words.

conditioned inhibition In classical conditioning, the conditioning of a decrease in CRs to a CS. Conditioned inhibition can be observed only when the conditioned response is apparent, so that there is a baseline of CRs that can be reduced by the inhibitory association.

conditioned place preference A training procedure in which animals are rewarded when they occupy a particular location in the environment and subsequently prefer to be in that location.

conditioned reflex In classical conditioning, the learned reaction triggered by the conditioned stimulus.

conditioned response (CR) In classical conditioning, a behavioral response, similar in form to the unconditioned response, that is evoked by the conditioned stimulus after being paired with the unconditioned stimulus.

conditioned stimulus (CS) In classical conditioning, the initially neutral stimulus that, when appropriately paired with the unconditioned stimulus, comes to elicit the conditioned response.

confabulation The production of elaborate false memories.

confounding variable An unintended independent variable that coincides with the intended independent variable and could affect the dependent variable.

consolidate (consolidation) To undergo an active process through which a new and initially changeable or labile memory becomes permanent.

context-dependent memory The phenomenon in which a memory is best retrieved when testing occurs in the same environment or state in which learning originally occurred.

contextual conditioning Development of an association between the environmental background and the CS–US association in which conditioning occurs.

control group A set of subjects who are treated exactly like the experimental group except for the absence of a particular manipulation of the independent variables that characterize the question under study.

cued recall A protocol for testing memory in which subjects are given a moderate degree of prompting, such as the category of information to be remembered or a part of the item to be recalled.

cumulative response In the free operant protocol, a method of recording behavioral responses in terms of the running sum over time.

delay cells In a working memory task, neurons that fire throughout the delay period when a sample stimulus must be remembered for subsequent recognition testing.

delay conditioning A classical conditioning procedure that involves presentation of the CS for a short period, usually less than one second, with the US presented during the last part of the CS period.

dendrites Extensions of the neuron membrane that receive information from other neurons.

dependent variable An experimental variable, typically a behavioral or biological response generated by the subject, that the experimenter measures.

digit span The number of digits a subject can immediately recall following presentation of a list.

discrimination The ability to acquire a conditioned response to one stimulus and no response to a similar but distinguishable stimulus.

dishabituation Recovery of a previously habituated behavioral response that typically occurs when a new stimulus that generates the same response is presented.

disinhibition Following extinction of classical conditioning, the reappearance of a CR in response to another, typically arousing, stimulus.

double dissociation An experimental observation in which two treatments (typically two types of brain damage) are shown to have separate and distinct effects. In brain imaging research, a double dissociation is established when two separate tasks are shown to produce changes in activation in two distinct brain areas—e.g. Task A affects area A but not area B, while task B affects area B but not area A.

dysexecutive syndrome A pattern of abnormalities associated with damage to the prefrontal cortex, characterized by an inability to contemplate current and recalled events or to interpret the validity and implications of those experiences to draw reasonable conclusions.

emotional memory The acquisition of attractions and aversions to otherwise neutral stimuli.

emotional system The brain system that processes affective information.

encoding The occurrence of memory representation.

episodic buffer A system within working memory that stores the sequence of events composing a recent experience; a later addition to Baddeley's original working memory model.

episodic memory The capacity to consciously recollect specific past events.

errorless learning A training procedure in which subjects are gradually trained to provide correct responses without the possibility of explicitly making a mistake.

excitatory postsynaptic potential (EPSP) An electrical potential in the postsynaptic element that brings the neuron closer to its threshold for generating an action potential.

exemplar An individual item within a category of similar items.

experimental group A set of subjects who are given a manipulation of the independent variables that characterize an operational definition of a mental phenomenon under study.

extinction The gradual disappearance of a learned response when the US ceases to follow the CS.

extradimensional shift In discrimination learning, learning the reward values of novel stimuli made up of multiple dimensions, and switching attention to a different stimulus dimension than was used in a previous discrimination problem.

false memory A claim of remembering an event that did not actually occur.

familiarity A conscious sense that a stimulus or situation has been previously experienced.

firing The generation of an action potential by a neuron.

first-order conditioning Classical conditioning resulting from a direct pairing of, and association between, a CS and a US. It contrasts with second-order conditioning, in which the first-order CS is used in the place of the US to produce conditioning to another CS.

fixation A form of memory consolidation that involves the stabilization of molecular structure changes within cells and synapses that occurs over minutes or hours.

fixed interval (FI) schedule An instrumental conditioning protocol in which reinforcement is delivered following the first response after a particular amount of time since the last reinforcement.

fixed ratio (FR) schedule An instrumental conditioning protocol in which reinforcement is given after a particular number of responses.

flashbulb memories Exceptionally strong memories for unique emotional or arousing events.

forgetting Loss of memories over time.

forgetting curve Analysis that measures the rate at which information is lost over time.

free operant An instrumental conditioning protocol in which the subject controls when it executes a response that delivers rewards (or avoids punishments) without experimenter intervention.

free recall A protocol for testing memory in which a subject is given minimal information with which to retrieve memories—typically merely a request to recall recently studied materials.

generalization The tendency of a learned response to be evoked by a stimulus similar to the conditioning stimulus.

graceful degradation Gradual rather than catastrophic decay of function when part of a distributed network model of memory is compromised.

habit A voluntary behavior that is brought about and influenced by reinforcers (rewards and punishments) presented predictably after the behaviors.

habituation The capacity to ignore inconsequential repetitive stimuli.

hippocampal system A system composed of the hippocampus and the immediately surrounding cortex connected to many cortical areas. This system is essential to cognitive memory.

hippocampus A part of the cerebral cortex in the temporal lobe that, in evolutionary terms, was one of the first cortical areas to develop. The hippocampus is essential to cognitive memory.

imagery The creation of sensory (usually visual) images of words or other items to elaborate memory content for the items.

independent variable An experimental variable that the experimenter determines independent of the subject's control.

inferotemporal cortex A part of the cerebral cortex of the temporal lobe that processes complex visual information and is essential to object identification and memory.

inhibitory postsynaptic potential (IPSP) An electrical potential in the postsynaptic element that takes the neuron further away from its threshold for generating an action potential.

instrumental conditioning A behavioral protocol in which rewards or punishments that follow a particular behavior alter the probability of that behavior being expressed.

interference Irrelevant materials that distract from the intended learning materials and can strongly influence memory retention.

interim responses Behaviors that occur in the middle of the interval between reinforcers, whose incidence can also be altered by a correlation with subsequent reinforcers.

interneurons Neurons that receive and send signals within a local region in the nervous system.

interstimulus interval (ISI) In classical conditioning, the time between the onset of the CS and the onset of the US.

intertrial interval (ITI) In classical conditioning, the time between successive presentations of the CS and US.

intradimensional shift In discrimination learning, learning the reward values of novel stimuli made up of multiple dimensions while maintaining attention to only one stimulus dimension.

intrusion error On a memory test, an incorrect response that involves incorrectly or inappropriately reusing a test item experienced earlier.

latent inhibition A classical conditioning phenomenon in which poor conditioning to a neutral stimulus occurs when that stimulus is presented repeatedly without a US before subsequent conditioning trials.

Law of Effect The hypothesis, proposed by Thorndike, that rewards and punishments, respectively, strengthen or weaken stimulus–response associations, increasing or decreasing the likelihood that a behavior will be repeated.

Law of Regression The hypothesis, proposed by Ribot, that the likelihood that a particular memory will be lost due to injury is inversely related to the time elapsed between the event to be remembered and the injury.

learned helplessness An acquired feeling of futility, or a passive response indicative of such feelings, in a situation where one has no control over the incidence of a negative reinforcer.

learning The process through which we alter our skills, change our dispositions, add to our knowledge, and generally benefit or suffer from experience.

level of processing The way in which material is analyzed—from superficial physical qualities of the stimulus to deep levels of its meaning.

long-term depression (LTD) A cellular mechanism for weakening connections between neurons, decreasing the excitatory postsynaptic potential and the likelihood of an action potential generated by activation of a synapse.

long-term potentiation (LTP) A cellular mechanism for strengthening connections between neurons, thereby increasing the excitatory postsynaptic potential and the likelihood of an action potential generated by activation of a synapse.

matching law In instrumental conditioning, the production of a consistent pattern of multiple responses that maximizes the rewards.

memory The expression of learning in alterations of performance across a broad range of daily activities.

meta-memory A self-assessment of how much one is aware of remembering particular information.

module In distributed network models of memory, a processing unit that corresponds to one type of information, such as visual or auditory, or serves a particular function, like input or output.

motor neurons Neurons that have many branching dendrites; each motor neuron has a single axon that extends over a long distance to send signals to muscles.

motor program A preprogrammed behavioral sequence that is initiated complete with sequencing and timing of its elements.

motor systems Systems of the brain that support movement and motor coordination.

neuron doctrine The hypothesis that the brain is composed of discrete nerve cells that are the essential units of information processing.

neurons The basic information processing cells in the nervous system.

neurotransmitters Chemicals that transmit a signal from one neuron to another across the synaptic cleft and activate the synaptic potential in the dendrite of the next neuron.

nonassociative learning Forms of learning, including habituation and sensitization, that do not involve a specific association between a stimulus and its consequences or behavioral responses.

operational definition An observable behavioral or physiological measure of a hypothetical mental function.

organology The theory, proposed by Gall, that independent psychological traits are supported by specialized brain organs.

parahippocampal region A set of cortical areas surrounding the hippocampus and composing a part of the hippocampal system.

partial reinforcement effect A phenomenon in instrumental conditioning in which irregular incidence of rewards following behaviors leads to greater persistence of the response during extinction.

perceptual learning The improvement in perception of categories of stimuli that we are required to discriminate.

perceptual memory The unconscious formation and representation of specific previously experienced stimuli and the expression of these representations by unconscious changes in performance of tasks involving those stimuli. Perceptual memory involves learning and remembering specific sensory stimuli.

perceptual priming Repetition-produced facilitation of identification or other processing of the sensory qualities of a stimulus.

perceptual skill learning Improvement in the ability to detect, discriminate, and classify sensory stimuli of a particular category. Perceptual skill learning is a general capacity for sensory analysis, not memory for a specific stimulus.

perseveration In the Wisconsin Card Sorting Test and other memory tasks, the tendency to continue to use a rule or strategy when it is no longer appropriate; also the continued processing of information obtained earlier.

phonological loop In Baddeley's model of working memory, a system that stores and manipulates speech-based information.

postsynaptic element A specialized area of the dendrite or cell body with receptors for neurotransmitters.

prefrontal cortex The area in front of the motor cortex that supports thinking and planning.

presynaptic element The enlarged end of an axon in which transmitters are manufactured and released across the synaptic cleft to another neuron.

primacy effect In serial recall, superior recall of items at the beginning of the list, usually attributed to lack of interference from preceding items.

primary reinforcer See *reinforcer*.

principal neurons Neurons that have a highly organized set of dendrites and axons that may connect with local cells or extend many millimeters to send signals to another brain region.

proactive interference The negative influence of materials learned before a target item on subsequent memory for the target item.

probability matching In instrumental conditioning, a pattern of responses in which subjects select each of several choices in proportion to their rate of success.

procedural learning The acquisition of reflexive behaviors and habits.

prosopagnosia A type of agnosia that causes an inability to recognize faces.

prototype A simple model of a category of items that shares the basic features of all the items.

rapid reacquisition Following extinction of classical conditioning, the reappearance of a CR with very few CS–US presentations.

receiver operating characteristics (ROCs) An analytic method that measures the ability to identify items from a previously studied list under varying levels of confidence or bias in making the recognition judgment.

recency effect In serial recall, superior recall of items at the end of the list, usually attributed to items' availability in short-term memory.

receptors Specialized molecular structures in the postsynaptic element that receive neurotransmitters and generate synaptic potentials.

recognition A protocol for testing memory in which a subject is shown the item to be remembered, usually along with other items not studied, and is asked to identify whether each item was among those studied.

recollection The ability to bring to consciousness the circumstances of a previous experience.

reference system A particular perspective view within a survey representation.

reflex arc A simple brain circuit in which a sensory stimulus leads to a specific, involuntary muscular or behavioral response.

reinforcer (or **primary reinforcer**) Rewards or punishments that alter the incidence of behaviors they follow.

reinforcer devaluation A procedure through which the attractive value of a reinforcer is changed after instrumental learning has occurred. This procedure can reduce subsequent conditioned responses involving that reinforcer.

release from proactive inhibition A phenomenon in serial recall in which performance increases when subjects switch from lists of one category to another.

reorganization A form of consolidation that involves alterations of our knowledge networks through complex interactions between brain structures lasting for weeks to years after learning experiences.

repetition priming The facilitation of identification or other processing of specific stimulus materials to which one has been recently exposed.

Rescorla–Wagner model A classical conditioning model proposing that the effectiveness of the US depends on the extent to which its occurrence and magnitude differ from the subject's expectation based on experience, such that conditioning requires a mismatch between the subject's expectancy of the US and the actual experience of the US.

response chaining An instrumental conditioning protocol in which animals are gradually conditioned to execute a sequence of operant behaviors, only the last of which results in reward presentation.

resting potential A natural electrical potential, or difference in charge, between the inside and outside of a cell membrane.

retention The maintenance of information in memory over time.

reticular theory of brain circuitry The hypothesis that the brain's wiring involves a fixed network of fine wires, like a spider's web.

retrieval The process of searching for and finding a stored memory.

retrieval cues Stimuli available at the time of retrieval that are derived from information that surrounded the target item during encoding and assist success in retrieval.

retroactive interference The negative influence of materials learned after a target item on subsequent memory for the target item.

retrograde amnesia Loss of memories formed prior to the onset of amnesia.

reverberation In Hebb's hypothesis, the repeated recycling of information around a cell assembly. Hebb proposed that this process embodied and sustained the transient memories initially activated in the cerebral cortex.

route A specific path from one location in the environment to another.

schema A preexisting knowledge structure into which new memories are incorporated.

secondary reinforcer A stimulus that, after being associated with a reinforcer, takes on a key property of the reinforcer in altering the incidence of behaviors it follows.

second-order conditioning A classical conditioning protocol in which initially a first-order conditioned response is developed by pairing of a CS with a US; then presentation of the first-order CS is preceded by another CS, resulting in conditioning of the CR to the second CS.

self-ordering task An object recognition task in which the subject determines the initial order in which items are initially selected and then must remember the order of the choices.

semantic memory Accumulated world knowledge that is not tied to any particular learning event and is subject to conscious recollection.

sensitization An increase in awareness of and responsiveness to arousing or emotional stimuli.

sensory cells Cells that have specialized dendrite endings to receive signals from sensory organs, including (but not limited to) those in the eyes, ears, nose, skin.

sensory preconditioning A classical conditioning protocol in which two CSs are paired repeatedly before any conditioning that pairs one of the CSs and the US. The occurrence of preconditioning is reflected in production of the CR to the CS that was not directly paired with the US.

sensory systems Systems of the brain that process perceptual information.

serial patterns An instrumental conditioning protocol in which subjects are trained to perform a particular series of behavioral actions to receive rewards.

serial position curve An analysis of serial recall that measures the likelihood that each successive list item is remembered.

serial probe recognition task A procedure for testing working memory in which, on each trial, a list of items is initially presented; then following a variable delay, memory for the item at a particular position in the list is tested. Performance is measured in terms of accuracy at different positions in the list.

serial recall In memory for a list of items, the accuracy of recall for each item depending on its position in the list.

shaping An instrumental conditioning procedure that gradually modifies the behavior of an animal (or human) toward a desired response by rewarding behaviors that are increasingly similar to the desired response.

short-term memory Information that is encoded and can be immediately recalled—usually seven plus or minus two items.

short-term sensory store A representation of perceptual information from which single items can be retrieved for a brief period (seconds) following presentation of an array of items.

simultaneous conditioning A classical conditioning protocol in which the CS and US are presented at the same time. This protocol is used to examine whether the timing of conditioned and unconditioned stimuli is critical for learning the association between them.

Skinner box A chamber in which animals are trained in the free operant protocol.

source memory Memory of where and when information was acquired.

spontaneous recovery Reappearance of a conditioned response following the passage of time.

state-dependent learning An example of context-dependent memory in which the retrieval performance of subjects who learn under the influence of a drug or alcohol is typically better when they are tested in the same state of mind.

stimulus detection The ability to acquire expertise in perceiving stimulus features in difficult tasks such as aligning or orienting fine line stimuli.

stimulus–response (S–R) association Linkage of the representations of a sensory stimulus (S) and a behavioral response (R).

striatal subsystem A motor system in which the striatum receives input from the entire cerebral cortex and projects to parts of the thalamus specialized for motor control; these connections form loops back to the premotor and motor cortex and the prefrontal association cortex. This system supports the acquisition and expression of habits.

striatum A set of subcortical nuclei that controls posture and movement. The striatum helps to coordinate a set of movements to execute a specific objective, such as walking or grasping; this system helps us learn habitual movement patterns and physical skills.

subvocal speech A system in working memory that supports the ability to consciously verbalize words without speaking aloud.

superstitious learning Behaviors whose incidence changes as a result of being correlated with subsequent reinforcers, even when the subjects are unaware of any causal relationship between the action and its consequences.

survey A map-like overview of knowledge about the environment.

synapse The connection between two neurons, including three main components: the presynaptic element, the postsynaptic element, and the synaptic cleft.

synaptic cleft A small gap between the presynaptic element and postsynaptic element through which a neurotransmitter diffuses.

synaptic potentials Electrical signals of synapses and dendrites that are relatively small and variable in size; they decrease as they travel along the dendrites toward the cell body.

synaptic vesicles Tiny encapsulated packets within the presynaptic element that contain neurotransmitters.

systems Circuits interconnected to form pathways for information to flow through the brain. Distinct systems represent different types of physical stimuli (like vision and hearing) and allow emotional responses, thinking, and coordinated action.

taste aversion learning A classical conditioning protocol in which ingestion of a novel food is followed by gastrointestinal illness, resulting in a subsequent aversion to that food.

temporally graded retrograde amnesia Retrograde amnesia that causes greater loss of memories for events that occurred recently before a trauma than for events that occurred more remotely in the past.

terminal responses Behaviors that naturally occur just before the occurrence of a reinforcer—such as orienting to the place where food is delivered—whose incidence is most likely to change as a result of coinciding with the reinforcer.

token economy A behavior modification system based on operant conditioning principles, in which individuals earn tokens for performing or not performing specific behaviors, and the tokens can subsequently be exchanged for reinforcers.

trace conditioning A classical conditioning protocol in which the CS terminates before the US is presented, leaving a gap (or trace interval) between the CS and US when no stimulus is present.

unconditioned response (UR) In classical conditioning, the automatic reaction triggered by the unconditioned stimulus.

unconditioned stimulus (US) In classical conditioning, the stimulus that triggers an innate reflexive behavioral response.

variable interval (VI) schedule An instrumental conditioning protocol in which the minimum time interval between rewarded responses varies randomly but has a constant average period.

variable ratio (VR) schedule An instrumental conditioning protocol in which the number of responses required before the reward varies randomly but has a constant average value.

visuospatial sketchpad In Baddeley's model of working memory, a system that stores and manipulates visual or spatial information.

Wisconsin Card Sorting Test A procedure for testing working memory in which subjects must sort cards in a deck according to a rule that changes from time to time. The key working memory demand is to keep track of the current rule and switch the rule when necessary.

word stem completion A test of verbal repetition priming in which subjects initially study a list of words, then see the first three letters of each word and try to complete it.

working memory The cognitive processes that support holding information in mind temporarily while manipulating or actively rehearsing it.

REFERENCES

Adolphs, R. (2002). Neural systems for recognizing emotion. *Current Opinion in Neurobiology, 12,* 169–177.

Adolphs, R., Tranel, D., Damasio, H., & Damasio, A. (1994). Impaired recognition of emotion in facial expressions following bilateral damage to the human amygdala. *Nature, 372,* 669–672.

Adolphs, R., Tranel, D., Damasio, H., & Damasio, A. R. (1995). Fear and the human amygdala. *The Journal of Neuroscience, 15,* 5879–5891.

Aggleton, J. P., & Shaw, C. (1996). Amnesia and recognition memory: A reanalysis of psychometric data. *Neuropsychologia, 34,* 51–62.

Alvarez, P., & Squire, L. R. (1994). Memory consolidation and the medial temporal lobe: A simple network model. *Proc. Nat. Acad. Sci. USA, 91,* 7041–7045.

Anderson, J. R. (1982). Acquisition of cognitive skill. *Psychological Review, 89,* 369–406.

Aristotle. (350 B.C.). *On memory and reminiscence.* (J. I. Beare, Trans.). Retrieved February 3, 2003, from http://www.knuten.liu.se/~bjoch509/works/aristotle/memory.txt.

Atkinson, R. C., & Shiffrin, R. M. (1968). Human memory: A proposed system and its control processes. In K. W. Spence & J. T. Spence (Eds.), *The psychology of learning and motivation: Advances in research and theory* (pp. 89–195). New York: Academic Press.

Baddeley, A. D. (1986). *Working memory.* Oxford: Oxford University Press.

Baddeley, A. D. (1998). Recent developments in working memory. *Current Opinion in Neurobiology, 8,* 234–238.

Baddeley, A. D. (2000). The episodic buffer: A new component of working memory. *Trends in Cognitive Sciences, 4,* 417–423.

Baddeley, A. D., & Hitch, G. (1974). Working memory. In G. A. Bower (Ed.), *The psychology of learning and motivation, vol. 8* (pp. 47–89). New York: Academic Press.

Baddeley, A. D., & Warrington, E. K. (1970). Amnesia and the distinction between long- and short-term memory. *Journal of Verbal Learning and Verbal Behavior, 9,* 176–189.

Bahrick, H. P., & Phelps, E. (1987). Retention of Spanish vocabulary over eight years. *Journal of Experimental Psychology: Learning, Memory and Cognition, 13,* 344–349.

Bartlett, F. C. (1932). *Remembering.* London: Cambridge University Press.

Bayley, P. J., Hopkins, R. O, & Squire, L. R. (2003). Successful recollection of remote autobiographical memories by amnesic patients with medial temporal lobe lesions. *Neuron, 38,* 135–144.

Bayley, P. J., & Squire, L. R. (2002). Medial temporal lobe amnesia: Gradual acquisition of factual information by nondeclarative memory. *Journal of Neuroscience, 22,* 5741–5748.

Beale, J. M., & Keil, F. C. (1995). Categorical effects in the perception of faces. *Cognition, 57,* 217–239.

Bechera, A., Tranel, D., Hanna, D., Adolphs, R., Rockland, C., & Damasio, A. R. (1995). Double dissociation of conditioning and declarative knowledge relative to the amygdala and hippocampus in humans. *Science, 269,* 1115–1118.

Bend, M., & Nordin, S. (1997). Perceptual learning in olfaction: Wine tasters versus controls. *Physiology and Behavior, 62,* 1065–1070.

Berendt, J. (1973, November). Where were you? *Esquire.*

Berke, J. D., & Hyman, S. E. (2000). Addiction, dopamine, and the molecular mechanisms of memory. *Neuron, 25,* 515–532.

Berman, D. E., Hazvi, S., Rosenblum, K., Seger, R., & Dudai, Y. (1998). Specific and differential activation of mitogen-activated protein kinase cascades by unfamiliar taste in the insular cortex of the behaving rat. *Journal of Neuroscience, 18,* 10037–10044.

Biederman, I., & Shiffar. (1987). Sexing day-old chicks: A case study and expert systems analysis of a difficult perceptual learning task. *Journal of Experimental Psychology: Learning, Memory, and Cognition, 13,* 640–645.

Birrell, M., & Brown, V. J. (2000). Medial frontal cortex mediates perceptual attentional set shifting in the rat. *Journal of Neuroscience, 20,* 4320–4324.

Bliss, T.V. P., & Lomo, T. (1973). Long-lasting potentiation of synaptic transmission in the dentate area of anesthetized rabbits following stimulation of the perforant path. *Journal of Physiology (London), 232,* 331–356.

Bontempi, B., Laurent-Demir, C., Destrade, C., & Jaffard, R. (1999). Time-dependent reorganization of brain circuitry underlying long-term memory storage. *Nature, 400,* 671–674.

Bransford, J. D., & Franks, J. J. (1971). The abstraction of linguistic ideas. *Cognitive Psychology, 2,* 331–350.

Bransford, J. D., & Johnson, M. K. (1973). Contextual requisites for understanding: Some investigations of comprehension and recall. *Journal of Verbal Learning and Verbal Behavior, 11,* 717–726.

Breiter, H. C., Etcoff, N. L., Whalen, P. J., Kennedy, W. A., Rauch, S. L., Buckner, R. L., Strauss, M. M., Hyman, S. E., & Rosen, B. R. (1996). Response and habituation of the human amygdala during visual processing of facial expression. *Neuron, 17,* 875–887.

Breland, K., & Breland, M. (1961). The misbehavior of organisms. *American Psychologist, 16,* 681–684.

Breland, K., & Breland, M. (1966). *Animal behavior.* New York: Macmillan.

Brewer, W. F. (1988). Qualitative analysis of the recalls of randomly sampled autobiographical events. In M. M. Gruneberg, P. E. Morris, & R. N. Sykes (Eds.), *Practical aspects of memory: Current research and issues* (pp. 263–268). New York: Wiley.

Brewer, W., & Treyens, J. C. (1981). Role of schemata in memory for places. *Cognitive Psychology, 13,* 207–230.

Brown, J. (1958). Some tests of decay theory of immediate memory. *Quarterly Journal of Experimental Psychology, 10,* 12–21.

Brown, M. W., & Aggleton, J. P. (2001). Recognition memory: What are the roles of the perirhinal cortex and hippocampus? *Nature Reviews Neuroscience, 2,* 51–61.

Brown, R., & Kulik, J. (1977). Flashbulb memories. *Cognition, 5,* 73–99.

Brown, R., & McNeill, D. (1966). The "tip of the tongue" phenomenon. *Journal of Verbal Learning and Verbal Behavior, 5,* 325–337.

Bryant, P. E., & Trabasso, T. (1971). Transitive inferences and memory in young children. *Nature, 232,* 456–458.

Buckner, R. L., Kelley, M., & Petersen, S. E. (1999). Frontal cortex contributes to human memory formation. *Nature Neuroscience, 2,* 311–314.

Buckner, R. L., & Wheeler, M. E. (2001). The cognitive neuroscience of remembering. *Nature Reviews Neuroscience, 2,* 624–634.

Bunsey, M., & Eichenbaum, H. (1996). Conservation of hippocampal memory function in rats and humans. *Nature, 379,* 255–257.

Burnham, W. M. (1903). Retroactive amnesia: Illustrative cases and a tentative explanation. *American Journal of Psychology, 14,* 382–396.

Cahill, L., & McGaugh, J. L. (1995). A novel demonstration of enhanced memory associated with emotional arousal. *Consciousness and Cognition, 4,* 410–421.

Cahill, L., & McGaugh, J. L. (1998). Mechanisms of emotional arousal and lasting declarative memory. *Trends in Neuroscience, 21,* 273–313.

Cahill, L., Haier, R. J., Fallons, J., Alkire, M. T., Tang, C., Keator, D., Wu, J., & McGaugh, J. L. (1996). Amygdala activity at encoding correlated with long-term free recall of emotional information. *Proceedings of the National Academy of Sciences, 93,* 8016–8021.

Cajal, S. Ramón y. (1894). La fine structure des centres nerveux. *Proceedings of the Royal Society of London, B55,* 444.

Capaldi, E. J., Verry, D. R., & Davidson, T. L. (1980). Memory, serial anticipation pattern learning, and transfer in rats. *Animal Learning and Behavior, 8,* 575–585.

Carew, T. J., Walters, E. T., & Kandel, E. R. (1981). Associative learning in *Aplysia*: Cellular correlates supporting a conditioned fear hypothesis. *Science, 211,* 501–504.

Caso, L. L., Haxby, J. V., & Martin, A. (1999). Attribute-based neural substrates in temporal cortex for perceiving and knowing about objects. *Nature Neuroscience, 2,* 913–919.

Chao, L. L., Haxby, J. V., & Martin, A. (1999). Attribute-based neural substrates in temporal cortex for perceiving and knowing about objects. *Nature Neuroscience, 2,* 913–919.

Chase, W. G., & Simon, H. A. (1973). Perception in chess. *Cognitive Psychology, 4,* 55–81.

Christian, K. M., & Thompson, R. F. (2003). Neural substrates of eyeblink conditioning: Acquisition and retention. *Learning and Memory, 11,* 427–455.

Cho, Y. H., Beracochea, D., & Jaffard, R. (1993). Extended temporal gradient for the retrograde and anterograde amnesia produced by ibotenate entorhinal cortex lesions in mice. *Journal of Neuroscience, 13,* 1759–1766.

Cho, Y. H., & Kesner, R. P. (1996). Involvement of entorhinal cortex or parietal cortex in long-term spatial discrimination memory in rats: Retrograde amnesia. *Behavioral Neuroscience, 110,* 436–442.

Claparède, E. (1911/1951). Recognition and "me"ness. In D. Rapaport (Ed.), *Organization and pathology of thought* (pp. 58–75). New York: Columbia University Press. (Reprinted from *Archives de Psychologies, 11* (1911), 79–90.)

Clark, R. E., & Squire, L. R. (1998). Classical conditioning and brain systems: The role of awareness. *Science, 280,* 77–81.

Clark, R. E., & Squire, L. R. (1999). Human eyeblink classical conditioning: Effects of manipulating awareness of stimulus contingencies. *Psychological Science, 10,* 14–18.

Clark, R. E., West, A. N., Zola, S. M., & Squire, L. R. (2001). Rats with lesions of the hippocampus are impaired on the delayed nonmatching-to-sample task. *Hippocampus, 11(2),* 176–186.

Clark, R. E., Zola, S. M., & Squire, L. R. (2000). Impaired recognition memory in rats after damage to the hippocampus. *Journal of Neuroscience, 20,* 8853–8860.

Clayton, N., & Dickenson, A. D. (1998). Episodic-like memory during cache recovery by scrub jays. *Nature, 395,* 272–274.

Cohen, J. D., Perlstein, W. M., Braver, T. S., Nystrom, L. E., Noll, D. C., Jonides, J., & Smith, E. E. (1997). Temporal dynamics of brain activation during a working memory task. *Nature, 386,* 604–607.

Cohen, N. J. (1984). Preserved learning capacity in amnesia: Evidence for multiple memory systems. In N. Butters & L. R. Squire (Ed.), *The neuropsychology of memory* (pp. 83–103). New York: Guilford Press.

Cohen, N. J., & Squire, L. R. (1980). Preserved learning and retention of a pattern-analyzing skill in amnesia: Dissociation of knowing how and knowing that. *Science, 210,* 207–210.

Cohen, N. J., Ryan, J., Hunt, C., Romine, L., Wszalek, T., & Nash, C. (1999). Hippocampal system and declarative (relational) memory: Summarizing the data from functional neuroimaging studies. *Hippocampus, 9(1),* 83–98.

Colegrove, F. W. (1899). Individual memories. *American Journal of Psychology, 10,* 228–255.

Collins, A. M., & Quillian, M. R. (1969). Retrieval time from semantic memory. *Journal of Verbal Learning and Verbal Behavior, 8,* 240–247.

Collins, A. M., & Quillian, M. R. (1972). Experiments on semantic memory and language comprehension. In L. W. Gregg (Ed.), *Cognition in learning and memory* (pp. 117–147). New York: Wiley.

Conway, J. K. (Ed.). (1995). *Flashbulb memories.* Hillsdale, NJ: Earlbaum.

Corkin, S. (1984). Lasting consequences of bilateral medial temporal lobectomy: Clinical course and experimental findings in H. M. *Seminars in Neurology, 4,* 249–259.

Corkin, S. (2002). What's new with the amnesic patient H. M.? *Nature Reviews Neuroscience, 3,* 153–159.

Corkin, S., Amaral, D. G., González, R. G., Johnson, K. A., & Hyman, B. T. (1997). H. M.'s medial temporal lobe lesion: Findings from magnetic resonance imaging. *Journal of Neuroscience, 17,* 3964–3979.

Courtney, S. M., Ungerleider, L. G., Kell, K., & Haxby, J. V. (1997). Transient and sustained activity in a distributed neural system for human working memory. *Nature, 386,* 608–611.

Craik, F. I. M., & Lockhart, R. S. (1972). Levels of processing: A framework for memory research. *Journal of Verbal Learning and Verbal Behavior, 11,* 671–684.

Craik, F. I. M., & Tulving, E. (1975). Depth of processing and the retention of words in episodic memory. *Journal of Experimental Psychology: General, 104,* 268–294.

Crombag, H. F. M., Wagenaar, W. A., & Van Koppen, P. J. (1996). Crashing memories and the problem of "source monitoring." *Applied Cognitive Psychology, 10,* 95–104.

Damasio, A. R. (1989). Time-locked multiregional retroactivation: A systems-level proposal for the neural substrates of recall and recognition. *Cognition, 33,* 25–62.

Damasio, A. R., Eslinger, P. J., Damasio, H., Van Hoesen, G. W., & Cornell, S. (1985). Multimodal amnesic syndrome following bilateral temporal and basal forebrain damage. *Archives of Neurology, 42,* 252–259.

Damasio, H., Grabowski, T. J., Tranel, D., Hichwa, R. D., & Damasio, A. R. (1996). A neural basis for lexical retrieval. *Nature, 380,* 499–505.

Darwin, C. J., Turvey, M. T., & Crowder, R. G. (1972). The auditory analogue of the Sperling partial report procedure: Evidence for a brief auditory storage. *Cognitive Psychology, 3,* 255–267.

Davachi, L., Mitchell, J. P., & Wagner, A. D. (2003). Multiple routes to memory: Distinct medial temporal lobe processes build item and source memories. *Proceedings of the National Academy of Sciences, 100,* 2157–2162.

Davachi, L., & Wagner, A. G . (2002). Hippocampal contributions to episodic encoding: Insights from relational and item-based learning. *Journal of Neurophysiology, 88,* 982–990.

Davis, M. (1994). The role of the amygdala in emotional learning. *International Review of Neurobiology, 36,* 225–266.

Davis, H. P., & Squire, L. R. (1984). Protein synthesis and memory: A review. *Psychological Bulletin, 96,* 518–559.

Day, M., Langston, R., & Morris, R. G. M. (2003). Glutamate receptor mediated encoding and retrieval of paired associate learning. *Nature, 424,* 205–209.

DeGroot, A. D. (1966). Perception and memory versus thought: Some old ideas and recent findings. In B. Kleinmuntz (Ed.), *Problem solving.* New York: Wiley.

Dias, R., Robbins, T. W., & Roberts, A. C. (1996). Dissociation in prefrontal cortex of affective and attentional shifts. *Nature, 380,* 69–72.

Disterhoft, J. F., Kronforst, M. A., Moyer, J. R., Thompson, L. T., Van der Zee, E. A., & Weiss, C. R. (1996). Hippocampal neuron changes during trace eyeblink conditioning in the rabbit. In J. R. Bloedel, T. J. Ebner, & S. P. Wise (Eds.), *The acquisition of motor behavior in vertebrates* (pp. 143–174). Cambridge, MA: MIT Press.

Dobbins, I. G., Foley, H., Schacter, D. L., & Wagner, A. D. (2002). Executive control during episodic retrieval: Multiple prefrontal processes subserve source memory. *Neuron, 35,* 989–996.

Downing, P. E., Jiang, Y., Shuman, M., & Kanwisher, N. (2001). A cortical area selective for visual processing of the human body. *Science, 293,* 2470–2473.

Dudai, Y. (2004). The neurobiology of consolidations, or how stable is the engram? *Annual Review of Psychology, 55,* 51–86.

Dudchencko, P., Wood, E., & Eichenbaum, H. (2000). Neurotoxic hippocampal lesions have no effect on odor span and little effect on odor recognition memory, but produce significant impairments on spatial span, recognition, and alternation. *Journal of Neuroscience, 20,* 2964–2977.

Duff, M. C., Hengst, J., Tranel, D., & Cohen, N. J. (2005). Development of shared information in communication despite hippocampal amnesia. *Nature Neuroscience, 9,* 140–146.

Duncan, C. P. (1949). The retroactive effect of electroshock on learning. *Journal of Comparative and Physiological Psychology, 42,* 32–44.

Dusek, J. A., & Eichenbaum, H. (1997). The hippocampus and memory for orderly stimulus relations. *Proceedings of the National Academy of Science, U.S.A., 94,* 7109–7114.

Eacott, M. J., & Norman, G. (2004). Integrated memory for object, place, and context in rats: A possible model of episodic memory? *Journal of Neuroscience, 24,* 1948–1953.

Ebbinghaus, H. (1885/1913). *Memory: A contribution to experimental psychology.* New York: Dover.

Eich, J. E. (1980). The cue-dependent nature of state-dependent retrieval. *Memory and Cognition, 8,* 157–173.

Eichenbaum, H., Clegg, R. A., & Feeley, A. (1983). A reexamination of functional subdivisions of the rodent prefrontal cortex. *Experimental Neurology, 79,* 434–451.

Eichenbaum, H., & Cohen, N. J. (2001). *From conditioning to conscious recollection: Memory systems of the brain.* New York: Oxford University Press.

Eichenbaum, H., Dudchenko, P., Wood, E., Shapiro, M., & Tanila, H. (1999). The hippocampus, memory, and place cells: Is it spatial memory or memory space? *Neuron, 23,* 1–20.

Eichenbaum, H., Otto, T., & Cohen, N. J. (1994). Two functional components of the hippocampal memory system. *Brain and Behavioral Sciences, 17,* 449–518.

Eichenbaum, H., Stewart, C., & Morris, R. G. M. (1990). Hippocampal representation in spatial learning. *Journal of Neuroscience, 10,* 331–339.

Ekstrom, A. D., Kahana, M. J., Caplan, J. B., Fields, T. A., Isham, E. A., Newman, E. L., & Fried, I. (2003). Cellular networks underlying human spatial navigation. *Nature, 425,* 184–187.

Eldridge, L. L., Knowlton, B. J., Furmanski, C. S., Brookheimer, S. Y., & Engel, S. A. (2000). Remembering episodes: A selective role for the hippocampus during retrieval. *Nature Neuroscience, 3,* 1149–1152.

Elgersma, Y., & Silva, A. J. (1999). Molecular mechanisms of synaptic plasticity and memory. *Current Opinion in Neurobiology, 9,* 209–213.

Epstein, R., & Kanwisher, N. (1998). A cortical representation of the local visual environment. *Nature, 392,* 598–601.

Epstein, R., Graham, K. S., & Downing, P. E. (2003). Viewpoint-specific scene representations in the human parahippocampal cortex. *Neuron, 37,* 865–876.

Epstein, R., & Kanwisher, N. (1998). A cortical representation of the local visual environment. *Nature, 392,* 598–601.

Ericsson, A., & Chase, W. G. (1982). Exceptional memory. *American Scientist, 70,* 607–615.

Everitt, B. J., Dickinson, A., & Robbins, T. W. (2001). The neuropsychological basis of addictive behavior. *Brain Research Reviews, 36,* 129–138.

Everitt, B. J., & Robbins, T. W. (1992). Amygdala–ventral striatal interactions and reward-related processes. In J. P. Aggleton (Ed.), *The amygdala: Neurobiological aspects of emotion, memory, and mental dysfunction* (pp. 401–429). New York: Wiley-Liss.

Farah, M. J. (2004). *Visual agnosia.* Cambridge: MIT Press.

Farah, M. J., & McClelland, J. L. (1991). A computational model of semantic memory impairment: Modality specificity and emergent category specificity. *Journal of Experimental Psychology: General, 120,* 339–357.

Fenn, K. M., Nusbaum, H. C., & Margoliash, D. (2003). Consolidation during sleep of perceptual learning of spoken language. *Nature, 425,* 614–616.

Fisher, R. P., & Geiselman, R. E. (1992). *Memory-enhancing techniques for investigative interviewing: The cognitive interview.* Springfield, IL: Charles C. Thomas.

Finger, S. (2000). *Minds behind the brain: A history of the pioneers and their discoveries.* New York: Oxford University Press.

Fortin, N. J., Agster, K. L., & Eichenbaum, H. (2002). Critical role of the hippocampus in memory for sequences of events. *Nature Neuroscience, 5,* 458–462.

Fortin, N. J., Wright, S. P., & Eichenbaum, H. (2004). Recollection-like memory retrieval in rats is dependent on the hippocampus. *Nature, 431,* 188–191.

Frankland, P.W., Bontempi, B., Talton, L. E., Kaczmarek, L., & Silva, A. J. (2004). The involvement of the anterior cingulate cortex in remote contextual fear memory. *Science, 304,* 881–883.

Freedman, D. J., Riesenhuber, M., Poggio, T., & Miller, E. K. (2001). Categorical representation of visual stimuli in the primate prefrontal cortex. *Science, 291,* 312–316.

Freedman, D. J., Riesenhuber, M., Poggio, T., & Miller, E. K. (2003). A comparison of primate prefrontal and inferior temporal cortices during visual categorization. *Journal of Neuroscience, 23,* 5235–5246.

Frey, U., & Morris, R. G. M. (1997). Synaptic tagging and long-term potentiation. *Nature, 385,* 533–536.

Fuster, J. M. (1995). *Memory in the cerebral cortex: An empirical approach to neural networks in the human and nonhuman primate.* Cambridge, MA: MIT Press.

Gaffan, D., & Harrison, S. (1987). Amygdalectomy and disconnection in visual learning for auditory secondary reinforcement by monkeys. *Journal of Neuroscience, 7,* 2285–2292.

Gallagher, M., & Holland, P. C. (1994). The amygdala complex: Multiple roles in associative learning and attention. *Proceedings of the National Academy of Sciences, 91,* 1171–1776.

Garcia, J., & Ervin, F. R. (1968). Gustatory-visual and telereceptor-cutaneous conditioning—adaptation in internal and external milieus. *Communications in Behavioral Biology Part A, 1,* 389–415.

Gauthier, I., Skudlarski, P., Gore, J. C., & Anderson, A. W. (2000). Expertise for cars and birds recruits brain areas involved in face recognition. *Nature Neuroscience, 3,* 191–197.

Gauthier, I., Tarr, M. J., Anderson, A. W., Skudlarski, P., & Gore, J. C. (1999). Activation of the middle fusiform "face area" increases with expertise in recognizing novel objects. *Nature Neuroscience, 2,* 568–573.

Gabrieli, J. (1995). Contribution of the basal ganglia to skill learning and working memory in humans. In J. C. Houk, J. L. Davis, & D. G. Beiser (Eds.), *Models of information processing in the basal ganglia* (pp. 227–294). Cambridge, MA: The MIT Press.

Gabrieli, J. D. E., Brewer, J. B., Desmond, J. E., & Glover G. H. (1997). Separate neural bases of two fundamental memory processes in the human medial temporal lobe. *Science, 276,* 264–266.

Gabrieli, J. D., Fleischman, D. A., Keane, M. M., Reminger, S. L., & Morrell, F. (1995). Double dissociation between memory systems underlying explicit and implicit memory in the human brain. *Psychological Science, 6*, 76–82.

Gabrieli, J. D. E., Milberg, W., Keane, M., & Corkin, S. (1990). Intact priming of patterns despite impaired memory. *Neuropsychologia, 28*, 417–427.

Gaffan, D. (1994). Scene-specific memory for objects: A model of episodic memory impairment in monkeys with fornix transection. *Journal of Cognitive Neuroscience, 6*, 305–320.

Garcia, J., & Koelling, R. A. (1966). Relation of cue to consequence in avoidance learning. *Psychonomic Science, 4*, 123–124.

Gilbert, C. D. (1994). Early perceptual learning. *Proceedings of the National Academy of Sciences, 91*, 1195–1197.

Giovanello, K. S., Schnyer, D. M., & Verfaellie, M. (2003). A critical role for the anterior hippocampus in relational memory: Evidence from an fMRI study comparing associative and item recognition. *Hippocampus, 14*, 5–8.

Giovanello, K. S., Verfaellie, M., & Keane, M. M. (2003). Disproportionate deficit in associative recognition relative to item recognition in global amnesia. *Cognitive, Affective, and Behavioral Neuroscience, 3*, 186–194.

Glenberg, A. M., Smith, S. M., & Green, C. (1977). Type I rehearsal: Maintenance and more. *Journal of Verbal Learning and Verbal Behavior, 16*, 339–352.

Glisky, E. L., Schacter, D. L., & Tulving, E. (1986). Learning and retention of computer-related vocabulary in memory-impaired patients: Method of vanishing cues. *Journal of Clinical and Experimental Neuropsychology, 8(3)*, 292–312.

Godden, D., & Baddeley, A. D. (1975). Context-dependent memory in two natural environments: On land and under water. *British Journal of Psychology, 66*, 325–331.

Goldman-Rakic, P. S. (1995). Cellular basis of working memory. *Neuron, 14*, 477–485.

Goldman-Rakic, P. S. (1996). The prefrontal landscape: Implications of functional architecture for understanding human mentation and the central executive. *Philosophical Transactions of the Royal Society of London, B351*, 1445–1453.

Goldstone, R. L. (1998). Perceptual learning. *Annual Review of Psychology, 49*, 585–612.

Goodglass, H., Kelin, P., Carey, P., & Jones, K. (1966). Specific semantic word categories in aphasia. *Cortex, 2*, 74–89.

Gormezano, I., Prokasy, W. F., & Thompson, R. F. (Eds.). (1987). *Classical conditioning* (3rd ed.). Hillsdale, NJ: Erlbaum.

Goshen-Gottstein, Y., Moscovitch, M., & Melo, B. (2000). Intact implicit memory for newly formed verbal associations in amnesic patients following single study trials. *Neuropyschology, 14*, 570–578.

Graf, P., Mandler, G., & Haden, P. E. (1982). Simulating amnesic symptoms in normal subjects. *Science, 218*, 1243–1244.

Graf, P., Squire, L. R., & Mandler, G. (1984). The information that amnesic patients do not forget. *Journal of Experimental Psychology: Learning, Memory, and Cognition, 10*, 164–178.

Grafton, S. T., Hazeltine, E., & Ivry, R. (1995). Functional mapping of sequence learning in normal humans. *Journal of Cognitive Neuroscience, 7*, 497–510.

Graybiel, A. M. (1995). Building action repertoires: Memory and learning functions of the basal ganglia. *Current Opinion in Neurobiology, 5*, 733–741.

Graybiel, A. M., Aosaki, T., Flaherty, A. W., & Kimura, M. (1994). The basal ganglia and adaptive motor control. *Science, 265,* 1826–1832.

Griffiths, D., Dickinson, A., & Clayton, N. (1999). Episodic memory: What can animals remember about their past? *Trends in Cognitive Sciences, 3,* 74–80.

Gustavson, C. R., Garcia, J., Hankins, W. G., & Rusiniak, K. W. (1974). Coyote predation control by aversive conditioning. *Science, 184,* 581–583.

Guy, S. & Cahill, L. (1999). The role of overt rehearsal in enhanced conscious memory for emotional events. *Consciousness and Cognition, 8,* 114–122.

Hamann, S. B., Ely, T. D., Grafton, S. T., & Kilts, C. D. (1999). Amygdala activity related to enhanced memory for pleasant and aversive stimuli. *Nature Neuroscience, 2,* 289–293.

Hampson, R. E., Pons, T. P., Stanford, T. R., & Deadwyler, S. A. (2004). Categorization in the monkey hippocampus: A possible mechanism for encoding information into memory. *Proceedings of the National Academy of Sciences, 101,* 3184–3189.

Hart, J. T. (1967). Memory and memory-monitoring processes. *Journal of Verbal Learning and Verbal Behavior, 6,* 685–691.

Haxby, J. V., Gobbini, M. I., Furey, M. L., Ishai, A., Schouten, J. L., & Pietrini, P. (2001). Distributed and overlapping representations of faces and objects in ventral temporal cortex. *Science, 293,* 2425–2430.

Healy, M. R., Light, L. L., & Chung, C. (2005). Dual process model of associative recognition in young and older adults: Evidence from receiver operating characteristics. *Journal of Experimental Psychology: Learning, Memory, and Cognition, 31,* 768–788.

Hebb, D. O. (1949). *The organization of behavior.* New York: Wiley.

Heckers, S., Zalezak, M., Weiss, A. P., Ditman, T., & Titone, D. (2004). Hippocampal activation during transitive inference in humans. *Hippocampus, 14,* 153–162.

Heit, G., Smith, M. E., & Halgren, E. (1988). Neural encoding of individual words and faces by the human hippocampus and amygdala. *Nature, 333,* 773–775.

Henke, K., Buck, A., Weber, B., & Wieser, H. G. (1997). Human hippocampus establishes associations in memory. *Hippocampus, 7,* 249–256.

Herrnstein, R. J. (1990). Levels of stimulus control: A functional approach. *Cognition, 37,* 133–166.

Hock, H. S., Smith, L. B., Escoffery, L., Baters, A., and Field, L. (1989). Evidence for the abstractive encoding of superficial position information in visual patterns. *Memory and Cognition, 17,* 490–502.

Holdstock, J. S., Mayes, A. R., Roberts, N., Cezayirli, E., Isaac C. L., O'Reilly, R. C., & Norman, K. A. (2002). Under what conditions is recognition spared relative to recall after selective hippocampal damage in humans? *Hippocampus, 12(3),* 341–351.

Holyoak, K. J., & Thagard, P. (1995). *Mental leaps: Analogy in creative thought.* Cambridge, MA: MIT Press.

Hulse, S. H., & Campbell, C. E. (1975). "Thinking ahead" in rat discrimination learning. *Animal Learning and Behavior, 3,* 305–311.

Hyde, T. S., & Jenkins, J. J. (1973). Recall of words as a function of semantic, graphic, and syntactic orienting tasks. *Journal of Verbal Learning and Verbal Behavior, 12,* 471–480.

Ishai, A., Ungerleider, L. G., Martin, A., Schouten, J. L., & Haxby, J. V. (1999). Distributed representation of objects in the human ventral visual pathway. *Proceedings of the National Academy of Sciences, 96,* 9379–9384.

Ivkovich, D., Collins, K. L., Eckerman, C. O., Krasnegor, N. A., & Stanton, M. E. (1999). Classical delay eyeblink conditioning in 4- and 5-month-old human infants. *Psychological Science, 10,* 4–8.

Jacobson, S. F., Wolfe, J. B., & Jackson, T. A. (1935). An experimental analysis of the frontal association areas in primates. *Journal of Nervous and Mental Disease, 82,* 1–14.

Jacoby, L. L. (1983). Remembering the data: Analyzing interactive processes in reading. *Journal of Verbal Learning and Behavior, 22,* 485–508.

Jacoby, L. L. (1999). Ironic effects of repetition: Measuring age-related differences in memory. *Journal of Experimental Psychology: Learning, Memory, and Cognition, 25,* 3–22.

James, W. (1890/1918). *The principles of psychology.* New York: Holt.

Jenkins, H. M., & Moore, B. R. (1973). The form of the autoshaped response with food or water reinforcers. *Journal of the Experimental Analysis of Behavior, 20,* 163–181.

Johnson, M. K., Kim, J. K., & Risse, G. (1985). Do alcoholic Korsakoff's syndrome patients acquire affective reactions? *Journal of Experimental Psychology: Learning, Memory, and Cognition, 11,* 27–36.

Johnston, R. E. (1993). Memory for individual scent in hamsters (*Mesocritcetus auratus*) as assessed by habituation methods. *Journal of Comparative Psychology, 107,* 201–207.

Johnston, R. E., & Jernigan, P. (1994). Golden hamsters recognize individuals, not just individual scents. *Animal Behavior, 48,* 129–136.

Jonides, J., & Smith, E. E. (1997). The architecture of working memory. In M. D. Rugg (Ed.), *Cognitive neuroscience* (pp. 243–276). Hove East Sussex: Psychology Press.

Kamin, L. J. (1968). "Attention-like" processes in classical conditioning. In M. R. Jones (Ed.), *Miami Symposium on the prediction of behavior: Aversive stimulation* (pp. 9–31). Miami, FL: University of Miami Press.

Kanwisher, N. (2000). Domain specificity in face perception. *Nature Neuroscience, 3,* 759–763.

Kanwisher, N., McDermott, J., & Chun, M. M. (1997). The fusiform face area: A module in human extrastriate cortex specialized for face perception. *Journal of Neuroscience, 17,* 4302–4311.

Kapp, B. S., Whalen, P. J., Supple, W. F., & Pascoe, J. P. (1991). Amygdaloid contributions to conditioned arousal and sensory information processing. In J. Aggleton (Ed.), *The amygdala: Neurobiological aspects of emotion, memory, and mental dysfunction* (pp. 229–254). New York: Wiley-Liss.

Karni, A. (1996). The acquisition of perceptual and motor skills: A memory system in the adult human cortex. *Cognitive Brain Research, 5,* 39–48.

Karni, A., & Sagi, D. (1991). Where practice makes perfect in texture discrimination: Evidence for primary visual cortex plasticity. *Proceedings of the National Academy of Sciences, 88,* 4966–4970.

Karni, A., Tanne, D., Rubenstein, B. S., Askenasy, J. J. M., & Sagi, D. (1994). Dependence on REM sleep of overnight improvement of a perceptual skill. *Science, 265,* 679–682.

Kelley, A. (2004). Memory and addiction: Shared neural circuitry and molecular mechanisms. *Neuron, 44,* 161–179.

Keppel, G., Postman, L., & Zavortnik, B. (1968). Studies of learning to learn: VIII. The influence of massive amounts of training upon the learning and retention of paired associate lists. *Journal of Verbal Learning and Verbal Behavior, 7,* 790–796.

Kermadi, I., & Joseph, J. P. (1995). Activity in the caudate nucleus of monkeys during spatial sequencing. *Journal of Neurophysiology, 74,* 911–933.

Kesner, R. P., Gilbert, P. E., & Barua, L. A. (2002). The role of the hippocampus in memory for the temporal order of a sequence of odors. *Behavioral Neuroscience, 116,* 286–290.

Kesner, R. P., & Jackson-Smith, P. (1992). Neurobiology of an attribute model of memory: Role of prefrontal cortex. In I. Gormezano and E. A. Wasserman (Eds.), *Learning and memory: The behavioral and biological substrates* (pp. 251–273). Hillsdale, NJ: Lawrence Erlbaum.

Kesner, R. P., Wasler, R. D., & Winzenried, G. (1989). Central but not basolateral amygdala mediates memory for positive affective experiences. *Behavioral Brain Research, 33,* 189–195.

Kilpatrick, L., & Cahill, L. (2003). Amygdala modulation of parahippocampal and frontal regions during emotionally influenced memory storage. *Neuroimage, 20,* 2091–2099.

Kim, J. J., Clark, R. E., & Thompson, R. F. (1995). Hippocampectomy impairs the memory of recently, but not remotely, acquired trace eyeblink conditioned responses. *Behavioral Neuroscience, 109,* 195–203.

Kim, J. J., & Fanselow, M. S. (1992). Modality-specific retrograde amnesia of fear. *Science, 256,* 675–677.

Kintsch, W., & Buschke, H. (1969). Homophones and synonyms in short-term memory. *Journal of Experimental Psychology, 80,* 403–407.

Kleinsmith, L. J., & Kaplan, S. (1963). Paired associate learning as a function of arousal and interpolated interval. *Journal of Experimental Psychology, 65,* 190–193.

Kluver, H., & Bucy, P. (1937). "Psychic blindness" and other symptoms following bilateral temporal lobectomy in rhesus monkeys. *American Journal of Physiology, 119,* 352–353.

Knowlton, B. J., Mangels, J. A., & Squire, L. R. (1996). A neostriatal habit learning system in humans. *Science, 273,* 1399–1401.

Knowlton, B. J., Ramus, S. , & Squire, L. R. (1992). Intact artificial grammar learning in amnesia. *Psychological Sciences, 3(3),* 172–179.

Knowlton, B. J., & Squire, L. R. (1993). The learning of categories: Parallel brain systems for item memory and category knowledge. *Science, 262,* 1747–1749.

Kolb, B., & Robbins, T. (Eds.). (2003). The rodent prefrontal cortex. *Behavioural Brain Research, 146(1).*

Kreiman, K., Kock, C., & Fried, I. (2000a). Category-specific visual responses of single neurons in the human medial temporal lobe. *Nature Neuroscience, 3,* 946–953.

Kreiman, K., Kock, C., & Fried, I. (2000b). Imagery neurons in the human brain. *Nature, 408,* 357–361.

Kritchevsky, M., Chang, J., & Squire, L. R. (2004). Functional amnesia: Clinical description and neuropsychological profile of 10 cases. *Learning and Memory, 11,* 213–226.

Krupa, D. J., Thompson, J. K., & Thompson, R. F. (1993). Localization of a memory trace in the mammalian brain. *Science, 260,* 989–991.

Kunst-Wilson, W. R., & Zajonc, R. B. (1980). Affective discrimination of stimuli that cannot be recognized. *Science, 207,* 557–558.

Lashley, K. S. (1950). In search of the engram. *Symposia of the Society of Experimental Biology, 4,* 454–482.

Lashley, K. S. (1951). The problem of serial order in behavior. In L. A. Jeffress (Ed.), *Cerebral mechanisms in behavior.* New York: John Wiley.

Lechner, H. A., Squire, L. R., & Byrne, J. H. (1999). 100 years of consolidation: Remembering Müller & Pilzecker. *Learning and Memory, 6,* 77–87.

LeDoux, J. E. (1992). Brain mechanisms of emotion and emotional learning. *Current Opinion in Neurobiology, 2,* 191–197.

LeDoux, J. E. (1996). *The emotional brain.* New York: Simon and Schuster.

LeDoux, J. E., Cicchetti, P., Xagoris, A., & Romanski, L. M. (1990). The lateral amygdaloid nucleus: Sensory interface of the amygdala in fear conditioning. *The Journal of Neuroscience, 10,* 1062–1069.

Lee, I., & Kesner, R. P. (2003). Time-dependent relationship between the dorsal hippocampus and the prefrontal cortex in spatial memory. *Journal of Neuroscience, 15,* 1517–1523.

Levi, D. M., & Polat, U. (1996). Neural plasticity in adults with amblyopia. *Proceedings of the National Academy of Sciences, 93,* 6830–6834.

Light, L. L. (1991). Memory and aging: Four hypotheses in search of data. *Annual Review of Psychology, 42,* 333–376.

Linton, M. (1975). Memory for real-world events. In D. A. Norman & D. E. Rumelhart (Eds.), *Explorations in cognition* (pp. 376–404). San Francisco: W.H. Freeman.

Loftus, E. F., & Palmer, J. C. (1974). Reconstruction of automobile destruction: An example of the interaction between language and memory. *Journal of Verbal Learning and Verbal Behavior, 13,* 585–589.

Loftus, E. F., & Pickrell, J. E. (1995). The formation of false memories. *Psychiatric Annals, 25,* 720–725.

Louie, K., & Wilson, M. A. (2001). Temporally structured replay of awake hippocampal ensemble activity during rapid eye movement sleep. *Neuron, 29,* 145–156.

Luria, A. R. (1968). *The mind of a mnemonist.* New York: Basic Books.

Lynch, K. (1960). Image of the city. Cambridge, MA: MIT Press.

MacLean, P. D. (1949). Psychosomic disease and the "visceral brain": Recent developments bearing on the Papez theory of emotion. *Psychosom. Med., 11,* 338–353.

Maguire, E. A. (2001). Neuroimaging studies of autobiographical event memory. *Philosophical Transactions of the Royal Society of London, Series B: 356,* 1441–1452.

Maguire, E. A., Burgess, N., Donnett, J. G., Frackowiak, R. S. J., Frith, C. D., & O'Keefe, J. (1998). Knowing where and getting there: A human navigational network. *Science, 280,* 921–924.

Maguire, E. A., Frackowiak, R. S. J., & Frith, C. D. (1997). Recalling routes around London: Activation of the right hippocampus in taxi drivers. *Journal of Neuroscience, 17,* 7103–7110.

Maguire, E. A., & Frith, C. D. (2004). The brain network associated with acquiring semantic knowledge. *NeuroImage, 22,* 171–178.

Maguire, E. A., Vharga-Khadem, F., & Mishkin, M. (2001). The effects of bilateral hippocampal damage on fMRI regional activations and interactions during memory retrieval. *Brain, 124,* 1156–1170.

Maine de Biran, P. (1804/1929). *The influence of habit on the faculty of thinking.* Baltimore: Williams & Wilkins.

Manns, J. R., Hopkins, R. O., Reed, J. M., Kitchener, E. G., & Squire, L. R. (2003). Recognition memory and the human hippocampus. *Neuron, 37,* 171–180.

Manns, J. R., Hopkins, R. O., & Squire, L. R. (2003). Semantic memory and the human hippocampus. *Neuron, 38,* 127–133.

Manns, J. R., & Squire, L. R. (1999). Impaired recognition memory on the Doors and People Test after damage limited to the hippocampal region. *Hippocampus, 9(5),* 495–499.

Martin, A., Wiggs, C. L., Ungerleider, L. G., & Haxby, J. V. (1996). Neural correlates of category-specific knowledge. *Nature, 379,* 649–652.

Martin, S. J., Grimwood, P. D., & Morris, R. G. M. (2000). Synaptic plasticity and memory: An evaluation of the hypothesis. *Annual Review of Neuroscience, 23,* 649–711.

Mauk, M. D. (1997). Roles of cerebellar cortex and nuclei in motor learning: Contradictions or clues. *Neuron, 18,* 343–346.

Mayes, A. R., Holdstock, J. S., Isaac, C. L., Hunkin, N. M., & Roberts, N. (2002). Relative sparing of item recognition memory in a patient with adult-onset damage limited to the hippocampus. *Hippocampus, 12(3),* 325–340.

McAlonan, K., & Brown, V. J. (2003). Orbital prefrontal cortex mediates reversal learning and not attentional set shifting in the rat. *Behavioural Brain Research, 146,* 97–103.

McClelland, J. L., McNaughton, B. L., & O'Reilly, R. C. (1995). Why are there complementary learning systems in the hippocampus and neocortex? Insights from the successes and failures of connectionist models of learning and memory. *Psychological Review, 102,* 419–457.

McClelland, J. L., & Rumelhart, D. E. (Eds.). (1986). *Parallel distributed processing: Explorations of the microstructure of cognition. Vol. 2: Psychological and biological models.* Cambridge, MA: MIT Press.

McCloskey, M. E., & Glucksberg, S. (1978). Natural categories: Well-defined or fuzzy sets. *Memory and Cognition, 6,* 462–472.

McDonald, R. J., & White, N. M. (1993). A triple dissociation of memory systems: Hippocampus, amygdala, and dorsal striatum. *Behavioral Neuroscience, 107,* 3–22.

McDonald, R. J., & White, N. M. (1994). Parallel information processing in the water maze: Evidence for independent memory systems involving dorsal striatum and hippocampus. *Behavioral Neural Biology, 61,* 260–270.

McGaugh, J. L. (1966). Time-dependent processes in memory storage. *Science, 153,* 1351–1358.

McGaugh, J. L. (2000). Memory: A century of consolidation. *Science, 287,* 248–251.

McGaugh, J. L., Cahill, L., & Roozendaal, B. (1996). Involvement of the amygdala in memory storage: Interactions with other brain systems. *Proceedings of the National Academy of Sciences, 93,* 13508–13514.

McGaugh, J. L., McIntyre, C. K., & Power, A. E. (2002). Amygdala modulation of memory consolidation: Interaction with other brain systems. *Neurobiology of Learning and Memory, 78,* 539–552.

McGeogh, J. A., & McDonald, W. T. (1931). Meaningful relation and retroactive inhibition. *American Journal of Psychology, 43,* 579–588.

McGonigle, B. O., & Chalmers, M. (1977). Are monkeys logical? *Nature, 267,* 694–696.

Miller, E. K. (2000). The prefrontal cortex and cognitive control. *Nature Reviews Neuroscience, 1,* 59–65.

Miller, E. K., Erickson, C. A., & Desimone, R. (1996). Neural mechanisms of visual working memory in prefrontal cortex of the macaque. *Journal of Neuroscience, 16,* 5154–5167.

Mineka, S., Davidson, M., Cook, M., & Keir, R. (1984). Observational conditioning of snake fear in rhesus monkeys. *Journal of Abnormal Psychology, 93,* 355–372.

Mink, J. W. (1996). The basal ganglia: Focused selection and inhibition of competing motor programs. *Progress in Neurobiology, 50,* 381–425.

Mishkin, M., & Delacour, J. (1975). An analysis of short-term visual memory in the monkey. *Journal of Experimental Psychology: Animal Behavior Processes, 1,* 326–334.

Moar, I. T. (1978), as discussed in A. D. Baddeley. (1999). *Essentials of human memory.* Hive, UK: Psychology Press, Ltd.

Moita, M. A. P., Moisis, S., Zhou, Y., LeDoux, J. E., & Blair, H. T. (2003). Hippocampal place cells acquire location-specific responses to the conditioned stimulus during auditory fear conditioning. *Neuron, 37,* 485–497.

Morris, R. G. M. (1984). Developments of a water-maze procedure for studying spatial learning in the rat. *Journal of Neuroscience Methods, 11,* 47–60.

Morris, R. G. M. (2001). Episodic-like memory in animals: Psychological criteria, neural mechanisms, and the value of episodic-like tasks to investigate animal models of neurodegenerative disease. *Philosophical Transactions of the Royal Society of London, Series B: Biological Sciences, 356,* 1453–1465.

Morris, R. G. M., & Frey, U. (1997). Hippocampal synaptic plasticity: Role in spatial learning or the automatic recording of attended experience? *Philosophical Transactions of the Royal Society of London, Series B: Biological Sciences, 352,* 1489–1503.

Morris, R. G. M., Garrud, P., Rawlins, J. P, & O'Keefe, J. (1982). Place navigation impaired in rats with hippocampal lesions. *Nature, 297,* 681–683.

Moscovitch, M. (1992). Memory and working-with-memory: A component process model based on modules and central systems. *Journal of Cognitive Neuroscience, 4,* 257–267.

Moyer, J. R., Deyo, R. A., & Disterhoft, J. F. (1990). Hippocampectomy disrupts trace eyeblink conditioning in rabbits. *Behavioral Neuroscience, 104,* 243–252.

Müller, G. E., & Pilzecker, A. (1900). Experimentelle beiträge zur lehre vom gedächtnis. *Z. Psychol. Ergnzungsband, 1,* 1–300.

Mumby, D. G., Gaskin, S., Glenn, M. J., Scharamek, T. E., & Lehmann, H. (2002). Hippocampal damage and exploratory preferences in rats: Memory for objects, places, and contexts. *Learning and Memory, 9,* 49–57.

Mumby, D. G., Wood, E. R., & Pinel, J. P. (1992). Object recognition memory is only mildly impaired in rats with lesions of the hippocampus and amygdala. *Psychobiology, 20,* 18–27.

Murray, E. A. (1996). What have ablation studies told us about the neural substrates of stimulus memory? *Seminars in the Neurosciences, 8,* 13–22.

Murray, E. A., & Mishkin, M. (1998). Object recognition and location memory in monkeys with excitotoxic lesions of the amygdala and hippocampus. *Journal of Neuroscience, 18,* 6568–6582.

Musen, G., Shimamura, A. P., & Squire, L. R. (1990). Intact text-specific reading skill in amnesia. *Journal of Experimental Psychology: Learning, Memory, and Cognition, 6,* 1068–1076.

Musen, G., & Squire, L. R. (1993). On implicit learning of novel associations by amnesic patients and normal subjects. *Neuropsychologia, 7,* 119–135.

Nader, K., Schafe, G. E., & LeDoux, J. E. (2000). Fear memories require protein synthesis in the amygdala for reconsolidation after retrieval. *Nature, 406,* 722–726.

Nauta, W. J. H. (1971). The problem of the frontal lobe: A reinterpretation. *Journal of Psychiatric Research, 8,* 167–187.

Naya, Y., Yoshida, M., & Miyashita, Y. (2001). Backward spreading of memory retrieval signal in the primate temporal cortex. *Science, 291,* 661–664.

Neisser, U. (1982). *Memory observed.* San Francisco: W. H. Freeman.

Nemanic, S., Alvarado, M. C., & Bachevalier, J. (2004). The hippocampal/parahippocampal regions and recognition memory: Insights from visual paired comparison versus object delayed non-matching in monkeys. *Journal of Neuroscience, 24,* 2013–2026.

O'Kane, G., Kensinger, E. A., & Corkin, S. (2004). Evidence for semantic learning in profound amnesia: An investigation with patient H. M. *Hippocampus, 14,* 417–425.

O'Keefe, J., & Dostrovsky, J. (1971). The hippocampus as a spatial map; Preliminary evidence from unit activity in the freely moving rat. *Brain Research, 34,* 171–175.

O'Keefe, J., & Nadel, L. (1978). *The hippocampus as a cognitive map.* New York: Oxford University Press.

Olton, D. S. (1984). Comparative analyses of episodic memory. *Brain and Behavioral Sciences, 7,* 250–251.

Olton, D. S., Becker, J. T., & Handlemann, G. E. (1979). Hippocampus, space, and memory. *Brain and Behavioral Sciences, 2,* 313–365.

Olton, D. S., Collison, C., & Werz, M. A. (1977). Spatial memory and radial maze performance in rats. *Learning and Motivation, 8,* 289–314.

O'Reilly, R. C., & Rudy, J. W. (2001). Conjunctive representations in learning and memory: Principles of cortical and hippocampal function. *Psychological Reviews, 108,* 311–345.

Otto, T., & Eichenbaum, H. (1992). Complementary roles of orbital prefrontal cortex and the perirhinal–entorhinal cortices in an odor-guided delayed nonmatching to sample task. *Behavioral Neuroscience, 106,* 763–776.

Packard, M. G., Cahill, L., & McGaugh, J. L. (1994). Amygdala modulation of hippocampal-dependent and caudate nucleus-dependent memory processes. *Proc. Natl. Acad. Sci., 91,* 8477–8481.

Packard, M. G., Hirsh, R., & White, N. M. (1989). Differential effects of fornix and caudate nucleus lesions on two radial maze tasks: Evidence for multiple memory systems. *The Journal of Neuroscience, 9,* 1465–1472.

Packard, M. G., & Knowlton, B. J. (2002). Learning and memory functions of the basal ganglia. *Annual Review of Neuroscience, 25,* 563–593.

Packard, M. G., & McGaugh, J. L. (1992). Double dissociation of fornix and caudate nucleus lesions on acquisition of two water maze tasks: Further evidence for multiple memory systems. *Behavioral Neuroscience, 106,* 439–446.

Packard, M. G., & McGaugh, J. L. (1996). Inactivation of hippocampus or caudate nucleus with lidocaine differentially affects expression of place and response learning. *Neurobiology of Learning and Memory, 65,* 65–72.

Packard, M. G., & Wingard, J. C. (2004). Amygdala and "emotional" modulation of the relative use of multiple memory systems. *Neurobiology of Learning and Memory, 82,* 243–252.

Paller, K. A. (1997). Consolidating dispersed neocortical memories: The missing link in amnesia. *Memory, 5,* 73–88.

Papez, J. W. (1937). A proposed mechanism of emotion. *Archives of Neurology and Psychiatry, 7,* 217–224.

Pascual-Leone, A., Grafman, J., Clark, K., Stewart, M., Massaquoi, S., Lou, J., & Hallett, M. (1993). Procedural learning in Parkinson's disease and cerebellar degeneration. *Annals of Neurology, 34,* 594–602.

Pasternak, T., & Greenlee, M. W. (2005). Working memory in primate sensory systems. *Nature Reviews Neuroscience, 6,* 97–107.

Pavlov, I. P. (1927). *Conditioned reflexes.* New York: Oxford University Press.

Peigneux, P., Laureys, S., Fuchs, S., Collette, F., Perrin, F., Reggers, J., Phillips, C., Degueldre, C., Del Fiore, G., Aerts, J., Luxen, A., & Maquet, P. (2004). Are spatial memories strengthened in the human hippocampus during slow wave sleep? *Neuron, 44,* 535–545.

Penick, S., & Solomon, P. R. (1991). Hippocampus, context, and conditioning. *Behavioral Neuroscience, 105,* 611–617.

Perrett, S. P., Ruiz, B. P., & Mauk, M. D. (1993). Cerebellar cortex lesions disrupt learning-dependent timing of conditioned eyelid responses. *Journal of Neuroscience, 13(4),* 1708–1718.

Peterson, L. R., & Peterson, M. (1959). Short-term retention of individual items. *Journal of Experimental Psychology, 58,* 193–198.

Petrides, M. (1995). Impairments on nonspatial self-ordered and externally ordered working memory tasks after lesions of the mid-dorsal part of the lateral frontal cortex in the monkey. *Journal of Neuroscience, 15,* 359–375.

Phillips, R. G., & LeDoux, J. E. (1992). Differential contribution of amygdala and hippocampus to cued and contextual fear conditioning. *Behavioral Neuroscience, 106,* 274–285.

Piaget, J. (1928). *Judgment and reasoning in the child.* London: Kegan, Paul, Trench, and Trubner.

Pillemer, D. B. (1998). *Momentous events, vivid memories.* Cambridge, MA: Harvard University Press.

Pitman, R. K., Sanders, K. M., Zusman, R. M., Healy, A. R., Cheema, F., Lasko, N. B., Cahill, L., & Orr, S. P. (2002). Pilot study of secondary prevention of posttraumatic stress disorder with propranolol. *Biological Psychiatry, 51,* 189–192.

Poldrack, R. A., Prabakharan, V., Seger, C., & Gabrieli, J. D. E. (1999). Striatal activation during cognitive skill learning. *Neuropsychologia, 13,* 564–574.

Polster, M. R., Nadel, L., & Schacter, D. L. (1991). Cognitive neuroscience analyses of memory: A historical perspective. *Journal of Cognitive Neuroscience, 3,* 95–116.

Port, R. L., Mikhail, A. A., & Patterson, M. M. (1985). Differential effects of hippocampectomy on classical conditioned rabbit nictitating membrane response related to interstimulus interval. *Behavioral Neuroscience, 99,* 200–208.

Postle, B. R. (2006). Working memory as an emergent property of the mind and brain. *Neuroscience, 139,* 23–38.

Postma, A., Jager, G., Kessels, R. P., Koppeschaar, H. P., & van Honk, J. (2004). Sex differences for selective forms of spatial memory. *Brain and Cognition, 54,* 24–34.

Poucet, B. (1993). Spatial cognitive maps in animals: New hypotheses on their structure and neural mechanisms. *Psychological Review, 100,* 163–182.

Preston, A. R., Shrager, Y., Dudukovic, N. M., & Gabrieli, J. D. E. (2004). Hippocampal contribution to the novel use of relational information in declarative memory. *Hippocampus, 14,* 148–152.

Quinn, G., & McConnell, J. (1996). Irrelevant pictures in visual working memory. *Quarterly Journal of Experimental Psychology, 49A*, 200–215.

Rainer, G., Rao, C., & Miller, E. K. (1999). Prospective coding for objects in the primate prefrontal cortex. *Journal of Neuroscience, 19*, 5493–5505.

Ranganath, C., Johanson, M. K., & D'Esposito, M. (2000). Left anterior prefrontal activation increases with demands to recall specific perceptual information. *Journal of Neuroscience, 20*, RC108.

Ranganath, C., Yonelinas, A. P., Cohen, M. X., Dy, C. J., Tom, S. M., & D'Esposito, M. D. (2003). Dissociable correlates of recollection and familiarity with the medial temporal lobes. *Neuropsychologia, 42*, 2–13.

Rao, S. C., Rainer, G., & Miller, E. K. (1997). Integration of what and where in the primate prefrontal cortex. *Science, 276*, 821–824.

Rauch, S. L., Whalen, P. J., Shin, L. M., McInerney, S. C., Macklin, M. L., Lasko, N. B., Orr, S. P., & Pitman, R. K. (2000). Exaggerated amygdala response to masked face stimuli in posttraumatic stress disorder: A functional MRI study. *Biological Psychiatry, 47*, 769–776.

Recanzone, G. H., Merzenich, M. M., & Jenkins, W. M. (1992). Frequency discrimination training engaging a restricted skin surface results in an emergence of a cutaneous response zone in cortical area 3a. *Journal of Neurophysiology, 67*, 1057–1070.

Recanzone, G. H., Schreiner, C. E., & Merzenich, M. M. (1993). Plasticity in the frequency representation of primary auditory cortex following discrimination training in adult owl monkeys. *Journal of Neuroscience, 13*, 87–103.

Reed, J. M., & Squire, L. R. (1998). Retrograde amnesia for facts and events: Findings from four new cases. *Journal of Neuroscience, 18*, 3943–3954.

Reed, J. M., Squire, L. R., Patalano, A. L., Smith, E. E., & Jonides, J. (1999). Learning about categories that are defined by object-like stimuli despite impaired declarative memory. *Behavioral Neuroscience, 113*, 411–419.

Reinitz, M. T., Verfaellie, M., & Milberg, W. P. (1996). Memory conjunction errors in normal and amnesic subjects. *Journal of Memory and Language, 35*, 286–299.

Rescorla, R. A. (1973). Effect of US habituation following conditioning. *Journal of Comparative and Physiological Psychology, 82*, 137–143.

Rescorla, R. A. (1988). Behavioral studies of Pavlovian conditioning. *Annual Review of Neuroscience, 11*, 329–352.

Rescorla, R.A. (1988). Pavlovian conditioning: It's not what you think it is. *American Psychologist, 43*, 151–160.

Rescorla, R. A., & Wagner, A. R. (1972). A theory of Pavlovian conditioning: Variations in the effectiveness of reinforcement and nonreinforcement. In A. H. Black & W. F. Prokasy (Eds.), *Classical conditioning II: Current research and theory* (pp. 64–99). New York: Appleton.

Ribot, T. A. (1882). *The diseases of memory.* New York: Appleton.

Rioult-Pedotti, M.-S., Friedman, D., Hess, G., & Donoghue, J. P. (1998). Strengthening of horizontal cortical connections following skill learning. *Nature Neuroscience, 1*, 230–234.

Ripps, L. J., Shoeben, E. J., & Smith, E. E. (1973). Semantic distance and the verification of semantic relations. *Journal of Verbal Learning and Verbal Behavior, 12*, 1–20.

Robbins, T. W., & Everitt, B. J. (1992). Functions of dopamine in the dorsal and ventral striatum. *Seminars in Neuroscience, 4,* 119–128.

Roberts, A. C., Robbins, T. W., & Weiskrantz, L. (Eds). (1996). Executive and cognitive functions of the prefrontal cortex. *Philosophical Transactions: Biological Sciences, 351.*

Roberts, W. A. (2002). Are animals stuck in time? *Psychological Bulletin, 128,* 473–489.

Roediger, H. L. (1990). Implicit memory: Retention without remembering. *American Psychologist, 45,* 1043–1056.

Rogan, M. T., Staubli, U. V., & LeDoux, J. E. (1997). Fear conditioning induces associative long-term potentiation in the amygdala. *Nature, 390,* 604–607.

Roitblat, H. L., Pologe, B., & Scopatz, R. A. (1983). The representation of items in serial position. *Animal Learning and Behavior, 11,* 489–498.

Rosch, E. (1973). Natural categories. *Cognitive Psychology, 4,* 328–349.

Rosch, E., & Mervis, C. B. (1975). Family resemblances: Studies in the internal structure of categories. *Cognitive Psychology, 7,* 573–605.

Rosenkilde, C .E. (1979). Functional heterogeneity of the prefrontal cortex in the monkey: A review. *Behavioral and Neural Biology, 25,* 301–345.

Rubin, D. C., & Schulkind, M. D. (1997). The distribution of autobiographical memories across the lifespan. *Memory and Cognition, 25,* 859–866.

Sacks, O. (1985). *The man who mistook his wife for a hat.* New York: Summit.

Sage, J. R., & Knowlton, B. J. (2000). Effects of US devaluation on win–stay and win–shift radial maze performance in rats. *Behavioral Neuroscience, 114,* 295–306.

Salmon, D. P., & Butters, N. (1995). Neurobiology of skill and habit learning. *Current Opinion in Neurobiology, 5,* 184–190.

Schacter, D. L. (1987). Implicit memory: History and current status. *Journal of Experimental Psychology: Learning, Memory, and Cognition, 13,* 501–518.

Schacter, D. L. (2001). *The seven sins of memory.* Boston: Houghton Mifflin.

Schacter, D. L., Alpert, N., Savage, C. R., Rauch, S. L., & Albert, M. (1996). Conscious recollection and the human hippocampal formation: Evidence from positron emission tomography. *Proceedings of the National Academy of Sciences, 93,* 321–325.

Schacter, D. L., & Buckner, R. L. (1998). Priming and the brain. *Neuron, 20,* 185–195.

Schiltz, C., Bodart, J. M., Dubois, S., Dejardin, S., Michel, C., Roucoux, A., Crommelinck, M., & Orban, G. A. (1999). Neuronal mechanisms of perceptual learning: Changes in human brain activity with training in orientation discrimination. *NeuroImage, 9,* 46–62.

Schmidt, R. A. (1988). *Motor control and learning: A behavioral emphasis* (2nd ed). Champagne, IL: Human Kinetics Publishers.

Schmolck, H., Buffalo, E. A., & Squire, L. R. (2000). Memory distortions develop over time: Recollections of the O. J. Simpson trial verdict after 15 and 32 months. *Psychological Sciences, 11,* 39–45.

Schon, K., Hasselmo, M. E., Lopresti, M. L., Tricarico, M. D., & Stern, C. E. (2004). Persistence of parahippocampal representation in the absence of stimulus input enhances long-term encoding: A functional magnetic resonance imaging study of subsequent memory after a delayed match-to-sample task. *Journal of Neuroscience, 24,* 11088–11097.

Schultz, W. (2006). Behavioral theories and the neurophysiology of reward. *Annual Review of Psychology, 57,* 87–115.

Schultz, W., Apicella, P., & Ljungberg, T. (1993). Responses of monkey dopamine neurons to reward and conditioned stimuli during successive steps of learning a delayed response task. *Journal of Neuroscience, 13,* 900–913.

Schultz, W., Apicella, P., Romo, R., & Scarnati, E. (1995). Context-dependent activity in primate striatum reflecting past and future behavioral events. In J. C. Houk, J. L. Davis, & D. G. Beiser (Eds.), *Models of information processing in the basal ganglia* (pp. 11–28). Cambridge, MA: MIT Press.

Schultz, W., Tremblay, L., & Hollerman, J. R. (2000). Reward processing in primate orbitofrontal cortex and basal ganglia. *Cerebral Cortex, 10,* 272–284.

Scoville, W. B., & Milner, B. (1957). Loss of recent memory after bilateral hippocampal lesions. *Journal of Neurology, Neurosurgery, and Psychiatry, 20,* 11–12.

Seitz, R. J., & Roland, P. E. (1992). Learning of sequential finger movements in man: A combined kinematic and positron emission tomography (PET) study. *European Journal of Neuroscience, 4,* 154–165.

Seitz, R. J., Roland, P. E., Bohm, C., Greitz, T., & Stone-Elander, S. (1990). Motor learning in man: A positron emission tomographic study. *Neuroreport, 1,* 57–66.

Seligman, M. E. P. (1975). *Helplessness: On depression, development, and death.* San Francisco: W. H. Freeman.

Seligman, M. E. P., & Maier, S. F. (1967). Failure to escape traumatic shock. *Journal of Experimental Psychology, 74,* 1–9.

Shallice, T., & Warrington, E. K. (1970). Independent functioning of verbal memory stores: A neuropsychological study. *Quarterly Journal of Experimental Psychology, 22,* 261–273.

Shelton, A. L., & Gabrieli, J. D. E. (2002). Neural correlates of encoding space from route and survey perspectives. *Journal of Neuroscience, 22,* 2711–2717.

Shelton, A. L., & McNamara, T. P. (2001). Systems of spatial reference in human memory. *Cognitive Psychology, 43,* 274–310.

Sherrington, C. S. (1906). *The integrative action of the nervous system.* New Haven, CT: Yale University Press.

Shettleworth, S. J. (1975). Comparative studies on memory in food storing birds. In E. Alleva, A. Fasolo, H. Lipp, L. Nader, & L. Ricceri (Eds.), *Behavioral brain research in natural and seminatural settings: Possibilities and perspectives* (pp. 159–192). Dordrecht: Kluwer.

Shimamura, A. P. (1995). Memory and frontal lobe function. In M. S. Gazzaniga (Ed.), *The cognitive neurosciences* (pp. 803–813). Cambridge, MA: MIT Press.

Shimamura, A. P., Janowsky, J. S., & Squire, L. R. (1990). Memory for the temporal order of events in patients with frontal lobe lesions and amnesic patients. *Neuropsychologia, 28,* 803–813.

Shimizu, E., Tang, Y-P., Rampon, C., & Tsien, J. Z. (2000). NMDA receptor dependent synaptic reinforcement as a crucial process for memory consolidation. *Science, 290,* 1170–1174.

Siegel, J. M. (2001). The REM sleep–memory consolidation hypothesis. *Science, 294,* 1058–1063.

Simons, J. S., & Spiers, H. J. (2003). Prefrontal and medial temporal lobe interactions in long-term memory. *Nature Reviews Neuroscience, 4,* 637–648.

Skinner, B. F. (1938). "Superstition" in the pigeon. *Journal of Experimental Psychology, 38,* 168–172.

Slamecka, N. J., & Graf, P. (1978). The generation effect: Delineation of a phenomenon. *Journal of Experimental Psychology: Learning, Memory and Cognition, 4,* 592–604.

Small, S. A., Nava, A. S., Perera, G. M., DeLaPaz, R., Mayeux, R., & Stern, Y. (2001). Circuit mechanisms underlying memory encoding and retrieval in the long axis of the hippocampal formation. *Nature Neuroscience, 4,* 442–449.

Small, W. S. (1901). Experimental study of the mental processes of the rat II. *American Journal of Psychology, 12,* 206–239.

Smith, C. (2001). Sleep states and memory processes in humans: Procedural versus declarative. *Sleep Medicine Reviews, 5,* 491–506.

Smith, E. E., Jonides, J., & Koeppe, R. A. (1996). Dissociating verbal and spatial working memory using PET. *Cerebral Cortex, 6,* 11–20.

Solomon, P. R. (1980). A time and a place for everything? Temporal processing views of hippocampal function with special reference to attention. *Physiological Psychology, 8,* 254–261.

Sperling, G. A. (1960). The information available in brief visual presentation. *Psychological Monographs, 74,* 498.

Spiridon, M., & Kanwisher, N. (2002). How distributed is the visual category information in the human occipito-temporal cortex? An fMRI study. *Neuron, 35,* 1157–1165.

Squire, L. R., & Kandel, E. R. (1999). *Memory: From mind to molecules.* New York: Freeman & Co.

Squire, L. R., Knowlton, B., & Musen, G. (1993). The structure and organization of memory. *Annual Review of Psychology, 44,* 453–495.

Squire, L. R., & Zola, S. M. (1998). Episodic memory, semantic memory, and amnesia. *Hippocampus, 8(3),* 205–211.

Staddon, J. E. R., & Simmelhag, V. L. (1971). The "superstition" experiment: A reexamination of its implications for the principles of adaptive behavior. *Psychological Review, 78,* 3–43.

Stark, C. E. L., Bayley, P. J., & Squire, L. R. (2002). Recognition memory for single items and for associations is similarly impaired following damage to the hippocampal region. *Learning and Memory, 9,* 238–242.

Stark, C. E. L., & Squire, L. R. (2001). Simple and associative recognition in the hippocampal region. *Learning and Memory, 8,* 190–197.

Steele, R. J., & Morris, R. G. M. (1999). Delay-dependent impairment in matching-to-place task with chronic and intrahippocampal infusion of the NMDA-antagonist D-AP5. *Hippocampus 9,* 118–136.

Steinmetz, J. E. (1996). The brain substrates of classical eyeblink conditioning in rabbits. In J. R. Bloedel, T. J. Ebner, & S. P. Wise (Eds.), *The acquisition of motor behavior in vertebrates* (pp. 89–114). Cambridge, MA: The MIT Press.

Steinmetz, J. E. (1999). A renewed interest in human classical eyeblink conditioning. *Psychological Science, 10,* 24–25.

Stern, C. E., Corkin, S., Gonzalez, R. G., Guimaraes, A. R., Baker, J. R., Jennings, P. J., Carr, C. A., Sugiura, R. M., Vedantham, V., & Rosen, B. R. (1996). The hippocampal formation participates in novel picture encoding: Evidence from functional MRI. *Proceedings of the National Academy of Science, USA, 93,* 8660–8665.

Stevens, J. (1988). An activity theory approach to practical memory. In M. N. Gruneberg, P. E. Morris, & R. N. Sykes (Eds.), *Practical aspects of memory: Current research and issues. Vol. 1. Memory in everyday life* (pp. 335–341). Chichester, UK: Wiley.

Stevens, A., & Coupe, P. (1978). Distortions in judged spatial relations. *Cognitive Psychology, 10,* 422–437.

Stickgold, R. (2005). Sleep-dependent memory consolidation. *Nature, 437,* 1272–1278.

Stickgold, R., LaTanya, J., & Hobson, J. A. (2000). Visual discrimination learning requires sleep after training. *Nature Neuroscience, 3,* 1237–1238.

Stickgold, R., Malia, A., Maguire, D., Roddenberry, D., & O'Connor, M. (2000). Replaying the game: Hypnagogic images in normals and amnesics. *Science, 290,* 350–353.

Stickgold, R., Whidbee, D., Schirmer, B., Patel, V., & Hobson, J. A. (2000). Visual discrimination task improvement: A multi-step process occurring during sleep. *Journal of Cognitive Neuroscience, 12,* 246–254.

Tallal, P., Miller, S. L., Bedi, G., Byma, G., Wang, X., Nagarajan, S. S., Schreiner, C., Jenkins, W. M., & Merzenich, M. M. (1996). Language comprehension in language learning impaired children improved with acoustically modified speech. *Science, 271,* 81–84.

Tang, Y.-P., Shimizu, E., Dube, G. R., Rampson, C., Kerchner, G. A., Zhuo, M., Liu, G., & Tsien, J. Z. (1999). Genetic enhancement of learning and memory in mice. *Nature, 401,* 63–69.

Tarr, M. J., & Gauthier, I. (2000). FFA: A flexible fusiform area for subordinate-level visual processing automatized by expertise. *Nature Neuroscience, 3,* 764–769.

Teasdale, J. D., & Russell, M. L. (1983). Differential effects of induced mood on the recall of positive, negative, and neutral words. *British Journal of Clinical Psychology, 22,* 163–171.

Teng, E., & Squire, L. R. (1999). Memory for places learned long ago is intact after hippocampal damage. *Nature, 400,* 675–677.

Thompson, C. P. (1982). Memory for unique personal events: The roommate study. *Memory and Cognition, 10,* 324–332.

Thompson, R. F., & Kim, J. J. (1996). Memory systems in the brain and localization of a memory. *Proceedings of the National Academy of Sciences, 93,* 13438–13444.

Thorndike, E. L. (1898). Animal intelligence: An experimental study of the associative processes in animals. *Psychological Monographs, 2.*

Thorndyke, P. W., & Hayes Roth, B. (1982). Differences in spatial knowledge acquired from maps and navigations. *Cognitive Psychology, 14,* 560–589.

Timberlake, W., & Lucas, G. A. (1989). Behavior systems and learning: From misbehavior to general principles. In S. B. Lein & R. B. Mower (Eds.), *Contemporary learning theories: Instrumental conditioning and the impact of biological constraints on learning* (pp. 237–275). Hillsdale, NJ: Erlbaum.

Tobias, B. A., Kihlstron, J. F., & Schacter, D. L. (1992). Emotion and implicit memory. In S.-A. Christianson (Ed.), *The handbook of emotion and memory: Research and theory.* Hillsdale, NJ: Earlbaum.

Tolman, E. C. (1932/1951). *Purposive behavior in animals and men.* Berkeley: University of California Press.

Tranel, D., & Damasio, A. R. (1985). Knowledge without awareness: An autonomic index of facial recognition by prosopagnosics. *Science, 228,* 1453–1454.

Tulving, E. (1983). *Elements of episodic memory*. New York: Oxford University Press.

Tulving, E. (2002). Episodic memory: From mind to brain. *Annual Review of Psychology, 53,* 1–25.

Tulving, E., & Markowitsch, H. J. (1998). Episodic and declarative memory: Role of the hippocampus. *Hippocampus, 8(3),* 198–203.

Tulving, E., & Schacter, D. L. (1990). Priming and human memory systems. *Science, 247,* 301–306.

Tulving, E., Schacter, D. L., & Stark, H. A. (1982). Priming effects in word-fragment completion are independent of recognition memory. *Journal of Experimental Psychology: Learning, Memory, and Cognition, 8,* 336–342.

Tulving, E., & Thomson, D. M. (1973). Encoding specificity and retrieval processes in episodic memory. *Psychological Review, 80,* 352–373.

Turriziani, P., Fadda, L., Caltagirone, C., & Carlesimo, G. A. (2004). Recognition memory for single items and associations in amnesia patients. *Neuropsychologia, 42,* 426–433.

Underwood, B. J. (1957). Interference and forgetting. *Psychological Review, 64,* 49–60.

Uylings, H. B. M., Groenewegen, J. H., & Kolb, B. (2003). Do rats have a prefrontal cortex? *Behavioural Brain Research, 146,* 3–17.

Vaiva, G., Ducrocq, F., Jezequel, K., Averland, B., Lestavel, P., Brunet, A., & Marmar, C. R. (2003). Immediate treatment with propranolol decreases posttraumatic stress disorder two months after trauma. *Biological Psychiatry, 54,* 947–949.

Vargha-Khadem, F., Gadin, D. G., Watkins, K. E., Connelly, A., Van Paesschen, W., & Mishkin, M. (1997). Differential effects of early hippocampal pathology on episodic and semantic memory. *Science, 277,* 376–380.

Verfaellie, M., Koseff, P., & Alexander, M. P. (2000). Acquisition of novel semantic information in amnesia: Effects of lesion location. *Neuropsychological, 38,* 484–492.

Wais, P. E., Wixted, J. T., Hopkins, R. O., & Squire, L. R. (2006). The hippocampus supports both the recollection and the familiarity components of recognition memory. *Neuron, 49,* 459–466.

Walker, M. P., & Stickgold, R. (2005). It's practice, with sleep, that makes perfect: Implications of sleep-dependent learning and plasticity for skill performance. *Clinical Sports Medicine, 24,* 301–317.

Wallis, J. D., Anderson, K. C., & Miller, E. K. (2001). Single neurons in prefrontal cortex encode abstract rules. *Nature, 411,* 953–956.

Warrington, E. K. (1996). Studies of retrograde memory: A long-term view. *Proceeding of the National Academy of Sciences (United States of America), 93,* 13523–13526.

Warrington, E. K., & Shallice, T. (1984). Category-specific semantic impairments. *Brain, 107,* 829–854.

Wasserman, E. A., & Miller, R. R. (1997). What's elementary about associative learning? *Annual Review of Psychology, 48,* 573–607.

Watanabe, T., Nanez, J. E., Koyama, S., Mukai, I., Liederman, J., & Saskai, Y. (2002). Greater plasticity in lower-level than higher-level motion processing in a passive perceptual learning task. *Nature Neuroscience, 5,* 1003–1009.

Watanabe, T., Nanez, J. E., & Saskai, Y. (2001). Perceptual learning without perception. *Nature, 413,* 844–848.

Watson, J. B. (1913). Psychology as the behaviorist views it. *Psychological Reviews, 20,* 158–164.

Weinberger, N. M., Javid, R., & Lepan, B. (1993). Long-term retention of learning-induced receptive field plasticity in the auditory cortex. *Proceedings of the National Academy of Sciences, 90,* 2394–2398.

Whishaw, I. Q., & Douglas, D. G. (2003). On the origins of autobiographical memory. *Behavioural Brain Research, 138,* 113–119.

Williams, L. (1977). The perception of stop consonant voicing by Spanish–English bilinguals. *Perception and Psychophysics, 21,* 289–297.

Willingham, D. B., & Koroshetz, W. J. (1993). Evidence for dissociable motor skills in Huntington's disease patients. *Psychobiology, 21,* 173–182.

Wilson, F. A. W., Scalaidhe, S. P., & Goldman-Rakic, P. S. (1993). Dissociation of object and spatial processing domains in primate prefrontal cortex. *Science, 260,* 1955–1958.

Wilson, I. A., Gallagher, M., Eichenbaum, H., & Tanila, H. (2006). Neurocognitive aging: Prior memories hinder new hippocampal encoding. *Trends in Neurosciences, 29,* 662–670.

Winocur, G. (1992). A comparison of normal old rats and young adult rats with lesions to the hippocampus or prefrontal cortex on a test of matching-to-sample. *Neuropsychologia, 30,* 769–781.

Wirth, S., Yanike, M., Frank, L. M., Smith, A. C., Brown, E. N., & Suzuki, W. A. (2003). Single neurons in the monkey hippocampus and learning of new associations. *Science, 300,* 1578–1581.

Wood, E., Dudchenko, P. A., & Eichenbaum, H. (1999). The global record of memory in hippocampal neuronal activity. *Nature, 397,* 613–616.

Wood, E., Dudchenko, P., Robitsek, J. R., & Eichenbaum, H. (2000). Hippocampal neurons encode information about different types of memory episodes occurring in the same location. *Neuron, 27,* 623–633.

Woodruff-Pak, D. S. (1999). New directions for a classical paradigm: Human eyeblink conditioning. *Psychological Science, 10,* 1–3.

Woodruff-Pak, D. S., Papka, M., & Ivry, R. B. (1996). Cerebellar involvement in eyeblink classical conditioning in humans. *Neuropsychology, 10,* 443–458.

Wright, A. W., Santiago, H. C., Sands, S. F., Kendrick, D. F., & Cook, R. G. (1985). Memory processing of serial lists by pigeons, monkeys, and people. *Science, 229,* 287–289.

Yonelinas, A. P. (2001). Components of episodic memory: The contribution of recollection and familiarity. *Philosophical Transactions of the Royal Society of London, Series B: Biological Sciences, 356,* 1363–1374.

Yonelinas, A. P. (2002). The nature of recollection and familiarity: A review of 30 years of research. *Journal of Memory and Language, 46,* 441–517.

Yonelinas, A. P., Kroll, N. E. A., Quamme, J. R., Lazzara, M. M., Sauvé, M. J., Widaman, K. F., & Knight, R. T. (2002). Effects of extensive temporal lobe damage or mild hypoxia on recollection and familiarity. *Nature Neuroscience, 5,* 1236–1241.

Zajonc, R. (1968). Attitudinal effects of mere exposure. *Journal of Personality and Social Psychology, Monograph Supplement, 9,* 1–27.

Zohary, E., Celebrini, S., Britten, K. H., & Newsome, W. T. (1994). Plasticity that underlies improvement in perceptual performance. *Science, 263,* 1289–1292.

Zola, S. M., Squire, L. R., Teng, E., Stefanacci, L., Buffalo, E. A., & Clark, R. E. (2000). Impaired recognition memory in monkeys after damage limited to the hippocampal region. *Journal of Neuroscience, 20,* 451–463.

Zola-Morgan, S., & Squire, L. R. (1990). The primate hippocampal formation: Evidence for a time-limited role in memory storage. *Science, 250,* 288–290.

Zubin, J., & Barrera, S. E. (1941). Effect of electroconvulsive therapy on memory. *Proceedings of the Society of Experimental Biology and Medicine, 48,* 596–597.

ART AND PHOTO CREDITS

PHOTOGRAPHS

p. 9, 1.2: © Ros Drinkwater/Alamy; **p. 13, 1.3:** © Bettmann/Corbis; **p. 17, 1.4:** Bettmann/Corbis; **p. 66, 2.11:** Reprinted from Posner, M. I. and Raichle, M. E., *Images of Mind*, reprinted by Permission of Henry Holt and Company 1997; **p. 91, 3.2:** Courtesy Infant Studies Centre, University of British Columbia, Vancouver, B.C. Canada; **p. 94, 3.3A:** Courtesy of Robert Johnson, Cornell University; **p. 116, 4.1:** This article was published in *Cognition*, Vol. 57, Beale, J. M. & Keil, F. C., Categorical Effects in the Perception of Faces, *Cognition*, 217–239, Copyright Elsevier, 1995; **p. 195, 6.3 (both):** Photo Researchers, Inc.; **p. 239: 7.9:** WDCN/Univ. College London/Photo Researchers, Inc.; **p. 280, 8.9:** Schacter, D. L., Alpert N., Savage C. R., Rauch S. L., and Albert M., Conscious recollection and the human hippocampal formation: evidence from positron emission tomography. *Proceedings from the National Academy of Sciences U.S.A.* 1996 January 9; 93(1): 321–325, Copyright 1996 National Academy of Sciences, U.S.A.; **p. 281, 8.10A:** From Preston et al., (2004) Hippocampal contribution to the novel use of relational information in declarative memory, *Hippocampus, 14,* 148–152, Reprinted with permission of Wiley-Liss, Inc., a subsidiary of John Wiley & Sons, Inc.; **8.10B:** From Heckers, S. et al., (2004) Hippocampal activation during transitive inference in humans, *Hippocampus, 14,* 153–162. Reprinted with permission of Wiley-Liss, Inc., a subsidiary of John Wiley & Sons, Inc; .**p. 312, 9.5A:** Reprinted by permission from Macmillan Publishers Ltd: From Elderidge, L. L. et al., (2000). Remembering episodes: A selective role for the hippocampus during retrieval. *Nature Neuroscience, 3,* 1149–1152; **p. 319, 9.8:** Courtesy Ian Cannel and Nicky Clayton, University of Cambridge; **p. 329, 9.12:** From Amy L. Shelton and John D. E. Gabrieli, Neural Correlates of Encoding Space from Route and Survey Perspectives, *The Journal of Neuroscience*, April 1, 2002, 22(7): 2711–2717. Reprinted with permission of *The Journal of Neuroscience*; **p. 347, 10.4:** Reprinted by permission from Macmillan Publishers Ltd.: From "A neural basis for lexical retrieval" Hanna Damasio, Thomas J. Grabowski, Daniel Tranel, Richard D. Hichwa & Antonio R. Damasio. *Nature,* 380: 499–505 (11 April 1996); **p. 351, 10.5:** Reprinted by permission from Macmillan Publishers Ltd: Gauthier, I. et al. Activation of the middle fusiform "face area" increases with expertise in recognizing novel objects. *Nature Neuroscience, 2,* 568–573; **p. 356, 10.8:** Reprinted by permission from Macmillan Publishers Ltd: Corkin, S. (2002) What's new with the amnesic patient H. M.? *Nature Reviews Neuroscience,* Feb; 2(2): 153–60; **p. 379, 11.5:** Reprinted by permission from Macmillan Publishers Ltd: Teng, E. & Squire, L. R. 1999. Memory for place learned long ago is intact after hippocampal damage. *Nature,* 400: 675–677; **p. 413, 12.14:** From Freedman et al. Categorical Representation of Visual Stimuli in the Primate Prefrontal Cortex, *Science,* New Series, Vol. 291. No. 5502 (Jan. 12, 2001), pp. 312–316. Reprinted with Permission of AAAS.

FIGURES

CHAPTER 1

p. 19, 1.5: After Figure 1 in Thorndike, E. L. (1898). *Animal intelligence: An experimental study of the associative processes in animals.* Psychological Review Monograph Supplement 2 (4, Whole No. 8); **p. 25, 1.6:** After Tolman, E. C. (1932/1951). *Purposive behavior in animals and men.* Berkeley, CA: University of California Press; **p. 32, 1.8:** Data from Bechera, A., Tranel, D., Hanna, D., Adolphs, R., Rockland, C., & Damasio, A. R. (1995). Double dissociation of conditioning and declarative knowledge relative to the amygdala and hippocmapus in humans. *Science, 269,* 1115–1118.

CHAPTER 2

p. 42, 2.1: Modified from Figure 41 in Ramón y Cajal, S. (1988). *Cajal on the cerebral cortex: An annotated translation of the complete writings.* (J. DeFelipe & E. G. Jones, Ed. and Trans.) New York: Oxford University Press; **p. 57, 2.8:** Modified from Figure 3-1 in Eichenbaum, H. (2002). *The cognitive neuroscience of memory.* New York: Oxford University Press; **p. 59, 2.9A–B:** Modified from Nicoll, R. A., Kauer, J. A., & Malenka, R. C. (1988). The current excitement in long-term potentiation. *Neuron, 1,* 97–103; **2.9C–D:** Modified from Figure 3-4 in Eichenbaum, H. (2002). *The cognitive neuroscience of memory.* New York: Oxford University Press; **p. 61, 2.10C–E:** Data from Steele, R. J., & Morris, R. G. M. (1999). Delay-dependent impairment in matching-to-place task with chronic and intrahippocampal infusion of the NMDA-antagonist D-AP5. *Hippocampus, 9,* 118–136; **p. 72, 2.16A:** Modified from Figure 2.14 in Enns, J. T. (2004). *The thinking eye, the seeing brain.* New York: Norton; **2.16B:** Modified from Figure 15.3 in Gazzaniga, M. S., Ivry, R. B., & Mangun, G. R. (2002). *Cognitive neuroscience* (2nd ed). New York: Norton; **p. 75, 2.17:** Modified from Figure 10-1 in Eichenbaum, H. (2002). *The cognitive neuroscience of memory.* New York: Oxford University Press; **p. 77, 2.18:** Modified from Figure 11-2 in Eichenbaum, H. (2002). *The cognitive neuroscience of memory.* New York: Oxford University Press; **p. 78, 2.19:** Modified from Figure 1 in Eichenbaum, H. (2000). A cortical-hippocampal system for declarative memory. *Nature Reviews Neuroscience, 1,* 41–50.

CHAPTER 3

p. 94, 3.3B: Data from Johnston, R. E. (1993). Memory for individual scent in hamsters (*Mesocritcetus auratus*) as assessed by habituation methods. *Journal of Comparative Psychology, 107,* 201–207; **p. 95, 3.4B:** Data from Johnston, R. E., & Jernigan, P. (1994). Golden hamsters recognize individuals, not just individual scents. *Animal Behavior, 48,* 129–136; **p. 98, 3.5A:** Squire, L. R. & Kandel, E. R. Figure: The gill withdrawal reflex in *Aplysia,* from *Memory: From mind to molecules.* New York: Freeman; **3.5B:** Modified from p. 40 of Squire, L. R. & Kandel, E. R. *Memory: From mind to molecules,* p. 37. Reprinted by permission; **p. 99, 3.6:** Squire, L. R. & Kandel, E. R. Figure: The circuit for habituation of the gill withdrawal reflex, from *Memory: From mind to molecules,* p. 40. Reprinted by permission; **p. 100, 3.7:** Modified from p. 43 of Squire, L. R. & Kandel, E. R. *Memory: From mind to molecules.* New York: Freeman; **p. 103, 3.8:** Modified from Figure 2-6 in Eichenbaum, H. (2002). *The cognitive neuroscience of memory.* New York: Oxford University Press; **p. 104, 3.9:** Modified from Figure 2-7 in Eichenbaum, H. (2002). *The cognitive neuroscience of memory.* New York: Oxford University Press.

CHAPTER 4

p. 117, 4.2: Modified from Figure 11.8 in Fahle, M., & Poggio, T. (2002). *Perceptual learning.* Cambridge, MA: MIT Press; **p. 119, 4.3:** Modified from Figure 3 in Schiltz, C., Bodart, J. M., Dubois, S., Dejardin, S., Michel, C., Roucoux, A., Crommelinck, M., & Orban, G. A. (1999). Neuronal mechanisms of perceptual learning: Changes in human brain activity with training in orientation discrimination. *NeuroImage, 9,* 46–62; **p. 121, 4.4A–B:** Stickgold, James, & Hobson: Figure reprinted by permission from Macmillan Publishers Ltd. from "Visual Discrimination Learning Requires Sleep After Training," *Nature Neuroscience,* Vol. 3, No. 12, pp. 1237–1238 (2000). Copyright © 2000, Nature Publishing Group; **p. 122, 4.5:** After Weinberger, N. M., Javid, R., & Lepan, B. (1993). Long-term retention of learning-induced receptive field plasticity in the auditory cortex. *Proceedings of the National Academy of Sciences, U.S.A., 90,* 2394–2398; **p. 124, 4.6:** Modified from Recanzone, G. H., Schreiner, C. E., & Merzenich, M. M. (1993). Plasticity in the frequency representation of primary auditory cortex following discrimination training in adult owl monkeys. *The Journal of Neuroscience, 13,* 87–103; **p. 126, 4.7:** Modified from Watanabe, T., Nanez, J. E., & Saskai, Y. (2001). Perceptual learning without perception. *Nature 413,* 844–848. **p. 129, 4.9:** Modified from Cohen, N. J., & Squire, L. R. (1980). Preserved learning and retention of a pattern-analyzing skill in amnesia: Dissociation of knowing how and knowing that. *Science, 210,* 207–210; **p. 132, 4.10:** Data from Jacoby, L.L. (1983). Remembering the data: Analyzing interactive processes in reading. *Journal of Verbal Learning and Behavior, 22,* 485–508; **p. 134, 4.11:** Tuber, Milner, & Corkin: Series of 5 Successively More Complete Line Drawings of an Airplane. This article was published in *Neuropsychologia,* 6, Tuber, Milner, & Corkin, "Further Analysis of the Hippocampal Amnesic Syndrome," Copyright © Elsevier 1968. Reprinted with permission; **p. 135, 4.12:** Data from Graf, P., Squire, L. R., & Mandler, G. (1984). The information that amnesic patients do not forget. *Journal of Experimental Psychology: Learning, Memory, and Cognition, 10,* 164–178; **p. 136, 4.13:** After Gabrieli, J. D. E., Milberg, W., Keane, M., & Corkin, S. (1990). Intact priming of patterns despite impaired memory. *Neuropsychologia, 28,* 417–427; **p. 139, 4.14:** Tulving & Schacter: 4 Block-Like Objects (possible (upper) and impossible (lower)). From "Priming and Human Memory Systems," *Science,* Vol. 247, pp. 301–306 (1990). Copyright © 1990 by American Association for the Advancement of Science. Reprinted with permission from AAAS.

CHAPTER 5

p. 152, 5.3: After Figure 1 in Trapold, M. A., & Spence, K. W. (1960). Performance changes in eyelid conditioning as related to motivational and reinforcing properties of the UCS. *Journal of Experimental Psychology, 59,* 209–213; **p. 154, 5.5:** After Figure 4-6 in Mazur, J. E. (2002). *Learning and behavior* (5th ed). Upper Saddle River, NJ: Prentice Hall; **p. 157, 5.6:** After Moore, J. (1972) Stimulus control: Studies of auditory generalization in rabbits. In A. H. Black and W. F. Prokasy (Eds.), *Classical conditioning II: Current theory and research.* New York: Appleton-Century-Crofts; **p. 163, 5.8:** After Figure 4-4 in Mazur, J. E. (2002). *Learning and behavior* (5th ed). Upper Saddle River, NJ: Prentice Hall; **p. 167, 5.9:** Modified from p. 61 in Squire, L. R., & Kandel, E. R. *Memory: From mind to molecules.* Freeman; **p. 170, 5.11 (top):** Modified from Figure 1 in Thompson, R. F., & Krupa, D. J. (1994). Organization of memory traces in the mammalian brain. *Annual Review of Neuroscience, 17,* 519–549; **5.11 (bottom):** After Krupa, D. J., Thompson, J. K., & Thompson, R. F. (1993). *Science, 260,* 989–991; **p. 173, 5.12:** Modified from Figure 5.2 in Steinmetz J. E. (1996). The brain substrates of classical eyeblink conditioning in rabbits. In Bloedel, J. R., Ebner, T. J., & Wise, S. P. (Eds.), *The acquisition of motor behavior in vertebrates,* pp. 89–114. Cambridge, MA: MIT Press; **p. 175, 5.13A:** Data from Smith, J. C., & Roll, D.L. (1967). Trace conditioning with X-rays as an aversive stimulus. *Psychonomic Science, 9,* 11–12; **5.13B:** Data from Figure 1 in Garaic, J., Ervin, F. R., & Koelling, R. A. (1966). Learning with prolonged delay of reinforcement. *Psychonomic Science, 5,* 121–122.

CHAPTER 6

p. 204, 6.5: Modified from Figure 2 in Kelley, A. E. (2004). Memory and addiction: Shared neural circuitry and molecular mechanisms. *Neuron, 44,* 161–179; **p. 206, 6.6:** Data from Packard, M.G., Hirsh, R., White, N. M. (1989). Differential effects of fornix and caudate nucleus lesions on two radial maze tasks: Evidence for multiple memory systems. *The Journal of Neuroscience, 9,* 1465–1472; **p. 210, 6.7:** Knowlton et al.: Weather Prediction Game—Probability of Sunshine. From "A Neostriatal Habit Learning System in Humans," *Science,* Vol. 273, pp. 1399–1402 (1996). Reprinted with permission from AAAS; **p. 214, 6.8:** Modified from Figure C-3 in Schultz, W. (2006). Behavioral theories and the neurophysiology of reward. *Annual Review of Psychology, 57,* 87–115; **p. 215, 6.9:** Modified from Figure 8 in Kermadi, I., & Joseph, J. P. (1995). Activity in the caudate nucleus of monkey during spatial sequencing. *Journal of Neurophysiology, 74,* 911–933.

CHAPTER 7

p. 232: 7.5: Cahill et al.: Figure reprinted by permission from Macmillan Publishers Ltd. from "β-Adrenergic Activation and Memory for Emotional Events," *Nature,* Vol. 371, Issue 6499, pp. 702–704 (1994). Copyright © 1994, Nature Publishing Group; **p. 236, 7.7:** Modified from Figure 11-2 in Eichenbaum, H. (2002). *The cognitive neuroscience of memory.* New York: Oxford University Press; **p. 240, 7.10:** Modified from Figure 1 in LeDoux, J. E. (1992). Brain mechanisms of emotion and emotional learning. *Current Opinion in Neurobiology, 2,* 191–197; **p. 241, 7.11:** After Figure 4 in Bechara, A., Tranel, D., Hanna, D., Adolphs, R., Rockland, C., & Damasio, A. R. (1995). Double dissociation of conditioning and declarative knowledge relative to the amygdala and hippocampus. *Science, 269,* 1115–1118; **p. 244, 7.12:** Modified from Figure 3 in Gallagher, M. & Holland, P. (1994). The amygdala complex: Multiple roles in associative learning and attention. *Proceedings of the National Academy of Sciences, U.S.A., 91,* 11771–11776; **p. 246, 7.13:** Modified from Figure 2 in Gallagher, M. & Holland, P. (1994). The amygdala complex: Multiple roles in associative learning and attention. *Proceedings of the National Academy of Sciences, U.S.A., 91,* 11771–11776.

CHAPTER 8

p. 258, 8.1: Adapted from Corkin, S., Amaral, D. G., Gonzalez, R. G., Johnson, K. A., & Hyman, B. T. (1997). H. M.'s medial temporal lobe lesion: Findings from magnetic resonance imaging. *The Journal of Neuroscience, 17,* 3964–3980; **p. 265, 8.3:** After Figure 1 in Craik, I. M., & Tulving, E. (1975). Depth of processing and retention of words in episodic memory. *Journal of Experimental Psychology, 104,* 268–294; **p. 267, 8.4:** Data from Hyde, T., & Jenkins, J. J. (1973). Recall for words as a function of semantic, graphic, and syntactic orienting tasks. *Journal of Verbal Learning and Verbal Behavior, 12,* 471–480; **p. 270, 8.5:** Data from Ebbinghaus, H. (1964). *Memory: A contribution to experimental psychology* (H. A. Ruger & C. E. Bussenius, Trans.). New York: Dover. (Original work published 1913); **p. 272, 8.6:** Data from Keppel, G., Postman, L., & Zavortnik, B. (1968). Studies of learning to learn: VIII. The influence of massive amounts of training upon the learning and retention of paired associate lists. *Journal of Verbal Learning and Verbal Behavior, 7,* 790–796; **p. 274, 8.7:** Data from Table 1 in Godden, D. and Baddley, A. D. (1975). Context dependent memory in two natural environments: On land and under water. *British Journal of Psychology, 66,* 325–33; **p. 278, 8.8B:** Data from Milner, B., Corkin, S., & Teuber, H. L. (1968). Further analysis of the hippocampal amnesic syndrome: 14-year follow-up study of H. M. *Neuropsychologia, 6(3),* 215–234; **p. 284, 8.11:** Data from Morris, R. G. M., Garrud, P., Rawlins, J. P, & O'Keefe, J. (1982). Place navigation impaired in rats with hippocampal lesions. *Nature, 297,* 681–683; **p. 285, 8.12:** After Figure 1 in Muller, R. (1996). A quarter century of place cells. *Neuron, 17,* 979–990; **p. 288, 8.14:** Data from Eichenbaum, H., Stewart, C., Morris, R. G. M. (1990). Hippocampal representation in spatial learning. *The Journal of Neuroscience, 10,* 331–339; **p. 289, 8.15:** Modified from Figure 3 of Wood, E., Dudchenko, P., Robitsek, J. R., & Eichenbaum, H. (2000). Hippocampal neurons encode information about different types of memory episodes occurring in the same location. *Neuron, 27,* 623–633; **p. 290, 8.16B–C:** Data from Bunsey, M., & Eichenbaum, H. (1996). Conservation of hippocampal memory function in rats and humans. *Nature, 379,* 255-257.

CHAPTER 9

p. 305, 9.2: After Yonelinas, A. P. (2001). Components of episodic memory: The contribution of rec-ollection and familiarity. *Philosophical Transactions of the Royal Society of London, Series B: Biological Sci-ences, 356,* 1363–1374; **p. 308, 9.3:** After Figure 1 in Giovanello, K. S., Verfaellie, M., & Keane, M. M. (2003). Disproportionate deficit in associative recognition relative to item recognition in global amne-sia. *Cognitive, Affective, and Behavioral Neuroscience, 3(3),* 186–194; **p. 309, 9.4:** After Figure 5 in Yoneli-nas, A. P. (2001). Components of episodic memory: The contribution of recollection and familiarity. *Philosophical Transactions of the Royal Society of London, Series B: Biological Sciences, 356,* 1363–1374; **p. 312, 9.5B:** Reprinted by permission from Macmillan Publishers Ltd: From Elderidge, L. L. et al., (2000). Remembering episodes: A selective role for the hippocampus during retrieval. *Nature Neuro-science, 3,* 1149–1152; **p. 316, 9.6:** Data from Zola, S. M., Squire, L. R., Teng, E., Stefanacci, L., Buf-falo, E. A., & Clark, R. E. (2000). Impaired recognition memory in monkeys after damage limited to the hippocampal region. *The Journal of Neuroscience, 20,* 451–463; **p. 318, 9.7:** Data from Fortin, N. J., Wright, S. P., & Eichenbaum, H. (2004). Recollection-like memory retrieval in rats is dependent on the hippocampus. *Nature, 431,* 188–191; **p. 321, 9.9A–D:** Steele & Morris: Figure 1 from "Delay dependent impairment in matching-to-place task with chronic and intrahippocampal infusion on the NMDA-antagonist D-AP5," *Hippocampus,* Vol. 9, No. 2, pp. 118–136 (1999). Copyright © 1999, Wiley-Liss, Inc. Reprinted with permission of Wiley-Liss, Inc., a subsidiary of John Wiley & Sons, Inc.; **p. 323, 9.10B:** Data from Fortin, N. J., Agster, K. L., & Eichenbaum, H. (2002). Critical role of the hippocampus in memory for sequences of events. *Nature Neuroscience, 5,* 458–462; **p. 326, 9.11:** After Wood, E., Dudchenko, P. A., & Eichenbaum, H. (1999). The global record of memory in hippocampal neuronal activity. *Nature, 397,* 613–616.

CHAPTER 10

p. 335, 10.1: Modified from Collins, A. M., & Quillian, M. R. (1969). Retrieval time from semantic memory. *Journal of Verbal Learning and Verbal Memory, 8,* 240–247; **p. 342, 10.2:** Alan D. Baddeley: Figures 8.2 and 8.3 in *Essentials of Human Memory,* pp. 158–159. Copyright © 1999 by Psychology Press, a member of the Taylor & Francis Group; **p. 353, 10.6:** Knowlton, Ramus, & Squire: Figure from "Intact Artificial Grammar Learning in Amnesia: Dissociation of Classification Learning and Explicit Memory for Specific Instances," *Psychological Science,* Vol. 3, Issue 3, pp. 172–179 (1992). Copy-right © 1992, Blackwell Publishing, Ltd. Reprinted by permission of the publisher; **p. 354, 10.7:** J. M. Reed et al.: Figure 1 from "Learning About Categories That Are Defined by Object-Like Stimuli Despite Impaired Declarative Memory," *Behavioral Neuroscience,* Vol. 113, No. 3, pp. 411–419 (1999).

CHAPTER 11

p. 370, 11.2: Modified from Figure 2.5A in Hebb, D. O. (1949). *The organization of behavior.* New York: Wiley; **p. 382, 11.6B:** Data from Zola-Morgan, S., & Squire, L. R. (1990). The primate hip-pocampal formation: Evidence for a time-limited role in memory storage. *Science, 250,* 288–290; **p. 383, 11.7B:** Data from Kim, J. J., & Fanselow, M. S. (1992). Modality-specific retrograde amnesia of fear. *Science, 256,* 675–677; **p. 384, 11.8B:** Data from Kim, J. J., Clark, R. E., & Thompson, R. F. (1995). Hippocampectomy impairs the memory of recently, but not remotely, acquired trace eyeblink con-ditioned responses. *Behavioral Neuroscience, 109,* 195–203; **p. 385, 11.9B:** Data from Cho, Y. H., Bera-cochea, D., & Jaffard, R. (1993). Extended temporal gradient for the retrograde and anterograde amnesia produced by ibotenate entorhinal cortex lesions in mice. *The Journal of Neuroscience, 13,* 1759–1766; **p. 389, 11.10:** After Alvarez, P., & Squire, L. R. (1994). Memory consolidation and the medial temporal lobe: A simple network model. *Proceedings of the National Academy of Sciences, U.S.A., 91,* 7041–7045; **p. 391, 11.11:** McClelland et al.: Figures from "Why are there complementary learn-ing systems in the hippocampus and neocortex? Insights from the successes and failures of connec-

NAME INDEX

Adolphs, R., 238
Aggleton, J. P., 307, 317
Alvarez, P., 388, 389
Anderson, J. R., 202
Aristotle, 12
Atkinson, R. C., 404, 405

Baddeley, A. D., 274, 406, 408, 410, 412, 419
Bahrick, H. P., 270
Barrera, S. E., 368
Bartlett, F. C., 24, 25
Bayley, P. J., 358, 378, 380
Beale, J. M., 115
Bechera, A., 31, 240
Bend, M., 113
Berendt, J., 230
Berke, J. D., 211
Biederman, I., 118
Birrell, M., 426
Bliss, T. V. P., 57
Bontempi, B., 393
Bransford, J. D., 268, 275
Breiter, H. C., 238
Breland, K., 187
Breland, M., 187
Brewer, W. F., 298
Brown, J., 403
Brown, M. W., 317
Brown, R., 230, 272
Brown, V. J., 426
Bryant, P. E., 261
Buckner, R. L., 138, 434
Bucy, P., 238
Bunsey, M., 291, 358
Burnham, W. M., 368, 371

Burns, R., 314
Buschke, H., 406
Butters, N., 208

Cahill, L., 231, 249, 250
Cajal, S. Ramón y, 41
Campbell, C. E., 200
Capaldi, E. J., 200
Carew, T. J., 166
Chalmers, M., 262
Chao, L. L., 351
Chase, W. G., 267, 276
Cho, Y. H., 385, 386
Christian, K. M., 169
Claparéde, E., 221
Clark, R. E., 177, 317
Clayton, N., 318, 319
Cohen, J. D., 432
Cohen, N. J., 128, 129, 259, 260, 261, 311, 313
Colegrove, F. W., 230
Collins, A. M., 335, 336
Conway, J. K., 229
Corkin, S., 257, 277, 278, 355, 377
Coupe, P., 344
Courtney, S. M., 433
Craik, F. I. M., 265
Crombag, H. F. M., 303

Damasio, A. R., 221, 222, 346, 392
Darwin, C. J., 400
Davachi, L., 312
Davis, H. P., 373
Davis, M., 225, 238
Day, M., 320

DeGroot, A. D., 267
Delacour, J., 315
Dias, R., 424
Dickenson, A. D., 318, 319
Disterhoft, J. F., 176
Dobbins, I. G., 434
Dostrovsky, J., 283
Douglas, D. G., 314
Downing, P. E., 349
Dudai, Y., 373
Dudchencko, P., 317, 413
Duncan, C. P., 368
Dusek, J. A., 291, 358

Ebbinghaus, H., 16, 269, 299
Eich, J. E., 274
Eichenbaum, H., 259, 287, 291, 313, 317, 327, 352, 358, 392
Ekstrom, A. D., 325
Eldridge, L. L., 311
Elgersma, Y., 372
Epstein, R., 328, 349
Ericsson, A., 276
Ervin, F. R., 175
Everitt, B. J., 211, 227

Fanselow, M. S., 382
Farah, M. J., 339, 340, 347
Fenn, K. M., 120, 387
Finger, S., 41, 49, 63, 65
Fisher, R. P., 303
Fortin, N. J., 317, 322
Frankland, P. W., 394
Franks, J. J., 275
Freedman, D. J., 431, 432

Subject Index